# Management for Professionals

More information about this series at http://www.springer.com/series/10101

Robert Kepczynski • Alecsandra Dimofte •
Raghav Jandhyala • Ganesh Sankaran •
Andrew Boyle

# Implementing Integrated Business Planning

## A Guide Exemplified With Process Context and SAP IBP Use Cases

Springer

Robert Kepczynski
Zurich, Switzerland

Alecsandra Dimofte
SAP Switzerland
Regensdorf, Switzerland

Raghav Jandhyala
SAP LABS LLC
Tempe, Arizona, USA

Ganesh Sankaran
Ingolstadt, Germany

Andrew Boyle
SAP LABS LLC
Tempe, Arizona, USA

ISSN 2192-8096 ISSN 2192-810X (electronic)
Management for Professionals
ISBN 978-3-319-90094-0 ISBN 978-3-319-90095-7 (eBook)
https://doi.org/10.1007/978-3-319-90095-7

Library of Congress Control Number: 2018941554



Cover illustration: eStudio Calamar, Berlin/Figueres

Printed on acid-free paper

This Springer imprint is published by the registered company Springer International Publishing AG part of Springer Nature.
The registered company address is: Gewerbestrasse 11, 6330 Cham, Switzerland

# Preface

The idea of this book came to light after one of the Integrated Business Planning workshops under impactful transformation program. My colleagues Mariel Ramirez, Emmanuel Bieth, and Badra Touddert have encouraged me to put planning knowledge and experience on paper, so that global and country implementation stakeholders could benefit from it. We shared the same opinion that this book may help many other companies to have a better start in their IBP journey.

I gathered ideas about planning and integration of finance and discussed it with few people with whom I used to work with, and that is why, I have asked Raghav Jandhyala, Alecsandra Dimofte, Ganesh Sankaran, and at the final stage Andrew Boyle to join this project. We talked to many customers and our work colleagues and came to the conclusion that we want to write a book about integrated business planning enabled on SAP IBP but not as configuration guide. We wanted to contextualize IBP with process description and then connect to SAP IBP use cases. The main focus of this book is process context translated into IBP use cases. This book is a continuation of Integrated Business Planning (Kepczynski et al. 2018).

Once the book was pretty much ready, we asked chemical company Regional S&OP Manager and large food and beverages company Solution Architect to provide content review.

Content would not be ready without our colleagues, who provided project support and managed figures and references. Therefore, we would like to thank Federico Sasso, Ivan Kostakev, Vladimir Dorodnitsyn, Giulio Zunino, and Tommaso Nardi for their contribution. Last but not least, we were lucky to have Alexei Koifman as true IBP book supporter.

Let us know what you think about the book. Enjoy the reading.

Zurich, Switzerland — Robert Kepczynski

## Reference

Kepczynski, R., Jandhyala, R., Sankaran, G., & Dimofte, A. (2018). *Integrated business planning – How to integrate planning processes, organizational structures & capabilities, and leverage SAP IBP technology*. Springer.

# Contents

# About the Authors

## Authors

**Robert Kepczynski** has more than 20 years of experience in supply chain management and technology. Robert does assess, design, and implement people capability models and process design and delivers efficient technology solutions. Robert specializes in supply chain planning processes and technology. Robert took business roles in:

- Plant supply/production planning and sequencing, inventory and materials management, warehouse and duty operations, and costing and budgeting
- Market IBP & S&OP and distribution planning
- Regional & global S&OP, sales forecasting, demand planning and demand management, and process ownership

Robert did lead x-functional transformation programs delivering functional optimization and differentiation. Robert contributed to the 2nd in the world SAP IBP implementation, which have started in 2013 and proved that Robert has the head, heart and hands for IBP.

**Alecsandra Dimofte (Ghita)** works for SAP where she started as a supply chain management consultant. Alecsandra was involved in several IBP/S&OP implementation projects which allowed her to play different roles, from integration consultant to functional design lead. Alecsandra contributed to the development of the S&OP practice within her delivery unit and to the growth of the IBP online community by active participation in the space dedicated to IBP.

**Raghav Jandhyala** is a Senior Director of Product Management at SAP for SAP IBP responsible for sales and operations planning and unified planning processes and best practices in IBP. Raghav has over 16 years of experience in different fields like supply chain management, retail, and banking along with a strong technical background in development and adoption of business applications. Raghav held various roles in his career as business consultant, development architect, solutions manager, and product manager. Raghav is responsible for developing the road map for S&OP solution and works with multiple IBP customers for new innovations and as a trusted advisor for their global rollouts.

**Ganesh Sankaran** is a supply chain management technology practitioner. Ganesh helps clients solve business problems and generate value from their supply chain processes, particularly in the planning domain. Ganesh possesses a skill set that combines deep theoretical insights into SCM and rich implementation experience in SAP solutions further enriched by around 7 years of prior software development experience.

**Andrew Boyle** is part of the team at SAP Product Management focused on order-based planning for IBP. Andrew has nearly 20 years of experience working with SAP enterprise software systems, mainly within the supply chain management space. Andrew held various roles in his career as SAP customer, instructor, pre-sales engineer and architect, solutions manager, and product manager.

## Reviewers

**Regional S&OP Manager** at a large chemical company—He has more than 30 years of experience in supply chain management, logistics, and information technology, and he is currently a supply chain and logistics manager for a global manufacturer of differentiated chemical products. He has a solid background in IT solutions and has led design and implementation of S&OP from site to global level.

**Solution Architect** in supply chain planning at a very large food and beverages products company, where he is helping to shape a multi-year process renovation program centered on SAP IBP. He has 15 years of experience designing software solutions for supply chain planning, having previously worked in the packaging, chemicals, and machinery manufacturing sectors in Switzerland, the United States, Sweden, and South Africa. Previously, he worked as a software developer at SAP in Germany.

## Project Support

**Federico Sasso** focuses on logistics processes and particularly in production planning and material management area. He completed his master thesis on outlier detection and correction for seasonal and intermittent products. In IBP he focuses on statistical forecasting and data analysis. Special thanks to Federico, who helped us to make this book happen.

**Ivan Kostakev** has over 3 years of shop-floor experience in the manufacturing industry, both as a logistics manager and as a project engineer. He specializes in integrated business planning.

**Vladimir Dorodnitsyn** brings experience in the design, implementation, and integration of SAP EWM and SAP ERP. He works in the domain of supply chain planning with strong focus on integrated business planning including both business and technology transformation topics.

**Giulio Zunino** has gained insights into the automation of cross-industry production processes and in the automotive industry as a whole. Here, he particularly focused on ways to address the new challenges that the digitalization of the production processes is causing.

**Tommaso Nardi** works in supply chain management practice. Over the past few years, Tommaso has developed a deep understanding and hands-on knowledge of supply chain planning and operational transformations in the life sciences sector.

# Move Away from Disconnected Planning 1

## 1.1 Disconnected Planning Diagnosis

We have seen that broadly understood planning processes happen over short-, mid- and long-term horizon. Many used to call those processes as operational, tactical, and strategic planning processes. Short-term operational planning processes happen over 4–12-week horizon, tactical planning processes cover up to 3 years, and strategic planning processes shape business even up to 10-year horizon.

If we take a closer look into those three planning horizons, we have come to the conclusion that planning processes executed in respective time horizon were characterized differently by:

- Objective
- Impact
- Stakeholders decision power (position in the company hierarchy)
- Stakeholders degree of connection to operational execution or strategic directives
- Frequency
- Granularity
- Time bucket
- Degree of embedding financials into decision-making process
- Degree of embedding product/technology information into decision-making process
- Degree of embedding of customer/market information into decision-making process
- Industry needs
- Systems and technology support

Since those characteristics are different for each of the planning type, many companies face enormous amount of challenges to integrate planning processes under one coherent framework called Integrated Business Planning. Companies struggle to unlock value of those planning processes being integrated and managed

 
R. Kepczynski et al., *Implementing Integrated Business Planning*, Management for Professionals, https://doi.org/10.1007/978-3-319-90095-7_1

holistically. In order to understand how to integrate planning processes, let's attempt to describe them one by one as per strategic, tactical, and operational planning.

**Strategic Planning** We have realized that companies have one strategic planning process which defines business direction and strategy for long-term horizon and the other one which was focused on strategic assets/products but impacting mid-term horizon. Both processes were highly important and had high impact on company performance.

We have seen that strategic planning which set company direction was executed on annual base (sometimes twice a year) and was normally led by business development or business planning team. Let us call this process as **annual business planning**.

We have seen that strategic planning process that is focused on strategic assets/products was executed on a monthly basis and was typically led by senior supply chain planning managers. Let us call this process as **monthly strategic product/assets planning**.

**Annual Business Planning** This process addresses a global view on business development and business strategy where strategic initiatives affecting technology investments, market positioning and developments, and channel growth are captured, discussed, reconciled, and monetized.

On the demand side, this process addresses issues associated with introduction of new sales channels, entering new markets, and competitor's trends.

On the supply side, this process addresses internal or external manufacturing footprint assessment, investments in operations, warehousing, and long-term capacity challenges to be solved with internal or external manufacturing/tolling/3–4PL/CAPEX discussion. Quite often as part of this process, large technology shifts or extensions are being discussed. Length of strategic horizon is much aligned to R&D of the products or technologies.

On the financial side, this process addresses financial risk and opportunities like exchange rate fluctuations, macroeconomic trends, and impact of potential acquisitions and mergers.

This process is typically executed once per year and does cover inputs from various functions considering up to 10-year future horizon. Process is being led or managed by global senior management of the company which have decision power to make changes in company strategy and approve strategic initiatives but do not hands on influence short-term execution.

Experts who support execution of this process prepare data and analysis on aggregated level like product lines or business lines, regional or global scope, and profit or cost center groups. Normally data is being prepared on annual bucketing and mainly in monetary terms.

Decision-making process fundamentally is based on evaluation of assumptions and pros/cons discussion of the financial impact on future company performance. Decision-making process in essence is about developing "what-if" business risk and opportunity scenarios and aims to visualize to the management scenario impacts like

CAGR (compound annual growth rate). The output of this process was communicated to various functions in the organizations including local management.

**Monthly Strategic Product/Assets Planning** This process addresses regional or global and mid- to long-term view on strategic products, raw materials, and assets. Examples of those could be:

- Active ingredients in the chemical industry
- Active pharma ingredients (drug substances) in the pharma and healthcare industry
- Steel in kitchen appliances
- Seed varieties in the agriculture industry

Those strategic products are very often linked to high cost contribution in the final products, sometimes even above 70%. This process regularly generates impact and improves transparency on monthly tactical S&OP process executed on country to global level but where products discussed have higher form of customization. Link between strategic products planning and tactical S&OP enables organizations to reach objective of:

- Raising awareness
- Managing feasibility of tactical SOP plans realization in better way
- Analyzing projected performance against budget on a regional/country/product family level

Typically, this process was executed in a mix of the so-called top-down (by marketing as demand for strategic form of the product) and bottom-up (by supply chain as demand based on consumption of strategic form of the product), where two streams of inputs are being compared and reviewed.

This process runs on monthly basis with monthly time bucketing for horizon of up to 5–7 years.

Key stakeholders who lead and manage the monthly strategic product planning are typically on level of functional manager on global and regional level, mostly from marketing and supply chain. Typically they are not accountable for business strategy but have influence and provide inputs to annual business planning.

Decision-making process fundamentally is based on evaluation of demand inputs and unconstrained and constrained supply planning linked to supply propagation to countries/markets. Fair share of profitability is often used as criterion to allocate strategic form of the product to demand locations. Allocation in tactical horizon is supported with "what-if" business risk and opportunity scenarios which aim to visualize the impact of budget realization and operating profit on the company as a whole and its business units (markets, countries).

This process and stakeholders have stronger impact on execution of the country/market operational plans.

**Tactical Planning/Sales and Operations Planning** This process addresses a country-regional-global view on product, demand, supply, financial and volumetric reconciliation (integrated reconciliation meeting), and sign-off by management (S&OP meeting). It does focus on addressing issues associated with top-line revenue and volumetric projections, definition of country or product group or channel price tactics, bottom-line profits exposed from constraints, gaps to budget, financial elements projection (like exchange rates), and alignment to strategic initiatives. It is a main process which impact realization of operating plans like budget.

Process is very cross-functional and, since it's executed from local to global level, stakeholders can have different accountability and impact on execution. Main process objective is to deliver balanced plan in volume and value with documented assumptions. The process is not focused on resolving very short-term issues but rather focused on how to achieve business objectives for the current year and current year plus one.

Decision-making process consolidates inputs through product-demand-supply-reconciliation to management review meeting. In each of the steps "what-if" business scenario planning is used to model risk and opportunities. Very often scenarios go across process steps like for tender demand to supply and integrated reconciliation or for a new product launch to demand, supply, and financial impact assessment.

Data which was being used had a monthly granularity on various levels on product and commercial-geographical hierarchy. Process on country/market level was often executed on SKU/product group/sales zone/country level. Process on regional/global level was reviewed on product lines/country/group of country level. Process on site level was executed mainly on key manufacturing assets or key strategic product level. Time bucketing was typically monthly, with specific focus on subtotaling like:

- Year to date, year to go, and full year
- Weeks, months, quarters, and years which help to quickly assess situation

We have observed that time horizon of this process varies from current year to current year plus 2.

In the last few years, we have observed that tactical S&OP process is more and more tightly integrated with financial planning, but this is not yet very common. There are a lot of companies which run their S&OP process in volume only and disconnected from financials.

Tactical S&OP process in many industries is linked tightly at minimum once per month with operational planning. Tactical S&OP sets detailed framework for operational planning in which it is even further optimized and resolved especially in demand-supply balancing but on more granular level.

S&OP has many forms, variations, and definitions but let us bring one from leading practitioner:

Sales and Operations Planning is communication and decision making process:

- To balance demand and supply
- To set plans for volume that will guide the detail mix and
- To integrate financial, product development and operating plans

(Gray 2006)

**Operational Planning** This process addresses in country, very often in country/sales zone demand and supply imbalances. This process was very down to earth and operated with resources and assets which were available at a certain point in time for short horizon. We have seen that operational planning was introduced in the companies when monthly S&OP process was not granular enough to solve demand-supply imbalances driven by product type or channel. We observed various frequencies of this process from daily to weekly to bi-weekly. What we have found very interesting is that this process was switched on and switched off during the year especially in case of:

- Highly seasonal products
- Limited life products and offers
- Short peak seasons
- Large promotional campaigns
- Customer-specific products
- Commodity business

This means that operational planning can be driven by product or industry characteristics.

We have observed that time horizon of this process varies from few days up to 12–16 weeks.

Operational planning focuses to EXTRACT THE BIGGEST VALUE FROM AVAILABLE MATERIALS, MANPOWER, MACHINES, AND MONEY. THESE FOUR DIMENSIONS MAY BE CALLED "4M."

Data which was typically needed had a very high granularity, very often order level (sales/production, inventory) on daily/weekly bucketing. Due to the amount of highly granular information, exception management did play an important role in the process.

Participants/contributors of operational planning process were very hands-on experts in the organization, subject matter experts who were "doing the job."

You can understand operational planning as sort of optimization to tactical S&OP. There was tight integration between those two processes ensured by especially aligned calendar of activities. At minimum once per month, outputs of operational planning were integrated into tactical S&OP. The operational process was executed typically on a single meeting where product, customer, demand, supply, and financial information were available to make short-term decisions. Even though this process was tightly connected to execution, you still can look at

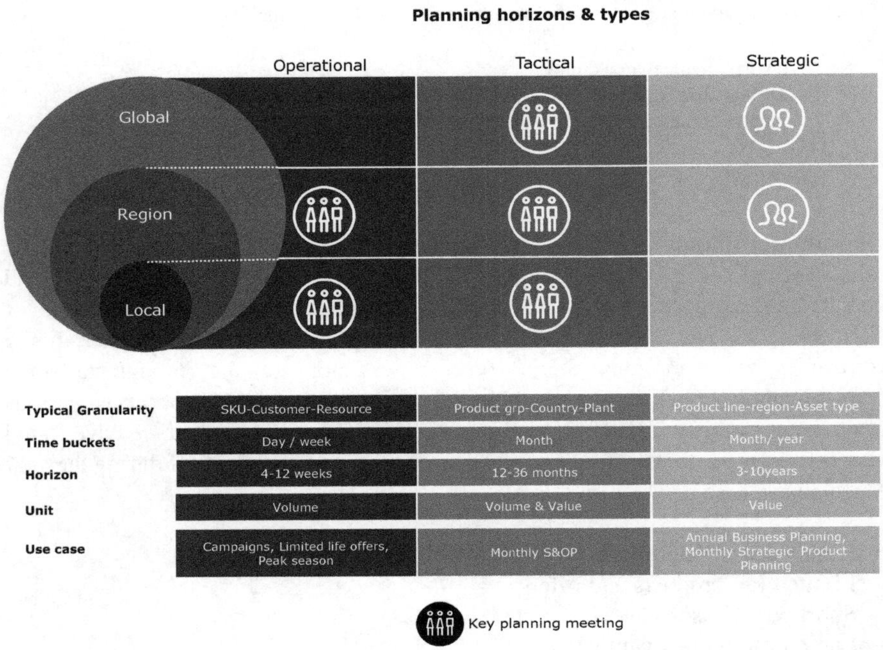


**Fig. 1.1** Planning horizons-types-levels and their key characteristics

it as execution steering, a way to get alignment with framework defined in tactical S&OP. We have seen that operational planning can be done within country on sales zone level or across countries but then driven by brand/product group tactics and specifics.

## View Across All Planning Types

In Fig. 1.1, you see summary of observations about key characteristics linked to planning types, horizons, and levels. We have observed very often that many organizations struggle to connect those planning processes because of their differences and lack of focus on organizational and technology aspects.

What we have found very interesting is that activities in all planning types can be mapped against well-recognized sales and operations planning process dimensions. Just a reminder—S&OP have the following process dimensions (Fig. 1.2):

- Product
- Demand
- Supply
- Reconciliation (integrated reconciliation)
- S&OP

**Planning horizons & types**

| S&OP process dimensions | | Operational | Tactical | Strategic |
|---|---|---|---|---|
| | Product / Customers / Services Review | Order based changes in product packaging | New product launches and withdrawals<br>Product transfers | New technologies introductions<br>Technology transfers |
| | Demand Review | Order types<br>Sensed demand<br>Sensed forecast | Forecast on detail and aggregated level in volume and value | Demand trends<br>New markets<br>New sales channels |
| | Supply Review | Existing inventories<br>Firm Supply | Planned safety stock<br>Optimized supply plans<br>Fair share / profitable allocations | Planned supply capabilities<br>Internal & external manufacturing |
| | Reconciliation in volume and value (Pre-SO&OP) | Detail balancing and demand fulfilment prioritization | Volumetric and value E2E reconciliation & simulations<br>Mid term financial risk & opportunities | Financials risks & opportunities<br>CAGR, long term operating profits |
| | S&OP meeting (sign off authorization) | Experts | Managers | Senior Management |

**Fig. 1.2** Planning types versus S&OP process dimensions

Observations about planning types and S&OP process step were visualized in Fig. 1.2. As we can see on above figure, activities across all planning types can be mapped against same S&OP process dimensions, but they have different objective, focus, and stakeholders. We are bringing up mapping of activities across all planning processes to illustrate that they have similarities. Those similarities should be leveraged when putting all of planning types into one coherent business management and planning environment called Integrated Business Planning.

## 1.2 How to Operate Integrated Business Planning

### 1.2.1 Design and Operate IBP in Holistic Way, Extend S&OP

**Integrate Design**

Different planning types are often not integrated therefore companies have big challenges to:

- Operationalize their strategies
- Connect strategic, tactical, and operational planning with execution
- Anticipate and/or react on changes in performance or business environment
- Understand business risk and opportunities
- Allocate and leverage right investments in processes, people, and technology to maximize company profit

To understand what IBP is and to address those pain points, we wanted to share some hints about integrated design enabling connection to what drives and enables successful IBP transformation.

The word which makes a difference in the term Integrated Business Planning is "Integrated." In this chapter, we will define key dimensions of integrated design (see Fig. 1.3).

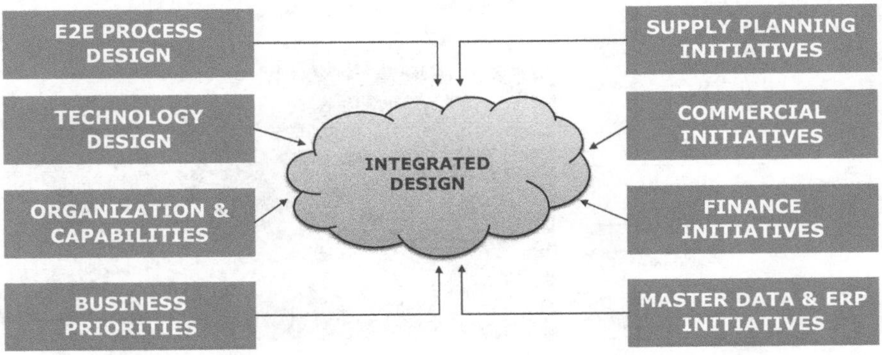


**Fig. 1.3** Integrated design for IBP

What makes integration so important and challenging is that all above dimensions coexist and cofunction like in living ecosystem. Connecting them, finding right trade-offs is what makes a difference and impact to your business performance and to expand competitive advantage to your business in the digital era.

**Business Priorities** Knowing your pain points and inefficiencies is of indisputable value for the organization which want to do something with it. We have faced misinterpretation of pain caused by organizational unit pushing for change. One example was a company that wanted to improve supply planning but had the true pain point of lack of integration between functions, lack of sales engagement in S&OP process, and lack of transparency as regards financial information, resulting in huge variations and firefighting in supply. Some say knowing business priorities is like knowing your enemy; if you know them, you have a chance to make a successful change.

**Organizational Design and Integration** We can define organizational design and integration as:

- Organizational structures
- Roles and responsibilities
- Competencies and skills
- Capability to influence and change way of working to enable integration between processes and to remove walls and obstacles, which are needed to make IBP happen on local (market), production site, regional, and global level for strategic, tactical, and operational planning

There are two major organizational integration flows:

- Horizontal integration between S&OP process steps and operational and strategic planning process steps
- Vertical integration across organizational levels

Here are some hints to consider in organizational design:

- Define global organizational structure which ensures country, regional, and global levels are connected by reporting lines and positions.
- Introduce differentiated seniority and differentiated competencies to ensure connection between strategic, tactical, and operational processes on various levels (country, site, region, global).
- Embed differently focused demand planning and demand management to ensure certain competency are in place to execute tasks with various functions like product, sales, marketing, finance, supply, IT, and management.
- Embed finance role across all S&OP process dimensions with clear background in controlling and not accounting.
- Connect demand planning, demand management, and finance with respect to the integrated process steps to help the whole organization to analyze and recommend what to do and how to connect risks and opportunities in product, demand, supply, and finance.
- Build and extend existing capabilities to shift from supply chain-driven volumetric process to cope with financial elements as integral part of IBP process framework.

Under organizational integration, we should understand as well:

- Change management
- Change governance implications on transformation

When driving change, you will need to find out what responsibilities/authority transformation "project" and "line" organization should have. Does configuration where "line" organization owns change and results, but "project" organization owns design and enables transformation, sounds logical to you?

You should define governance and accountability in the transformation program which will reflect the interests/goals of both "project" and "line" organizations. You may think to look at it from the early beginning of the transformation journey.

Take it as friendly hint based on many "gray hair" experiences and invest appropriate amount of efforts into "people factor."

We have paraphrased a quote from Steve Jobs and came up with

**DESIGN IS NOT A WORD DOCUMENT OR POWER POINT BUT THE WAY PROCESS, ORGANIZATION, SYSTEM OPERATES IN BUSINESS**

Which makes a lot of sense to many of our customers. We bring this up to connect it to organizational design and lines of responsibilities; e.g., the organizational unit co-responsible for design (normally part of "project" organization) should be at least co-responsible for how it works in business (with "line" organization) and maybe co-accountable for business case delivery (see Fig. 1.4).

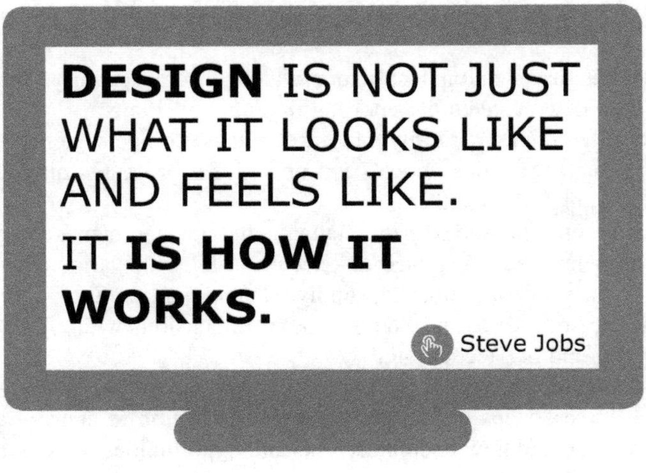


**Fig. 1.4** Design is not how it looks but how it works in business

**E2E Process Design and Integration** Can be understood as:

- Set of activities to achieve expected and agreed IBP outcomes (e.g., unconstrained forecast and constrained plan in volume and value, "top-line" revenue, "bottom-line" profit, risk, and opportunities with verified assumptions on each level of the organization).
- IBP outputs which need to be leveraged in other adjacent processes (e.g., integrated business plan in value used in financial processes and system to project P&L)
- IBP inputs from adjacent processes (e.g., average sales price, shipments, invoices)
- Design principles (e.g., demand review meeting is about signing off realistic unconstrained (free from supply constraints) forecast for current and next year which need to be available globally on work day 5, or integrated business plan represents actuals in the past and constrained volume and value projection until end of current year plus one, with incorporated risk and opportunities available on work day 10)
- Globally aligned and synchronized calendar of activities across strategic, tactical, and operational planning processes (e.g., in tactical planning in week 2, integrated business plan has to be defined with input with recent updates from operational planning)
- Globally aligned and synchronized calendar of milestones of activities, e.g., consensus forecast being agreed by work day 5
- Understanding of how strategic process outputs will influence and connect in bidirectional way tactical processes
- Understanding of how tactical process outputs will influence and connect in bidirectional way operational planning processes
- Understanding how financial, commercial, supply, and demand processes will interact in order to generate integrated business plan
- Finally understanding how operational planning processes should be linked to execution processes

Enabling process integration in a large-scale company is not a trivial task, mainly due to fact that those companies do not have homogenous business models. What makes it hard to do is that one needs to find balance and trade-offs between flexibility expressed in process variants linked to different business models and process standardization/harmonization required to manage them on global level. Let us try to explain this problem further. Would you apply the same rules and same process step timelines to countries which are small in your revenue portfolio and which do not have sophisticated capabilities and skills in place versus the countries with big revenue, complex and demanding process, and sophisticated competencies? This is what we meant when we talked about balancing flexibility with standardization; this is when we think alignment on process milestone, design principles, and objectives are sufficient. A more tailored approach in process design is needed then. In highly heterogeneous conglomerates of business models, alignment on having key milestones in the process is crucial, but experience says that "one size does not fit all." Do not try to control everything; it does not make sense these days. Size, importance, maturity, and degree of integration of a specific business model in the whole operating model could make a difference in the definition of end-to-end process design, transformation, and implementation approach.

End-to-end IBP design should take care of touch points with adjacent processes. Let us bring few examples of those touch points and decisions which need to be reflected in IBP design principles.

- When and how to integrate sales prices for forecast valuation
- What currency exchange rates should be used
- When and how to integrate costs for profit calculations
- When supply systems in short horizon will deliver reliable optimized 3 months schedule
- When and how data should be bidirectionally exchanged with ERP system for detail supply scheduling and supply execution
- Does sales community need to update account plans or forecast in SAP IBP or CRM system
- Will integrated business plan be on "net" level
- What should be the source system of material master data attributes and how and when in the process they should be integrated
- What should be the source system of customer and commercial hierarchy master data attributes and how and when they should be integrated in the process
- What should be the source system for financial master data attributes and how they should be integrated

**Initiatives Integration** Could be understood as a set of activities leading to understating interactions required between IBP and finance, commercial, supply, master data, or even ERP initiatives. Connecting with other initiatives at least on design principles and integration principles is a minimum. In large organization knowing what "left" and "right" hand is doing is not that easy. Initiatives integration will help you to:

- Avoid duplication of work in process design
- Make integration between processes coherent
- Get understanding of complexity and importance of each other function input
- Define required inputs and align implementation timelines
- Sequence design and implementation plans
- Understand and address initially contradicting designs
- Understand cost and value realization impact potentially causes by lack of alignment between process areas and initiatives

**Technology Design and Integration** Today's business models are complex, data availability grows exponentially, and system landscapes are not homogenous anymore. The Integrated Business Planning platform should enable data and system integration. You should understand what you have and define what is needed already as part of preparation to transformation or initial phase of it. System integration may form even up to 30% of implementation costs.

Technology design and integration could be defined in two layers:

- In the first layer, you should understand technology landscape affecting Integrated Business Planning, define systems which need to be integrated and platforms on which they operate now and in the future, and understand improvement initiatives affecting systems to be integrated as part of IBP solution. This activity normally should happen before or in initial phase of the transformation program.
- In the second layer, you should be able to define data model and detail data integration requirements to support end-to-end process design. This activity normally happens in process design phase of the transformation program.

In some companies due to poor quality of data or very heterogeneous IT landscape, special project stream was formed to address not only master data but transactional data challenges. You may consider to position such stream as part of technology.

**Operate IBP in Holistic Manner**

Let us connect this to integrated design:

- Integrated design approach will help you to make IBP happening and navigate via inevitable changes in scope, focus, stakeholders, and business environment and address key pain points of disconnected planning.
- Integrated design helps to find out what Integrated Business Planning can mean for your company.

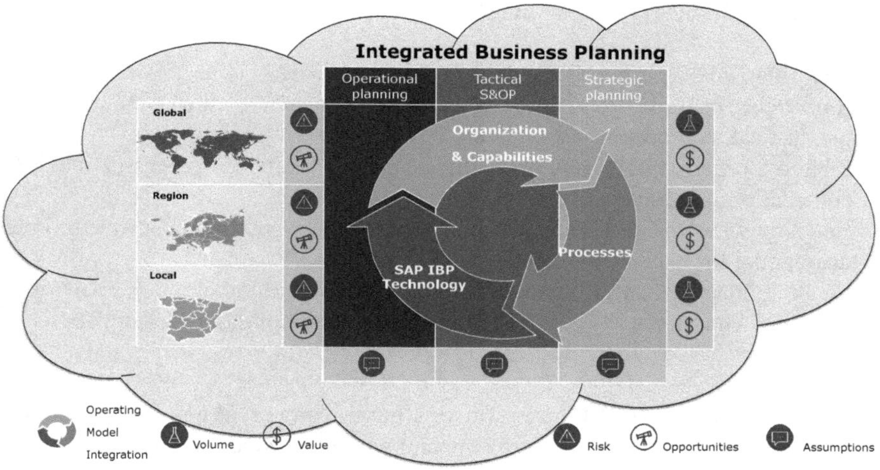


**Fig. 1.5** Holistic way to operate Integrated Business Planning enabled on SAP IBP

Figure 1.5 was made to illustrate that with Integrated Business Planning we connect:

- All planning process, e.g., strategic, tactical, and operational
- Volume and value inputs
- Risk and opportunities described by assumptions
- All levels from local market and production and distribution plants to regional and global level
- All dimensions of operating model (process, people, technology)

Connecting strategic, tactical, and operational process will **improve your business**.

Connecting volume with value will **make planning important**.

Connecting risk and opportunities in IBP will **make planning real**.

Connecting local, regional, and global level will make **IBP stakeholders as team**.

Connecting operating model dimension will help you **make IBP happen**.

**Extend S&OP**

S&OP operating without integration to other planning processes and without value-added extensions like financial integration or end-to-end "what-if" business risk and opportunity simulations could hinder possibility to achieve competitive position in dynamic, complex marketplace. More tailored products and more sophisticated services require higher adaptability and flexibility in planning processes, all based on richer sets of source data and larger number of source systems. Clear rationale behind maturing S&OP and extending it is to cope with market dynamics and constant changes.

Integrated Business Planning transformation can be understood as:

- Maturing and extending S&OP with IBP value drivers
- Embedding matured S&OP into IBP operating framework which connects strategic, tactical, and operational planning processes
- Enabling organizational and capability connection between processes into IBP coherent organization
- Enabling with SAP IBP technology integration of various data sources into one data model for discussed planning processes
- Enabling management of volume and financial information in one framework
- Enabling end-to-end "what-if" business risk and opportunity simulations in volume and value

Why do we highlight IBP transformation in this chapter? We wanted to explain that making your S&OP process more mature with new value drivers is a major but not the only element in IBP transformation.

For the purpose of this book, we wanted to characterize IBP as follows (this does not mean we want to challenge existing terminology):

**INTEGRATED BUSINESS PLANNING IS A BUSINESS MANAGEMENT PROCESS WHICH AIMS TO CONNECT STRATEGIC, TACTICAL, AND OPERATIONAL PLANNING ON LOCAL (MARKETS, SITES), REGIONAL (INCL. PRODUCTION SITES), AND GLOBAL LEVEL, TO ASSESS RISK AND OPPORTUNITIES, TO VERIFY ASSUMPTIONS, AND TO GENERATE WITH CROSS-FUNCTIONAL COLLABORATION A FEASIBLE INTEGRATED BUSINESS PLAN IN VOLUME AND VALUE.**

We see quite a confusion or freedom in interpretation of what Integrated Business Planning is, whether it is just a new term for S&OP, whether this is S&OP with financials, etc. As highlighted in the IBF article by Bowe, some of the above value drivers should have been accelerating well-established and mature S&OP process. Unfortunately, transformation projects often poorly address these. Also, there is no institution to define S&OP reference standards like SCOR/APICS (Bower 2012).

Let us keep Integrated Business Planning as term in the business and let us not throw it away; do not neglect the value it created for companies needing a second chance for their S&OP and especially for those who see that IBP can help them to connect strategic, tactical S&OP, and operational planning process on organizational and technology dimension.

Based on the discussions with our customers, prospects, and colleagues and on our own experience, we have listed key value drivers which should be considered when maturing your S&OP process to make it fit into IBP holistic business management process framework (see Fig. 1.6).

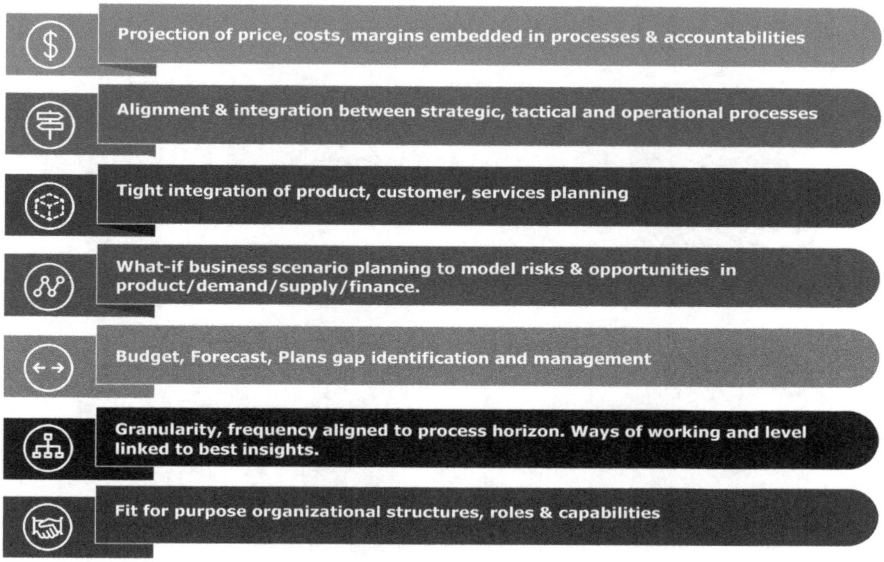


**Fig. 1.6** S&OP value drivers enabling step change into IBP framework. Revised based on (Palmatier and Crum 2013)

### 1.2.2 Build Capabilities to Integrate and CoE to Sustain Change

**Roles and Capabilities Which Integrate**

A fundamental part of IBP's success lies in building fit-for-purpose organizational structures and competencies. We see demand planner, demand manager, and finance controller as key roles to ensure process and organizational integration. Even though they need to focus on vertical and horizontal integration of strategic, tactical, and operational planning, integration of S&OP process steps stays essential (Fig. 1.7). Identified focus area implies stronger integration and better overlap of capabilities between those roles opposite to work in silo.

We see that those three roles cover whole spectrum of the process integration needed in IBP. Finding the right talent becomes a challenge then.

**IBP Center of Expertise Which Sustains Change**

Understanding how to sustain change in your organization should be on the top of your agenda. We are not saying how to reach a go-live but how to embed changes in the process and in people's behaviors. It is a topic which addresses the importance of company culture. The Integrated Business Planning Center of Expertise could make transformation adaptable to changing business environment and could take ownership to introduce and sustain change in processes, organizational structures, capabilities, and technology.

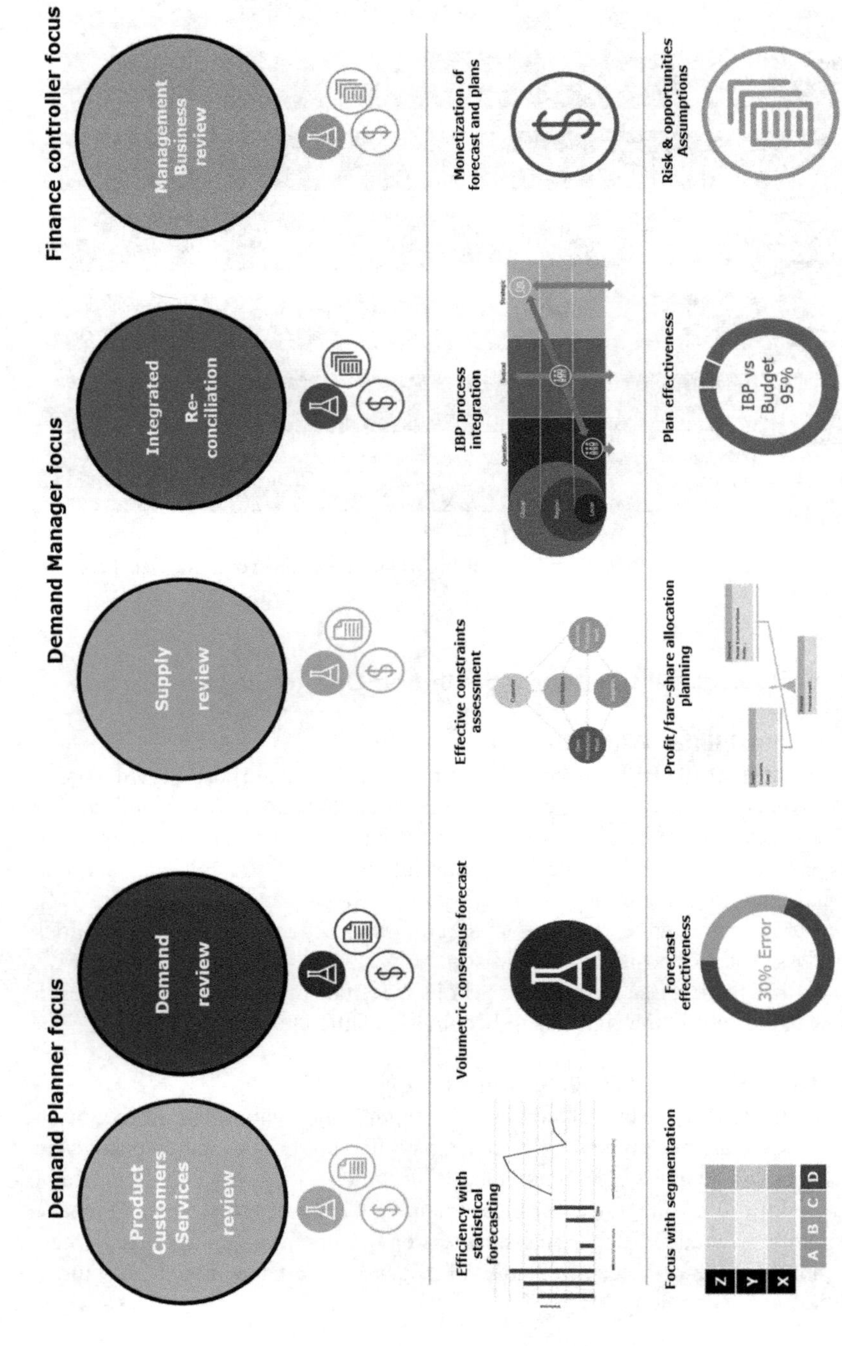


**Fig. 1.7** Demand planner, demand manager, and finance controller integration focus in IBP

It has been proven by many studies that ca. 70% of the transformation programs did not deliver what was intended. Many problems with the realization of these programs come from the failure associated with the lack of a change sustainability framework and the lack of leadership and/or management support. There are many reasons for this: some important ones are the resistance to change and the lack of proper management buy-in. Transformation is often treated as an extra task for "line" organization senior management, tasks which are often not being measured. This makes it easy for the responsible person to agree to anything but apply "my" ways of working. When driving change, personal connection becomes critical, and the same goes for sustainability of change in organization. You should know what is in it for you, right? That is what business line experts and leaders expect to understand. We should understand some common pitfalls that transformation programs fall into:

- Make a change which is not lived
- Implement change without influencing behaviors
- Neglect relationship between "project" and "line" organization
- Lack of focus on cross-functional process excellence
- Lack of focus on knowledge sharing
- Lack of focus on proper documentation

This is exactly what IBP CoE should focus on. Sustainability of transformation is mainly focused on people; therefore, the IBP Center of Expertise should focus its efforts on:

- Process improvement or lead transformation
- Transparency regarding project information and objectives
- Coordinating learning and development of various stakeholder groups
- Building education framework and knowledge sharing platform
- Continuous improvements by design
- Process governance
- Talent management

The IBP Center of Expertise should leverage cross-functional expertise from:

- Demand planning
- Finance
- Supply and operations
- Sales and marketing
- IT/system

Let us start from how to organize an Integrated Business Planning CoE. In most cases, there is a possibility to leverage existing excellence teams and form the IBP CoE as a "virtual" one but led and organized by an IBP champion.

The other approach could be to form the IBP CoE as an organizational unit which truly holds IBP transformation and improvements together on a global scale (Fig. 1.8).

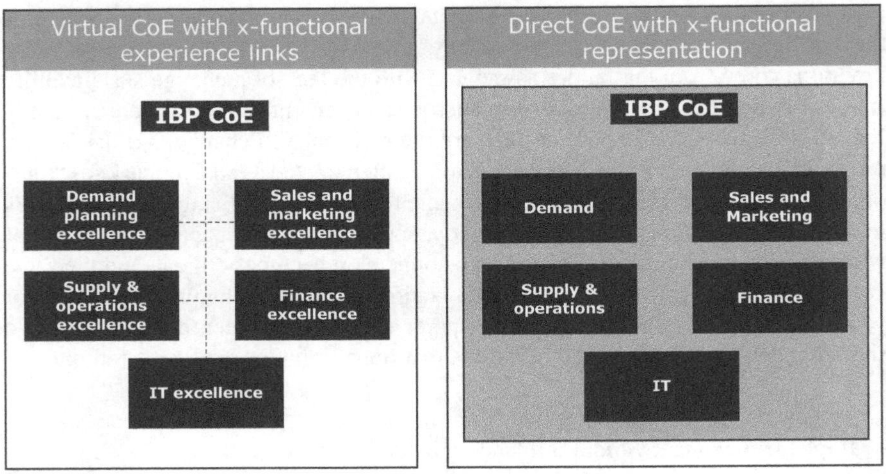


**Fig. 1.8** IBP Center of Expertise (excellence) virtual vs direct model

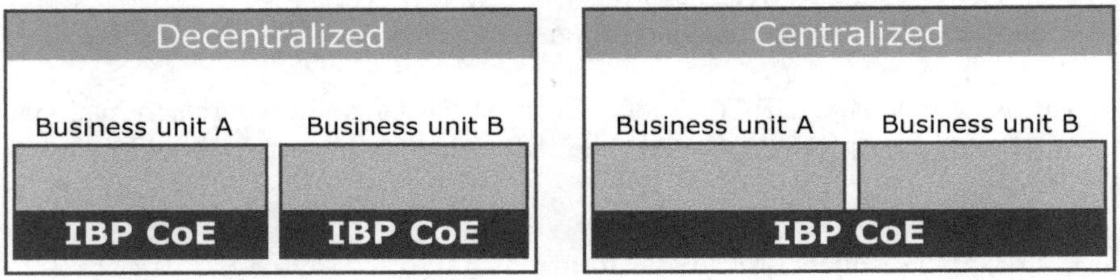


**Fig. 1.9** IBP CoE decentralized vs centralized model

Which one is the better approach? There is no single, universal answer. You need to decide what you want to achieve or what is really possible to be achieved with an IBP transformation program and then pick a model which matches those expectations. Running CoE as a soft virtual link between existing functionally focused expertise teams may work, but it all depends on the IBP champions and teams. In the other model, you are less dependent on the interactions between the experts managed by different functional managers and driven by different KPIs. In both models, the challenge of business operating model transformation stays the same.

You may think to adopt IBP CoE approach as (Fig. 1.9):

– Centralized, where IBP CoE will overarch business units
– Decentralized, where IBP Coe will be business unit specific

The centralized approach is good in homogenous, relatively small or less complex organizations. The decentralized model may be good in large, heterogeneous, and very distinctive business models operated under the same formal umbrella. If

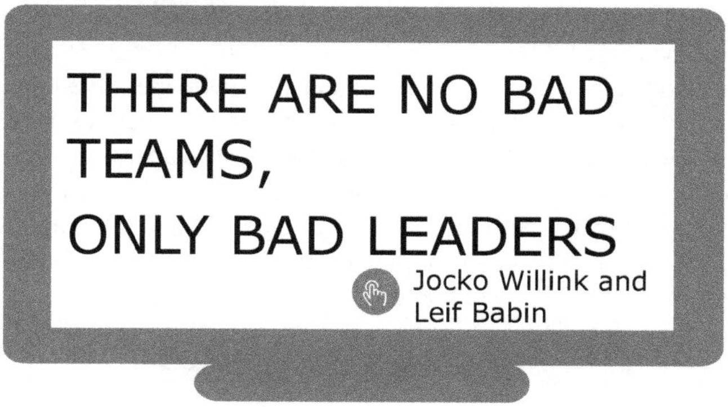


**Fig. 1.10** There are no bad teams only bad leaders

you go for decentralized model, you would invest time to find synergies between business units and take as much efforts as required to unify the IBP CoE.

Let us scratch the surface of the challenges linked to deployment of CoE concept. You should define and agree with your senior management what kind of responsibilities IBP CoE should have. What do we mean by that? There should be a clear split of responsibilities between the organizational unit which run the processes and the one which takes care of transformation and improvements. We see CoE as responsible for the design, understood as in Fig. 1.4. Design is not how it looks but how it works in business, yet departments who run specific parts of IBP should be accountable for the results.

As we have highlighted above, demand and forecasting excellence may be integrated virtually into IBP CoE but still should be understood as:

- Mix of people with high statistical skills (demand analytics) and people who work closely to market businesses (demand planners)
- Demand analytics as useful and meaningful input and KPIs to the demand planners, so that they can make the right adjustments
- Not to rely on gut feelings but on the right amount of competences mix
- Position demand champions to drive the journey to become demand driven (Chase 2016)

Finally there were many books written about leadership, but exposing its importance in few words takes a talent; see Fig. 1.10.

### 1.2.3 Build Holistic Transformation Road Map

A transformation project should start from the knowledge of the as-is situation. This is obvious, yet it is essential to make a step back and do it right. You need to assess your as-is maturity and the state of IBP from an organizational, capability, process, and system perspective. Framework explained here (is used by leading consulting company) helps you go through the steps leading to the development of road map and business case (Fig. 1.11).

The assessment can be done on both qualitative and quantitative inputs. Combining both normally leads to the most valuable insights. The assessment should be done against the following "dimensions": objective (business priorities), process, organization, performance management, and technology. These dimensions may have a different maturity, and therefore very often a differentiated approach should be followed. Selected dimension or part of the process may have different gap; therefore, approach to bridge gap could be different; see Fig. 1.12.

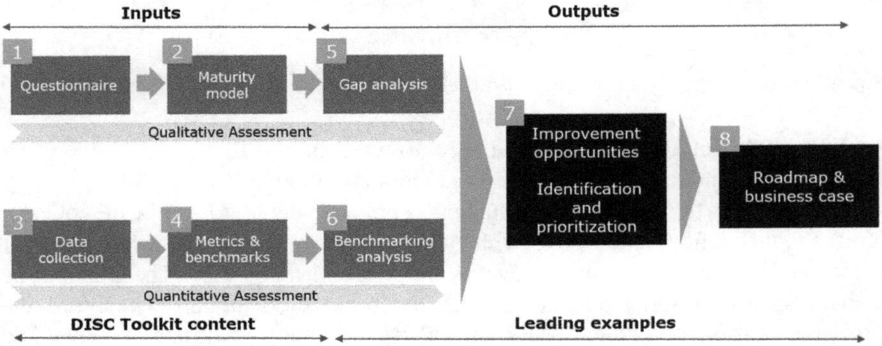


**Fig. 1.11** Key elements of Deloitte integrated supply chain assessment framework

| Criteria | Current state | Gap between current state and target state | | | | Target state |
|---|---|---|---|---|---|---|
| | | Lagging | Developing | Performing | Leading | |
| Forecasting Primary data input | Currently invoice data netted with return is being used. | ○ | | ● | | Total historical orders classified by deviation from customer expectation will be used as primary data input<br>Data for base line will be separated for risk & opportunities |
| Forecasting Organization | Demand planning roles & responsibilities are mixed supply planning, lack of demand planning excellence, lack of demand planning champion | ○ | | | ● | Organizational structures, positioning, roles and responsibilities will be aligned globally<br>Demand planning excellence led by experienced forecasting champion will be embedded in Integrated Business Planning center of expertise. |
| Forecasting Capabilities | Lack of statistical forecasting capabilities and data processing & management for PoS signal | ○ | | ● | | Build statistical forecasting in house capabilities supported in interim stage with external service. Not required to build PoS data processing skills. |

○ Current State ● Target State

**Fig. 1.12** Gap analysis—current vs target state examples

The assessment should be done against the following "dimensions": objective, process, organization, performance management, and technology. These dimensions may have a different maturity, and therefore, very often a differentiated approach should be followed (Amber and Debashis 2015).

The completeness of the maturity assessment is vital. You should assess and prepare output in selected maturity assessment approach. Check in particular if your organization structure fits the purpose, if capabilities are allocated in the right places, if the processes are robust, and if the technology can be put in the hands of users and key users. Ultimate outcome of assessment is identification of opportunities, prioritization, business case, and high-level deployment plan.

Keeping above in mind, we can emerge into Integrated Business Planning. We start with a detailed view on SAP IBP technology overview, and then we proceed to strategic, tactical S&OP, and operational planning processes explained with SAP IBP use cases.

# Enable IBP with SAP Integrated Business Planning 2

## 2.1 SAP IBP Applications Overview

**SAP Integrated Business Planning** is a real-time supply chain planning solution purpose built to profitably meet future demand by optimizing the supply chain. Built natively on SAP HANA and deployed in cloud, SAP IBP provides the flexibility, agility, and performance to meet complex planning requirements of the next-generation supply chain. SAP IBP is used by many customers in strategic, tactical, and operational planning on a unified integrated data model supporting sales and operation planning, demand planning, inventory optimization, response and supply, and control tower. Together with robust planning algorithms, real-time simulations, what-if analysis, dashboards and analytics, alerts, embedded social collaboration, and data integration with external sources, SAP IBP is the state of the art planning solution.

Each of the applications brings specific value to support business process, to make them more efficient and effective. There are not interfaces between the applications they all work on same HANA database.

In Fig. 2.1 you will find short description of each application and an overview.

SAP IBP is a cloud system and comes with integration capabilities. You may integrate data and system to design and implement comprehensive planning framework. Sources of information may vary from flat files to many applications providing data needed in Integrated Business Planning process. Data is being integrated into HANA database where all configuration and rules are being defined. Key users and end users interact with the system through various user interfaces. Main user interface is MS Excel with special IBP plug-in. Users can leverage Web UI analytics. Process collaboration is facilitated with SAP JAM; this instrument which is embedded in SAP IBP helps users to connect, make decisions, and interact. Key users may be granted with access to configuration of functional rules, e.g., ABC/XYZ segmentation, demand prioritization enabled with SAP Fiori technology. We have seen very often that key users in special Web UI apps configure



R. Kepczynski et al., *Implementing Integrated Business Planning*, Management for Professionals, https://doi.org/10.1007/978-3-319-90095-7_2

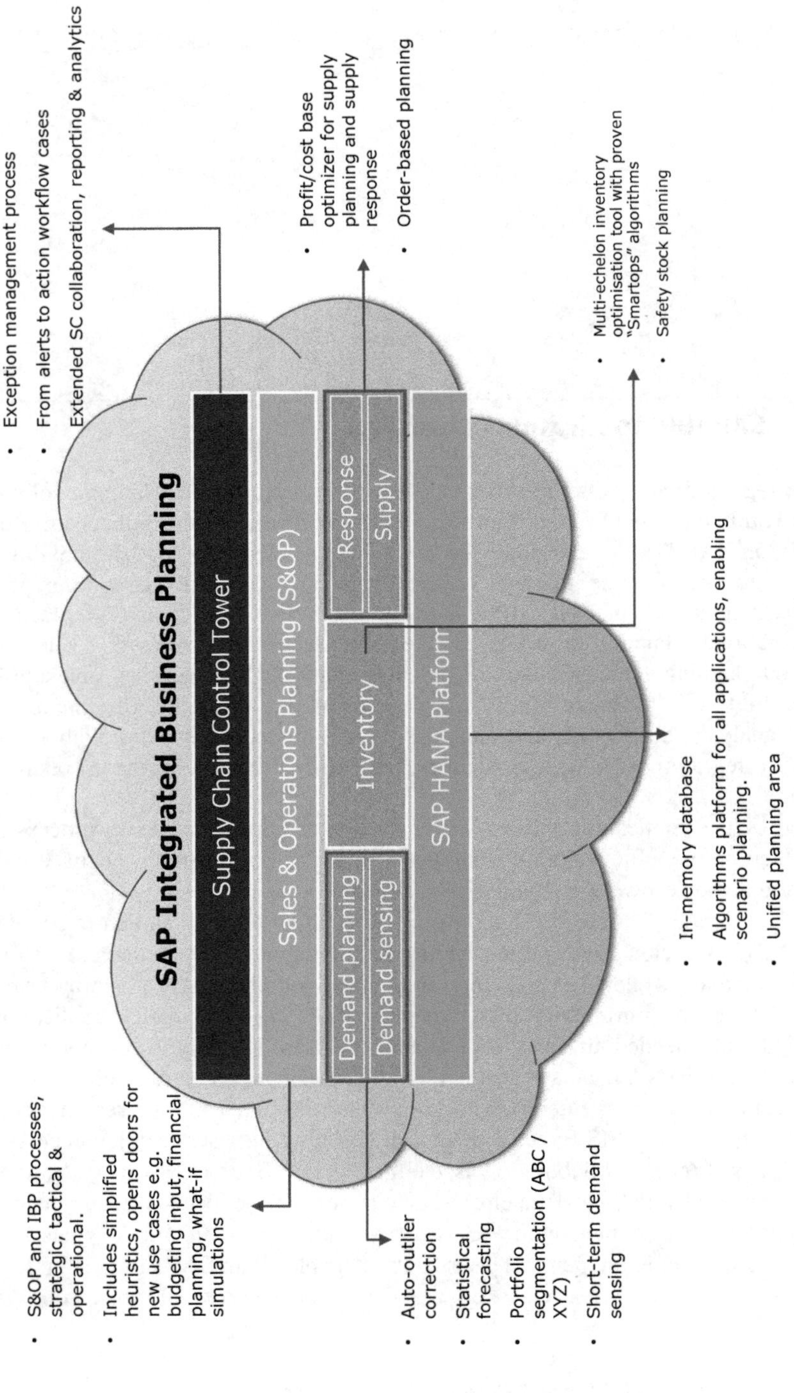


**Fig. 2.1** SAP IBP applications overview

functionality and it brings tool closer to business. At the end user, interfaces are fit for purpose. See Fig. 2.2 for visualization of the SAP IBP.

## 2.2 Model Processes

### 2.2.1 Balance Global Process Framework and Local Variants

We want to start deep dive into SAP IBP from process modeling. Small and big companies struggle to find the right balance between process harmonization and flexibility. What we have seen works best is certain framework in place which covers organizational structures and competencies, common process milestones and outputs, and same robust technology.

To orchestrate a business process across multiple cross-functional units, a well-coordinated SAP IBP process management capability can be leveraged. In Fig. 2.3 you can see an example of high-level process steps in S&OP process.

How companies face the problem of process standardization and harmonization? Let us bring well-recognized company. Unilever has built a central standard framework for demand planning process, composed of baseline generation by demand management, cross-functional forecast enrichment, and consensus approach. They have recognized the need to introduce light process variance across markets. Unilever predicts that within 10 years, demand in emerging markets will exceed the one in developed ones, which exposes challenges in demand planning if not addresses early enough. They wanted to adapt to each country's particularities in terms of market size/maturity and of local employees skills, consider which measure impacts demand shaping activities. Hybrid approach was introduced where some process framework elements did exist like high-level forecasting process flow based on statistical forecasting with cross-functional inputs and a consensual demand plan built after a "forecast alignment meeting" but still decentralized bit tailored way (Blosch and Uskert 2011).

What makes S&OP different is implementation. Implementing globally S&OP has many nuances, and a truly understanding and commitment toward S&OP is needed, and naïve thinking about reproducing globally what has been achieved locally must be avoided. Global S&OP cannot be mandated but only fully understood. S&OP process may be implemented globally, regionally, and locally. Coordination and integration among the levels is guaranteed monthly by management business review meetings and key interaction between stakeholders (Palmatier and Crum 2003).

With those two examples in mind, let us understand how we can leverage SAP IBP functionality.

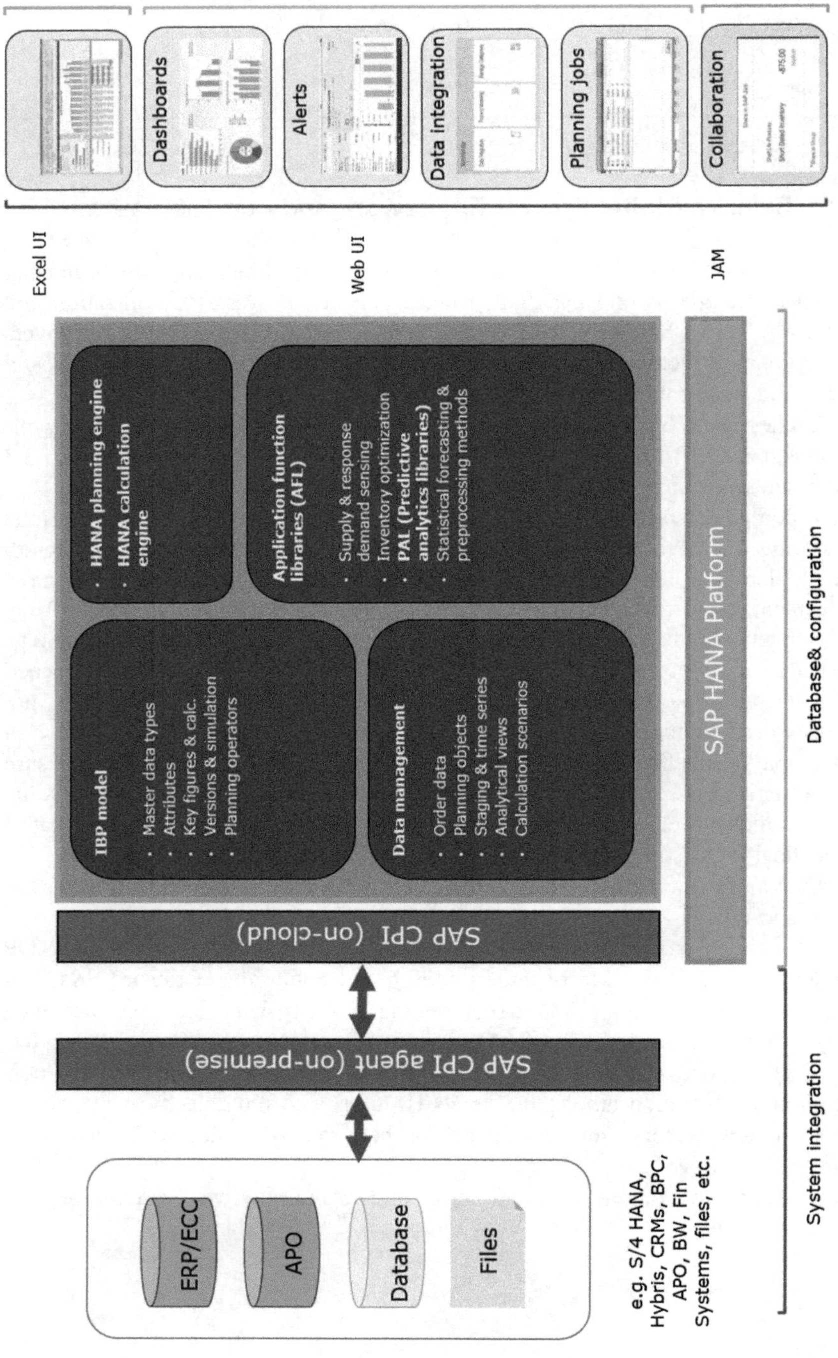


**Fig. 2.2** SAP IBP—from data integration to user interfaces

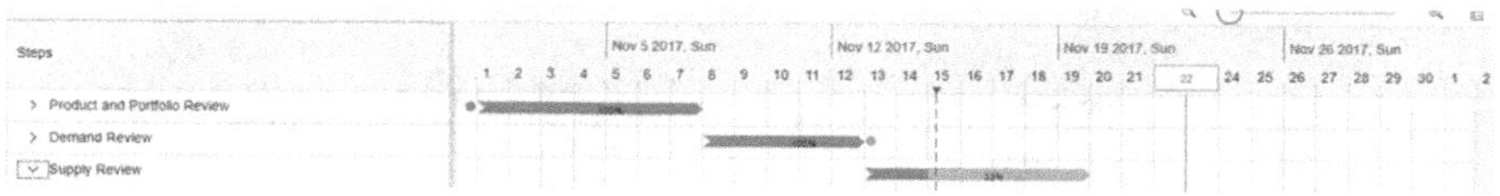

**Fig. 2.3** SAP IBP—S&OP process chevrons

### 2.2.2 Visualize and Monitor Process

In the global process templates, we should define the following process characteristics:

- Agreed IBP process steps.
- Milestones and durations for the process steps.
- Global process owners who monitor progress and adherence to milestones.
- Global agenda which can be modified locally/regionally in every cycle. Maybe even regional agenda should be developed.
- Global tasks which can be modified locally/regionally.
- Expected results of the meeting, e.g., documented assumptions, need to be stored in collaboration platform and visible globally.

Once the process template is defined, we can release it on regularly basis to create, e.g., monthly instances. It will allow you to monitor and visualize every S&OP cycle on every level. You can use IBP dashboard for that. Process charts can be created for each process instance and added to the IBP dashboard to view and to track the progress of each process. The dashboard can show one or more active IBP processes at the same time to view at a global level all the regional or business units' specific processes. Figure 2.4 shows the important aspects of the process monitoring and visualization.

Associated with the process dashboard are as follows:

1. Tasks app where tasks for the logged in user can be viewed and completed from Web UI as well in Excel UI
2. Collaboration in JAM where collaborative groups, feeds, decisions, and documents can be maintained

The process instance displayed in the IBP dashboard shows at a glance all the process steps and their associated start/end dates, status, and progress percentage. Associated with each step is the monitoring of which users are participating in the process step, what tasks have been assigned to whom, and which users have completed the tasks and who are behind. Process instances can be supplemented with planning-related charts together in a dashboard; see Fig. 2.5. Process steps in S&OP and tasks are visible in one dashboard.

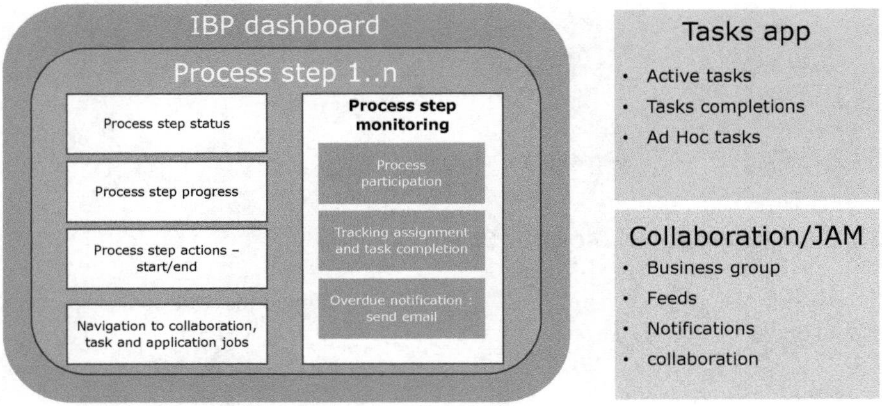


**Fig. 2.4** IBP process on the dashboard—concept

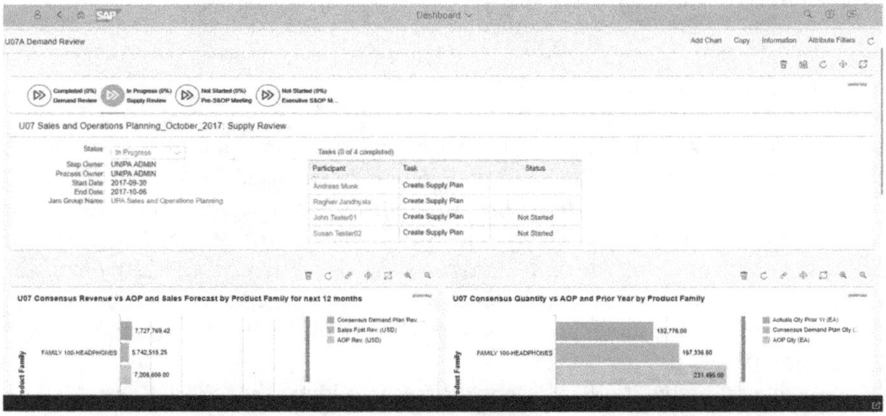


**Fig. 2.5** Process instance on SOP dashboard

**Process Step Status** The process step has status not started/in progress or completed (see Fig. 2.6). The step can be set to in progress or completion manually or through process automation. Process automation is triggered by rules you define.

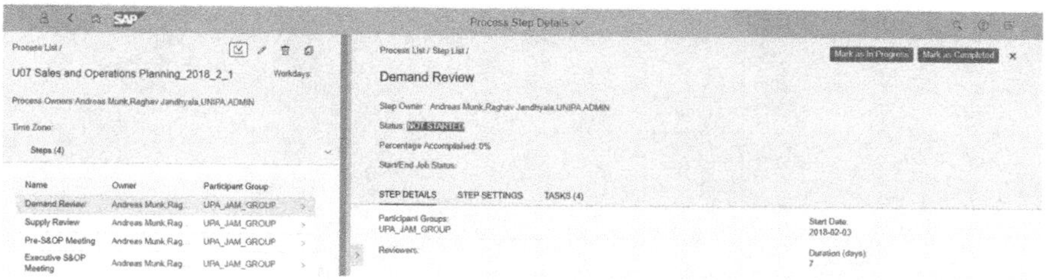


**Fig. 2.6** Process step status

**Process Step Actions** When the process step is set to in progress, there are two actions that can happen:

1. Users that are part of the process step's group who are assigned to a task first get invited to the collaboration JAM group if they are already not part of the JAM group.
2. JAM tasks get generated automatically to all the users who are assigned to work on task in the process step definition.

Users get email notification that tasks have been assigned to them when the process step is started. These tasks are visible in the tasks Fiori apps and Excel UI (see Fig. 2.7) or in JAM group task. Tasks as defined in JAM group on Web UI are visible to users where they normally execute their meaning in Excel UI of SAP IBP.

If there are any application jobs that are associated with the start or end of the process step, these get triggered as well. User can navigate from the process step to the application job that was triggered as part of the process step status change (see Fig. 2.8).

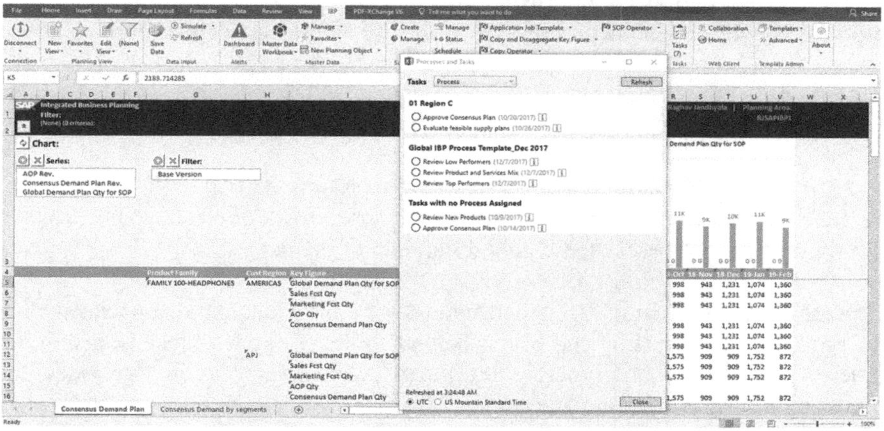


**Fig. 2.7** Tasks completion in Excel

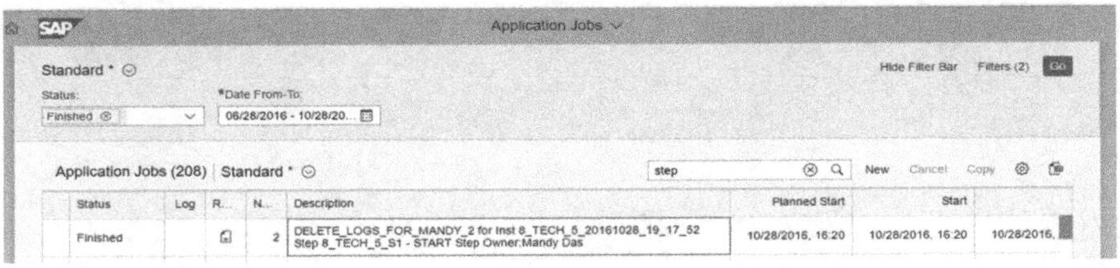

**Fig. 2.8** Application jobs linked to process steps

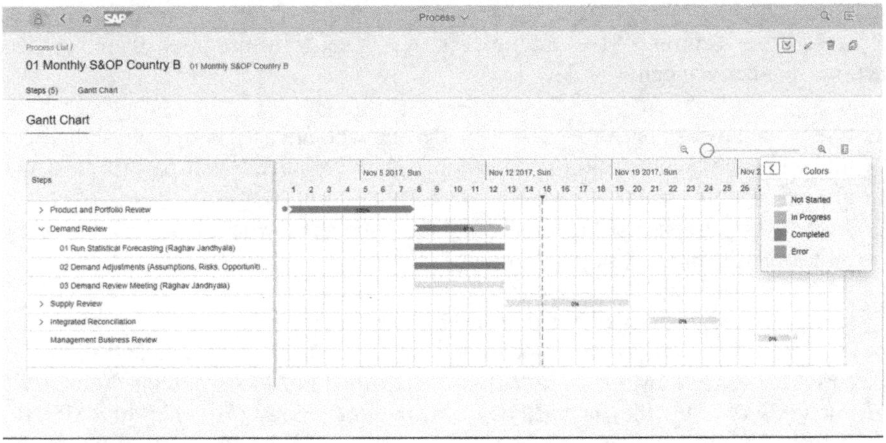

**Fig. 2.9** Progress of process step

**Process Step Progress** When a step is started, it will have a starting progress of 0%, and tasks are dispatched to the participants. As users complete the tasks, the progress on the process step keeps increasing until it reaches 100% completion. The step progress is indicated in the progress bar (Fig. 2.9) on the Gantt chart representation.

**Navigations** From process step, user can navigate to other application areas which include:

1. JAM collaboration group associated with the process step
2. Tasks application area to view and complete open tasks or create ad hoc tasks
3. Application jobs associated with the start/end of the process step

**Process Step Monitoring** To understand how the individual tasks associated with the process are progressing and who is behind on the tasks and to take an action for timely completion of the process, the process step monitoring area provides the necessary information to the process step owners.

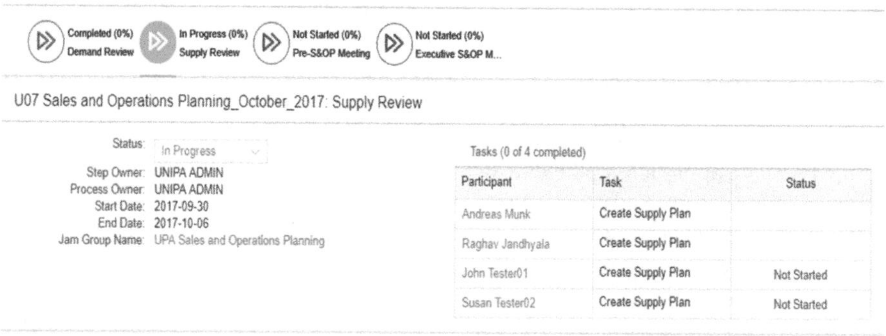


**Fig. 2.10** Process step owners

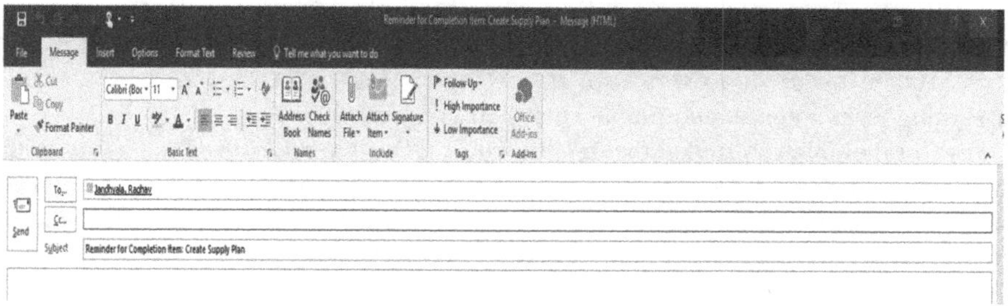


**Fig. 2.11** Email notifications

As shown in Fig. 2.10, the step monitor lists the participants and the tasks assignment, status of the individual JAM tasks, and overall completion status of the tasks. If there are any process step status exceptions, for example, step start date occurred and prior step is not yet completed, it will display delayed status.

From the process monitoring area, the process step owner can take the necessary action to notify the participants who are behind on completion of the tasks. When the email link is selected for the participant, an email option opens with the default information to complete the tasks to which the process step owner can add additional information and send (Fig. 2.11).

**Notifications and Reminders**

For effective collaboration, process management in IBP provides functionality to send email notifications and reminders to the involved participants for the following cases:

1. Email notifications for tasks are sent from JAM to the participants when a process step is set to in progress.
2. If the user is not yet part of the JAM collaboration group, an email notification is sent to join the group.
3. Further, based on the JAM notification settings, participants get a reminder when the tasks are approaching the due date or when new tasks are created and assigned from JAM.
4. Process step owners can send reminder emails for participants that are due on tasks completion.

### 2.2.3 Manage Tasks

Tasks in IBP are actionable business activities that are assigned to process step participants. These are required to be completed for the process to move forward. In S&OP process with several cross-functional business groups and hundreds of users, it is vital to make sure every user is participating in an orchestrated process by assigning tasks to users and monitoring their completions.

Process templates provide the default list of tasks that are carried out along with their assignment in every step of the process. These tasks get initiated as JAM tasks when the process step is set to in progress. There are different responsibilities related to tasks based on the roles of the users in a process (Fig. 2.12).

**Process Owners/Step Owners**

| Actions | IBP application area |
|---|---|
| Define default set of tasks for a process step with assignments | Process template |
| Monitor tasks progress. | Process dashboard, Manage Process Fiori App |
| Easily identify which tasks are holding the process and notify the task owner for timely completion | Process step monitoring |
| Add ad-hoc tasks relevant for the planning cycle. | Tasks application |
| Re-assign tasks if the participant is unavailable or cannot complete on time. | JAM tasks |

**Fig. 2.12** Process owner actions

| Actions | IBP application area |
|---|---|
| View open tasks and their deadline | Tasks App / Excel -Add In / JAM |
| Complete tasks | Tasks App / Excel -Add In / JAM |
| Set reminders for tasks completions | JAM tasks |
| Add ad-hoc tasks | Tasks app |
| View previously completed tasks | JAM tasks |

**Fig. 2.13** Task owner actions

**Task Owners**
Task owners have the following options to work with (Fig. 2.13).

**IBP Tasks Application**
Tasks application in IBP provides an easy access for task owners to view and complete their open tasks. A navigation is provided to the JAM task (see Fig. 2.14) for the user to add further details to the tasks, start collaboration with others users, set up reminders, and adjust the tasks dates as required.

In the tasks app, user can choose to complete the task. If there are automation settings associated with the step, for example, end process step when tasks are completed, it is immediately invoked if the task being completed is the very last task in the process step.

In addition to viewing and completing tasks, the task app also provides the capability to add ad hoc tasks to a process step of a running process instance. This is applicable in cases where for a process cycle some additional tasks beyond the tasks that are defined in the template need to be completed.

These ad hoc tasks can then be assigned to one or more participants of the process step along with a due date. These ad hoc tasks can also be added to the overall process progress which means the progress for the process step also takes into consideration the completion of the ad hoc tasks.

**Tasks Management in Excel**
After the process templates have been defined for a process, say monthly IBP S&OP, a recurrence or instance of a process is run each month. In manage process Fiori app, the monthly processes can be instantiated for the defined process template. When a process with several process steps is in progress, tasks are automatically created and assigned to the respective participants of the task of the process steps. Typically, in IBP, the persons who are completing the tasks are planners who are mostly working

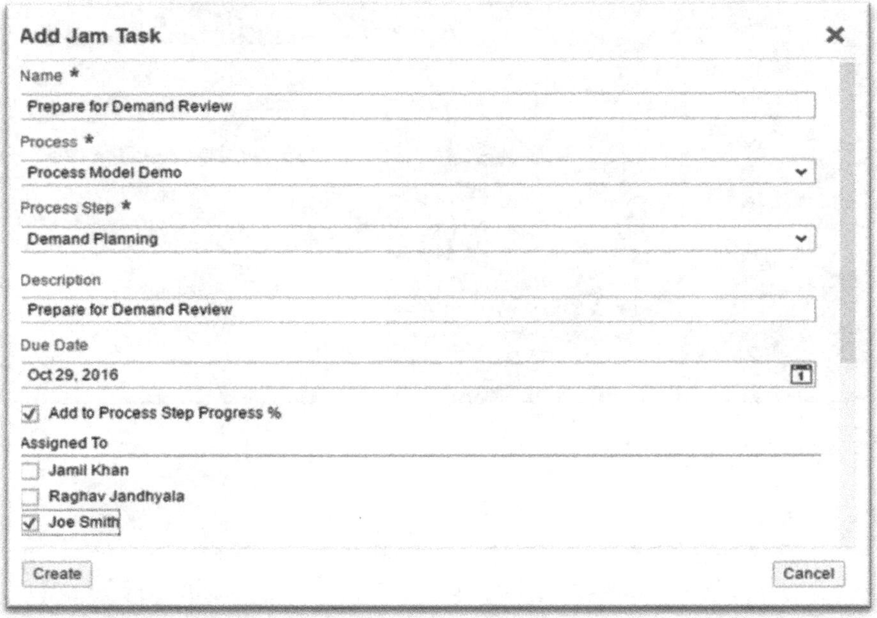


**Fig. 2.14** JAM task

on planning tasks in Excel. SAP IBP Excel add-in provided the tasks monitoring and completion collaboration, so planners do not need to jump between screens and view/complete all relevant activities in Excel.

SAP Excel add-in includes a tasks tab in the IBP ribbon. It provides a notification of all open tasks for the logged in user. Users can view their open tasks and filter by due date, priority, or process to which the tasks belong. These tasks can then be completed directly in Excel (Fig. 2.15).

Users can further view the status of the process to which the task belongs by clicking on the information icon (see Fig. 2.16).

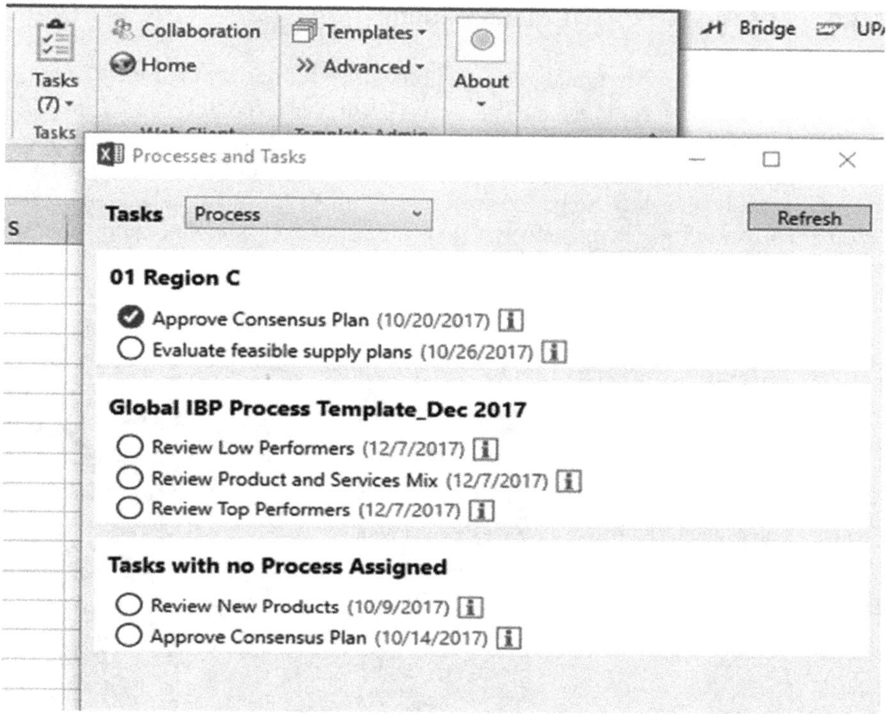


**Fig. 2.15** Tasks in Excel UI are there for user where action happens

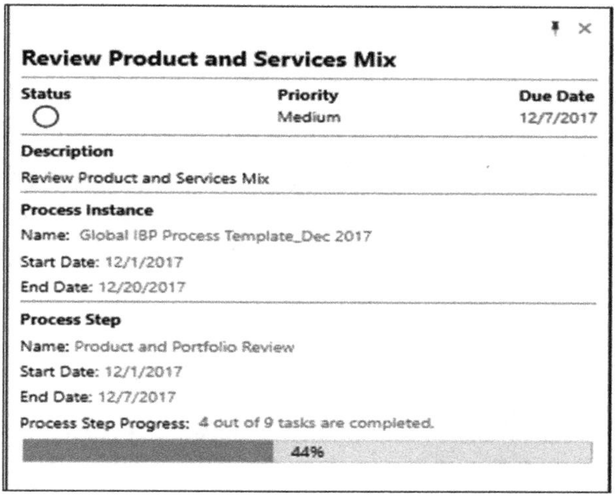


**Fig. 2.16** Task status helps planners to evaluate data on which they action upon

### 2.2.4 Automate Process Management

Most of the tactical/operational planning processes follow a monthly or weekly process cadence. For example, in IBP, you can define a monthly S&OP process template and instantiate a process instance for S&OP cycle each month. A process instance can have multiple process steps with different set of tasks and application jobs associated with each step. Therefore, it is important to have a harmonized automation of the process instances so that they start and complete automatically based on the criteria defined by the process owners (Fig. 2.17).

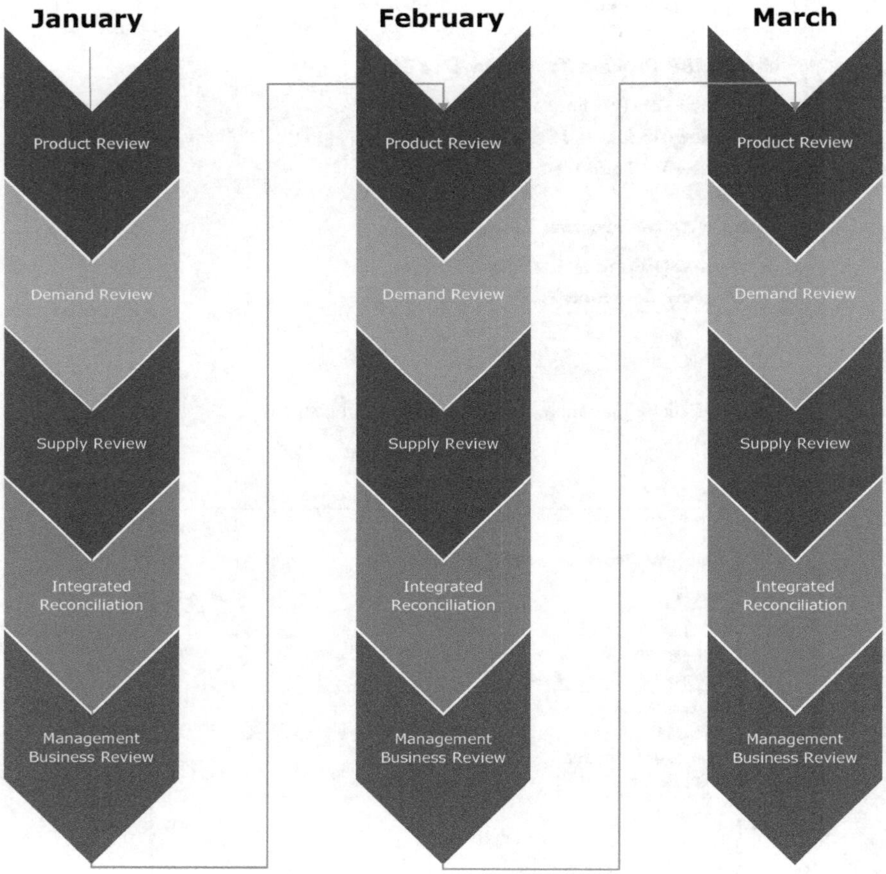


**Fig. 2.17** In country S&OP process automation

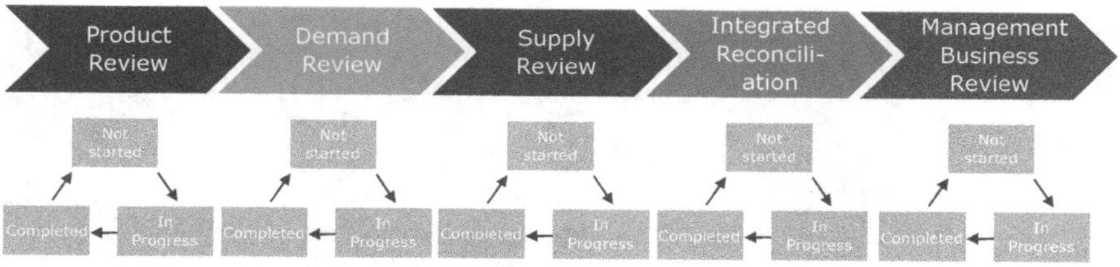


**Fig. 2.18** Multiple process step status

There can be several processes that are running together in parallel, based on the automation criteria defined for the processes. Take, for example, global IBP process, where processes can be slightly different for each country. Each country-specific process can be automated to run independently based on dates or other predefined criteria.

In SAP IBP, every process step in a process has the following status lifecycle: not started, in progress, and completed (see Fig. 2.18).

Process automation can be configured for each process step of a process template which defines how the step should start or end. Each process step has the following settings:

- Start and end dates
- Tasks [optional]
- Application job associated with start or end of the process step [optional]

**Automation Based on Dates**

Process execution could adhere to specific dates, e.g., integrated reconciliation should start on workday 12.

**Automation Based on Tasks Completion**

Steps can be automated to end when the tasks that were created within process steps are completed.

**Automation Based on Application Jobs Completion**

Steps can also be automated to execute when an application job associated with step start or step end is complete. For example, the end step can be reached only when application job associated with start step is completed; the next step can start only when application job associated with the previous end step is completed.

For example (Fig. 2.19), a step is set to start when the start date is reached and end when all tasks are completed. Further, application jobs, e.g., statistical forecast, is associated with step start, and copy consensus to final consensus is defined in end step.

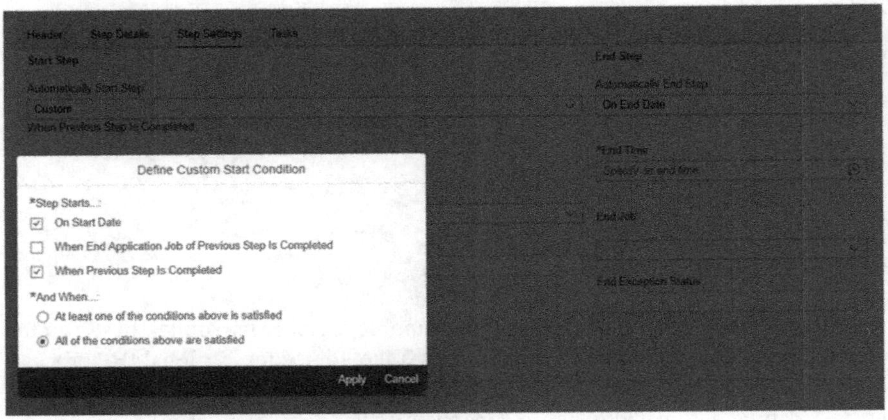


**Fig. 2.19** Process automation definition

## Step Start Automation Criteria

The steps can be automated to start based on the criteria defined by the process step owner. Steps can be started by start date only, by completion of previous step only, and by completion of previous step application job (see Fig. 2.20). They can further be set up based on any "and/or" combinations of the above criteria.

For example, in a monthly S&OP process which has the five process steps, product review, demand review, supply review, integrated reconciliation, and management business review, the start steps can be defined with different start step conditions (see Fig. 2.21).

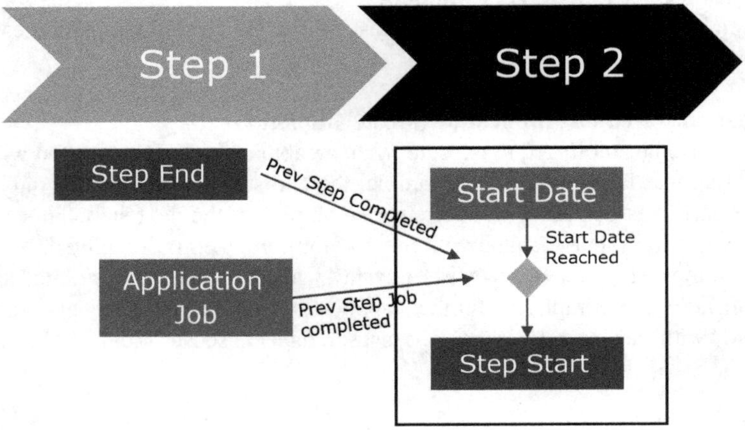


**Fig. 2.20** Start date—process step automation rules

| Process Step | Start Step Condition |
|---|---|
| **Product Review** | Start on 1st workday of every month |
| **Demand Review** | Start on 5th workday of every month **OR** when Product Review Step is completed. |
| **Supply Review** | Start on 10th workday of every month **AND** when application Job of Prior Step is completed. (e.g. at end of Demand Review Step – a Copy Operator will copy Demand plan as input to Supply Plan) |
| **Integrated Reconciliation** | Start on 12th workday of every month **AND** when prior step Supply Review is completed |
| **Management Business Review** | Start on 20th workday of every month. |

**Fig. 2.21** Start date conditions

### Step End Automation Criteria

The end step can be configured by the process step owner to end based on the following criteria: when end date has reached, when tasks associated with the start step are completed, and when application job associated with the start step is completed. Additionally, they can also be set up based on any "and/or" combinations of the above criteria, and still the step can be set to completion manually by the process step owner if needed (Fig. 2.22).

For example, in a five-step monthly S&OP process, the process automation for ending of the steps can be defined in the following ways (Fig. 2.23).

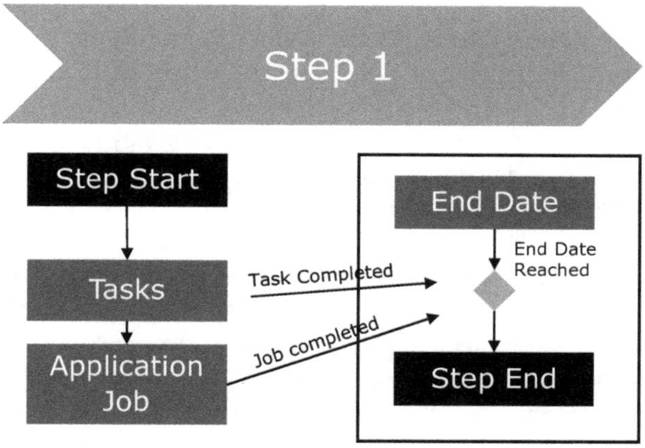


**Fig. 2.22** End date—process step automation rules

| **Process Step** | **End Step Condition** |
|---|---|
| **Product Review** | When Tasks are completed |
| **Demand Review** | End on 9th workday of every month **OR** when Tasks are completed |
| **Supply Review** | End on 16th workday of every month **AND** when Tasks are completed |
| **Integrated Reconciliation** | End on 18th workday of every month **OR** when Tasks are completed |
| **Management Business Review** | End on 20th workday of every month. |

**Fig. 2.23** End date conditions

### 2.2.5 Orchestrate Batch/Application Jobs

Integrated Business Planning brings together processes of different periodicities, frequency of execution, and planning actions which can be on demand like entering a forecast by planners or batch job oriented like running data load, running snapshots, and running statistical forecasts. All of it has to be put together into coherent process.

Batch jobs in IBP can be run in the following ways:

1. Run immediately or schedule from Excel add-in
2. Run immediately or schedule from Web UI application jobs
3. Run immediately when a certain process stage is reached

Typically, application jobs are scheduled to run based on dates and can be scheduled in the IBP application jobs Web UI. However, if the application job execution needs to be tied to a business process that can start or end based on completion of process steps and not just the dates, then they can be orchestrated as part of the process management capabilities.

Different countries may have different numbers of working days, and the application job execution should be based on these predefined process calendars. In such cases as well, the application jobs execution can be orchestrated as part of process execution.

The example below shows process orchestration of application jobs for weekly demand planning processes. Application jobs can be associated with the start or end of process steps and are orchestrated when the process step is started or completed based on the criteria defined by process step owner. For example, run statistical forecasting job can be automated when the previous step gathers and cleansed historic data is completed (Fig. 2.24).

Another such example is monthly S&OP process. The process steps can be automated based on dates, task completions, and application job completions. In the example below, the supply review step can be automated to start on the workday 7 and when the demand review step is completed.

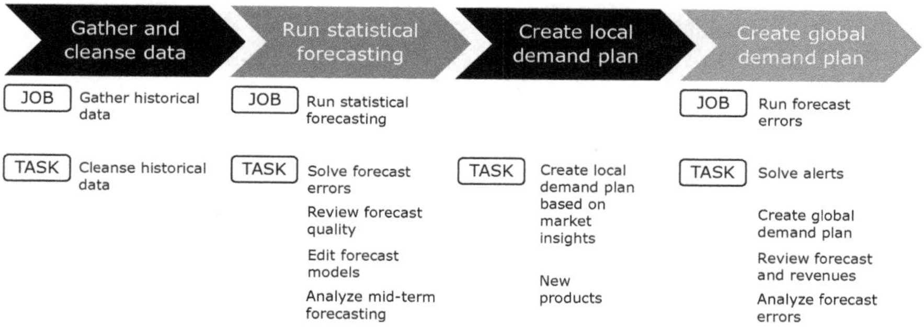


**Fig. 2.24** Process orchestration based on tasks/jobs

If the demand review step is not completed on time, the supply review step and the corresponding run supply operator job will not start until the demand review step is completed (Fig. 2.25).

Another example of such orchestration is IBP to Ariba supplier collaboration for forecast commit process (Fig. 2.26).

The buyer on IBP would run a supply plan and generate supplier forecast and send it to the supplier on Ariba Network. Supplier receives the forecast and commits to the forecast. Buyer receives the forecast commit and runs the supply plan to generate the feasible plan based on the new forecast commits (maybe be constrained). In all the above steps, the application jobs for supply planning and data sharing can be associated with the process steps, and upon completion of these application jobs, the steps progress automatically to complete a business process.

Figure 2.27 shows an example of process orchestration where, for demand review step, an application job template, statistical forecasting, is assigned to the start step.

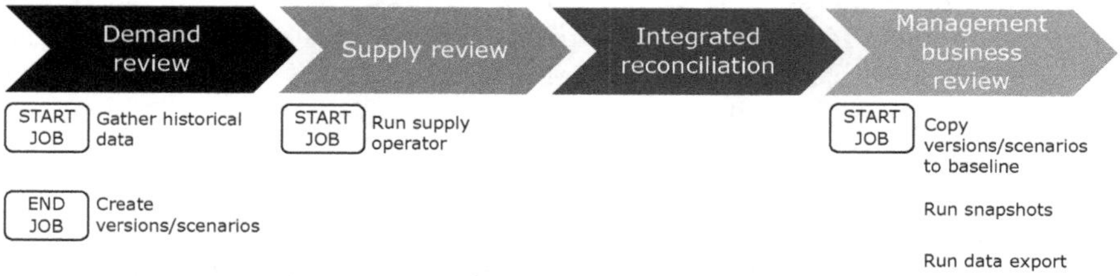


**Fig. 2.25** Process orchestration based on jobs/operators/steps

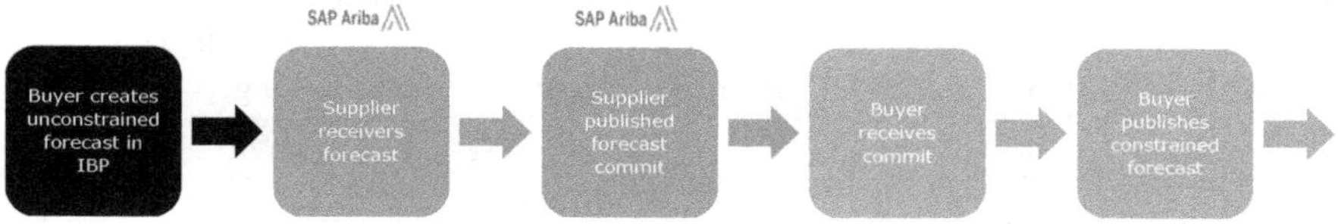


**Fig. 2.26** Cross systems process orchestration SAP IBP—SAP Ariba

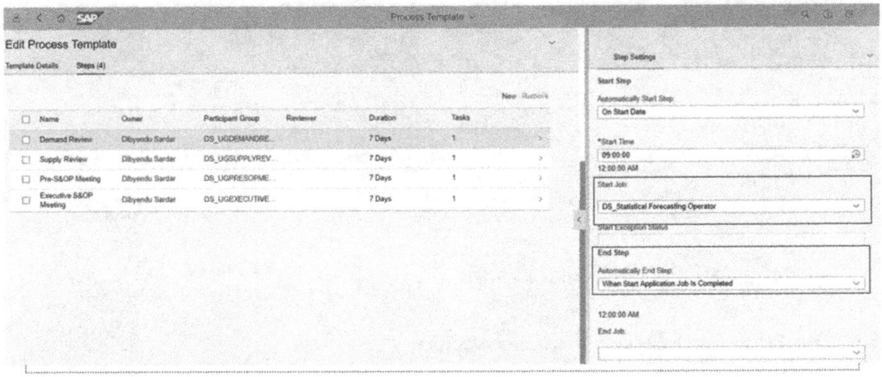

**Fig. 2.27** Process orchestration settings in SAP IBP based on jobs/operators/steps

The automation is defined for this step such that the step always starts on start date at 9am and ends when the associated application job is completed (see Fig. 2.27).

The above examples show how application jobs can be associated with process steps, and their execution is dependent on the completion status of a process step, unlike just the date-based criteria when executed from application jobs in Web UI and/or scheduled from IBP Excel add-in.

## 2.3 Facilitate Collaboration

### Collaboration in Integrated Business Planning

The three main pillars of an IBP process are people, process, and data and technology (Fig. 2.28). The people aspect of IBP drives the core of the planning process. Even when there are good processes and technologies in places, if the people involved are not organized in proper structures, have no adequate competencies, do not collaborate, and have no transparency and trust, this could lead the IBP process to be unsuccessful and could lead IBP to be operated in noneffective and non-efficient way.

### Why Collaboration Is Necessary in IBP?

IBP is a planning process which is cross-functional, cross business units, and lines of business with tens to hundreds of users driving toward one plan that profitably meets demand and supply, aligning with the strategic objectives of a company. Therefore, it is very important that all the stakeholders involved in this harmonized business process are engaged and make collaborative decisions based on transparency of information. Collaboration in the IBP process provides the following:

1. Collaboration across cross-functional teams
2. Recording decisions and actions
3. Documentation of storage and sharing

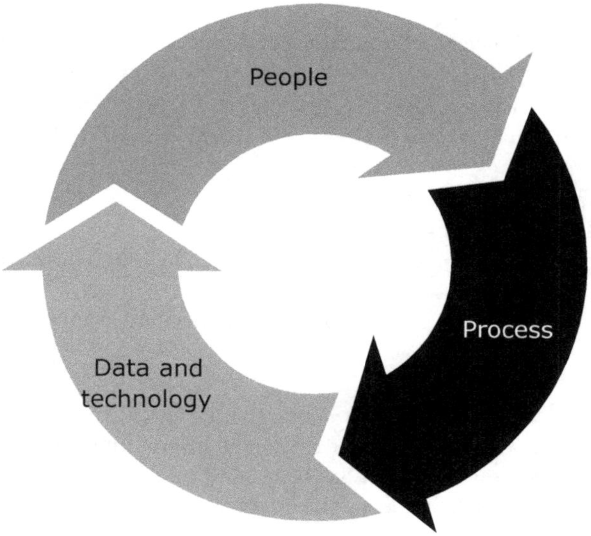


**Fig. 2.28** Coherent operating model

4. Collaborative decision-making
5. Better communication
6. Transparency of information
7. Easier user onboarding and higher user adoption

Nowadays social collaboration is part of everyday life with user-friendly, easy-to-adopt collaborative platforms like Facebook, Twitter, Messenger, etc.; the need for collaboration quickly moves also to the enterprise platform where collaboration and social media engagement is necessary for the business community.

Companies are measured by how they engage their internal communities and customers. Internally it is important to align cross different functional groups, on how the departmental plans achieve the strategic growth plans of the company. In a typical setup, the board and leadership team are responsible for defining the strategic direction of the company. These strategic goals are then translated to the strategic, tactical, and operational goals of the company. For example, company sets a goal for top-line revenue increase of 20% over the next 3 years. This translates to R&D goals of accelerating new product launches, sales targets of reaching new markets and customers/upselling, technology team goals of driving toward new solutions and to reduce infrastructure costs, etc. We observed very often that strategic, tactical, operational plans followed by execution are not transparent and that departments work in silos thereby hindering the overall growth of the company. The need for a well-established collaboration enabled via technology platform where people are engaged, objectives and information are transparent, and decisions are made jointly can significantly increase growth and improve cost management.

**Collaboration in SAP IBP**

SAP IBP provides the necessary functionality and tools for a collaborative planning process. SAP JAM is the social collaboration platform that is embedded and seamlessly integrated in the SAP IBP application. Collaboration in IBP is achieved by the following:

1. Embedded JAM collaboration
2. Process management integrated with JAM
3. Collaborative sharing of content: IBP Excel planning views, analytics, and scenarios
4. Case management for alerts in supply chain control tower application

**JAM Collaboration**

SAP JAM is an enterprise social collaboration platform that is heavily used for collaboration across various groups, to exchange information, share document, etc. This is a well-proven platform that has been used by several customers to connect internal and external stakeholders to exchange information and collaborate on important activities.

SAP JAM is a cloud-based enterprise collaboration with seamless connectivity on mobile devices providing structured collaborative tools like ranking, forums, tasks, etc. for collaborative decision-making.

SAP IBP uses SAP JAM providing JAM collaborative functionality directly embedded in IBP application. Single sign-on and direct navigation to JAM from IBP provide users the seamless collaboration across all areas of IBP application. In the IBP launchpad (Fig. 2.29), the collaboration Fiori app provides a direct navigation to JAM collaboration where the logged in user can see both the public and private collaboration groups that he/she is part of.

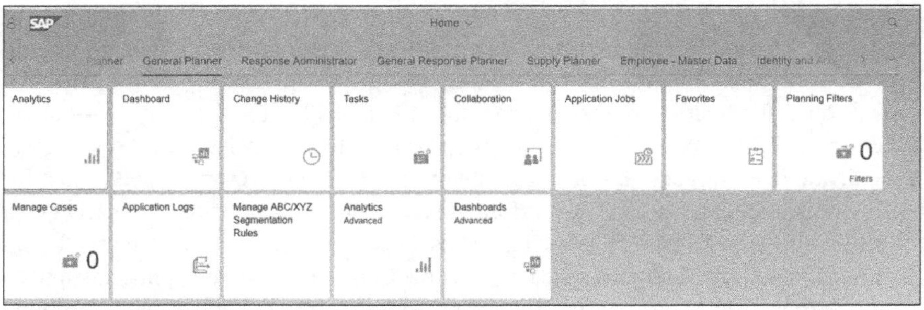


**Fig. 2.29** IBP launchpad with collaboration app

### 2.3.1 SAP Use Case: End-to-End Collaboration

Though there are several scenarios for collaboration in IBP, we start with a collaboration scenario in demand review step. Demand managers/planners identify a gap between the consensus forecast and annual operating plan (targets) and work with various stakeholders across sales, marketing, supply, and finance to close the gap to the target and present results for decision-making in the management business review meeting.

Let us put the following business process scenario to illustrate how you could leverage collaboration functionalities.

**1. Demand Review**

Demand manager and demand planner collaborate with sales, supply, and finance team to close the gaps to meet AOP targets. Monthly IBP process in USA is in progress for the May cycle and focuses on horizon until end of the current year plus up to 2 years ahead. To manage the collaboration across several stakeholders, a JAM group has been created, and the stakeholders have been invited to the group. Demand planner John identifies that the consensus forecast is far off from AOP targets set by the company. John uses SAP IBP and JAM to collaborate and evaluate options for the solution (Fig. 2.30).

In the demand review step of IBP process, huge gap between consensus demand plan revenue and annual operating plan is identified. John posted through JAM a feed providing visibility of the situation to other stakeholders involved in the planning process.

John up front has defined JAM group for demand review or S&OP review as a private group with specially invited participants (see Fig. 2.31). A JAM group

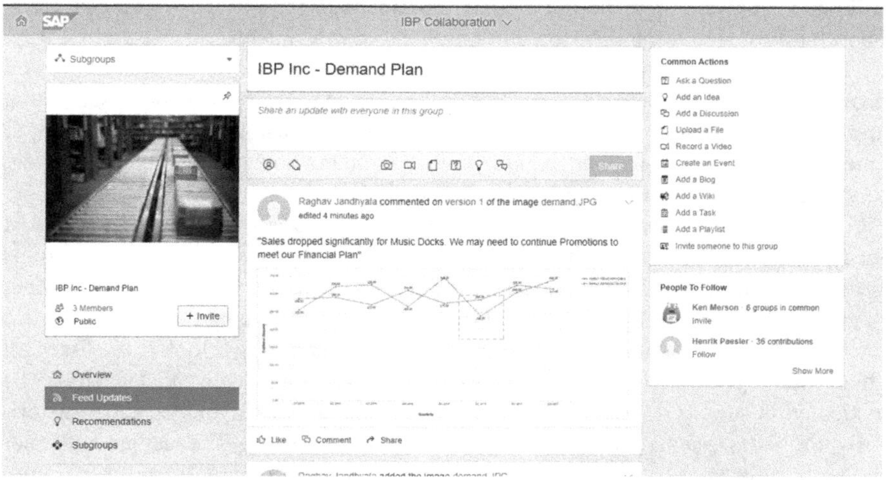


**Fig. 2.30** SAP JAM collaboration portal—demand review

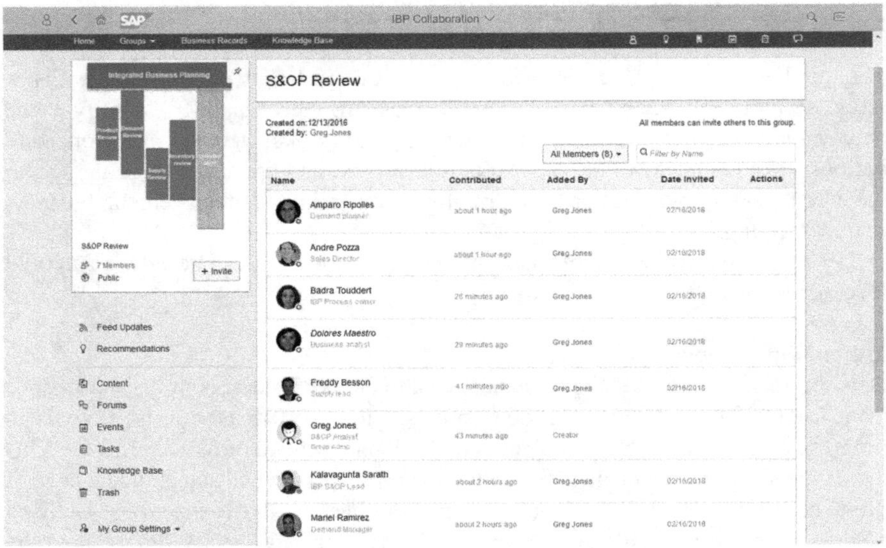


**Fig. 2.31** SAP JAM demand review group

organizes all the required collaboration activities among the involved users by sharing and broadcasting information.

After the feed is posted to the JAM group with the chart showing the gap, users get notified immediately. They can provide their feedback/comments on how to resolve the current issue. In this case Jeff from sales posted the note that there is an opportunity for large deal happening with a new retailer in Q2 that could be potentially incorporated into the demand plan. On first glance this could be a good solution to close a gap, but sales bias, commercial, supply, and financial risks/ opportunities need to be accounted before a decision is made.

The sales planner makes the quantitative adjustments to the sales forecast qty and provides qualitative notes and summary of the change in the reason codes dialog that appears when changes to the plan are saved. On the reason code dialog, the user enters the reasons for the change along with a comment and chooses the JAM group to whom this information needs to be shared (Fig. 2.32).

Upon saving the reason code and comments get available instantly in the JAM feed for the JAM group to which the feed has been posted. Users in the JAM groups get instantly notified about changes to the plan. They can see in the JAM feed when the change was made, by whom and the date/time for the change.

After the end of the sales input cycle, the demand planner can look at the list of all changes and can finally arrive at a new consensus demand plan that needs to be evaluated in supply review. Before doing so, demand planner analyzes that historically the sales planner has had bias in his sales numbers. The demand planner therefore adjusts the consensus plan by taking into consideration the sales input bias. New updates are then posted to the JAM feed and all stakeholders are informed.

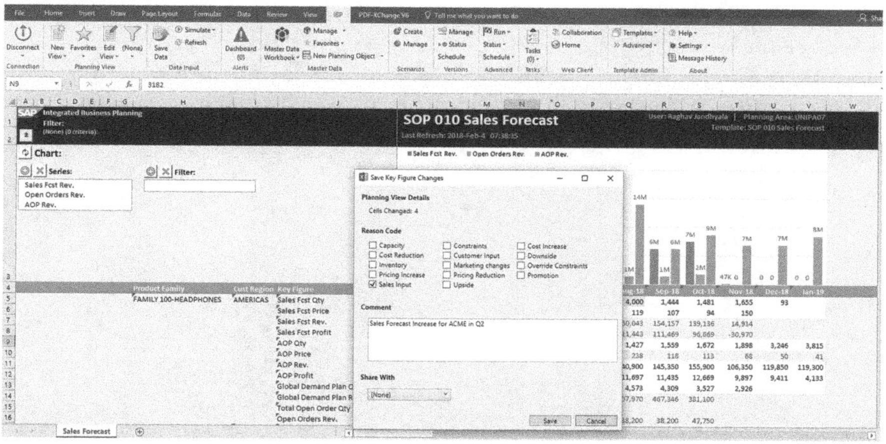


**Fig. 2.32** SAP JAM sharing changes and reason codes in sales input

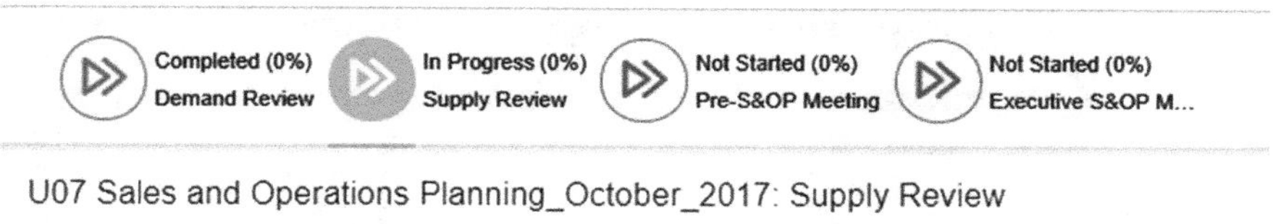


**Fig. 2.33** SAP JAM supply review

## 2. Transition to Supply Review

The IBP process management capability is tightly integrated with JAM. Each process step is associated with a JAM group, and tasks are associated, assigned as JAM tasks, for all participants for the tasks when the process step starts.

When demand planner completes the last task of arriving at agreed consensus demand plan, whether from completing the task in JAM or IBP tasks application, the process step then goes to completion, and the next process step gets started (Fig. 2.33). As a next step in the planning process is the supply review step, it gets started, and the associated tasks are assigned as JAM tasks for the supply review step participants.

## 3. Scenario Sharing

Demand manager with supply planner will further evaluate several plans and their supply impact without impacting the baseline. Demand manager creates a scenario called sales increase and shares it (Fig. 2.34).

In the supply review step, the demand plan input which is an unconstrained plan is checked for supply feasibility. Several constraints in the supply are considered like nondelivery costs to customer, customer sourcing, lead times, capacity, and material constraints to come up with a supply plan that is realistic and feasible. In the supply review with scenario planning, supply planner discusses with demand manager

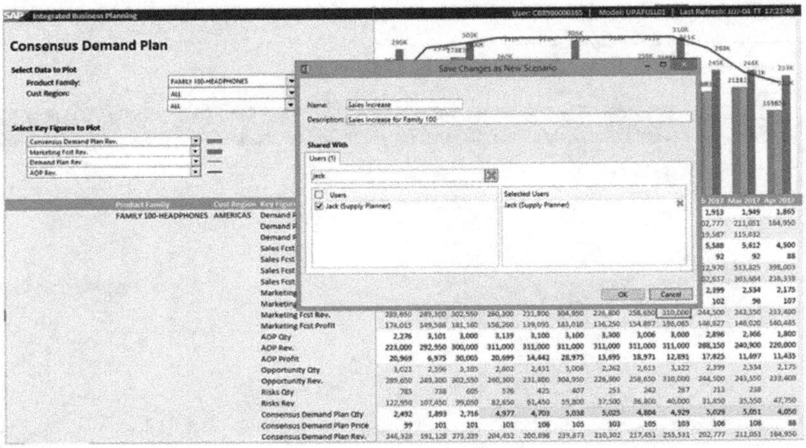


**Fig. 2.34** Collaboration in supply planning, create and share scenario

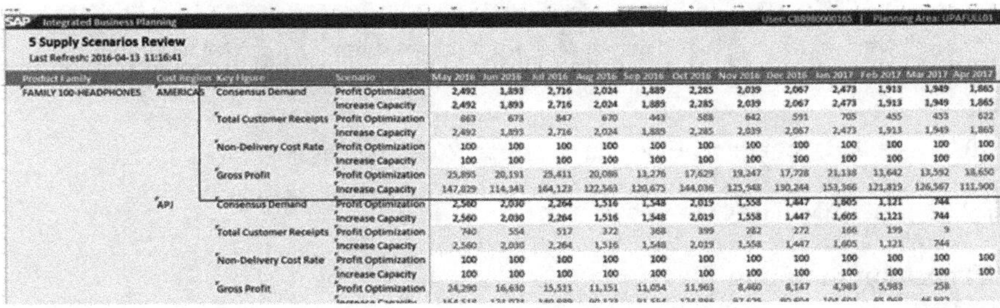


**Fig. 2.35** Collaboration in supply scenario planning

impact on the gross profit from increasing capacity vs pre-building (profit optimization); see Fig. 2.35.

It was agreed to evaluate holistically scenarios in integrated reconciliation process steps.

**4. Validating Options**

After the demand review and supply review steps are completed, the next process step is the integrated reconciliation where the demand, supply, and financial reconciliation happens. Stakeholder had an ambition to capture risk and opportunities and finalize proposal for management decision. Here JAM plays an important role in allowing of structured collaboration across the stakeholders by providing several decision-making tools like polls, decisions, pro/con table, ranking, and comparison table (Fig. 2.36).

As a preparation for the integrated reconciliation meeting, the supply options to meet the gap between AOP target and consensus demand plan are evaluated, and each participant can add to the pros/cons for the list of options. Finally, a ranking

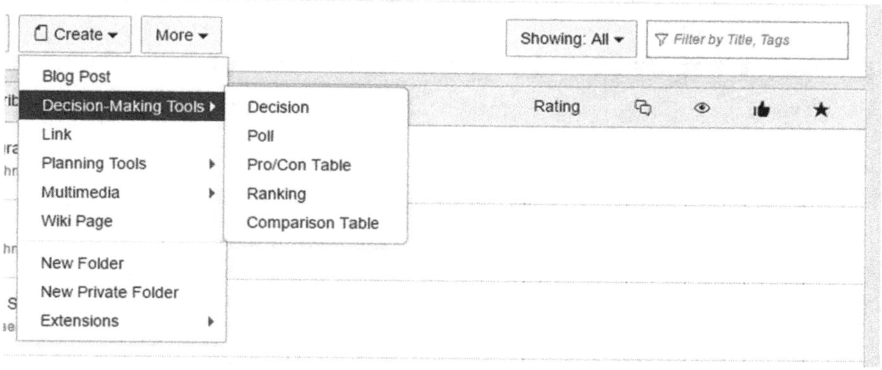


**Fig. 2.36** JAM decision-making collaboration tools

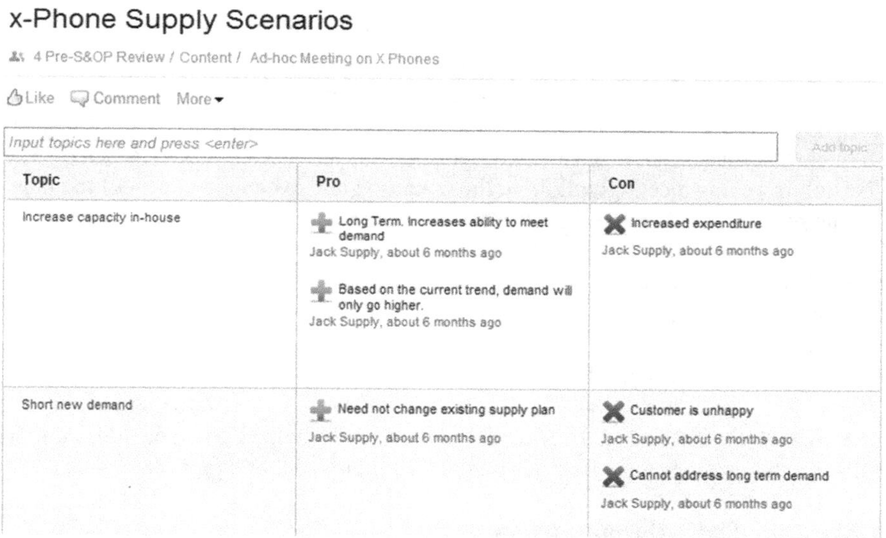


**Fig. 2.37** SAP JAM collaboration in pros and cons decision matrix

tool would allow participants to rank their options. These activities are then instantly available in the JAM feed which allows all stakeholders to get a clear understanding of how a decision was made, what factors were taken into consideration, and who were involved in the decision process thereby providing a transparency on the decision-making process (see Fig. 2.37).

**5. Management Review Meetings and Decisions**

The next step in the process is the management meeting. Using the JAM collaboration tool, the S&OP process coordinator sets up the meeting with an agenda and list of

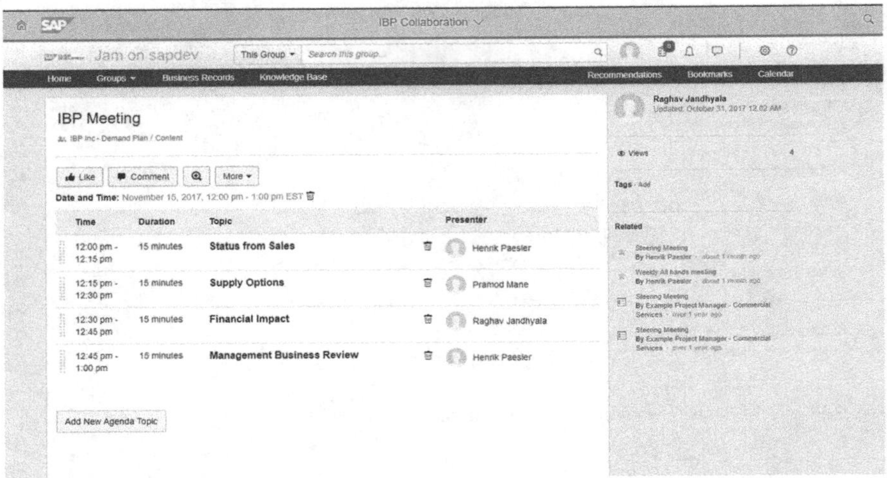


**Fig. 2.38** Agenda for management business review meeting (IBP meeting)

documents that need to be reviewed during the IBP meeting. In our scenario, the leadership team across all departments attends this meeting to decide on the final plan taking into consideration the risks, opportunities, and assumptions captured. The decision from this meeting will drive the operation and execution aspect of the plan.

The meeting has been set up with the following agenda:

- Review sales forecast
- Review supply options
- Assess financial impact
- Decision and approval of plans (see Fig. 2.38)

SAP IBP with embedded JAM collaboration tools helped to make decision in collaborative manner with full transparency of inputs and assumptions.

**6. Store and Share Documentation**

The final step in the process after the management business review is to capture all the decisions, actions, meeting notes, and documents. The decisions and documents from the IBP meetings for each of the planning cycles can be stored in the flexible folder structure that can be defined for the users to easily find and access information (see Fig. 2.39). Access can be controlled.

All the decision that were taken and the planning processes can be easily accessed from this section thereby increasing transparency and information communication.

After completion of the management business review (old S&OP meeting) step, the plan should be promoted from the simulative version/scenario to the baseline version and this plan taken as final (see Fig. 2.40).

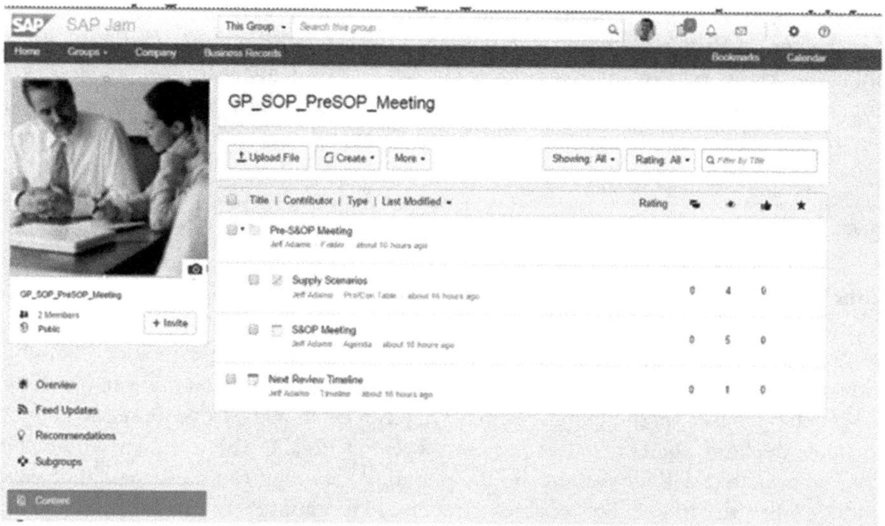


**Fig. 2.39** Store S&OP cycle documentation

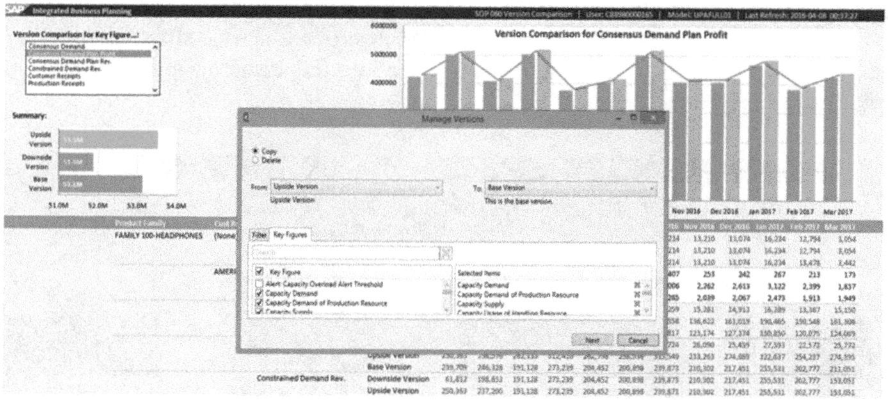


**Fig. 2.40** Promoting planning scenario/version into base line

SAP JAM provides a good collaboration platform for IBP. The multiple work groups, which can be dynamically created, allow for context-driven communication and conversation between members, share ideas, provide comments, respond to questions, and interact with other members right in the planning tool. With so much information that is tracked, it is also very important to find the information quickly. The content search feature in JAM provides a free-form search to instantly access any content. JAM augments the planning process with its rich set of tools to provide a qualitative input to otherwise quantitative-driven plans.

With any collaborative tools, the success of its adoption depends on the ease to use the tool, self-service with no trainings, seamless connectivity, and embedded collaboration as part of the planning tools. SAP IBP meets both the planning and collaboration done right from one place thereby increasing the user adoption and increasing collaboration across the team and company.

## 2.4 Share Content and Manage Cases

**Sharing Content in SAP IBP**

In addition to the embedded collaboration using JAM in IBP, several planning contents in IBP can be shared across users or user groups. These include planning views, scenarios, alerts, analytics, and dashboards. For example, a favorite planning view created based on planning view template can be shared by one demand planner to other demand planner and user group (see Fig. 2.41). The users to whom the content is shared will have access to the planning view and can view the data based on their visibility filters. This enables a better collaboration between users, where all the shared information is available in one system without having to download, email, and view offline copies of information that can become stale over time. Template planning view could have different level on which data is displayed, but planner can have different need to look on data for different products groups.

Custom alerts used in IBP supply chain control tower can be shared, providing instant access of alerts, and collaborate on exceptions that occur during planning (see Fig. 2.42).

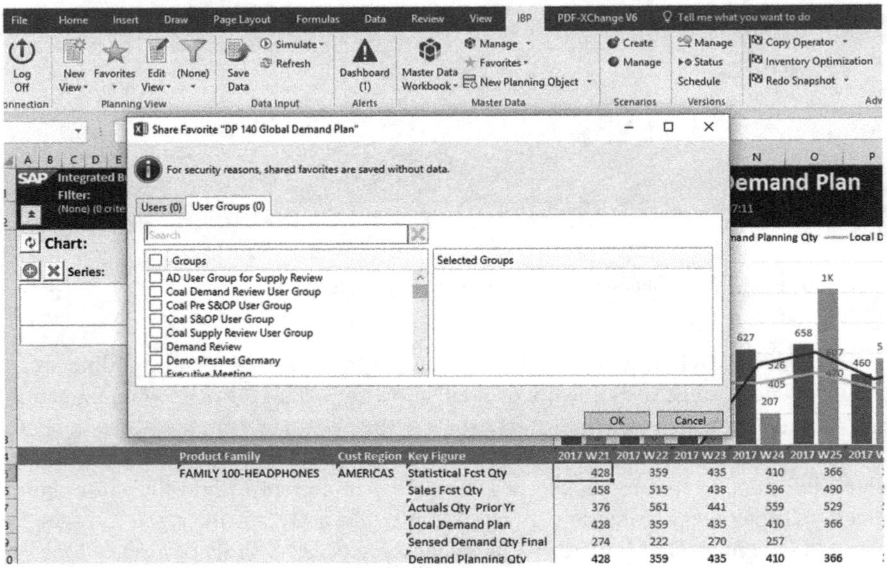


Fig. 2.41 Favorite planning view sharing

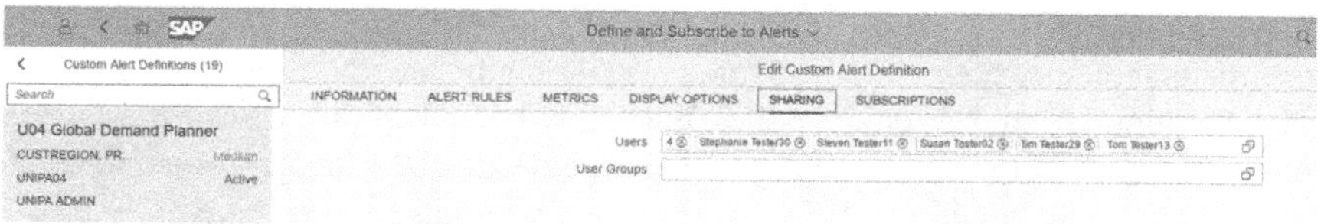


**Fig. 2.42** Sharing custom alerts

Further, dashboards and analytics can be shared as well. It is quite a common case that key business user or process owner creates default analytics and dashboards which can be shared with other stakeholders. The users who have access to the shared content can view the shared analytics/dashboards and save as a copy and modify to their individual preferences. A key user for demand planning could create charts helping in forecast analysis, forecast vs actuals, forecast errors by product family, etc. These can be shared within demand planners community. Dashboards and analytics further allow users to opt out of the shared content.

**Shared Content Management**

Amount of content which can be shared can grow heavily therefore; it is important to manage on a periodic basis the shared content. SAP IBP provides a Fiori app to maintain and manage the shared content. When an owner of the shared content leaves the organization, the shared content associated with that user can be granted ownership to a substitute user. Further content which is no longer active can be deleted and content like planning view favorites, analytics, dashboards, and alerts can be shared/unshared with users/user groups in the content administration app (see Fig. 2.43).

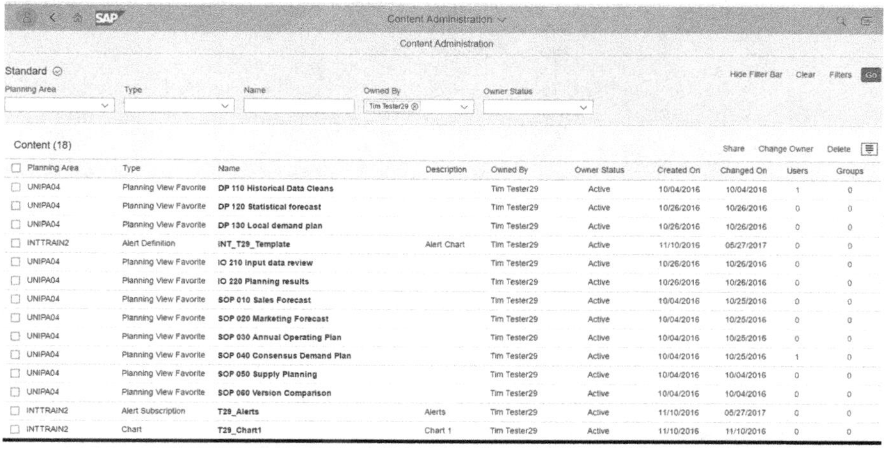


**Fig. 2.43** Shared content administration

**Case Management**

Case management which is part of supply chain control tower allows collaboration and resolution of supply chain issues that have been identified from the custom alerts. Case management app in SAP IBP encapsulates all the information relevant to solve issue and maintain a log of all actions that were taken to resolve an issue.

Users can track one or more alerts in a case, take snapshots of the data, add comments, and track changes to the case in case history. Cases have a lifecycle and status for users to focus on the most important ones (see Fig. 2.44). These cases can also be assigned to several users or user groups to collaborate and resolve the case.

Cases can also be shared to the JAM group to provide visibility on the cases that are being worked on. The link provided in the feed navigates directly to the relevant case (see Fig. 2.45).

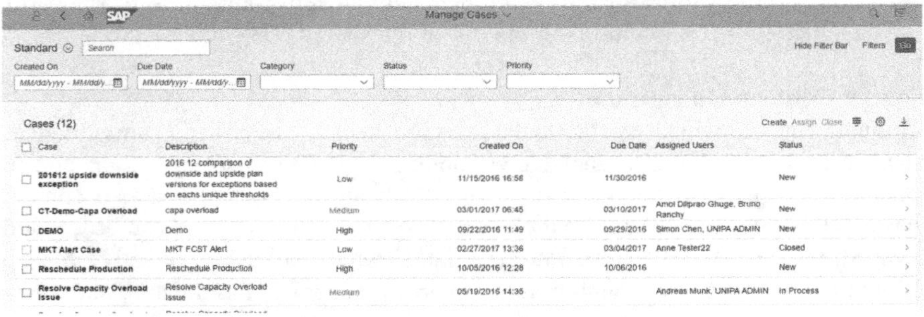


**Fig. 2.44** Case management overview list

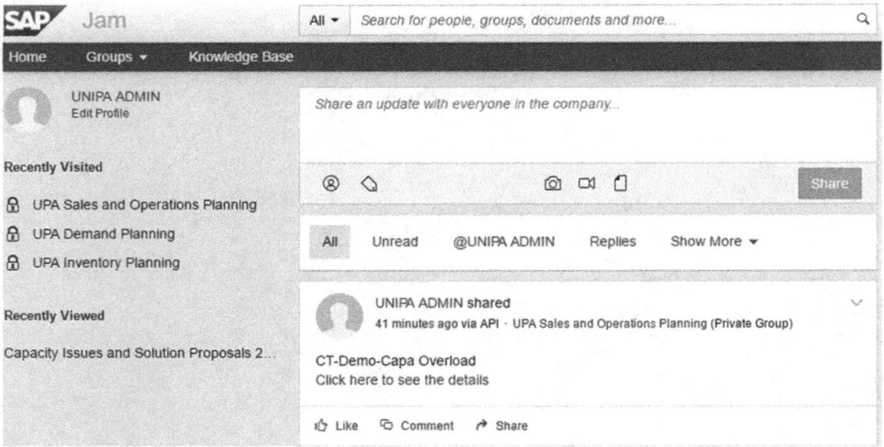


**Fig. 2.45** Case shared in JAM feed

## 2.5 Capture Assumptions, Review Change History

### 2.5.1 Assumptions

Many companies that have succeeded in their planning processes have realized that the plans are only as good based on the qualitative information that drives the quantitative numbers. Therefore, the assumptions that drive the change are as important to be captured as the changes to the numbers.

The numbers alone are not sufficient to be captured. The qualitative input that drives the numbers should be captured, and plan and their changes should be based on assumptions. Oliver Wight suggests using assumptions and only plan changes when there is a documented assumption behind the change.

Assumptions and the business drivers are unique to a company, and the different categories of assumptions vary by different industries. Common assumption categories include market conditions, growth assumptions, competition assumptions, performance assumptions, etc.

These assumptions are then associated with a certain planning hierarchy, for example, at a brand level or category/region level where they are more relevant. Assumptions can keep changing for each planning period, and therefore the planning numbers are also changed and tracked together with the changing assumptions.

**Link to Risks and Opportunities**

Risks and opportunities are important aspects of every review step in IBP. There are characters of risks and opportunities that need to be captured and evaluated in a planning tool, so that their effect is clear. Characteristics like probability and change drivers are qualitative information that needs to be tracked as part of the planning process. In a planning process, the risks and opportunities can be managed as separate key figures, scenarios that are considered in the overall business plan. The individual risk and opportunities can be modeled as an event, and different scenarios can be planned based on it. Often risks and opportunities are derived from the assumptions and changes to the assumptions. Those assumptions can be captured through the collaborative tools described earlier. Both risks and opportunities can be defined at different planning levels of hierarchy. As a result of the review meetings, values can be adjusted based on discussion and collaborative, transparent way of working with assumptions. These can be recorded in the JAM collaboration of IBP for documentation, traceability, and transparency.

**Why Track Changes Besides Audit?**

IBP is a collaborative planning process where plenty of users are engaged in providing inputs to the respective quantitative plans, at different levels of hierarchy based on some particular assumptions. A consolidation of all the changes (which could potentially be in hundreds to thousand changes for a planning cycle) and the reasons behind the changes, considering all the risks and opportunities, translate to a single plan that is agreed across the cross-functional units and vetted as the plan that needs to be executed.

Therefore, it is important that all users are making changes to the plan at the level they can and the changes made do not deviate their thresholds for changes. Those thresholds may be very relevant when working on aggregated level. The planning system should be able to track all the changes and provide a simple interface for planners to quickly analyze what changes are contributing to the highest impact and what are the reasons behind those changes. For example, in a sales forecasting process, the sales managers quickly need to analyze which sales representatives are contributing to the largest volume changes.

Other reasons are for audit purpose to understand which user made such changes and to track which users are not contributing toward the forecast.

**Reason Codes**

Reason codes in IBP can be defined to categorize the qualitative information for the plan changes. There are predefined reason codes in SAP IBP; however, you can choose to manage and maintain your own reason codes. These reason codes become available when there are changes made to forecasts and plans. For example, when user makes changes to consensus demand plan qty and saves, get a pop-up window to select the reason code along with commentary (see Fig. 2.46). This will give qualitative information and reason behind the changes to the plan. Similarly, when the user runs a planning operator in batch mode from Excel or maintains master data in Excel, the reason code dialog appears to capture the information behind the action that changes the data in the system.

The share with lists the JAM collaboration groups to which the user is associated. In the above case where a sales forecast is made, the following choices are made: reason code (sales input) and comment (projection of 150 units and shared with

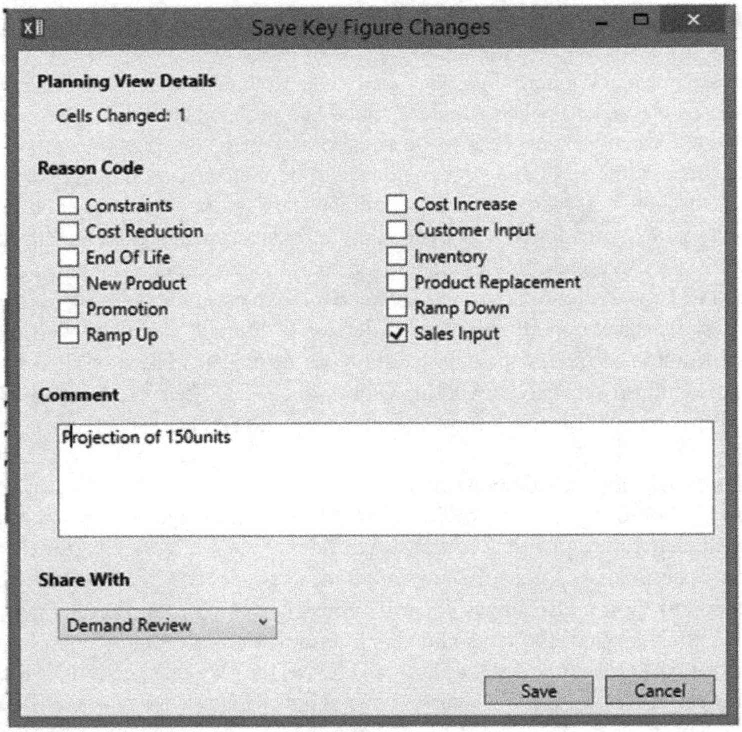


**Fig. 2.46** Reason code

demand review JAM group). When the user saves changes, the above qualitative information for the change is stored in the database for later reporting on the changes. This could serve as another way to capture assumptions.

### 2.5.2 Change History, Comments

When change history is enabled, key figures can be configured to be tracked. This enables to view the changes in change history report in IBP Excel view and the Web UI. When the IBP system has JAM collaboration enabled, the changes to data immediately appear as feed within JAM enabling other users in the JAM group to note the changes in the plan (Fig. 2.47).

During a planning cycle, there can be hundreds of users making changes to the forecasts across different planning levels and time horizons. In some organizations it is primarily important to track key figures that are manually updated during a plan cycle with information such as:

1. Who made the change
2. When was the change made
3. What was the value before change
4. What is the value after change
5. What is the reason code behind the change
6. What comments are associated with the change

This information will help planners to report on impact of changes and actual changes.

In SAP IBP, changes in particular key figure representing process step can be made at any planning level. In the example below, the key figure sales forecast qty is modified at aggregated product family and customer level. There were ten cells highlighted with changes (see Fig. 2.48).

When the data is stored in the back end, it gets disaggregated to about 100 cells at the lowest level of product and customer, and the changes are tracked at this lowest level (see Fig. 2.49). This allows to do an impact or effect view of changes at any aggregate level of hierarchy.

**Fig. 2.47** History of changes in JAM feed

SAP Integrated Business Planning

**Changes made to highlighted cells and saved: Total cell changes at aggregated level : 10**

**Planning View Additional Filters:** Change Date Range ; Reason Code

| Product Family | Customer | Key Figure | Jan | Feb | Mar | Apr | May | Jun |
|---|---|---|---|---|---|---|---|---|
| PF1 | C1 | Sales Forecast Qty | 150 | 150 | 150 | 150 | 150 | 100 |
| | C2 | Sales Forecast Qty | 200 | 200 | 200 | 200 | 200 | 200 |
| PF2 | C2 | Sales Forecast Qty | 300 | 350 | 350 | 350 | 350 | 350 |

**Fig. 2.48** Change history on aggregated level

SAP Integrated Business Planning

**When viewed at detailed level: Total Cell changes : 100**

| Product | Product Family | Customer | Key Figure | Jan | Feb | Mar | Apr | May | Jun |
|---|---|---|---|---|---|---|---|---|---|
| PF1 | P1 | C1 | Sales Forecast Qty | 30 | 30 | 30 | 30 | 30 | 20 |
| | P2 | C1 | Sales Forecast Qty | 30 | 30 | 30 | 30 | 30 | 20 |
| | P3 | C1 | Sales Forecast Qty | 30 | 30 | 30 | 30 | 30 | 20 |
| | P4 | C1 | Sales Forecast Qty | 30 | 30 | 30 | 30 | 30 | 20 |
| | P5 | C1 | Sales Forecast Qty | 30 | 30 | 30 | 30 | 30 | 20 |
| PF1 | P1 | C2 | Sales Forecast Qty | 40 | 40 | 40 | 40 | 40 | 40 |
| | P2 | C2 | Sales Forecast Qty | 40 | 40 | 40 | 40 | 40 | 40 |
| | P3 | C2 | Sales Forecast Qty | 40 | 40 | 40 | 40 | 40 | 40 |
| | P4 | C2 | Sales Forecast Qty | 40 | 40 | 40 | 40 | 40 | 40 |
| | P5 | C2 | Sales Forecast Qty | 40 | 40 | 40 | 40 | 40 | 40 |
| PF2 | P11 | C2 | Sales Forecast Qty | 30 | 35 | 35 | 35 | 35 | 35 |
| | P12 | C2 | Sales Forecast Qty | 30 | 35 | 35 | 35 | 35 | 35 |
| | P13 | C2 | Sales Forecast Qty | 30 | 35 | 35 | 35 | 35 | 35 |
| | P14 | C2 | Sales Forecast Qty | 30 | 35 | 35 | 35 | 35 | 35 |
| | P15 | C2 | Sales Forecast Qty | 30 | 35 | 35 | 35 | 35 | 35 |
| | P16 | C2 | Sales Forecast Qty | 30 | 35 | 35 | 35 | 35 | 35 |
| | P17 | C2 | Sales Forecast Qty | 30 | 35 | 35 | 35 | 35 | 35 |
| | P18 | C2 | Sales Forecast Qty | 30 | 35 | 35 | 35 | 35 | 35 |
| | P19 | C2 | Sales Forecast Qty | 30 | 35 | 35 | 35 | 35 | 35 |
| | P20 | C2 | Sales Forecast Qty | 30 | 35 | 35 | 35 | 35 | 35 |

**Fig. 2.49** Change history on detail level

For example, user can make change to different key figures at multiple planning levels and save data. This gets represented as one change ID and can be viewed in change history view.

Suppose users make each of the following changes in simulation run and finally saves all the data:

- Sales forecast qty for product (P1) and customer (C1) for Aug 2017 and Sept 2017
- Sales forecast qty for product family (PF1) and customer (C2) for June and July 2017
- Consensus forecast qty for customer region (R1) for Sept 2017

When the data is saved to back end, it gets a change ID representing all the above changes and data disaggregated and stored at the lowest level of the key figure. The change also records the level at which the change was made along with other change information like user, data, reason codes, and comments.

Change history and comments reporting in IBP provide the following capability:

- Show the effect of changes in a planning view
- Show the actual changes
- Navigation form planning view to change history view

**Change History Effect/Impact Report**

The change history impact or effect of changes report shows the effect of the changes at any user-defined aggregation level for the selected key figures. The effect view allows to see changes for any key figures associated with the key figure for which change history is tracked. We can see the impact of sales forecast revenue based on the changes to the sales forecast qty. Any key figures that are dependent on the sales forecast qty key figure can be viewed to analyze the impact of the change.

In the change history effect view, user can choose the time range for the changes by providing the start and end date time and like in planning view select other parameters. Further settings in change history allow to view the before and after values, differences, and % change difference. The resultant report (see Fig. 2.50) helps understand the following:

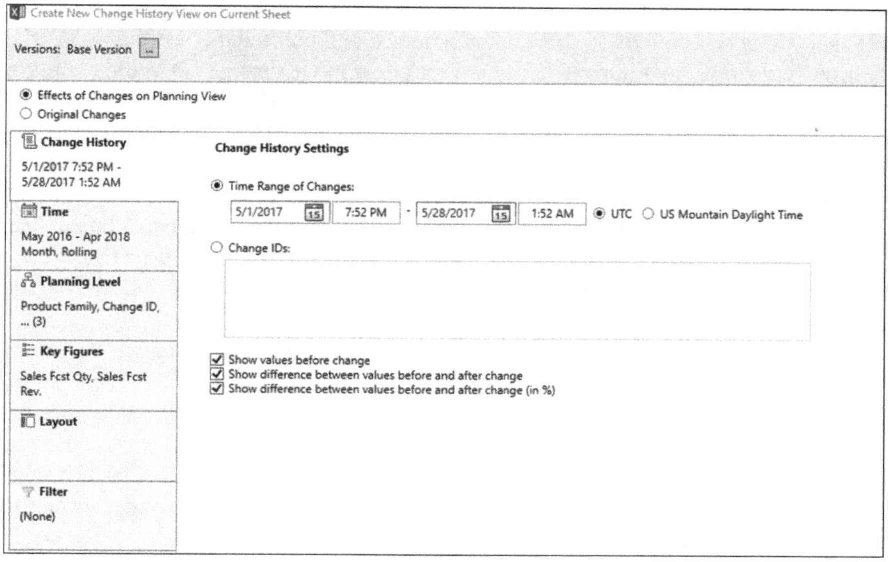


**Fig. 2.50** Change history view parameters

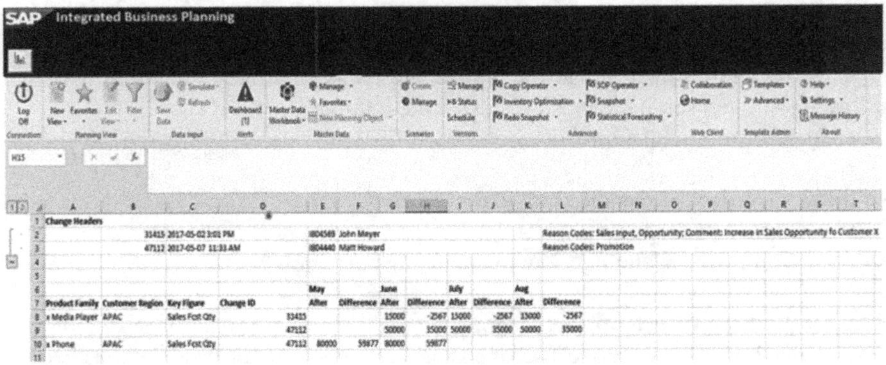

**Fig. 2.51** Change history detail

- Knowing impact of the changes and how relevant is that impact
- What changes led to the impact during the planning cycle and who/when was it performed
- What was the reason/logic for the change

The resulting change history impact report then aggregates all the change values at selected product family and customer region and for each of those planning combinations for the selected key figure sales forecast qty and provides a breakdown of the changes in the form of change ID. The change history header lists all the changes along with the user, dates, reason codes, and comments (see Fig. 2.51).

You can choose to aggregate by changes, i.e., remove change ID in the planning view. The planning view then shows the value of the key figure aggregated across all the changes that were performed during the selected change history time interval.

The change history view can be saved as a favorite and shared with other users, just like any other planning view. Since the change history view is another planning view, all the properties of the planning view like flexible layout can also be applied to the change history view. User can choose to layout the results as desired, so they can easily filter and sort on the information for faster analysis (see Fig. 2.52), for example, sort the changes by the impact on sales revenue.

As part of the analysis of the changes, you can also filter the changes based on reason code and the user (see Fig. 2.53).

In addition user can filter for one particular change and check its impact on associated key figures at different aggregation levels. The change IDs presented in the change history effect view can comprise of several changes made at different planning levels. To view more details about the change, SAP IBP provides a change history original changes view.

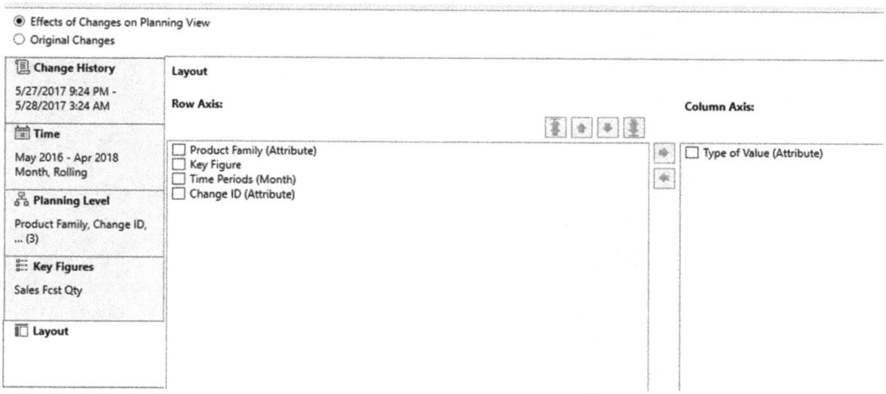


**Fig. 2.52** Change history view flexibility

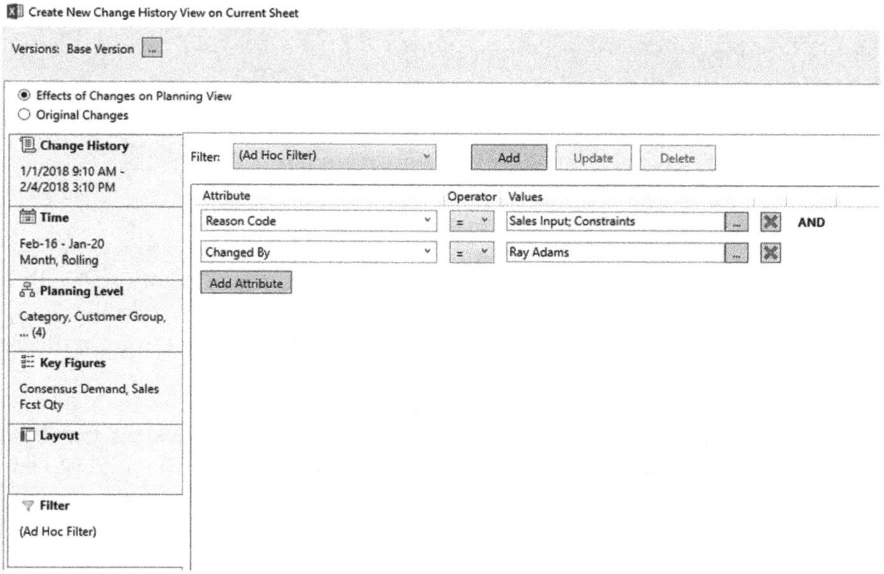


**Fig. 2.53** Filtering change history

## Original Changes View/Summary of Changes

The actual changes report available in IBP Excel add-on provides the list of changes along with details about the planning levels and filters associated with the change during the time the change was saved. Unlike the effect view that can be viewed at user-defined aggregate level, the original changes view displays the planning levels and time periods associated with the change, and therefore the planning levels and

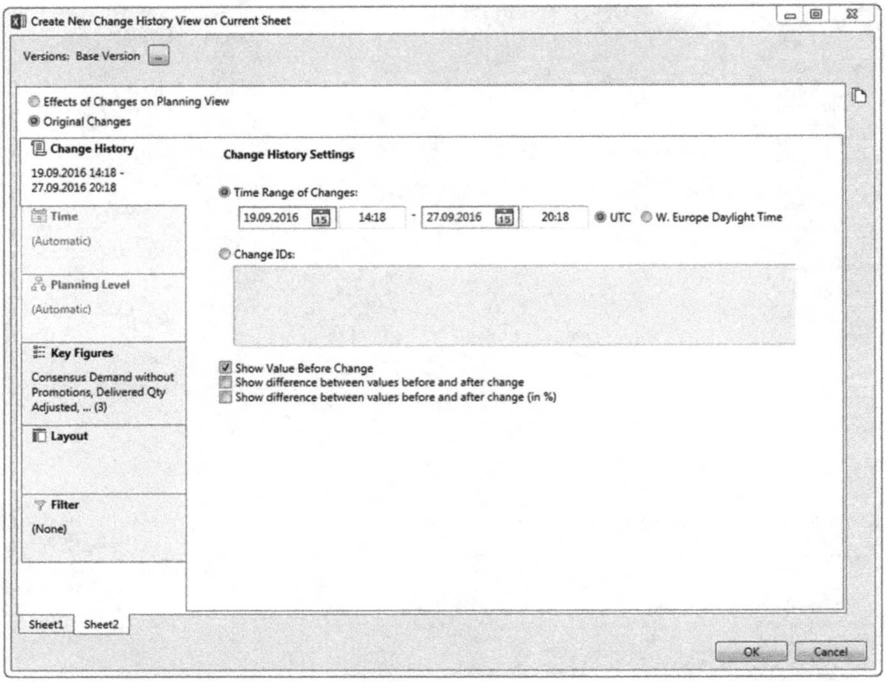


**Fig. 2.54** View changes on original level

time periods are not selectable. Only the key figures that change history enabled are allowed to be selected. Filters can be used to narrow down the results (see Fig. 2.54). For example, show all changes associated with product family PF1 and key figure sales forecast qty for the last week.

The system automatically fetches the planning levels and the time periods associated with the change. Further information like filters, conversions that were selected during the time the change was made, are also displayed. The original view can also be thought of as a point in time report, because it provides all the information about the planning view settings when the change was made.

The resulting view (see Fig. 2.55) shows the original changes, where two users made changes to plan data resulting in two change IDs. Change ID 31415 made by user John has changes across two planning levels across different key figures. Sales forecast qty was updated at product/customer level from Jun to Aug in simulation followed by sales forecast qty and consensus demand qty updates at product/customer region level for different time periods. When these two sets of changes were saved, user provided the reason codes and comments which resulted in saving the changes to the back end with a change ID 31415.

Similar to the change history effect view, the change history original view can also be filtered for reason codes and user. Further the layout can be changed that helps planner to perform quick analytics on the changed data. IBP also provides a

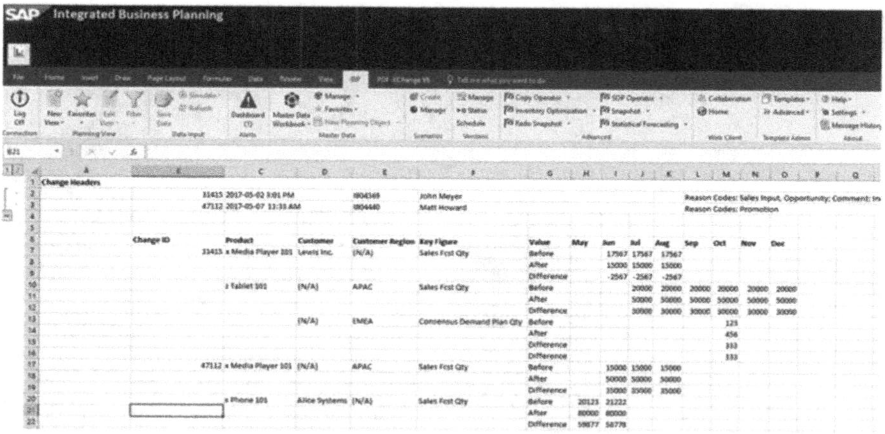

**Fig. 2.55** Original changes view

Web UI-Fiori app for change history which has similar functionality as the change history effect view in IBP Excel add-on. It provides the capabilities to download the change history with comments as a CSV file. This can be used for more sophisticated analysis of change history data offline in Excel like pivoting for aggregation by reason codes, top five changes, last five changes, etc.

## 2.6 Model Data and Planning Area

A planning model in IBP provides the following capabilities to support different business processes:

1. Highly flexible configuration
2. Pre-configured standard leading practices content
3. Calculations and algorithms

A planning model in an Integrated Business Planning covers planning processes with different periodicities, planning levels at which plans are run, and different levels at which data is stored.

An IBP solution typically addresses process and data integration across various systems or applications. These processes can have different granularities of the planning hierarchies and time periods. Furthermore, the processes can have different frequency of execution. The above example shows a planning process with short-, mid-, and long-term planning, with the focus varying from days to weeks, weeks to months, and months to years. There can be several different user roles accessing different aspects of an integrated process where demand planners focus on volume at

Fig. 2.56 Integrated Business Process

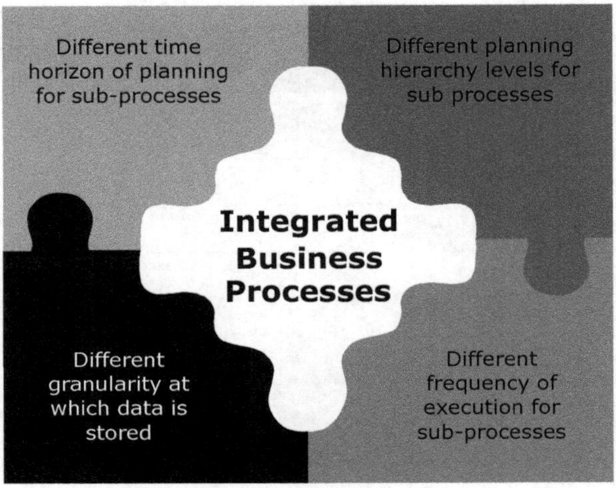


detailed level of product/customer, whereas finance would have a view on value from detail to aggregated business units/category levels.

In SAP IBP, a unified planning model covers business process and data, across different application modules like demand, S&OP, control tower, inventory, supply, and response. The integrated planning process is a harmonized execution of multiple processes with the characteristics as listed in Fig. 2.56.

**Integrated Business Processes** do connect different subprocesses covering strategic, tactical, and operational planning in one coherent, transparent, and manageable process. These three process dimensions could be understood as:

- Strategic view on long-term planning:
  - Strategic sales and operation planning
  - Long-range business planning
  - Network design and policy setting
- Tactical view on midterm to long-term planning:
  - Monthly sales and operation planning
  - Demand planning and demand management
  - Inventory optimization
  - Supply planning, allocations planning
- Operational view on short- to midterm planning:
  - Demand sensing
  - Demand shaping
  - Order confirmations and supply priorities

The above integrated process can have a huge time horizon span. It may start from the operational planning which covers up to 8 weeks, through the tactical planning which covers from 3 to 36 months, and finally to the strategic planning which often goes even beyond a 5 years horizon.

The above planning process operates on different planning hierarchy levels and time periods:

- S&OP process is usually viewed and run at an aggregated product family and country/region level
- Demand planning at monthly or weekly—product, customer, and location level
- Demand sensing at daily—product, customer, and location level
- Exception management on daily product-location level or KPIs like perfect order fulfillment executed on order level of sales, orders, and deliveries

Furthermore, these processes operate on a different granularity at which the data is stored. Processes can have different granularities at which the data is stored for the underlying data involved in the process:

- Statistical forecasting quantity at monthly product/location
- Marketing forecast stored at monthly product line level
- Finance plan at quarterly product family and regional Level
- Sales force forecast at monthly product/customer level
- Supply plan key figures like capacities at resource location level

Finally those subprocesses operate at a different frequency, e.g.:

- Strategic sales and operation planning on a yearly frequency
- Tactical sales and operation planning at a monthly frequency
- Demand planning, inventory optimization from a weekly frequency
- Demand sensing and control tower from a daily frequency

The underlying supply chain model and the planning engine provide the needed flexibility to meet the planning and analytical needs of each exemplary user as shown in Fig. 2.57.

The artifacts of the underlying supply chain planning model that supports the business processes include the following:

1. IBP-configured model: a flexible configuration to define the supply chain planning model with key figures, planning hierarchies, versions, and planning operators
2. Algorithms libraries available in HANA:
   (a) Application Function Libraries (AFL): sophisticated planning algorithms, e.g., supply planning heuristics and optimization and multistage inventory optimization that run natively on HANA
   (b) Predictive Analytics Library (PAL): used by IBP for the statistical forecasting methods
3. HANA planning and calculation engine of the underlying SAP HANA platform
4. Data management: generated data model based on the pre-configured planning model that supports time series and order-based models

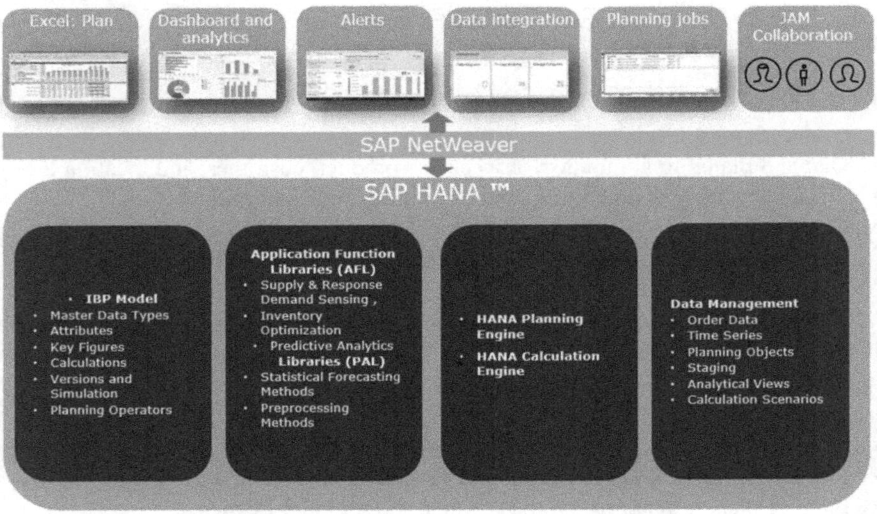


**Fig. 2.57** SAP IBP on HANA

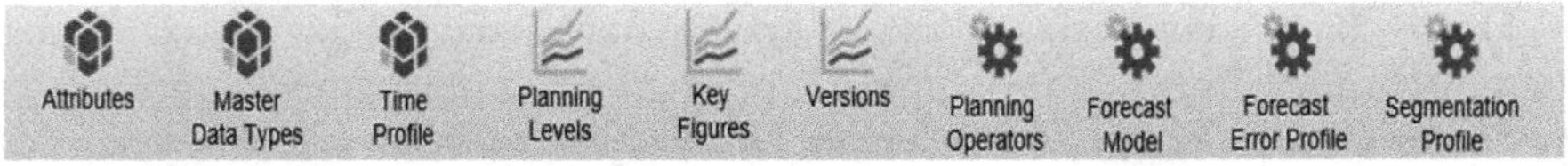


**Fig. 2.58** SAP IBP—planning area configuration dimensions

Let us define fundamentals of SAP IBP data modeling.

Planning area in SAP IBP is a set of configuration elements that defines the data structure of a unified and Integrated Business Planning process. It brings together essential elements of planning processes like planning time periods and planning horizons and planning hierarchies, key figures, scenarios, and versions. Planning area may contain many plan datasets—one actual dataset and many version datasets. In IBP, the planning area artifacts like tables, views, calculation scenarios, and permissions are generated upon activation. These then form the basis for planning processes like data loads, calculations, planning views, planning operators, etc. (see Fig. 2.58).

A planning area is run natively in HANA within the planning and calculation engine. This allows for faster calculations where the data and calculations are run in-memory.

In SAP IBP, the key figures are stored and/or calculated. The calculated key figures have calculations on the stored key figure with several intermediate calculations at different levels of hierarchies. Only the stored key figures are stored in the HANA in-memory database, and the calculations behind the calculated key figures are executed on the fly whenever user queries such key figures from Excel, analytics, planning operators, etc. On the fly aggregation is performed on the stored

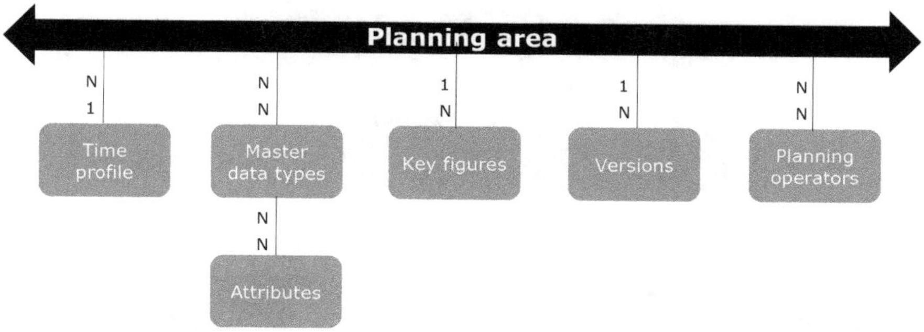


**Fig. 2.59** SAP IBP—planning area (N 1 describes many to many relationship)

data and in-memory utilizing the power of SAP HANA, so there is no need to store aggregates or intermediate calculation results.

**Elements of a Planning Area**
The following illustration (Fig. 2.59) shows the primary entities of a planning area. A planning area is representative of multidimensional cube with several hierarchies of master data dimensions, time dimension, key figures, and versions. A planning area is composed of multiple key figures. Each key figure has a base planning level which represents the primary master data key structures. For example, sales forecast is stored at planning level that has product ID and customer ID as root characteristics along with time level as month. There can be several planning operators that can be associated with the planning area which operate on the data, e.g., statistical forecasting, supply planning heuristics, snapshots, etc. A master data type can be associated with one or more planning areas giving the flexibility to model a unified planning area or several planning areas sharing master data.

## 2.6.1 Master Data Attributes

Master data types are the primary dimensions of the planning data defining the structure of the master data that needs to be planned, e.g., customer, location, product, and resource are some of the main data categories. Key figures or measures are based on the master data, e.g., consensus forecast is planned at product and country master data dimensions.

Master data type has one or more attributes that represent the data type and semantics of a data field, e.g., product ID. Master data types can have one or more primary keys of data along with several associated attributes.

Attributes of a master data can have hierarchy of data, e.g., product family and brand are hierarchical attributes of a product. Examples of hierarchies are shown below (Fig. 2.60).

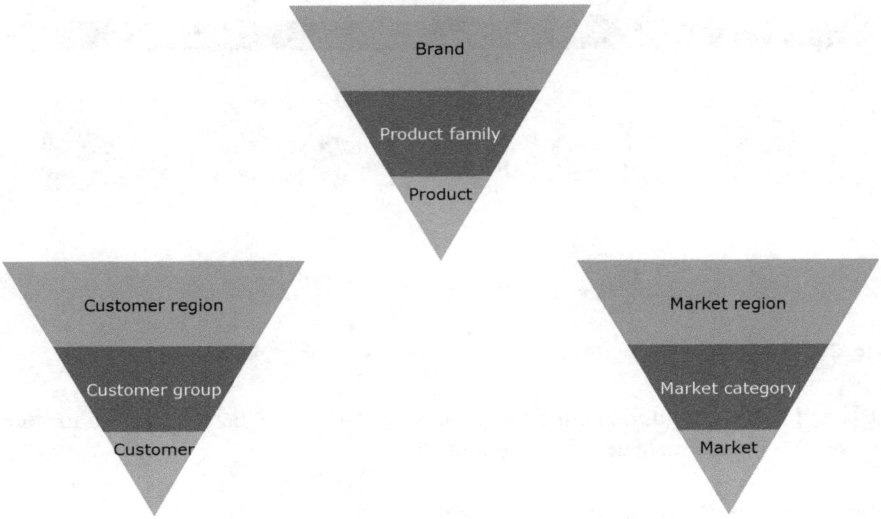


**Fig. 2.60** Master data types

**Types of Master Data Types**

A master data type in IBP can be defined as simple, compound, reference, virtual, or external master data types (Fig. 2.61). These types of master data types give flexibility to model different dimensions of data along with their referential integrity.

**Simple Master Data Type** These are primary dimensions of data which contain the main entities for planning. Examples include product, customer, location, resources, etc. Simple master data types typically have a single key which represents the ID of primary object (Fig. 2.62), e.g., PRDID is a key of simple master data type PRODUCT.

**Compound Master Data Type** This is used to store attributes that belong to multiple master data type keys, e.g., in the master data type PRODUCT CUSTOMER, the market family and market segment are attributes of the combination of customer and product. There is a foreign key relationship between the keys of the compound and the referenced master data types with individual keys (Fig. 2.63). Compound master data like product/customer may be used to derive plant in complex supply chain models. In source system like S/4, we may use customer info record, so to this combination plant is attached or we may create plant derivation based on sales order line where product is linked to customer and supply plant.

**Reference Master Data Type** This is a master data type that refers to another master data type. It does not contain actual master data but simply refers to the data contained in its underlying master data type. It is required when the underlying data is the same but can play different semantic roles and you want to avoid loading the

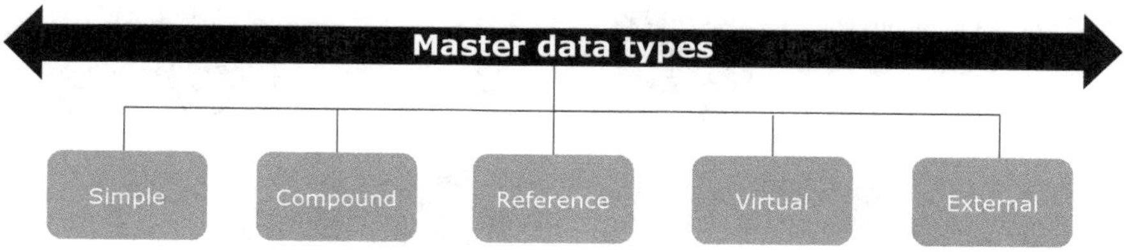


**Fig. 2.61** Master data types

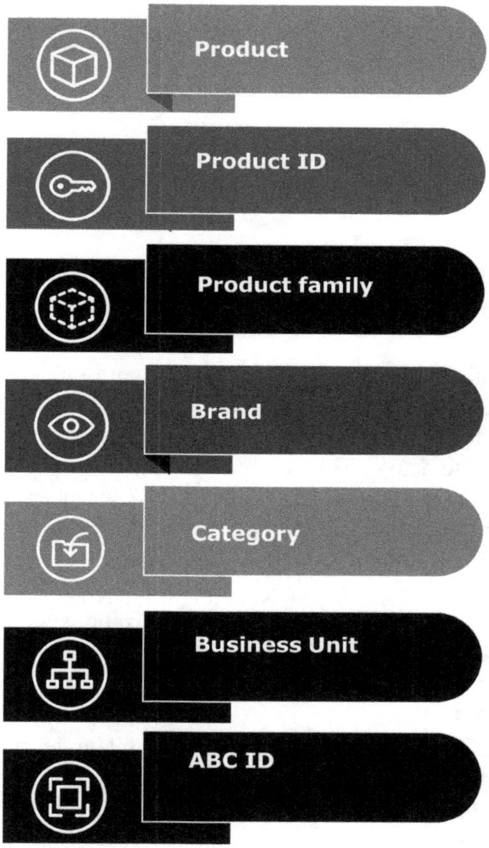


**Fig. 2.62** Simple master data types examples

same data twice (Fig. 2.64). For example, consider "product" and "component." So one could model "product" as an independent master data type, whereas "component" could become a reference master data type, which refers to master data type "product."

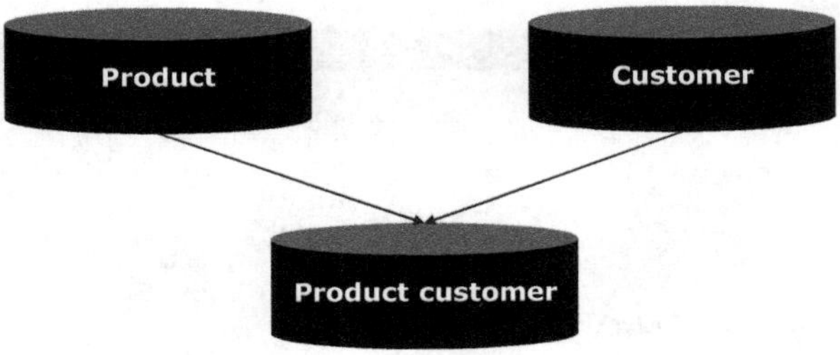


**Fig. 2.63** Compound master data

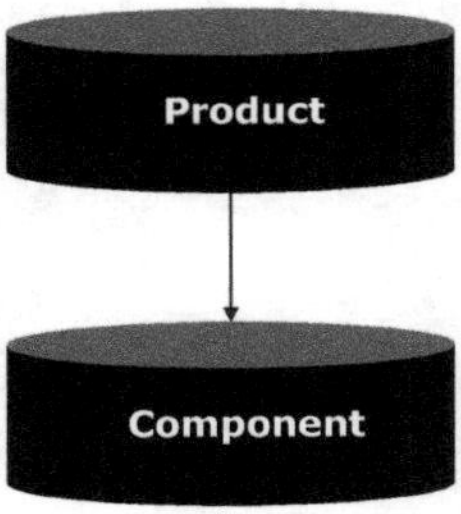


**Fig. 2.64** Reference master data

**Virtual Master Data Type** This is used to join two or more master data types with a join condition. This is usually used when an attribute of one master data type should be available for another. For example, the master data type "product customer group" has an attribute active. This attribute should be available for all customers belonging to the customer group. To achieve this, we need to join the product customer group and customer master data types. The join is on customer group attribute (Fig. 2.65). Virtual master data type doesn't store data but models a relationship between other master data types. This type of master data type can help to minimize and default a lot of value in organizations which are not changing their fundamental structures very often.

**External Master Data Type**

SAP Integrated Business Planning can handle and integrate master data when the content comes from an external database. Before you can use the external master data types, the database tables they retrieve their content from must be integrated from SAP ERP to SAP HANA database tables inside SAP Integrated Business Planning. The integration runs in batch mode.

You may ask yourself how master data types are being used in the IBP planning area. The supply chain model for Integrated Business Planning contains master data types which are typically imported from system of record like SAP S/4 or special ones created in IBP for planning purposes.

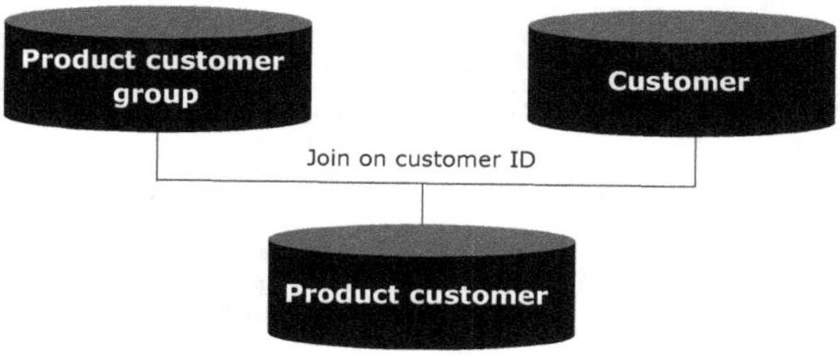


**Fig. 2.65** Virtual master data

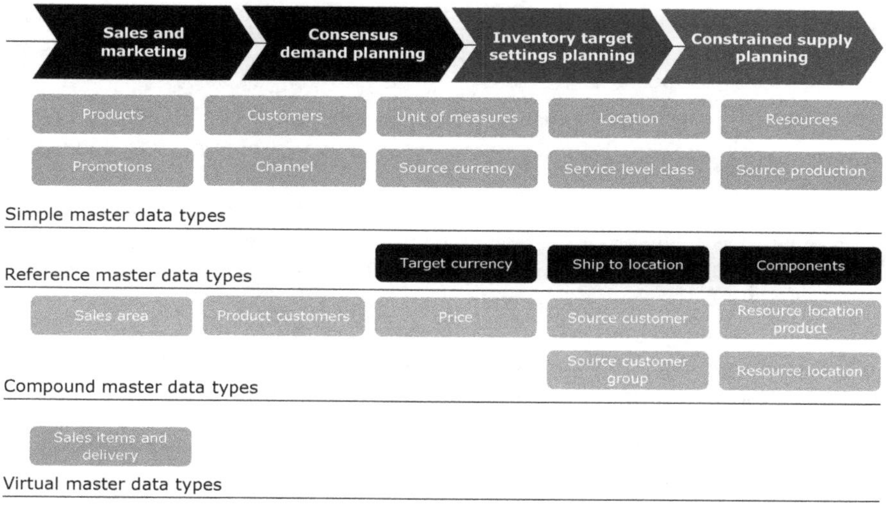


**Fig. 2.66** Master data types linked to process steps

Figure 2.66 shows a simple planning process across demand, inventory, and supply planning steps along with integrated financials. At each level of the planning process, there are different master data types that are used in this process.

Products, unit of measure, and currency conversions are common across all processes; however, channel, sales area, and customers are typically used in the demand processes.

For the data to be consistent across all planning processes, several types of master data types are used:

- Simple master data types are used for the primary master data like products, customers, and locations.
- Compound master data types are used for combinations of primary master data types, for example, product/customer with market-/country-related attributes and resource location with capacity-related attributes.

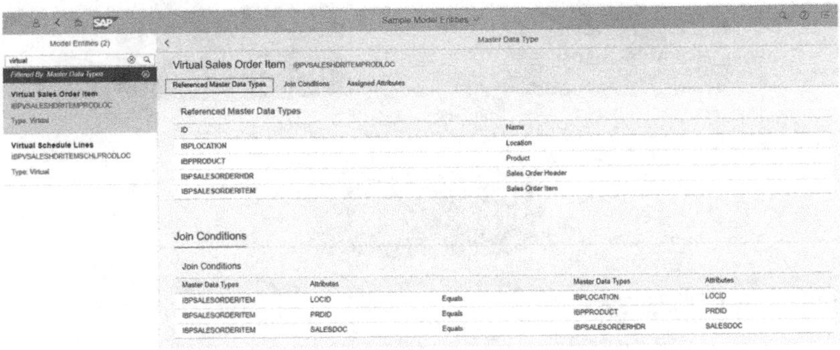


**Fig. 2.67** Virtual master data example

- Reference master data types like target currency, ship-to location, and components refer to the primary master data type's currency, location, and product, respectively.
- Virtual master data types perform a join between several master data types, e.g., sales items and delivery master data type used in supply chain control tower join between primary master data types of sales order header, sales order item, schedule lines, product, and location.

Virtual master data, for example, sales order items, can be loaded in IBP control tower as master data with virtual join son sales order header, product, and location master data types (see Fig. 2.67).

### 2.6.2 Time Profiles

A time profile is the time component of the key figure dimension and defines the time horizon for planning, time aggregate levels, and their hierarchy along with the planning time horizons for each level. Time levels define the various levels of time buckets in which data can be managed. Examples of different time profile levels are years, quarters, months and weeks, technical weeks, and days. The timeline is an ordered sequence of non-overlapping buckets or "periods."

Further, hierarchies can be defined for time profiles. Time profile hierarchy starts from the lowest level (e.g., daily) to the higher levels (e.g., week, monthly, quarter, year) (see Fig. 2.68). A time profile is a flexible configuration element but needs to be defined for a planning area representing the business process framework. Based on the business requirements, time profile could vary on the periods, horizons, and levels.

| Week | 33 | 34 | 35 | 36 | 37 | 38 | 39 | 40 | 41 | 42 | 43 | 44 | 45 | 46 | 47 | 48 | 49 | 50 | 51 | 52 | 1 | 2 | 3 |
|---|---|---|---|---|---|---|---|---|---|---|---|---|---|---|---|---|---|---|---|---|---|---|---|
| Month | Aug | | Sep | | | | | Oct | | | | Nov | | | | Dec | | | | | Jan | | |
| Quarter | Q3 | | | | | | | Q4 | | | | | | | | | | | | | Q1 | | |

**Fig. 2.68** Calendar

| Month | June | | | | | July | | | | | August | | | | | |
|---|---|---|---|---|---|---|---|---|---|---|---|---|---|---|---|---|
| Calendar Week | CW 23 | CW 24 | CW 25 | CW 26 | CW 27 | | CW 28 | CW 29 | CW 30 | CW 31 | | CW 32 | CW 33 | CW 34 | CW 35 | CW 36 |
| Technical Week | TW 23 | TW 24 | TW 25 | TW 26 | TW 27a | TW 27b | TW 28 | TW 29 | TW 30 | TW 31a | TW 31b | TW 32 | TW 33 | TW 34 | TW 35 | TW 36a |
| Factor | 5 | 5 | 5 | 5 | 2 | 3 | 5 | 5 | 5 | 5 | 0 | 5 | 5 | 5 | 5 | 1 |

**Fig. 2.69** Weeks and technical weeks

**Types of Calendars: 4-4-5 Calendar**

As we see there are 4 weeks in October and November and 5 in December, and that is why calendar type is 4-4-5.

Further, time profiles allow the modeling of time profile levels with multiple parents (e.g., technical weeks where a calendar week can be overlap between 2 months) and intermediate levels without parents (e.g., calendar weeks).

**Calendar with Split Weeks Across Months**

In IBP, the time profiles support technical weeks or week to month split where a calendar week overlaps between 2 months (Fig. 2.69).

In such cases a period factor attribute can be defined in the time profile which indicates how the value should disaggregate from an aggregated time level. This feature will be very useful in integration of tactical S&OP executed on monthly buckets with operational planning executed in weeks.

## 2.6.3 Key Figures and Planning Levels

Key figures represent values of data on combination of time level and planning attributes. Key figures are sometimes also called measures and hold transactional data like price, quantity, value, ratio, etc. Key figures can be imported into the IBP system, calculated, and/or manually edited. Some examples of key figures include sales forecast, marketing forecast, consensus unconstrained forecast, projected inventory, or actual data such as sales orders and shipment history.

Each stored key figure has a base planning level which defines the keys at which the data is stored, e.g., sales forecast is by month, product ID, and customer ID.

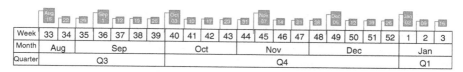

Figure 2.70 shows the properties of a key figure. A planning area can contain multiple key figures which are the key elements of planning in a business process. The key figures have several properties like aggregation, disaggregation, calculation definitions, and display settings. These key figures are classified as per Fig. 2.70. Some key figures can be tracked for changes if needed. Some key figures which are used in planning algorithms (planning operators) have fixed semantics.

Let us describe few types of key figures:

- **Stored key figures:** Data is stored in this type of key figure at a defined base planning level. All stored key figures are editable or are imported into the system (e.g., actuals qty).
- **Calculated key figures:** Values in this type of key figure are always calculated based on user-defined formula (e.g., "Revenue = Qty * Price"). This type of key figure is usually not editable. However, to support use cases such as defaulting, a key figure can be both editable and stored.
- **Alert key figures:** These are key figures with user-defined criteria that monitor and manage execution of business plans. They can only have values of 0 or 1, meaning that the alert itself is either ON or OFF. Alerts typically check conditions on other key figures such as target revenue vs consensus revenue > 10%

**Planning levels** are a set of attributes that enable users to analyze and plan at different levels of data. As an example, PRODCUST planning level is defined as product/customer and will allow for data analysis that is tied to both the product, customer, and combinations of both and their associated attributes (e.g., the *demand* for a product could be a function of a specific customer and type of product itself).

Key figure calculations (calculated key figures) are done at a defined planning level, which can be different from the level that a user requests to view the key figure (Fig. 2.71). A planning area typically includes key figures of multiple planning levels, and these can be linked with calculations often resulting in key figures at additional planning levels (Fig. 2.72).

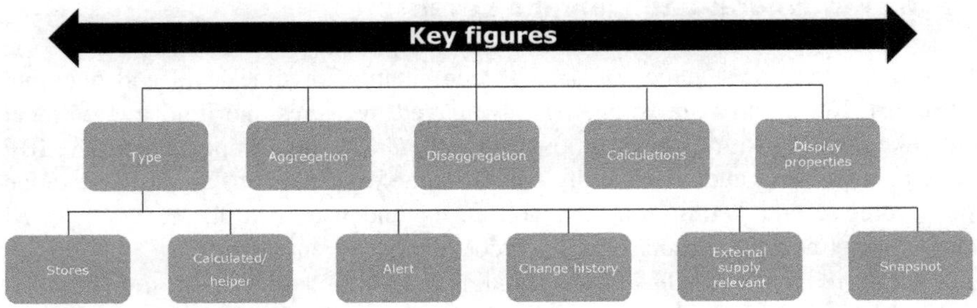


**Fig. 2.70** Key figure types

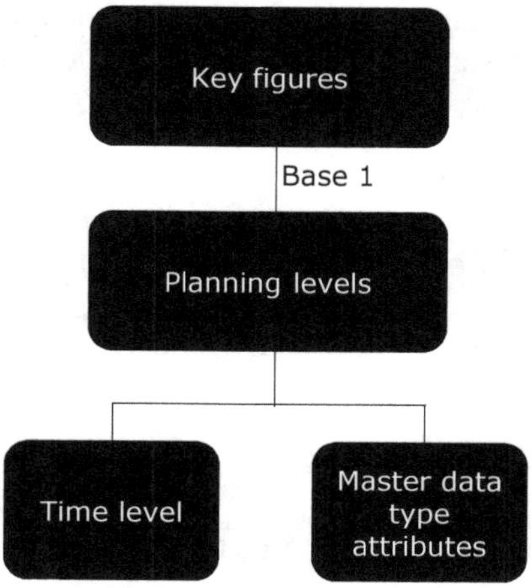


**Fig. 2.71** Key figure to planning level, time, and master data

| Planning process | Typical plan levels | Typical key figures |
|---|---|---|
| Consensus demand | Product | Sales, marketing, finance, demand and consensus qty, price and revenue |
| Capacity planning | Locations-resources | Unconstrained load, constrained load, capacity limit |
| Scenario comparison | Product family | Gross profit, constrained demand plan rev & qty, projected inventory cost |
| Sales representative forecast | Customer-product | Sales forecasts qty & rev, Opportunities qty and rev |
| Sales manager forecasts | Sales rep, product family | Sales manager qty & rev, sales qty and rev opportunities and target qty and rev. |
| New product introduction | Product , product lifecycle status | Marketing qty, price, rev |
| Integrated business plan and inventory | Product family | Consensus demand plan, constrained demand plan, inventory target qty, projected inventory qty |
| Sourcing from locations | Product , customer location | Consensus demand plan, demand by location qty, sourcing ratio |
| Total material qty | Product, components | Consensus demand, production req, dependent material qty, total material qty |

**Fig. 2.72** Planning processes and typical levels and key figures

Data across different planning levels enable integration between highly granular operational plan (SKU/customer/location/day) and tactical plan (product/customer/month) to strategic (product line/country/month).

### 2.6.4 Planning and Copy Operators and Versions and Scenarios

There are few main instruments in SAP IBP which help to manage planning and dataflows:

- Planning operator
- Copy operator
- Versions and scenarios (we will describe their usage in the planning process)

In Fig. 2.73 we illustrate how, when in the Integrated Business Planning process, planning operators, copy operators, and versions/scenarios can be used.

**Planning Operators**

Planning operators in IBP perform specialized functions beyond what is possible through key figure calculations, e.g., cross-period calculations for demand sensing, supply heuristics, and optimizer, just to name a few. Each planning operator has unique sets of parameters that drive the operations of a planning operator on the dataset.

Planning operators can be run in simulate mode or batch mode, e.g., statistical forecasting can be run in simulate mode, whereas the copy operator which copies data from source to target key figures can only be run in batch mode. The planning operators are associated to a planning area. These planning operators can further be scheduled as application jobs or to be triggered from planning view in Excel user interface.

In IBP, the planning operators are an integral part of the planning process, e.g., as part of demand planning process, you would run a statistical forecast which uses the forecasting operators. After the demand plans are finalized, these are approved and stored as backups for performance measurement or deviation current versus previous cycle calculation in another key figure using a copy operator. As part of the data lifecycle, you run a purge on the key figures which are, for example, older than 2 years. This is done using a purge key figure operator.

The planning operators supported by IBP (Fig. 2.74) can be broadly classified into the following categories:

1. Specialized planning functions like the copy operator, disaggregation operator, snapshots operator, and grouping of operators. These are usually done in batch model and operate on a large set of data. For example, the snapshot operator performs copy of the current values of the key figure into snapshot or backup key figures and performs cascading of snapshots. This later allows performing waterfall analysis reports on the data.

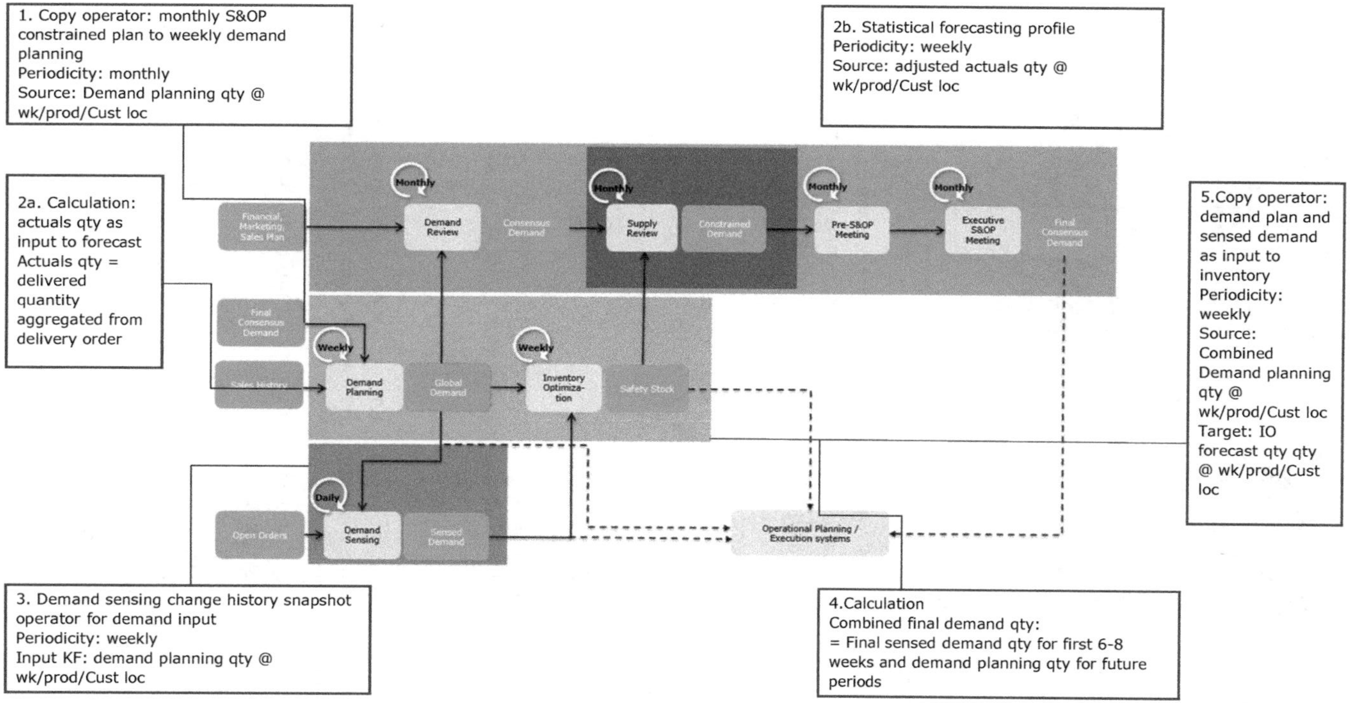


**Fig. 2.73** Planning operators and copy operators in the process

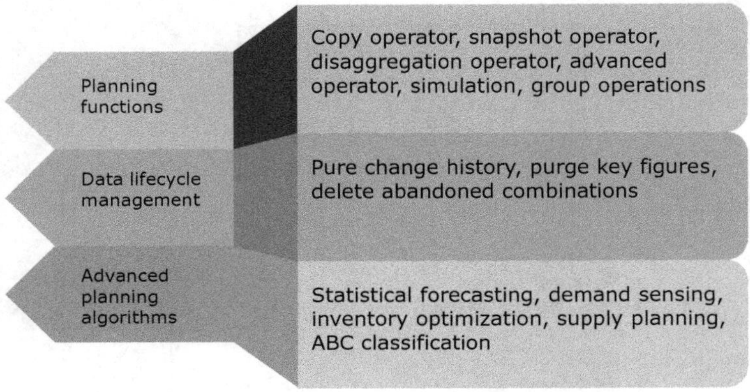


**Fig. 2.74** IBP Operators

2. The planning operators supporting data lifecycle management are run only in batch mode. These operate on mass data and perform data cleanup like purge key figures or key figures with change history beyond a specified period. Advanced operations like deleting abandoned combinations perform data operations to delete data that does not conform the defined model. For example, master data is deleted but the time series records exist.
3. Advanced planning algorithms and functions can typically support both batch and simulation mode, depending on the type of the planning requirement. They have specialized logic and algorithms to perform complex calculations with defined business rules. In IBP, the advanced planning algorithms like statistical forecasting use the HANA Predictive Analytical Library. Supply planning, inventory optimization, and other functions like forecast error methods are built as Application Function Libraries that run natively in HANA.

**Copy Operators**

Copy operator copies data between source and target key figures for the defined set of parameters. A copy operator can have one or more sets of source and target key figures including duration for which data should be copied, the offsets, and attribute filter criteria. Copy operator uses the data integration function when copying data from source to target key figures (Fig. 2.75).

The following are the typical use cases of copy operator in a planning process.

Consider a simple process between demand review and supply review. The output of the demand review process is the consensus unconstrained forecast and serves as the input to the supply planning process, e.g., for rough cut capacity planning.

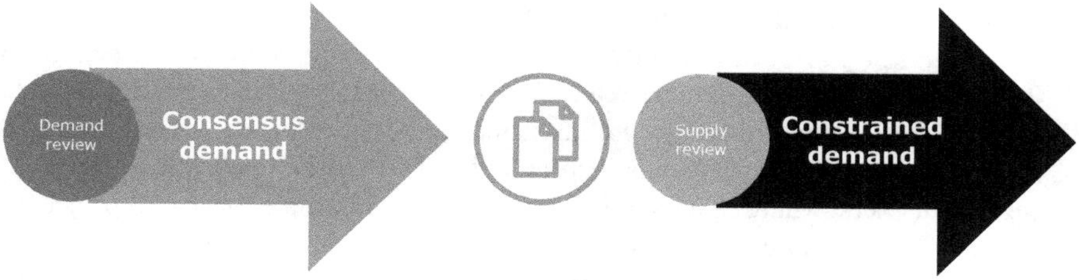


**Fig. 2.75** Copy operator concept

### Copy Operator Use Cases

1. Handover of planning data between processes across different planning levels
   For example, the output of a consensus demand planning process is the consensus unconstrained forecast qty. This key figure then becomes an input to the consensus demand qty at product/customer level or independent demand at product/location used in supply planning. The demand planning process in IBP can be very different for each business model, e.g., some have consensus demand at product/customer level and others at product/customer/sales organizational level. The output of the demand process then needs to be aggregated at a level that supply planning can use it as input. This is possible by using a copy operator that copies data between key figures having different base planning levels.
2. Approval process to finalize a plan
   The output of the IBP process culminating in the management review meeting needs to be stored and locked from modifications, while the plan is being worked on for the next cycle. In such cases the output of a certain stage of a process can be copied into a stored key figure which can only be edited by certain roles. The copy operator can also serve as the approval function that can be executed by certain user roles to copy the result of the approved plan into a stored key figure marked as the final approved plan. Another example of such a use case is the use of copy operator as pre-fill. In bottom up forecasting approach sales representatives, forecast can be copied and pre-filling sales lead forecast, where sales leads updated only his entries but based on up-to-date sum of sales reps forecasts; see chapter Sales Inputs (Bottom-Up) for details.
3. Backup of key figures
   The final plans from each planning cycle needs to be stored in backup key figures so that they can be used for plan-to-plan comparison to analyze forecast accuracy, plan adherence, and waterfall comparison. Several plans that are confirmed in an IBP are usually snapshotted or backed up into another key figure. Examples includes saving sales forecast qty, final integrated business plan qty, revenue, or profit, from each planning run/S&OP cycle. Copy operator provides flexibility in defining target key figures to be used for copy along with grouping of several sources to target key figures for copy. This can be scheduled at regular intervals or run ad hoc by planners whenever an important stage in a planning cycle is complete.

4. Clear key figures values or pre-fill key figures between planning runs

   Certain key figures need to be cleared before the next planning cycle begins so that the data fields for input are ready for input for next cycle. Examples include adjusted key figures like adjusted statistical forecast, adjusted sensed demand, adjusted deliveries, etc. The copy operator can also be used to clear key figures in certain buckets where a value is not expected. Example on-hand projected inventory in certain cases; some pre-fill key figures are required based on some complex calculations on key figures. Some examples include copying time shifted prior year sales history to current year, to achieve year-over-year comparison. This can be achieved using copy operator offset and duration function.
5. Time series data management—fill time periods and create combinations

   It is important for a planning process that the data required for planning is available for the planning periods and the combinations exist in the system to be used by in the process. Copy operator provides functionality to fill empty time series entries for a key figure with null values or extend the time series for key figures to future periods. The copy operator uses data integration functionality. That means when the copy operation is performed between key figures that have different planning levels, then the planning combinations get created if not already available for the base planning level of the target key figure.

**Versions and Scenarios**

Performing "what-if" scenario planning and defining alternative plans to manage business risk and opportunities are an important capability of SAP Integrated Business Planning system. Often in an IBP process, several alternate plans need to be evaluated based on the different assumptions. These alternative plans should coexist just like the baseline plans but provide flexibility to do ad hoc or streamlined analysis for decision-making without affecting planning data and sometimes even master data of the base version.

These alternative plans could have different business purposes where some are more focused on evaluating long-term strategic planning situations, some are more focused on evaluating options for tactical S&OP, and some are more focused for collaborations on current plans. SAP IBP provides two options for "what-if" scenario constructs, namely, "versions" and "user-defined scenarios." The section below explains the purpose of each and how versions and scenarios together can be used for evaluating alternate plans.

**Versions**

Versions are alternate plans of data where several assumptions are evaluated and uncertainties are factored in to come up with, e.g., the most profitable and feasible plan. When a planning area is created containing the master data and key figures, these by default become part of a "baseline version." As part of configuration, alternate versions can be defined, for example, "upside" and "downside" scenarios. Each version can have their unique set of key figures or can share key figures from the "base version." For example, on-hand inventory or historical sales do not change between versions, so these can be defined in a version to have data referring to a base version. By default, master data is shared across all versions in a planning area. However, based on the type of alternate plans to be evaluated per the business needs, version can be defined with version-dependent master data in which case the master data must be loaded to a specific version.

Versions are configuration entries, and like a planning area base version, the artifacts like tables, views, etc. are generated during planning area activation. Therefore, it is required to know up front and define the version that needs to be used in a planning process. Further a clear definition of what key figures should be included in a version must be predefined along with settings of version-dependent or version-independent master data making it less flexible for changes unless planning area is activated. A planning area can have one or more versions, and each version can share master data or have version-specific master data. The data model or planning area provides all the necessary functionality and user access such that the alternate plans can coexist with the baseline plan without affecting data in the base version.

Versions are very often used in IBP processes. Examples of use cases and their usage are the following:

1. Versions for evaluating strategic plans with version-specific master data, for example, evaluating long-term decisions about adding a new plant or launching a new product line: In most of these situations, the data required for planning does not exist in the source systems. This data need to be created and maintained to evaluate long-term strategy and its financial impact. Therefore, versions with version-dependent master data are defined as part of the planning area setup. Such versions are saved and validated for longer periods of time to support the strategic decisions.
2. Versions for evaluating tactical plans: In reconciliation pre-management business review meetings, often alternate versions are evaluated and compared. In most cases such versions share same master data and evaluate results of plans based on several different assumptions on data. Examples include an upside version where all opportunities $> 50\%$ are included part of consensus forecast, or evaluating supply shortage situations by adding additional own manufacturing capacity, or meeting the demand with alternate sources of supply such as a contract manufacturer/toller. The results of the versions in terms of revenue and margin projections are usually reviewed in the pre-management business review meetings to provide suggestions and inputs to the management S&OP review meeting.

Versions also have a data lifecycle where key figure data can be copied between versions and deleted from a version. Copy key figures from base version to upside version filtered by user selected key figures and attribute values. That means the version can be operated on all or subset of data. All planning operations like copy, snapshot, statistical forecasting, supply planning, etc. can be performed on versions, similar to base version. Further versions can be scheduled as application jobs. A use case of such is that during the beginning of a planning cycle, the upside version data

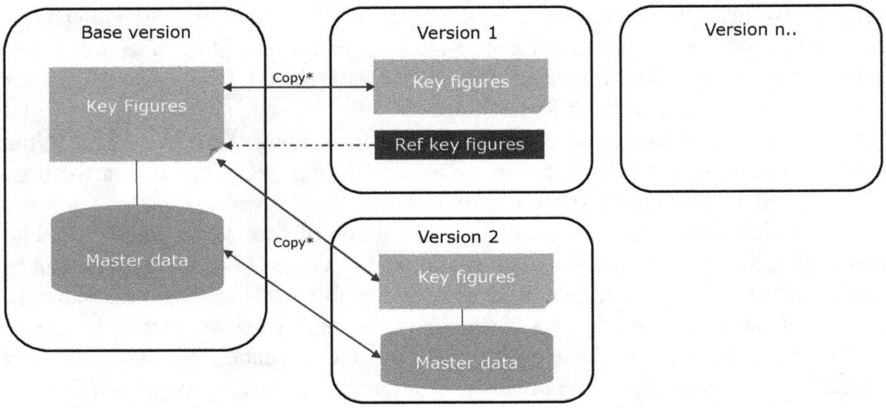


**Fig. 2.76** Versions in data model

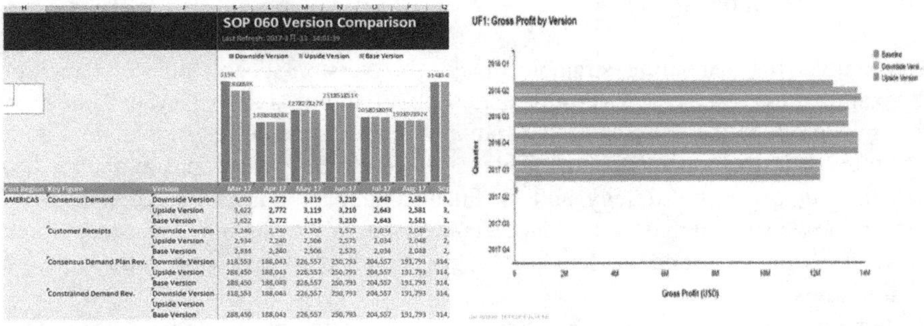


**Fig. 2.77** Versions comparison

from the previous cycle is deleted followed by a copy of data from baseline to the upside version.

As shown in the picture above (Fig. 2.76), a planning area has base version (which holds all the master data and key figures) and one or more configured versions. These versions can share master data with base or can have their own version-dependent master data. The version management in IBP provides capabilities to copy of key figure and master data between versions along with deletion of a version data. These can be executed directly in Excel.

End users can easily compare plans between base version and other versions by selecting versions in Excel planning views and Web UI analytics and dashboards (Fig. 2.77).

## User-Defined Scenarios

Unlike versions that are pre-configured and available to all users, the user-defined scenarios can be created by end users as part of the planning process to evaluate

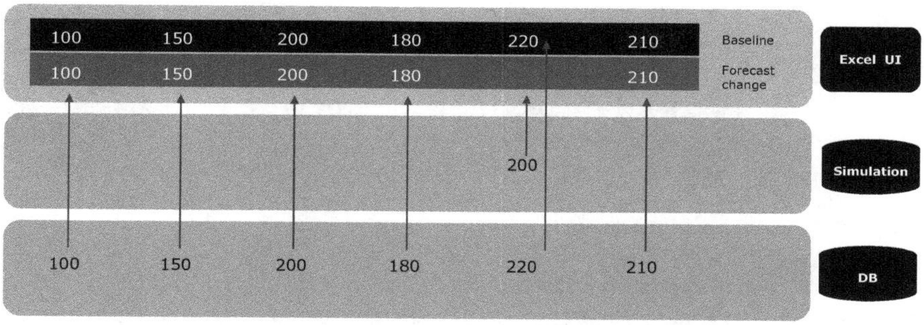


**Fig. 2.78** Scenarios in data model

multiple scenarios in parallel to the base plan. The results of a simulation can be stored by end users in its own scenario. Scenarios provide an own workspace for the planners to work on the plan. These scenarios are deltas on top of the baseline plan and can be managed without affecting the base plan.

Scenarios in IBP can be defined on a base version or configured versions or a combination of both. Scenarios are private to the user who defined them and can be shared with other users for collaborative decision-making. Typically, in a planning process, a planner works on several changes to the data based on planning assumptions and works on validating these multiple assumptions and collaborating with other users before making the change final. These final changes are then promoted to the baseline plan.

### Deltas in User-Defined Scenarios

User-defined scenarios only store the delta of the changes to the key figure values. It provides a see-through mechanism where all other values come from the baseline plan, except the key figure values which are updated in a scenario. For example, the key figure value is changed from 220 to 200 and saved in a scenario. All other values of this key figure come from the baseline version (Fig. 2.78).

This provides the flexibility and performance to perform what-if analysis because only the deltas are stored in the simulation which avoids duplication of non-changed data.

### User-Defined Scenarios Management

All user-defined scenarios can be created and managed in Excel user interface of IBP where it is most relevant (Fig. 2.79). These include sharing scenario with other users, promoting a scenario to baseline, resetting scenario to its original state, and deleting and duplicating a scenario.

Scenarios can be selected in Excel and analytics to compare and analyze planning results between scenarios, for example, customer demand and the constrained demand together with the gross profit for two alternate scenarios—profit optimization and increase capacity (Fig. 2.80).

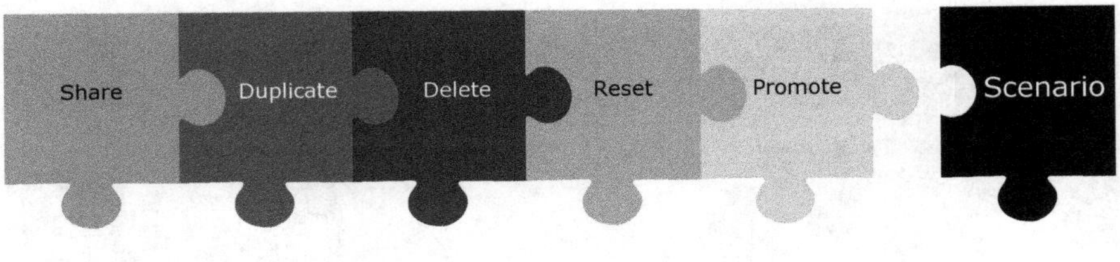


**Fig. 2.79** Management of scenarios

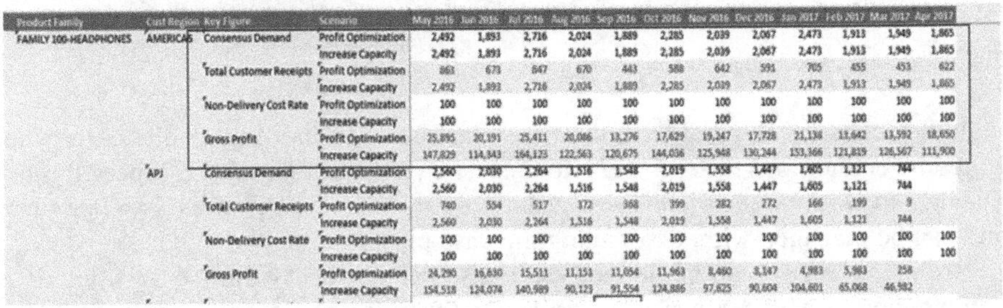

| Product Family | Cust Region | Key Figure | Scenario | May 2016 | Jun 2016 | Jul 2016 | Aug 2016 | Sep 2016 | Oct 2016 | Nov 2016 | Dec 2016 | Jan 2017 | Feb 2017 | Mar 2017 | Apr 2017 |
|---|---|---|---|---|---|---|---|---|---|---|---|---|---|---|---|
| FAMILY 100-HEADPHONES | AMERICAS | Consensus Demand | Profit Optimization | 2,492 | 1,893 | 2,716 | 2,024 | 1,889 | 2,285 | 2,039 | 2,067 | 2,473 | 1,913 | 1,949 | 1,865 |
| | | | Increase Capacity | 2,492 | 1,893 | 2,716 | 2,024 | 1,889 | 2,285 | 2,039 | 2,067 | 2,473 | 1,913 | 1,949 | 1,865 |
| | | Total Customer Receipts | Profit Optimization | 863 | 673 | 847 | 670 | 443 | 588 | 642 | 591 | 705 | 455 | 453 | 622 |
| | | | Increase Capacity | 2,492 | 1,893 | 2,716 | 2,024 | 1,889 | 2,285 | 2,039 | 2,067 | 2,473 | 1,913 | 1,949 | 1,865 |
| | | Non-Delivery Cost Rate | Profit Optimization | 100 | 100 | 100 | 100 | 100 | 100 | 100 | 100 | 100 | 100 | 100 | 100 |
| | | | Increase Capacity | 100 | 100 | 100 | 100 | 100 | 100 | 100 | 100 | 100 | 100 | 100 | 100 |
| | | Gross Profit | Profit Optimization | 25,895 | 20,191 | 25,411 | 20,086 | 13,276 | 17,629 | 19,247 | 17,728 | 21,138 | 11,642 | 13,592 | 18,650 |
| | | | Increase Capacity | 147,829 | 114,343 | 164,125 | 122,563 | 120,675 | 144,036 | 125,948 | 130,244 | 133,366 | 121,819 | 126,567 | 111,900 |
| | APJ | Consensus Demand | Profit Optimization | 2,560 | 2,030 | 2,264 | 1,516 | 1,548 | 2,019 | 1,558 | 1,447 | 1,605 | 1,121 | 744 | |
| | | | Increase Capacity | 2,560 | 2,030 | 2,264 | 1,516 | 1,548 | 2,019 | 1,558 | 1,447 | 1,605 | 1,121 | 744 | |
| | | Total Customer Receipts | Profit Optimization | 740 | 554 | 517 | 372 | 368 | 399 | 282 | 272 | 166 | 199 | 9 | |
| | | | Increase Capacity | 2,560 | 2,030 | 2,264 | 1,516 | 1,548 | 2,019 | 1,558 | 1,447 | 1,605 | 1,121 | 744 | |
| | | Non-Delivery Cost Rate | Profit Optimization | 100 | 100 | 100 | 100 | 100 | 100 | 100 | 100 | 100 | 100 | 100 | 100 |
| | | | Increase Capacity | 100 | 100 | 100 | 100 | 100 | 100 | 100 | 100 | 100 | 100 | 100 | 100 |
| | | Gross Profit | Profit Optimization | 24,290 | 16,630 | 15,511 | 11,151 | 11,054 | 11,963 | 8,460 | 8,147 | 4,983 | 5,983 | 258 | |
| | | | Increase Capacity | 154,518 | 124,074 | 140,989 | 90,123 | 91,554 | 124,886 | 97,625 | 90,604 | 104,601 | 65,068 | 46,982 | |

**Fig. 2.80** Scenario example

## Versions and Scenarios Comparison

In the following table, you will find the summary of differences between version and scenarios (Fig. 2.81).

Versions and user-defined scenarios complement each other to providing high level of flexibility for real-time "what-if" analysis in IBP process. The benefits of such include the following:

1. What-if analysis can be run on all or selected dataset.
2. Real-time analysis and calculation of profitability and revenue projections of the alternate plans.
3. Faster what-if analysis of changing assumptions and evaluating impact on the plan in a separate workspace from the baseline plan.
4. Single data model that supports multiple versions and scenarios and base version to coexist without affecting the base plan.
5. User permissions are applied to the data they can view and manage.
6. Lifecycle to copy, promote, and delete versions and scenario.
7. High usability and efficiency in management business review meetings by presenting the alternate plans in easy to use and visualize analytical charts and Excel planning views.

| | Versions | User defined scenarios |
|---|---|---|
| Purpose | Copies of planning dataset from base version | Saved simulation of planning data on top on versions( incl base) |
| Use case | Evaluate long term revenue and margin projection on adding a new product line | Evaluate impact on change in price or increase in demand for a customer. |
| Visibility | All users who have access to versions | Planning user who created the scenario and to whom the scenario is shared |
| Creation | Pre-defined as part of planning area configuration | Created on the fly in a planning process. |
| Who manages creation and changes | Planning area admin | Planning user who created |
| Data copy | Full copies of data | Deltas from baseline |
| Master data | Version dependent master data can be configured or share master data from base version | Shares same data as base version |

**Fig. 2.81** Versions vs scenarios

### 2.6.5 Calculations, Defaulting, Conversions, and Flexible Views on Data

**Calculations**

IBP provides highly flexible model configuration to define the planning model that meets the customers' business process. The experts can define key figure with the right levels of aggregation and disaggregation along with calculations at different planning hierarchies. The key figures that are displayed in the Excel planning views or the analytics are aggregated based on the user's request for data at a user-defined aggregation level of attributes and time. An example is where in a consensus demand planning view, the data is viewed at months, product family, and customer region across several key figures including demand plan qty, sales, marketing finance, and consensus (Fig. 2.82). However, each of the underlying key figures can be stored or calculated key figures defined at different granularity levels of attributes and time (or planning levels). The calculations defined on these key figures dictate how these key figures should be aggregated when queried by the user.

Figure 2.83 shows an example of calculations that are built by aggregating and calculations of key figures from several other calculations at different planning levels.

The above example shows that when consensus demand revenue key figure is queried by user, then at run time all the underlying calculations are executed on the fly and displayed to the user. It is common in an IBP model to have few stored key

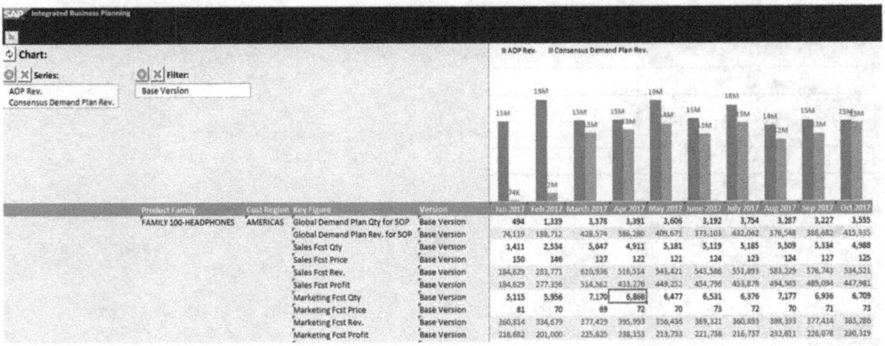


**Fig. 2.82** Calculation display in the view

figures and several calculated key figures whose results are calculated only when the user requests for it.

There are several patterns of key figure calculations that are possible, of which a few which are typically used in a planning process are defined below.

### Calculations Across Multiple Planning Levels

A simple example for this is consensus demand revenue = consensus demand qty * price. However, the input key figures can be stored or calculated at different planning levels:

*Consensus demand qty* is stored at month, product, and customer level and *price* at quarter, product family, customer, and currency level.

When calculating the *consensus demand revenue*, these key figures at different planning levels get joined based on the common attributes as shown in Fig. 2.84.

Another example is marketing forecast qty = promotions qty + marketing adjustment.

*Promotions quantity* is at month/product/customer and event level, whereas *marketing adjustment* and *marketing forecast qty* are at month/product/customer level. The calculation involves two steps aggregation and addition (Fig. 2.85):

1. *Promotions qty* at month/product/customer = SUM (promotions qty at month product/customer event)
2. *Marketing forecast qty* at month/product/customer = *promotions qty* at month product/customer + *marketing adjustment* at month/product/customer

### Price and Cost Key Figures Aggregations Using Weighted Average Calculations

When aggregating price and cost key figures, the most common aggregation method is an average. However, it does not give a correct picture to planners as the underlying revenue contribution based on the price and quantity of each product is

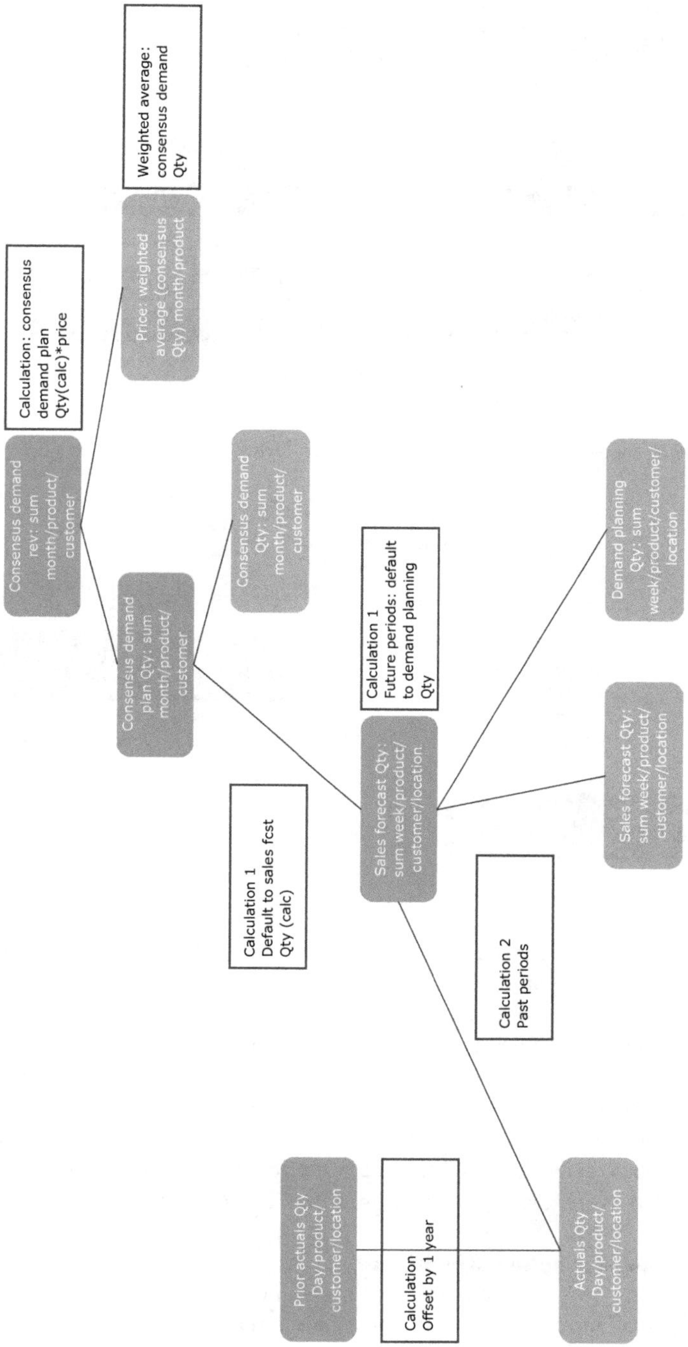


**Fig. 2.83** Key figure connection tree

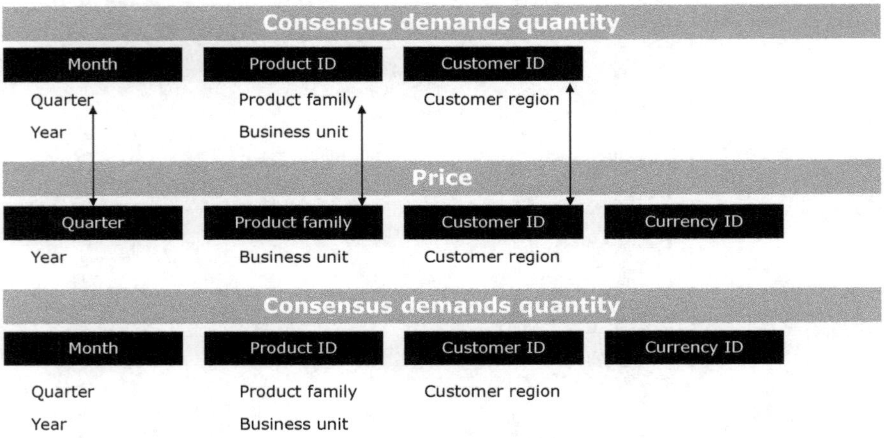


**Fig. 2.84** Key figure calculation with different planning levels

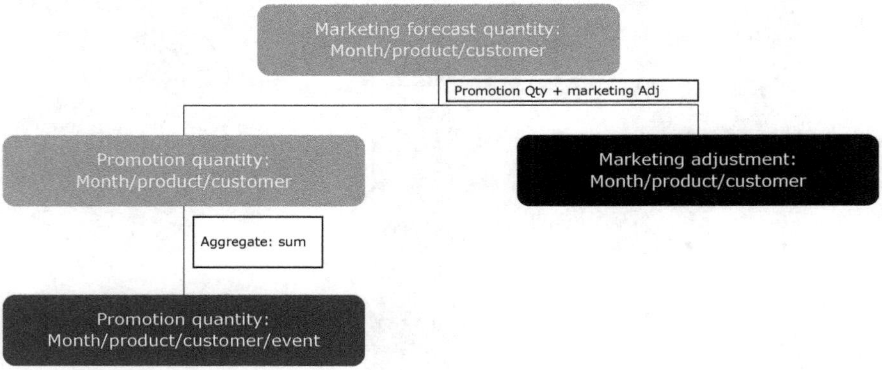


**Fig. 2.85** Calculation with aggregation and addition

not considered. The underlying products may have high forecast volumes at lower price and low forecast volumes at higher price. Therefore, to get a more accurate picture of the price, a weighted average calculation of the price based on the weighted contribution of forecast to the overall revenue is considered.

At the base level, revenue is calculated as forecast * price. When user requests for this price value at an aggregated level, this calculated revenue is aggregated along with the aggregated forecast, and then a ratio of the aggregated revenue over aggregated forecast gives the weighted average price. Figure 2.86 shows an example of how weighted average price calculation differs from the average price.

### Default to Value of Another Key Figure

In several business process scenarios, it is a common requirement that a key figure refers to values of another key figure value unless manual overrides are made. For example, sales forecast qty defaults to statistical forecast qty and sales forecast qty

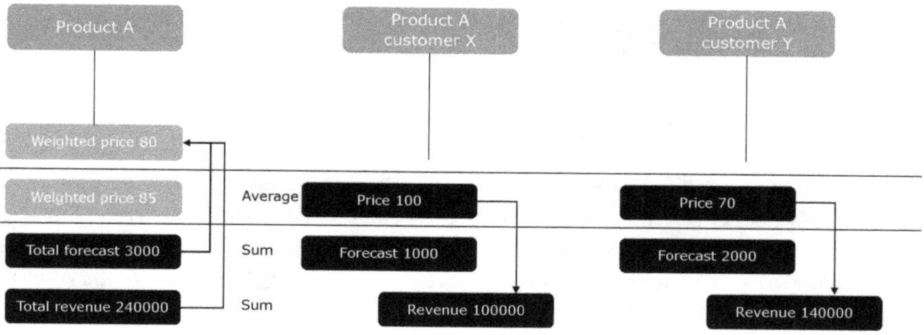


**Fig. 2.86** Weighted calculation

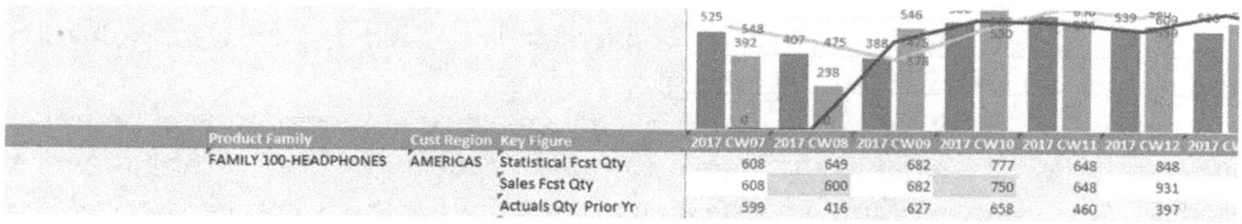


**Fig. 2.87** Defaulting key figure calculation

can be overridden with its own values. Such key figures are both stored and calculated key figures. The stored value of the key figure holds the value that has been imported into the system or entered in the Excel user interface by the user. The calculated value of the key figure at a planning level checks if the stored key figure value is empty and only then defaults to the other key figure (Fig. 2.87).

In Fig. 2.87 the sales forecast qty defaults to the statistical forecast qty in week CW07 and overridden manually in week CW08.

The logical calculation looks like the following:

Sales forecast qty at week PRODCUST [calculated] = If (sales forecast qty at week PRODCUST [stored] is 0 or empty), then statistical forecat qty at week PRODCUST [stored] is sales forecast qty at week PRODCUST [stored]

There can also be a defaulting chain defined for key figures as shown in Fig. 2.88.

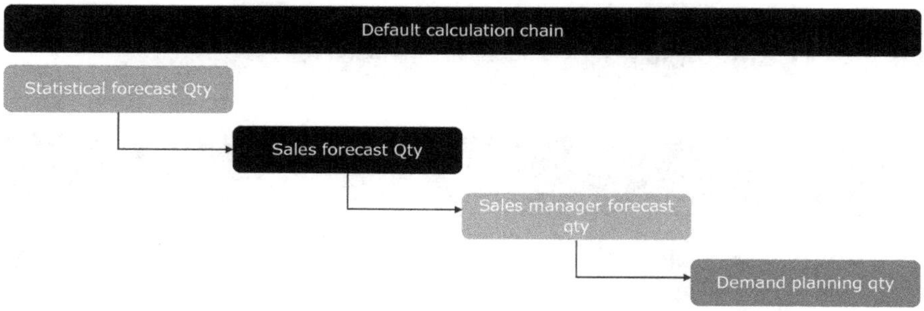


**Fig. 2.88** Key figure defaulting chain

## 2.6.6 Value and Volume Conversions Using Currency and Unit of Measure Conversions

### Currency Conversion for Finance Key Figures

The valuation of key figures like revenue, profit, price, cost, etc. associated with a plan can be viewed in a planning view or analytics in the target currency chosen by the business user. For example, the sales plans across different countries with their local currencies need to be converted to the target currency for reporting or management business reviews when viewing across all regions. The flexibility to account for projected changes in exchange rates and its impact on finance plans should be immediately visible for what-if analysis. Therefore, the currency conversion model in IBP provides the required flexibility to handle conversions across various currencies and exchange rates to have a global view on the finance data. Exchange rate variations can be simulated by modeling exchange rates as key figures. By choosing different target currency, the conversion is applied on the fly and valuation displayed in target currency (Fig. 2.89).

Logical definition: *Sales forecast revenue* is planned at month/product/customer currency, where currency is the source currency of the *sales forecast revenue* for a product and customer. Currency conversion for *sales forecast revenue* is calculated as sales forecast revenue at month/product/customer currency and currency to = sales forecast revenue at month/product/customer currency * exchange rate at currency to.

### Unit of Measure Conversions for Volume Key Figures

Many volume key figures in IBP like sales forecast qty, opportunity qty, and consensus demand qty represent quantities that need to be aggregated from plans at different base units of measure to a common target unit of measure. Like currency conversions, the units of measure conversion also apply the UOM conversion factor to the base key figure (Fig. 2.90).

However, the units of measure conversions are typically dependent on the product and are mostly constant, i.e., don't vary by time. In Fig. 2.91, each product has a base unit of measure. The UOM conversion master data type represents the conversion factor from product UOM to the target UOM. Conversion factor modeled as master data attribute is then time-independent attribute.

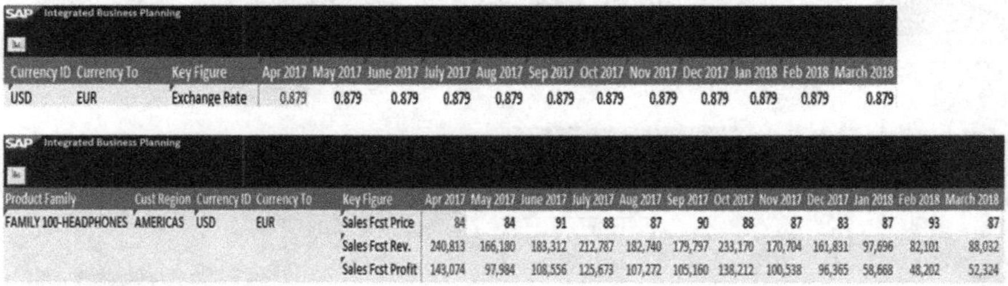
SAP Integrated Business Planning

| Currency ID | Currency To | Key Figure | Apr 2017 | May 2017 | June 2017 | July 2017 | Aug 2017 | Sep 2017 | Oct 2017 | Nov 2017 | Dec 2017 | Jan 2018 | Feb 2018 | March 2018 |
|---|---|---|---|---|---|---|---|---|---|---|---|---|---|---|
| USD | EUR | Exchange Rate | 0.879 | 0.879 | 0.879 | 0.879 | 0.879 | 0.879 | 0.879 | 0.879 | 0.879 | 0.879 | 0.879 | 0.879 |

SAP Integrated Business Planning

| Product Family | Cust Region | Currency ID | Currency To | Key Figure | Apr 2017 | May 2017 | June 2017 | July 2017 | Aug 2017 | Sep 2017 | Oct 2017 | Nov 2017 | Dec 2017 | Jan 2018 | Feb 2018 | March 2018 |
|---|---|---|---|---|---|---|---|---|---|---|---|---|---|---|---|---|
| FAMILY 100-HEADPHONES | AMERICAS | USD | EUR | Sales Fcst Price | 84 | 84 | 91 | 88 | 87 | 90 | 88 | 87 | 83 | 87 | 93 | 87 |
| | | | | Sales Fcst Rev. | 240,813 | 166,180 | 183,312 | 212,787 | 182,740 | 179,797 | 233,170 | 170,704 | 161,831 | 97,696 | 82,101 | 88,032 |
| | | | | Sales Fcst Profit | 143,074 | 97,984 | 108,556 | 125,673 | 107,272 | 105,160 | 138,212 | 100,538 | 96,365 | 58,668 | 48,202 | 52,324 |

**Fig. 2.89** Exchange rates for value key figures

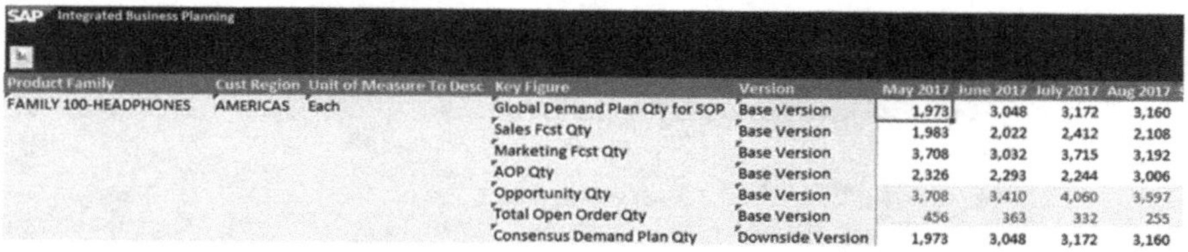

| Product Family | Cust Region | Unit of Measure To Desc | Key Figure | Version | May 2017 | June 2017 | July 2017 | Aug 2017 |
|---|---|---|---|---|---|---|---|---|
| FAMILY 100-HEADPHONES | AMERICAS | Each | Global Demand Plan Qty for SOP | Base Version | 1,973 | 3,048 | 3,172 | 3,160 |
| | | | Sales Fcst Qty | Base Version | 1,983 | 2,022 | 2,412 | 2,108 |
| | | | Marketing Fcst Qty | Base Version | 3,708 | 3,032 | 3,715 | 3,192 |
| | | | AOP Qty | Base Version | 2,326 | 2,293 | 2,244 | 3,006 |
| | | | Opportunity Qty | Base Version | 3,708 | 3,410 | 4,060 | 3,597 |
| | | | Total Open Order Qty | Base Version | 456 | 363 | 332 | 255 |
| | | | Consensus Demand Plan Qty | Downside Version | 1,973 | 3,048 | 3,172 | 3,160 |

**Fig. 2.90** Unit of measure conversion

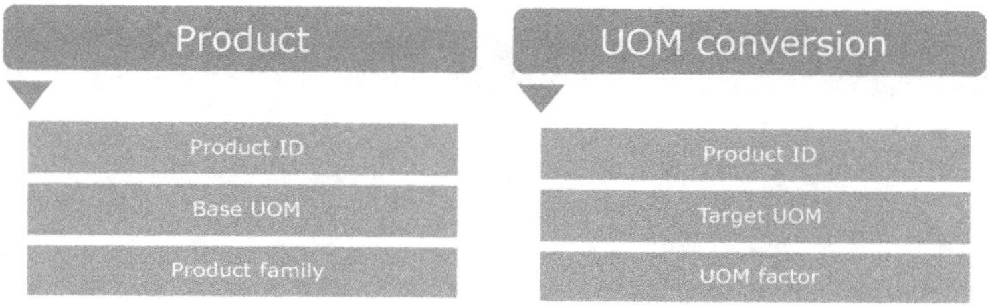


**Fig. 2.91** Unit of measure conversion assignment

The logical calculation is as follows for UOM conversion of source key figure *sales forecast qty:*

*Sales forecast qty* at month/product/customer target UOM = *sales forecast qty* at month product/customer * *UOM factor* at product target UOM

**Currency and UOM Conversions for Price and Cost Key Figures**

Most price and cost key figures are value-based key figures for a unit qty, e.g., average selling price (ASP) = $5/unit. Therefore, both currency and units of measure conversion need to be applied to the key figure calculations where UOM conversion factor is time-independent value and varies by product, whereas currency conversion is based on the time-varying currency conversion factor between source and target currencies.

The logical calculation of price key figure conversion is as follows (Fig. 2.92):

1. Perform UOM conversion

   *Sales forecast price* at month/product/customer currency target UOM = *sales forecast price at month/product/customer currency * UOM factor at product target UOM*
2. Perform currency conversion

   *Sales forecast price* at month/product/customer currency target UOM = *sales forecast price at month/product/customer currency target UOM * exchange rate at product target UOM* currency

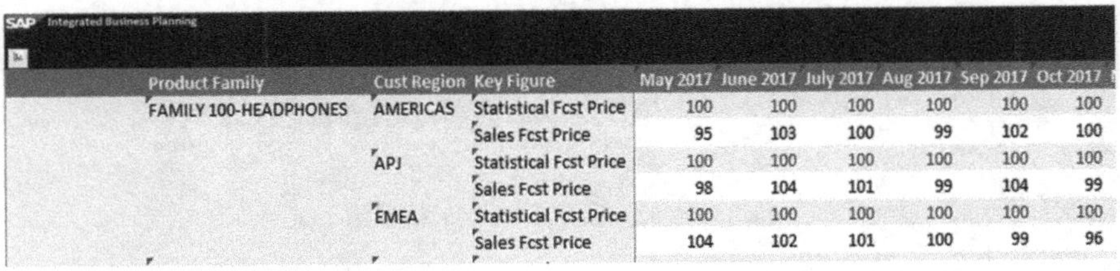

SAP Integrated Business Planning

| Product Family | Cust Region | Key Figure | May 2017 | June 2017 | July 2017 | Aug 2017 | Sep 2017 | Oct 2017 |
|---|---|---|---|---|---|---|---|---|
| FAMILY 100-HEADPHONES | AMERICAS | Statistical Fcst Price | 100 | 100 | 100 | 100 | 100 | 100 |
| | | Sales Fcst Price | 95 | 103 | 100 | 99 | 102 | 100 |
| | APJ | Statistical Fcst Price | 100 | 100 | 100 | 100 | 100 | 100 |
| | | Sales Fcst Price | 98 | 104 | 101 | 99 | 104 | 99 |
| | EMEA | Statistical Fcst Price | 100 | 100 | 100 | 100 | 100 | 100 |
| | | Sales Fcst Price | 104 | 102 | 101 | 100 | 99 | 96 |

**Fig. 2.92** Unit of measure and currency conversion

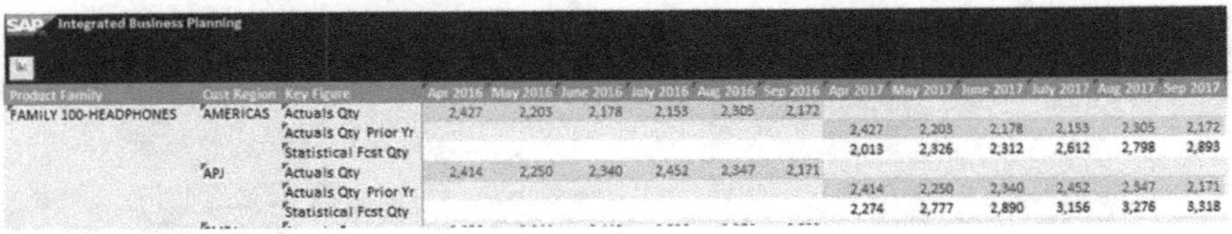

SAP Integrated Business Planning

| Product Family | Cust Region | Key Figure | Apr 2016 | May 2016 | June 2016 | July 2016 | Aug 2016 | Sep 2016 | Apr 2017 | May 2017 | June 2017 | July 2017 | Aug 2017 | Sep 2017 |
|---|---|---|---|---|---|---|---|---|---|---|---|---|---|---|
| FAMILY 100-HEADPHONES | AMERICAS | Actuals Qty | 2,427 | 2,203 | 2,178 | 2,153 | 2,305 | 2,172 | | | | | | |
| | | Actuals Qty Prior Yr | | | | | | | 2,427 | 2,203 | 2,178 | 2,153 | 2,305 | 2,172 |
| | | Statistical Fcst Qty | | | | | | | 2,013 | 2,326 | 2,312 | 2,612 | 2,798 | 2,893 |
| | APJ | Actuals Qty | 2,414 | 2,250 | 2,340 | 2,452 | 2,347 | 2,171 | | | | | | |
| | | Actuals Qty Prior Yr | | | | | | | 2,414 | 2,250 | 2,340 | 2,452 | 2,347 | 2,171 |
| | | Statistical Fcst Qty | | | | | | | 2,274 | 2,777 | 2,890 | 3,156 | 3,276 | 3,318 |

**Fig. 2.93** Year-over-year actuals

## Year-Over-Year: Show Prior Year Values in Current Year Using Period Shifting, Time, and Attribute Transformations

Attribute transformations in IBP provide the flexibility to transform an attribute value. These could be attributes of time dimensions or the planning dimensions. For example, we can time shift the months by 12 periods to view the actuals qty of last year "over" the current year. This helps in the demand planning process to compare current year values to the last year before making some planning data adjustments or to perform variance analysis (Fig. 2.93).

Logical calculation of the above can be defined as follows:

PERIODID0 (monthly period) at transformed month/product/customer = PERIODID0 + 12 (input KF: actuals qty at month/product/customer).

That means we have a new transformed planning level which is same as month/product/customer but in this planning level, the month is shifted by 12 periods. When actuals qty key figure is viewed at this transformed planning level, then the last year value is displayed in the current year.

Same can be applied to attributes to transform value of one attribute to another, for example, in the demand planning bill of material modeling to calculate dependent and independent demand of a product.

## Actuals in Past Periods for Sales Forecast Qty: Using Time Periods Calculations

Some of the commonly used time-related calculations on key figures are as follows:

For past periods of sales forecast qty, use actuals qty, and for future periods, use the stored/editable value of sales forecast qty (Fig. 2.94).

The input key figure actuals qty can be at a different planning level say week, product, location, and customer. This first needs to be aggregated to month/product/customer level, and then the calculations are performed at that level:

SAP Integrated Business Planning

| Product Family | Cust Region | Key Figure | Jan 2017 | Feb 2017 | March 2017 | Apr 2017 | May 2017 | June 2017 | July 2017 | Aug 2017 |
|---|---|---|---|---|---|---|---|---|---|---|
| FAMILY 100-HEADPHONES | AMERICAS | Actuals Qty | 2,220 | 2,010 | 2,080 | | | | | |
| | | Sales Forecast Qty | 2,220 | 2,010 | 2,080 | 2,427 | 2,203 | 2,178 | 2,153 | 2,305 |

**Fig. 2.94** Past from actuals and future from forecast

SAP Integrated Business Planning

| Product Family | Cust Region | Key Figure | Jan 2017 | Feb 2017 | March 2017 | Apr 2017 | May 2017 | June 2017 | July 2017 | Aug 2017 | Sep 2017 | Oct 2017 | Nov 2017 | Dec 2017 |
|---|---|---|---|---|---|---|---|---|---|---|---|---|---|---|
| FAMILY 100-HEADPHONES | AMERICAS | Actuals Qty | 2,220 | 2,010 | 2,080 | | | | | | | | | |
| | | Sales Forecast Qty | 2,220 | 2,010 | 2,080 | 2,427 | 2,203 | 2,178 | 2,153 | 2,305 | 2,172 | 2,382 | 2,062 | 2,250 |
| | | YTD Sales | | | | 6,310 | | | | | | | | |
| | | YTG Sales | | | | 17,705 | | | | | | | | |

**Fig. 2.95** YTD, YTG

If (month < current month, actuals qty, sales forecast qty).

### Year-to-Date and Year-to-Go

Sales volume is calculated and displayed in the current year based on actuals and forecast (see Fig. 2.95).

The calculation model is as follows:

1. YTD sales at month/product/customer = If (year = current year and month < currency month then actuals qty) otherwise empty value
2. Aggregate and drop months to get time-independent YTD sales value
   YTD sales at product/customer = SUM (YTD sales at month/product/customer)
3. Add back the time dimension by joining on any time-related key figure
   *YTD sales* at current month/product/customer = If (month = current month then *YTD sales* at product/customer) otherwise empty value. Input, sales qty at month/product/customer
   YTD; YTG is very useful to quickly analyze your forecast and plans.

### Period-to-Period Comparison of a Key Figure Using Time Profile Attributes

Typically, during planning there are several analyses of data performed at different levels of hierarchies of time and planning attributes. One of such use case is to perform period-to-period comparison of key figures. For example, show quarter-to-quarter comparisons, month-to-month comparison, or year-to-year comparisons of actual sales. This gives insights into the data and allows to drill down and analyze further to provide quantitative insights for planning and decision-making.

IBP provides time profiles to which time attributes can be added. These time profile attributes, for example, month in year, quarter in year, etc., can then be added as regular planning attributes in the planning views or analytics to perform period-to-period comparisons.

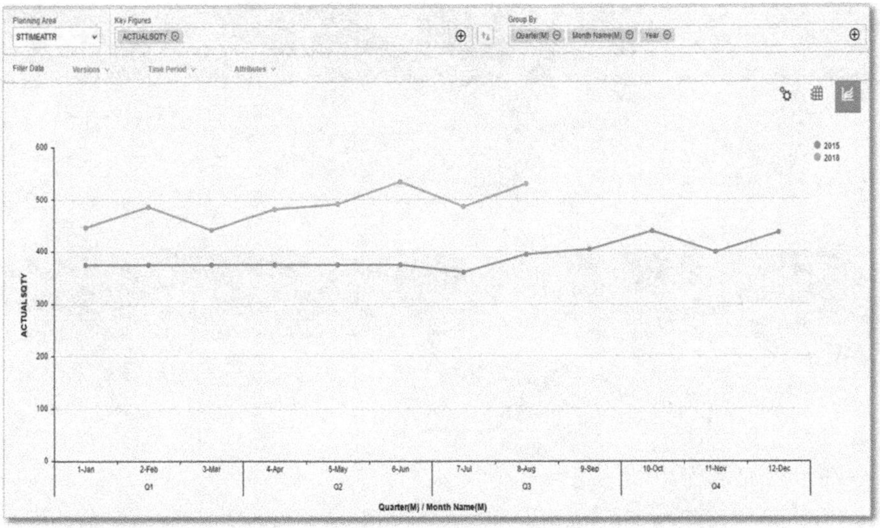


**Fig. 2.96** Time profile attributes (month over month example) in analytics

As shown in Fig. 2.96, month-to-month comparison of each quarter for actual sales and year-to-year comparison by month in analytics are few of the examples possible using time profile attributes.

### Product Mix Configuration Using Split Factor Configuration

Some of the other modeling patterns possible with IBP are split factor configuration where an aggregated key figure value say KF1 can be calculated at lower planning level based on the proportional factors of an input key figure KF2 when aggregated to planning level of KF1.

Example includes finding the sales qty mix by doing a contribution of sales qty of each product to the aggregated product family (Fig. 2.97).

### Last Period Aggregation

If we take key figure cumulative sales as a running total of sales forecast qty for each period, when this key figure is aggregated to quarters, the value of the last month of each quarter for cumulative sales should be carried over to the value in the quarter bucket as shown in Fig. 2.98.

### Flexible Time Axis: Telescopic View of Planning Data

With the management of planning data across strategic, tactical, and operation plans spanning different time horizons of years, quarters, months, weeks, and up to daily level, it is important for planners to manage their view based on a telescoping view of data across time. This means viewing short-term horizon in weeks for next 12 weeks following by midterm to long-term horizon in months followed by the long-term horizon in quarters and years.

SAP Integrated Business Planning

| Product Family | Product ID | Customer ID | Key Figure | Jan'16 | Feb'16 | Mar'16 | Apr'16 | May'16 |
|---|---|---|---|---|---|---|---|---|
| IBP | IBP-110 | (None) | Sales Qty Mix | 61% | 64% | 64% | 61% | 63% |
| | | 101 | Sales Qty | 1,000 | 1,100 | 1,100 | 1,000 | 1,200 |
| | | 102 | Sales Qty | 250 | 250 | 250 | 250 | 250 |
| | IBP-120 | (None) | Sales Qty Mix | 20% | 17% | 19% | 24% | 20% |
| | | 101 | Sales Qty | 400 | 350 | 400 | 500 | 450 |
| | IBP-130 | (None) | Sales Qty Mix | 20% | 19% | 17% | 15% | 17% |
| | | 102 | Sales Qty | 400 | 400 | 350 | 300 | 400 |

**Fig. 2.97** Split factors

SAP Integrated Business Planning

| Product ID | Customer ID | Key Figure | Apr 2017 | May 2017 | June 2017 | July 2017 | Aug 2017 | Sep 2017 | Oct 2017 | Nov 2017 | Dec 2017 |
|---|---|---|---|---|---|---|---|---|---|---|---|
| IBP-100 | 17100001 | Sales Fcst Qty | 200 | 200 | 200 | 200 | 200 | 200 | 200 | 200 | 200 |
| | | Cumulative Sales | 800 | 1,000 | 1,200 | 1,400 | 1,600 | 1,800 | 2,000 | 2,200 | 2,400 |

SAP Integrated Business Planning

| Product ID | Customer ID | Key Figure | Q2 2017 | Q3 2107 | Q4 2017 |
|---|---|---|---|---|---|
| IBP-100 | 17100001 | Sales Fcst Qty | 600 | 600 | 600 |
| | | Cumulative Sales | 1,200 | 1,800 | 2,400 |

**Fig. 2.98** Cumulative aggregations per last period of the quarter

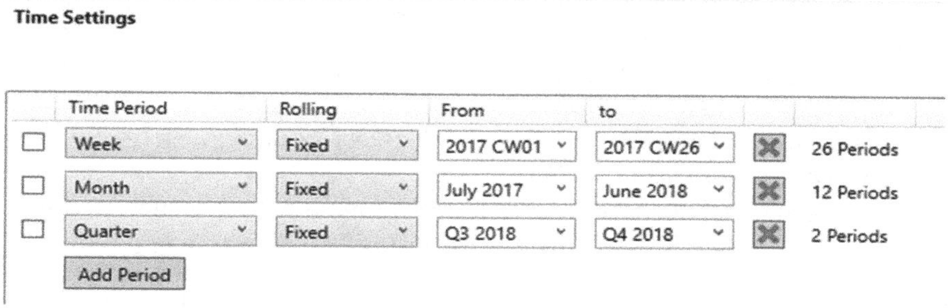


**Fig. 2.99** Time profiling Excel planning view

Such flexibility is provided in IBP planning views where the time settings of a planning view can be maintained to create a telescopic view (Fig. 2.99).

The above settings then get respected in the planning view showing data across time periods (Fig. 2.100).

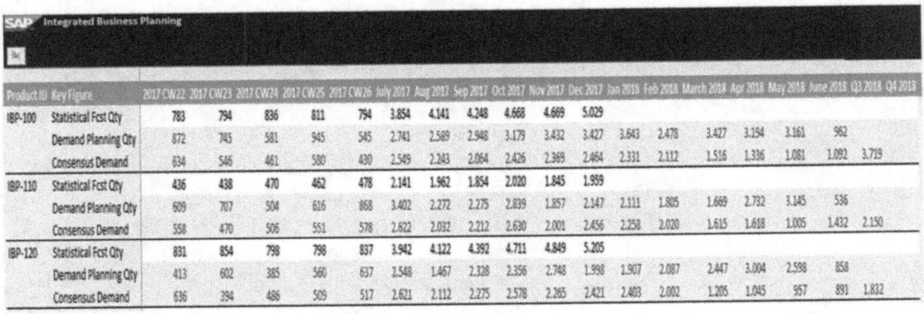


| Product ID | Key Figure | 2017 CW22 | 2017 CW23 | 2017 CW24 | 2017 CW25 | 2017 CW26 | July 2017 | Aug 2017 | Sep 2017 | Oct 2017 | Nov 2017 | Dec 2017 | Jan 2018 | Feb 2018 | March 2018 | Apr 2018 | May 2018 | June 2018 | Q3 2018 | Q4 2018 |
|---|---|---|---|---|---|---|---|---|---|---|---|---|---|---|---|---|---|---|---|---|
| IBP-100 | Statistical Fcst Qty | 783 | 794 | 836 | 811 | 794 | 3.854 | 4.141 | 4.248 | 4.668 | 4.669 | 5.029 | | | | | | | | |
| | Demand Planning Qty | 872 | 745 | 581 | 945 | 545 | 2.741 | 2.589 | 2.948 | 3.179 | 3.432 | 3.427 | 3.643 | 2.478 | 3.427 | 3.194 | 3.161 | 962 | | |
| | Consensus Demand | 634 | 546 | 461 | 580 | 430 | 2.549 | 2.243 | 2.064 | 2.426 | 2.369 | 2.464 | 2.331 | 2.112 | 1.516 | 1.336 | 1.081 | 1.092 | 3.719 | |
| IBP-110 | Statistical Fcst Qty | 436 | 438 | 470 | 462 | 478 | 2.141 | 1.962 | 1.854 | 2.020 | 1.845 | 1.959 | | | | | | | | |
| | Demand Planning Qty | 609 | 707 | 504 | 616 | 868 | 3.402 | 2.272 | 2.275 | 2.839 | 1.857 | 2.147 | 2.111 | 1.805 | 1.669 | 2.732 | 3.145 | 536 | | |
| | Consensus Demand | 558 | 470 | 506 | 551 | 578 | 2.622 | 2.032 | 2.212 | 2.630 | 2.001 | 2.456 | 2.258 | 2.020 | 1.615 | 1.618 | 1.005 | 1.432 | 2.150 | |
| IBP-120 | Statistical Fcst Qty | 831 | 854 | 798 | 798 | 837 | 3.942 | 4.122 | 4.392 | 4.711 | 4.849 | 5.205 | | | | | | | | |
| | Demand Planning Qty | 413 | 602 | 385 | 560 | 637 | 2.548 | 1.467 | 2.328 | 2.356 | 2.748 | 1.998 | 1.907 | 2.087 | 2.447 | 3.004 | 2.598 | 858 | | |
| | Consensus Demand | 636 | 394 | 486 | 509 | 517 | 2.621 | 2.112 | 2.275 | 2.578 | 2.265 | 2.421 | 2.403 | 2.002 | 1.205 | 1.045 | 957 | 891 | 1.832 | |

**Fig. 2.100** Telescopic view in Excel UI

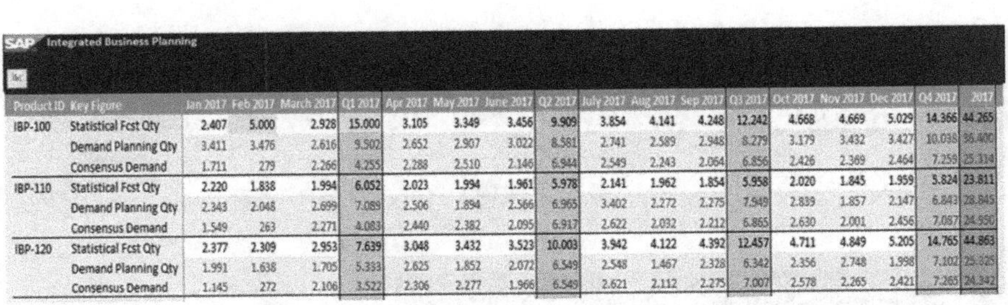


| Product ID | Key Figure | Jan 2017 | Feb 2017 | March 2017 | Q1 2017 | Apr 2017 | May 2017 | June 2017 | Q2 2017 | July 2017 | Aug 2017 | Sep 2017 | Q3 2017 | Oct 2017 | Nov 2017 | Dec 2017 | Q4 2017 | 2017 |
|---|---|---|---|---|---|---|---|---|---|---|---|---|---|---|---|---|---|---|
| IBP-100 | Statistical Fcst Qty | 2.407 | 5.000 | 2.928 | 15.000 | 3.105 | 3.349 | 3.456 | 9.909 | 3.854 | 4.141 | 4.248 | 12.242 | 4.668 | 4.669 | 5.029 | 14.366 | 44.265 |
| | Demand Planning Qty | 3.411 | 3.476 | 2.616 | 9.502 | 2.652 | 2.907 | 3.022 | 8.581 | 2.741 | 2.589 | 2.948 | 8.279 | 3.179 | 3.432 | 3.427 | 10.038 | 36.400 |
| | Consensus Demand | 1.711 | 279 | 2.266 | 4.255 | 2.288 | 2.510 | 2.146 | 6.944 | 2.549 | 2.243 | 2.064 | 6.856 | 2.426 | 2.369 | 2.464 | 7.259 | 25.314 |
| IBP-110 | Statistical Fcst Qty | 2.220 | 1.838 | 1.994 | 6.052 | 2.023 | 1.994 | 1.961 | 5.978 | 2.141 | 1.962 | 1.854 | 5.958 | 2.020 | 1.845 | 1.959 | 5.824 | 23.811 |
| | Demand Planning Qty | 2.343 | 2.048 | 2.699 | 7.089 | 2.506 | 1.894 | 2.566 | 6.965 | 3.402 | 2.272 | 2.275 | 7.949 | 2.839 | 1.857 | 2.147 | 6.843 | 28.845 |
| | Consensus Demand | 1.549 | 263 | 2.271 | 4.083 | 2.440 | 2.382 | 2.095 | 6.917 | 2.622 | 2.032 | 2.212 | 6.865 | 2.630 | 2.001 | 2.456 | 7.087 | 24.950 |
| IBP-120 | Statistical Fcst Qty | 2.377 | 2.309 | 2.953 | 7.639 | 3.048 | 3.432 | 3.523 | 10.003 | 3.942 | 4.122 | 4.392 | 12.457 | 4.711 | 4.849 | 5.205 | 14.765 | 44.863 |
| | Demand Planning Qty | 1.991 | 1.638 | 1.705 | 5.333 | 2.625 | 1.852 | 2.072 | 6.549 | 2.548 | 1.467 | 2.328 | 6.342 | 2.356 | 2.748 | 1.998 | 7.102 | 25.325 |
| | Consensus Demand | 1.145 | 272 | 2.106 | 3.522 | 2.306 | 2.277 | 1.966 | 6.549 | 2.621 | 2.112 | 2.275 | 7.007 | 2.578 | 2.265 | 2.421 | 7.265 | 24.342 |

**Fig. 2.101** Subtotaling in Excel UI

The time settings of a planning view can be further set up to show subtotals of data by time, i.e., show months planning data along with rolled up quarters and yearly sums. This setting applies to all key figures in the planning view as shown in the template. This could be thought of overlaying individual monthly, weekly, and yearly planning views together (Fig. 2.101).

User does not configure data model. User has a lot of flexibility to define his or hers ways of working without intervention of IT department. SAP IBP is more self-service oriented than any previous planning SAP tool. Main user interface of SAP IBP is Excel UI (Fig. 2.102).

In the implementation process, either you start from predefined templates (example shown above) or you modify them or you start from scratch.

SAP IBP is oriented in large for "self-service." User can create their own ways of working aligned to insights by themselves. Users can create out of default project or SAP template their own favorite where they can change and adjust how they interact with system and data.

**Time Horizon and Periodicity** User can select how they display data on time axis per their needs. This feature will help you to have details on shorter horizon and aggregation in long term (Fig. 2.103).

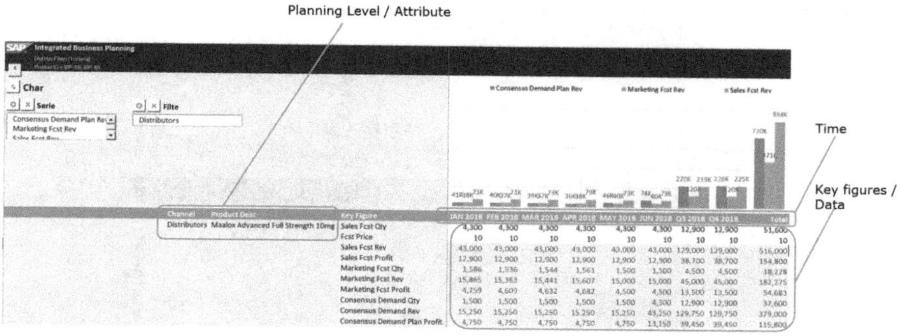

**Fig. 2.102** SAP IBP—Excel UI planning screen overview

**Time Settings**

| What to Show | | Label for Total | Time Period | | Rolling | | From | | to | | | |
|---|---|---|---|---|---|---|---|---|---|---|---|---|
| ☐ | Periods ⌄ | | Month ⌄ | | Rolling ⌄ | | JAN 2018 ⌄ | | JUN 2018 ⌄ | | ✖ | 6 Periods |
| ☐ | Periods ⌄ | | Quarter ⌄ | | Rolling ⌄ | | Q3 2018 ⌄ | | Q4 2018 ⌄ | | ✖ | 2 Periods |
| ☐ | Total ⌄ | Total | Year ⌄ | | Rolling ⌄ | | 2018 ⌄ | | 2018 ⌄ | | ✖ | 1 Period |
| | Add Period | | | | | | | | | | | |

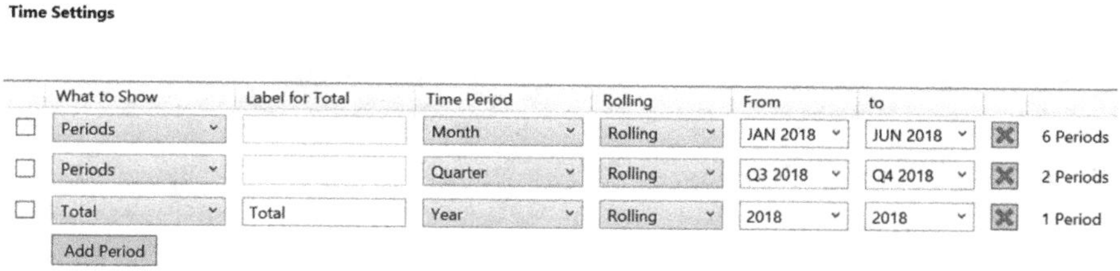

**Fig. 2.103** SAP IBP—time dimensions in Excel planning view

**Key Figures** Data are shown in quantities or values and totals and displayed in the view. Some key figures are stored like sales forecast qty, and some are calculated like sales forecast revenue. Further key figures have properties of what can be edited and what can be view only.

**Planning Levels** The key figures are viewed and edited at any chosen level of data, e.g., product family and customer region. These are the planning levels at which the data is viewed and can be edited. However, each of these key figures could be defined at different base levels like sales qty is defined at product/customer and month level.

User interacts with data in similar way like in MS Excel pivot table (Fig. 2.104).

User can select *versions and scenarios* which represents alternate plans (Fig. 2.105).

User can define subtotaling on planning level, so they can work on detail and see immediately impact on the total (Fig. 2.106).

Subtotaling is configured by user and can be stored in favorite or template (Fig. 2.107).

We would like to bring user experience comparison brought by our colleague (Fig. 2.108).

Knowing how to operate pivot table, you may get very good starting point on how to operate data in SAP IBP.

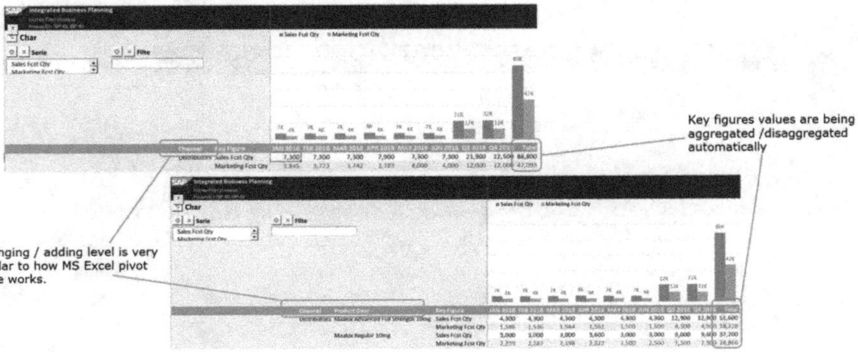


**Fig. 2.104** SAP IBP and Microsoft Excel pivot table analogy

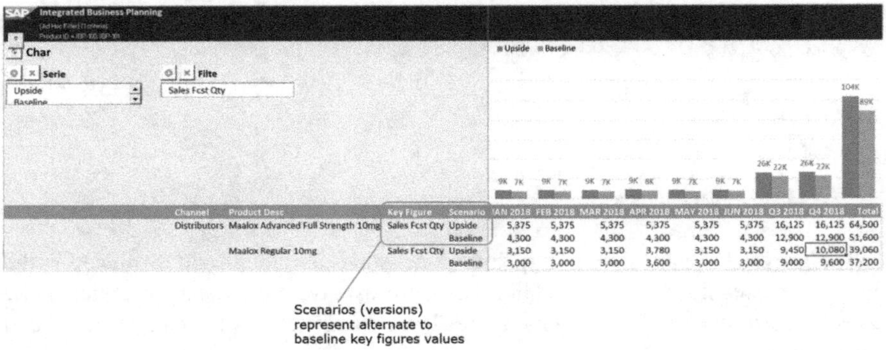


| Channel | Product Desc | Key Figure | Scenario | JAN 2018 | FEB 2018 | MAR 2018 | APR 2018 | MAY 2018 | JUN 2018 | Q3 2018 | Q4 2018 | Total |
|---|---|---|---|---|---|---|---|---|---|---|---|---|
| Distributors | Maalox Advanced Full Strength 10mg | Sales Fcst Qty | Upside | 5,375 | 5,375 | 5,375 | 5,375 | 5,375 | 5,375 | 16,125 | 16,125 | 64,500 |
| | | | Baseline | 4,300 | 4,300 | 4,300 | 4,300 | 4,300 | 4,300 | 12,900 | 12,900 | 51,600 |
| | Maalox Regular 10mg | Sales Fcst Qty | Upside | 3,150 | 3,150 | 3,150 | 3,780 | 3,150 | 3,150 | 9,450 | 10,080 | 39,060 |
| | | | Baseline | 3,000 | 3,000 | 3,000 | 3,600 | 3,000 | 3,000 | 9,000 | 9,600 | 37,200 |

**Fig. 2.105** SAP IBP—scenario display in Excel UI

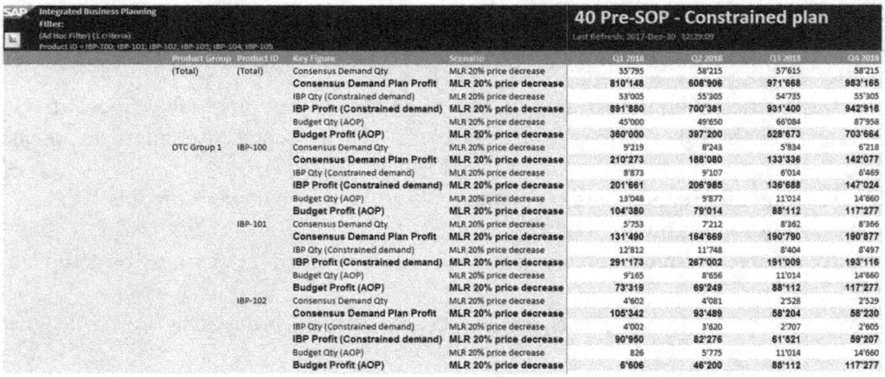


| Product Group | Product ID | Key Figure | Scenario | Q1 2018 | Q2 2018 | Q3 2018 | Q4 2018 |
|---|---|---|---|---|---|---|---|
| (Total) | (Total) | Consensus Demand Qty | MLR 20% price decrease | 55'795 | 58'215 | 57'615 | 58'215 |
| | | **Consensus Demand Plan Profit** | **MLR 20% price decrease** | **810'148** | **608'906** | **971'668** | **983'165** |
| | | IBP Qty (Constrained demand) | MLR 20% price decrease | 53'005 | 55'305 | 54'735 | 55'305 |
| | | **IBP Profit (Constrained demand)** | **MLR 20% price decrease** | **891'880** | **700'381** | **931'400** | **942'918** |
| | | Budget Qty (AOP) | MLR 20% price decrease | 45'000 | 49'650 | 66'084 | 87'958 |
| | | **Budget Profit (AOP)** | **MLR 20% price decrease** | **360'000** | **397'200** | **528'673** | **703'664** |
| OTC Group 1 | IBP-100 | Consensus Demand Qty | MLR 20% price decrease | 9'219 | 8'243 | 5'834 | 6'218 |
| | | **Consensus Demand Plan Profit** | **MLR 20% price decrease** | **210'273** | **188'080** | **133'336** | **142'077** |
| | | IBP Qty (Constrained demand) | MLR 20% price decrease | 8'873 | 9'107 | 6'014 | 6'469 |
| | | **IBP Profit (Constrained demand)** | **MLR 20% price decrease** | **201'661** | **206'985** | **136'688** | **147'024** |
| | | Budget Qty (AOP) | MLR 20% price decrease | 13'048 | 9'877 | 11'014 | 14'660 |
| | | **Budget Profit (AOP)** | **MLR 20% price decrease** | **104'380** | **79'014** | **88'112** | **117'277** |
| | IBP-101 | Consensus Demand Qty | MLR 20% price decrease | 5'753 | 7'212 | 8'362 | 8'366 |
| | | **Consensus Demand Plan Profit** | **MLR 20% price decrease** | **131'490** | **164'669** | **190'790** | **190'877** |
| | | IBP Qty (Constrained demand) | MLR 20% price decrease | 12'812 | 11'748 | 8'404 | 8'497 |
| | | **IBP Profit (Constrained demand)** | **MLR 20% price decrease** | **291'173** | **267'002** | **191'009** | **193'116** |
| | | Budget Qty (AOP) | MLR 20% price decrease | 9'165 | 8'656 | 11'014 | 14'660 |
| | | **Budget Profit (AOP)** | **MLR 20% price decrease** | **73'319** | **69'249** | **88'112** | **117'277** |
| | IBP-102 | Consensus Demand Qty | MLR 20% price decrease | 4'602 | 4'081 | 2'528 | 2'529 |
| | | **Consensus Demand Plan Profit** | **MLR 20% price decrease** | **105'342** | **93'489** | **58'204** | **58'230** |
| | | IBP Qty (Constrained demand) | MLR 20% price decrease | 4'002 | 3'620 | 2'707 | 2'605 |
| | | **IBP Profit (Constrained demand)** | **MLR 20% price decrease** | **90'950** | **82'276** | **61'521** | **59'207** |
| | | Budget Qty (AOP) | MLR 20% price decrease | 826 | 5'775 | 11'014 | 14'660 |
| | | **Budget Profit (AOP)** | **MLR 20% price decrease** | **6'606** | **46'200** | **88'112** | **117'277** |

**Fig. 2.106** Subtotaled product group coupled with working ability on product (example)

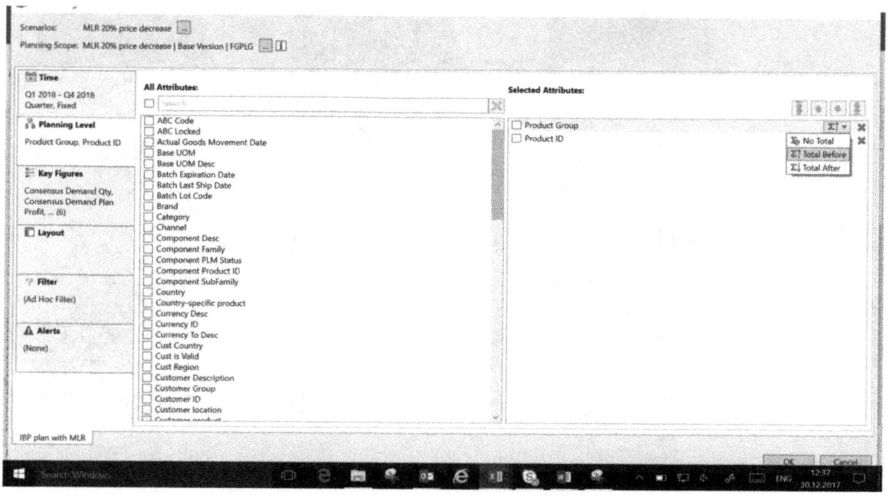

Fig. 2.107 Subtotaling on planning level

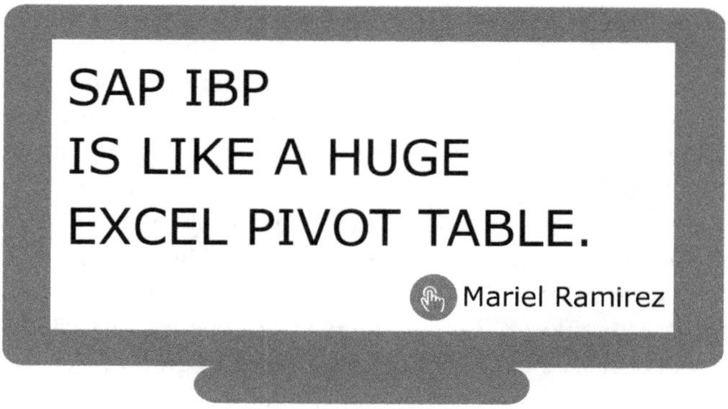


Fig. 2.108 SAP IBP like MS Excel pivot table

### 2.6.7 Access Control

One of the core capabilities of any planning solution is to provide access to the right set of data and functions to the business users accessing the system. For example, a demand planner John has access to all planning data in the regions of North America and product line A and can perform certain business functions like running statistical forecasting, viewing and managing forecast errors, etc.

A global IBP process can be managed in a single IBP system which can manage the necessary data and functional authorizations across multiple business roles, multiple business units, or multiple business lines. Such a system provides all the

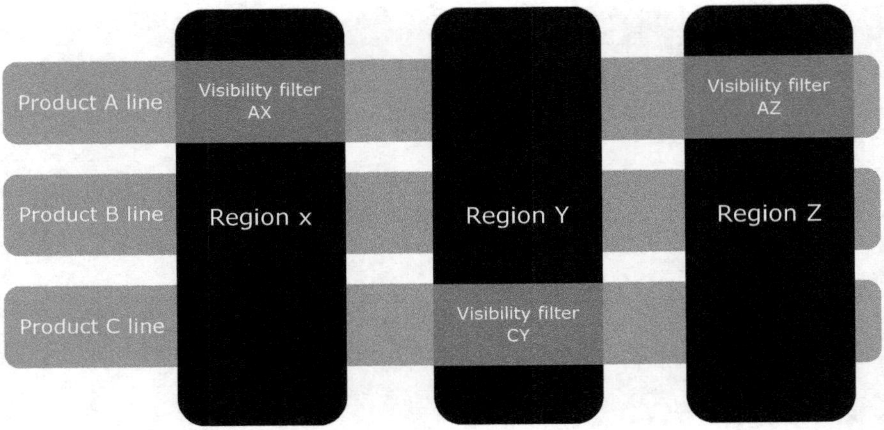


**Fig. 2.109** Visibility filters

necessary access controls and flexibility ensuring that the data does not get accessed or modified by the users who should not have access in first place.

The first step in ensuring that the users have access to the right set of data is through visibility filters.

Visibility filters control the data, i.e., master data, and key figure values that can be accessed by end users by defining conditions on the master data attributes for a planning area. For example, by creating a visibility filter for attribute product family = PF1 of product master data type and assigning it to user John, John can only access the planning data related to the product family PF1. This is a simple case; however, in real-life scenarios, customers have a multidimensional access controls for their planners across multiple attributes. For example, a planner can have access to product line A and region X. Further, there can be conditions such that a user has access to a product line A across all regions, except region Z. See Fig. 2.109 for visibility filter creation across two planning attributes.

With the above setup, the IBP application ensures that whenever the master data is accessed by the user in any parts of the application, like in Excel planning views, analytics, forecast assignments, master data maintenance, etc., only the data that the user can view and edit is available. Visibility filters can be assigned to the users or user groups or business roles in IBP.

A key figure value that is calculated and displayed in IBP to a user will have the visibility filter of the user applied. The visibility filters are applied to all the input stored key figures that are part of the resultant calculated key figure. This ensures that the right data is retrieved for the input key figures before calculations are performed such that users don't get access to data as a result of intermediate calculations (Fig. 2.110).

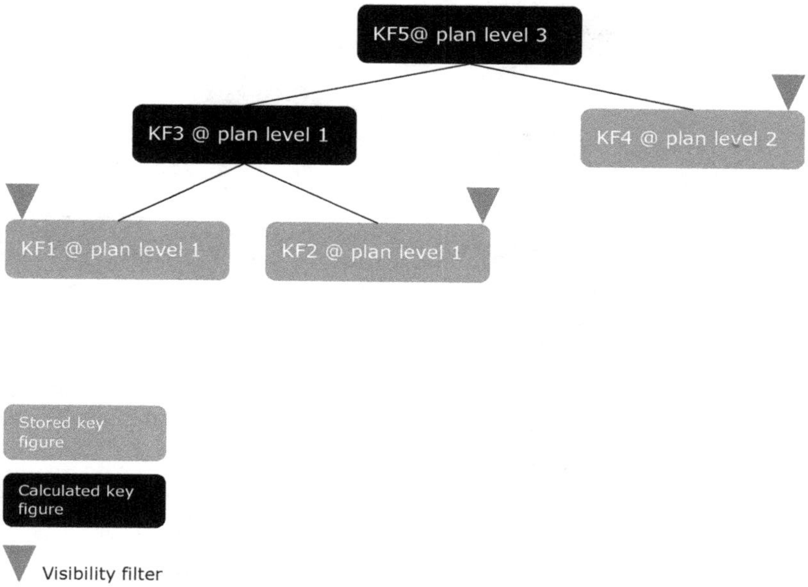


**Fig. 2.110** Visibility filters vs calculations

**IBP Permission Model**

Permissions for user to access certain data for key figures and certain functionality are managed in IBP through the constructs of user, user groups, business role, business catalogs, restrictions, and visibility filters as shown in Fig. 2.111.

**Users** These are the business users in IBP system that work on business data and perform business functions, for example, John Smith—demand planner for product line A

**User Groups** User groups can be defined in IBP to combine a set of users who participate in a collaboration activity, for example, NA demand planner user groups. Many functions in IBP such as visibility filters can be assigned to a user group. Further, dashboards, user-defined scenarios, and alerts can be shared with user groups. User groups also participate in process collaboration as part of process management capability in IBP

**Business Catalogs**

Business catalogs are business functions that give access to certain Fiori apps in IBP. For example, a demand planner typically needs access to the catalogs, such as manage forecast models, assign forecast models, analyze promotions, etc., to manage demand planning activities. The catalogs are pre-delivered in certain groups like demand planner, general planner, basic functions, etc. When defining a role, these

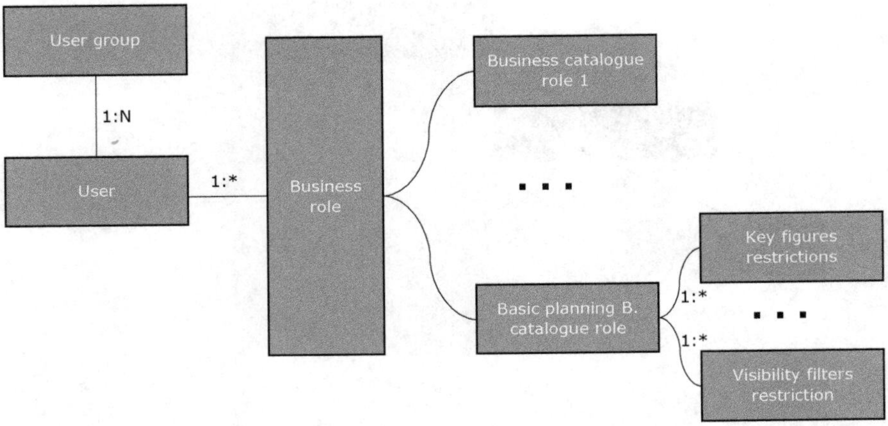


**Fig. 2.111** IBP permission model

catalogs are assigned to the role. Depending on what catalogs are assigned to a role for a user, the Fiori launchpad in IBP shows the Fiori apps relevant for that user.

Following are the pre-delivered catalogs for demand planner group in IBP:

- Manage forecast models
- Assign forecast models
- Analyze promotions
- Manage product lifecycle
- Manage forecast error calculations—demand planning
- Manage ABC/XYZ segmentation rules

**Business Roles**

Business roles in IBP bring together the required data access and functional access that can be assigned to one or more business users. For example, a company may have global demand planner role with certain set of functions—to perform basic planning functions, statistical forecasts, forecast errors, etc.—and access to certain sets of key figures that are relevant for demand planning (statistical forecast, consensus demand, demand forecast accuracy, consensus revenue, etc.) and certain set of data assigned from visibility filter.

Further, IBP provides few out of the box business roles templates with predefined catalogs that can be used a starting point for defining business roles. These include:

- Account planner
- Administrator
- Configuration expert
- Demand planner
- Inventory planner

- Supply chain analyst
- Supply planner

## 2.7 Integrate Data and Systems

In the *Integrated Business Planning* book (Kepczynski et al. 2018), we provided an overview of the current integration technologies that are facilitating the data transfer between SAP/non-SAP systems and IBP. In this chapter we explore more technical context of integration.

Let us start from an overview mapping the integration technologies with the IBP processes/modules (Fig. 2.112).

Integrated Business Planning framework brings together various processes that can be part of the extended supply chain management to facilitate the cross-functional cross companies' alignment and collaboration.

Key aspect of planning is to connect systems and information in efficient way to enable organization to understand and leverage data in business decisions, driving the organization to a competitive advantage.

The integration needs are very different from one company to another, depending on the organizations' size, degree of processes and technology standardization across locations or division, and industry specifics. When it comes to SAP IBP, the integration content is also driven by the licensed modules that are under the implementation scope.

To minimize the data integration challenge, SAP Integrated Business Planning solution comes with complementary integration technologies that will facilitate the organizations' journey in collecting/sending data from/to multiple sources. These integration technologies include:

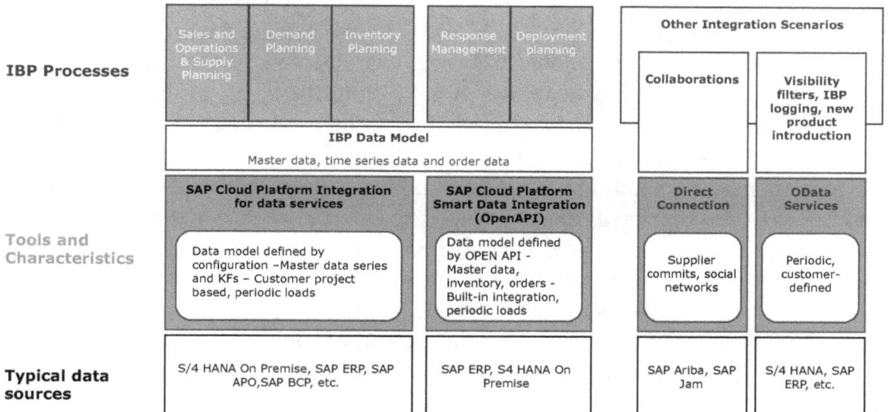


**Fig. 2.112** IBP integration technologies

- SAP Cloud Platform Integration for data services (formerly known as SAP HANA Cloud Integration for data services or HCI-DS)
- Open API based on SAP Cloud Platform Smart Data Integration (known as SDI)
- cXML message for integration with SAP Ariba Network
- RESTful web service for integration with SAP JAM collaboration
- Manual integration with CSV files

Decision tree in Fig. 2.113 depicts that each integration tool fits in connection with processes and data types such as master data, orders, etc.

There are two main integration areas:

- Batch and time series planning which is relevant for most of the IBP modules such as IBP for demand, inventory, sales and operation planning, control tower, or supply (part of supply and response)
- Near real-time and order integration for order-based planning required by IBP response

**Cloud Platform Integration for Time Series Data**

Time series integration is facilitated by SAP Cloud Platform Integration for data services. This multi-tenant cloud solution enables organizations to safely extract, transform, and load (ETL) data from source systems to IBP tables via HTTPS protocol. It comes with a simplified and intuitive web-based user interface that allows to drag and drop objects in order to define data mappings and create transformation flows.

In Fig. 2.114 we see the high-level architecture for integrating times series IBP with other on-premise solutions, SAP or non-SAP. It is easy to observe where SAP Cloud Platform Integration for data services comes into play taking the middleman role.

On the left side, we have the SAP Data Services Agent for SAP Cloud Platform Integration, which is installed behind the firewall of the customer's environment. The agent role is to provide secured connectivity and data transfer from on-premise source to the target in the cloud. The agent is able to operate without firewall exceptions, and the communication is always from the agent to the cloud which means that also when we send data from IBP to on-premise, the agent will initiate the transfer. On the right side, we have the SAP Cloud Platform Integration for data services application, where the interfaces build and management takes place. Once the data has been extracted, transformed (if required), and mapped to the target, it gets loaded into IBP staging table. From here the IBP application starts the post processing activities to evaluate whether data is consistent or not. If yes, the data is moved to the core table and immediately available for access; if not, data is being rejected, and a rejection report can be retrieved from Data Integration Jobs app.

SAP IBP provides flexible integration content based on SAP Cloud Platform Integration for data services, ready-to-use interfaces that serve as a starting point for inbound (data is loaded to IBP) and outbound (data is extracted from IBP) data transfers. The templates are designed to meet the most common requirements of a

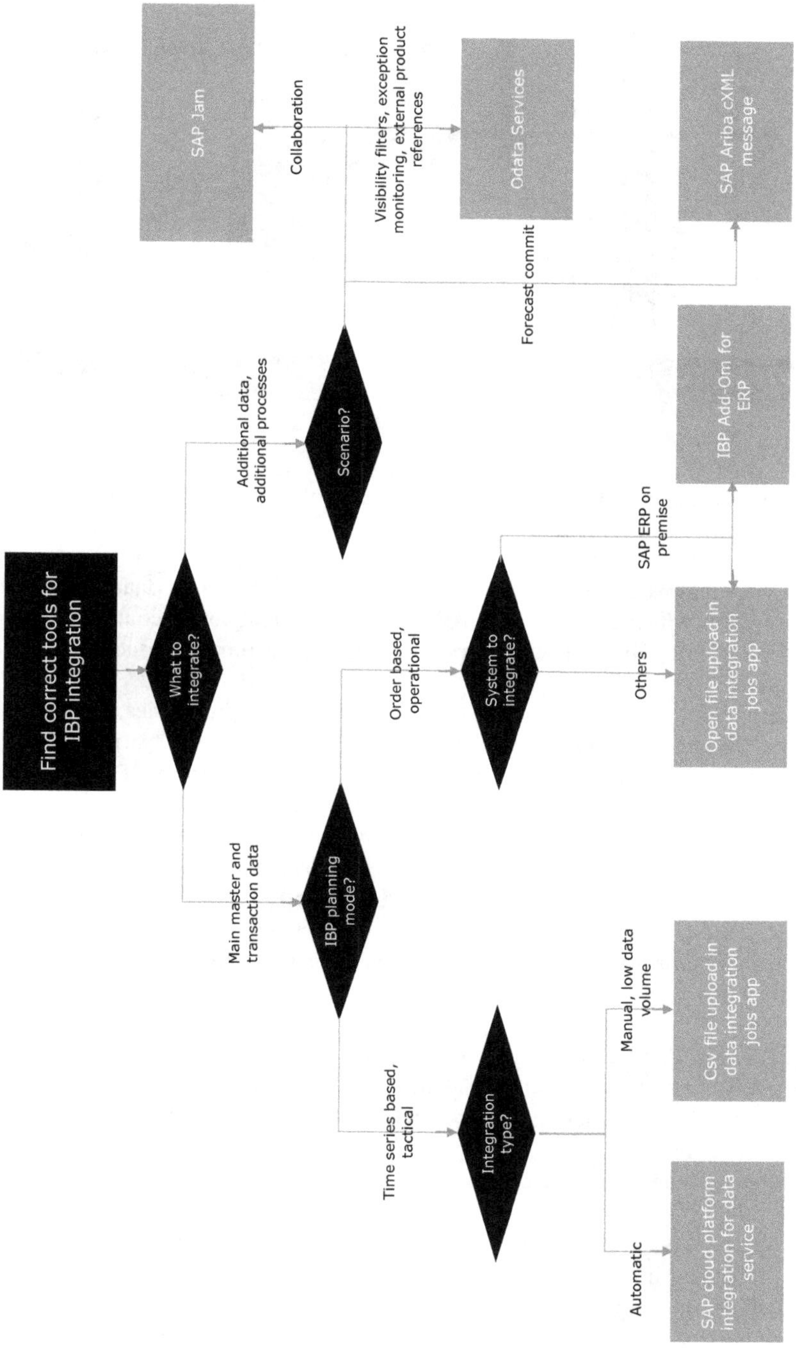


**Fig. 2.113** IBP communication/integration decision tree

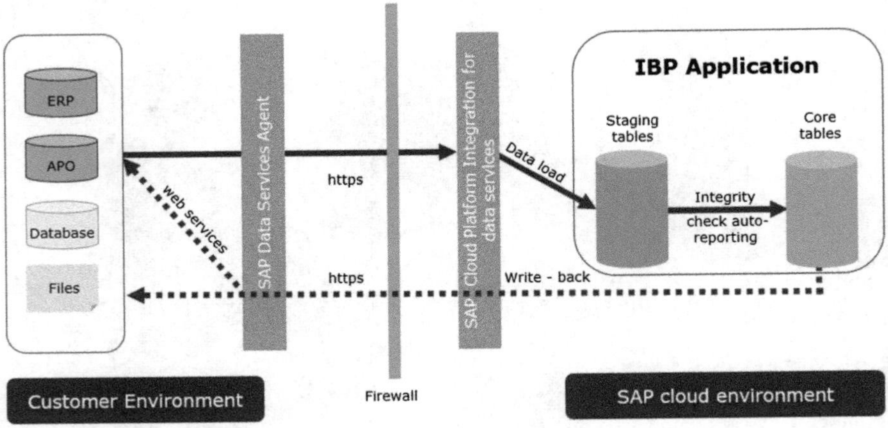


**Fig. 2.114** Overview of integration with SAP IBP

SAP Integrated Business Planning implementation project. These templates can be classified in the following groups:

- Master data templates that provide content to transfer master data from the leading system which can be SAP ERP or APO. The templates' content covers various master data objects such as product, location, customer, product-location, or resources.
- Key figure templates that are used to transfer transactional time series data. They cover key figures like initial inventory, actuals, sales forecast price that is extracted from SAP ERP or capacity limit, and consumption from APO.
- General purpose templates don't provide any data extraction, transformation, or mapping content but contain some variables that are required by IBP to process data after source data has reached the staging table, e.g., $G_PLAN_AREA, which must contain the planning area value as defined in IBP.

SAP Cloud Platform Integration for data services has the following transformation capabilities:

- Query: Retrieve dataset from single or multiple source and apply transformation.
- Target query: Last transform in the dataflow. Load data in target.
- Aggregation: Perform data aggregation based on specific input columns, e.g., sum, avg, and max.
- ABAP query: Generate ABAP code to retrieve dataset and executed on the source system
- ABAP aggregation: Perform aggregation inside SAP application
- Custom ABAP: Allow you to use you own ABAP Code to return data to CPI.
- XML map: Produce hierarchical structure as output, based on input schema.
- XML batch: Group the XML wows in batches for improved performance.
- Web service.

What we would advise as part of project preparation is the following:

- Analyze the business requirements.
- Have a good understanding of the planning model in IBP (e.g., identify the key of each master data table, identify the root attributes of each planning level where key figures must be loaded).
- Identify the source tables and fields to read data from.
- Map the source data with the target data: does the data definition between source and target match? Identify any mapping that requires data transformation first.

Data is extracted from the source using a dataflow as seen in Fig. 2.115 which defines the extraction logic such as join conditions, filters, sort, group by, look ups, if statements, field mappings, and many other.

In this example you can see an ABAP dataflow joining two source objects, the extractor 9ACA_DSTD_080 holding transactional data with the table T009B in order to retrieve data according to the correct fiscal period maintained there. There are different transform queries in between the join condition and the source objects to apply transformations at field level such as filters which are all executed in the source application highlighted by the rectangular shape. Once the transformation is completed and reached the ABAP endpoint, data is streamed from source to cloud where CPI again offers the option for adding further transform queries which are now being processed with the help of the CPI agent and then mapped to the target table SOP_STAGGING_KFTAB_ABPZ1PASOPTST.

Dataflows are then used by higher-level objects called tasks or processes. These are used to group one or more dataflows in an execution sequence.

Tasks contain the following information:

- Name, description, and project they belong to
- Source and target data stores to be used in the task's dataflows
- One or more dataflows
- Pre-/postload scripts and global variables applicable to dataflows in the task

Processes share the same properties as tasks. In addition to that SAP IBP offers, greater flexibility in ordering the load sequence of dataflows by grouping them in sequence or parallel allows the user to include dataflows from different source systems.

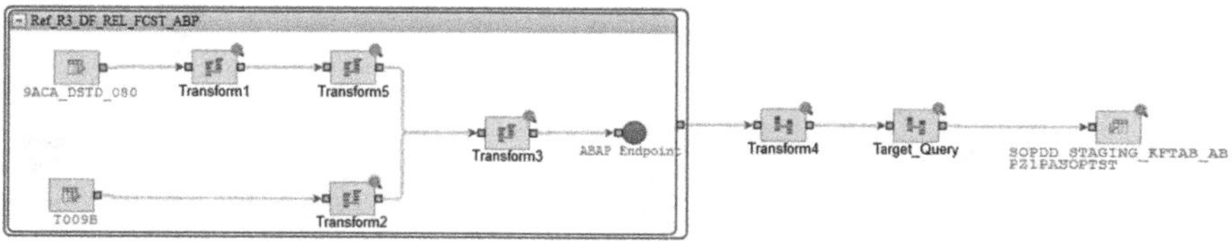


**Fig. 2.115** SAP CPI for data services—data transformation flow

You can also choose not to go with SAP Cloud Platform Integration for data services and use instead an on-premise ETL tool. With this approach, the other tool can extract data into flat files which are then loaded to IBP via HTTPS protocol using the Data Integration Jobs app. However, we don't recommend this option for production environment, and we would restrict it for the beginning of an implementation project or for a proof of concept/pilot project where data load is limited to most representative samples. Moreover, SAP Cloud Platform Integration for data services has the advantage of providing an end-to-end visibility over the integration flow which a different ETL tool cannot support as the integration would be split and intermediated by flat files.

**Cloud Platform Integration for Order Data**

Moving beyond time series planning, SAP Cloud Platform Smart Data Integration (SDI) is used to integrate data to the response application. Demand prioritization, gating factor analysis, or what-if simulations, they all require master and transactional data mainly on order level that come from external systems, SAP or non-SAP.

SDI is a native technology part of HANA database that can access, provision, replicate, and transform data for loading in SAP HANA on-premise or cloud. The data movement happens almost in real time with high speed and decreased latency due to in-memory processing.

Similar to SAP Data Services Agent, part of SAP Cloud Platform Smart Data Integration (SDI) has the Data Provisioning Agent which provides secured connectivity to the HANA database where the IBP application runs. The connectivity, metadata browsing, and data access are done through the Data Provisioning Adapter which is hosted by the Data Provisioning Agent, which can be SAP delivered or custom.

The overview of the integration between IBP response management and external systems is shown in Fig. 2.116. On the left side, we have the data sources which can be

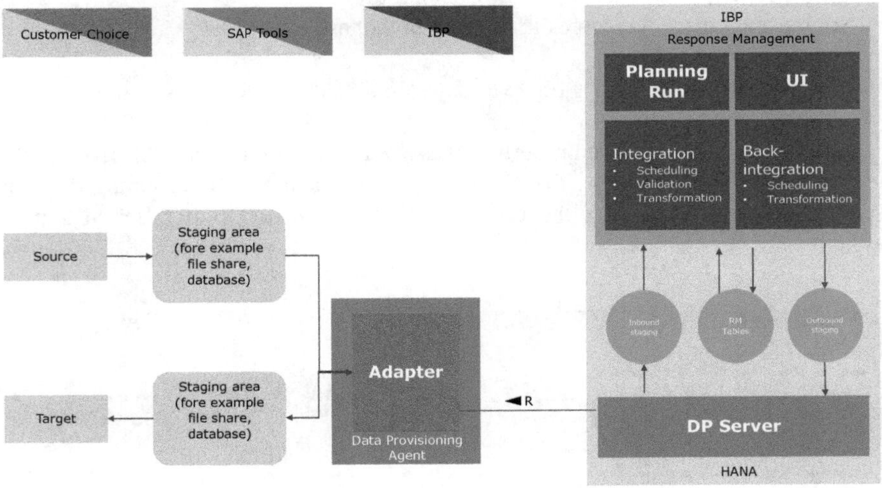


**Fig. 2.116** SAP IBP response application integration overview

SAP or non-SAP (Oracle, DB2, SQL Server, etc.). Data is extracted from these systems and stored into a staging area which can be a database or a shared file. From here the data will be sent to the response management system through the data adapter.

When the integration is with SAP ERP, you can use the SAP ERP supply chain integration add-on for SAP Integrated Business Planning. The add-on supports to gather, transform, and store the data in the database tables from where it can be accessed for integration with IBP. The connectivity between SAP ERP and IBP is enabled by the SAP Cloud Platform Smart Data Integration (SDI), while the data transfer is triggered and handled via an application job in the response application using open API.

The add-on also supports the outbound integration from IBP and creates orders in ERP based on what is received from IBP.

One can transfer the following data types from ERP to IBP:

- Master data such as locations, transportation lanes, or materials
- Transaction data like storage location stock, vendor consignment stock, and orders (planned orders, production orders, sales order, etc.)

**Cloud Platform Integration for Communication**

Now that we have reviewed the two main integration technologies, let's go back to the integration decision tree and focus on the right side of it where we have the integration with SAP JAM and SAP Ariba. These integrations are handled through the communication management app which enables you to establish secure communication with other systems (Fig. 2.117).

Once the communication partners and users are created, we need to define the communication arrangements that provide technical information about the authorizations, authentications methods, and inbound and outbound services that are needed for the communication.

For the integration with SAP Ariba Network, the integration scope—what data, at what granularity, and with who to share—is defined in the data sharing management app (Fig. 2.118). For example, we see below that part of the data sharing plan, there are two data sharing arrangements, with supplier 101 and supplier 102. What data is shared with these suppliers is defined in the mappings section, and each supplier is assigned with an own visibility filter.

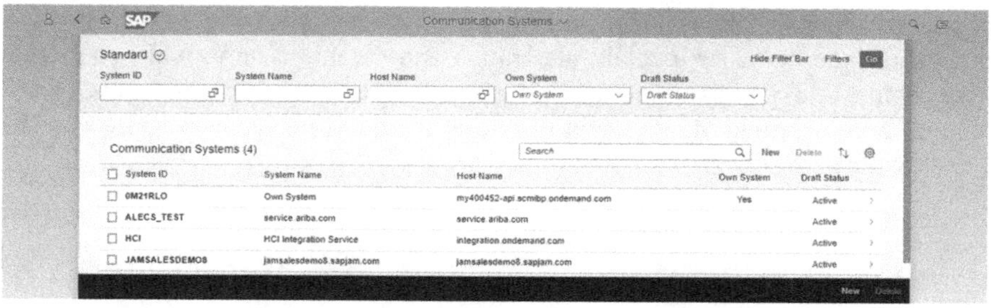


**Fig. 2.117** SAP IBP communication management app

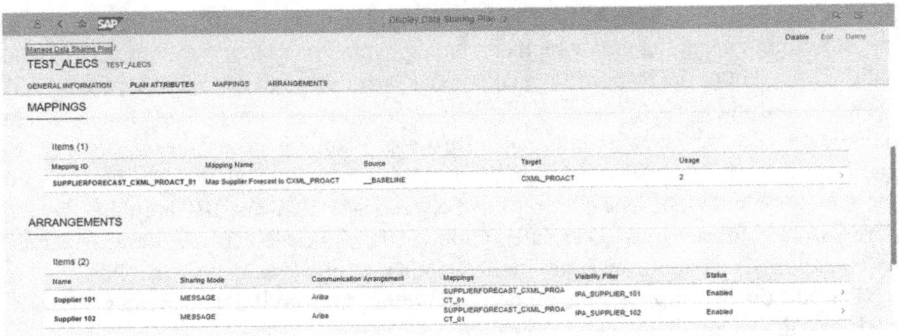


**Fig. 2.118** SAP IBP data sharing management app

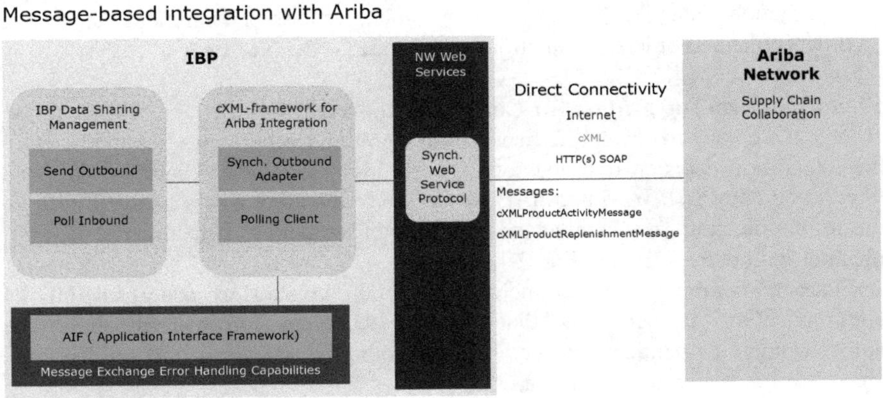


**Fig. 2.119** Message-based communication SAP IBP—SAP Ariba

Based on the information provided in this app, an cXML message is generated and integrated to Ariba. The cXML is a protocol created by Ariba based on the XML schemas to support business documents transfer.

Taking the example of the integration between SAP IBP and SAP Ariba Network, we see that data is being transferred over the Internet as a cXML message—commerce extensible markup language, protocol created by Ariba (Fig. 2.119).

Later in the book, we explain integration and communication with other SAP systems like SAP Hybris Cloud for Customers, SAP Business Planning and Consolidation, or SAP Trade Management (Trade Promotion Management and Customer Business Planning).

# 3 What and How to Monetize Forecasts and Plans

One of the key value drivers for Integrated Business Planning process is tight financial integration or even embedding of financial planning into the process. Financials might have basic and some more advance degree of integration or inclusion. Finance and pricing organization integrated in the process will change the way we look at it. All depends how far your organization would like to use IBP as process to manage business and not just planning. Strengths of integration and inclusion rules will determine how important IBP will be for your management and how important it will be for management of business models.

Some of the activities which are those days done by finance are done typically outside of S&OP framework and with some delay to the S&OP process calendar of activities. This is still part of disconnected planning. Activities like forecast price analysis including price flexibility, margin, and cost simulation and its impact on forecasts and plans very often are done after S&OP plan was submitted. Unfortunately we have seen it many times that financial flow becomes parallel to S&OP or even competes with S&OP. Management instead of looking on whole business in integrated way will be looking at volume and associated assumptions first and then on financial figures with most probably different assumptions, not shared and agreed with all key stakeholders and even worse maybe with different volumetric projections. If you keep finance aside, your organization naturally will generate second set of figures. Second set of figure is a major threat to any planning process, organization gets confused, and measurements are not reliable since its not aligned cross stakeholders. It can become a planning "matrix" in which it is hard to find what the truth is. We have realized that second set of figure generates an illusion of control, but in reality it does disconnect whole planning.

Financial elements and financial planning integration can serve as vital component to enable monetization of the forecasts and plans in terms of projections top-line revenue, bottom-line profit, and gap exposure to budget. Finance needs to perform needed activities linked to prediction of prices, costs, margin, and currency exchange rates with other stakeholders like demand manager and marketing, supply chain, and operations as per defined S&OP calendar of activities to meet objective of having



R. Kepczynski et al., *Implementing Integrated Business Planning*, Management for Professionals, https://doi.org/10.1007/978-3-319-90095-7_3

financials fully embedded in the process. Apart from projections of price, costs, and margin, there are other financial components which we have seen fully integrated in IBP process framework like projections of currency exchange rates, planning inventory write-off provisions, return provisions, license revenue fees, other sources of revenue, and many others.

Financial forecasting can be integrated with S&OP. One way of establishing a direct connection from S&OP to financial forecasting is to use driver-based planning such as activity-based budgeting (ABB). There should be S&OP scorecards to support controlling planning activities in S&OP. In more detail, theories emphasize the importance of including planning accuracy and other measures impacted by the process in the S&OP scorecards in order to become fact-based decision-making. It seems that having financial measures incorporated helps to focus attention of stakeholders (Heinonen 2009).

Demand manager and finance controller should define exactly what financial planning and measurement elements will be incorporated in IBP, how and when planning and measurement activities will be done, what sources of information will be used, and how outcomes will be used and communicated. They should have an objective to generate "one set of figures which drive business." Imagine how powerful IBP can become by making financials fully integrated. While integration is a true "beauty," some say it's a "beast" of IBP.

Figure 3.1 illustrates selected financial controller activities against S&OP process steps. As you can see, financial implications are on every process step. Financial elements of IBP should be positioned as fundamental element and equally important to volume. We see that demand manager and financial controller should organizationally and process wise ensure that discussions on decisions are always including finance. We have seen that many big organizations have commercial finance, supply chain and operations finance, and management reporting roles. Demand manager would need to connect them all into relevant activities. We know that it would not be easy and time-consuming, but alternative of keeping planning and management of the business not connected becomes a motivation to act. You can relate to integrated design concept which we have introduced in the other IBP book (Kepczynski et al. 2018).

Why do we want to do it like that? Purpose is very clear; we want to achieve a maturity state where SAP IBP is if not a single source then a main source of information for Integrated Business Planning to provide all relevant information to manage "one set of figures" as input to manage planning and business.

Note that monetization of forecasts and plans can trigger some disturbance which you need to consider. Financial pressures at the end of the accounting cycles increase instability and excitement in the supply chain and business management activities, fostering anxiety to get good numbers (SM Thacker and Associates 2007).

Still we wanted to call finance out as chapter to illustrate its importance and value on selected use cases. In many other chapters of this book, you will find use cases, reference, or examples on how to use financial elements in your IBP.

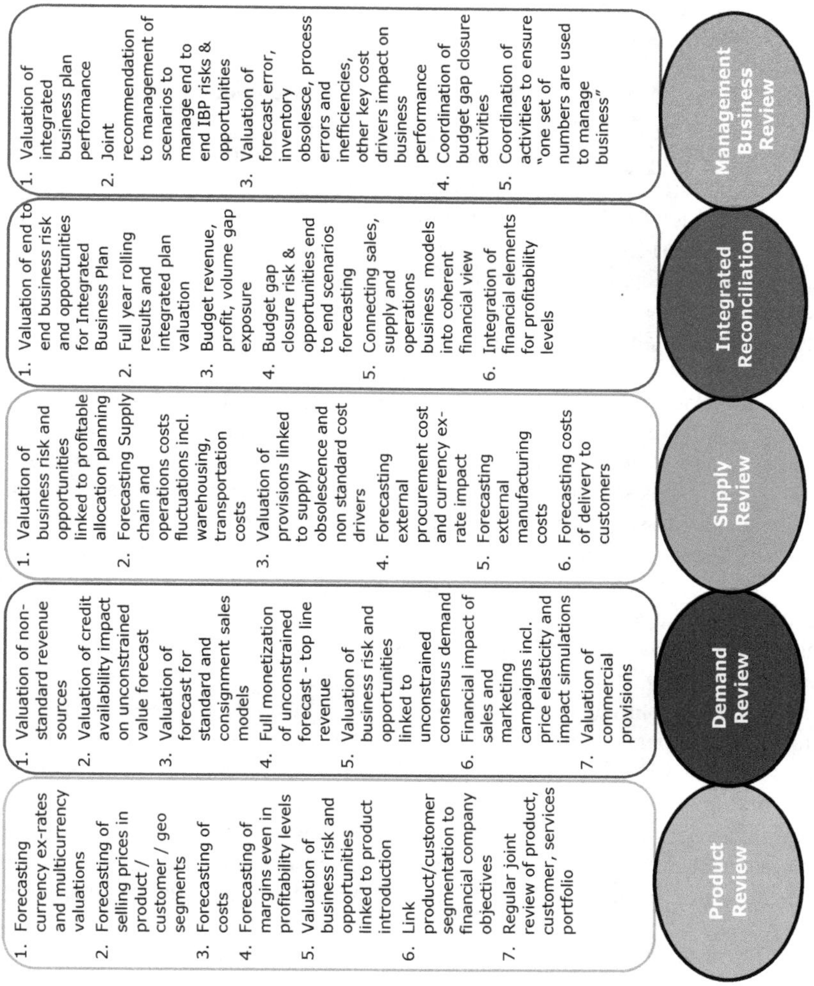


**Fig. 3.1** Finance controller in IBP—extract of selected activities

## 3.1 Forecasting Sales Price, COGS, and Margin

Monetization of forecasts and plans needs to answer the questions: What do you forecast to sell? What do you plan to supply? Does your business sell or supply money (euros, dollars) to your customers? Industrial companies typically sell products and services and then make money on it! There are many reasons why you should not start IBP from forecast value, but you should monetize your volumetric forecasts and plans. It is mainly due to challenging and:

- Often very wrong conversions of monetary assumptions into volumetric assumptions
- Wrong product mix established from monetary starting point
- Lack of transparency of integrating volume and value
- Focus on financial risk and opportunities instead of end-to-end trade-offs and cross-functional risks and opportunities
- Bias toward financial forecasting instead of market- and demand-driven forecasting
- Bias toward financial versus business planning and management

Forecasting price, COGS, and margin are often connected to volumetric side of the process. We have seen business where correlation between price and volume of sales is extremely strong, but that was not given in all the cases. We have seen business highly exposed to fluctuation of transportation, warehousing, and product costs. Those businesses struggled to predict their pricing policies and margins. Integrated Business Planning process framework should give you an opportunity to project price, cost, and margin and connect it to volumes. Looking on IBP as plan to manage business, you should connect cost/revenue drivers into it.

Figure 3.2 illustrates how financial elements can be mapped against end-to-end process from revenue through main cost drivers. Jointly finance controller and demand manger should map financial elements which are exposed to risk and opportunities in order to manage their predictions as part of IBP process. Model which is visualized above may be very relevant for differentiated response or response optimized around profits where management of cost elements is critical. This particular optimization scenario is rather a domain of supply manager, but demand manager and finance controller should be aware since they drive development of integrated business plan. Cost optimization logic is built into the supply optimizer.

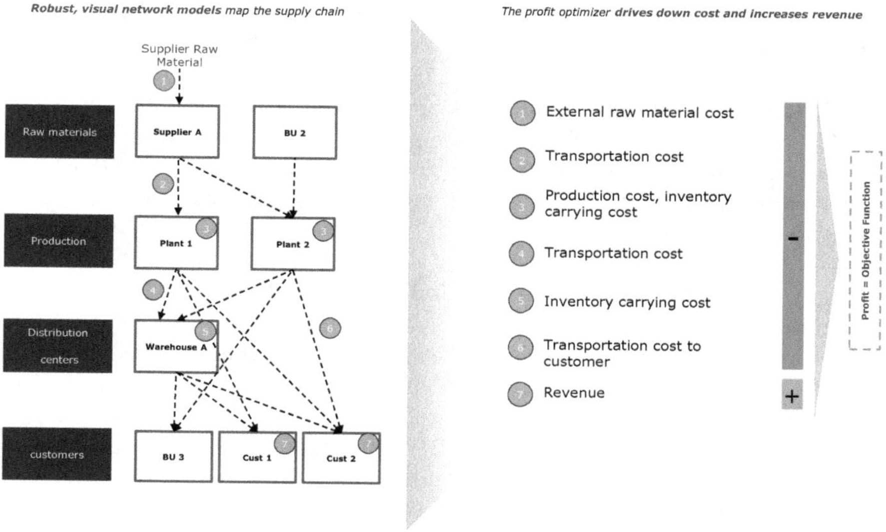


**Fig. 3.2** Predicting financial elements of the supply chain in IBP

## 3.1.1 SAP Use Case: Pricing and Cost Tactics

Initial price and forecasted price entries/changes, could be managed on fairly aggregated level. In Fig. 3.3, the forecasted price was adjusted on country- and product-quarter level.

Forecast selling price may be integrated from source system and then adjusted within IBP process and if needed sent back to source system. Management of the forecasted price could be done on level of commercial/finance master data hierarchy which makes sense. We have seen price policies being introduced per country, channel, product group, and even package type.

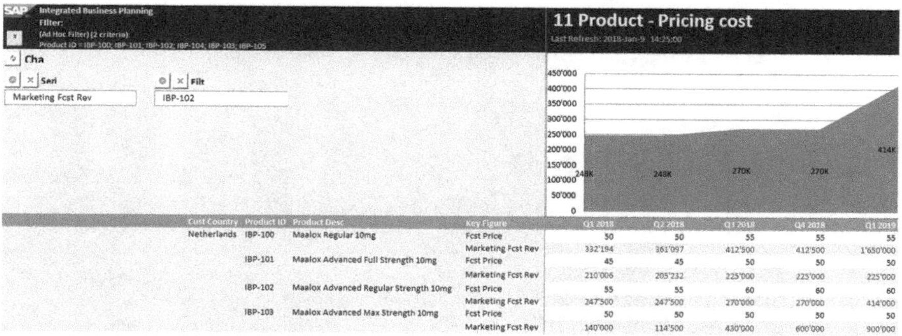


**Fig. 3.3** Forecasted sales price

Initial product cost in this use case was managed on product-location level. Finance controller with other stakeholders was forecasting changes of it on quarterly basis and capturing decision in unit cost key figure. As you see on Fig. 3.4 for simplicity reasons, we have captured cost as 30 for all products and locations.

We have seen very often that cost of the product was integrated from source and master system, but process of forecasting cost changes was initiated in IBP. Having those two initial set of data (price and cost) in place, let us further elaborate on how it was used in the process.

### Country "Top-Line" Revenue Projection with Introduction of Price Tactics Associated to Country Sales Channel

As we have discussed, initial average or blended sales price could be integrated from source system and used in IBP. If we assume that your IBP process requires information on SKU/country level, then we need to feed in this information. This is a very static approach, while normally IBP drives the whole thing into direction to embed and leverage capability to simulate price changes and visualize impact of it on any level of commercial and financial hierarchy. Why simulate price changes? Purpose of it is to incorporate your tactics in the market in the process. It is a way to operationalize integration between operational planning including campaigns and tactical S&OP aligned to strategic planning. It was needed to cope with forecasting and planning on aggregated and detailed level at the same time. IBP process might require simulation of future price and product mix changes on lower level than SKU/country. Process wise it is very common that in some sales channels and sales zone or areas, you would need to apply different price tactics and maybe even forecast different distribution costs to compete against local competitors. System wise SAP IBP helps you to achieve that with configurable disaggregation/aggregation and scenario planning. In Fig. 3.5 we notice that initial forecasted sales price of 50 was changed in Q1 and Q2 2018 into 45, but change was introduced on channel and not whole-country level. In this particular country, sales were done via distributors, directly e-commerce, but tactics was supposed to be applied only for distributors. You may apply this example to introduction of forecasted sales price on

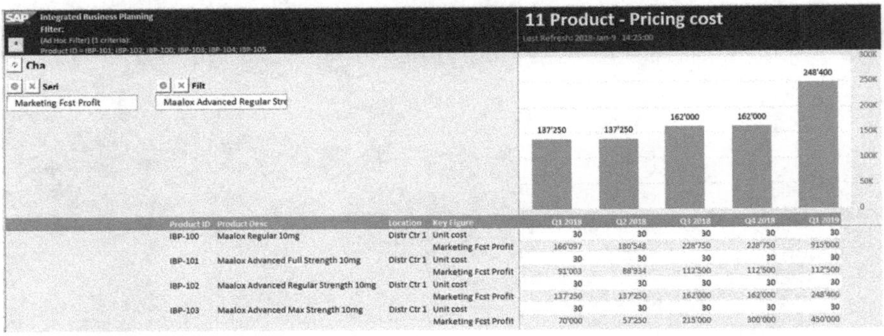


**Fig. 3.4** Forecasted product costs

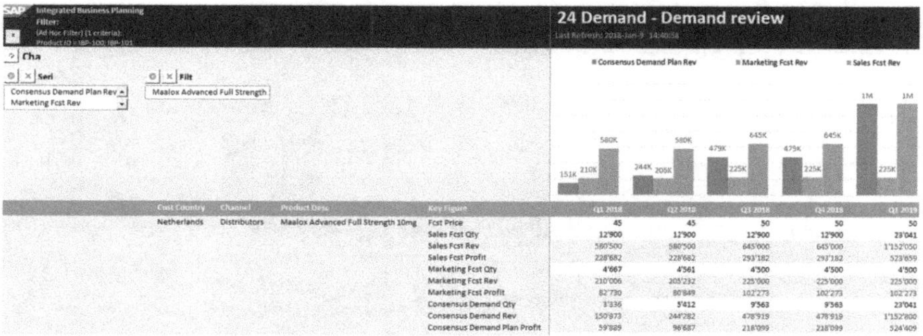


**Fig. 3.5** Country and sales channel forecasted pricing policy

customer group, product group, sales leader, or even customer if it makes in the process and if enabled key figure calculations and aggregation/disaggregation.

In this particular project, Fcst price key figure was used to calculate all revenue key figures, e.g., sales team input in sales fcst rev, marketing fcst rev, and consensus demand plan rev. On the other hand, we have seen customer who required more complex process. They wanted to introduce sort of consensus process for forecasting sales price where functions like sales, marketing, and finance were proposing forecasted sales price and those inputs were subject to make decision. Once decision was taken and captured in the system, agreed forecasted sales price was used to calculate consensus demand plan rev.

### Country "Bottom-Line" Profit Projection Incl. Projections of COGS Changes and Linked to Price Tactics Associated to Sales Channel

Price tactics introduced in the Netherlands was driven by commercial reasons but was not fully considering opportunities to improve cost base. Overall this may still be a simplified example since in reality most of the factors impacting risk and opportunities may come to play at the same time. Let us visualize case where we introduce projected cost reduction for certain group of products in few locations. In this case logistic department was under huge pressure to reduce cost and has opened up a tender for transportation services and selected partner which offer far more competitive conditions (incl. lower cost). They have planned to introduce the change of transportation company distribution center by distribution center and rollout it to whole country gradually for whole Europe. Costs decrease was captured in the special scenario and reflected as reduction from 30 to 25 (compare Fig. 3.4 with Fig. 3.6).

Country S&OP team was able to consider this change in their integrated reconciliation process steps. They were able to make decision if it makes sense to apply change, compared to base scenario. Similar use cases might be applicable to deployment of projected COGS changes, etc. from region to country, of course if those attributes are reflected in geographical dimensions of IBP data model.

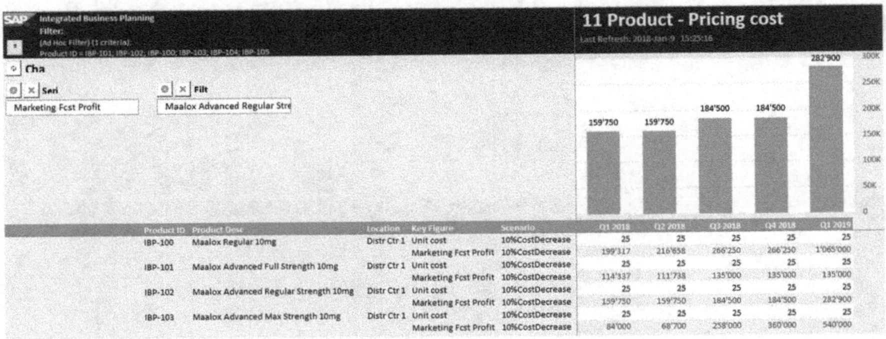


**Fig. 3.6** Scenario based forecasted cost reduction

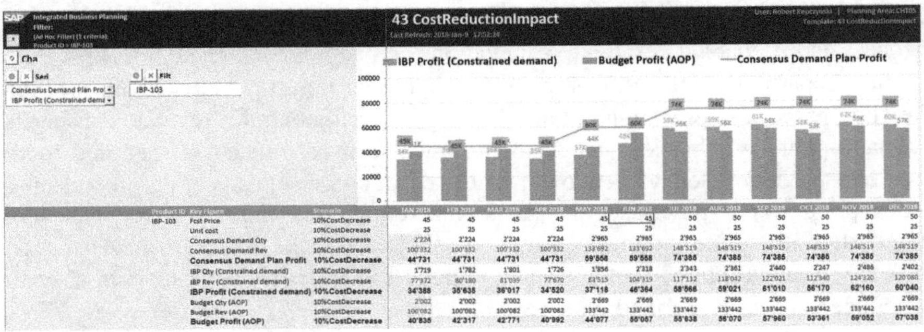


**Fig. 3.7** Forecasted prices and cost change impact on projected revenue and profit

Demand manager and finance controller defined that profit changes calculated based on price change and COGS change are visualized on scenario which needed to be discussed with management (Fig. 3.7).

Demand manager and finance controller connected price tactics in Q1 and Q2 2018 with cost reduction in scenario called 10% cost decrease. Budgeted qty, revenue, and profit were the same like for base scenario, but revenue driven by price change and profit driven by cost change were updated (Fig. 3.7). It was decided that demand manager and finance controller will prepare all the pros and cons (see Fig. 3.8).

Stakeholders should be presented with time-based view on any level needed, e.g., product ID and even on much aggregated level. Finance organization wanted to present to management profitability levels which did incorporate fixed costs and management overheads (Fig. 3.9). Those costs were integrated from SAP Business Planning and Consolidation (BPC) into SAP IBP and were captured in fixed cost and management overhead key figures. Based on data integrated from BPC, new profit level calculations were introduced in IBP profit level 2 and IBP profit level 3. SAP BPC is a tool where many companies prepare their budget or consolidate financial results of the whole group; it is not part of IBP but separate financial tool. This way

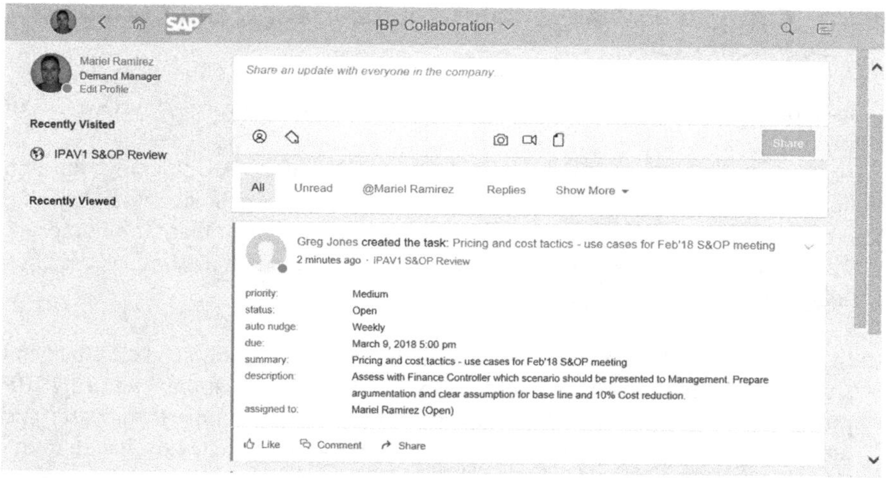


**Fig. 3.8** SAP JAM price and cost simulation action

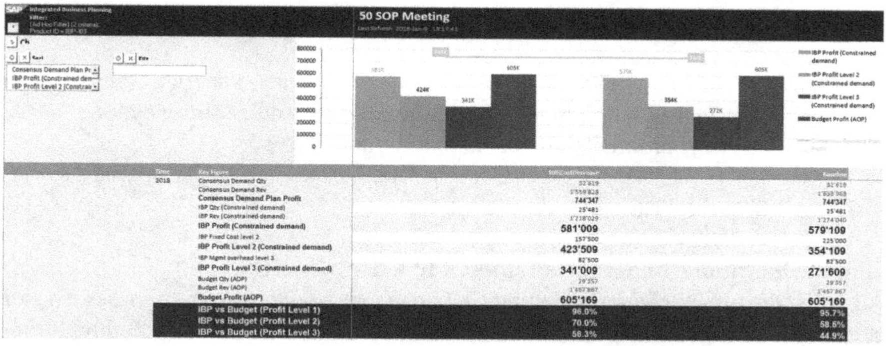


**Fig. 3.9** Profit level scenario comparison

of looking at financial data was specific to particular specific customer which we worked with.

As you see, difference starts to be obvious when we compare IBP profit ratios to budget profits which reflect product costs, price change, and reduction of fixed costs. The way data is presented in the screen is very flexible and normally can be adjusted by users or key users without intervention of IT.

## 3.2 Currency Exchange Rates, Multicurrency, and Currency Fluctuation

Is question which currency exchange rates to use in your IBP process framework still valid? Yes it is.

IBP covers time span of the next few weeks in operational planning, through tactical S&OP in the current and next year up to a few years in strategic planning. You can expect different currency exchange rate projections in that time frame.

There are few reasons why you may want to consider forecasting of currency exchange rates in your IBP processes:

1. In countries where currency goes through disturbance. Commercial and financial risks can be captured in simulations of exchange rate fluctuations impacting IBP process outputs (projected revenues, profit). You may compare forecasts and plans in budget currency exchange rate or with rolling currency exchange rate.
2. When your time horizon overlaps current and currently year + 1 and you would like to align currency exchange rates from the budgeting into next year IBP.
3. When you run strategic multiyear high level plan, so average projected currency exchange rate could be used.
4. When you sell your products in domestic market and run export sales to other currency zones.
5. When you purchase any form of your product (raw material, semifinished product, finished product) in significant amount from other currency.
6. When you set your targets in local and corporate currency.

Let us go case by case a bit deeper into it.

**Global Operations in Markets Exposed to Currency Risks**

Ad 1: On the top of leading operating exchange rate, you may need to assess risks of currency exchange rate fluctuations impacting your end result in local and reporting currency. Reporting currency is the one which is used by division, global, or corporate. You can make your currency exchange rate scenario dependent, and then you could maintain different currency exchange rates for simulations and assess simulation impact. Period-dependent currency exchange rates may be a valid solution if you import products other than local currency and you need to simulate or plan currency exchange rate changes but as well if you want to simulate profit in corporate currency. At the end objective would be to assess impact on your financial performance exposed to exchange rate risks/fluctuations.

**Planning Overlapping Current and Next Year's Budget Year**

Ad 2: In many countries, typically around August, budgeting process becomes important for commercial and marketing organization. If your tactical S&OP processes has 2-year horizon, maybe you should think of currency exchange rates alignment in your budgeting process with your IBP process for next year. In current year currency exchange rates can be maintained in external systems and imported into IBP. Until budget exchange rates are agreed for next year, you may use currency exchange rate projections provided by finance, but once next year's budget exchange rates are agreed, you can import them into IBP but affecting only relevant periods. You can achieve that with setting up currency exchange rates as period-specific key figure to store different values per month.

**Strategic Planning for Multiyear Horizon**

Ad 3: Long-term strategic IBP process may span over 5–7-year horizon and is normally executed on aggregated level. For such a long horizon, you may need to consider to use "multiple" currency exchange rates:

- From current year IBP
- Next year's budget
- Long-term projections of currency exchange rates for years 3, 4, and 5

You may update currency exchange rate for long-term projections on aggregated level and use disaggregation method which copies required value down to lowest level. We have seen that process of forecasting currency exchange rates was either aligned with corporate treasury department, management reporting, or finance management team.

**Forecasting Export Sales or Sales in Other Currency Zones**

Ad 4: In business models where you have production and inventory in euro zone but sales to non-euro zone, management of forecasted currency exchange rate in tactical S&OP will be very beneficial. You may think to integrate initial currency exchange rates from your treasury or financial system and manage forecasting on rolling base as part of IBP process. Forecast entered and assessed in non-euro zone country will store in local currency but as well recalculated to corporate currency. It will be needed for finance controllers and management to have full transparency of revenues and profits in both currencies.

**Planning Procurement from Other Currency Zones**

Ad 5: There is almost an imperative to manage currency exchange rate forecast and its impact on revenue, profit projections in case in your product portfolio there are:

- Finished products especially branded for you by subcontractor and external manufacturer in another currency zone.
- Key raw material which drives cost of finished product is imported from nonlocal currency zone.
- Late customization of the generic product is done in the other currency zone.

In the above case material costs, the finished product will depend on purchase costs which you may need to have in another than local currency.

**Setting Up Targets in Local and Corporate Currency**
Ad 6: We have seen cases where management had defined targets in monetary terms but in local currency they operated but as well in corporate currency they had to submit their results and plans. Management will make currency exchange rate topic very important by then.

Critical element of selecting right currency exchange rates for IBP processes is aligned with finance and management reporting teams who set up rules and control financial and reporting systems. Financial data have to match between your SAP IBP and financial systems/management reporting system. On the other hand, you need to have flexibility to simulate currency exchange rates because of reasons listed above. You need to put a process in place to coordinate forecasting of currency exchange rates with global or central finance team.

Forecasting currency exchange rates is needed to address business risk and opportunities linked to it. We have found common in above use cases that you need to have clear governance, activities assigned to finance or treasury team but as part of S&OP calendar of activities and in IBP process. Ultimate goal would be to integrate forecasting of this financial element as integral part of the IBP process.

### 3.2.1 SAP Use Case: Forecasting Currency Exchange Rates

One of our customers had significant amount of sales in countries with relatively high currency risks. In this process they wanted to capture specific currency exchange rate fluctuations in upside and downside version. Version will enable automatic calculation of value key figures and comparison between them. We had a rule to keep things stable in base version until decision will be taken and assessed in upside and downside version. Process of development of version-dependent currency exchange rates was supported by user-specific scenarios. Versions were stored in data model, but scenarios were used to facilitate collaboration in developing decision to define specific values of currency exchange rates. We were supported by what-if analysis to assess risks and opportunity of it. Keeping scenarios and versions in the system will help you to be more transparent, enabling better visibility to make better decisions. We always advise to store assumptions which were taken into versions/scenarios.

Once you will capture relevant currency exchange rate scenarios, you could easily connect them to key figures which can help you evaluate an impact. In Fig. 3.10 we see differences in revenue expressed in US dollars with currency exchange rates in Brazilian real and Russian ruble. You may need in result of agreed currency exchange rates to define new pricing policies to recover losses in case of drop of your currency, or you may want to sell more of products produced from raw materials bought on preferred currency exchange rate. Simulations may trigger many actions and involve many stakeholders, which we would recommend to track with scenario-dependent actions in SAP JAM.

SAP Integrated Business Planning — Exchange Rate Simulations

| Currency ID | Currency Description | Currency To Desc | Key Figure | Version | 2018 | 2019 | 2020 |
|---|---|---|---|---|---|---|---|
| BRL | Brazilian Real | U.S. Dollar | Exchange Rate | Baseline | 0.330 | 0.360 | 0.390 |
| | | | | Upside | 0.350 | 0.380 | 0.410 |
| | | | | Downside | 0.323 | 0.345 | 0.380 |
| | | | Sales Forecast Revenue | Baseline | 586K | 662K | 831K |
| | | | | Upside | 622K | 699K | 873K |
| | | | | Downside | 573K | 635K | 809K |
| RUB | Russian Ruble | U.S. Dollar | Exchange Rate | Baseline | 0.017 | 0.021 | 0.026 |
| | | | | Upside | 0.018 | 0.022 | 0.029 |
| | | | | Downside | 0.017 | 0.020 | 0.025 |
| | | | Sales Forecast Revenue | Baseline | 1,033K | 1,152K | 1,424K |
| | | | | Upside | 1,096K | 1,216K | 1,497K |
| | | | | Downside | 1,010K | 1,105K | 1,387K |

**Fig. 3.10** Forecasting currency exchange risks

## 3.3 Product Introduction and Sample Valuation

Valuation of product planning and product review process is mainly associated but not limited to projections of sales volume and sales revenue for new product introduction.

Demand manager should align with product marketing/portfolio managers on any risk associated to delays of introduction of the product in the market. Delays should be reflected on the volumetric side and value side. Their business is more regulated than the others; therefore some formal external processes may be not in your full control but would need to be planned. It means that new product should have forecasted price, cost, and margin, introduction dates, and introduction volume. Any delays in product introduction day must be reflected in the forecast and plan. Introduction of new product will impact volume and value side of Integrated Business Plan.

We have seen many industries where introduction of new products was supported with samples. Samples in most of the cases are free of charge, but they still need to be available. You should consider to capture sample volume if they are significant. Your IBP technical design will be able to ensure that samples are only impacting volume side of Integrated Business Plan and not revenue side. Scale of using samples to boost your sales varies cross industries; we have seen a chemical company which had a separate "supply chain" for managing samples.

As part of forecasting new products, its revenue, profit, and volumetric plans need to be developed. The errors in profit forecast are often much higher than in sales forecasts (Armstrong 2002).

### 3.3.1 SAP Use Case: Sample Valuation

Forecasting of samples may be linked to forecasting of new products. Depending how substantial samples would be, you may have various technical scenarios which can support business requirement. In this scenario we see delay in introduction of the new product from initially planned phase in January 2018 into February 2018. We see that for scenarios volume go hand in hand with values. Exceptions are samples which were not taken into revenue stream represented in marketing fcst rev.

In Fig. 3.11 we see that sample forecast quantity are being provided manually but as percentage of marketing forecast qty. Percentage was bigger in initial months of sales. Forecast "sales" of samples captured in sample forecast quantity was not interfering revenue stream captured in marketing forecast revenue. Revenue wise this was free-of-charge stream; cost wise it was still significant and worth to plan production and consider to affect margin. What we have done with sample quantity is that we have planned production for those volumes as well. Meaning in consensus forecast, qty samples were included only on volumetric side but not revenue.

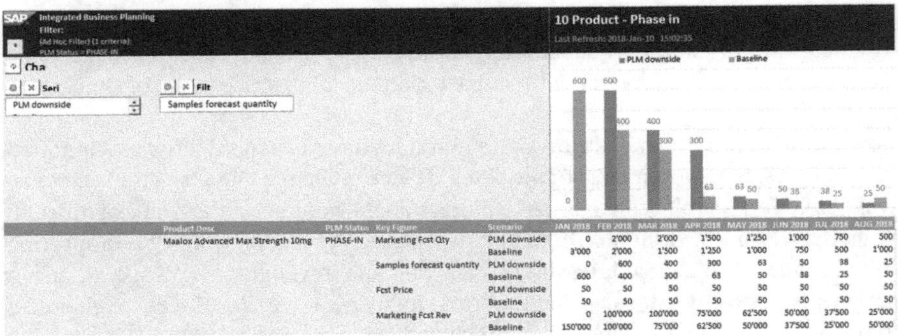


| Product Desc | PLM Status | Key Figure | Scenario | JAN 2018 | FEB 2018 | MAR 2018 | APR 2018 | MAY 2018 | JUN 2018 | JUL 2018 | AUG 2018 |
|---|---|---|---|---|---|---|---|---|---|---|---|
| Maalox Advanced Max Strength 10mg | PHASE-IN | Marketing Fcst Qty | PLM downside | 0 | 2'000 | 2'000 | 1'500 | 1'250 | 1'000 | 750 | 500 |
| | | | Baseline | 3'000 | 2'000 | 1'500 | 1'250 | 1'000 | 750 | 500 | 1'000 |
| | | Samples forecast quantity | PLM downside | 0 | 600 | 400 | 300 | 63 | 50 | 38 | 25 |
| | | | Baseline | 600 | 400 | 300 | 63 | 50 | 38 | 25 | 50 |
| | | Fcst Price | PLM downside | 50 | 50 | 50 | 50 | 50 | 50 | 50 | 50 |
| | | | Baseline | 50 | 50 | 50 | 50 | 50 | 50 | 50 | 50 |
| | | Marketing Fcst Rev | PLM downside | 0 | 100'000 | 100'000 | 75'000 | 62'500 | 50'000 | 37'500 | 25'000 |
| | | | Baseline | 150'000 | 100'000 | 75'000 | 62'500 | 50'000 | 37'500 | 25'000 | 50'000 |

**Fig. 3.11** Forecasting new products coupled with samples

## 3.4 Credit Availability and Nonstandard Revenues

**Aggregated Credit Availability**

In many businesses credit control plays an important role in being successful. Monitoring credit exposure and credit availability becomes more and more not only operational and execution process but as well input used in tactical S&OP planning.

How could we understand available credit information in IBP? We would rather propose to think of credit availability information as input to perform sanity check in demand review preparation. In markets where there are some challenges with currency and customers which have problems with cash flow, you will be automatically exposed to commercial constraint expressed in credit availability information.

In demand review preparation where you develop proposal for unconstrained forecast in value, I would recommend to consider high-level information about credit availability. It would help you to understand if your unconstrained market potential is really unconstrained.

You should compare available credit for your customer base on aggregated level with consensus forecast in value Fig. 3.12. For planning purposes we do not recommend to bring credit availability data on highly granular level.

If credit availability is higher than consensus forecast, then you are on safe side, but if it is lower, some actions may be needed:

- Organize more granular information (customer/sales representative/customer service) from your finance/credit department
- Define actions leading to contacting customers to pay amount which will increase credit availability

Corrective actions normally will take some time to introduce and turn into change of credit availability. In the meantime demand planner should help organization to identify and adjust consensus unconstrained forecast in volume and value.

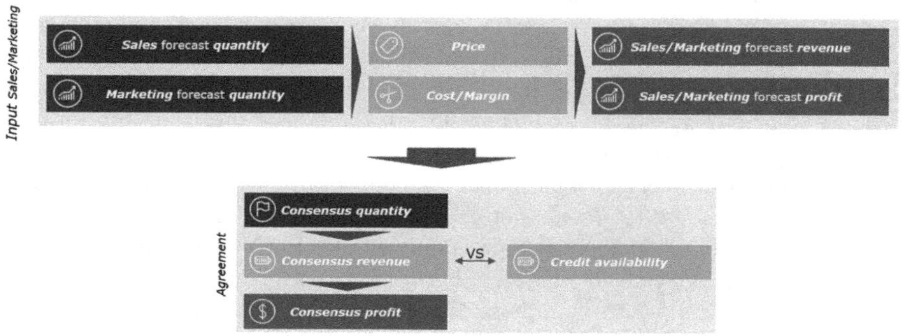


**Fig. 3.12** Consensus forecast revenue vs credit availability

In other words in this use case, forecast was constrained in some way with commercial constraints.

**Nonstandard Revenue Drivers**

Demand review process should deliver information on volumetric side but as well value side of demand. Considering that we talk about IBP as process to manage business and not just forecasting and planning, we want to bring example from the other project. In business model company had standard revenue stream linked to product and services but as well nonstandard ones. Let us shortly discuss other sources of revenue which could be reflected in your IBP process and data model like:

- License fees
- Royalties
- Franchise fees
- Advisory services
- Financing services
- Data fees

Sometime those items might be substantial in terms of value. We have seen that some of them are hard to predict since they are not a core business. It will become vital to find right and relevant knowledge in the company about those revenue sources and incorporate relevant stakeholders in monthly process. What else to do with cases when it is hard to predict accurately or on product level?

We could define those sources of revenue as key figures separately by sources or at least as lump sum. You should find and assign accountability to predict them to person who would be in possession of the best insights in terms of magnitude and phasing.

In many companies those sources of revenue may be reflected in financial items/ product ID. You should leverage as much as possible of those in your model. In case it is not possible to use existing elements of material hierarchy, you may need to create your own but specific to SAP IBP and aligned if required to finance system nomenclature/coding.

From knowing what nonstandard revenue sources will be forecasted and by whom, you need to move to next action and define on which level of commercial/ geographical hierarchy those nonstandard revenue sources will be captured and how they should affect country projections or above country projections. Some of those revenue sources may not be assignable to sales area and sale zone but only to country, region, or even only global level. In this case you need to define with finance appropriate level and what should disaggregation do with it. We have seen it working to create separate process steps which were focused to capture nonstandard revenue sources, but this process step was fully aligned to IBP calendar of activities and coordinated by demand manager. From technology side, you could define special SAP IBP template where those either specific (depending on significance) or lump sum nonstandard revenues will be captured and taken into consideration in value side of Integrated Business Plan.

### 3.4.1 SAP Use Case: Consensus Revenue Sanity Check with Credit Availability

Sanity check for realistic level of consensus demand revenue may be done on aggregated country level. User may be notified with "conditional formatting" enabled by key users as part of tailoring global templates to local needs. We can introduce ratio to compare consensus revenue with credit availability and assign color coding to focus our attention on exceptions. As we have discussed previously, it does not make any sense to look on credit availability on every single customer, but in the template above, we can see totals and details on same screen. We see credit availability versus consensus revenue on customer but all countries level as well (total); see Fig. 3.13.

It becomes obvious that overall assessment of the forecast revenue realization is driven by the Netherlands where we have Customer 2 driving huge revenue. Working on aggregated and detail level in same view makes it easier for the planner. Credit availability information may be integrated with use SAP cloud integration platform from master system in which we execute and manage credit risks.

In this particular template, we wanted to have a quick look on nonstandard sources of revenue as well; therefore we have included license forecast revenue. Nonstandard sources of revenue should be entered on level aligned to best insights of person accountable for projections. As you noticed this particular key figure was not entered in volume and then valuated but entered directly in value. In this particular project, nonstandard sources of revenue were automatically included in consensus revenue forecast. When using IBP process as process to manage your business, your consensus revenue forecast should integrate all relevant revenue sources.

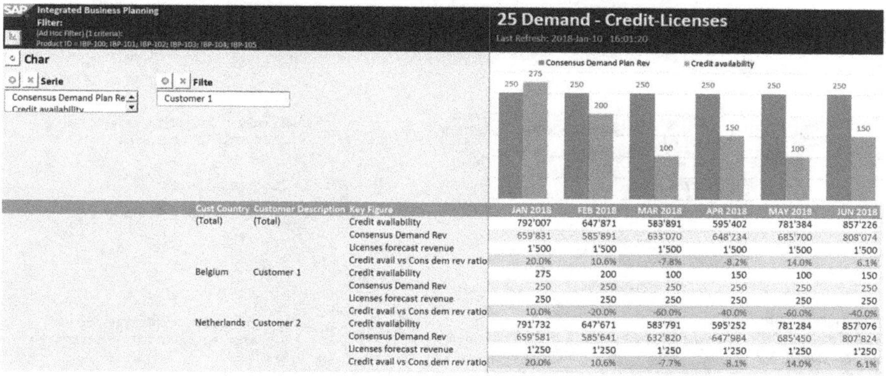


| Cust Country | Customer Description | Key Figure | JAN 2018 | FEB 2018 | MAR 2018 | APR 2018 | MAY 2018 | JUN 2018 |
|---|---|---|---|---|---|---|---|---|
| (Total) | (Total) | Credit availability | 792'007 | 647'871 | 583'891 | 595'402 | 781'384 | 857'226 |
| | | Consensus Demand Rev | 659'831 | 585'891 | 633'070 | 648'234 | 685'700 | 808'074 |
| | | Licenses forecast revenue | 1'500 | 1'500 | 1'500 | 1'500 | 1'500 | 1'500 |
| | | Credit avail vs Cons dem rev ratio | 20.0% | 10.6% | -7.8% | -8.2% | 14.0% | 6.1% |
| Belgium | Customer 1 | Credit availability | 275 | 200 | 100 | 150 | 100 | 150 |
| | | Consensus Demand Rev | 250 | 250 | 250 | 250 | 250 | 250 |
| | | Licenses forecast revenue | 250 | 250 | 250 | 250 | 250 | 250 |
| | | Credit avail vs Cons dem rev ratio | 10.0% | -20.0% | -60.0% | -40.0% | -60.0% | -40.0% |
| Netherlands | Customer 2 | Credit availability | 791'732 | 647'671 | 583'791 | 595'252 | 781'284 | 857'076 |
| | | Consensus Demand Rev | 659'581 | 585'641 | 632'820 | 647'984 | 685'450 | 807'824 |
| | | Licenses forecast revenue | 1'250 | 1'250 | 1'250 | 1'250 | 1'250 | 1'250 |
| | | Credit avail vs Cons dem rev ratio | 20.0% | 10.6% | -7.7% | -8.1% | 14.0% | 6.1% |

**Fig. 3.13** Consensus revenue forecast sanity check with credit availability

## 3.5 Consignment Sales Forecast Valuation

Many business models are not only based on standard way of selling product but e-commerce or consignment sales. Financial side of consignment sales model is pretty different from standard/direct sales model. You should consider to develop special process flows and integrate them into IBP process. Let us illustrate main difference between standard and consignment flow on Fig. 3.14.

Standard forecasting flow is straightforward since its one-step process. Orders are being realized, shipment booked, and invoiced created. Invoice reflects change of ownership. In demand-driven forecasting approach discussed later in the book, we highlight which data input to use as primary input for your forecasting process. Leading practices say it should be the one closest to customer demand and in this case invoice is not the one. Stream number 1 on Fig. 3.14 is based on sales orders which are not perfect but acceptable data input into the forecasting. In this flow financial side of consensus forecast could be assumed in same period as required or confirmed period of sales orders. We can roughly assume there is no misalignment in terms of timing between sales order required date/confirmed date and date of revenue. In many businesses there is a special process like collective invoicing, but let us put that aside.

Consignment forecasting flow consists of two major process steps. First process step is filling up of customer consignment location from Company A. Second step is consumption of the goods by customer which are at consignment location combined with reconciliation of stock and consumption with Company A. This activity once agreed between parties will generate revenue based on invoice for consumption of the product. In this model customer pays, so your company A generates revenue for products which are consumed only. Consignment location stock level would need to be validated on regular basis and integrated on regular basis. In this case implication of forecasting revenue is quite substantial, since you should forecast consignment

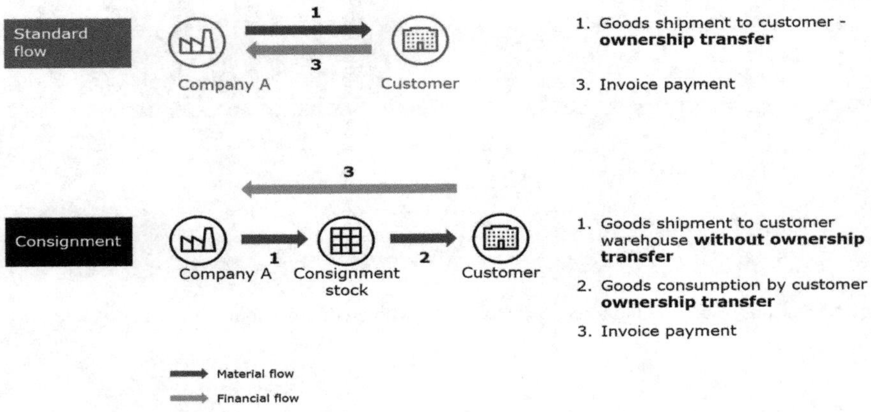


**Fig. 3.14** Consignment versus standard forecasting flow

location fill-up in volume to be used by supply chain and operations functions (see flow number 1 in Fig. 3.14) and you should forecast revenue based on consumption of the stock by customer from consignment location (see flow number 2 in Fig. 3.14). This process is not easy to forecast and plan since you need to balance stock information and invoiced data and fill up to predict revenue which will be recognized from consignment consumption. Consignment fill-up forecast in volume is not aligned normally to consignment consumption forecast in revenue. There is gap which is taken in reality by consumption of stock. More details about this process are explained in SAP use case later in the book.

## 3.6 Nonstandard Cost Drivers/Provisions

**Forecasting Provisions**

Integrated Business Plan should cover as much as possible of cost drivers in order to have the most complete financial side of the plan. In some business models, there are processes to predict volumetric side and value side (provision) of:

- Product returns
- Inventory obsolescence

They may be very substantial in cost and volume. We have experienced the case where returns were ca. 6% of business unit revenue or where obsolescence for certain product groups could be even up to 20% of inventory. If it is that much substantial, you should consider to incorporate it in your IBP process framework.

In here we briefly discuss forecasting of provisions linked to commercial returns, but further in the book when we will discuss shelf life planning, we will touch base on provision linked to projected obsolescence.

Projections of returns maybe associated with your commercial policies about returns. Demand manager should align with commercial and finance organization on that topic. Volumetric side of the forecasting returns may be used as input to calculate carry-over inventory in supply planning, input to calculate return transportation needs, and input to calculate quality needs to retest products. On financial side of commercial returns, we will talk about provisions. Provision in simplistic term may be understood as reserve of the money in "your pocket" which will negatively affect your financial result. You may use IBP process to generate provisions/accrual projections. We have seen two types of commercial returns:

1. Seasonal returns from the channel
2. Ongoing/continuous returns from the channel

End of the peak season commercial returns may be projected based on % of typical return rate based on the past data. Your company may have a policy about end of peak season returns for finished products, e.g., for product line A, we allowed X% or return after peak season. If you have that information, try to leverage it in the process and SAP IBP. In "apple-to-apple" rule, we set aside value of same type, meaning actuals for returns aside with forecast for returns. Data input (actuals) and output (forecast) could be stored on different key figures but need to form logical unit. Here comes a bit more complexity; data input for forecasting returns and provision will be affected by how your order-to-cash process is executed and configured in your transactional system. Just pay attention to classification of returns in your order-to-cash process. Once you know O2C process details, you would need to extract only those return types which are relevant for your IBP.

You may build return and provisions in bottom-up or top-down approach. Always try to balance efforts to provide input vs magnitude of forecasted returns, and last but not the least, assign it to organizational unit which possesses best insights about the process. We have seen that customer service and marketing were informed the best about returns and return policies.

### 3.6.1 SAP Use Case: Forecasting Returns and Provisions

In the example below, returns are forecasted based on bottom input from sales representatives and sales area leaders with reconciliation provided by product managers (marketing). Sales team provides input in so-called bottom-up approach and marketing more top-down; both inputs are reviewed by demand manager and finance manager. Based on reconciled figures, finance will calculate provisions accordingly. In the example below, we want to forecast commercial returns related to end of the sales peak season which ends up in February 2018.

In bottom-up input for returns, sales team might have very good insights about level of return since they are contacting customers on regular basis. They have provided their input in volumetric form per sales area, product ID, and customer group (Fig. 3.15).

Top-down input for returns was provided by marketing department (product managers). They were safeguards of the company policies about % of accepted returns. Marketing provides return % rate which is linked to consensus forecast qty to calculate proposal of forecasted returns (Fig. 3.16).

As we see return % were provided by product group and not specific customer.

Once both inputs are captured then in the demand review meeting, there was discussion point to reconcile, align on forecasted commercial returns at the end of the season, and monetize it in provisions. Demand planner and finance controller prepared template where inputs from sales and marketing were visualized and consensus returns were recorded (Fig. 3.17).

Automatically return provisions were calculated based on 100% of price and consensus returns qty. You may have in your company different rules, but that is an example of how process which required special attention due to its size was defined.

Similar approach might be designed for returns which are not associated to end of the peak season or campaign but which happen regularly. Our advice is to apply appropriate approach (top down, bottom up) based on magnitude of returns in your business.

SAP Integrated Business Planning

| Sales Area | Prd Group | Cust Group | SKU | Key Figure | Jan"18 | Feb"18 |
|---|---|---|---|---|---|---|
| North | Group 100 | CA01 | IBP-100 | Sales Area Returns | 400 | 900 |
| | | | IBP-110 | Sales Area Returns | 800 | 1,200 |
| | | | IBP-120 | Sales Area Returns | 600 | 1,000 |
| South | Group 100 | CA01 | IBP-100 | Sales Area Returns | 0 | 1,200 |
| | | | IBP-120 | Sales Area Returns | 0 | 800 |
| | Group 200 | CU02 | IBP-210 | Sales Area Returns | 500 | 2,400 |

**Fig. 3.15** Commercial returns forecasting input from sales team

SAP Integrated Business Planning

| Prd Group | Key Figure | Jan"18 | Feb"18 |
|---|---|---|---|
| Group 100 | Return % rate | 5% | 12% |
| | Consensus Demand Fcst | 18,000 | 29,000 |
| | Forecasted Returns | **900** | **3,480** |
| Group 200 | Return % rate | 4% | 10% |
| | Consensus Demand Fcst | 8,000 | 17,000 |
| | Forecasted Returns | **320** | **1,700** |

**Fig. 3.16** Commercial returns forecasting input from marketing team

SAP Integrated Business Planning

| Prd Group | Key Figure | Jan"18 | Feb"18 |
|---|---|---|---|
| Group 100 | Consensus Demand Fcst | 18,000 | 29,000 |
| | Forecasted Returns | 900 | 3,480 |
| | Sales Area Returns | 1,800 | 5,100 |
| | Consensus Returns | **1,200** | **4,000** |
| | Sales Fcst Price | $3 | $3 |
| | Consenus Returns Accruals | $3,600 | $12,000 |
| Group 200 | Consensus Demand Fcst | 8,000 | 17,000 |
| | Forecasted Returns | 320 | 1,700 |
| | Sales Area Returns | 500 | 2,400 |
| | Consensus Returns | **400** | **2,000** |
| | Sales Fcst Price | $4 | $4 |
| | Consenus Returns Accruals | $1,600 | $8,000 |

**Fig. 3.17** Commercial returns forecasting—consensus

## 3.7 Integrated Business Plan: Full Year and Budget Gap

Integrated Business Plan has two perspectives: volumetric and financial. Both of them for most of the components are connected but some not. In Fig. 3.18 we see development of volumetric and value inputs per process steps, starting from product review and finished on integrated business plan agreed in management review meeting. Many of the process steps are lined to risks and opportunities scenario planning which should be explained with documented assumptions.

All the process comes together in integrated reconciliation where end-to-end scenario planning is usually used to support preparation of recommendation for management. In the last process step, we approve final integrated business plan. This plan should be from design perspective on the same conceptual level like budget. What we mean by that is if budget is on "net sales" level, then final plan should be as well. We wanted to achieve comparability of the plan to budget to expose gaps in performance (see Fig. 3.18).

Integrated business plan from financial perspective could cover:

- Consolidated top-line revenue projection
- Consolidated bottom-line profit projection
- Gap to budget

Very often you want to see on rolling base and updated information about whole-year projected performance against the budget. In order to do that, you would need to design properly key figures which sum up actuals from the past and integrated business plan in current and future months. Key figure configured that way could be compared any time with budget, but it would be even better if it would enable to show budget gaps on any product, commercial and geographical attribute of the data model (Fig. 3.19).

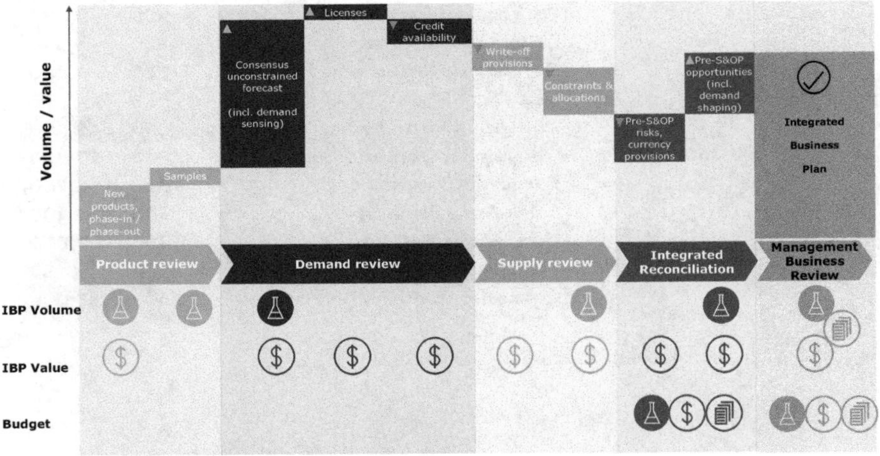


**Fig. 3.18** Integrated Business Planning waterfall

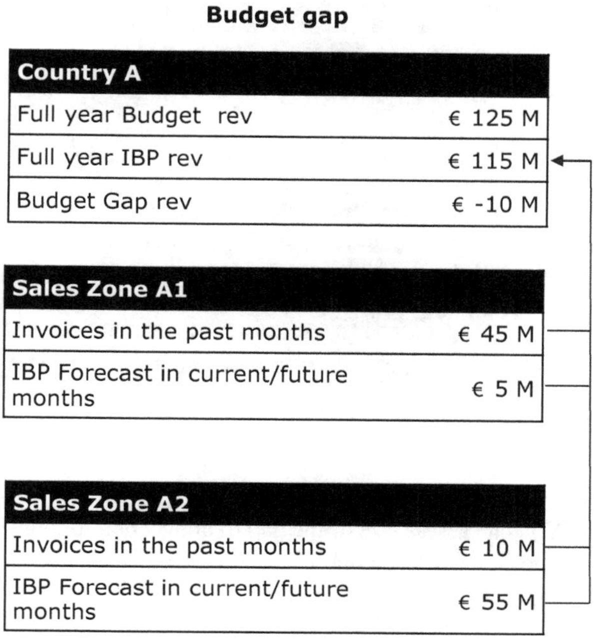
Budget gap
Country A
Full year Budget rev
€ 125 M
Full year IBP rev
€ 115 M
Budget Gap rev
€ -10 M
Sales Zone A1
Invoices in the past months
€ 45 M
IBP Forecast in current/future months
€ 5 M
Sales Zone A2
Invoices in the past months
€ 10 M
IBP Forecast in current/future months
€ 55 M

**Fig. 3.19** IBP vs budget revenue gap exposure

### 3.7.1 SAP Use Case: Integrated Business Plan Versus Budget

Visualization of IBP vs budget can be done on time series or even better as single ratio showing current year performance. In the view on Fig. 3.20, we see that data is totaled product group level but as well in time dimension per quarter and full year, but at the same time you can see all details on product ID level. Amazing thing about it is that you can work on both levels from the same screen you may enter adjustments on aggregated on detail level and aggregation/disaggregation will work for you automatically.

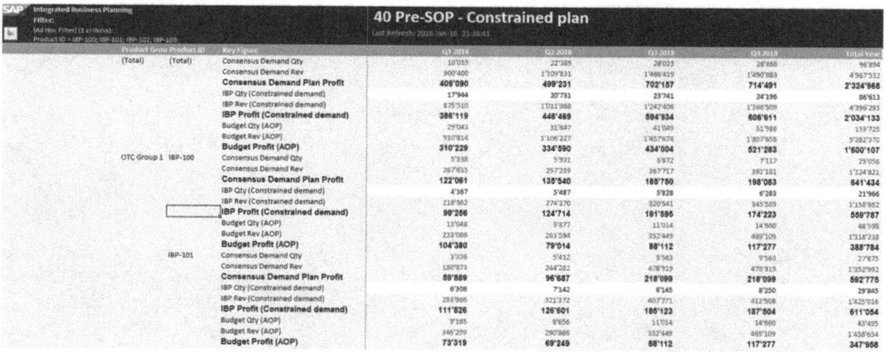


**Fig. 3.20** Aggregated and detail budget gap exposure on quantity, revenue, profit

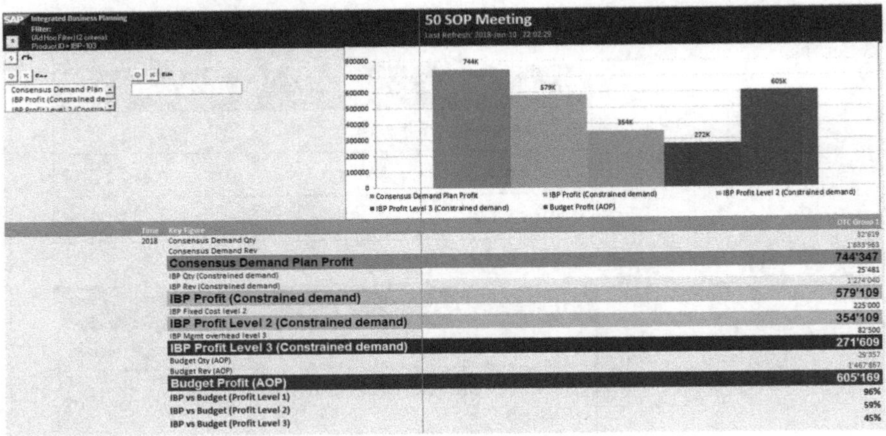


**Fig. 3.21** Full-year IBP to budget comparison

You can assess size of the gap to budget and rolling IBP plan in volume, revenue, and profit. If data model will allow, you could expose gap to budget and later on manage gap closure on any level of commercial, product, and geographical hierarchy.

On the other hand, you may prepare worksheet in management review meeting template which shows key financial data for the whole year (Fig. 3.21). It can show profitability levels for valid operating baseline scenario.

# Keep an Eye on Long Term Horizon with Strategic Planning

# 4

## 4.1 Annual Business Planning

Annual business planning is far more future-oriented process than tactical S&OP. Annual business planning is a long-term process where business strategies are being discussed and agreed. Strategies support long-term vision of the company, e.g., double the size of the company by 2025 and become market leader.

Annual business planning requires senior leader in the organization to drive it and senior position to integrate results of annual business planning with tactical S&OP or budgeting process. You need senior "leader" and senior "integrator," while integrator should be closer to functional area, e.g., marketing, finance, etc. We have seen marketing senior manager who was responsible for "demand side" of business growth as "integrator" and general. We see that the ability to connect and communicate with senior roles in R&D, business development/strategic marketing, manufacturing management, and SC&O is essential for "leader role," but the ability to capture decisions and assumptions in form which can be used in S&OP process is essential for "integrator role."

One of the key differences between annual business planning and tactical S&OP is linked to strategic initiatives. Strategic initiatives on market, channel, technology, research and development, supply chain and operation network drive business forward and drive development. Once we have seen it working, we have recognized that simulating business impact of strategic initiatives more than other aspects of IBP requires cross-functional coordination and end-to-end consideration. The other key difference is that business development of marketing department, typically leads that process and integration with tactical S&OP.

In strategic planning for annual business planning, many drivers may seem to be hard to grasp and hard to make them tangible. This is why capturing and analysis of assumptions play essential role in seeking consensus between senior stakeholders.

If we loosely compare annual business planning with process steps from S&OP, we may find on first glance a lot of similarities (see Fig. 4.1).

 
R. Kepczynski et al., *Implementing Integrated Business Planning*, Management for Professionals, https://doi.org/10.1007/978-3-319-90095-7_4

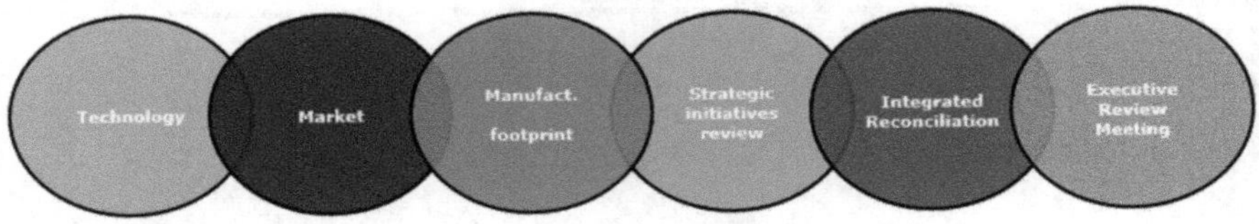


**Fig. 4.1** Annual business planning similarities to tactical S&OP steps

Dimension of product review is normally exchanged with technology; demand review with markets, channels, and product categories; and supply review with holistic manufacturing and operations footprint. Then new review is added focused on strategic initiatives, and finally we close process with integrated reconciliation and senior executives review.

As we have learned, strategic planning for annual business planning is a process which can be designed and built on company-specific and strategic requirements. You may differentiate what business drivers to include and how to model their impact on volumetric and financial side of IBP. We visualize strategic planning on waterfall chart (see Fig. 4.2).

Some of the waterfall components have revenue and cost side, e.g., acquisition of local competitor or new sales channel, but for simplification reason, we have demonstrated it on waterfall like that. It is more about the concept we wanted to visualize and not exact science or not exact business model. All the uncertainty associated to major process steps can be as well mapped if there is a way to quantify them.

Strategic planning has a different pace and routine compared to tactical S&OP. It takes a long time to organize all inputs to build long-term strategic business model. Time wise we have seen that annual business planning was finalized once per year, and it did happen around budgeting period. This time positioning ensured and reinforced interaction between tactical S&OP, budgeting, and strategic planning, since next year's strategic plan, tactical S&OP, and budget should be aligned. We have seen organization where those three sets of figures for same next year were different in budget, in tactical S&OP, and in annual business plan update. Differences were substantial, but they should not be substantial.

It is important that those plans will have defined integration time frame and organizational integration role discussed earlier (see Fig. 4.3).

You may see that integration between all of the above process flows is essential, essential to avoid complete misalignment and ·desynchronization of plans, assumptions, and objectives which should drive business from global senior executive management level who set direction to the ones in the country organizations, plants who make it happen.

We have seen many times that company has country-specific or even overall growth plan expressed mainly by key financial indicators. Your annual business planning may tend to reference those plans if it can be comparable, e.g., by 2025 example chemical company should be 15 billion, with increased market share,

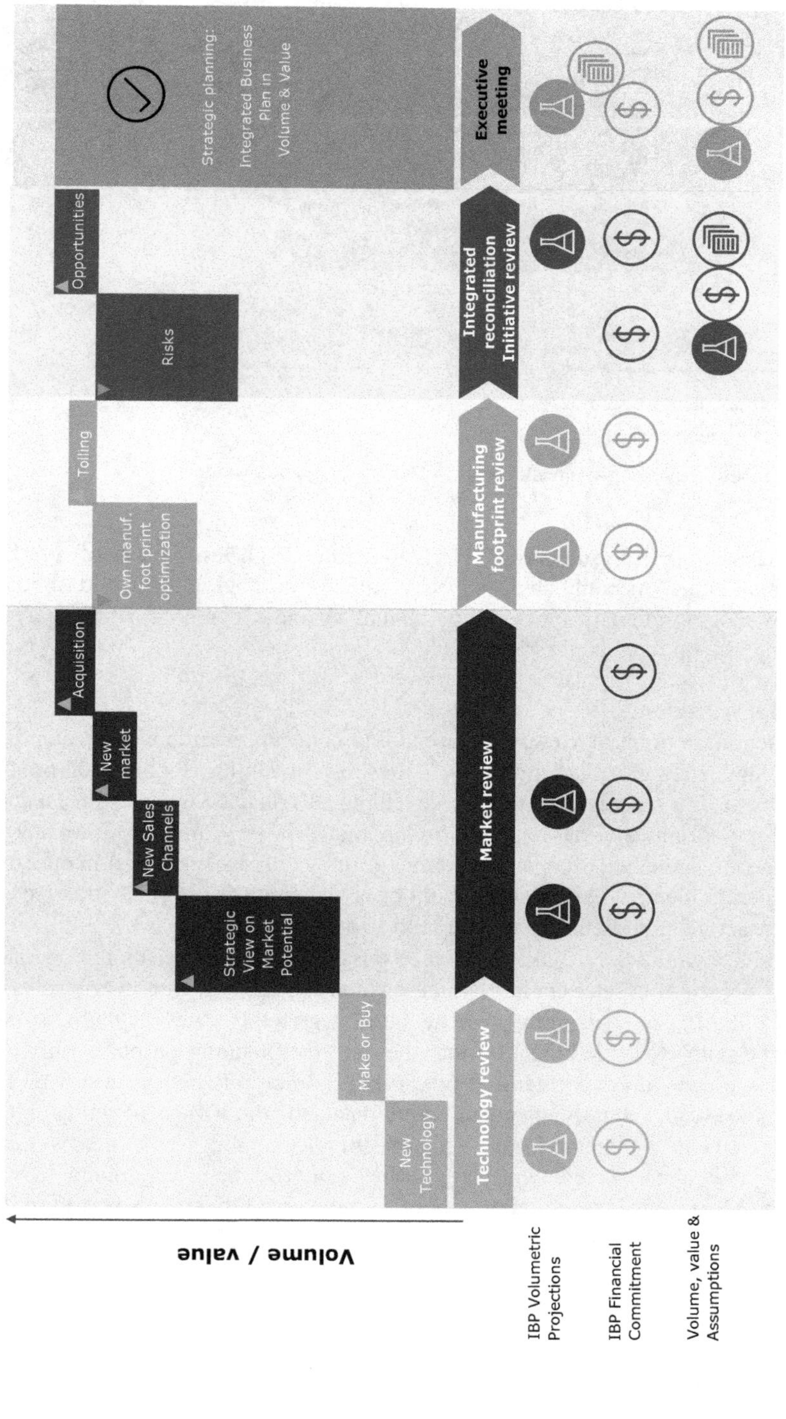


**Fig. 4.2** Strategic planning—simplified IBP waterfall

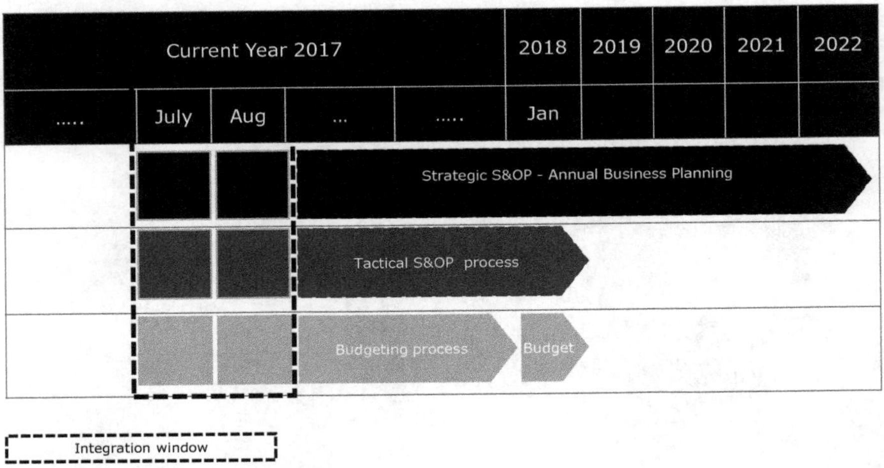


**Fig. 4.3** Strategic planning—annual business planning integration window

improved profitability, and strong R&D pipeline. High-level view of strategic growth plan indicators could be displayed together on strategic executive dashboard.

We will highlight key elements of annual business planning which may be important for you to consider and review.

**Technology/Product**

From integration point of view, it is essential to connect research and development pipeline into strategic planning—annual business planning. Pipeline of product development or even new technology development could be modeled in business risk and opportunities' what-if scenario planning. It is very often the case that we would need to simulate an impact of product form which does not exist in operative planning enthronement, e.g., development of new formulations, bulk, strategic raw materials, active ingredients, steel, and seed varieties.

Our advice would be to make as much as possible of not yet existing in operative planning objects through standard structures and hierarchies. It is worth to make effort to bring key new planning elements into Integrated Business Planning system but maybe with clear identification that they are for planning purposes only. We should not create "dummy" items if possible; it is more efficient to use SAP IBP capability to create version-dependent master data and assign those planning objects to "real elements of hierarchies," e.g., existing technology. If it makes sense, maintain new hierarchy elements, e.g., when you add new technology to your portfolio. Make some assumptions about assignments, share those assumptions with strategic planning stakeholders, but make it happen.

Other way to achieve similar result is to use one of the attributes of your data model to distinguish if planning object is for simulation or operative planning purposes. This parameter may be maintained directly in SAP IBP or derived from your source system.

**Markets/Demand**

Let us start from the differences of this process step in strategic planning-annual business planning and tactical S&OP:

- Less or no involvement from sales team.
- Inputs and analysis are done on high aggregation like product line/business line. It is not unusual to organize demand review by product categories and channels.
- Annual and quarterly bucketing.
- Geographical/commercial level on country or higher, e.g., country group and region.
- Stronger focus on monetized growth view expressed in compound annual growth rate (CAGR).

CAGR is compound annual growth rate normally displayed over a few years' horizon, assuming in certain extended constant growth. Strength of this measure is behind the fact that it is easy to understand: CAGR = (Ending value/Beginning value) ^ (1/n)−1.

You can design and implement this measure in your IBP. When testing or building your formula in IBP, you may confront it with results achieved in this simple CAGR calculator:

http://www.investopedia.com/calculator/cagr.aspx.

Assumptions about long-term demand plans are mostly shared and reconciled between regional, global, and country marketing organizations.

**Manufacturing Footprint/Supply Operations**

"Integrator" role discussed earlier should ensure that key information about manufacturing and supply operations plans are being captured:

- Introduction of new production assets or investment in existing assets to increase throughput
- Introduction of new tolling and packaging assets
- Optimization of manufacturing footprint decreasing ability to produce volume but increasing capability to decrease COGS and become more profitable
- Consolidation of production plants
- Production acquisitions
- Extensions of external or contract manufacturing

Annual business planning may require own production plants being mapped but as well external manufacturing/contract manufacturing. Simulation capabilities of SAP IBP support in easy way creation of master data objects like plants and new production lines and make them version dependent and used for planning purposes. It could mean that in your long-term projections, you would need to organize capacity and output information from your suppliers. SAP IBP helps a lot in simulating above especially with so-called versions which enable master data to be version dependent.

Typical consideration for annual business planning is to make clear guidance on “make or buy.” For certain parts of your portfolio as response to your growth ambition, you may want to consider:

- Increase of contract/externa manufacturing
- Bring manufacturing “back” since it may become too strategic to outsource

You could consider sourcing type as the element of your simulations and implement it in your IBP data model.

Long-term supply availability in essence is typically visualized on annual bucketing or quarterly bucketing but in practice calculated as market review on monthly basis. Long-term supply availability could be:

- Calculated with the use of SAP IBP S&OP heuristics or SAP IBP response and supply
- Projected with the use of simple formula with the use of calculated key figures
- Integrated with the use of HCI from any ERP system or flat files
- Provided manually

You can leverage system in the degree you want and you are ready for.

**Integrated Reconciliation and Strategic Initiative Review**
Reconciliation between market demand views, manufacturing view, and long-term financial view is the best way to explain strategic scenarios. In integrated reconciliation we connect all those views. We have seen very undervalued management of currency exchange rates for long-term planning; therefore please refer to monetization of forecast and plans chapter. “Integrator role” should contact treasury or finance department to get their view on forecasted exchange rate for corporate currency (e.g., USD).

Strategic initiatives which might be brought into IBP can vary a lot, but we have seen initiative which was about building a new plant to support sales growth in profitable manner in big emerging BRIC/BRICSA market (Brazil, Russia, India, China, South Africa, and Argentina). How should you tackle that topic? Let us bring few use cases to illustrate what we talk about.

### 4.1.1 Strategic Forecasting and Planning in Agriculture

**Agriculture Context**
Plant breeding, simply stated, is about developing crop varieties with a view to improving crop production. Given the importance of crop production in ensuring food security, plant breeders perform a very crucial role in society (see Fig. 4.4).

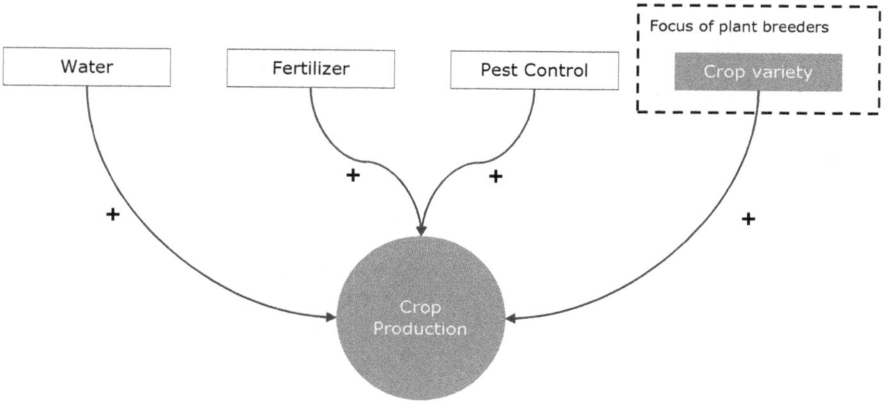


**Fig. 4.4** Factors influencing crop productivity and the particular focus of plant breeders (adapted from Poehlman 1987)

Crop productivity depends on various factors (see above). Among these factors, the particular focus of plant breeders is crop variety—that is, they endeavor to develop superior varieties by improving plant heredity (Poehlman 1987). To achieve productivity improvements, plant breeders rely on a bevy of disciplines that include agronomy, botany, plant genetics, crop physiology, plant pathology, entomology, plant biochemistry, and statistics (Poehlman 1987). Combining these various disciplines requires a clear strategy. The strategy of plant breeding can be summarized; thus (Poehlman 1987):

- Recognize morphological traits and physiological and pathological responses important for adaptation, yield, and quality of crops.
- Evaluate genetic potential for these traits in strains being assessed.
- Search sources of genes that contribute to favorable traits.
- Combine genetic potential into an improved variety or cultivar (cultivated variety).

Besides strong expertise in the scientific disciplines listed above, strong supply chain planning capabilities are also equally essential for successful execution of the strategic elements outlined above. Given the length of the development cycle of a variety (spanning several years; more on this later), strategic planning plays a very important role in ensuring that the varieties developed by the plant breeder pass the litmus test—which is wide acceptance by farmers.

To understand the importance of strategy and strategic planning, let's start by delineating the role of a typical plant breeder. In a supply chain involving seed growers or seed producers, plant breeder, and end customers (farmers or even license partners), Fig. 4.5 lists the responsibilities of each of these stakeholders:

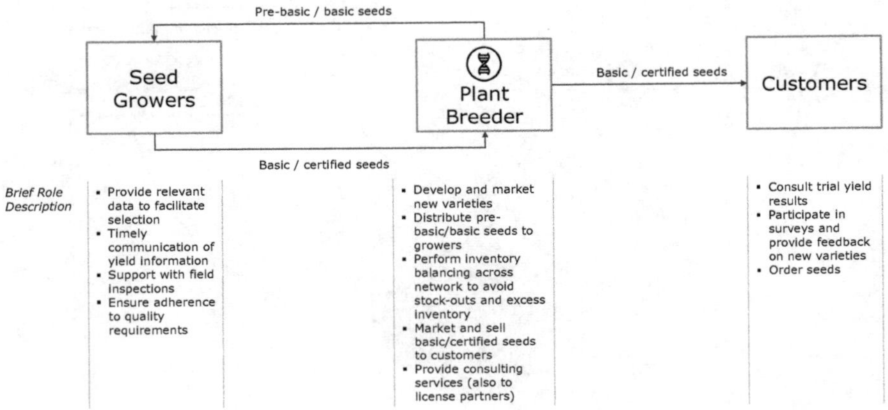


**Fig. 4.5** Typical responsibilities of different stakeholders in a plant breeder's supply chain

The key activities of a plant breeder (from Fig. 4.5) are provided below:

- Develop and market new varieties
- Distribute pre-basic/basic seeds[1] to growers
- Perform inventory balancing across network to avoid stock-outs and excess inventory
- Market and sell basic/certified seeds to customers
- Provide consulting services (also to license partners)

Most of these activities require long-term focus and thereby imply a long planning horizon. The need for a long horizon is best appreciated with an explanation of how the "product" (certified seeds in most cases) comes to be. Certified seeds, which for the most part are the greatest contributor of revenues for a plant breeder, start their life as breeder seeds. Breeder seeds are sown, and basic or foundation seeds are harvested, which are sown and harvested as certified seeds that are in turn treated, packed, and sold to end customers. Each "sow-grow-harvest" cycle is typically a year-long affair (longer for certain biennial crops such as beets). The evolution of a seed from breeder seed to certified seed is illustrated below in Fig. 4.6.

Planning activities not only have to account for the long planning horizon owing to the development lifecycle of a seed but also need to account for the crop calendar. Based on timing of planting and harvesting, crops can be classified into spring and winter crops. Crop calendar for typical crop types is depicted in Fig. 4.7.

Taking an example of a crop type, say winter wheat, it is clear from the illustration that seeds are planted around October and are harvested around August the following year. This implies that to ensure adequate supply of certified seeds for the

[1]Seeds are classified, broadly, according to their lifecycle stage into pre-basic, basic, and certified seeds. This is described further in Fig. 4.3.

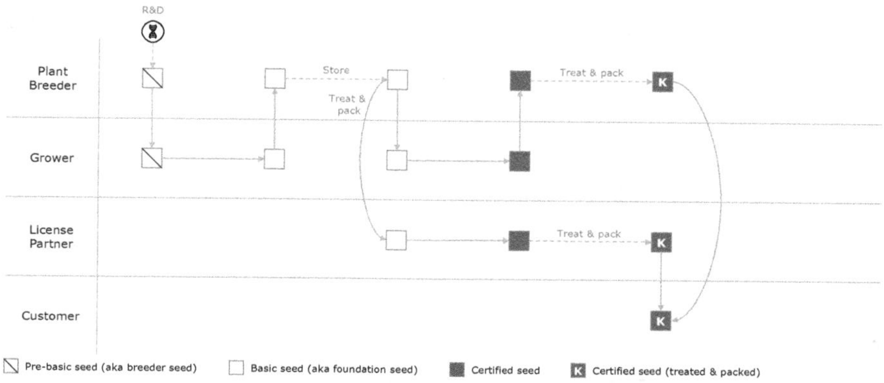


**Fig. 4.6** Seed evolution

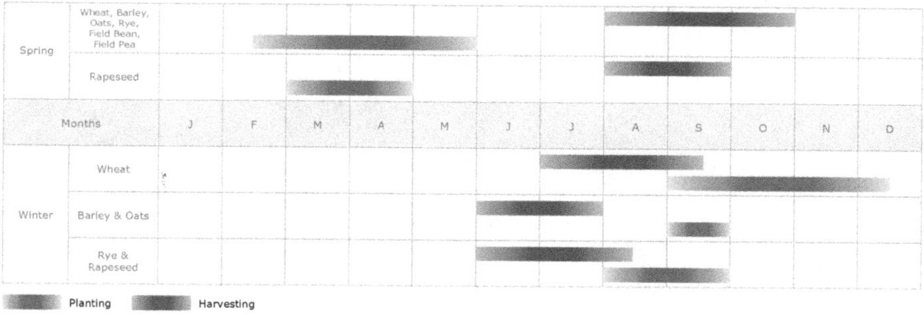


**Fig. 4.7** Winter and spring crop calendars

sales campaign of a given year, basic seeds should be available in sufficient quantities (accounting also for yield variability and other uncertainties) the previous year. The same goes for pre-basic seeds (or breeder seeds) the year before. We are talking about a multiyear production process, and a robust long-term, strategic planning is paramount for the success of a variety.

### Strategic Planning Process at a Plant Breeder

We have so far discussed the importance of strategic planning for a plant breeder. Strategic planning activities are not ends in themselves but only a means to an end, which is ensuring adequate product availability during the sales campaign in order to meet revenue and profitability targets. Given the rigidity of the production lead time, botanically speaking, product availability is given top billing by plant breeders as it has a direct bearing on market share. To better appreciate the role of strategic planning, let's extend the scope of planning to include tactical and operational activities as well and map them to a cone that goes from long-term to short-term activities as one navigates from left to right (see Fig. 4.8). For example, developing

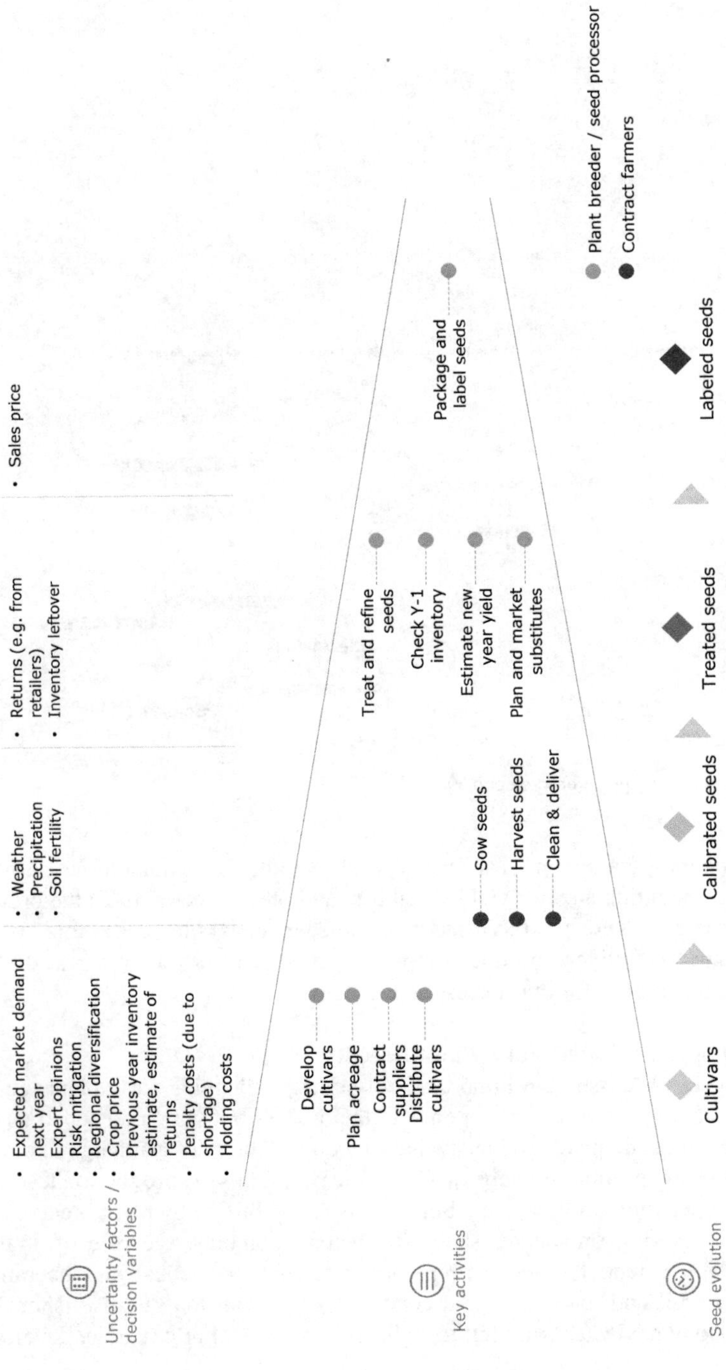


**Fig. 4.8** Seed planning hierarchy/cone

cultivated varieties (cultivars) is a very strategic activity with long-term significance and implications that occupies a position on the far left of the cone, whereas packaging and labeling of seeds to be sold to end customers are operational activities that sit on the far right. The success of activities that have operational focus (like packaging and labeling) is largely based on the effectiveness of planning activities that have preceded it.

The illustration also provides an overview of key uncertainty factors corresponding to the activities along the cone. As one can see, strategic and long-term activities are accompanied by higher uncertainties such as commodity prices, estimates of carry-over inventory, demand side and supply side risks, climatic conditions, etc.

Synthesizing the aspects of planning scope and crop calendars discussed above, one can think of a process framework such as the one shown in Fig. 4.9 that not only encompasses activities along the three planning regimes (strategic, tactical, and operational) but also accounts for time frames stipulated by crop calendars. In the illustration, the length of the chevron represents the planning horizon. The colored bars on the chevrons indicate the typical time window when the planning activities are executed. All of the planning activities have volumetric as well as value or financial focus (therefore the # and $ remark within parentheses). As one can see, the timing of the planning activities is tied to crop calendar—the top-half represents activities linked to spring crops, and the bottom-half corresponds to winter crops.

The process framework suggested is logically grouped into three sets of activities, namely, long-term sales planning, production planning, and multiplication planning.

Sales planning focuses on determining independent demand (end-customer demand) for varieties in the plant breeder's portfolio over the next 4–5 fiscal years, with particular focus on the forthcoming sales season. Production planning takes the results of sales planning as the key input and ascertains what needs to be produced by taking into consideration supply elements such as carry-over inventory, expected receipts, and additional demand elements such as inventory targets, factored in to account for different uncertainty factors (e.g., yield and climatic factors). Finally, net production demands are handed down to multiplication planning, where selection of seed producers that will grow the varieties for which there is a positive net demand is performed.

We'll now discuss each of the three planning processes (sales, multiplication, and supply/production plan) of the suggested process framework in turn and see how IBP is particularly suited to handle the requirements imposed by these processes.

**Long-term Sales Planning**

Before we get to the long-term aspect of planning activities in sales planning, let's briefly dwell on the execution aspects to frame the planning activities in their proper context.

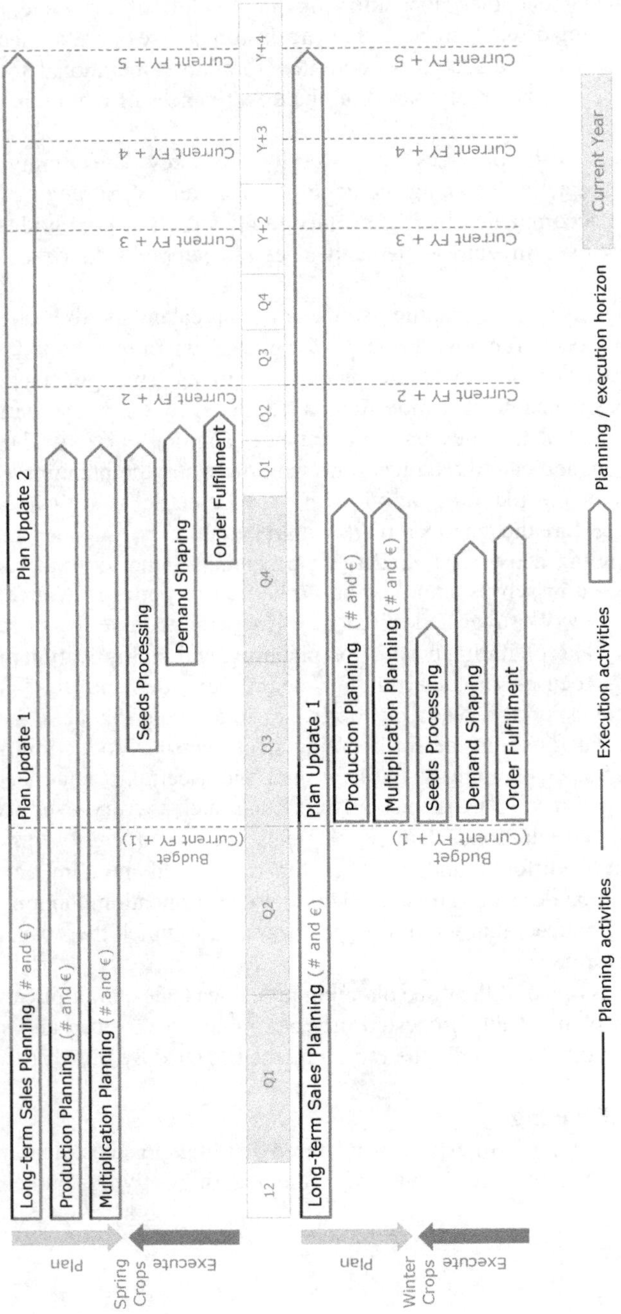


**Fig. 4.9** Seeds strategic to operational planning

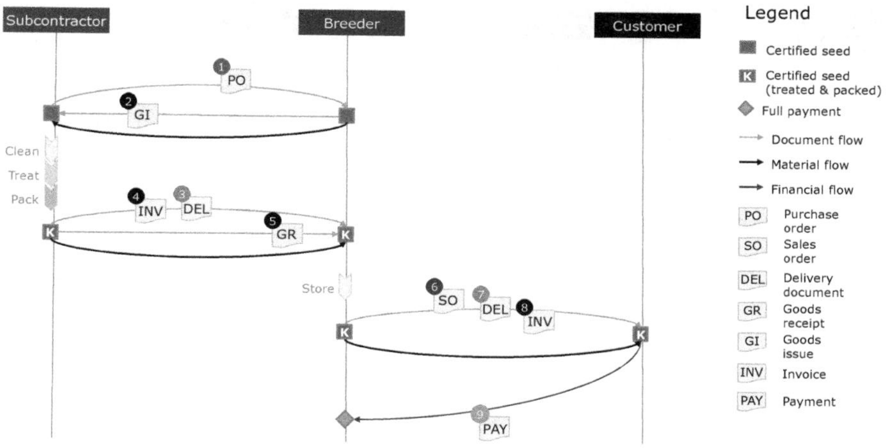


**Fig. 4.10** Process flow—selling certified seeds

We will discuss two typical flows—selling of certified seeds and collecting license revenues or royalties for sale of basic seeds to license partners.[2]

**Sales of Certified Seeds** The operational flows (physical, document, and value) are illustrated in Fig. 4.10.

The steps involved are:

1. Breeder purchases cleaning, treatment, and packaging services for certified raw seeds from subcontractor.
2. Breeder distributes certified raw (uncleaned) seeds to subcontractor.
3. Subcontractor delivers clean certified seeds in treated and packed condition to breeder.
4. Subcontractor invoices breeder for its services.
5. Breeder receives finished seeds from subcontractor.
6. Finished (treated and packaged certified seeds) are sold to customer, i.e., farmers.
7. Breeder delivers finished seeds to customer.
8. Breeder invoices customer.
9. Customer pays breeder for delivered seeds.

[2]In this process, plant breeders sell basic seeds to license partners who transform these (either by themselves or in partnership with seed producers) to certified seeds. Plant breeders are then owed royalties for certified seeds sold to end customers.

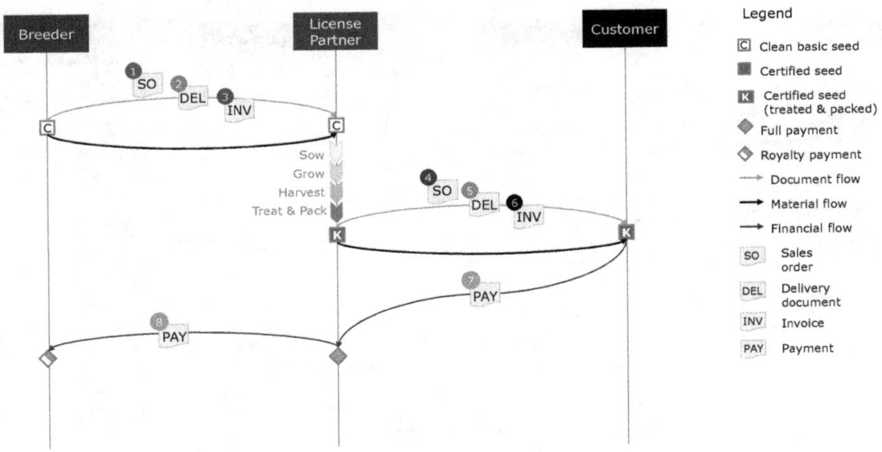


**Fig. 4.11** Process flow—license sales

**License Sales** The operational flows are illustrated in Fig. 4.11.

The steps involved here are:

1. Breeder sells basic seeds to license partner.
2. Breeder delivers basic seeds to license partner.
3. Breeder invoices license partner for the basic seeds.
4. License partner sells certified seeds to customers.
5. License partner delivers certified seeds to customer.
6. License partner invoices customer for the certified seeds.
7. Customer pays license partner for the certified seeds.
8. License partner pays breeder royalties from the selling of certified seeds to its customers.

As we have framed the context of planning activities (the desired result that the plant breeder wants to achieve), let's turn to the planning steps that need to happen in order to ensure operational excellence.

For planning the two types of businesses discussed above (selling of certified seeds, license sales), corresponding planning activities can be categorized, based on approach, into top-down planning and bottom-up planning.

Top-down planning involves starting with an estimation of the overall market potential for certified seeds and systematically working out that portion of the market that is accessible for the plant breeder to sell its own varieties. On the other hand, bottom-up planning relies heavily on the know-how of the sales team regarding the overall market and customers for the plant breeder's varieties. The sales teams provide their opinion on demand for varieties at different levels of granularity depending on their individual expertise and area of focus. These plans are collated, and consensus is achieved to generate a bottom-up sales plan. Comparisons between top-down and bottom-up plans can be illuminating as they might provide insights such as:

- Gap between addressable market and top-down or bottom-up sales plan—opportunities for improving market footprint.
- Gaps between top-down and bottom-up sales plan: incorrect or misaligned assumptions in terms of realistic market potential or ground realities (along the dimensions of market, customer, or product) that have not been adequately accounted for in top-down planning.
- The process framework suggested also includes updates to plans that happen at predefined timeframes during a fiscal year. Comparisons between planning versions (e.g., budget versus budget update made later in the year) can provide additional insights. For instance, an emergence or widening of gap between addressable market and sales plan as the year progresses can be indicative of operational issues such as poor inventory record accuracy (on-hand was overestimated), insufficient consideration of uncertainty factors, below par field inspection results, etc.

The approaches are graphically summarized in Fig. 4.12.

**Long-Term Supply/Production Planning**

Similar to sales planning, let's start by understanding the operational flows involved in production planning. We'll do so by focusing on one of the many operational processes, albeit a very important one, that of distribution of basic seeds required for multiplication, which then would yield certified seeds. The steps are visualized in Fig. 4.13 and listed below:

1. Breeder sells basic seeds to seed grower.
2. Breeder delivers basic seeds to seed grower.
3. Breeder invoices seed grower for the basic seeds.
4. Breeder purchases certified seeds from seed grower.

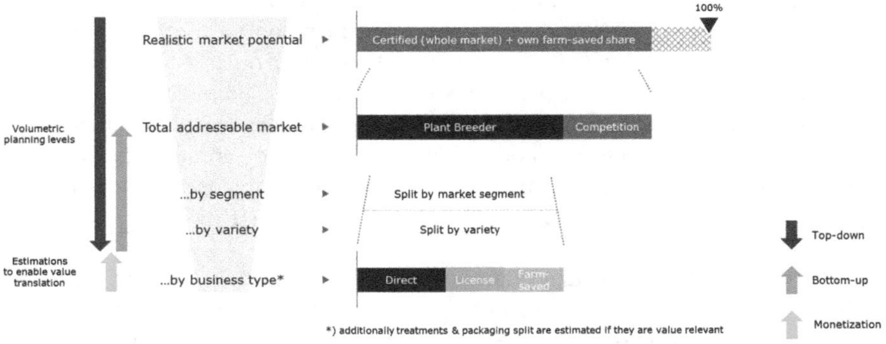


**Fig. 4.12** Seed's long-term sales planning concepts

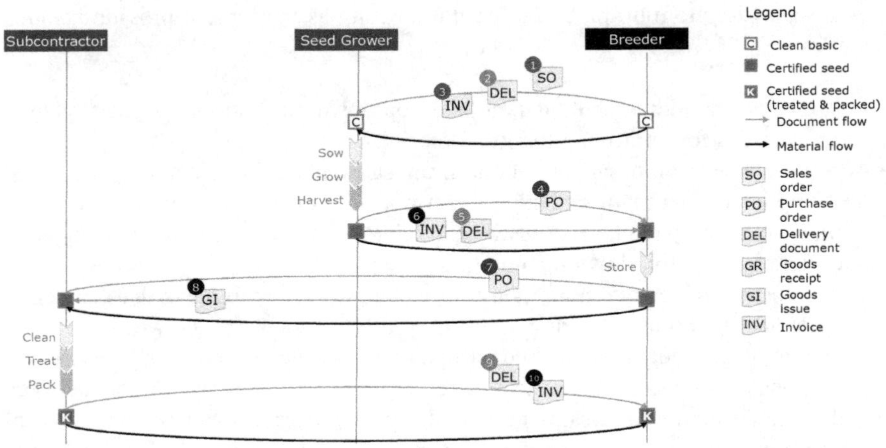


**Fig. 4.13** Process flow—production of basic seeds

5. Seed grower delivers raw certified seeds to breeder and, if requested, delivers raw certified seeds directly to subcontractor for cleaning.
6. Seed grower invoices breeder for raw certified seeds.
7. Breeder purchases cleaning of raw certified seeds and may also include treatment and packaging.
8. Breeder delivers raw certified seeds to subcontractor. If the seed grower delivers directly, this step is skipped.
9. Subcontractor delivers clean certified seeds to breeder after cleaning process; seeds may also be treated and packaged.
10. Subcontractor invoices breeder for cleaning (and optionally treatment and packaging) of seeds.

The implication of the above-described operational steps, from a planning perspective, is that requirements for basic seeds need to be determined accurately and efficiently based on sales demands for certified seeds while adequately accounting for various uncertainty factors. This requires consideration of all relevant demand and supply elements to calculate net production volumes in order to ascertain if there is a deficit that needs to be satisfied either through own multiplication or through procurement (external/internal vendor). In IBP, the various generations of the seeds can be represented as levels in a product bill of material, and various factors (such as yield, loss, and multiplication) can be modeled as output/component coefficients. A representation of a hybrid variety as a bill of material (BOM) is presented in Fig. 4.14.

With the independent demand for certified seeds (level 0 of the BOM) and the BOM structure as inputs, the S&OP operator of IBP is well placed to derive dependent demands across all BOM levels while considering supply nodes and additional demands at each of the levels as it propagates demand in a top-down fashion.

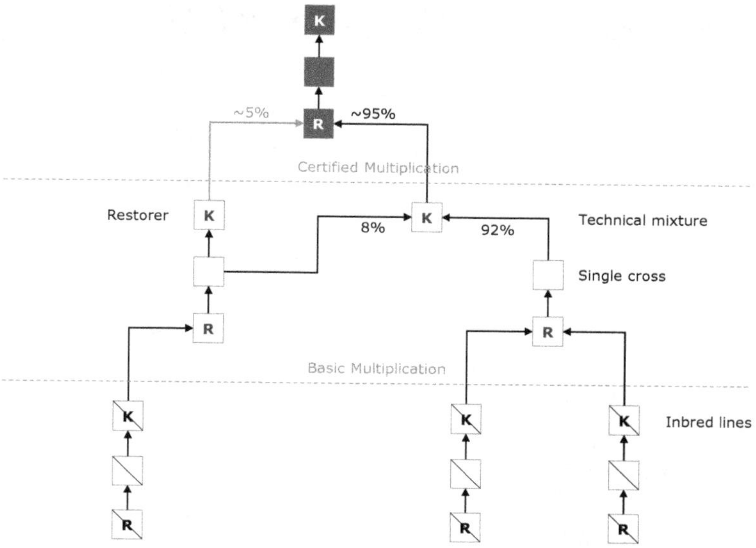


**Fig. 4.14** Bill of material for hybrid crop

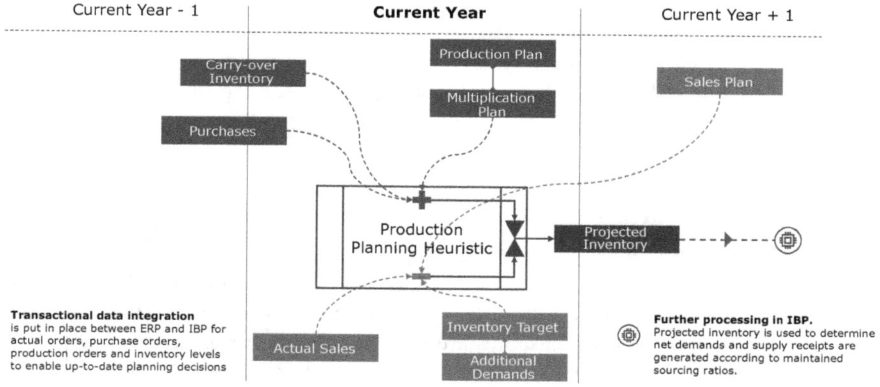


**Fig. 4.15** Schematic diagram for seed supply/production planning inputs

A simplified schematic diagram that illustrates how the heuristic algorithm calculates net demand by considering supply and demand elements is shown in Fig. 4.15. Also note that lead times can be modeled in the production master data to denote the time taken for the transition from one seed generation/classification (e.g., basic) to the next (certified). Of course, lead times for treatment, packaging, etc. can also be modeled, but these pale in comparison to the length of the crop's growth phase and therefore do not hold a high-data modeling significance. As per previous figure, K stands for certified seed and R for restorer.

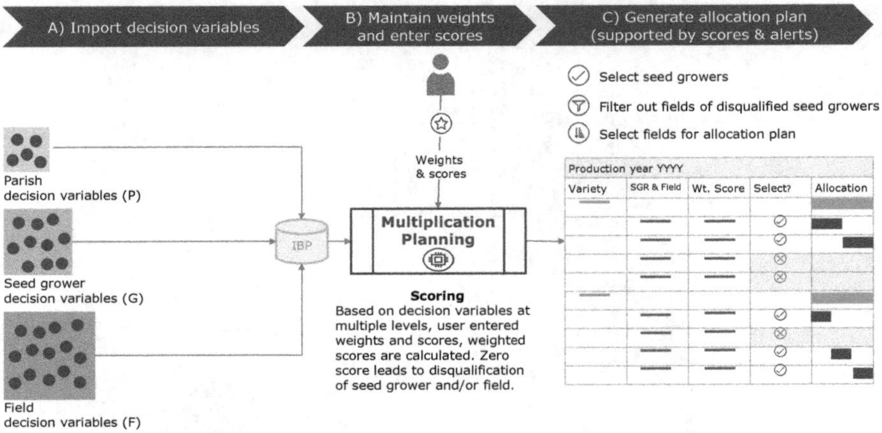


**Fig. 4.16** Seed multiplication process

## Multiplication Planning

The process of multiplication planning starts once net production demands for raw seeds of a particular seed classification or generation are known (say, raw certified seeds) and ends with all demands having been allocated to seed growers or fields (choice of seed growers or fields is stipulated by the desired granularity of planning).

The process is facilitated in the system by modeling decision variables on various levels of detail that helps evaluate the suitability of seed growers or fields for different varieties for which demands need to be allocated. This process is conceptually illustrated in Fig. 4.16.

In the model depicted, decision variables are grouped into three logical clusters—field, seed grower, and parish decision variables. Parish (a small geographical area) decision variables are for climatic and region-specific data that are not linked directly to varieties to be grown or fields. Some examples are data pertaining to temperature, rainfall, humidity, hailstorms, suitability for earliness of harvest, vernalization, water sufficiency, etc. Seed grower variables are for storing data for decision support that are linked to, as the name suggests, seed growers—this could be soft factors such as qualitative ranking, harvesting and processing techniques employed, certifications (EU or OECD), but then as well more quantitative factors such as field inspection and quality results in the past. The last group is for decision variables associated with a field such as preceding crop, pre-preceding crop, field acreage, yield, distance to neighboring crop, etc. Note that the planning level for both seed grower and field decision variables includes crop type.

As shown in the conceptual illustration, based on decision variables and weights administered for those decision variables—signifying their relative importance—scoring is done by the planner. Based on scores entered, weighted scores are calculated, and an allocation is proposed by the system based on weighted scores (proposal for allocation in % = total field score/grand total of field scores * 100). A score of zero has a special meaning as it disqualifies a field from selection.

Additionally, based on seed grower decision variables, a seed grower can be either selected or deselected for further consideration. Disqualification of a seed grower disqualifies all fields in her/his control. Finally, based on field scores and selection of seed growers, final assignment of varieties to fields and quantity assignments are done to complete the process.

Here are some decision variables in multiplication planning process:

- Pre-crop and pre-pre-crop
- Distance to neighboring crop
- Available acreage for sowing
- (Historical) results of field inspection
- Raw material quality results
- Yield performance
- Relationship with plant breeder
- Monthly rainfall
- Days of snow
- Days of hailstorm
- Temperature
- Humidity

### 4.1.2 SAP Use Case: Sales Planning, Multiplication Planning, and Production Planning

**Long-Term Sales Planning**

In this section we describe some salient implementation aspects of the sales planning process in IBP. In Fig. 4.17 key functional enablers in IBP that make it well suited for implementing the sales planning process described are listed.

**Top-down Planning of Realistic Market Potential**

A planning view that enables top-down planning of realistic market potential is visualized in Fig. 4.18.

Various inputs such as estimated acreage (for planting) for seeds of a given crop type (combination of crop and season—winter wheat in the example), sowing rate, and estimated share of certified seeds are modeled as input key figures. These inputs are used to generate a proposal for realistic market potential for certified seeds in volume (1). Additionally, plant breeder's share of farm-saved seeds is estimated and translated into volume (2). The sum of (1) and (2) are proposed as the total market for certified seeds including plant breeder's own share of farm-saved seeds. This proposal can be adjusted by the user (3). In the chart, system-calculated realistic market potential is compared to user overrides, and gaps between the two are called out (4), (5).

| Sales planning: functional requirement | IBP functional enabler |
|---|---|
| Step-wise resolution of realistic market potential into demand for varieties in the plant breeder's portfolio | • Data model and planning levels that enable different granularities for data storage<br>• Ability to flexibly define key figure calculations: for example, realistic market potential is a product of inputs such as estimated acreage for a given crop, sowing rate (for instance, in KG per hectare), estimate of certified seeds and farm-saved seeds[3] share<br>• Excel and web-based visualizations that help draw insights quickly (see description of types of gaps in the section about top-down and bottom-up planning)<br>• Defaulting logic: ease of definition of defaulting rules for generation of system proposal based on historical data and defaulting to this in case no manual inputs are provided |
| Gathering of inputs from various stakeholders for bottom-up planning | • Anytime, anywhere nature of working with Excel UI<br>• Collaborative features such as case management and scenario and version management<br>• Seamless integration of exceptions in Excel views to enable collation of inputs at different levels of granularity to create a consensus sales plan<br>• Point about defaulting logic mentioned above applies here as well |
| Translation of volumetric plans into value | • Ease of integration of volumetric as well as monetary inputs in the planning data model<br>• Flexible key figure definitions for calculation of revenue, COGS, contribution margin etc. to immediately assess impact of volumetric plans |

**Fig. 4.17** Sales planning key SAP IBP enablers

#### Breakdown of Realistic Market Potential First into Estimates by Market and Quality Classification and Subsequently into Share by Variety

A planning view that enables top-down planning of addressable market is visualized in Fig. 4.19.

Realistic market potential estimated for the crop type in the earlier step is broken down into estimates by market and quality classification (1), (2). In the case of market classification—which is a function of usage—winter wheat (in the USA, as it is the country in our example) is classified into categories such as hard winter, soft

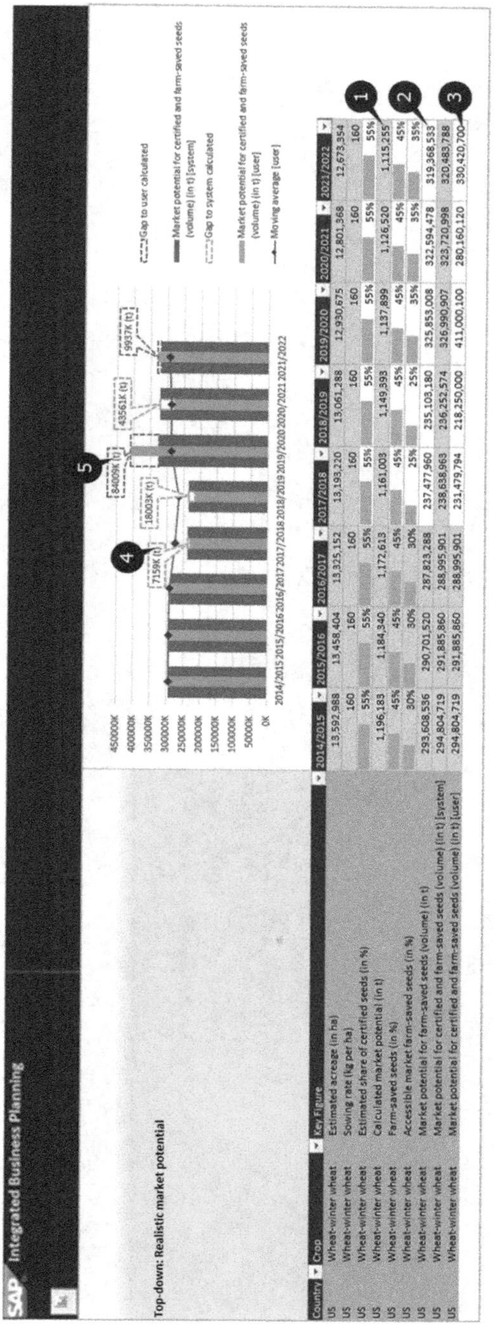


| Country | Crop | Key Figure | 2014/2015 | 2015/2016 | 2016/2017 | 2017/2018 | 2018/2019 | 2019/2020 | 2020/2021 | 2021/2022 |
|---|---|---|---|---|---|---|---|---|---|---|
| US | Wheat-winter wheat | Estimated acreage (in ha) | 13,592,988 | 13,458,404 | 13,325,152 | 13,193,220 | 13,061,288 | 12,930,675 | 12,801,368 | 12,673,354 |
| US | Wheat-winter wheat | Sowing rate (kg per ha) | 160 | 160 | 160 | 160 | 160 | 160 | 160 | 160 |
| US | Wheat-winter wheat | Estimated share of certified seeds (in %) | 55% | 55% | 55% | 55% | 55% | 55% | 55% | 55% |
| US | Wheat-winter wheat | Calculated market potential (in t) | 1,196,183 | 1,184,340 | 1,172,613 | 1,161,003 | 1,149,393 | 1,137,899 | 1,126,520 | 1,115,255 |
| US | Wheat-winter wheat | Farm-saved seeds (in %) | 45% | 45% | 45% | 45% | 45% | 45% | 45% | 45% |
| US | Wheat-winter wheat | Accessible market farm-saved seeds (in %) | 30% | 30% | 30% | 25% | 25% | 35% | 35% | 35% |
| US | Wheat-winter wheat | Market potential for farm-saved seeds (volume) (in t) | 293,608,536 | 290,701,520 | 287,823,288 | 237,477,960 | 235,103,180 | 325,853,008 | 322,594,478 | 319,368,533 |
| US | Wheat-winter wheat | Market potential for certified and farm-saved seeds (volume) (in t) [system] | 294,804,719 | 291,885,860 | 288,995,901 | 238,638,963 | 236,252,574 | 326,990,907 | 323,720,998 | 320,483,788 |
| US | Wheat-winter wheat | Market potential for certified and farm-saved seeds (volume) (in t) [user] | 294,804,719 | 291,885,860 | 288,995,901 | 231,479,794 | 218,250,000 | 411,000,100 | 280,160,120 | 330,420,700 |

**Fig. 4.18** Seed sales planning—forecasting crop realistic market potential

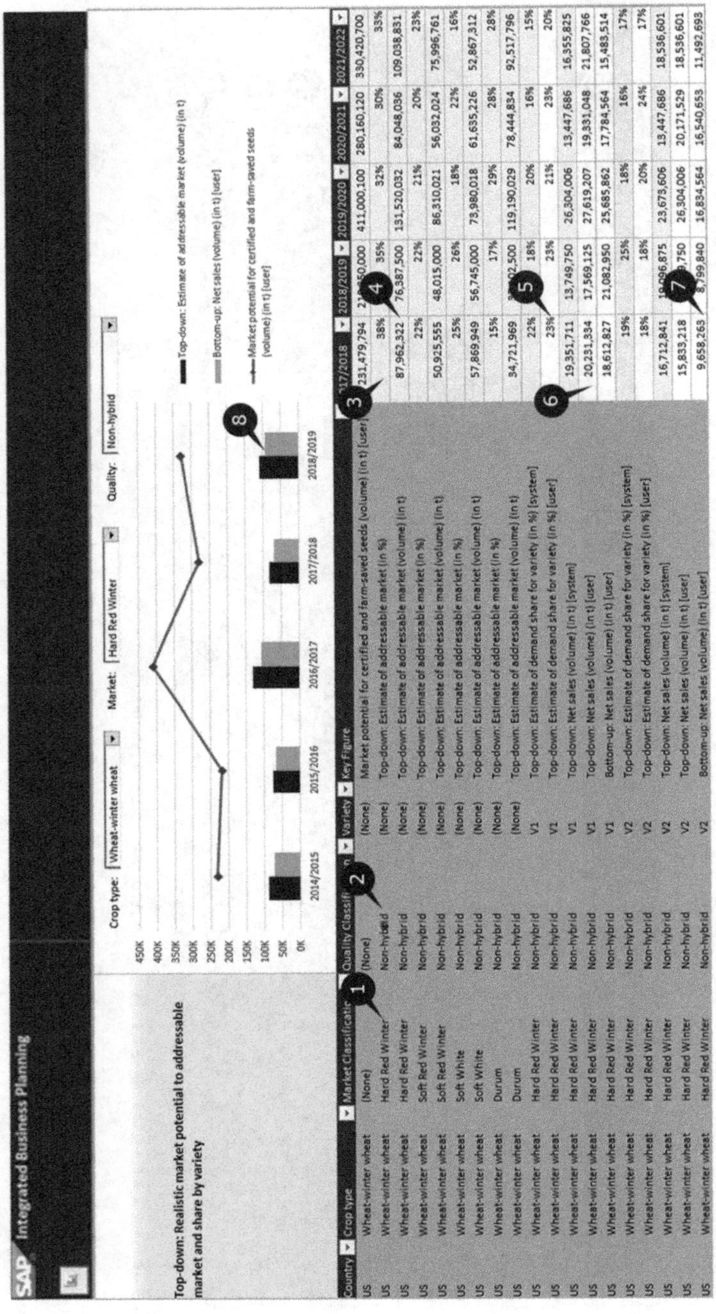


**Fig. 4.19** Seed sales planning—forecasting market share by variety

winter, soft white, and durum. Quality classification is more of a product-inherent aspect, and in the case of wheat, there are two classes: non-hybrid and hybrid. The system calculates a certain percentage share based on historical data. This is translated into a volume key figure by multiplying the percentage with the realistic market potential (3), (4). However, users are able to override system defaults, both percentage-wise and volumetrically (5), (6). Results of bottom-up planning can also be integrated into the view (7) to offer a comparison to top-down estimates and can lead to meaningful insights when compared (8).

### 4.1.2.1 Long-Term Supply/Production Planning

**Derivation of Dependent Demands Based on Independent Sales Demands for Certified Seeds**

Planned sales demands (dependent customer demands) for farmers/customers in the US are the primary input for planning (see Fig. 4.20). These demands are pegged to the supplying location—called customer facing WH 01—the USA in the example (1). Based on the sourcing rule for the warehouse, that is, the supplying location identified in IBP's master data, demands are pegged to the supplying location. It is supplying plant 01—the USA in this example. These are seen as dependent location demands. Once all demands for finished products are known, additional demands are corrections which are considered and netted against stocks and other receipts to calculate net demand. In our example, an inventory correction is done (2), and additional independent demands are planned (3) leading to a net demand as indicated by (4). As one can see, these net demands are passed on to certified semifinished goods (SFG). As the component coefficient is one, there is a 1:1 translation. This process continues, and SFG demands are propagated to the raw material (RM). Here, the translation is not 1:1 as there is a loss factor considered—so, more RM is required to account for cleaning loss. Finally, raw material demands are netted against receipts—in our example, there are purchase orders for RM, which are netted to calculate the final net demand that is apt for multiplication (9).

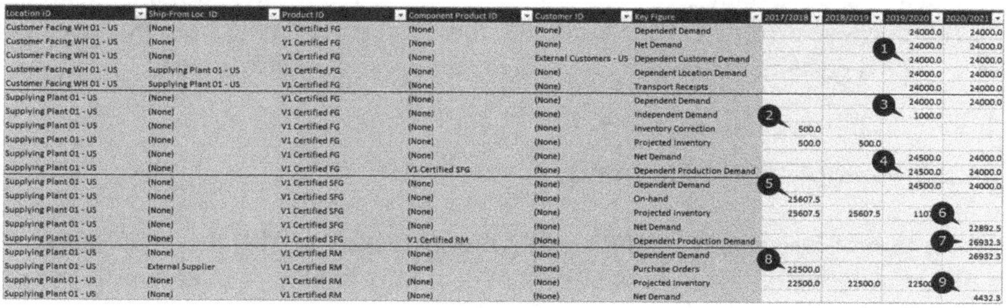

| Location ID | Ship-From Loc. ID | Product ID | Component Product ID | Customer ID | Key Figure | 2017/2018 | 2018/2019 | 2019/2020 | 2020/2021 |
|---|---|---|---|---|---|---|---|---|---|
| Customer Facing WH 01 - US | (None) | V1 Certified FG | (None) | (None) | Dependent Demand | | | 24000.0 | 24000.0 |
| Customer Facing WH 01 - US | (None) | V1 Certified FG | (None) | (None) | Net Demand | | | 24000.0 | 24000.0 |
| Customer Facing WH 01 - US | (None) | V1 Certified FG | (None) | External Customers - US | Dependent Customer Demand | | | 24000.0 | 24000.0 |
| Customer Facing WH 01 - US | Supplying Plant 01 - US | V1 Certified FG | (None) | (None) | Dependent Location Demand | | | 24000.0 | 24000.0 |
| Customer Facing WH 01 - US | Supplying Plant 01 - US | V1 Certified FG | (None) | (None) | Transport Receipts | | | 24000.0 | 24000.0 |
| Supplying Plant 01 - US | (None) | V1 Certified FG | (None) | (None) | Dependent Demand | | | 24000.0 | 24000.0 |
| Supplying Plant 01 - US | (None) | V1 Certified FG | (None) | (None) | Independent Demand | | | 1000.0 | |
| Supplying Plant 01 - US | (None) | V1 Certified FG | (None) | (None) | Inventory Correction | 500.0 | | | |
| Supplying Plant 01 - US | (None) | V1 Certified FG | (None) | (None) | Projected Inventory | 500.0 | 500.0 | | |
| Supplying Plant 01 - US | (None) | V1 Certified FG | (None) | (None) | Net Demand | | | 24500.0 | 24000.0 |
| Supplying Plant 01 - US | (None) | V1 Certified FG | V1 Certified SFG | (None) | Dependent Production Demand | | | 24500.0 | 24000.0 |
| Supplying Plant 01 - US | (None) | V1 Certified SFG | (None) | (None) | Dependent Demand | | | 24500.0 | 24000.0 |
| Supplying Plant 01 - US | (None) | V1 Certified SFG | (None) | (None) | On-hand | 25607.5 | | | |
| Supplying Plant 01 - US | (None) | V1 Certified SFG | (None) | (None) | Projected Inventory | 25607.5 | 25607.5 | 110 | |
| Supplying Plant 01 - US | (None) | V1 Certified SFG | (None) | (None) | Net Demand | | | | 22892.5 |
| Supplying Plant 01 - US | (None) | V1 Certified SFG | V1 Certified RM | (None) | Dependent Production Demand | | | | 26932.3 |
| Supplying Plant 01 - US | (None) | V1 Certified RM | (None) | (None) | Dependent Demand | | | | 26932.3 |
| Supplying Plant 01 - US | External Supplier | V1 Certified RM | (None) | (None) | Purchase Orders | 22500.0 | | | |
| Supplying Plant 01 - US | (None) | V1 Certified RM | (None) | (None) | Projected Inventory | 22500.0 | 22500.0 | 2250 | |
| Supplying Plant 01 - US | (None) | V1 Certified RM | (None) | (None) | Net Demand | | | | 4432.3 |

**Fig. 4.20** Seed conversion of sales demand to dependent demand

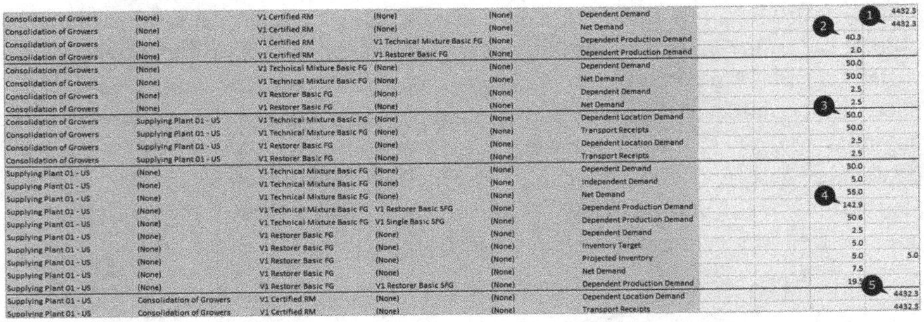

| | | | | | | | | | |
|---|---|---|---|---|---|---|---|---|---|
| Consolidation of Growers | (None) | V1 Certified RM | (None) | (None) | Dependent Demand | | | | 4432.3 |
| Consolidation of Growers | (None) | V1 Certified RM | (None) | (None) | Net Demand | | | | 4432.3 |
| Consolidation of Growers | (None) | V1 Certified RM | V1 Technical Mixture Basic FG | (None) | Dependent Production Demand | | | 40.3 | |
| Consolidation of Growers | (None) | V1 Certified RM | V1 Restorer Basic FG | (None) | Dependent Production Demand | | | 2.0 | |
| Consolidation of Growers | (None) | V1 Technical Mixture Basic FG | (None) | (None) | Dependent Demand | | | 50.0 | |
| Consolidation of Growers | (None) | V1 Technical Mixture Basic FG | (None) | (None) | Net Demand | | | 50.0 | |
| Consolidation of Growers | (None) | V1 Restorer Basic FG | (None) | (None) | Dependent Demand | | | 2.5 | |
| Consolidation of Growers | (None) | V1 Restorer Basic FG | (None) | (None) | Net Demand | | | 2.5 | |
| Consolidation of Growers | Supplying Plant 01 - US | V1 Technical Mixture Basic FG | (None) | (None) | Dependent Location Demand | | | 50.0 | |
| Consolidation of Growers | Supplying Plant 01 - US | V1 Technical Mixture Basic FG | (None) | (None) | Transport Receipts | | | 50.0 | |
| Consolidation of Growers | Supplying Plant 01 - US | V1 Restorer Basic FG | (None) | (None) | Dependent Location Demand | | | 2.5 | |
| Consolidation of Growers | Supplying Plant 01 - US | V1 Restorer Basic FG | (None) | (None) | Transport Receipts | | | 2.5 | |
| Supplying Plant 01 - US | (None) | V1 Technical Mixture Basic FG | (None) | (None) | Dependent Demand | | | 50.0 | |
| Supplying Plant 01 - US | (None) | V1 Technical Mixture Basic FG | (None) | (None) | Independent Demand | | | 5.0 | |
| Supplying Plant 01 - US | (None) | V1 Technical Mixture Basic FG | (None) | (None) | Net Demand | | | 55.0 | |
| Supplying Plant 01 - US | (None) | V1 Technical Mixture Basic FG | V1 Restorer Basic SFG | (None) | Dependent Production Demand | | | 142.9 | |
| Supplying Plant 01 - US | (None) | V1 Technical Mixture Basic FG | V1 Single Basic SFG | (None) | Dependent Production Demand | | | 50.6 | |
| Supplying Plant 01 - US | (None) | V1 Restorer Basic FG | (None) | (None) | Dependent Demand | | | 2.5 | |
| Supplying Plant 01 - US | (None) | V1 Restorer Basic FG | (None) | (None) | Inventory Target | | | 5.0 | |
| Supplying Plant 01 - US | (None) | V1 Restorer Basic FG | (None) | (None) | Projected Inventory | | | 5.0 | 5.0 |
| Supplying Plant 01 - US | (None) | V1 Restorer Basic FG | (None) | (None) | Net Demand | | | 7.5 | |
| Supplying Plant 01 - US | (None) | V1 Restorer Basic FG | V1 Restorer Basic SFG | (None) | Dependent Production Demand | | | 19.5 | |
| Supplying Plant 01 - US | Consolidation of Growers | V1 Certified RM | (None) | (None) | Dependent Location Demand | | | | 4432.3 |
| Supplying Plant 01 - US | Consolidation of Growers | V1 Certified RM | (None) | (None) | Transport Receipts | | | | 4432.3 |



**Fig. 4.21** Seed-dependent demand propagation

**Propagation of Certified Raw Material Demands to Seed Growers' Locations and Derivation of Demands for Input Materials (See Fig. 4.21)**
Once demands for raw certified seeds are known, these are passed to the seed growers (1). In the model shown, there is a location representing a consolidation of seed growers where all demands are initially consolidated. These are then allocated to individual fields or seed producers during multiplication planning (more on this in the last section). As per the BOM structure shown earlier, demands for raw material resolve into demands for basic seeds for the two components—technical mixture and restorer (2)—according to proportions defined in the BOM master data. These demands are passed back to the supplying location according to the location sourcing rule—seen as dependent location demands with the appropriate ship from location filled (3). These demands represent the quantity of basic seeds that need to be distributed to the seed growers in order to ensure adequate supply of certified seeds. The demands for technical mixture and restorer generate demands for their respective components, that of single semifinished and restorer semifinished (4). The process continues until demands are propagated all the way down or in case there is sufficient supply at any point that makes propagation unnecessary. In our example, we see there is a receipt element corresponding to the expected supply of raw certified seeds from the seed grower (5). From an execution standpoint, this will be converted to a purchase order, and if the planning was accurate and all uncertainties were sufficiently considered, these quantities should ensure coverage for expected customer demands for (treated and packed) certified seeds.

### 4.1.2.2 Multiplication Planning

**Evaluation of Decision Variables and Administration of Weights and Scores**
A planning view that enables assessment of decision variables and administration of scores based on those is visualized in Fig. 4.22.

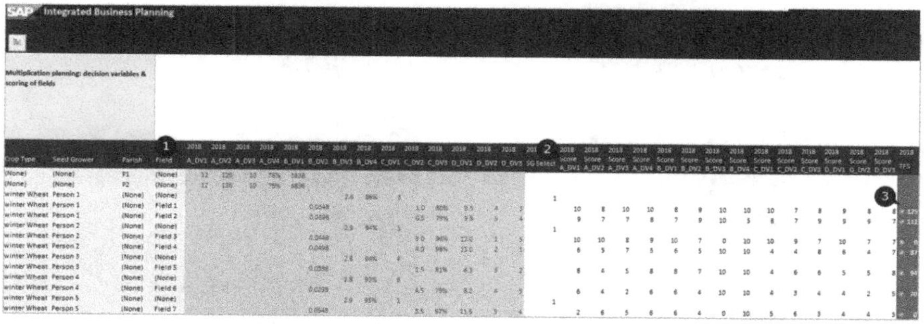


**Fig. 4.22** Seed multiplication decision variables review and scoring

Data for decision variables for the different clusters are loaded into IBP (1). These are assessed by the planner and scored (2). The scores are used to calculate a weighted total field score—weighted based on weight per decision variable administered as part of a periodic process.

Planning views for analysis of results of scores calculated automatically for one or more varieties and manual adaptation of those and final selection of fields (and allocation quantities thereof) are shown in Fig. 4.22 and Fig. 4.23.

Once field scores are calculated, allocations can be proposed on a field/variety level. The proposal is based on the ratio between the total field score for a field and the grand total of field scores across all fields for the given crop type (1). These percentages can be applied as a default when a field is chosen for a variety, which can then be reviewed and optionally adapted by the planner (2). A visualization of relative scores for different potential fields to choose from for a variety aids in the selection process (3).

**Selection of Fields and Allocation of Net Demands per Variety (See Fig. 4.24)**
Once scoring is done, the final step involves assigning fields to varieties. If planning a simpler variety or varieties where there is a limited selection of fields, earlier steps can be skipped for the sake of simplicity.

In this final step, all of the net production demands for the chosen varieties are aggregated on a virtual field called "consolidation of fields" (1), (2). Scores calculated in the earlier step can be shown to aid in the selection process. By selecting a field (3), system proposes an allocation based on field acreage and sowing rate (loaded as input variables). When a field is selected for one variety, it is automatically deselected for other varieties to avoid double allocation (4). Allocation quantities for the different fields for a given variety are summed up and compared to the to-be allocated quantities for that variety, which equals the net production

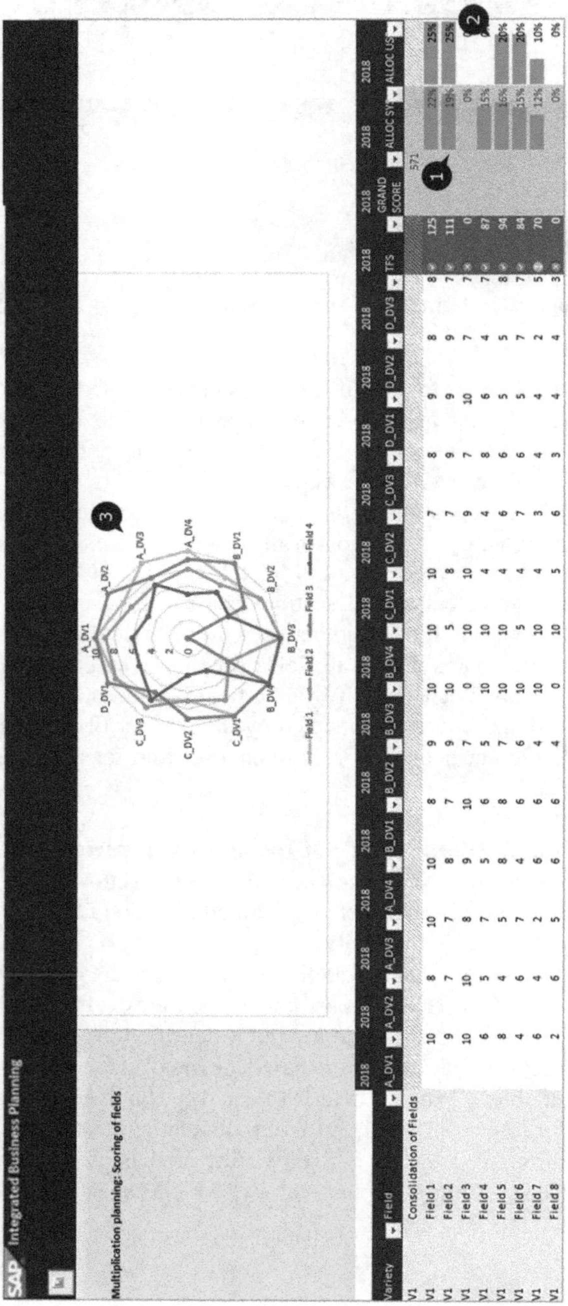


**Fig. 4.23** Seed fields' automatic scoring for multiplication planning

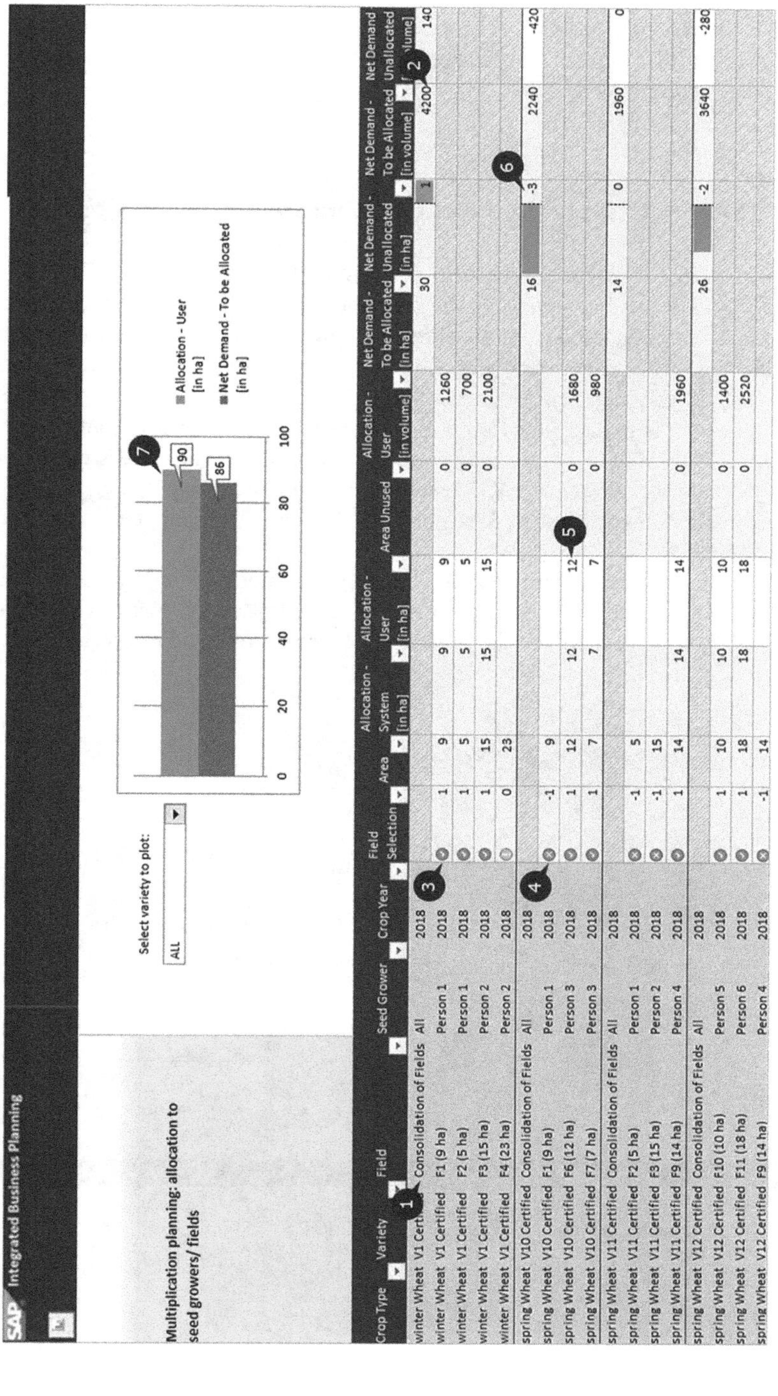


**Fig. 4.24** Allocation of multiplication to fields

demand (5), (6). A graphical summary shows a comparison of quantities to be allocated and what has already been allocated for a chosen variety or crop type. This can be useful to detect under-/over-allocations (7). This comparison is also supplemented with an alert.

### 4.1.3 SAP Use Case: Long-Term COGS Improvement Projections

Another example of business scenario for annual business planning is how to consider COGS reduction simulated in manufacturing and network optimization. Many companies initiate lean and six sigma programs to address waste, non-value-added activities, high cost of energy consumption, and lack of focus to become more "green". Those activities can be quantified and captured in your business model. What is important is to capture assumptions in order to give meaning to the figures.

In Fig. 4.25 we tried to visualize an example where there is automatic calculation between forecasted prices and COGS resulting in forecasted margin, e.g., forecasted price is editable (maybe loaded) key figure, COGS editable (maybe loaded), and margin calculated.

You may use scenario and version planning to model some variants which describe degree of confidence in expected COGS and price fluctuations. SAP IBP opens doors for you to map simple or complex business risk and opportunities.

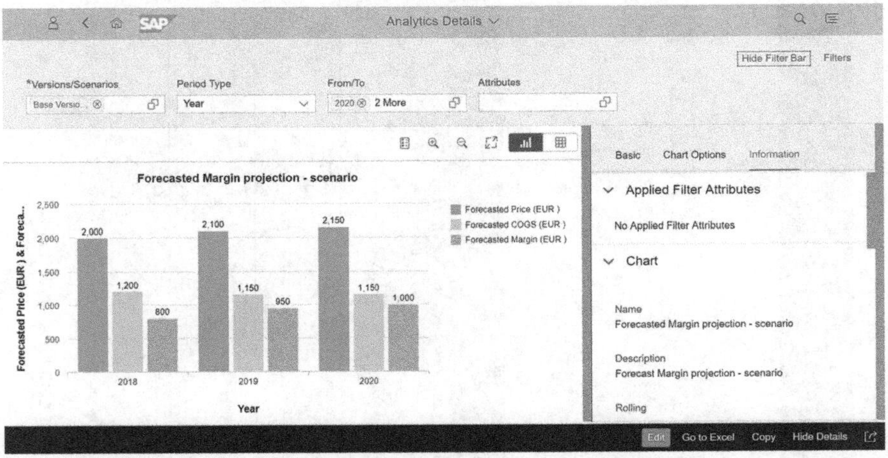


**Fig. 4.25** Annual business planning—price, COGS, margin

### 4.1.4 Strategic Initiatives in Long-Term Planning

As part of annual business planning process, several metrics can be used to measure the organization performance against its strategic goals. One of these is the compound annual growth rate (CAGR), which helps to assess the company's annual growth over a defined horizon of time. The CAGR is a straightforward KPI which provides one number for the growth rate using as input for the calculation of only few factors: the number of periods and a beginning and a final value that can be for any business measure like profits, revenue, or units sold.

Process needs to answer the basic question "How much business growth can we expect if":

- We launch a new product and new technology?
- We choose to extend the sales in a new country or region?
- We plan to extend the packaging capacity by adding a contract manufacturer in the supply chain network?

Starting from Fig. 4.26, it depicts the AS-IS and TO-BE simplified network diagram of a company that plans to extend its business footprint by creating a new sales channel and manufacturing network. We will see how Integrated Business Planning improves planning of strategic initiatives.

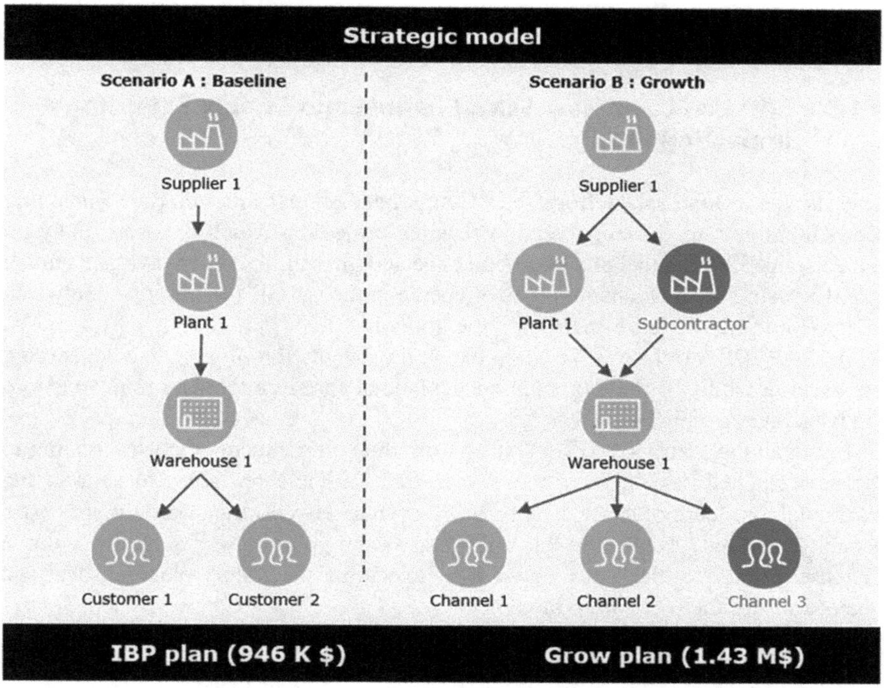


**Fig. 4.26** E2E strategic initiative modeled in SAP IBP

From business perspective we would like to model new sales channel, model growth associated to it, and translate this demand into capacity utilization for strategic horizon.

System wise we will leverage one of the key functionalities available in SAP IBP, namely, the version planning capability which is frequently used to manage alternate plans, for example, a risk (pessimistic)- and an opportunity (optimistic)-driven plan. While the data stays intact in the current plan (baseline), the end users can change and assess impact of various factors by running business process simulations in parallel versions. This parallel version can mirror or can be an extension of business model, supply chain network stored in the baseline version (the version where usually the current plan is held).

There are two ways to leverage SAP IBP in strategic planning. One way is to modify data in parallel versions or scenarios to simulate business risk and opportunities and compare them. The other way is to model changes in business model, network, portfolio, etc. on the top of modification of assumptions captured in data.

More business comprehensive strategic planning will use master data which is version dependent. To avoid issues with data consistency, we would leverage baseline master data and extend it with new nodes in parallel versions. Having a copy from baseline to the new version as a starting point will save considerable effort in preparing such a version. Then, we can extend the business model by adding master data for the new sales channel, new markets, new plants, new technology, etc.

### 4.1.5 SAP Use Case: New Sales Channel and Supply Extensions Impacting Profit

The snippet below, taken from the "Compound Annual Growth Rate" planning view, highlights the baseline version revenue projection which is based solely on the existing B2B channel and shows an expected growth of 10.14% average annual rate. Exposing the new channel—e-commerce in the CAGR calculation—shows an increase up to 26.45% for the same time horizon.

As SAP IBP interface is based on excel, the calculation of CAGR is leveraging the excel flexibility of having ad hoc calculations based on the data retrieved from the back end; see Fig. 4.27.

But attaining a 26% CAGR resulting from the volume increase corresponding to the new channel can only happen if there are available resources to support the additional production. How is the 26% revenue CAGR translated in the extra capacity required? To answer this question, we are going to propagate the volume increase throughout the entire network by executing the supply planning heuristic operator in parallel version to baseline.

Results of unconstrained long-term supply planning run grab our attention by alerting a capacity overutilization that goes up to 137% by year 2020 in Germany, manufacturing location 2 as per Fig. 4.28.

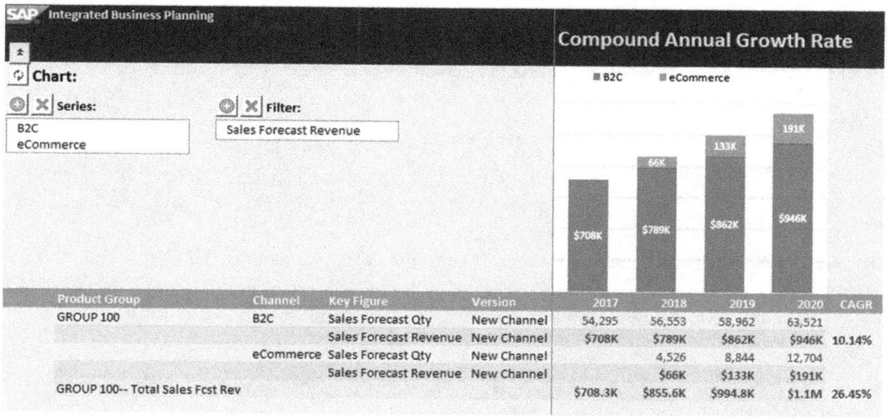


**Fig. 4.27** SAP IBP—new sales channel CAGR calculation

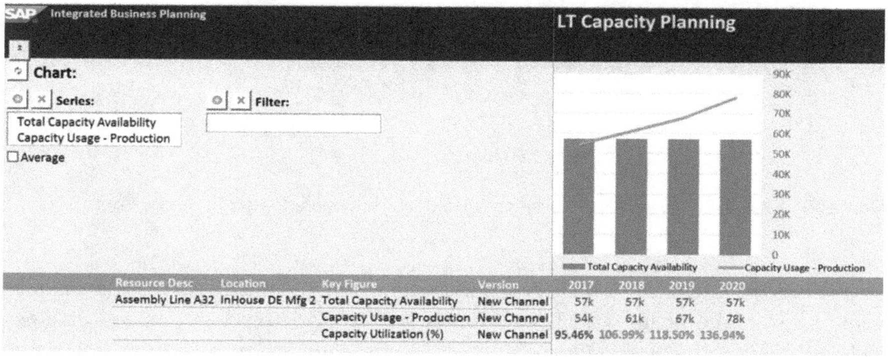


**Fig. 4.28** SAP IBP—strategic long-term capacity utilization projection

Further, the team has to evaluate how to deal with this bottleneck, perhaps an investment to increase the in-house capacity by adding night/weekend shifts. Another feasible option is to outsource a part of the production to a contract manufacturer (CMA).

Buyer has identified a CMA that can gradually increase its capacity and absorb the production that cannot be sustained in-house. As the CMA is based in a country with lower more competitive labor costs but highly qualified staff, we see the expected difference in average unit cost comparison between in-house production and outsourced production.

As we maintained the CMA in IBP as an own location, the planner can easily track what is the current load at the CMA against the available contracted capacity (see Fig. 4.29). We saved the CMA simulation as a scenario within the new channel version so that we can compare it against the baseline.

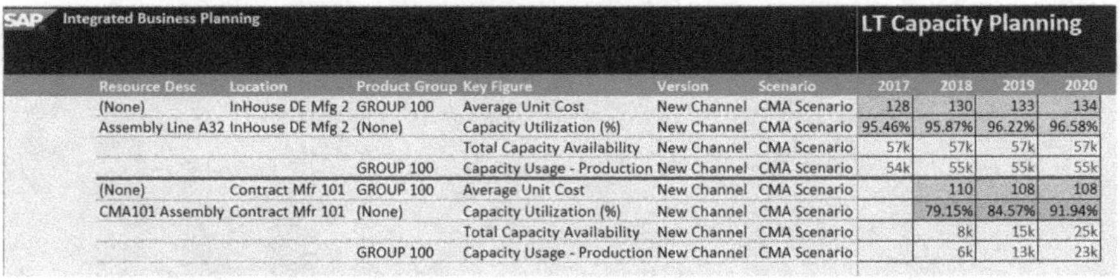

SAP Integrated Business Planning — LT Capacity Planning

| Resource Desc | Location | Product Group | Key Figure | Version | Scenario | 2017 | 2018 | 2019 | 2020 |
|---|---|---|---|---|---|---|---|---|---|
| (None) | InHouse DE Mfg 2 | GROUP 100 | Average Unit Cost | New Channel | CMA Scenario | 128 | 130 | 133 | 134 |
| Assembly Line A32 | InHouse DE Mfg 2 | (None) | Capacity Utilization (%) | New Channel | CMA Scenario | 95.46% | 95.87% | 96.22% | 96.58% |
| | | | Total Capacity Availability | New Channel | CMA Scenario | 57k | 57k | 57k | 57k |
| | | GROUP 100 | Capacity Usage - Production | New Channel | CMA Scenario | 54k | 55k | 55k | 55k |
| (None) | Contract Mfr 101 | GROUP 100 | Average Unit Cost | New Channel | CMA Scenario | | 110 | 108 | 108 |
| CMA101 Assembly | Contract Mfr 101 | (None) | Capacity Utilization (%) | New Channel | CMA Scenario | | 79.15% | 84.57% | 91.94% |
| | | | Total Capacity Availability | New Channel | CMA Scenario | | 8k | 15k | 25k |
| | | GROUP 100 | Capacity Usage - Production | New Channel | CMA Scenario | | 6k | 13k | 23k |

**Fig. 4.29** SAP IBP—own and contract manufacturing capacity planning (CMA)

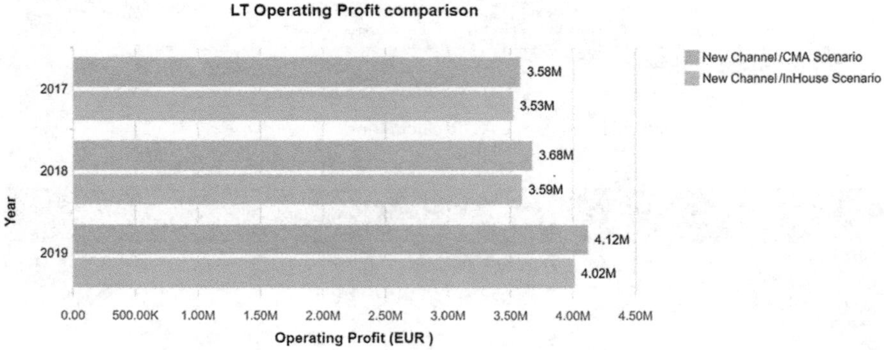


**Fig. 4.30** SAP IBP—in-house and contract manufacturing operating profit comparison

The CMA might seem a very good option, but there are also disadvantages associated: the company will lose from its flexibility to react to demand changes and will have to increase inventory levels as the contract manufacturer will come with greater lead times and lead time variability. To have an assessment of the impact on the inventory levels, the simulation could be continued using the IBP inventory operators. But we keep this example for a later chapter.

Wrapping the analysis for the strategic planning can be done using the analytics app to highlight a comparison between versions and/or scenarios (see Fig. 4.30). Looking at the comparison between the in-house and CMA as options for producing the extra volumes generated by the introduction of the new sales channel, we easily observe that the CMA scenario come with a higher operating profit.

Bringing together the AS-IS plan which is based only on the growth generated by the current B2B channel and the TO-BE plan based on the channel extension, we see the operating profit growth potential the organization has planned for as per Fig. 4.31.

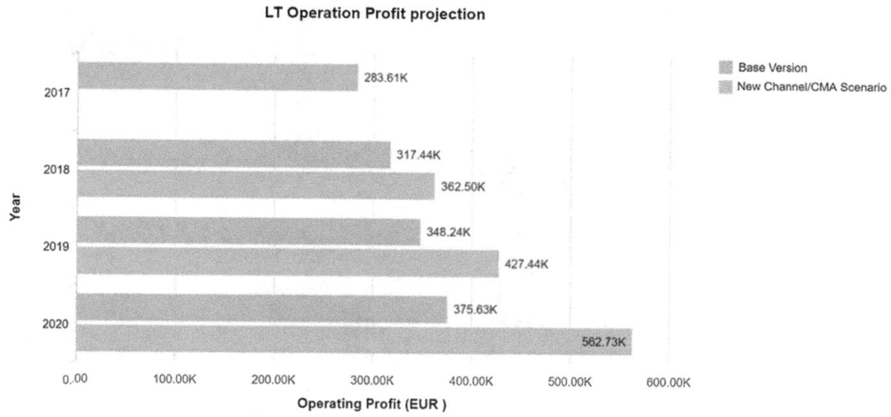


**Fig. 4.31** SAP IBP—AS-IS versus TO-BE operating profit comparison

## 4.2 Monthly Strategic Products Planning

Strategic planning has two faces. The one which will be described here has more intuitive connection to tactical S&OP. Strategic planning for monthly product planning is executed according to monthly drumbeat. It has direct link to tactical S&OP since availability of key/strategic products does influence ability to realize plans being agreed in tactical monthly S&OP from country to global level. In pharma industry this process is executed on active pharma ingredient or drug substance, in chemical companies on active ingredient level, in kitchen appliances on steel-type level, etc.

Please find few characteristics which describe why companies define strategic planning for monthly product planning as separate process:

- High-cost contribution of the strategic product in final product
- Long manufacturing lead time
- Critical impact on capacity and availability
- Long and significant new product implementation impact
- Limited manufacturing flexibility and compliance issues

This process is not only connected but has its aligned to S&OP its process steps. Process steps and SAP use case will be explained on chemical company active ingredient example.

**Product**

For this process you might need to focus your team on key raw materials, active ingredients, seed varieties, or steel which generate impact on global scale. In this

**Fig. 4.32** Strategic product segmentation

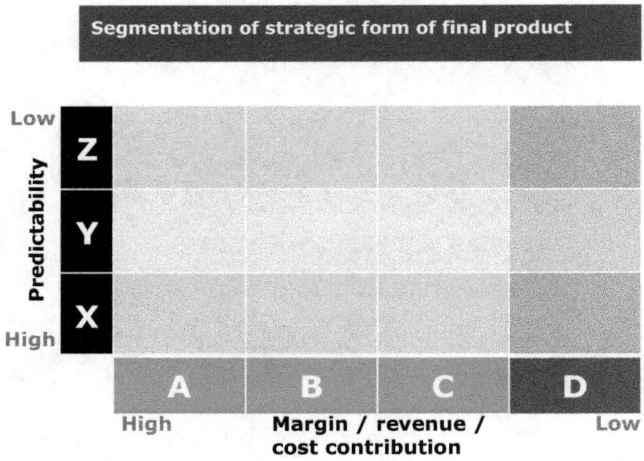


case you may need to introduce product segmentation concept on desired level in product/commercial hierarchy. You can use concept described in tactical S&OP as bidimensional segmentation ABC (D)/XYZ but for your active ingredients, steel, and seed variety on global scale (if it makes sense, see Fig. 4.32). Often the number of strategic products (raw materials) is limited and planners know by heart their cost/ revenue contribution but can be value added, e.g., in case of long history of acquisitions resulting in rich portfolio.

Once segmentation is being calculated, reviewed, and approved, you may use it in your allocation planning and demand review and update. In SAP IBP you would need to configure separate segmentation profile for strategic process. Level and other parameters would need to be adjusted as per need.

**Demand**

Demand side of strategic product planning consists of country forecast input converted from finished product into strategic product (later on called bottom up) and statistical forecast on active ingredient level (later called top down). Both inputs are being normally reconciled. You should consider how much of active ingredient you sell to the customers through B2B channel since this may be a significant demand driver. This happens often in chemical industry. Demand planner should ensure to capture all types of inputs and all types of demand.

In this case, when we have both selling models, statistical forecasting for active ingredient (top down) can use combined data input:

- Consumption transactions of active ingredient
- Direct sales of active ingredient via b2b channel

Horizon of forecast is normally up to 5–7 years, in monthly buckets, and at least based on 5 years of historical data. Demand review happens on monthly basis.

It would make sense to establish a monthly review and communication process for key raw materials/active ingredients (like in pharma or process industry) and establish integration with Tactical S&OP. How this could work?

On monthly basis active ingredient team from plant to global level should review independent demand generated based on aggregation of unconstrained market/country forecast provided on finished goods. This forecasted demand will be converted to active ingredient based on component usage stored in bill of materials. This data should be review versus previous release of the same set of figures and versus top-down active ingredient forecast which should be generated separately from market view. Top-down active ingredient statistical forecast might expose seasonality better, but it will be still without market trends being captured. Top-down forecast may be generated based on consumption of active ingredient. You would need to take care of that data which is being extracted from source system. Demand planner should ensure that comparison between market bottom-up input and statistical forecast top-down (e.g., on product/region level) is prepared, highlighted with supply planners for the constraints, defined timeline for the constraints, agreed with marketing "to whom to give" in case of shortages, and communicated the final allocation output to demand planners and demand managers in the markets.

**Supply**

Supply/manufacturing function needs to provide up-to-date information about availability and capacity bottlenecks for strategic form of the product. Horizon of capacity analysis spans normally from current and current year plus 1 and up to 5–7 years.

Supply information often leads to identification of constraints followed by allocation planning. You may want to run allocation of strategic products like active ingredient and steel to markets even though they may not even sell it, but they will have a visibility how much of their finished product forecasts and plans is impacted. We have seen that demand manager co-leads with marketing decision-making process to which markets allocate which strategic products.

### 4.2.1 Chemical Company Strategic Active Ingredient Monthly Planning

As part of integrated reconciliation, we wanted to describe of volumetric and financial information which takes place for strategic form of the product.

How strategic this process step is? Is this process sort of "mutation" of tactical S&OP but executed on global level for strategic raw materials/products? In a way it is, but since key raw material like active ingredient is a fundamental for whole supply chain, therefore it is strategic. We have seen similar processes executed for steel where its contribution in final product (stainless steel sink) was even above 90%. When you see that substantial contribution you start to ask yourself if you should forecast and plan finished goods or finished goods and steel, active ingredient. This is just to visualize to you that it depends on the business industry you may

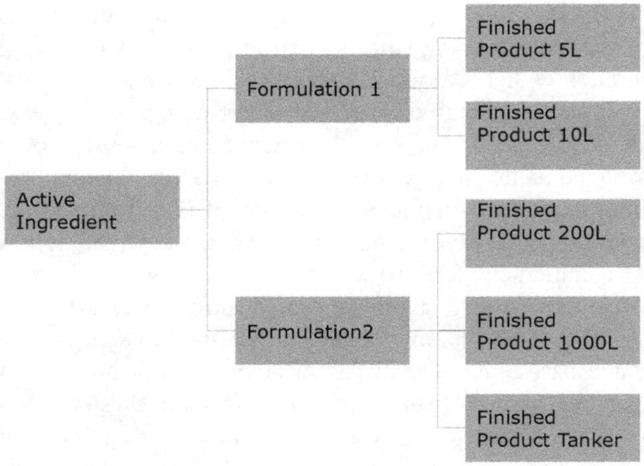


**Fig. 4.33** Active ingredient bill of materials

have already in place or you could think of establishing S&OP process for strategic products/raw materials/components.

We already learned that risk and opportunities can be linked to any pillar of S&OP process. We have already learned that risk and opportunities may be realized in SAP IBP through ease-of-use scenario planning or more comprehensive versions. Let us model scenario from chemical company.

Bill of material active ingredient (AI) is at the bottom but forms huge portion of the costs and defines availability of formulations and finished products made out of it (see Fig. 4.33). Bill of material will play vital role in one of the data streams/ subprocesses which generates input for final consensus AI forecast.

### 4.2.2 SAP Use Case: Key Raw Material/Active Ingredient Planning

We have observed that two streams of data and two subprocesses were generating information about active ingredient forecast. Those two sets of data were reconciled and analyzed and were adjusted in order to achieve consensus (see Fig. 4.34).

**Market Bottom Up**

Market bottom-up data stream is automatically generated by heuristic planning operator. It will take into consideration, e.g., component usage and stocks. Data can be monitored end to end for specific active ingredient on Web UI where analytics can help planner to spot changes or deviations from expectations (see Fig. 4.35).

Once situation is analyzed, planner can act upon it in the planning view. In the below example (Fig. 4.36), we see how the active ingredient forecast is generated by the explosion of the finished good's bill of material, capability available in the two time series supply planning operators.

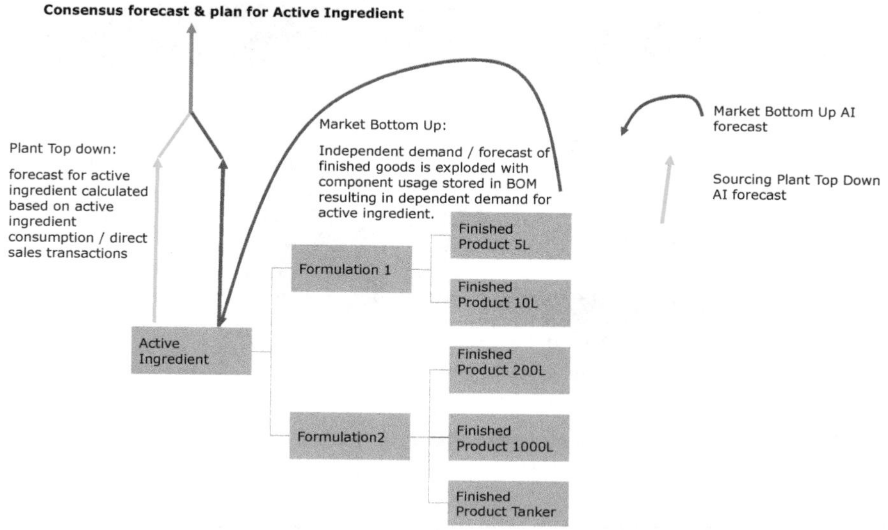


**Fig. 4.34** Active ingredient top-down and bottom-up forecasting and planning

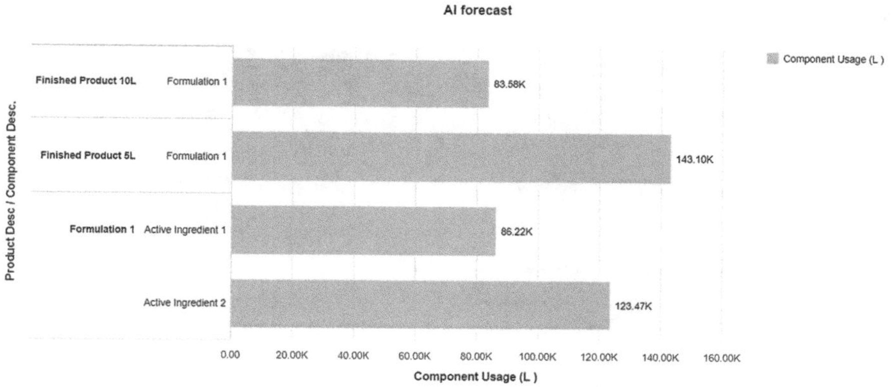


**Fig. 4.35** Active ingredient dependent demand forecast generated by BOM explosion

## Plant Top Down

As we have already mentioned earlier in this chapter, having the raw material planning driven by the finished good forecast might not be sufficient if we consider the direct sales of the active ingredient, a less precise accuracy of the finished good forecast or of the finished good forecast mix. Second data stream/subprocess can be generated based on active ingredient consumption and direct sales transactions. This particular data input needs to be integrated carefully from source system. Based on this combined dataset, we could generate statistical forecast (Fig. 4.37).

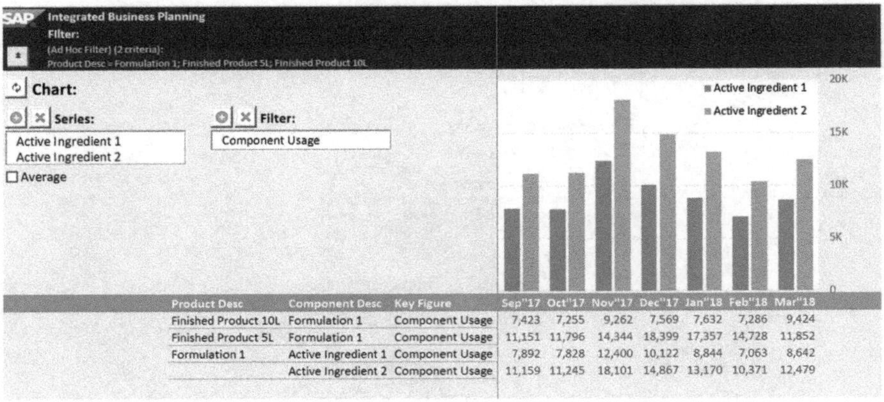


**Fig. 4.36** Active ingredient forecast calculated based on finished good market forecast and BOM component usage

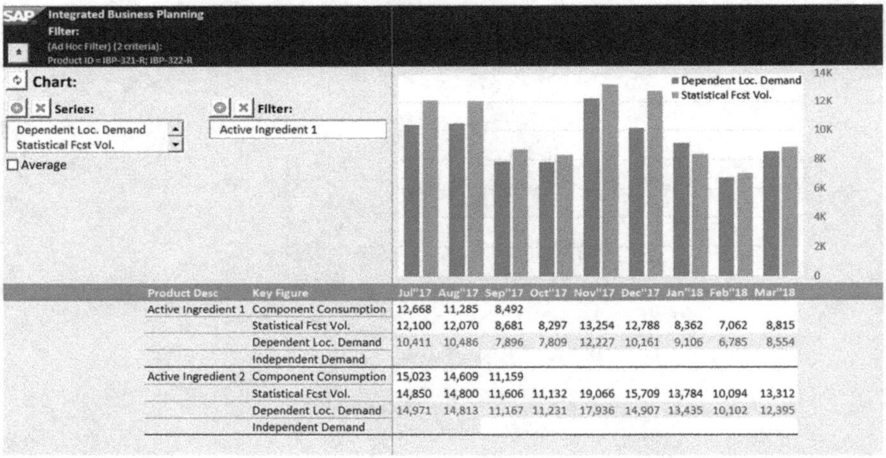


**Fig. 4.37** Active ingredient volume planning

Often happened that AI planner after consultation with global or regional marketing had to amend forecast; in this case independent demand key figure was used to store increase (Fig. 4.38).

## Consensus Forecast and Plan

Data from both streams, bottom up and top down, were compared and analyzed. Very often active ingredient planner did spot that markets did overestimated or underestimated heavily forecast of finished goods impacting strategic product. AI team with support of marketing department decided on final consensus forecast.

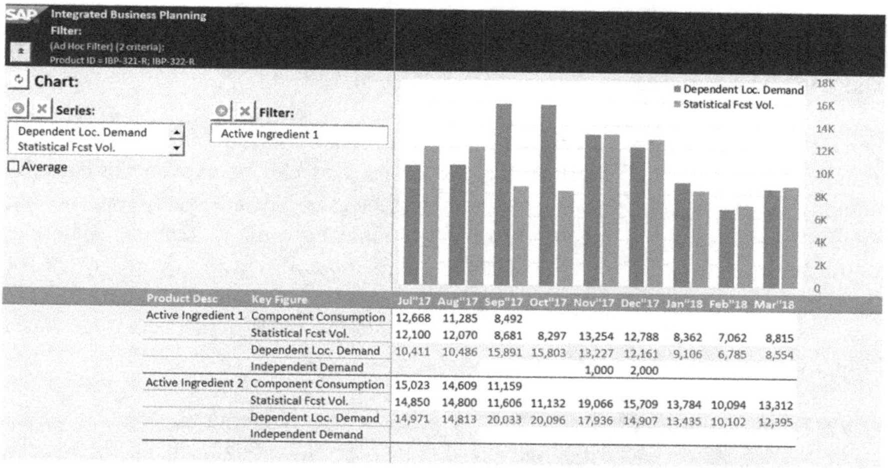


**Fig. 4.38** Adjusting AI forecast using the independent demand

Once consensus forecast was developed, constraint identification and supply planning were executed. Planner had to maximize business returns were planning AI campaigns. Marketing department helped to allocate future plans of active ingredient to markets to enable connection to local/market IBP process. It did help regional and market organization to connect Active Ingredient (AI) and markets. Key benefit was behind the fact that plans were more reliable and more realistic.

### 4.2.3 SAP Use Case: Integration of Strategic and Tactical Plans

SAP IBP provides unified platform where processes and data can be integrated between different process types from strategic planning to tactical S&OP to operational processes to execution. The integrated planning platform covers closed-loop integration of processes from the spectrum of long-term processes at aggregated planning levels to short-term processes at more detailed level. We look at several process types supported in SAP IBP and the integration of processes across these process types.

#### Strategic Planning

In strategic planning, the focus is on long-range planning for 3–5 years or beyond. The planning levels for a long-range plan are usually at a product line and hub level, and the planning time buckets are typically in quarters or yearly level. Some of the use cases for strategic planning include the following.

**Annual Business Planning** Strategic planning for annual business planning is performed usually once a year with a focus on strategic initiatives that are done for a long-term business plan of 5–10 years.

**Monthly Product Planning** Some strategic plans are performed monthly for product planning, for example, in chemical industries and active ingredient planning where the AI contributes to 70% of the product cost.

**Long-Range Capacity Planning** Strategic decisions based on analysis of the future demand can link new brand/series launch and can be expose the capacity situation in the existing factories. Sourcing decisions like adding a new factory, adding more capacity to existing resources, source from a new contract manufacturer, changing supplier for critical components are some of the decision that are made in the long-range planning. Long-range planning has an impact on the overall business and strategic direction of a company. Often CAPEX decisions are made from the results of the long-range plan.

**Long-Term Volume Planning** In this process, the planning is done in yearly buckets from years 3 to 5 beyond the S&OP planning horizon of up to 2 years. The future years are planned for long-term volume planning at an aggregated level, e.g., product category/region level. A base statistical forecast can be generated for the future 3–5 years based on the historical 3 years of forecasts and actual data aggregated at quarterly or yearly level. The planners can then adjust forecasts based on market assumptions and plan both volume and value forecasts considering prices, costs, projected revenue, and margins.

**Tactical S&OP** The focus of tactical S&OP process is planning for the next 3–24 months in a monthly bucket. The planning aggregation is usually at product family and customer region level. This could have bottom-up and top-down planning where the data for planning can be available at more granular level of product/customer or product/country level.

The planning for strategic planning and integration of the strategic planning plan to the tactical S&OP plan happens usually once a year around the budgeting cycle or the predefined planning periods for a customer. The planning process involves typically the following steps:

1. Aggregation from tactical to strategic for first 2 years
2. Strategic planning from 3–5 years
3. Disaggregate from strategic to tactical plan for Year 1 and Year 2 when the tactical planning horizon is reached

**Aggregation from Tactical to Strategic for the First 2 Years** The monthly S&OP plans which are planned for up to 2 years are rolled up to the aggregation level of strategic plan. This aggregated level can vary between each customer. For example, the strategic plan is at yearly level of product category and country. The aggregated attributes are usually a hierarchy of the product/customer or location.

**Strategic Planning for 3–5 Years**

After the tactical plan is aggregated to strategic plan level, data are copied into a new strategic forecast planning level, typically, at quarter/product category/region level. A baseline forecast can be achieved by performing a statistical forecast taking aggregated S&OP forecasts and actuals for past 3 years and projecting to future periods. Or planners can manually enter forecasts for the next 3–5 years for the planning data in the strategic planning level.

Suppose a product category has ten different products/SKUs in the current setup. In the future, we may not know how many products will be added or removed for this category. Further the forecasts about what products can be sold for what customers are not known. Therefore, the planning is done at an aggregate level knowing that the details won't be available or not required for the long-range planning. Further, new product categories can be introduced and planned in the strategic volume planning.

To keep the long-range planning separate from tactical and operations planning processes in IBP, the following modeling aspects can be considered:

1. Separate planning area: Strategic planning in a separate planning area with its own set of master data.
2. Same planning areas with different versions: Strategic planning in the same planning area as the tactical and operational planning area.
3. Same planning area with other planning processes. However, to keep the results separate from other planning processes, separate set of master data may be added and differentiated for supply planning using planning units.

**Disaggregate from Strategic to Tactical Plan for Year 1 and Year 2 when the Tactical Planning Horizon Is Reached**

After the strategic plans have been finalized for the long-term horizon, this needs to be translated to the tactical plans for Years 1 and 2 of the tactical planning horizon. The levels for disaggregation depend usually on levels at which the strategic plans are planned vs levels at which the tactical plans are planned. As an example, let's say the strategic plans for volume forecasts are planned at product category/region level. This needs to be disaggregated to the product and customer levels that are planned in the monthly S&OP plans assuming category and region are hierarchical attributes of product and customer, respectively.

The disaggregation can be based on certain rules, for example, split the strategic forecast to the monthly numbers based on the actuals of last year. This can be achieved as follows (Fig. 4.39):

1. Shift the actuals quantity by 1 year using Copy Operator and store in Key Figure Actuals 1 year offset.
2. Create a new stored Key Figure Strategic Plan Disagg which is stored at Product/Customer and Month Level and has Disagg Expression as Key Figure Actuals with 1 year offset. Make the Editable settings as system editable.

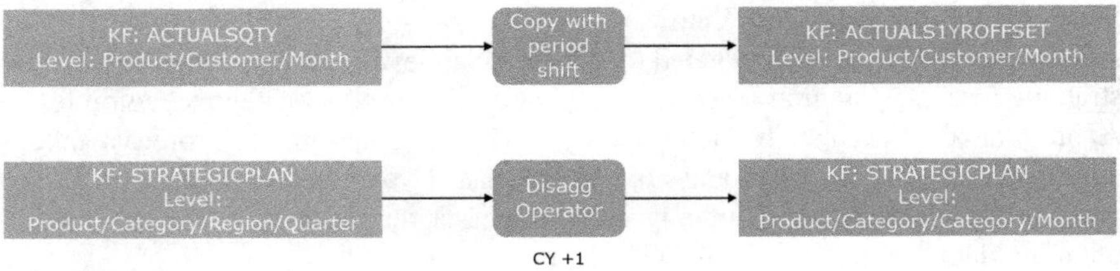


**Fig. 4.39** Strategic and tactical planning technical integration

3. Create a Disagg Operator which has Source Key Figure as strategic plan and Target Key Figure as Strategic Plan Disagg.
4. Create an application job with two steps: 1. copy operator to shift actuals and 2. Disagg Operator.

When this application job is scheduled to run once a year, the strategic plan is then disaggregated based on the actuals qty to the key Figure Strategic Plan Disagg.

As we see from above process, organizational and technical aspects should be addressed to ensure integration between strategic planning and tactical planning. On technology side, connection of planning levels described above becomes crucial.

# Ways to Improve Tactical S&OP

# 5

Tactical S&OP process can be visualized like in Fig. 3.18. In this big chapter, we bring to you a lot use cases which can help in your maturity assessment, design, and implementation.

## 5.1 Product, Customer, and Services Review

In this chapter you will find all the overview of activities performed by demand manager or demand planner to coordinate and ensure that new products, offering review, are included in IBP. Demand manager has a responsibility to facilitate integration with product/brand organization to optimize IBP.

Demand management and planning should help product/brand marketing to move toward a collaborative product and service design. This approach aims to reduce delivery cost and allow fundamental communications from the first steps among key stakeholders. In broad scope of methods in this approach, we may highlight key ones like:

- **Design for logistics** aims to optimize transportation costs and logistics business-related costs.
- **Universality** aims to sell the same product to multiple markets increasing volumes and reducing manufacturing costs without losing customers' loyalty.
- **Modularization** aims to share same components with different products having benefits from more cost-effective policies but not from customization.
- **Simplification** aims to remove complexity and shorten product design processes emphasizing collaboration and parallel working.
- **Design for manufacturing and assembly** aims to consider the manufacturability of the product cutting time length and reduce revisions.
- **Mass customization and postponement** aim to delay differentiation as soon as possible while increasing cost savings and trying to train new people for the new



R. Kepczynski et al., *Implementing Integrated Business Planning*, Management for Professionals, https://doi.org/10.1007/978-3-319-90095-7_5

tasks required when late customization will be demanded (APICS—module 2. G—Influencing and Prioritizing Demand 2015).

As you see from above, integration of new product development into IBP is crucial. This activity is very often underestimated in terms of workload required to achieve process integration. The way your company manages new product development may influence S&OP inputs and timelines. New product development like the other process steps has their own constraints from internal side touching base on organization and workload to external side touching base on compliance in registration of the products. Integration of new product development in pre-commercialization and commercialization phase requires a lot of coordination and focus from demand manager, product managers, and supply managers.

Let us list few aspects exposing key challenges for demand manager to integrate new product implementation in IBP:

- New product development (NPD) produces unrealistic plans that need to be reviewed during the monthly process as well as a high-level status report on NPD that must be discussed.
- NPD often hugely contributes to the final goal of a firm, and the importance of connecting key stakeholders and managerial skills has become essential to achieve integration.
- NPD resources are obliged to focus on day-to-day tasks and aligning on every stakeholder's objective rather than focusing on future opportunities and new product development (Palmatier and Crum 2003).

### 5.1.1 New Product Forecasting

In this section we focus on activities aiming to integrate new product introduction into Integrated Business Planning. Demand planning and management function should coordinate and ensure that product review key outputs are being integrated or even embed into IBP. What is the difference between integrate and embed? Integrate means, in this case, you take product development outputs like launch date and volume and use it in the process. Embed means you may simulate end-to-end impact when planning, e.g., commercialization phase of product introduction, and you may align dates, volume, and pricing to country in which product will be launched and analyze impact.

Product, services, customer review needed integration activities are very often underestimated in terms of workload and value it can generate for IBP. Integration of new product development in pre-commercialization and commercialization phase requires a lot of coordination and focus from demand manager, supply manager and product managers. New product development like the other process steps has their own constraints. There might be internal constraints touching base on organization and workload to external constraints or legislation to follow touching base on compliance in registration of the products.

Let us list a few challenges that are ahead of demand manager, supply manager, and product manager to integrate new product implementation into IBP:

- New product development can produce unrealistic plans, which need to be analyzed during the monthly process.
- New product development hugely contributes to the final company results; as a result soft and managerial skills must be at rendezvous to possibly satisfy many stakeholders!
- New product development resources are obliged to focus on day-to-day tasks rather than focusing on future opportunities and new product development (Palmatier and Crum 2003).

New products and services have long been looked at by companies as an invitation for a respite from price pressures and razor-thin product margins. New products and services open up a window of opportunity, although small (more on this later), to command higher margins and pursue top-line growth. With the rapid pace of innovation, the window of opportunity is forever shrinking. The picture isn't very pretty from a performance standpoint either. Sample consumer products industry (Steutermann and Suleski 2016) reports that multiplication of products has led to a 32% increase in active items since 2010. However, a revenue growth of a mere 3–4% during the same period has meant that sales per item have dropped by 22%. The already bleak picture is made worse when we consider studies that show forecast accuracy for new products after 1 year of introduction is around 50% (Kahn 2014).

So, what exactly are new products, and what makes planning them quite an intractable problem?

A new product can be an existing product for which the market footprint is expanding or a breakthrough innovation, so radically new, and for which practically the whole world is a market, with a lot of possibilities in between. This is illustrated in Fig. 5.1. The key dimensions are market reach (current to global) and product innovation (minor cost improvement/technical upgrade to breakthrough innovation). As noted, planning becomes harder as we cover more spectrums from left to right.

**What Makes the New Product Forecasting and Planning So Difficult?**
As briefly noted, planning becomes harder as one moves from left to right along the market growth and product innovation spectrums. The reason is, the further along one is from status quo, the less relevant are the current points of reference and, consequently, historical data. As the data gets sparse, focus needs to move beyond simply the use of quantitative techniques. Other tools and skills come to the fore in the context of new product forecasting (NPF).

We have been stressing the importance of integration in IBP (the "I" in IBP). New product forecasting is a poster child for a process that requires tight integration and coordination between various functions such as: new product development, supply chain design, supply chain planning, sales and marketing and finance. Sparseness of data also necessitates a high level of integration due to the increased relevance of

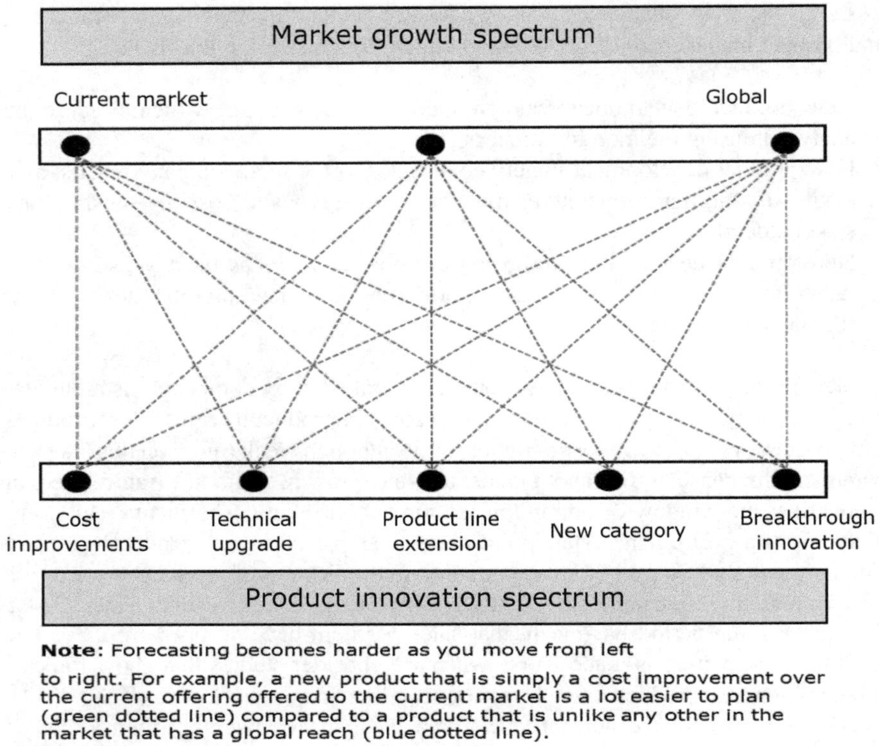


**Fig. 5.1** Market spectrum versus product innovation in new product implementation

business drivers (internal and external) influencing demand and supply of new products and qualitative inputs such as assumptions and expert opinions. A high level of involvement across the board implies a high degree of effort, but this is justified as new product launch is a high-risk/high-payoff endeavor where success or failure has implications on long run profitability of the firm as a whole.

The following list highlights some of the key characteristics of new products and challenges involved in forecasting them:

- Lack of historical data.
- Reliance on judgmental factors rather than hard number crunching.
- Impact of external factors (think Porter's five forces) (Porter and Millar n.d.).
- Impact of internal processes. For example, manufacturing processes may still be immature leading to lower yields. Suppliers are apt to be more unreliable if the components are new as well.
- Uncertainty around market positioning, promotional budget (that impacts demand).

- Interplay between products, also called cannibalization effects, can play a significant role in shaping demand for new products (and impacting demand for existing products).
- If level of innovation is high, companies have very limited opportunities for taking corrective actions if plans do not materialize.
- New product launches tend to be highly visible. If things go wrong, they receive wide coverage and the significance of failure gets amplified.

New product forecasting involves a tough balancing act between supply and demand. Based on an extensive research involving Intel, Moon (2013) and Erhun et al. (2007) argue that there are eight key risk factors across demand and supply categories that require management attention in order to execute product transitions successfully. These are:

1. Environmental indicators—for example
2. Macroeconomic factors and business cycles
3. Competition
4. Pricing
5. Timing of launch (e.g., in relation to relevant previous launch and/or planned future launches)
6. Marketing policies
7. Product capability
8. External alignment and internal execution

The breadth of factors that need to be properly considered highlights the importance of cross-functional integration. As such, collaboration provides a forum for sharing privileged information that may not be available to all parties involved (Erhun et al. 2007).

New product forecasting, as is evident from discussions so far, is a lot about entering unchartered waters and where "data does not speak loud and clear" (SuperforecastingTetlock). Therefore, there is a reliance on qualitative methods that are not so much about number crunching, and if it is quantitative, it is more about considering external factors that drive demand rather than historical time series. Qualitative methods generally require significant investments in time and effort, particularly with respect to data collection. The data that is collected and factors analyzed go toward diminishing the uncertainty and lending more credibility to predictions.

We need to acknowledge the diversity of data inputs in new product forecasting; the spread is far more pronounced in the case of new products compared to existing products. Insights gained from the Good Judgment Project (GJP) are quite pertinent here and provide useful guidelines for achieving excellence in NPF process. The GJP was funded by the National Intelligence Council (NIC). The key architects of the project ran a multiyear tournament, and their experience is documented in the book *Superforecasting: The Art and Science of Prediction* (Gardner and Tetlock 2015).

Diversity of inputs necessitates expertise across different areas. A key finding from GJP is that generalists outperform specialists. In new product forecasting, it is important to consider a variety of internal and external factors in order to not be blindsided by an overlooked aspect that ends up derailing plans. In the case of existing products, key factors are already embedded in historical data. In the case of new products, since historical time series data is sparse or nonexistent, relationship between key factors and future demands needs to be made explicit.

When opinions are involved, biases start to cloud judgment. A key insight from the GJP is that training for as little as 1 hour can improve accuracy by 14%. As new product forecasting relies heavily on qualitative inputs, it is important to have a good grasp of the key principles of probability and statistics to make planners mindful of common cognitive biases.

The importance of sharing information in order to disseminate privileged information, closely held, across all parties involved was discussed earlier. This brings us to the second insight, which is that teams outperform individuals. Collaboration is crucial to make judgments based on a combination of qualitative and quantitative information.

A complementary approach to improving the effectiveness of the overall new product development and introduction process is to try and reduce the reliance on forecasting. This involves becoming more responsive. Responsiveness will in turn help reduce the time span for speculative activities that are carried out *in anticipation* of demand by transitioning some of those to activities that can be carried out *in response* to actual demands.

The factors that impact new product forecasting are quite unique (vis-à-vis existing incumbent products) and require differentiated treatment when it comes to forecasting.

Figure 5.2 [adapted from Kahn (2014)] compares and contrasts old and new product forecasting along the dimensions of data, method, prediction interval, scenarios, and performance.

| | Old product forecasting | New product forecasting |
|---|---|---|
| Data | Historical data | Assumptions |
| Method | Statistical | Qualitative |
| Prediction interval | Narrow | Broad |
| Scenarios | Based on "near" certainties | Preventions and contingencies |
| Performance | Accuracy | Expected error |

**Fig. 5.2** Existing and new product forecasting features

At first the demand manager and supply manager through product review meetings should understand the nature of product introduction:

- Extension of existing portfolio, e.g., new packaging
- New portfolio but with similarities to existing one
- Completely new portfolio

Those three categories may have different implications: how to forecast, promote, plan supply, and assess risks and opportunities with use of scenario planning.

New product can be similar to one which exists already; it would make sense then to reuse sales data history of similar product to predict the future of the new one. Technique which is used is called "like modeling." We would recommend following consideration in your process and technical design:

- Original sales data
- Cleansed sales data

We advise to consider to copy original sales data from like to new product and then adjust data of the new product to reflect marketing insights. In cleansed sales data, you could perform any adjustments to seasonality, level, and trend and then use it as primary data input for statistical forecasting.

When talking about new product or like product forecasting, we should always consider master data perspective.

We briefly discuss key dimensions of NPF in turn.

**Data**

Availability of data is linked to newness of the product and targeted market segments. The further away the product and market characteristics of the new product are from its ancestor(s), the harder it is to use historical data for planning purposes. Data availability is also a function of the lifecycle stage of the product. Especially in the early stages, there's a need for focusing on analysis of external and internal factors (e.g., macroeconomic factors, competition, production capacity—particularly important if the constraint is more internal than external, etc.) that influence demand rather than historical time series of the variable being forecasted, which tends to be nonexistent to very sparse (link between lifecycle stage and data availability for use in quantitative methods is illustrated in Fig. 5.3).

Planning in the initial stages (1–3 in the illustration above) should provide answers to questions related to (Mulllick Satinder 1971):

- Resource requirements
- Allocation of funds for R&D, marketing activities, operational capabilities—manufacturing capacities, logistics, and the like
- Fit of new product in the existing portfolio

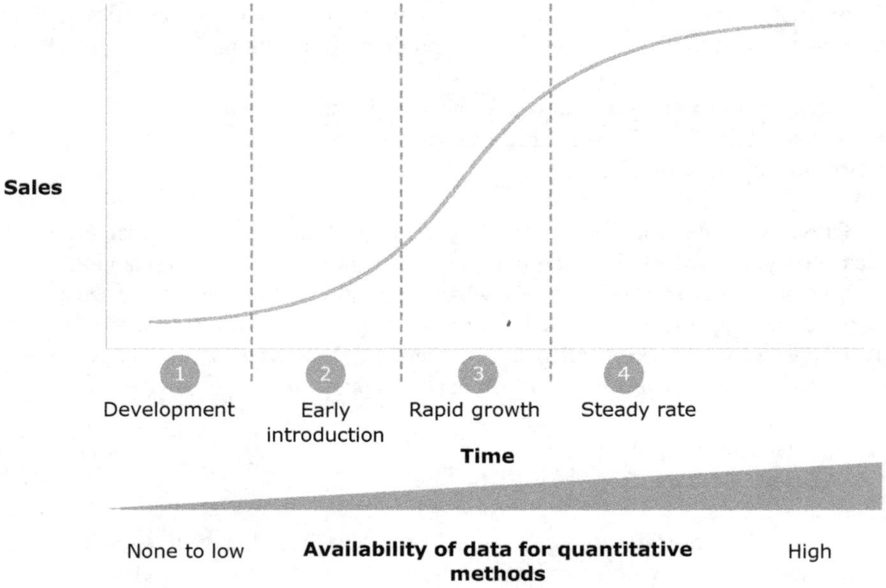


**Fig. 5.3** Product lifecycle stage and data availability for quantitative methods

- Timing of rapid growth phase and planning in case of need for additional manufacturing capacity
- Timing of growth settling into a steady rate

These decisions have far-reaching consequences and, therefore, justify investments in identification and use of the right methods to obtain good forecasts (Mulllick Satinder 1971).

**Method**
When data is hard to come by, reliance on qualitative methods increases. Here's a quick roundup of some of the most frequently used qualitative methods.

*Delphi Method* Expert opinions are sought through a series of questionnaires. Information garnered in the first round is used to design the next. Also, information acquired at the end of each round is disseminated to all participants (chiefly by incorporating them in the questionnaire for the subsequent round). This way, plans are made on the basis of a shared body of data. Delphi method helps avoid some common biases—for example, anchoring, which is a result of humans being excessively influenced by the first estimate or confirmation bias that is a result of seeking out only information that confirms preexisting notions or the bandwagon effect that is caused by an influential participant steamrolling (in many instances inadvertently) opinions of others.

*Panel Consensus* A group of experts collaborate to generate forecasts. The panel consists of experts drawn from different areas relevant to the task at hand—for example, economists, product design engineers, sales and marketing managers, supply chain managers, etc. Unlike the Delphi method, discussions among participants are encouraged, and the objective is to have them agree on a consensus plan. However, this approach is fraught with risk of biases (see description of Delphi method). Social factors also come into play—particularly hierarchical bias due to healthy debates being stymied by influential members (Reinmuth 1974). Therefore, the accuracy of this method tends to be poor (Mulllick Satinder 1971).

*Market Research* This method leverages insights from the constituency that has the most influence on demand for the new product—prospective customers. The scale of research depends on the number of potential customers and markets being targeted. This method is quite suitable if the scale is manageable or in instances where distributors can provide reliable inputs regarding customer behaviors (Reinmuth 1974).

*Historical Analogy* Unless the new product is so radically new that it inhabits a category of one, data from similar products (either your own or of your competition) can be used for forecasting.

SAP IBP offers like modeling which helps to manage product lifecycle. This functionality uses reference products, weighting factors to manage input data for like products when forecasting new one. The historical data is a weighted sum of the demands of the reference products which can then be used to statistically forecast the new product. The forecast start date that is maintained in the lifecycle profile determines the timing for switching from using demands for reference products to demands collected on the new product. The following technical SAP use case describes the use of this functionality. It also goes beyond like modeling and talks about how lifecycle data can be used to derive lifecycle statuses that aid in product segmentation and to provide visual cues to planners in planning views.

There are also some quantitative models that are available for NPF. Notable among those are a class of models called diffusion models. These models predict demands by modeling behaviors of two key categories of customers: innovators—early adopters that drive majority of the demands in the development and testing stages and imitators that drive demands in later stages and determine the maximum market share that the product can be expected to achieve. By modeling their behaviors, growth curves can be defined that aid in predicting demands. Diffusion models are more complex than qualitative models. One of the key reasons for higher complexity is the need for incorporating external variables. However, the payoff for higher complexity is lacking as they also have a poor track record (Kahn 2014).

**Prediction Interval** A prediction interval includes two components: a forecast range (pessimistic and optimistic estimates) and the probability that the true value will lie in that range. For a given probability, the breadth of the range depends on the expected forecast error.

The forecast range is calculated as follows:

$\text{Forecast}_{t+1} \pm z * \sqrt{\text{MSE}}$ where $\text{Forecast}_{t+1}$ is the forecast made at the end of the current period $t$ and MSE is the mean squared error.[1]

In the case of new products, the range tends to be broader as the uncertainty they are exposed to is greater. Therefore it stands to reason that processes that rely on new product forecasts put prevention and contingency strategies in place in accordance with the expected scale of error. Communicating prediction intervals help put contingencies in place for when plans don't materialize—that is when the true value of forecast deviates from the most likely value ($F_{t+1}$ in the formula above). For example, a contingency plan for the optimistic case materializing could be to subcontract production of demands that cannot be handled in-house. If instead of prediction intervals, a point forecast (a single value that represents the most likely outcome) was used, demands in excess of in-house capacity will go down as lost sales.

**Scenarios** For existing products, planning for unlikely outcomes typically takes the form of planning of safety inventory to hedge against uncertainty. For new products, this is normally not sufficient because of the uncertainty around the forecast as well as other risk factors (demand and supply). In order to be prepared for a range of outcomes, risk factors need to be assessed to generate a risk profile. Such a risk profile needs to form the basis for creation of risk scenarios and strategies for prevention and rescue (in case a scenario should come to pass).

Broadly speaking, outcomes can range from demand being higher or lower than expected and/or certain internal execution or external alignment problems leading to shortages. Interdependencies between the new product and existing products will also result in ripple effects that have the potential to significantly impact firm profitability.

If an assumption-based model has been used (assumptions, e.g., can be factors such as market size, core constituency, market share, buying intent, market coverage), it is important to have these assumptions clearly documented (Reinmuth 1974). Should any of these assumptions change, plans need to be redrawn, and potentially prevention strategies will have to be invoked, or contingency plans might have to be exercised to salvage the situation.

An example for an approach to modeling risk scenarios is depicted in Fig. 5.4. Key qualitative and quantitative inputs (expert opinions, assumptions, and historical analogy—like products) are used to generate a forecast range, make an assessment of risks and draw up a risk profile, and also to clarify interdependencies between the new and existing products. Finally, risk scenarios are created, informed by the risk assessment made earlier, that prescribe actions to take in the event of one or more risks becoming reality. Actions can be preventive in nature that are called upon to

[1]The square root of MSE is an approximation for standard deviation. This is based on the assumption that forecast errors are normally distributed with the mean of zero. The probability determines the $z$ value. For example, $z$ takes on the value ~1.64 for 95% probability. Therefore, the 95% prediction interval would be calculated by multiplying 1.64 and $\sqrt{\text{MSE}}$ (calculated using the test or holdout dataset).

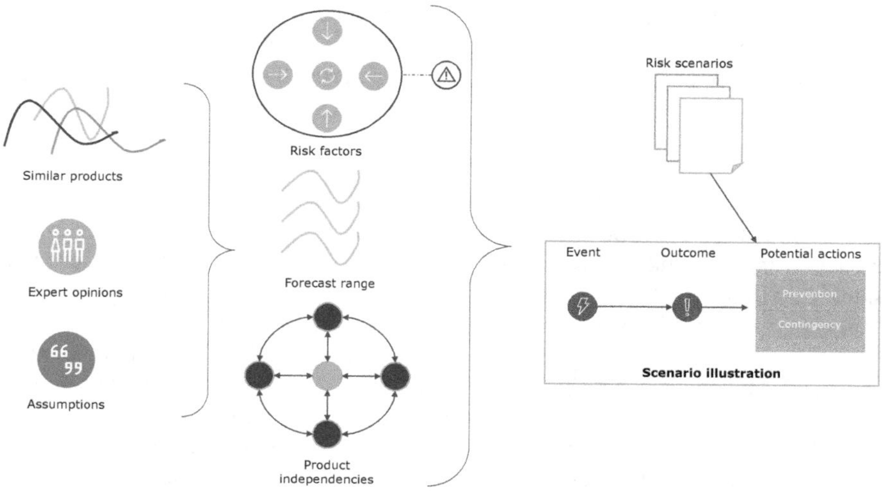


**Fig. 5.4** Modeling of scenarios—an illustration of key inputs and activities involved

avoid unfavorable outcomes or contingency measures (if prevention is not possible) in order to do damage control.

In the following SAP use case subchapters, we describe how scenarios can be modeled in IBP using versions. Scenarios fall into two broad categories:

There are scenarios that are ad hoc in nature and support planners in their day-to-day planning activities by allowing them to simulate effects of changes made in one or more key figures to overall plans.

Then there are scenarios that have much broader scope and relevance and are evaluated often, usually in a collaborative fashion. These are persisted in the database. In IBP terminology, the ad hoc scenarios are called simply "scenarios" and the persistent ones are called "versions." From a design perspective, scenarios do not need to be planned in advance and therefore do not involve any configuration activities. On the other hand, versions, as they represent plan alternatives, need to be planned in advance. Key questions of planning relevance are: what should be the different versions (e.g., optimistic, pessimistic, besides the base version)? What are the key figures that need to belong to one or more versions? Should there be version-specific master data, and if yes, which ones?

**Performance** The first rule of forecasting is that forecasts are always wrong. When it comes to new products, one could say that forecasts are significantly wrong. In the face of this reality, what becomes important is to be able to have a clear estimate of the expected scale of error and have preventive and contingency strategies in place when plans do not materialize. As data is quite sparse in the case of new products, it is essential to carefully analyze early data in the form of customer orders as they are quite invaluable as leading indicators of plan accuracy. Besides, close monitoring also provides an opportunity to steer outcomes rather than simply measuring them.

When monitoring data for new products, of particular importance are the inflection or tipping points—these refer to the timing of rapid growth and the timing of products settling into a steady state (after the rapid growth stage). Getting the timing right for these turning points can help ensure shortages and excess supply are avoided and can mean the difference between a successful launch and a failure.

If a statistical model is being used for new product forecasting (say, in with the help of like modeling), tracking signal is a useful technique to monitor validity of the model. If the tracking signal violates thresholds set, it might mean that there is a significant bias, which might point to the fact that a turning point has been reached. Tracking signal is calculated as the ratio of error total (cumulative) to mean absolute deviation. Using a useful property of MAD, which is that 1.25 * MAD approximates one standard deviation, threshold limits can be set for error total linked to standard deviation of forecast errors. As it is important to pick up on any shift in demand early enough, tight thresholds could be set (e.g., a tracking signal of $\pm 2.5$ translates to two standard deviations). If the threshold is violated by the total error, an exception can be triggered that draws human attention. Owing to their strategic importance, new products call for specifically designed metrics for performance measurement. Metrics need to be designed in such a fashion that timely intervention is possible to shape and not just observe outcomes. Gartner recommends a hierarchy of metrics for new product development and introduction (NPDI) that does just that (Burkett 2016). In their framework, there are three tiers—the top tier has metrics for forecast accuracy and return on innovation, the middle tier is focused on time to value metrics (around cash flow, revenue, and profit margins), and the ground-level lower tier is aimed at tracking NPDI status and post-launch performance.

### 5.1.2 SAP Use Case: Product Lifecycle Management

In IBP, the product lifecycle management app allows use of historical sales data from similar products for statistical forecasting. Let's say we have a new product IBP-103 that is similar in terms of demand characteristics to two products, namely, IBP-101 and IBP-102. Figure 5.5 shows how this scenario can be modeled assuming both predecessors can be assigned with equal weights.

Once weights and references are assigned, the historical data that will be used for forecasting the new product can be visualized using the simulation feature (as shown in Fig. 5.6). The default key figure that is used to read historical data of the referenced products is the one that has the business meaning "actual sales" assigned in the key figure configuration (labeled 1 in the illustration).

The date until which the historical data of the referenced product(s) will be used is set based on the forecast start date assigned to the new product. This date signifies the timing for use of new product's demands for forecasting. The start date for the new product is set on the level of what is called a launch dimension. This is an attribute that can be freely chosen. For example, this can be an attribute that denotes the market(s) where the product will be launched. Multiple entries can be added to

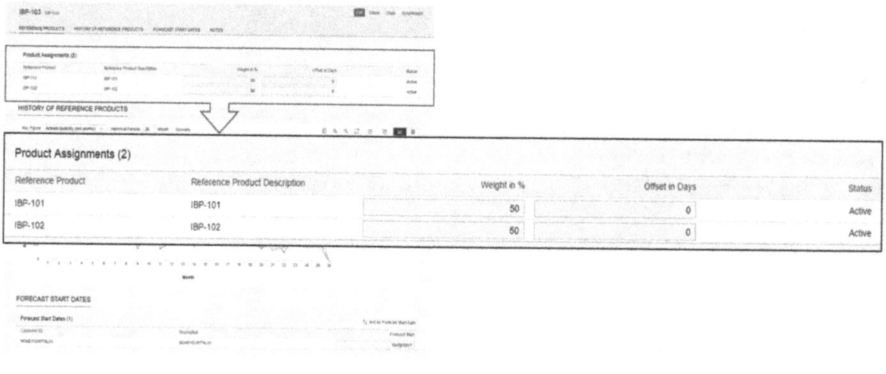


**Fig. 5.5** Assigning reference products in IBP's manage product lifecycle app

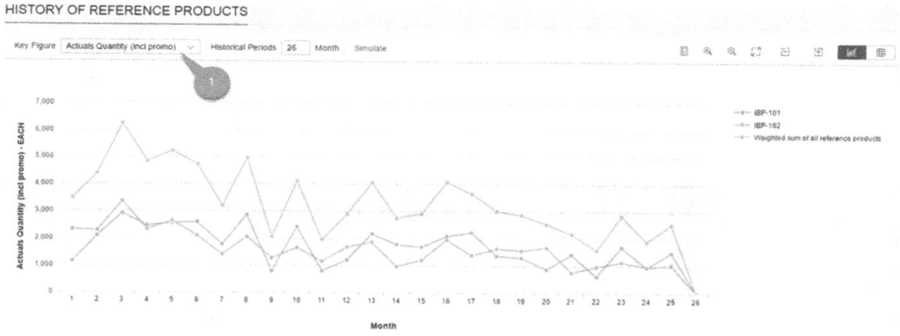


**Fig. 5.6** Simulating use of actual sales data of reference products

set potentially different start dates for different markets. Use of wildcard characters lets one maintain a certain default date and then as many additional entries with different start dates as there are exceptions (Fig. 5.7).

Once saved and active, use of lifecycle information for statistical forecasting is enabled by checking the appropriate option in the forecast model maintenance app (as shown in Fig. 5.8).

For the example discussed, the result of statistical forecast execution is shown in Fig. 5.9. Although there is no historical data, there is a statistical forecast (blue bars) generated based on the weighted sum of actual sales of the two referenced products.

To provide enhanced visibility to planners regarding new products, it might be worthwhile to define lifecycle statuses that correspond to the lifecycle stage of a product. As the forecast start date in the app is not accessible in key figure calculations, an approach is described below that involves use of a custom lifecycle master data type.

This approach clearly introduces redundancy in the form of an additional master data type that holds roughly the same data that is maintained in the lifecycle app.

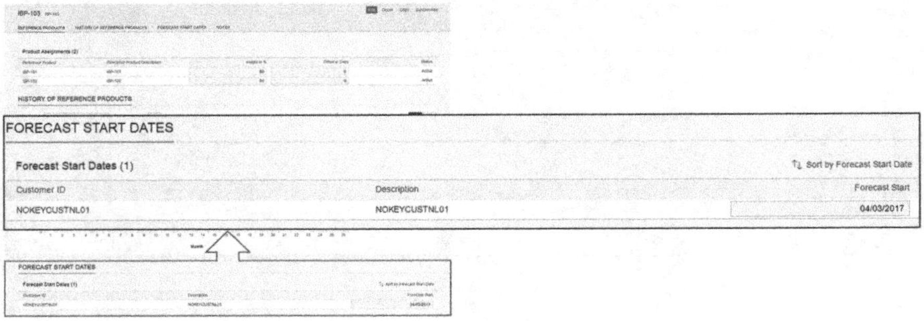


**Fig. 5.7** Setting forecast start date for the new product

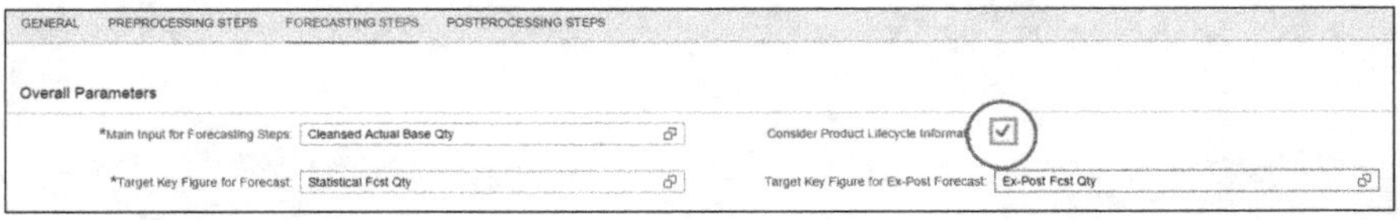


**Fig. 5.8** Ensuring lifecycle information is used for statistical forecasting

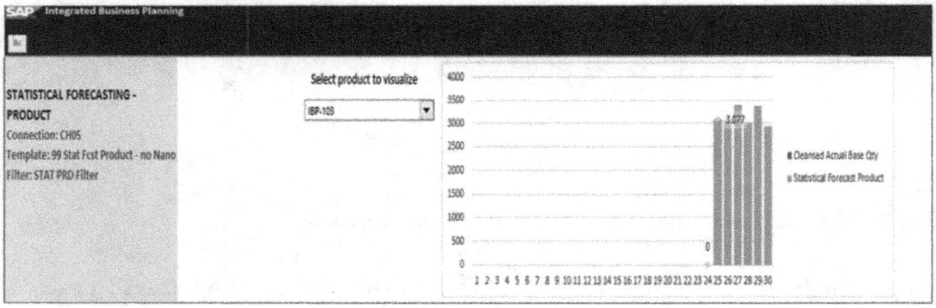


**Fig. 5.9** Result of statistical forecast execution on the new product

However, one could argue that the cost of this redundancy is offset by the benefits of being able to use this data in key figure calculations to define statuses for segmentation and provide visual clues to planners in planning views.

An example for lifecycle statuses is shown in Fig. 5.10. The statuses are derived based on the date difference between the phase-in or phase-out date (new product) and the system date (current date). For example, if a certain product has been phased-in and the start date is more than 12 months in the past, a status of "active normal" can be assigned. Or if a product is being phased out (phase-out date in the current period), a status of "phasing out" can be assigned.

The high-level prerequisites and steps needed to implement this feature are as follows:

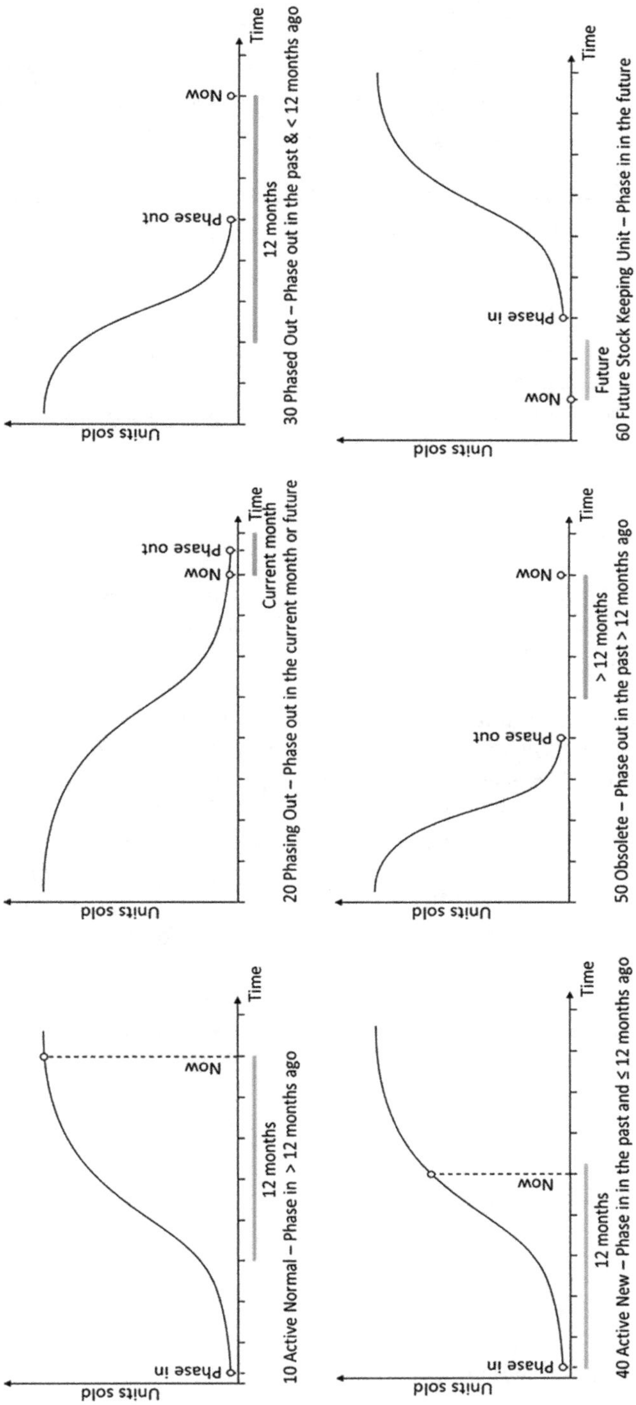


**Fig. 5.10** Examples for lifecycle statuses derived based on phase-in (forecast start) date

Key master data prerequisites:

- A lifecycle master data type (MDT) that has at least the following attributes: product ID, new product ID, phase-out and phase-in dates, and additional attributes as needed depending on the planning level on which product lifecycle data will be maintained.
- Two technical MDTs (for phase-in and phase-out dates, respectively). One is a simple MDT and the other is a reference of that simple MDT. These are used for mapping dates to period IDs (identifiers used in the time profile associated with the planning area)
- A virtual MDT to perform date lookup and retrieve the period ID corresponding to a certain date. The join condition is between the lifecycle MDT and the technical date lookup MDTs.
- A lifecycle status attribute that is included in the MDT where the key attributes match the planning level on which lifecycle maintenance is done (say, product and market).

In configuration you would need to take care of:

- A planning level (let's call it lifecycle) is created that includes the product (old), new product, and the period IDs (virtual MDT attributes) corresponding to the phase-out and phase-in dates.
- For a product being phased out, a key figure that is created on the lifecycle level is used to calculate the difference in number of periods between the current date and the phase-out date ("Ph Out Periods Diff" in Fig. 5.11). Similarly, for the product being phased in, difference in number of periods between the current date and the phase-in date is calculated in a different key figure ("Ph In Periods Diff" in Fig. 5.11). As can be seen from the example illustrated in Fig. 5.11, the current month (in bold) is April 2017, and therefore the number of periods until phase-in starts for the new product "103" is 0 (result shown in key figure "Ph In Periods Diff"), and the number of periods since phase-out is 1 for the old product (result shown in key figure "Ph Out Periods Diff").
- An attribute transformation is performed on the lifecycle attribute and statuses are derived based on predefined rules. The rules are formulated in terms of the time difference between the phase-in/phase-out dates and the current date (see Fig. 5.12). The transformed attribute should be part of planning levels of all key figures that are used in planning views where the lifecycle attribute is relevant.

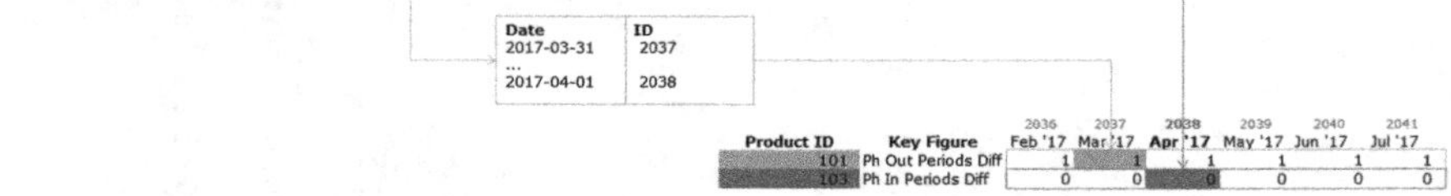

**Fig. 5.11** Calculating periods since or until phase-in or phase-out

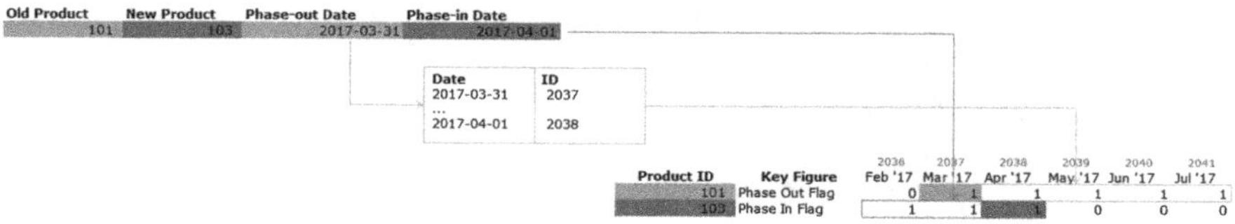


**Fig. 5.12** Phase-in and phase-out flag key figures for providing visual cues in planning views

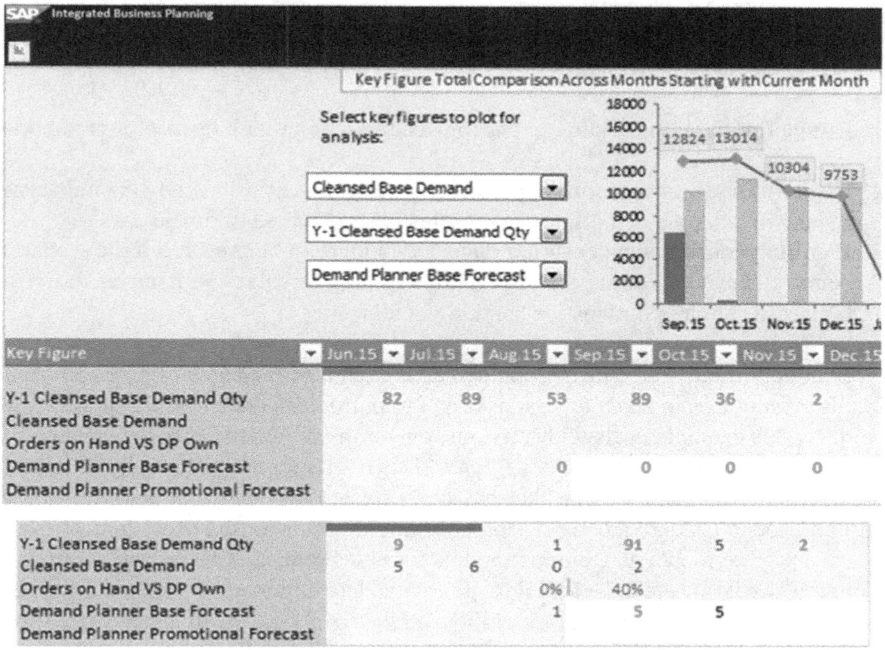


**Fig. 5.13** Red and blue lines as visual clues in planning views based on lifecycle dates

- Additionally, it might be useful to provide visual clues to planners in planning views to draw attention to products based on their lifecycle dates. For example, a red fill in a period indicates that the said period is greater than or equal to the phase-out date. Alternatively, a blue fill indicates that the said period is less than or equal to the phase-in date. This can be accomplished by configuring flag key figures as shown in. These key figures are used in conditional formatting (EPM formatting) to achieve the effect described. Formatting is also used to reduce to the font of the value to say one point in order to make the filled cells resemble a line drawn above the relevant key figures (Fig. 5.13).

Once identified, data may not be usable right away as market and economic factors driving demand (translated to penetration rate and ultimate penetration level that determine the shape of the growth curve) may be different between the new product and its ancestor(s). This requires adjustment of the data, for example, with the use of weighting factors.

### 5.1.3 SAP Use Case: New Product Forecasting and Planning, Risks, and Opportunities

In the following use case, new product introduction is used as the context to describe the use of scenarios (versions) to model risks and opportunities.

The example has three parts:

1. **Range forecast**: forecasting a range instead of a point with the use of prediction intervals.
2. **Risk/opportunity evaluation**: performing what-if analysis to study the impact of a specific outcome coming to pass, in this example, the optimistic case.
3. **Planning contingency**: ensuring plans are in place to be prepared if the scenario being evaluated becomes reality. This step also involves looking at the cost impact of multiple options for handling contingency.

If an opportunity (say, increase in demand) cannot be managed, it poses a risk—in this example, as in many others, risks and opportunities are two sides of the same coin. As this example deals with versions, one of the prerequisites is the creation of the versions and assignment of key figures. This is a configuration activity. We have modeled an optimistic version that has been created and exists in addition to the baseline version. There are no version-specific master data used even though it can be used, e.g., to model new production line for new product. All forecast and supply planning key figures (except actual transactional data imported into IBP) are flagged as version specific. That is, values of those in the optimistic version can differ from the baseline version (configuration in Fig. 5.14).

**Part 1: Range Forecast** As discussed earlier in the section about prediction intervals, for new products, it is often important to forecast a range of outcomes instead of simply a single data point given the elevated levels of uncertainty. The technique of prediction intervals works by calculating a range (best case > most likely > worst case) for a given probability. The breadth of the range depends on the estimated error (estimated using, say, mean squared error (MSE)). Let's assume that the product IBP_301 is similar to another product already in the company's portfolio. A statistical forecast is calculated using the similar product's historical data, and the MSE is used to estimate the standard deviation (√MSE), and using the standard normal distribution table, ranges for different probabilities are calculated.

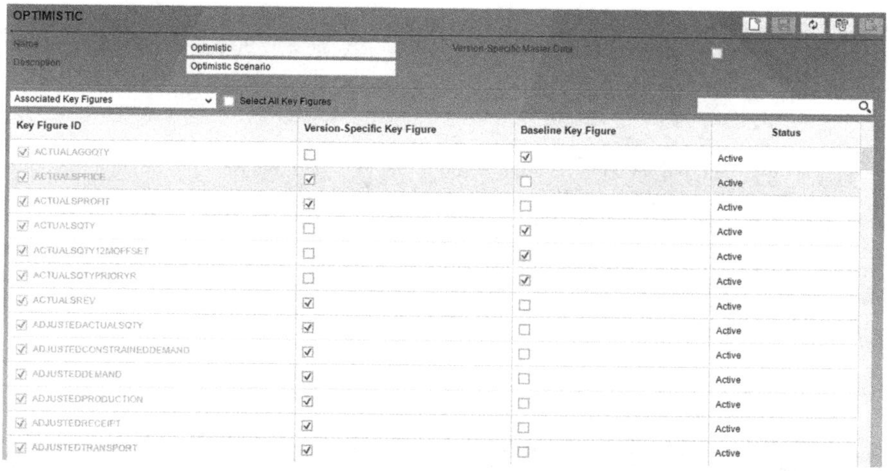


**Fig. 5.14** Configuration of versions

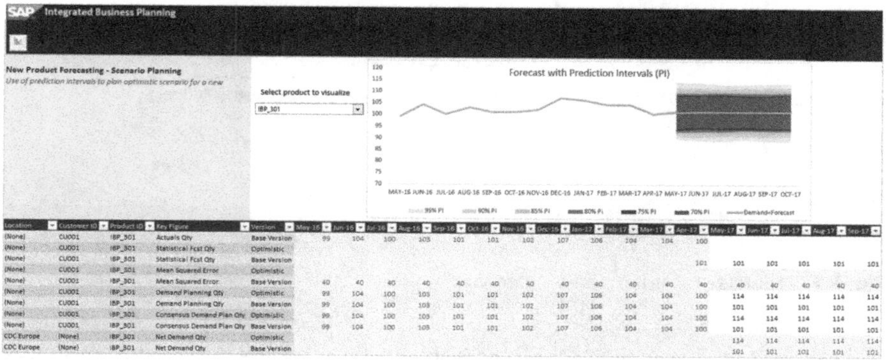


**Fig. 5.15** Range forecast using prediction intervals

This is visualized in the planning view[2] (see Fig. 5.15).

As one can see in Fig. 5.16, for 95% prediction interval, the forecast upper bound is around 114. This value is assumed to be the optimistic case or the best case. Therefore, the forecast of 114 units is stored in the optimistic version. The base version holds what is assumed to be the most likely outcome (the mean), which is 101 units—this is also the output of the statistical forecast.

---

[2]The graph was created in Excel using a two-step process. Step 1: using functions RAND and NORM.INV to simulate forecast values for various random probabilities. Step 2: using PERCENTILE function, calculate the lower and upper range for a given prediction interval (say, range between 2.5th percentile and 97.5th percentile gives the lower and upper bounds for 95% prediction interval).

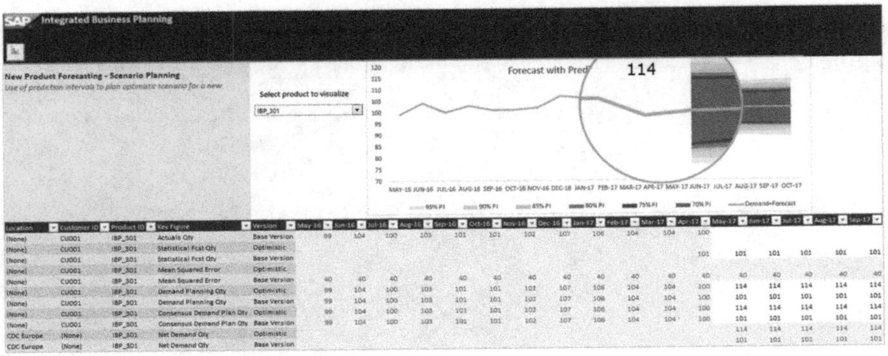


**Fig. 5.16** Choosing best case at a specific prediction interval as the optimistic forecast

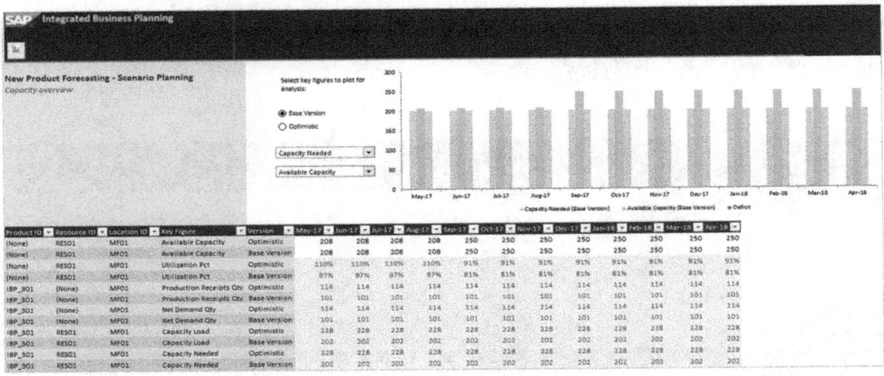


**Fig. 5.17** Results of heuristic run for base version

Let's assume further that these figures are not enriched any further and are simply transferred to the consensus forecast key figure "consensus demand plan qty," which is then the input to supply planning.

**Part 2: Risk Evaluation** The next step is an assessment of feasibility from a supply standpoint of meeting demands estimated in the multiple versions, each one representing a particular scenario (an embodiment of inputs such as risk factors, assumptions, product interdependencies, etc. as illustrated in Fig. 5.4). In our example, we have two versions: one where the forecast is estimated to be 101 units (baseline) and one where it is 114 units (optimistic).

We start by generating a supply plan by using the heuristic planning method, which assumes infinite capacity. All the relevant supply planning master data are maintained for the new product (IBP-301), and the results of the supply planning run in the baseline version are shown in Fig. 5.17. In this example, it is assumed that the

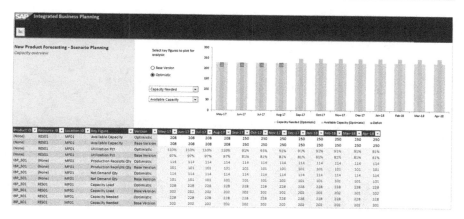

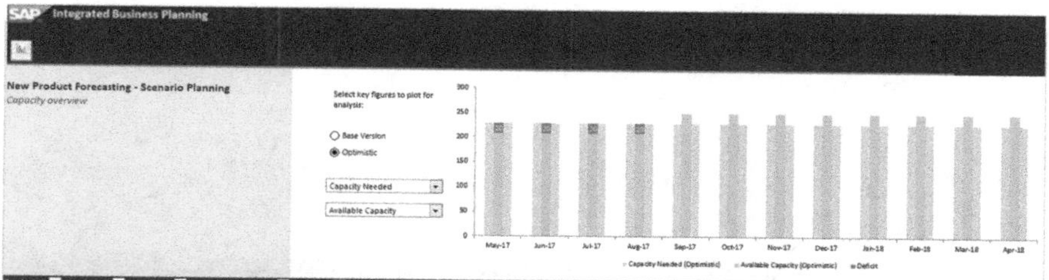


| Product ID | Resource ID | Location ID | Key Figure | Version | May-17 | Jun-17 | Jul-17 | Aug-17 | Sep-17 | Oct-17 | Nov-17 | Dec-17 | Jan-18 | Feb-18 | Mar-18 | Apr-18 |
|---|---|---|---|---|---|---|---|---|---|---|---|---|---|---|---|---|
| (None) | RES01 | MF01 | Available Capacity | Optimistic | 208 | 208 | 208 | 208 | 250 | 250 | 250 | 250 | 250 | 250 | 250 | 250 |
| (None) | RES01 | MF01 | Available Capacity | Base Version | 208 | 208 | 208 | 208 | 250 | 250 | 250 | 250 | 250 | 250 | 250 | 250 |
| (None) | RES01 | MF01 | Utilization Pct | Optimistic | 110% | 110% | 110% | 110% | 91% | 91% | 91% | 91% | 91% | 91% | 91% | 91% |
| (None) | RES01 | MF01 | Utilization Pct | Base Version | 97% | 97% | 97% | 97% | 81% | 81% | 81% | 81% | 81% | 81% | 81% | 81% |
| IBP_301 | (None) | MF01 | Production Receipts Qty | Optimistic | 114 | 114 | 114 | 114 | 114 | 114 | 114 | 114 | 114 | 114 | 114 | 114 |
| IBP_301 | (None) | MF01 | Production Receipts Qty | Base Version | 101 | 101 | 101 | 101 | 101 | 101 | 101 | 101 | 101 | 101 | 101 | 101 |
| IBP_301 | (None) | MF01 | Net Demand Qty | Optimistic | 114 | 114 | 114 | 114 | 114 | 114 | 114 | 114 | 114 | 114 | 114 | 114 |
| IBP_301 | (None) | MF01 | Net Demand Qty | Base Version | 101 | 101 | 101 | 101 | 101 | 101 | 101 | 101 | 101 | 101 | 101 | 101 |
| IBP_301 | RES01 | MF01 | Capacity Load | Optimistic | 228 | 228 | 228 | 228 | 228 | 228 | 228 | 228 | 228 | 228 | 228 | 228 |
| IBP_301 | RES01 | MF01 | Capacity Load | Base Version | 202 | 202 | 202 | 202 | 202 | 202 | 202 | 202 | 202 | 202 | 202 | 202 |
| IBP_301 | RES01 | MF01 | Capacity Needed | Optimistic | 228 | 228 | 228 | 228 | 228 | 228 | 228 | 228 | 228 | 228 | 228 | 228 |
| IBP_301 | RES01 | MF01 | Capacity Needed | Base Version | 202 | 202 | 202 | 202 | 202 | 202 | 202 | 202 | 202 | 202 | 202 | 202 |

**Fig. 5.18** Results of heuristic run for optimistic version

preferred source for the product is in-house production. Please note that the supply heuristic (or any planning algorithm like supply optimizer) can be run in multiple versions simultaneously.

As can be seen from the graph, the capacity available exceeds capacity needed for producing 101 units. So, baseline forecast, if this should in fact become reality, should not pose a problem in terms of available capacity to meet demands.

The optimistic version, however, brings up potential issues from a capacity feasibility standpoint. This is visualized in the planning view shown in Fig. 5.18. It is quite evident that in the first 4 months (May 2017 to July 2017), there is a deficit in capacity for 20 capacity units—in other words, a capacity overload of 10%. This poses a potential risk—please recall that 114 units represents the upper forecast range for a prediction interval of 95%. So, if one wants to be 95% assured of being able to meet demands for the given variability profile, which in our example is expressed through the MSE measure, one needs to have a contingency in place for this eventuality.

**Part 3: Planning Contingency** As in-house production is assumed to be the preferred source of supply, the first option that is explored is adding capacity in order to bridge the capacity deficit in the first 4 months. Let's also assume that we can only add capacity in increments of 20% and we'd like to evaluate the impact of doing so. Adding 20% more capacity would increase the fixed production cost. The cost calculations are shown and visualized in Fig. 5.19.

The operating profit is nothing but the difference between the consensus demand plan revenue and cost. For the optimistic case, for the first 4 months, the demand plan revenue is 114 * 70 (unit price), which is 7980 €. The cost equals fixed production cost + production cost rate * forecasted quantity, which is 8100 €. This represents a loss of 120 €, which is what we see in the graph.

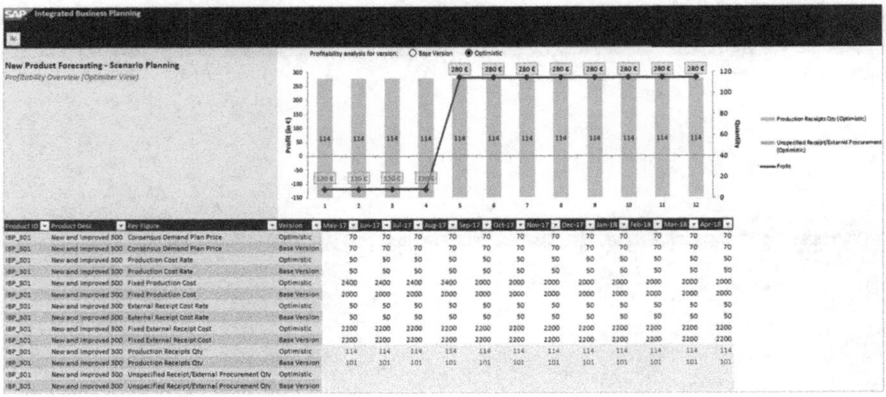


| Product ID | Product Desc | Key Figure | Version | May-17 | Jun-17 | Jul-17 | Aug-17 | Sep-17 | Oct-17 | Nov-17 | Dec-17 | Jan-18 | Feb-18 | Mar-18 | Apr-18 |
|---|---|---|---|---|---|---|---|---|---|---|---|---|---|---|---|
| IBP_301 | New and Improved 300 | Consensus Demand Plan Price | Optimistic | 70 | 70 | 70 | 70 | 70 | 70 | 70 | 70 | 70 | 70 | 70 | 70 |
| IBP_301 | New and Improved 300 | Consensus Demand Plan Price | Base Version | 70 | 70 | 70 | 70 | 70 | 70 | 70 | 70 | 70 | 70 | 70 | 70 |
| IBP_301 | New and Improved 300 | Production Cost Rate | Optimistic | 50 | 50 | 50 | 50 | 50 | 50 | 50 | 50 | 50 | 50 | 50 | 50 |
| IBP_301 | New and Improved 300 | Production Cost Rate | Base Version | 50 | 50 | 50 | 50 | 50 | 50 | 50 | 50 | 50 | 50 | 50 | 50 |
| IBP_301 | New and Improved 300 | Fixed Production Cost | Optimistic | 2400 | 2400 | 2400 | 2400 | 2000 | 2000 | 2000 | 2000 | 2000 | 2000 | 2000 | 2000 |
| IBP_301 | New and Improved 300 | Fixed Production Cost | Base Version | 2000 | 2000 | 2000 | 2000 | 2000 | 2000 | 2000 | 2000 | 2000 | 2000 | 2000 | 2000 |
| IBP_301 | New and Improved 300 | External Receipt Cost Rate | Optimistic | 50 | 50 | 50 | 50 | 50 | 50 | 50 | 50 | 50 | 50 | 50 | 50 |
| IBP_301 | New and Improved 300 | External Receipt Cost Rate | Base Version | 50 | 50 | 50 | 50 | 50 | 50 | 50 | 50 | 50 | 50 | 50 | 50 |
| IBP_301 | New and Improved 300 | Fixed External Receipt Cost | Optimistic | 2200 | 2200 | 2200 | 2200 | 2200 | 2200 | 2200 | 2200 | 2200 | 2200 | 2200 | 2200 |
| IBP_301 | New and Improved 300 | Fixed External Receipt Cost | Base Version | 2200 | 2200 | 2200 | 2200 | 2200 | 2200 | 2200 | 2200 | 2200 | 2200 | 2200 | 2200 |
| IBP_301 | New and Improved 300 | Production Receipts Qty | Optimistic | 114 | 114 | 114 | 114 | 114 | 114 | 114 | 114 | 114 | 114 | 114 | 114 |
| IBP_301 | New and Improved 300 | Production Receipts Qty | Base Version | 101 | 101 | 101 | 101 | 101 | 101 | 101 | 101 | 101 | 101 | 101 | 101 |
| IBP_301 | New and Improved 300 | Unspecified Receipt/External Procurement Qty | Optimistic | | | | | | | | | | | | |
| IBP_301 | New and Improved 300 | Unspecified Receipt/External Procurement Qty | Base Version | | | | | | | | | | | | |

**Fig. 5.19** Cost of organizing additional capacity in the first 4 months

What this means is if the optimistic case should become reality and we intend to satisfy demands by organizing additional capacity in order to satisfy them through in-house production, it will not be profitable.

Therefore, an alternative, which is external procurement, is explored as an option.

For evaluating this alternative, we use the supply optimizer algorithm. Profit maximization is chosen as the objective. Optimizer, as opposed to the heuristic algorithm, does not refer to quotas for assigning the source of supply.[3] To explore alternative sources of supply, we use the optimizer algorithm that attempts to maximize profit (which is the option we've assumed. Delivery maximization is the other option) by finding the most profitable combination of sourcing options.

The results of the optimizer run are visualized in Fig. 5.20. The variable costs for both in-house production and external procurement are the same. However, the fixed costs for external procurement are lower when compared to in-house production in the event that capacity has to be increased by 20% (2200 vs 2400). Inventory holding costs are deliberately set quite high to prevent production in excess of what is forecasted in a given period—this might be preferable in the case of new products that are particularly vulnerable to demand uncertainty. With this cost model, we see that the optimizer proposes external procurement in the optimistic scenario for the first 4 months instead of utilizing additional in-house capacity at a higher fixed cost. What is also noteworthy is that the unit price, which is set at 70 €, is high enough to not lead the optimizer to suggest nondelivery or late delivery of some of the demands. As a result, in the first 4 months, the profit is 80 €, and it goes up to 280 € when switching to in-house production starting month 5.

The approach described for contingency planning—that is, initial assessment using a heuristic method and subsequent exploration of options using supply

[3]For the benefit of the heuristic method, and given that in-house production is the preferred sourcing option, quotas were maintained in master data in such a way that 100% was allocated to in-house production.

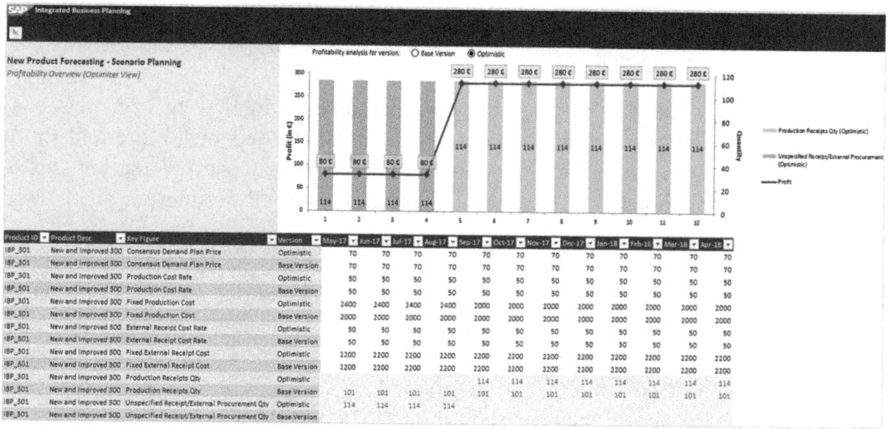


| Product ID | Product Desc | Key Figure | Version | May-17 | Jun-17 | Jul-17 | Aug-17 | Sep-17 | Oct-17 | Nov-17 | Dec-17 | Jan-18 | Feb-18 | Mar-18 | Apr-18 |
|---|---|---|---|---|---|---|---|---|---|---|---|---|---|---|---|
| IBP_301 | New and Improved 300 | Consensus Demand Plan Price | Optimistic | 70 | 70 | 70 | 70 | 70 | 70 | 70 | 70 | 70 | 70 | 70 | 70 |
| IBP_301 | New and Improved 300 | Consensus Demand Plan Price | Base Version | 70 | 70 | 70 | 70 | 70 | 70 | 70 | 70 | 70 | 70 | 70 | 70 |
| IBP_301 | New and Improved 300 | Production Cost Rate | Optimistic | 50 | 50 | 50 | 50 | 50 | 50 | 50 | 50 | 50 | 50 | 50 | 50 |
| IBP_301 | New and Improved 300 | Production Cost Rate | Base Version | 50 | 50 | 50 | 50 | 50 | 50 | 50 | 50 | 50 | 50 | 50 | 50 |
| IBP_301 | New and Improved 300 | Fixed Production Cost | Optimistic | 2400 | 2400 | 2400 | 2400 | 2000 | 2000 | 2000 | 2000 | 2000 | 2000 | 2000 | 2000 |
| IBP_301 | New and Improved 300 | Fixed Production Cost | Base Version | 2000 | 2000 | 2000 | 2000 | 2000 | 2000 | 2000 | 2000 | 2000 | 2000 | 2000 | 2000 |
| IBP_301 | New and Improved 300 | External Receipt Cost Rate | Optimistic | 50 | 50 | 50 | 50 | 50 | 50 | 50 | 50 | 50 | 50 | 50 | 50 |
| IBP_301 | New and Improved 300 | External Receipt Cost Rate | Base Version | 50 | 50 | 50 | 50 | 50 | 50 | 50 | 50 | 50 | 50 | 50 | 50 |
| IBP_301 | New and Improved 300 | Fixed External Receipt Cost | Optimistic | 2200 | 2200 | 2200 | 2200 | 2200 | 2200 | 2200 | 2200 | 2200 | 2200 | 2200 | 2200 |
| IBP_301 | New and Improved 300 | Fixed External Receipt Cost | Base Version | 2200 | 2200 | 2200 | 2200 | 2200 | 2200 | 2200 | 2200 | 2200 | 2200 | 2200 | 2200 |
| IBP_301 | New and Improved 300 | Production Receipts Qty | Optimistic | | | | | 114 | 114 | 114 | 114 | 114 | 114 | 114 | 114 |
| IBP_301 | New and Improved 300 | Production Receipts Qty | Base Version | 101 | 101 | 101 | 101 | 101 | 101 | 101 | 101 | 101 | 101 | 101 | 101 |
| IBP_301 | New and Improved 300 | Unspecified Receipt/External Procurement Qty | Optimistic | 114 | 114 | 114 | 114 | | | | | | | | |
| IBP_301 | New and Improved 300 | Unspecified Receipt/External Procurement Qty | Base Version | | | | | | | | | | | | |

**Fig. 5.20** Results of the optimizer run

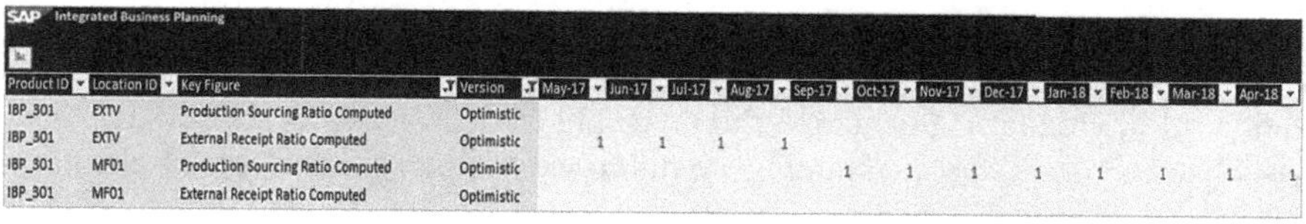


| Product ID | Location ID | Key Figure | Version | May-17 | Jun-17 | Jul-17 | Aug-17 | Sep-17 | Oct-17 | Nov-17 | Dec-17 | Jan-18 | Feb-18 | Mar-18 | Apr-18 |
|---|---|---|---|---|---|---|---|---|---|---|---|---|---|---|---|
| IBP_301 | EXTV | Production Sourcing Ratio Computed | Optimistic | | | | | | | | | | | | |
| IBP_301 | EXTV | External Receipt Ratio Computed | Optimistic | 1 | 1 | 1 | 1 | | | | | | | | |
| IBP_301 | MF01 | Production Sourcing Ratio Computed | Optimistic | | | | | 1 | 1 | 1 | 1 | 1 | 1 | 1 | 1 |
| IBP_301 | MF01 | External Receipt Ratio Computed | Optimistic | | | | | | | | | | | | |

**Fig. 5.21** Setting up supply quotas based on supply optimizer results

optimizer—might be quite appropriate for aggregate planning. A purpose configured optimizer, like the one described above, can perform the job of comparing multiple options with a specific criterion or criteria in mind—in our case, it was finding the right combination of supply sources that maximizes profit.

Assuming somewhere down the line the optimistic scenario becomes the most likely one and that it has to be promoted to the baseline scenario, a copy operation will need to be performed to copy the relevant key figures from the optimistic version to the base version. If for operational planning, heuristic method is used and the results of the optimizer run from a sourcing perspective need to be adopted by heuristic method, one could run a special algorithm that calculates quotas from the results of a supply plan. In the simple example discussed, the quota will be 100% for external procurement in the first 4 months and changing to 100% for in-house production starting from month 5. The quotas that are so calculated are stored in corresponding sourcing ratio key figures with a "COMP" (stands for computed) suffix (see Fig. 5.21 that shows the results of the algorithm that calculates quotas from the supply plan).

### 5.1.4 Focus Is a "King" and Exception Is a "Queen"

**Focus**

We have experienced that in complex commercial and marketing organizations, large supply networks focus and exception management becomes more and more important. Forecasting and planning should not be done with same attention across all products, all customers, all channels, all markets, and all production plants (see Fig. 5.22).

Segmentation is a process that is designed to help to differentiate and optimize ways of working, to maximize company position with their products, services for their customers and markets. Segmentation brings focus, structure in the process especially when business is complex and diversified.

Segmentation can bring focus on right things. Many companies face the challenge of the complexity of their portfolio, and service offering expands and expands and becomes more customized and more tailored. Working with same focus and on the same level of details will make you immerse in "deep dark ocean" of workload which will be not compensated with output value. You need to have few instruments which will help you to navigate within complexity of your business. Segmentation could serve as mechanism to align product, sales, marketing, and SC&O on prioritization rules. Product segmentation should be linked to desired process outputs. Let's visualize that on example, assuming we run in the company three types of planning:

1. Short-term operational planning, normally executed with high granularity in the market/country sporadically rolled up to global level
2. Midterm tactical planning, normally used an instrument to assess 4M (manpower, machine, materials, money) constraints, your manufacturing capabilities in 2–3 years' horizon visualized against strategic plans
3. Long-term strategic planning of strategic raw materials or base semifinished products like active ingredient in chemical industry seed variety in agriculture,

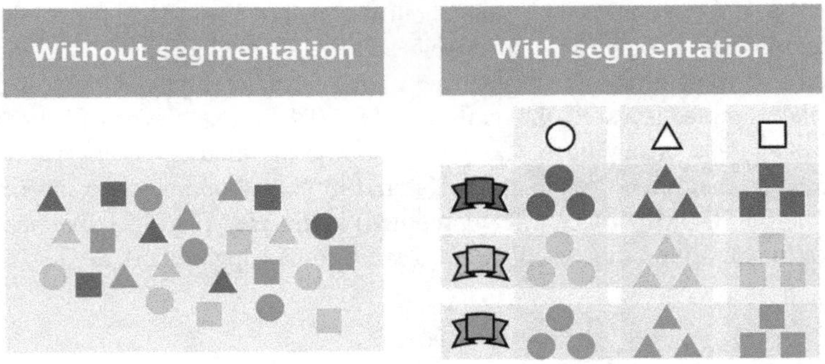


**Fig. 5.22** Segment or not to segment, this not a question!

steel in white goods manufacturer, and drug substance in pharmaceutical industry (Fig. 5.23)

Each planning type should have its own segmentation, but if bidimensional segmentation would be used, then measure behind ABC should be linked to objectives, e.g., profitable growth. Each planning process (operational, tactical, strategic) has its own characteristics, objectives, and stakeholders (Fig. 1.1); therefore it will need its own way to execute focus and not just with different thresholds for same measures but as well different measures (see Fig. 5.24).

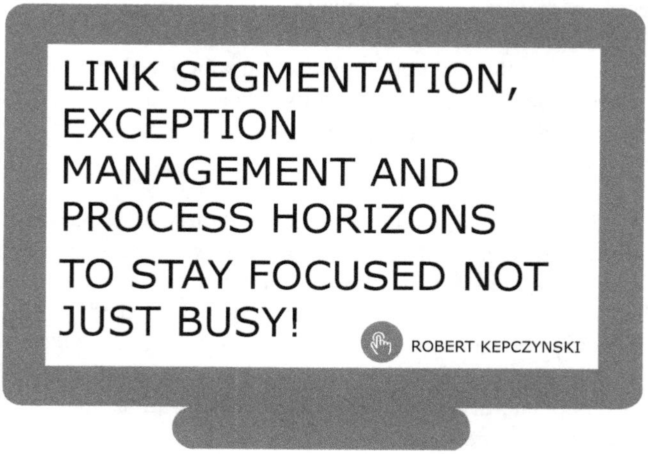


**Fig. 5.23** Stay focused not just busy!

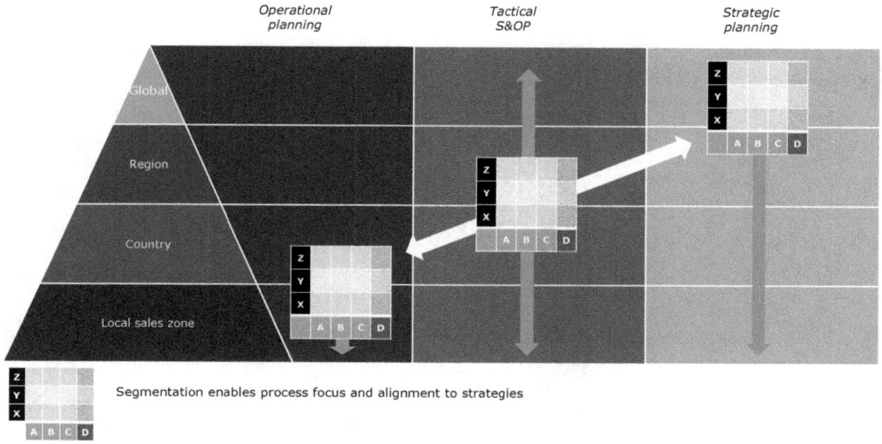


**Fig. 5.24** Segmentation per planning type

Segmentation should have a purpose linked to the process output you want to achieve:

- Improve focus in country-based finished good S&OP process and ability to visualize results on aggregated level region/global.
- Improve focus in region/country grp semifinished good tactical and strategic planning, and visualize results on any level.
- Improve focus in global/region key raw materials strategic products planning, and visualize results on any level.
- Improve focus in sales zone operational planning, with use of product segmentation weighted with customer segmentation.

In case there are functions in your organization which look on product strategies, cross those levels you may consider to link levels via additional weighting like global, regional weighting in local segmentation.

**Exception**

Tailored alerts linked to, e.g., product segmentation will bring to your process different degrees of efficiency. It will help to bring exception management into the operational game. Let us visualize exception management on the example. In Fig. 5.25 we see example of forecast error thresholds linked to the ABC/XYZ product segmentation. Thresholds will be used to trigger tailored alerts for demand planners as part of demand review meeting preparation. Similar approach can be achieved if you populate inventory forward cover measure against ABC/XYZ and set up special alerts for supply planners.

Alerts may be single measure/threshold driven, or you may want to combine them; see demand review preparation (Sect. 5.2.9).

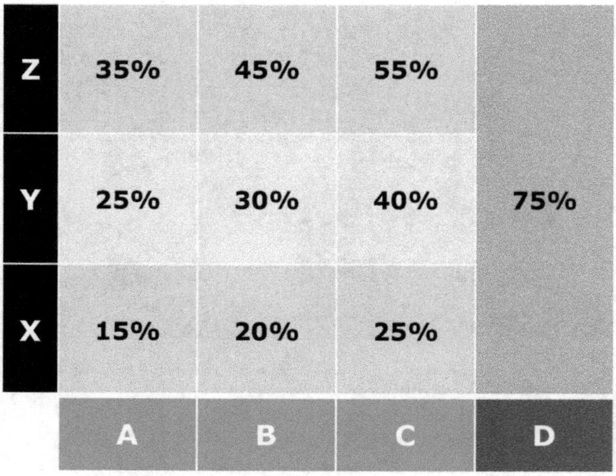


**Fig. 5.25** Portfolio segmentation alert thresholds

Is it easy to move that direction? We tend to validate everything. We tend to forget that exception management rules based on which system highlights deviations were agreed with process management teams and should be aligned to process and company strategies. Why we do not follow exception management, why we do not use them that often? One of the reasons we see is that in the past, technology was not easy to be understood by business. Business users did not have easy way to work, validate aggregated level while working with details driven by exceptions. Exception management can give you step change in process efficiency. You need to leverage and tailor exceptions to specific business process characteristic. Many processes would need to be automatized, e.g., for products with low-profit contribution and high predictability, you may automatize process of outlier detection, correction, and statistical forecast engine run. From alert to action! That's where you should go, and that's where SAP IBP system will help you to be. Here are some examples of exception management:

- Differentiated forecasting concept introduced in our first book (Kepczynski et al. 2018)
- Shelf life planning use case (Fig. 5.169)
- Consensus demand revenue sanity check (Fig. 3.13).

### 5.1.5 What and How to Segment

Definition of what and how to segment plays important role in making your process and technical design transparent. It can be used to align segmentation objectives with company business management objectives.

We can define segmentation based on the following parameters:

(a) Purpose/input vs output
(b) Measures used in segmentation
(c) Level
(d) Frequency
(e) Timing
(f) Horizon
(g) Thresholds
(h) Calculation method
(i) Process framework

**Ad (a) Input and Output Segmentation**

We can define two major types of segmentation:

- One which leads to define techniques for specific process
- The other which helps to define process segments

The first segmentation is done on process data inputs, the second on process data outputs (see Fig. 5.26).

*Data input segmentation:*

You might use product segmentation to categorize data input for statistical forecasting methods, which you would need to apply for specific datasets. Data input segment "X" with low variability would have special statistical forecasting algorithms compared to data input segment "Z" with high variability. This way of using segmentation will help you to select appropriate forecasting algorithms or even methods linked to specific product segments. This segmentation approach should be even closer linked to lifecycle of the product.

*Data output segmentation:*

You might use segmentation to define rules on how you should treat products in the process and visualize and link product segments to real and not planned performance which enables integration with other processes. Process data outputs are used in this method. Demand planning excellence may use this segmentation approach, e.g., once per year or so, to validate leading methods/forecasting techniques.

Above might look at first glance a bit contradictory to some publications, but we rather think is complementary to what was defined in leading literature. We would tend to use segmentation on your process outputs when you deal with business stakeholders and on process data inputs when you deal with data experts, data scientists, and statisticians. The purpose of using process data outputs is to link your segmentation to what process, people capabilities, and system functionality really delivers and not to what it supposed to deliver when data input is used. As

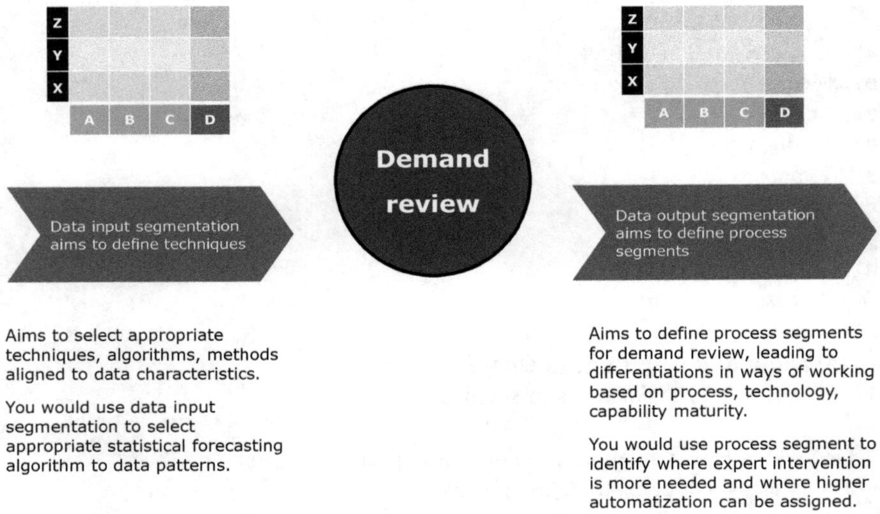


**Fig. 5.26** Data input or data output segmentation for demand review

example demand planners, demand manager would use this segmentation approach in process design.

Maybe another example will bring more clarity why we should distinguish segmentation for process inputs and process outputs. In one company we had a case that certain group of products with high variability in data input (shipments) had absolutely fantastic forecast performance in data output. In this case sales team with demand planning has arranged with customer (who was really advanced in forecasting) their forecast/sales order commitments which were driving consensus forecast for this product group. This forecast would have great performance but potentially very bad variability of data input (shipments). Data input segmentation would become not relevant for how you manage process, because process is not dependent always on data input (shipments) but to people and how you collaborate with partners.

Reference example says that strategy toward forecasting can differ depending on the classification of the demands; if 60% of the entire demand is erratic and lumpy, a good strategy would be to strengthen the service level and safety stock instead of improving the forecast accuracy (Demand Classification 2017).

What is definitely in common between those two segmentation methods is that both should have their clear purpose.

**Ad (b) Measures Used in Segmentation**

Measure for segmentation is extremely important. Measures used in segmentation should be linked to segmentation purpose and like for process output segmentation it should enable link to process or even company strategy.

**Ad (c) Segmentation Level**

Level on which product segmentation is executed should be linked to the process. In our case we can assume link between segmentation and planning type. Product segmentation for operational planning should be linked to level on which this process is commonly executed, e.g., product/customer/country. Segmentation should serve as instrument to optimize specific process which has determined parameters.

**Ad (d) Segmentation Frequency**

Frequency of running product segmentation should be linked to business characteristic. Let us give you an example of it; if we would have two big sales seasons during a year, most probably, we would run segmentation twice.

**Ad (e) Segmentation Timing**

Timing of the product segmentation process depends on business seasonality. You may look on timing of segmentation as, e.g., a way to align forecasting with budgeting process. If it is the case then, it would be a good idea to run segmentation before budgeting process and then use it in budgeting process.

**Ad (f) Segmentation Data Horizon**
Horizon of data used in product segmentation (past and future) should be relevant for frequency and timing being considered. Note that if you use bi- or multidimensional segmentation, then for each of the data, you should carefully define data horizon. You may use the following example: XYZ would use last year data to expose categorized demand variability, but ABC would use margin multiplied with consensus forecast for whole next year to categorize predicted profit contribution.

**Ad (g) Segmentation Thresholds**
Do not re-invent the wheel, and for, e.g., in ABC, use standard "Pareto" thresholds. In some businesses you may need to define exception segment like "D" where all exceptions to calculation would be stored. It could be very useful for marketing to identify product with negative margin or zero forecast sales (depending on the measure being used in segmentation). For XYZ you may use thresholds which would make sense for the measure chosen, e.g., mean absolute scaled error (MASE) class Z above 1 or weighted mean absolute percentage error (wMAPE) class Z above 60%.

**Ad (h) Segmentation Measure Calculation Method**
Select calculation linked to ABC or XYZ. For ABC in most of the cases, companies use either revenue or profit contribution. For XYZ many companies use wMAPE (weighted mean absolute percentage error), MASE (mean absolute scaled error), or variability of those measures (captured in coefficient of variation).

Let us bring some examples of segmentation use case from leading literature.

1. In AMR research study, portfolio segmentation is proposed to be used in the following way:
   (a) "Growth brands" where input from sales is very important
   (b) "Harvest brands" (mature products) where automatization with time series stat. forecasting is important
   (c) "Niche brands" where automatization "weighted combined" forecast plays vital role
   (d) New products: use attribute-based forecast (like products)/market research (Steutermann 2010)
2. Demand fulfillment is linked to the right positioning of inventory depending on the selected replenishment strategy: MTO, MTS, CTO, ETO, and ATS. Demand management should be involved when defining these strategies (Steutermann et al. 2012a).
3. Segmentation could drive definition of replenishment strategies toward the following configurations:
   (a) MTS: high volumes and low variety. Attention is focused on the finished product.
   (b) MTO: low volume and high variety.
   (c) ATO: great number of end items with a possibility of limited components.

(d) Late customization: to manage all the possible product options and to guarantee flexibility for product mixes and availability (APICS—module 3.D—Implementation of Demand Plans 2015).

4. Segmentation could be connected to supply, operations, customer service, and finance, because of the following key customer service challenges:
   (a) Poor forecast accuracy (70% of survey)
   (b) Lack of supply availability (61%)
   (c) Master data errors (55%)
   (d) Rush orders (42%),
   (e) Lack of alignment with sales regarding service levels (42%) (Steutermann 2016b)

Replenishment strategies can be determined with use of bidimensional product segmentation in the following way (Fig. 5.27):

**Ad (i) Segmentation Process Framework**

You may define process framework for product segmentation to achieve transparency, required stakeholder engagement. In one company segmentation was divided into preparation, review and sign off, implementation in the process and system, and regular usage. Each of the step in the process had an owner (Fig. 5.28).

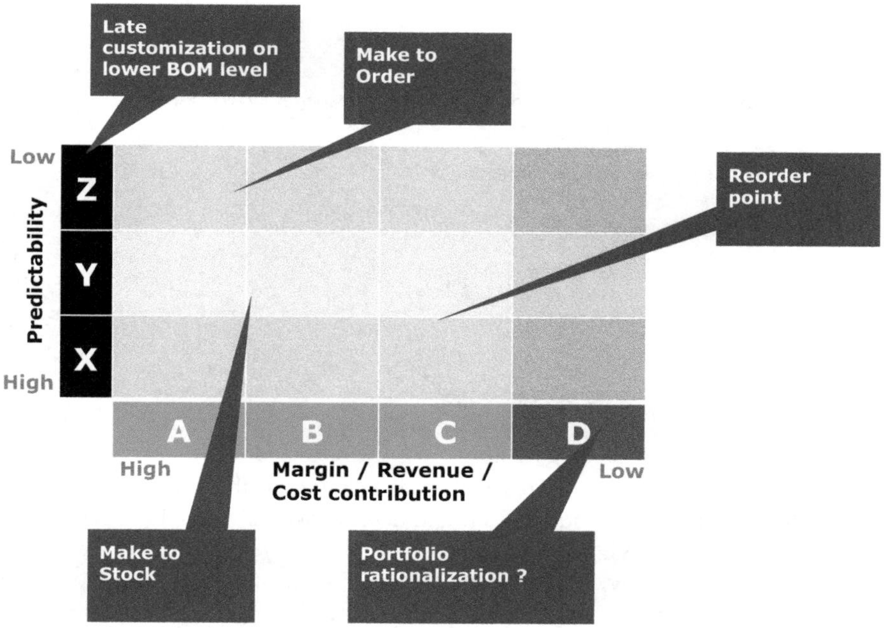


**Fig. 5.27** Segmentation used in simple approach to replenishment strategies definition

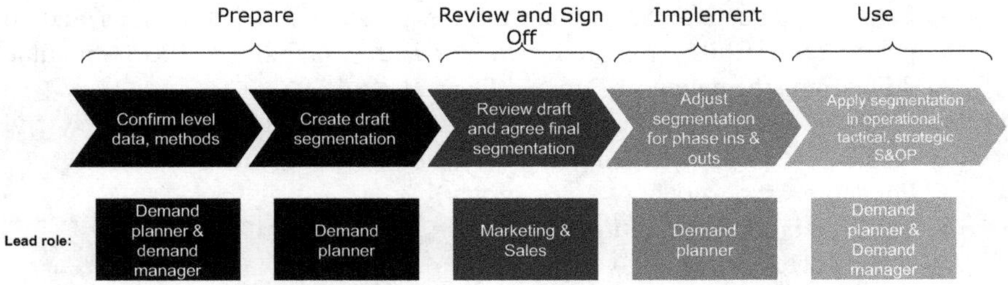


**Fig. 5.28** Segmentation process framework

| Step | Key activities | Lead role | Frequency |
|---|---|---|---|
| **Prepare** | Run automatic calculation<br>Verify data input & system configuration<br>Extract calculated segmentation for review | Demand Planner | Once per year / Season |
| **Review & Sign off** | Review if segmentation reflects desired reflection of strategic positioning or realistic market position | Portfolio Manager / Marketing | Once per year / Season |
| **Deploy** | Ensure validated and approved segmentation is being recorded in the system configuration<br><br>Apply new segmentation in next planning cycle | Demand Manager | Once per year / Season |

**Fig. 5.29** Segmentation process step explanation

Segmentation process framework highlighted above sets the process into a clear, easy-to-follow way to control, monitor, and deploy. We may detail it down in the following way (Fig. 5.29):

This process framework might be adapted to any planning type. We have seen that key to success of using segmentation was alignment with key stakeholders and assignment of ownership. In this particular company sign-off, accountability was in the hands of marketing organization.

### 5.1.6 Product Segmentation (ABC "D")

Product segmentation driven by single ABC dimension gives you an opportunity to align your process focus, e.g., to revenue growth. In this case product segmentation will be based on single measure. In SAP IBP terminology, segmentation will be based on one key figure for selected horizon. This key figure should represent business unit/country consensus unconstrained forecast value. We should not use data which is in the past but data which represents future. In this way you will avoid many amendments in segmentation and expose importance of consensus forecasting.

Let us go through key ABC segmentation considerations:

ABCD Consensus Unconstrained Forecast Value Proxy Benefits

- Align your segmentation to forecasted SKU market position for selected horizon.
- Drive focus based on revenue.
- Incorporate new products positioning based on their forecasted value.
- Leverage sales, marketing, demand planning insights, and knowledge captured in your consensus forecast.
- Enable selection of an appropriate horizon and time, which drives connection to your strategies and tactics incorporated in consensus forecast.
- Simplicity.

ABCD Level

- Geographical: Specific business unit/country.
- Example on country S&OP process, where the objective will be to facilitate their local process and improve focus on SKUs with high revenue contribution.
- Material hierarchy level: Sellable SKUs. Normally in company definition, there are SKUs which you do not sell; select the ones which you do sell and forecast. You may apply filters to select right portfolio for your segmentation.

ABCD Measure

- Consensus unconstrained forecast volume multiplied with forecasted sales price (probably average net sales price). This measure needs to be configured in your system first.

ABCD Thresholds (For Data Sorted Descending)

- $A$ products: $0\% \leq A \leq 80\%$.
- $B$ products: $80\% < B \leq 95\%$.
- $C$ products: $95\% < C \leq 100\%$.
- $D$ products: Nonmoving products where forecasted volume or forecasted price are set to zero or the ones decided my marketing to be withdrawn from your offering. This segment requires special attention (see Fig. 5.30).

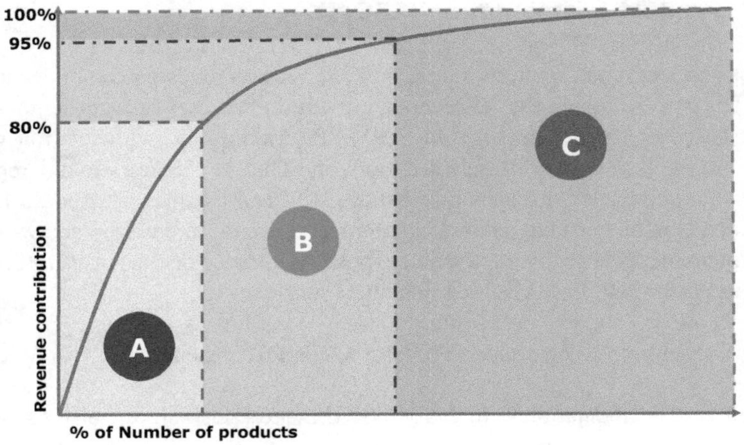


**Fig. 5.30** ABC segmentation based on revenue contribution

ABCD Timing

- Time: it would make sense to select period around which your forecasting might be used as input for next year budgeting process. It will help you to align in some way portfolio positioning between your annual budgeting and monthly forecasting process, in cycle which is relevant for your business.
- Example: in September company A does use consensus unconstrained forecast as primary input for their budgeting process. Agreed consensus forecast is being integrated with their budgeting application. You may consider to run portfolio segmentation in that period.

ABCD Horizon

- Horizon: it need to fit the purpose of reflecting forward looking picture but not the short, to be aligned to your strategic positioning.
- Example: if you are starting your budgeting period in August/September and use forecast as baseline input, it would make sense to use forecast from September current year until end of next year.
- Example: You may think as well to run portfolio segmentation before and after main season with horizon linked to in season and after season. You could select your season months and run product segmentation to support strategies and tactics defined for it and then after the season recalculate to change the focus.

ABCD Calculation

- Calculation would run for all sellable SKUs.
- Step 1 will calculate total revenue expressed in consensus forecast value key figure.

- Step 2 will calculate each SKU contribution and sort descending.
- Step 3 will assign and visualize value of ABCD in pre-configured earlier attribute for this segmentation.

ABCD Process

- See process framework for details.
- Based on calculated ABCD, your demand planning team needs to seek approval and maybe some amendments to segmentation with sales and marketing.
- Once agreement is achieved, it would need to be recorded in attribute which you would like to make editable for that purpose.
- Example: one calculated ABCD attribute and one editable ABCD attribute for which values are pre-filled based on calculated ABCD.

### 5.1.7 SAP Use Case: "ABCD" Revenue-Driven Product Segmentation

SAP IBP provides a comprehensive and easy-to-use Fiori app for defining segmentation profiles that contain configuration details and rules for classification. Segmentation profiles can be used for attributes available in the data model, e.g., material hierarchy attributes, customer hierarchy attributes, services, etc. Segmentation process may look like in Fig. 5.31.

In order to be able to leverage the capabilities of SAP IBP, the planning model structure has to comprise the segmentation characteristics that will allow classification to be executed as per the needs identified by the business:

- Which measure(s) is going to serve as basis for classification execution, e.g., revenue, profit contribution? Listing possible measures will help identifying the planning level where the characteristics must be assigned.
- What are the planning objects/levels that are going to be considered (e.g., product, customer, product-customer, etc.)? Answering this question will provide the basis for adapting the planning model by attaching the ABC attributes to the right master data object(s).

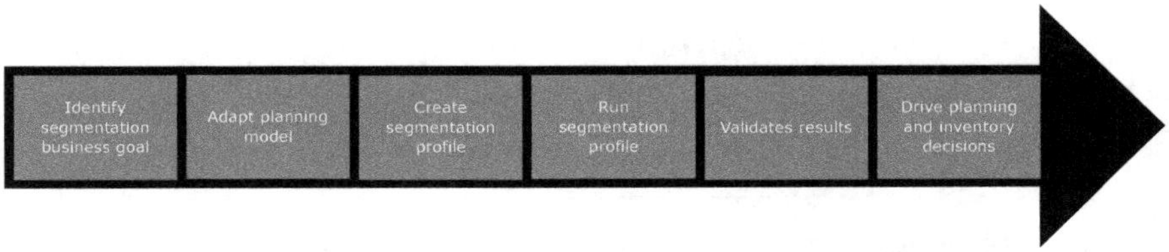


**Fig. 5.31** Segmentation steps

Once prerequisites (e.g., goals and level) are established, we can go ahead and define the segmentation profile. Each segmentation profile can be used in different planning types (operational, tactical, and strategic). You may have multiple segmentation profiles to support different processes on different organizational level.

Segmentation profiles have:

1. Input parameters:
   (a) Target attribute to store the results of segmentation
   (b) Input measure (key figure) based on which classification will run (Fig. 5.32)
2. Time setting:
   (a) Periodicity—defines the time level for calculation (e.g., consensus demand plan revenue weekly as minimum periodicity, but the calculation can run also on an aggregate level like month).
   (b) Define the time buckets (past, future, past and future) that form the calculation horizon.

3. Segmentation measure and thresholds to be considered.
4. Locking attribute—maintaining this attribute with value X will lock the planning object from being updated during segmentation run. This can be applicable for products with different behaviors that can be categorized by sales and marketing teams as "D" category: nonmoving products, end of life, exceptions, etc. (Fig. 5.33).

Applying the Pareto principle, the calculation logic behind ABC consists mainly in sorting the planning objects in decreasing sequence of their values and defining which the top, middle, and low classes are. This classification is executed based on one, out of four methods which are available at the definition level of the segmentation profile:

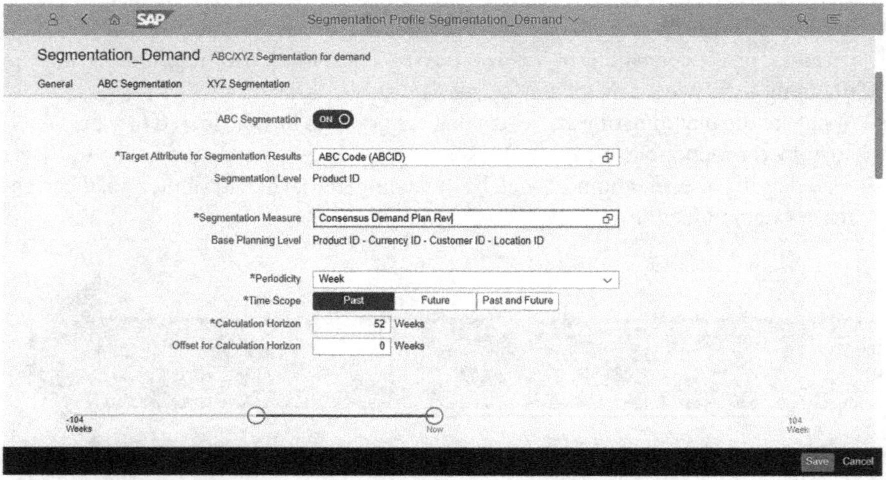


**Fig. 5.32** Product ABC segmentation—configuration step 1

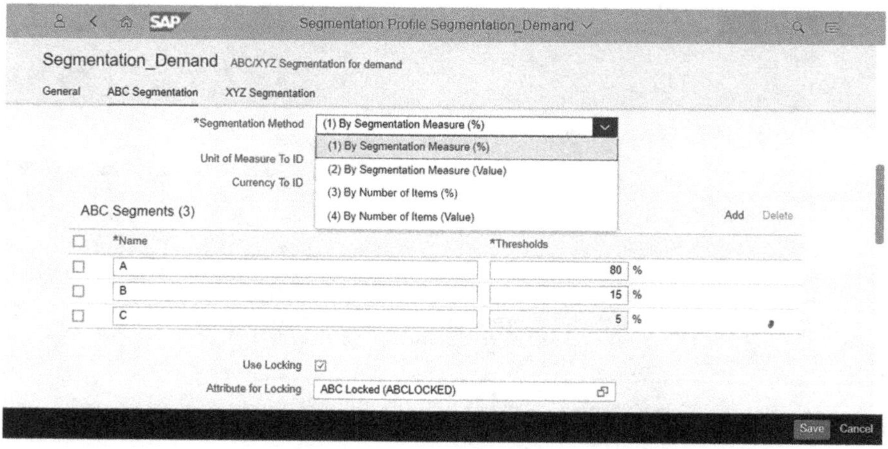


**Fig. 5.33** Product ABC segmentation—configuration step 2

- By segmentation measure (%)—segments are defined based on the relative cumulative value of each planning object to the overall value of the segmentation profile.
- By segmentation value—segments are defined based on the absolute value of each planning object to the overall value of the segmentation profile.
- By number of items (%)—segments are defined based on the relative number of items that sum up into the value of the segmentation profile.
- By number of items value—segments are defined based on the absolute number of items that sum up into the value of the segmentation profile (e.g., the top 30% or the top 3 should form class A).

Figure 5.34 exemplifies the above four methods on the same dataset, given that we provide as input the thresholds defined in the last row of the table.

ABC segmentation operator is usually scheduled as part of a regular tactical SOP process but can also be triggered ad hoc.

As segmentation results are stored at master data attribute level, being assigned to planning model, visualizing and analyzing ABC segmentation results in connection with complementary measures can be done using Excel and Fiori user interfaces.

One might define several segmentation profiles to cover multiple classifications needs from different areas of the business. We continue this chapter focusing on various examples where product and customer segmentation results can be used to drive demand planning strategy along with supply and inventory optimizations.

As "one size fits all" does not apply when you define product portfolio, having products divided by segments enables decision-makers to better target the elements that drive the revenue growth and adjust the business strategy per each tier.

In Fig. 5.35 we see a classification of consensus demand plan rev and consensus demand qty by product segments. When we drill down to A and B classes in a

| Product | FY Consensus Plan Rev. | Method 1 | Method 2 | Method 3 | Method 4 |
|---|---|---|---|---|---|
| IBP-300 | 332.2M$ | A | A | A | A |
| IBP-310 | 170.3M$ | A | A | A | A |
| IBP-210 | 158.5M$ | A | A | A | A |
| IBP-200 | 89.3M$ | A | B | A | B |
| IBP-220 | 65.8M$ | B | B | A | B |
| IBP-120 | 45.4M$ | B | B | B | B |
| IBP-110 | 34.1M$ | B | C | B | C |
| IBP-100 | 23.4M$ | C | C | B | C |
| IBP-320 | 18.4M$ | C | C | C | C |
| Total | 937.23M$ | | | | |

| | Method 1 | Method 2 | Method 3 | Method 4 |
|---|---|---|---|---|
| Method thresholds: | 0% ≤ A ≤ 80%<br>80% < B ≤ 95%<br>95% < C ≤ 100% | A - 660M$<br>B - 200M$<br>C - remaining | A - first 55% of items<br>B - next 35%<br>C - remaining | A - first 3 items<br>B - second best 3<br>C - remaining |

**Fig. 5.34** Product ABC segmentation comparison of thresholds methods

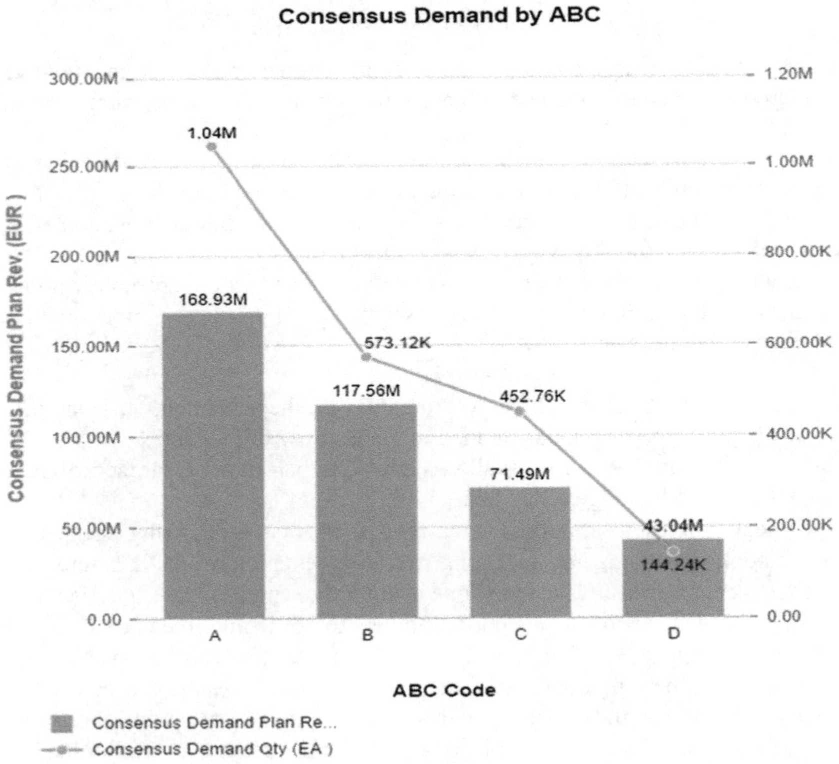


**Fig. 5.35** ABC per consensus forecast revenue and quantity

glance, we see the products that generate more than 80% of the revenue and find areas of improvements which would make an impact:

- What is the forecast quality of products from segment A?
- What is the ABC mix per product family?
- Are there opportunities to discontinue some C class products?
- How do segments react to various events?

Further, with the help of IBP Control Tower alerting capability, planners can define and subscribe to alerts that are generated and customized at segment level, e.g., different threshold points for alerting trigger.

### 5.1.8 Customer and Services Segmentation (ABC)

As not all customers are similar in the value they bring to your organization, segmenting them using ABC operator can help identifying the group that should be served with highest service and responsiveness level. Multiple measures can stay at the basis of analysis: generated revenue, expected revenue, gross profit contribution, etc.

We have seen a case where customer segmentation analysis triggered from S&OP process became an "eye opener" to change customer service approach. Marketing with management made decision which customers / customer group to serve with standard offering which with premium and which with surcharges. This approach could lead to further differentiation and optimization of your profits and efficiency. We have seen that customer segmentation was used in short-term operational planning process to allocate products in case of shortages to most important customers. This is not a theory; many companies do that.

You may attempt to segment your services by revenue, cost, and workload associated with it. In case, in your business model, services play important role and generate substantial revenue and cost or are simply critical to your offering, most probably it would make sense to forecast them and optimize planning and execution process through segmentation.

### 5.1.9 SAP Use Case: Customer Profit-Based Segmentation

Segmentation of customers may have many use cases, e.g., customer segmentation can drive a demand fulfillment prioritization rule in the supply run optimization.

Below, we see the profile that was defined for the customer segmentation. Therefore, the segmentation level is represented by the customer ID (Fig. 5.36). At the end of the segmentation process, the customers will be categorized based on the past 12 months of historical gross profit following a Pareto ABC distribution of 80-15-5.

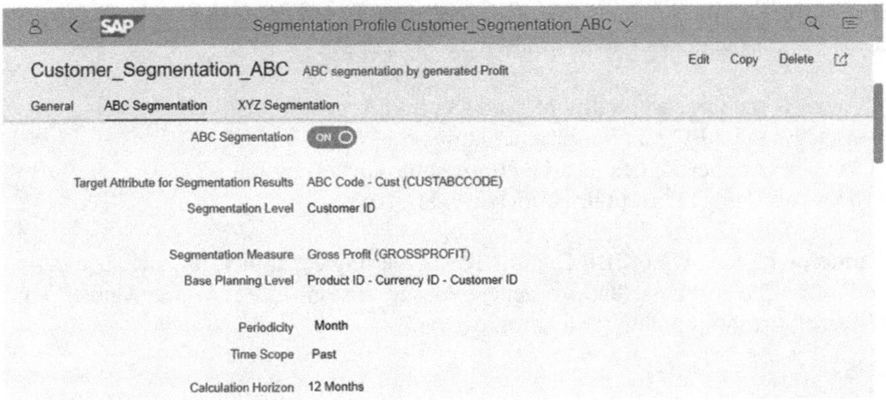


**Fig. 5.36** Customer segmentation ABC

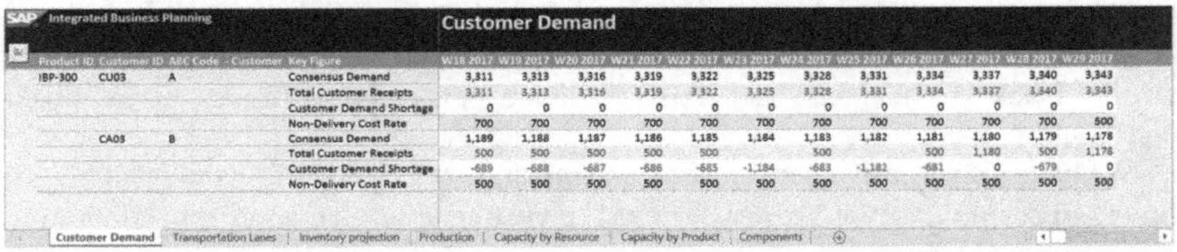


| Product ID | Customer ID | ABC Code - Customer | Key Figure | W18 2017 | W19 2017 | W20 2017 | W21 2017 | W22 2017 | W23 2017 | W24 2017 | W25 2017 | W26 2017 | W27 2017 | W28 2017 | W29 2017 |
|---|---|---|---|---|---|---|---|---|---|---|---|---|---|---|---|
| IBP-300 | CU03 | A | Consensus Demand | 3,311 | 3,313 | 3,316 | 3,319 | 3,322 | 3,325 | 3,328 | 3,331 | 3,334 | 3,337 | 3,340 | 3,343 |
| | | | Total Customer Receipts | 3,311 | 3,313 | 3,316 | 3,319 | 3,322 | 3,325 | 3,328 | 3,331 | 3,334 | 3,337 | 3,340 | 3,343 |
| | | | Customer Demand Shortage | 0 | 0 | 0 | 0 | 0 | 0 | 0 | 0 | 0 | 0 | 0 | 0 |
| | | | Non-Delivery Cost Rate | 700 | 700 | 700 | 700 | 700 | 700 | 700 | 700 | 700 | 700 | 700 | 500 |
| | CA03 | B | Consensus Demand | 1,189 | 1,188 | 1,187 | 1,186 | 1,185 | 1,184 | 1,183 | 1,182 | 1,181 | 1,180 | 1,179 | 1,178 |
| | | | Total Customer Receipts | 500 | 500 | 500 | 500 | 500 | | 500 | | 500 | 1,180 | 500 | 1,178 |
| | | | Customer Demand Shortage | -689 | -688 | -687 | -686 | -685 | -1,184 | -683 | -1,182 | -681 | 0 | -679 | 0 |
| | | | Non-Delivery Cost Rate | 500 | 500 | 500 | 500 | 500 | 500 | 500 | 500 | 500 | 500 | 500 | 500 |



**Fig. 5.37** Optimized supply differentiated by customer segmentation ABC

Thinking how to leverage the segmentation results, we will correlate the customer segmentation with the nondelivery cost rate, one of the costs that are used as input in the supply optimization operator. When implementing the supply optimizer, you can choose to go with the real costs or simulated costs that will drive the optimizer to compute a plan toward a certain pattern.

The nondelivery cost rate represents the cost of the lost revenue as it is defined as the cost per unit for the customer demand quantity that is not possible to be met by the supply plan. It can be equal with the sales price, or it can be augmented with some additional costs that would reflect the customer trust loss or image loss as a result of non-fulfilling customer demand and impacting the customer service level.

The product IBP-300 from below planning view screenshot has a differentiated nondelivery cost rate based on the customer segment. As the customer segment A has a higher nondelivery rate than customer from class B, in case of product availability constraint, the demand fulfillment will serve customer segment A with priority, as the penalty cost in case of non-fulfillment would be higher than for customer segment B (Fig. 5.37).

As highlighted in product segmentation ABC chapter, you can use any measure like revenue, profit, or cost contribution as proxy for customer segmentation.

### 5.1.10 Product Segmentation with Customer Weighting

We have seen that it was very important for many of our customers to know which categories of customers are behind product segments and if it should impact the way we operate planning processes, e.g., tactical allocation planning. Product segmentation weighted with customer importance was found as very helpful. Customer segmentation can be plugged into single or bidimensional product segmentation. Main purpose of merging segmentations is to better differentiate ways of working and if possible introduce differentiated response. You may use following process as reference (Fig. 5.38).

This type of weighted segmentation may have very good application in operational planning.

Let us explain you the concept in few steps:

1. We run product segmentation based on future/expected profit contribution.
2. We run customer segmentation based on future/expected profit contribution.
3. We run weighing of product segmentation based on customer ratio per product category, e.g., customer A class per product class C (see Fig. 5.39).

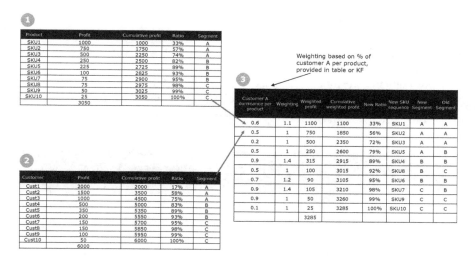

**Fig. 5.38** Weighting portfolio segmentation with customer segmentation

1

| Product | Profit | Cumulative profit | Ratio | Segment |
|---|---|---|---|---|
| SKU1 | 1000 | 1000 | 33% | A |
| SKU2 | 750 | 1750 | 57% | A |
| SKU3 | 500 | 2250 | 74% | A |
| SKU4 | 250 | 2500 | 82% | B |
| SKU5 | 225 | 2725 | 89% | B |
| SKU6 | 100 | 2825 | 93% | B |
| SKU7 | 75 | 2900 | 95% | B |
| SKU8 | 75 | 2975 | 98% | C |
| SKU9 | 50 | 3025 | 99% | C |
| SKU10 | 25 | 3050 | 100% | C |
| | 3050 | | | |

2

| Customer | Profit | Cumulative profit | Ratio | Segment |
|---|---|---|---|---|
| Cust1 | 2000 | 2000 | 17% | A |
| Cust2 | 1500 | 3500 | 58% | A |
| Cust3 | 1000 | 4500 | 75% | A |
| Cust4 | 500 | 5000 | 83% | B |
| Cust5 | 350 | 5350 | 89% | B |
| Cust6 | 200 | 5550 | 93% | B |
| Cust7 | 150 | 5700 | 95% | C |
| Cust8 | 150 | 5850 | 98% | C |
| Cust9 | 100 | 5950 | 99% | C |
| Cust10 | 50 | 6000 | 100% | C |
| | 6000 | | | |

Weighting based on % of customer A per product, provided in table or KF

3

| Customer A dominance per product | Weighting | Weighted profit | Cumulative weighted profit | New Ratio | New SKU sequence | New Segment | Old Segment |
|---|---|---|---|---|---|---|---|
| 0.6 | 1.1 | 1100 | 1100 | 33% | SKU1 | A | A |
| 0.5 | 1 | 750 | 1850 | 56% | SKU2 | A | A |
| 0.2 | 1 | 500 | 2350 | 72% | SKU3 | A | A |
| 0.5 | 1 | 250 | 2600 | 79% | SKU5 | A | B |
| 0.9 | 1.4 | 315 | 2915 | 89% | SKU4 | B | B |
| 0.5 | 1 | 100 | 3015 | 92% | SKU8 | B | C |
| 0.7 | 1.2 | 90 | 3105 | 95% | SKU6 | B | B |
| 0.9 | 1.4 | 105 | 3210 | 98% | SKU7 | C | B |
| 0.9 | 1 | 50 | 3260 | 99% | SKU9 | C | C |
| 0.1 | 1 | 25 | 3285 | 100% | SKU10 | C | C |
| | | 3285 | | | | | |

**Fig. 5.39** Weighting product segmentation with customer segmentation

### 5.1.11 SAP Use Case: Product Segmentation Weighted With Customer Segments

Another way of running the segmentation is to use a combination of product and customer segmentation, resulting into a product segmentation weighted by the customers that are driving the sales for those products. Once product and customer segmentation are executed separately, we need to define the ratio which represents the contribution of ABC customers per each product. This ratio is represented in Fig. 5.40 in the key figure Cust ABC dominance per Prod.

The ratio is one example of custom calculation that can be achieved from the key figure configuration menu. The logic is easy to implement, but it requires few intermediate calculations. In this example, we used the gross profit as input for the calculation as we needed to identify what is the customer segment contribution to the product gross profit.

First, we enhanced the key figure definition of the gross profit by adding an extra calculation which aggregates the gross profit across customers at product level (GROSSPROFIT@WKPRODCURR).

Then, we aggregated the gross profit into a helper key figure which is defined at a new planning level that contains the product ID and the customer segment as a root (GROSSPROFIT@WKPRODCUSTSEGCURR). This was technically required to be executed in a separate key figure, reason why we used a helper key figure—not needed for display in Excel UI.

Last we used the above aggregations of the gross profit key figure in the calculation definition of the ratio which is named Cust ABC dominance per Prod (GROSSPROFIT@WKPRODCUSTSEGCURR/GROSSPROFIT@WKPRODCURR).

Demand manager based on alignment with sales and marketing should define weighting which will be recorded and used to adjust base measure for ABC product segmentation. In system example above, it will be about adjusting gross profit used as segmentation measure.

Defined weighing can be specified as 1 in case we do not have many A class customers behind the products and can be above 1 if we have a lot of A class customers buying the product.

Once column "weighting" is updated, it will impact weighted gross profit column. Weighted gross profit will be the base measure in new product ABC segmentation profile created for that type of weighted segmentation.

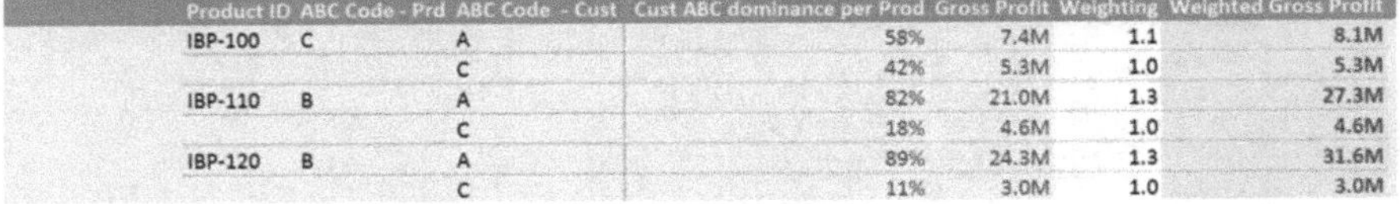

SAP Integrated Business Planning — Weighted Segmentation

| Product ID | ABC Code - Prd | ABC Code - Cust | Cust ABC dominance per Prod | Gross Profit | Weighting | Weighted Gross Profit |
|---|---|---|---|---|---|---|
| IBP-100 | C | A | 58% | 7.4M | 1.1 | 8.1M |
| | | C | 42% | 5.3M | 1.0 | 5.3M |
| IBP-110 | B | A | 82% | 21.0M | 1.3 | 27.3M |
| | | C | 18% | 4.6M | 1.0 | 4.6M |
| IBP-120 | B | A | 89% | 24.3M | 1.3 | 31.6M |
| | | C | 11% | 3.0M | 1.0 | 3.0M |

**Fig. 5.40** Product ABC segmentation weighted with customer segments (step 1)

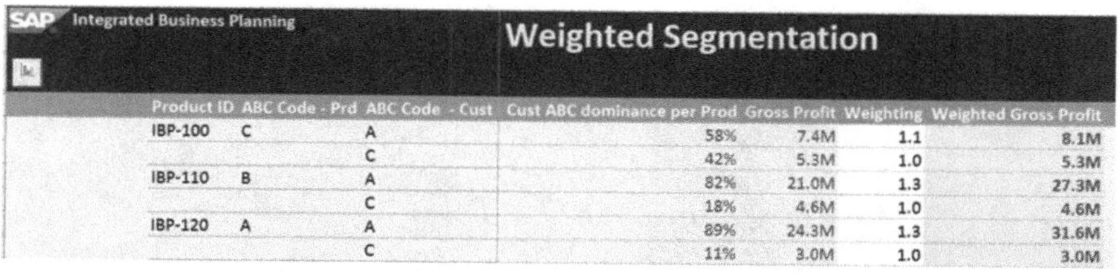

Integrated Business Planning

Weighted Segmentation

| Product ID | ABC Code - Prd | ABC Code - Cust | Cust ABC dominance per Prod | Gross Profit | Weighting | Weighted Gross Profit |
|---|---|---|---|---|---|---|
| IBP-100 | C | A | 58% | 7.4M | 1.1 | 8.1M |
| | | C | 42% | 5.3M | 1.0 | 5.3M |
| IBP-110 | B | A | 82% | 21.0M | 1.3 | 27.3M |
| | | C | 18% | 4.6M | 1.0 | 4.6M |
| IBP-120 | A | A | 89% | 24.3M | 1.3 | 31.6M |
| | | C | 11% | 3.0M | 1.0 | 3.0M |

**Fig. 5.41** Product ABC segmentation weighted with customer segments (step 2)

After customer weighting, product segmentation looks like in Fig. 5.41.

Notice change of classification for product IBP-120; compare Fig. 5.40 product ABC segmentation weighted with customer segments (step 1) and Fig. 5.41 product ABC segmentation weighted with customer segments (step 2).

### 5.1.12 Multidimensional E2E Supply Chain Segmentation

More advanced multidimensional segmentation may help you to define E2E differentiated response supported by replenishment strategies with optimized cost to serve ratio. ABC or ABC/XYZ segmentation models mentioned above were targeted to optimize dedicated part of IBP process or to optimize supply chain but in simple operations network. Model which could be defined with help of advanced analytics and advanced clustering techniques can open doors for end-to-end optimization of complex supply network. Advanced approach and modeling requires much more sophisticated set of skills, capabilities, and significantly larger amount of data.

Diagram in Fig. 5.42 illustrates approach to develop E2E supply chain segmentation with use of advanced analytics from data coming from unified data model, e.g., IBP data model. Unified data model will facilitate data integrity and data availability. Descriptive, diagnostic, and predictive analytics connected together will help you to understand options for SC strategies and predict their impact.

Few words about the model characteristics. Heart of the model is formed by attributes/variables which will be used in clustering analysis. Attributes should characterize real demand profiles and supply/operations processes which some of them you see on left-hand side of Fig. 5.42. Developing such a segmentation model is challenging. It would be fair to say and not to aim to deliver it in one step on global scale, but rather to try to organize proof of concept first. Complexity of data attributes being used in definition of E2E supply chain and operations strategies may substantially vary across industries and companies. Above model could be adapted to your environment and capabilities. One thing is for sure, which is substantially different to the other segmentation models, usage of such a model requires, on business side, high degree of cross-functional integration and consensus. Usage of such model on IT side requires solid data scientist capability to develop

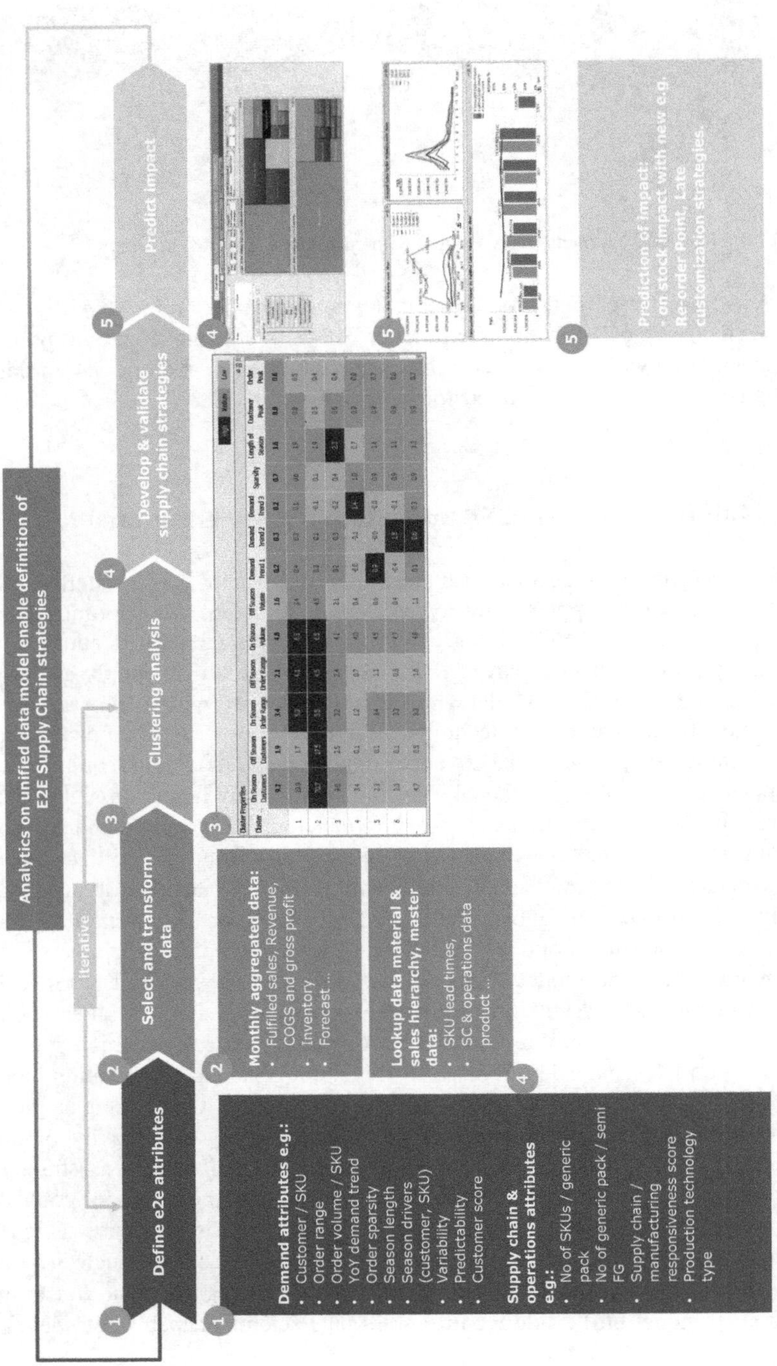


**Fig. 5.42** E2E supply chain segmentation with advanced analytics

clustering, define data discover options, and enable proper prediction of impact. Last but not the least, right leader and support are essential.

Advanced analytics initiative can help you to define what type of supply chain segmentation your business model should aim to operate. Knowing types of supply chain segmentation and their key characteristics is therefore important. Gartner (Davis 2011, 2012) defines and characterizes following supply chain segments:

- **No segmentation:** very short-term improvements with cost reductions only for local functional areas, mostly improving internal complexity with no clear targets and metrics.
- **Internal product/supply network:** employing the knowledge of SKU history (volume and variability) can lead to simple in certain extend agile responsive supply chain based on some differentiation in metrics targets.
- **Channel-back:** doing a backward value analysis starting from partners and markets, allowing then to segment the supply chain by such parameters as speed to market, predictability, availability, cost, etc. In this case channel requirements drive targets and objectives, where business case is about both customer satisfaction and revenue/profit growth.
- **End-user-back:** analyzing the trade-offs that end users value. These values include price, cost, on-shelf availability, value-added services, packaging, etc. The segmentation of supply chain is then done based on end-user "values," rather than based on geography or industry. This segmentation aims to balance planned cost/service trade-offs and create value for end user.

### 5.1.13 Product "Risks and Opportunities" and Assumptions

Risks and opportunities related to product review may influence many activities from demand shaping, integrated reconciliation, and supply availability to projected performance against the plan (budget). There might be various scenarios, e.g.:

- Registration of the product is delayed and how it impacts full-year result projection.
- Phase-in and phase-out have simple cannibalization of demand.
- New product trials block capacity on assets for other regular items.
- Tactical make-or-buy decision is needed to address exposed capacity gap vs unconstrained market forecast.

What you should consider when modeling in IBP process risk and opportunities related to product (Fig. 5.43):

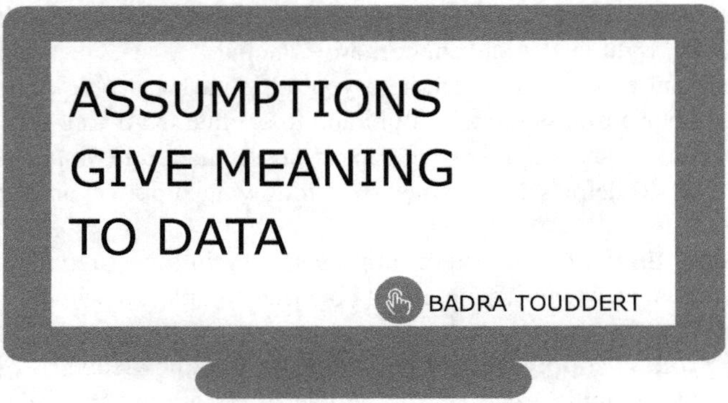


**Fig. 5.43** Assumptions give meaning to what-if analysis, to data

- Timing—of risk and opportunity.
- Level—(combination of material/commercial hierarchy) on which risk and opportunity will be captured.
- Make it up to date through demand planner connection to typical product stage gate review meetings.
- Make it part of the process by assigning accountability to product (portfolio) managers.

Assumptions in IBP scenario planning have same magnitude of importance as volumetric and value data. Let us focus on assumption being captured on qualitative input.

How to design the process to capture assumptions, how far we should be structured to allow easier analysis, how much we should be just descriptive—those are the questions you should raise in design. We highlight to you two out of many examples of how companies deal with capturing assumptions:

- Assumptions were structured according to definition provided by marketing. Structure was fully aligned to company business drivers which were normally updated as standard step in demand review. Assumptions visualization did present growth, stable, or decline trend over the years for specific level in organizational/material/commercial structure. Forecast updates gathered in qualitative input had to be linked to structure of business drivers (presented in the system as reason codes). This way of approaching the solution could open doors for analysis of forecast changes vs business drivers, and this ladies and gentlemen is already a value of its own.
- Assumptions were captured as free text mainly in demand review preparation process step. Assumptions were captured on various levels, e.g., SKU/country or customer or product line, but consolidated and distributed mainly to supply organization as standard deliverable of monthly demand review process step. Simple word template was used to capture assumption which then has been reviewed.

### 5.1.14 SAP Use Case: Product Phase-In Impacts Profit Projections

A successful Integrated Business Process review enables teams from various departments of the organization to achieve strategic alignment by helping each other to answer questions that arise in the decision-making process:

- Is it worth struggling to meet the extra demand—is it still profitable?
- Which sourcing decisions are optimizing the supply plan to drive the profit maximization?
- Do we achieve a break even sales volume for all products?

Business will understand what are the implications of various events that happen or might happen and not only the implications on the operational side but also on the financial performance. A mature process executed with the SAP IBP technology will reveal where are the performance gaps, facilitate the root cause identification and analysis, and provide support in the collaborative decision-making process.

Moving to an example which is meant to highlight how IBP can support profitability analysis, we start from the last integrated business plan where the phase-in calendar of a new enhanced product was agreed. This new product was developed on basis of an existing product but with market declining trend. To keep investment at minimum, the phase-in was planned in 6 months' time. Competition started an aggressive price reduction campaign for a similar product with the one we had in portfolio. It was observed that sales for an old product started to drop faster than expected. There were questions asked: What are the sales and marketing latest projections? Is there any action plan in place to cope with bigger gap to budget profits? If plans are confirmed, do we accept gap to budget? In this situation collaboration was essential, so a "case" was created to engage the sales and marketing teams (see Fig. 5.44).

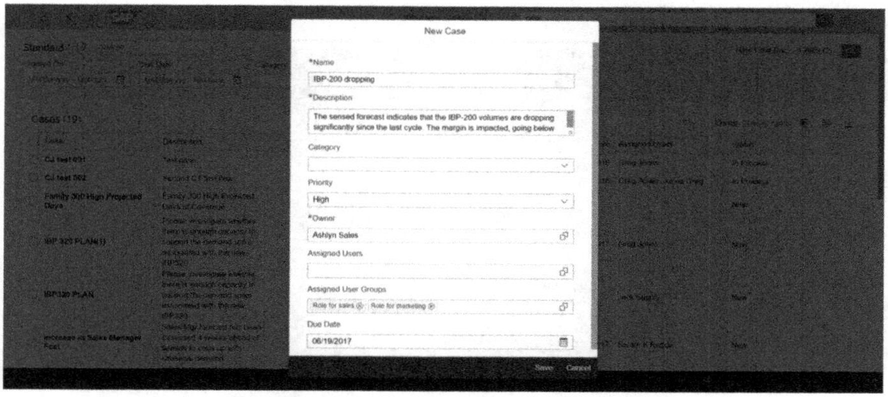


**Fig. 5.44** Supply chain control tower case

The sales representative needed to revise his projection and confirm the drop of the demand. This triggered a new consensus demand which was translated in margin decrease, moving the operating profit below the budgeted target and capacity sub-utilization.

Based on these new numbers, product manager with demand planner organized a meeting with sales, marketing, finance, and supply teams. They have asked themselves a question if there could be an option to utilize the extra capacity for the new product and bring forward the phase-in date? They all agree on the criticality of introducing the new product as this will offer a competitive advantage. The product was initially planned to hit the market in 6 months' time as one of the main component comes from an oversee supplier that has a long lead time. But there was an option to go for air freight delivery for few initial batches in parallel with sea freight delivery. Before checking with the supplier, they wanted to see the financial impact. For a better assessment, we chose to leverage the version capability of IBP:

- Base version shows the projection based on the current plan where the new product introduction is scheduled for February 2018.
- Accelerated version is computed based on the accelerated plan where the introduction of the IBP-210 is moved forward to November 2017.

Assumptions of the accelerated versions were the following:

- Margin is lower in the first months due to the special transportation mode.
- Shifting forward the release data with 3 months will cannibalize earlier the demand of IBP-200.
- Production needs to be planned accordingly to minimize the obsolete inventory levels of IBP-200.

We see in Fig. 5.45 that the accelerated version comes with better gross profit projection than in the current plan.

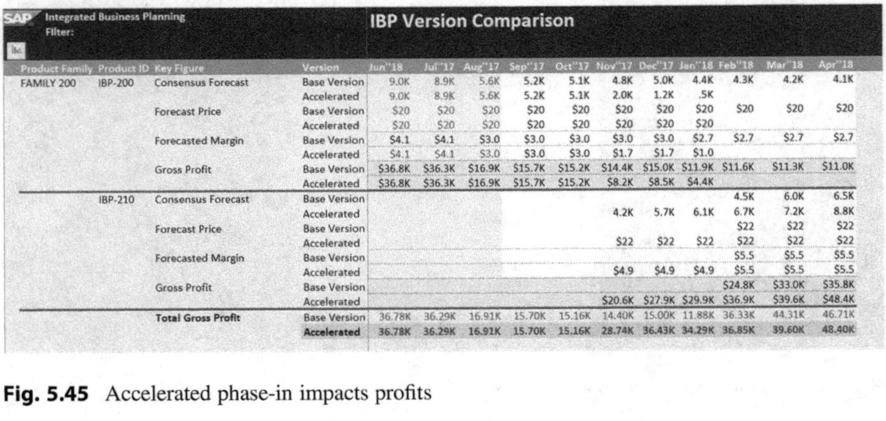
SAP Integrated Business Planning
Filter:
IBP Version Comparison

| Product Family | Product ID | Key Figure | Version | Jun"18 | Jul"17 | Aug"17 | Sep"17 | Oct"17 | Nov"17 | Dec"17 | Jan"18 | Feb"18 | Mar"18 | Apr"18 |
|---|---|---|---|---|---|---|---|---|---|---|---|---|---|---|
| FAMILY 200 | IBP-200 | Consensus Forecast | Base Version | 9.0K | 8.9K | 5.6K | 5.2K | 5.1K | 4.8K | 5.0K | 4.4K | 4.3K | 4.2K | 4.1K |
| | | | Accelerated | 9.0K | 8.9K | 5.6K | 5.2K | 5.1K | 2.0K | 1.2K | .5K | | | |
| | | Forecast Price | Base Version | $20 | $20 | $20 | $20 | $20 | $20 | $20 | $20 | $20 | $20 | $20 |
| | | | Accelerated | $20 | $20 | $20 | $20 | $20 | $20 | $20 | $20 | | | |
| | | Forecasted Margin | Base Version | $4.1 | $4.1 | $3.0 | $3.0 | $3.0 | $3.0 | $3.0 | $2.7 | $2.7 | $2.7 | $2.7 |
| | | | Accelerated | $4.1 | $4.1 | $3.0 | $3.0 | $3.0 | $1.7 | $1.7 | $1.0 | | | |
| | | Gross Profit | Base Version | $36.8K | $36.3K | $16.9K | $15.7K | $15.2K | $14.4K | $15.0K | $11.9K | $11.6K | $11.3K | $11.0K |
| | | | Accelerated | $36.8K | $36.3K | $16.9K | $15.7K | $15.2K | $8.2K | $8.5K | $4.4K | | | |
| | IBP-210 | Consensus Forecast | Base Version | | | | | | | | | 4.5K | 6.0K | 6.5K |
| | | | Accelerated | | | | | | 4.2K | 5.7K | 6.1K | 6.7K | 7.2K | 8.8K |
| | | Forecast Price | Base Version | | | | | | | | | $22 | $22 | $22 |
| | | | Accelerated | | | | | | $22 | $22 | $22 | $22 | $22 | $22 |
| | | Forecasted Margin | Base Version | | | | | | | | | $5.5 | $5.5 | $5.5 |
| | | | Accelerated | | | | | | $4.9 | $4.9 | $4.9 | $5.5 | $5.5 | $5.5 |
| | | Gross Profit | Base Version | | | | | | | | | $24.8K | $33.0K | $35.8K |
| | | | Accelerated | | | | | | $20.6K | $27.9K | $29.9K | $36.9K | $39.6K | $48.4K |
| | | **Total Gross Profit** | Base Version | 36.78K | 36.29K | 16.91K | 15.70K | 15.16K | 14.40K | 15.00K | 11.88K | 36.33K | 44.31K | 46.71K |
| | | | **Accelerated** | 36.78K | 36.29K | 16.91K | 15.70K | 15.16K | 28.74K | 36.43K | 34.29K | 36.85K | 39.60K | 48.40K |

**Fig. 5.45** Accelerated phase-in impacts profits

Based on this analysis, the buyer checked with the supplier where he is able to support the component delivery ahead of the initial schedule and ramp up his production with a faster pace. As the supplier confirms this flexibility, the accelerated version plan will be promoted/copied to the base version.

## 5.2 Demand Review

### 5.2.1 What Shall You Forecast

Did you ask yourself, what shall you forecast? The answer is quite easy; you should forecast what market demands!

Very often companies mix sales forecast (market demand), operational plan, and sales targets. Sales forecast is a demand projection, provided with a set of environmental assumptions. Operational plan is a set of operational actions required to reach sales forecast regardless of the outcome. Sales target are sales goals established to motivate sales and marketing staff (Mentzer and Moon 2004).

We should aim to become demand driven and should not neglect challenges behind degree of transformation, efforts which are required to achieve that. We have seen some companies which have stopped their journey and forecast what they will invoice or do not proceed further in their forecasting maturity. Why do companies do not move further, do not improve, and do not innovate in forecasting and demand planning? Let us list some of the reasons:

- Do not have a champion who is driving change from organizational, process, technology perspective. Very often champion is not aware of technology or heavily underestimates people "change" impact.
- Cannot align and agree with the changes between global and local organizations. Governance of the change is often not balanced between organizational, processes, and technology. Particular interests and not the common goal drive willingness to change.
- Do not recognize what talents are needed, where they are, and what skills are needed. Very often focus is given only to organization structure change but not capabilities and not sustainability.
- There is no awareness of digital technology like SAP IBP, which opens doors to different thinking and breaks barriers which blocked the integration between partners, e.g., use of point of sales data.
- Focus is on "installing" a change and not making it sustainable.
- Data input to forecasting process, e.g., invoice data, is labeled as demand, which is not correct. There are huge differences between invoice and real demand information (see Fig. 5.47)
- IBP process design does not cover impact and required change in connected process areas, e.g., order-to-cash process.

To understand what demand driven could mean, let us quickly go through the simplified supply chain/sales channel figure.

As we see in Fig. 5.46, there are many ways of how products get to end consumer, but essentially there are three categories of selling: sell-in, sell-out, and sell-through. We need to understand those concepts to define what you will forecast:

- Category of selling called sell-through describes what you actually have sold to your consumers.
- Sell-out as you see describes what your distributors/customers of your customers have sold.
- At the very beginning is how many you have shipped (sell-in) into your sales channels.

There are often supply chain configurations that you omit certain category of selling, e.g., you sell to consumers directly without sell-out. Sell-through and sell-in have normally a relationship; some describe it as ratio. The higher the ratio, the more inventory turnover you have. Very often in many industries, sell-in/sell-through arrangement between the businesses partners regulates how returns will be managed.

Let us detail relationship of type of selling and primary data input for forecasting.

In Fig. 5.47 we see correlation of type of customer, type of selling, primary data input for forecasting, transparence use of primary data input brings to organization, maturity/benefits which is needed and possible to achieve, and finally what relative forecast error we normally observe. You should observe this figure row by row and notice the direction of demand-driven transformation which points to consumers and consumer data.

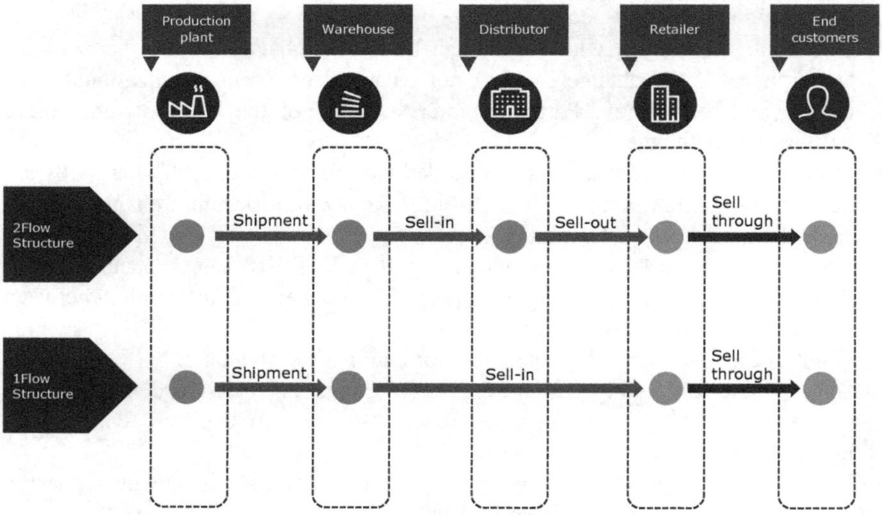


**Fig. 5.46** Sell-in, sell-out, sell-through

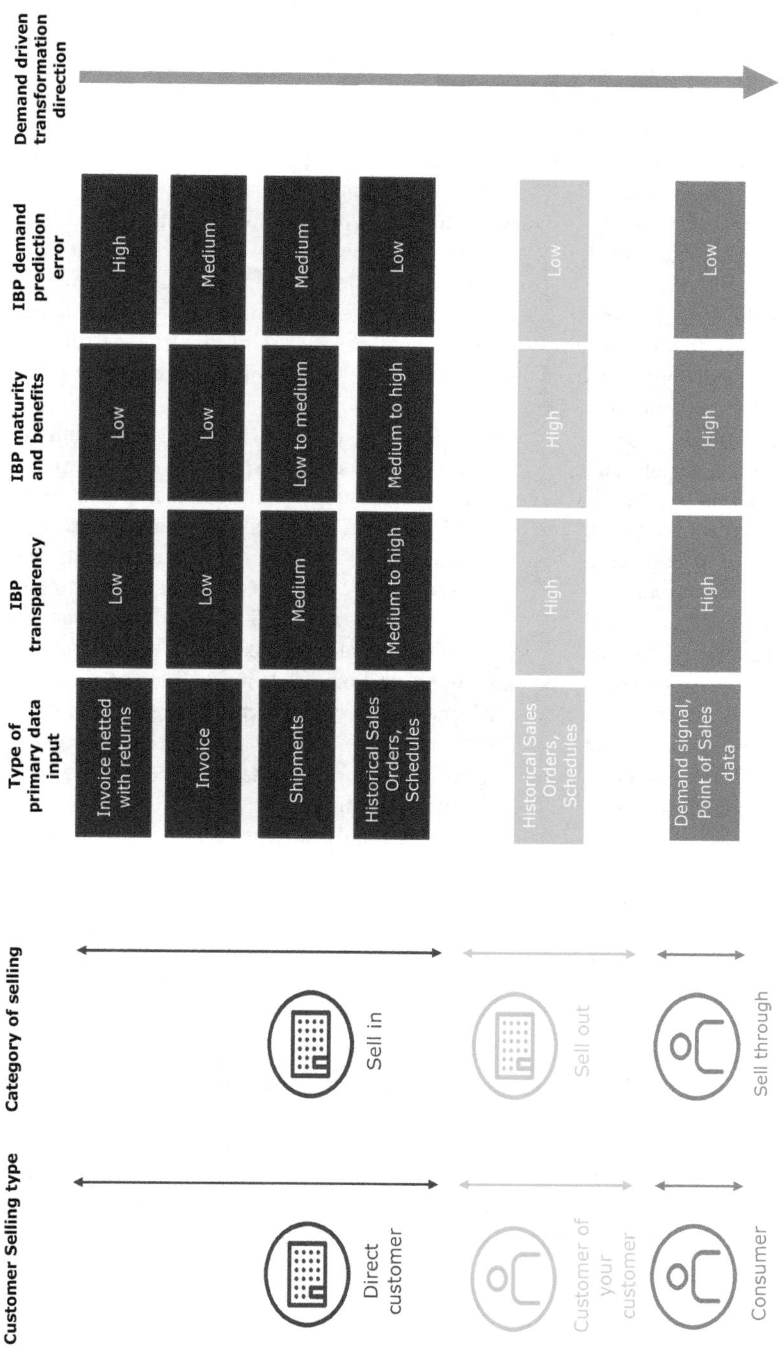


**Fig. 5.47** What shall you forecast, demand-driven transformation direction on forecasting data input example

In sell-in context, forecast should be viewed as a formal request from sales and marketing function to have the products, materials, and capacities available according to the quantity and, at the time that they anticipate the demand will occur from the customer, to ship the product to their premises (Watkins 2014).

Leading practices say that becoming demand driven improves your process performance, transparency, and responsiveness and finally improve shareholder value. Demand driven was proven and shown in many companies' tangible benefits.

In early stage of your transformation journey, you should understand what you forecast now and what you should forecast in the future, how to get where you want to be, and what impact transformation to become demand driven will you have on your organization, processes, and technology. Assessment of your as-is situation, design principles for the future, prioritization of changes, and governance sets the foundation of transformation. Do not proceed too far without foundation in place (see Sect. 1.2.3 for details).

Selection of primary forecasting data input can improve or reduce your opportunity to understand market signals, enable or limit the way you could response to it, and improve or reduce profitability. Selection of primary forecasting data input can create better alignment between functions involved in IBP or actually opposite. In many countries in Europe there is a saying "compare apple with apples", so data input in forecasting and forecasting process output are from same "busket". If we use invoice data as primary input, then we forecast what we invoice and not what market demands! We then forecast ability to invoice customers/distributors, but we do not forecast your potentials on the market! You actually forecast all your constraints supply and financials if you forecast what you invoice. Let us illustrate selection of data input for forecasting with short example:

Business unit management decided to use invoice data as primary forecasting input in IBP. From data perspective it gave them high confidence to be aligned with selected elements of management and finance reporting; from production and supply perspective, it did not give them information to plan when they should have product ready for sales; and from marketing perspective, it did not give them proper input information about what is their unconstrained market potential. What then have they achieved with selecting invoice? They achieved status quo! They have aligned with seven most expensive words in transformation programs:

***We have always done it that way***

Let us illustrate on data example what this decision really meant for end-to-end process.

In Fig. 5.48 we see data inputs layer per layer, from invoices netted with returns (credit notes) to demand quantity on the bottom. On the left-hand side, we see periods and quantities provided by specific data input type. If you select invoice netted with returns, you forecast 80 for next March assuming same level of sales, but actually comparing it to demand qty which says 10 in January and 120 in February makes a huge difference. It happens very often that use of invoice, shipment data is misunderstood as being demand driven or as right demand signal for forecasting

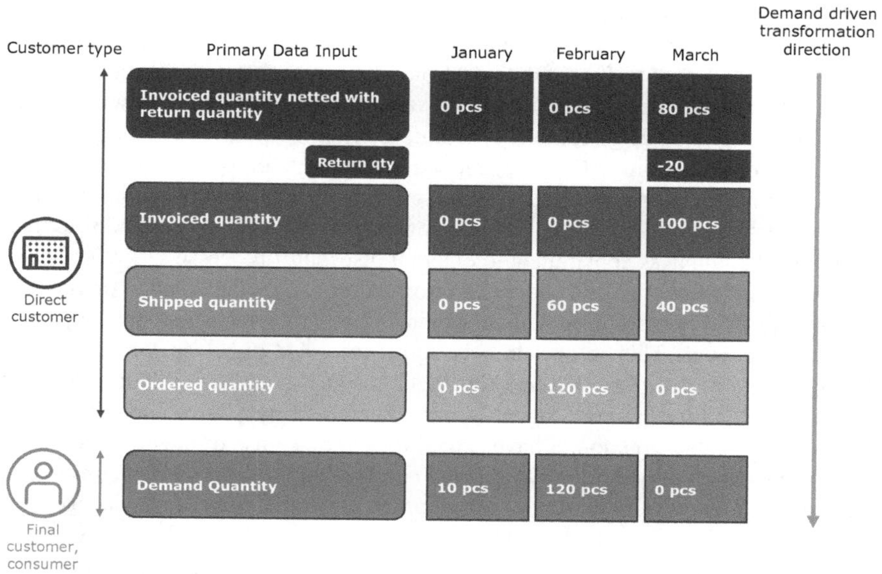


**Fig. 5.48** What you forecast if you select wrong data input

under IBP framework. You see from above figure that quantity which is needed can be differently interpreted depending on primary data input used in the process.

Let us have a bit more detail look how to understand primary data inputs for IBP (as per Fig. 5.48):

**Invoiced qty netted with return**—illustrates case where your main input for forecasting is aligned to financial flow and returns. In this case your data input is biased significantly by invoicing procedures and credit note process. Using this data as main input for forecasting would result in forecasting not what the customer wanted but when customer was invoiced on credit and debit side. Data Input is constrained to financial process constraints.

**Invoice qty**—illustrates case where debit invoices are being used as main data input for forecasting. It does form better signal than invoice netted with returns but still when used in forecasting would represent signal which is biased by internal company invoicing procedures. In this example internal rule says to invoice customer when all shipments from specific order are completed. This rule can substantially change volume assigned to time buckets. Data input is constrained to financial process.

**Shipped qty**—illustrates case where we have change from forecasting aligned to financial flow to material flow. Shipment was realized in two parts due to availability of material and transportation issues. This signal is biased by your internal supply and operations processes. Shortages of product availability and lack of proper transportation option are considered in the data. Data Input is constrained to supply/distribution process.

**Ordered qty**—illustrates case when we take historical orders captured in order-to-cash process. This approach would require to record what the customer really wanted and then classify exceptions from this requirement. Capturing what is needed and when it is needed requires solid order-to-cash process with proper classification of order lines and schedule lines. In this case customer required 120, out of which only 100 were shipped in two parts on periods not aligned to requirement. Signal may be slightly biased by your distributors' policies (direct customers, not consumers), but it is far better than previous invoice and shipment inputs. Data input is constrained to external distributor processes.

**Demand qty**—this is the best source of information to become demand driven, but normally it is not the only source which is used in forecasting unconstrained market demand. This information is combined with direct customers' orders which capture complete demand for direct customers and outputs of consensus demand planning process. Signal is not constrained by your company internal processes (unless you do not have capabilities to make use of the data). Signal is not constrained by your distributors and comes directly from market/consumers. As you see there are quite a few opportunities to improve inventory management when using this signal and reaching out beyond your direct (sell-in) customers. You can eliminate bull whip effect which still is so often big in supply networks.

Closer to demand riven you become better unconstrained forecast you predict. Use unconstrained forecast as input for supply and financial planning. On the other hand, identify gaps with business plan (budget), and define actions to close them (Crum and Palmatier 2003).

There are inevitable challenges on your demand-driven transformation journey which you should be aware of:

- Technology platform and people capabilities to enable collection, integration, analysis, and cleansing of data
- System functionality and people capabilities to enable use of data in forecasting process
- Capabilities to understand impact and correlation of sell-through and sell-in (direct customer data) in context of extended supply chain and value chain

We could think of Fig. 5.49 like context of demand-driven transformation journey.

Becoming demand driven is a journey; it requires strategic thinking and high transformation ability. Going that journey pays off!

Many examples proof that becoming demand driven is not done in one step due to the fact that each component of operating model (system, process, people capabilities) may have different maturity. You can consider transformation in steps. Those steps should not be executed for ages, focus on time to value, and bring change to life step-by-step.

Each step could consist of transformation in processes, systems, and people capabilities not just data which will be used. Our experience says that the lowest

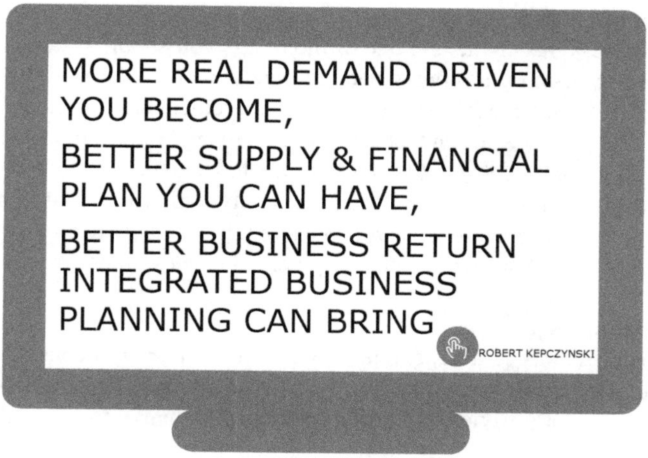


**Fig. 5.49** Becoming demand driven is essential in IBP transformation

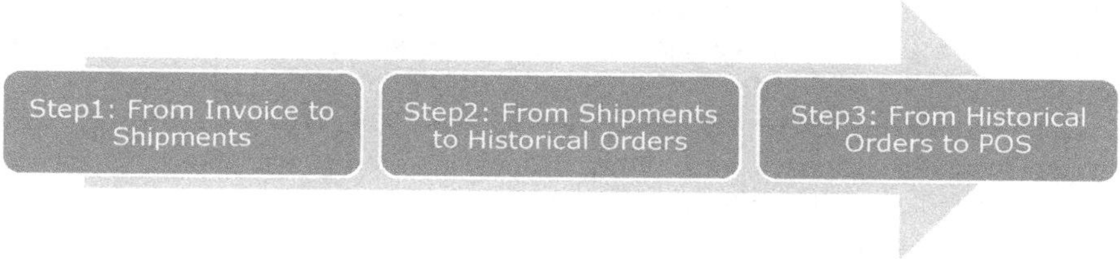


**Fig. 5.50** Demand-driven steps

degree of change is in step 1, and the highest degree of change and benefits may be achieved in step 3 (see Fig. 5.50).

### Transformation Step 1

Firstly, in order to address this challenge, one of the things you should consider to do is separate your debit from credit invoice data. Map what types of invoices are relevant and what are not (like intercompany invoices might not be relevant). Once you separate the types of invoicing, try to match it with the matching shipment data. We have seen that for some companies, it is easier to use invoiced netted with returns data, for the sake of comparison and may be to budget, but it is not the recommended approach on the path to become demand driven. Once done separation of type of invoices, assess and link your shipment data and if ok use it in forecasting. Separation of invoices leads to separation of shipments and return transactions.

**Transformation Step 2**

In order to address this challenge, one of the things you should consider to do is to assess if your order-to-cash process does capture the whole demand that customers required and if it does classify exceptions to requirements (differences in quantity, time, price). We have seen often that sales orders are not being captured if there is no stock or firmed supply plan, even though we have seen that sales orders were recorded already with requested dates and quantity which in reality reflected only what is possible (confirmed to achieve). We strongly advise to deep dive into order-to-cash process to find out what really shipment and sales order data shows to you.

**Transformation Step 3**

In order to address this challenge, one of the things you should consider to do is to move toward use of consumer data. Assess your capabilities and available information first. This is not a trivial step and requires solid change to normally available data and capabilities in your company if it did not exist before. What type of capabilities we talk about here, e.g., capability to connect to POS data, capability to recognize patterns in POS data, capability to use pattern recognition in demand sensing and then in consensus demand planning.

If your IBP assessment (see some hints in Sect. 1.2.3 Build holistic transformation road map) informs you that you can skip certain interim transformation steps to become demand driven faster, just do it! As we discussed earlier transformation depends highly on your order-to-cash process maturity.

Note from research, Demand sensing, by incorporating downstream (POS) data further increases accuracy and reduces demand latency and bullwhip effect. Companies reported reduced forecast error by 48% by switching from shipments to POS demand (Shamir 2013).

**Few Hints for Your Order-to-Cash Process Assessment**

As we have identified above, your order-to-cash process produces important information for IBP from demand planning and demand management perspective.

Let us illustrate what you may need to know before going into direction of using sales orders as input for your IBP:

- Do you capture all orders from customers?
- Do you capture all parameters requested by customer like when, what, how many?
- Are the sales orders entered into the system when you have product shortages?
- Does your order-to-cash process classify order lines or schedule lines in case there are exceptions from parameters requested by customer (qty, time, price)?
- Does your order-to-cash process have clear rules and reason codes for order line classifications?
- Does your order-to-cash process has formalized rules how customer service executes backorder rescheduling?
- Does your order-to-cash process leave sales orders with dates in the past?
- Is your order-to-cash process connected with available to promise?

- What objects are being used in ATP only availability or planned orders or requisitions as well?
- When in o2c process exactly your ATP is being executed (on order entry, shipments) and how (online, batch)?
- Do you use allocation quotations in your ATP process step?
- Do you measure OTIF and Do you measure OTIF vs requested, promised dates and volumes?
- Does your order intake have a pattern during the month, e.g., 70% orders are flowing in last week of the month? Does it vary by country?
- Do you transfer product from one customer location to the other with or without full reversing material and financial flows?

Answers to those exemplary questions should help you to understand IBP data input and decide in how many steps to plan journey to become demand driven. All three steps of transformation to become demand driven are touching your order-to-cash process maturity. O2C does feed IBP with data which would be used as basis of demand review and reconciliation process steps.

### 5.2.2 Demand Review Process Overview

Demand review process step is very important in the whole IBP and should deliver:

- Consensus unconstrained forecast volume and value
- Agreed risks and opportunities and captured assumptions

Diversification of forecasting inputs and levels would give you an opportunity to reconcile them and remove biases from specific group of stakeholders' method. Process design should aim to be balanced between efforts invested and performance. Process should be labor intensive only in areas where it is needed. Let us go through building blocks of demand review process. Demand review process has four main building blocks, which we see in Fig. 5.51.

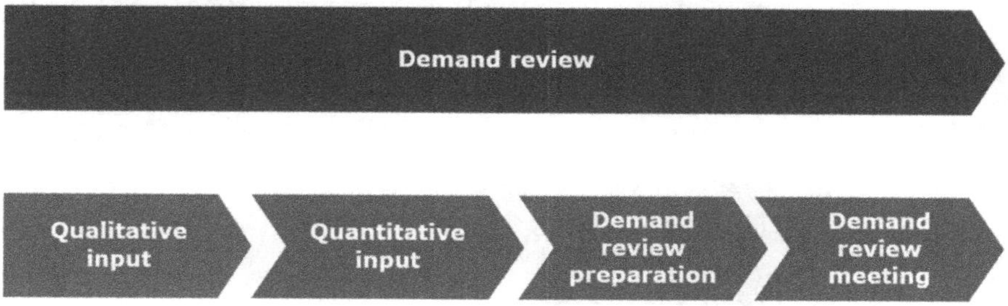


**Fig. 5.51** Demand review building blocks

All of the building blocks should coexist; you should not skip any of them, but you should shape how you leverage inputs in the process. We mean that qualitative input should be defined in relationship to quantitative inputs; you should aim to eliminate bias from one method or function as you go through process steps.

Qualitative method are in simple terms those provided manually by process stakeholders. You may design qualitative input to consist of input from:

- Sales
- Marketing
- Demand planning
- Business planning

You need to select relevant functions to provide inputs in order to remove bias if you have only one to work with. Collaboration between functions in demand review process helps to remove bias and to get aligned, reduces errors, and ensures transparency on assumptions where forecast was based on.

In Fig. 5.52 we see that qualitative inputs for sales team may be hierarchical and may start from sales representative who is in direct contact with customer. Sales representative inputs are being reviewed, adjusted, and approved by leaders, managers, and directors. You do not have to design sales input like that, but ensure input from sales is in your process and is reviewed against other functions inputs. Extensive sales input normally is defined like above when company does not have capabilities to build quantitative input (statistical forecasting) or when marketing and demand planning are not involved in forecasting since it is attributed purely to sales. This is not a leading practice to leave input to one function. Marketing and demand planning should provide their opinions and projections and capture them in respective forecast inputs. In the following demand review subchapters, we elaborate how you can design process to capture above inputs and eliminate bias.

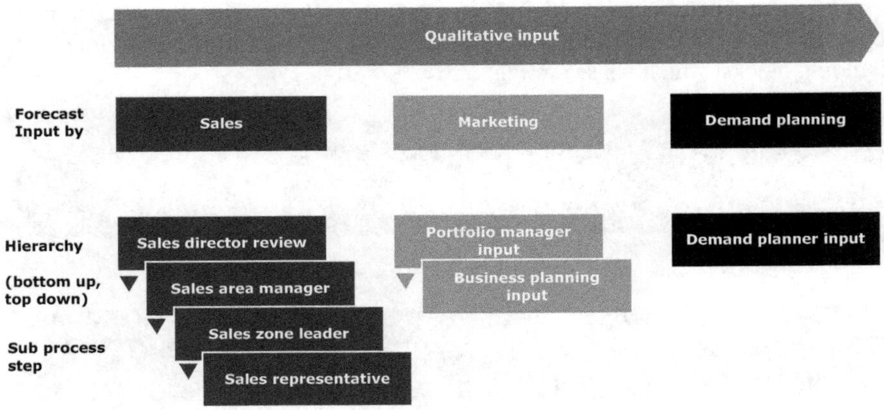


**Fig. 5.52** Qualitative input types—sales, marketing, and demand planning

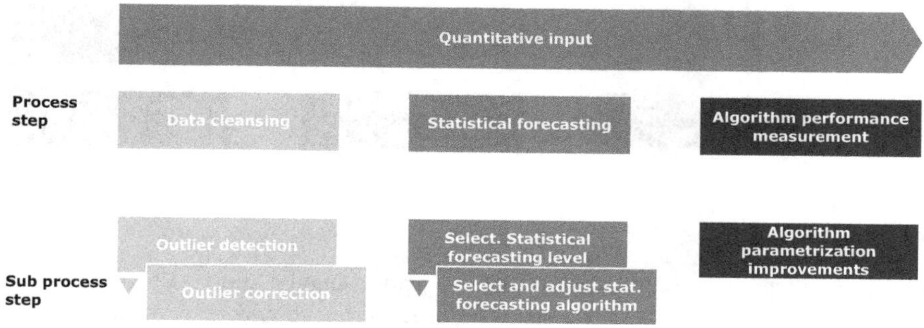


**Fig. 5.53** Quantitative input—statistical forecasting

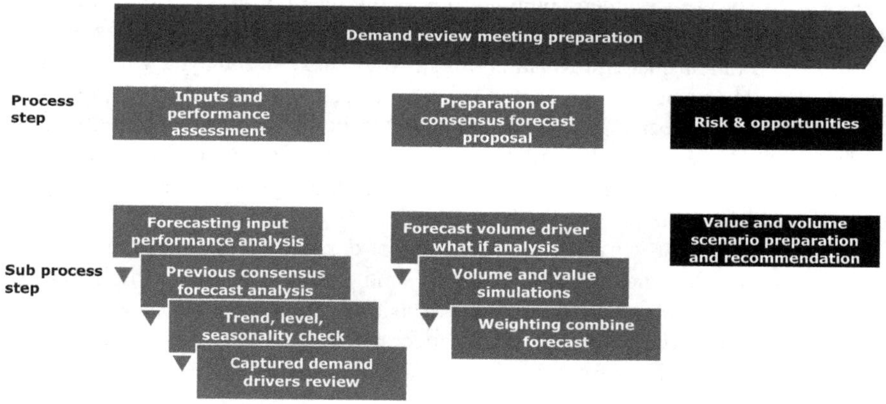


**Fig. 5.54** Demand review meeting preparation

Qualitative techniques are a valuable source for any forecaster, but the problem with qualitative forecasting techniques is that they are expensive. In general they require large amounts of time (Mentzer and Moon 2004).

In Fig. 5.53 we see building blocks of statistical forecasting. There are three main elements of it: data cleansing, statistical forecasting runs, and algorithm measurement and adjustments. We have seen many times that statistical forecasting was treated in companies as black box. You throw data in and expect magic to happen to have perfect results out. Well it does not work like that, as we see in many organizations which leveraged capabilities of the data scientist, functional capabilities of SAP IBP, analytical tools, and skills. In Fig. 5.53 we see very simplified process. It is proven by many organizations that investments of time, efforts, and skills in statistical forecasting may pay back and even exceed your expectations on what it could bring to improve forecast effectiveness and efficiency. In statistical forecasting, it is important to use cleansed data and appropriate algorithms, to be able to adjust algorithm parameters, and last not least to perform it on multiple levels.

In Fig. 5.54 we see high-level picture of the most important step in the process, demand review meeting preparation. Preparation is focused on inputs analysis,

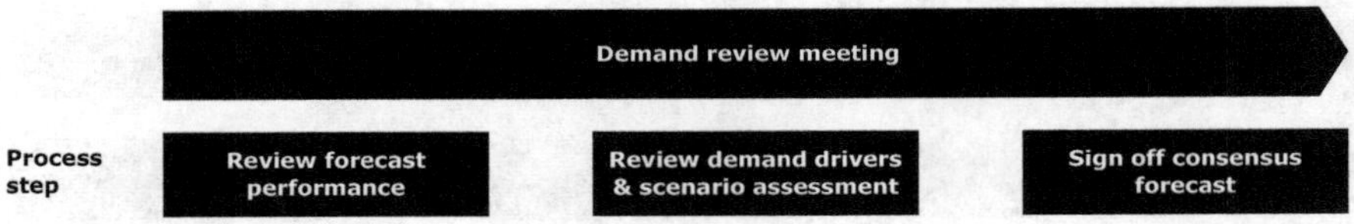


**Fig. 5.55** Demand review meeting

check, verifications, and simulations of, e.g., price change and its volume impact, capturing and validating assumptions. This process step should generate up to two to three scenarios in volume and value which propose consensus forecast and have clear assumptions. This process step takes into account qualitative and quantitative inputs and may use weighted combine forecasting method on top. Demand review meeting preparation should be done on SKU maybe location, country level. You should be confident that SKU data is ok, since the next step maybe will introduce changes to volume but on aggregated level; therefore you need good proportion of data on low level. Decision and recommendation should be data and fact driven.

Note that study shows 75% of UK firms still abuse judgmental overrides over analytics and data variables. Most of the time, gut feelings are wrong, and they do not adjust the baseline for good (Chase 2009).

Finally in Fig. 5.55 we see building blocks of demand review meeting.

Demand planner and demand manager should ensure proper participation of stakeholders who are authorized to make decisions which drive business.

In *Sales Forecasting Management*, Mentzer and Moon (2004) say that advantage of soliciting contributions from more than one person, of course, is that it can offset biases introduced into a forecast when the forecast is provided by one person. You should balance this approach with experience saying the more people touching the forecast, the more errors you have.

Qualitative inputs solely will not do any good in many industries. Combinations of methods and techniques will help you to achieve better results.

Process design should enable input gathering and review. Input should be as light and as quick as possible, to capture underlying assumptions and be focused on changes (Crum and Palmatier 2003).

In SAP IBP you can imagine that data will be displayed on total regional level with split per country (Fig. 5.56).

What would drive efficiency and effectiveness of demand review process, secret is behind this success formula (Fig. 5.57). We would like to highlight to you our own demand review success formula:

As you see from this formula, it is not additive but multiplicative. Success cannot be fully achieved if only one component drives demand review.

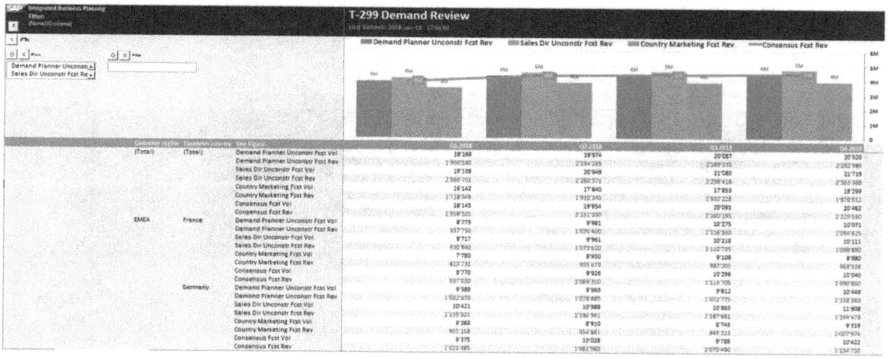


**Fig. 5.56** Consensus forecast volume and revenue, forecast inputs

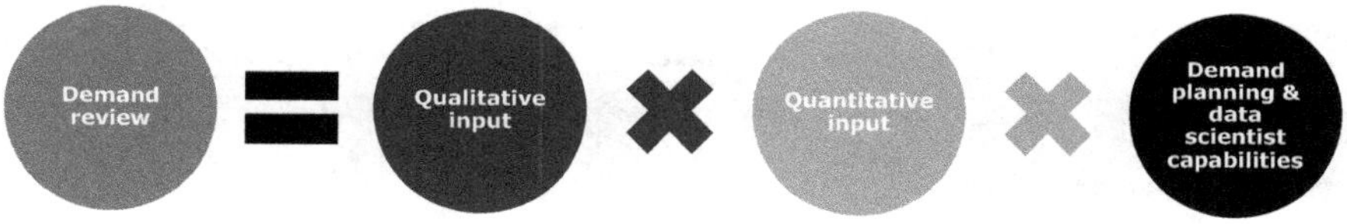


**Fig. 5.57** Demand review success formula

### 5.2.3 Sales Inputs (Bottom-Up)

Let's talk about how to organize sales input in the company described with following characteristics: the organization which have a few levels in sales team, organizations that are geographically in one country but split accountability by zones and areas, and organizations that have "one face to customer" in place. Sales representatives were obliged to visit and talk to customers often to gather their feedback and requirements. Sales representatives were supposed to get knowledge to understand market requirements and competition activities. We will use following hierarchy to explain you the model:

Sales country director → sales area manager → sales zone leader → sales representatives

Large sales community normally is supported by various functions like technical support. Support functions typically are not the ones to provide forecast input. Whole portfolio was able to be sold in the whole country; in some areas specific part of portfolio was dominating sales but with no special restrictions. Company took a decision to incorporate this organization in capturing forecast in IBP process. If we look at it from analytical perspective, we have four levels which provide forecast input or review. We would need to organize more than 300 people in sales team. All sales team organizational levels were present in commercial hierarchy and transactional system master data. This type of organization could be mapped in the demand review sub-process steps in the following manner:

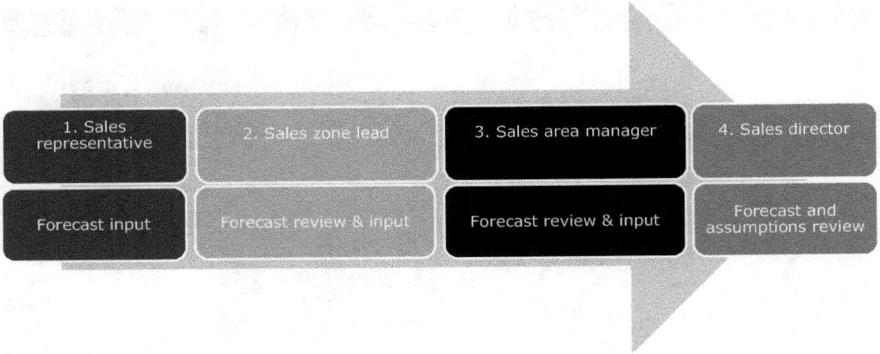


**Fig. 5.58** Bottom-up sales input in multilevel sales team

| Input type | Role | Typical input level | Typical unit | No of input providers |
|---|---|---|---|---|
| **1. Sales Rep**<br><br>**forecast review and input** | Sales Representative | Customer / SKU | Volume / month | 250 |
| **1. Sales Zone**<br><br>**forecast review and Input** | Sales Zone leader | Sales Rep/ Customer / Product grp | Volume / month | 50 |
| **1. Sales Area**<br><br>**forecast review and Input** | Sales Area manager | Sales Zone / Customer grp / Product grp | Volume & Value / month & year | 5 |
| **1. Country**<br><br>**forecast review** | Country Sales Director | Sales Area / Product line | Volume & Value/ month & year | 1 |

**Fig. 5.59** Example of large market sales team

We can call this way of capturing forecast input as bottom-up approach (Fig. 5.58). This approach is about building sales team projection from lowest level in organizational hierarchy which is in frequent contact with customer. As we go up in hierarchy, input should be more reviewed than entered, and errors should be reduced. We agreed a rule to not to overwrite each other's inputs but to manage inputs with dataflows between steps.

Sales team was defined as follows (Fig. 5.59).

## Input Schedule

Large organization like above would require sufficient amount of time to build sales team forecast input. It would be not feasible to start organizing sales team input only

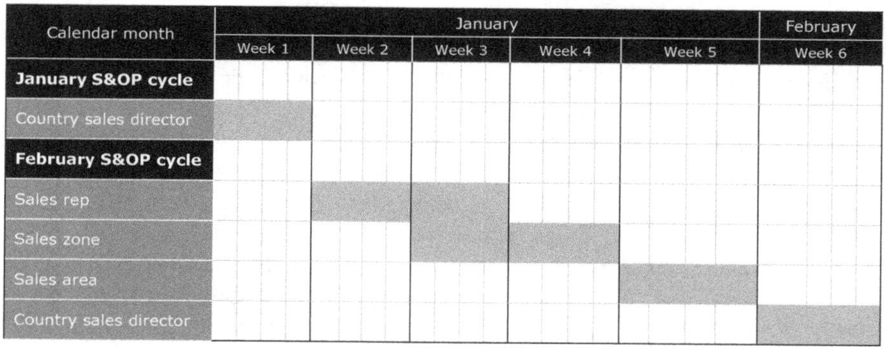

Calendar month
January
February
Week 1
Week 2
Week 3
Week 4
Week 5
Week 6
January S&OP cycle
Country sales director
February S&OP cycle
Sales rep
Sales zone
Sales area
Country sales director


**Fig. 5.60** Sales team forecast input and review schedule

when "the books" are closed and still align it to S&OP calendar of activities. S&OP cycle month is determined by the month in which final output will be signed off. In this case sales team would need to start earlier. What we mean by that is the following: February S&OP cycle would be started by sales team input in January. Sales team would need to have precise schedule (Fig. 5.60), for example, sales team schedule for February S&OP cycle.

As you see from this schedule, it is important to define start and end dates for each cycle for each input. It does not mean that you can enter forecast only in defined period. The above schedule is only to organize how we manage dataflows between sales representative input and sales leader input and sales area manager input to director level. Each of the inputs could be defined in the system as process step represented as template. Templates might be tailored in favorites by users to fit their needs. What you need to ensure is forecast is being built from bottom up according to the overall IBP schedule. Sales representatives start ca. around 2nd week of January for February cycle. Horizon of inputs in this case was current year and next year (so up to 2 years). We did not want to use process and tool to manage current month deviations from the forecast. Bottom-up inputs provided by sales should be leveraged in context of capturing customer buying behaviors as well as leverage it for purpose of having right proportions, which can be used in system disaggregation logic. Proportions will help us to easier introduce changes to forecast on aggregated level but with better more accurate way to disaggregate.

Each of the function providing input in forecasting process has its typical bias. Sales team may often:

- Have a perception that their forecast will influence their target, so they may under-forecast
- Over-forecast for the products which tend to have capacity constraints (Moon 2013)

You should consider to define targets for forecast error to be linked to qualitative inputs and demand review preparation where you should spot and address typical bias.

**Keeping Input Open for Updates**

According to our proposed schedule, copy of data between sales rep level and sales zone leader could happen in beginning of weeks 3 and 4. It does not mean that we close the system for sales representatives until next cycle. We want them to enter as much up-to-date information and still manage our large sales team process on various levels. We could propose that copy operator which is executed to pre-fill input from sales representative and sales zone leader will make a snapshot called "sales rep input snapshot." Sales representative snapshot key figure will represent copy of data taken on specific day of the month agreed as date on which they should finalize their forecast. This data can be used as pre-fill to sales zone lead. Sales representative input key figure is the one where sales representative can change forecast continuously, e.g., to prepare next cycle based on very recent customer visit in April. Data snapshot could be used for performance measurement purposes. Thanks to exception management capabilities of SAP IBP supply chain control tower, we can flag sales representative snapshot versus sales representative input continuous changes and deviations and address them in between the cycle process.

**Rationale Behind Protecting and Organizing Inputs**

As you have learned, we can separate and protect inputs in sales team as we go through organizational hierarchy. There are quite important reasons for it:

- Make people accountable for the input and ensure they know it is protected.
- Measure individual input to trigger tailored corrective actions.
- Measure all inputs separately to assess value of adjustments.

Demand planner should play vital role in organization of sales team bottom-up forecast input:

- Help sales team to organize themselves and execute tasks according to desired schedule.
- Help to vertically integrate sales team levels.
- Be involved in sales meetings and selected sales forecast reviews, e.g., sales area maybe zone but definitely country level.
- Help sales team to understand role of level, trend, and seasonality in information they provide.
- Help sales team how to understand measurement as input to self-driven continues process improvement.
- Regularly train and refresh knowledge about process and tool.
- Regularly improve his/her knowledge about portfolio and customers.
- Join from time to time sales representative at customer visit/meeting to feel what it is to be in front of customer and what it makes to understand and communicate with customer.
- Help to reassign forecast inputs between people in case changes in sales team occur.

### 5.2.4 SAP Use Case: Building Bottom-Up Sales Input

In our example we will capture inputs from sales representatives, adjust them on area level, and review the ones approved by commercial head/director.

Sales representatives are assigned to zone/area. They provide sales input on level which speaks to them. They do not have to work on level which is defined by somebody in headquarters thousands of kilometers from their accountability and market. They can select attributes and create favorites to manage forecast input for different types of customers in different ways, can enter on customer group, customer, product, and customer level by month by quarter, etc.

Current month forecast input may be supported with actual data from current and previous years, open sales orders, input from previous month, etc. (see Fig. 5.61).

When sales representatives accomplish their work, dataflows to next level to sales area manager who might want to see forecast on aggregated level. Sales manager may not start work from scratch, but his forecast can be pre-filled by sum of up-to-date inputs from sales representatives in his area. We will enable flow of data with copy operator, between key figures representing sales representative input to sales area input (see Fig. 5.62).

In this example whole data is being copied from sales representative input to sales area manager input, including proportions. It means that if sales area manager would like to change total sales area forecast volume on aggregated level, it will be disaggregated proportionally to lowest level but only in his key figure (sales are unconstrained forecast volume). We can model that each individual can only change his/her data; sales area manager would not be able to change sales representative input.

Sales area managers wanted to adjust total forecast on aggregated level first and then make some adjustments on particular sales representative level. Sales manager can easily spot differences between his inputs and sales representatives on total level or specific sales representative. Special conditional formatting or alert key figures can be used to highlight deviations from expectations. Color coding embedded in exception management helps to spot areas of attention quickly. Populating on the

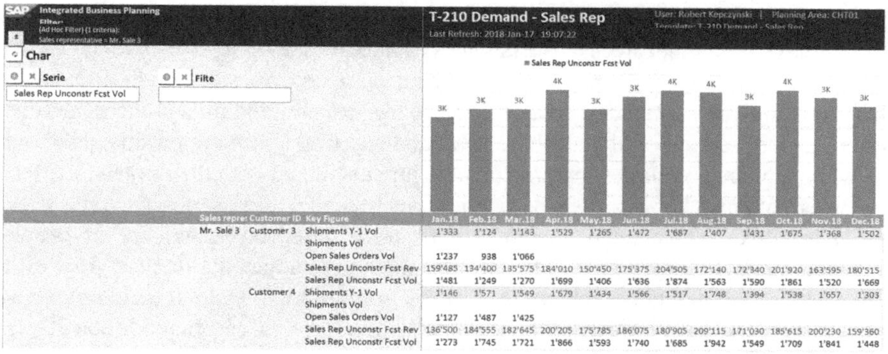


**Fig. 5.61** Sales representative input

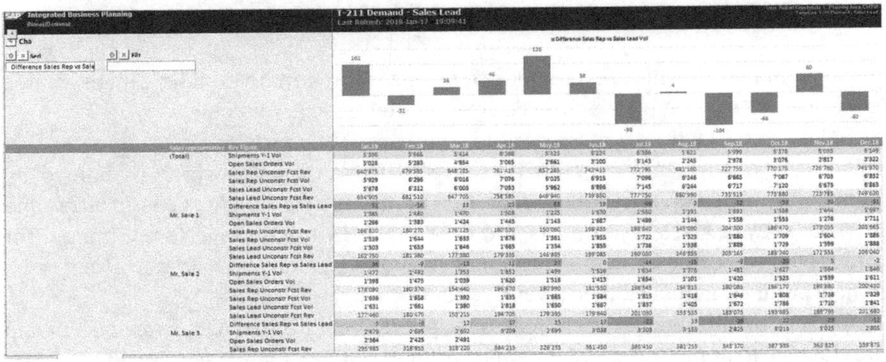


**Fig. 5.62** Sales area lead forecast input

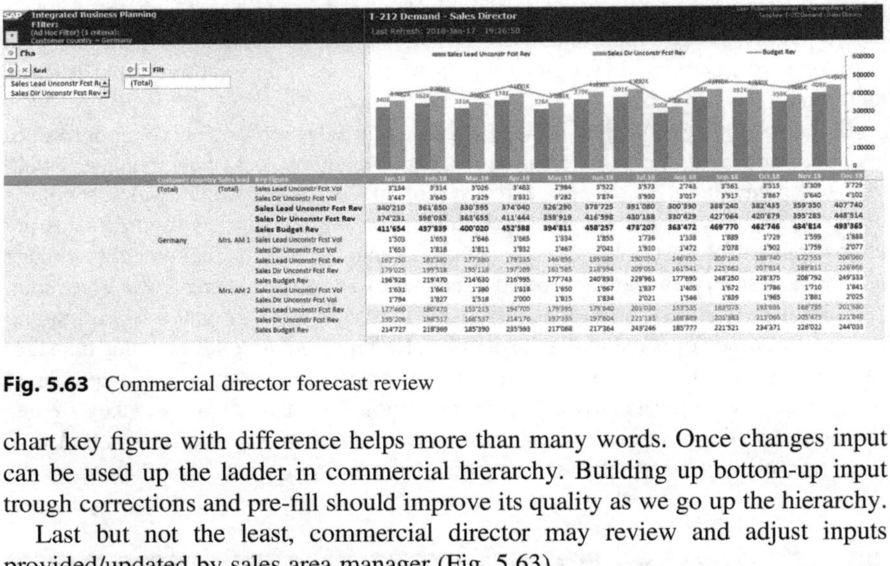


**Fig. 5.63** Commercial director forecast review

chart key figure with difference helps more than many words. Once changes input can be used up the ladder in commercial hierarchy. Building up bottom-up input trough corrections and pre-fill should improve its quality as we go up the hierarchy.

Last but not the least, commercial director may review and adjust inputs provided/updated by sales area manager (Fig. 5.63).

We have seen that forecast assessment is sometimes done to sales budget. In the case shown in Fig. 5.63, revenues are being compared to sales budget revenue. Directors look on aggregated data per sales leader country and total at the same time (there is total section on the attribute level and any time grouping on time axis).

Main advantage of sales input/qualitative input is linked with their potential effect on sales patterns. Inputs might be applied when neither time series nor regression analysis works. Then the prediction can be done based on experience of people working internally or externally. It is a valid method to adjust the forecast. However the accuracy of qualitative forecasting suffers from multiple factors, including complex nature of data, historical data bias, political issues, etc. (Mentzer and Moon 2004).

### 5.2.5 Marketing Input (Top-Down)

One of the key inputs in demand review process step is input and review provided by marketing. Marketing should:

- Balance short-term focus with long-term objectives.
- Find trade-offs between short-term goals and strategic long-term portfolio or market initiatives and plans.
- Provide input for phase-in and phase-outs.
- Provide inputs for management of product lifecycle codes.
- Identify inputs for business risks and opportunities.
- Provide unconstrained forecast on aggregate level.

Demand planning should interact with marketing to understand and ensure marketing activities are incorporated in relevant process steps of Integrated Business Planning. Because of this needed interactions, demand planner may need to be able to navigate in, e.g.:

- **Market research** which aims to gather market information to assess if customers will care about the product, to analyze them, and to refine and tailor suit the new product as a consequence
- **Demand generation** which is about transforming latent demand in real customer's needs, influencing them and making them realize the need for the new product
- **The 4 Ps of marketing:** product, price, placement, and promotions (APICS—module 2.G—Influencing and Prioritizing Demand 2015)

Portfolio manager, marketing manager is normally responsible for part of company portfolio organized by groups, families, lines, brands. In the following example, portfolio manager will be responsible for product line which represents product family, group, and specific packaging of SKUs on the country level.

An important question for which you need to find an answer is how independent marketing input should be from sales or demand planning inputs. Making marketing input more independent would be the best way to manage personal and organizational biases. You need to gather inputs which represent different points of view and projections. Technically this independence of marketing input could be realized by not pre-filling their forecast input by aggregated sales team input.

Marketing may provide in their forecast following bias which we should be aware off:

- Over-forecasting by product managers for new products, to support their new product initiatives
- Over-forecast to make sure production sufficient (Moon 2013)

All qualitative forecast inputs in tactical S&OP could have same technical planning level; this will enable team members to compare all inputs on any level of organizational, commercial, and product hierarchy. Bottom-up or top-down approach can leverage system functionality to work on level you want then and still be comparable. Type of approach (bottom-up, top-down) should be aligned to accountabilities and organizational structure.

How can we make marketing input more efficient? Marketing typically does not go SKU per SKU; therefore, for them top-down approach would be much more suitable. It means that marketing team does not build their forecast cross multiple levels in organization and from bottom up. Portfolio managers provide volumetric forecast in their accountability but on aggregated level. Portfolio manager works in example portfolio structure: product line→product family→product grp→SKU. They might tailor inputs to reflect change which they want to introduce on particular sales zone level, and, for that, only attribute has to be different.

### 5.2.6 SAP Use Case: Building Top-Down Marketing Input

In one of the organizations which we worked with, marketing was present on local/market level and regional level. Alignment between local and regional marketing happened on regular monthly basis as part of tactical S&OP process. As part of demand review in the country, local marketing did align regularly volume projection with regional team; this activity happened normally before market demand review. Country marketing provided forecast projections in volume which were monetized according to company rules. Once all countries accomplished this input, regional marketing reviewed total regional volume and value and compared them with sum of country inputs (see Fig. 5.64).

Regional marketing easily did spot that deviations between their projections and local projection continue from 2017. In current year 2018, they wanted to spot where biggest deviations occur and align with local marketing why differences occur.

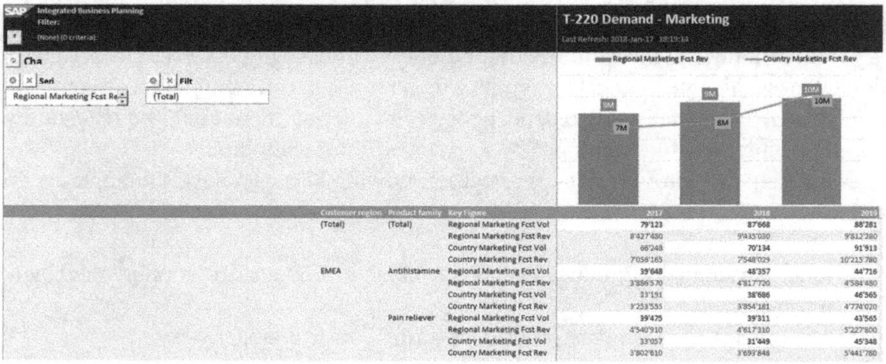


**Fig. 5.64** Regional marketing product line review of local marketing forecasts in annual buckets

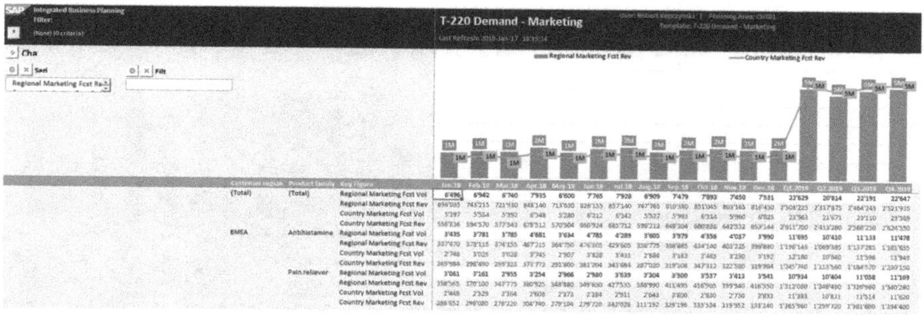


**Fig. 5.65** Regional marketing product line review of local marketing forecasts in monthly buckets current year

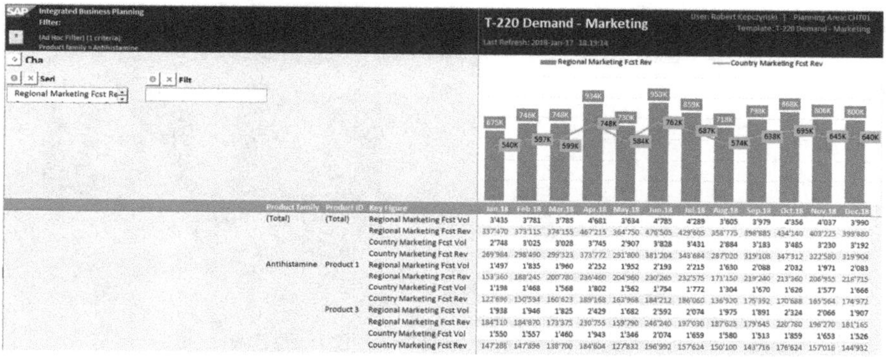


**Fig. 5.66** Regional marketing product line review on product level

Regional portfolio manager deep dived into product line forecast by month and recognized some differences on selected product lines (Fig. 5.65).

Regional manager did further analyze data on specific SKUs and in the meantime contacted local portfolio manager (Fig. 5.66).

Regional and local portfolio manager agreed to simulate specific changes in the forecast on country level for selected product line and specific products. They have created scenario where they have captured 30% increase on selected part of the range (Fig. 5.67).

Once they have compared, analyzed, and discussed assumptions behind base scenario and increased scenario, it was obvious to them that 2018 was underestimated on local level, but 30% increased scenario looked much better. They agreed that increased scenario should be used in demand review meeting in local S&OP (Fig. 5.68).

Above use case was possible to realize since data model and user interface flexibility enabled it. Interesting was that it was decided that disaggregation of local marketing forecast will be done with use of proportions from sales director final input. Sales team

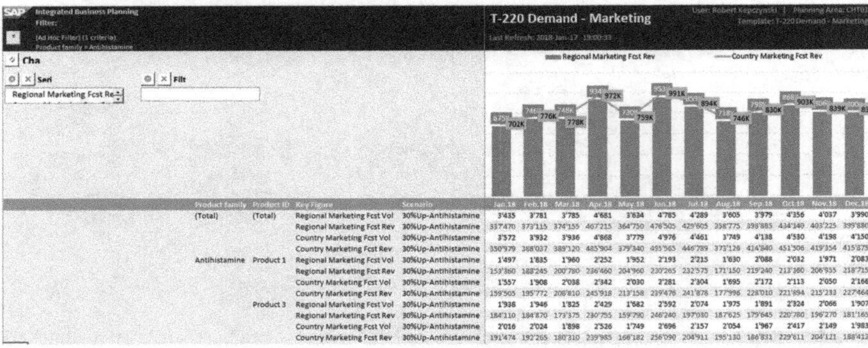


**Fig. 5.67** Regional marketing product line increases simulation on specific part of portfolio

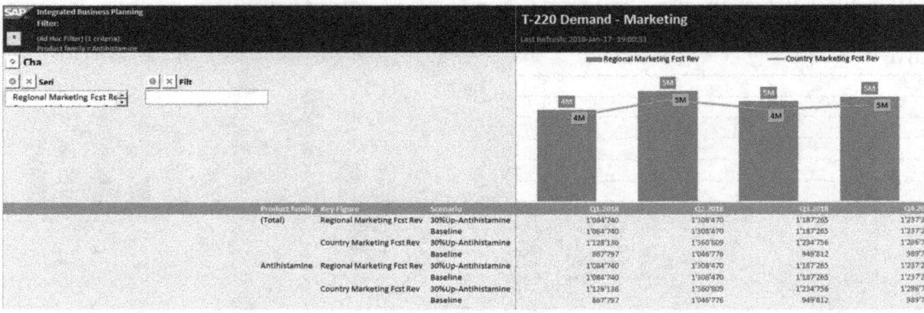


**Fig. 5.68** Regional marketing and local marketing scenario comparison

was supposed to be closest to customer; therefore, it made sense to use proportion from their input when disaggregating changes introduced on aggregated level.

You may want to tight up marketing input with sales input. Sales team forecast can pre-fill marketing portfolio manager input for further adjustments. Pre-fill of forecast from sales to marketing team has a bit of risk. Those departments have different insights, goals, and ways of working which are nothing else but true gold which should be extracted separately. Another risk is that if marketing will not do their job, you actually did not remove bias from sales forecast input.

### 5.2.7 Statistical Forecasting

Today, more than ever before, companies are under immense pressure to reduce costs, improve service levels, and decrease lead times in a marketplace that is witnessing diminishing customer loyalty, burgeoning product variety, shrinking product lifecycles, and increasing competition, just to name a few. Given these trends, it is not hard to imagine the high costs of markdowns and stock-outs endemic in the supply chains of today. In the face of these uncertainties, predicting demand has become that much more difficult. This is also one of the reasons why initiatives such as just-in-time and efficient consumer response, which focus on reducing uncertainty by developing the ability to quickly respond to the demands of the market, have gained traction. However, these initiatives do not eliminate the need for a forecast. At best, they complement a good forecast. Moreover, in the case of industries, where reducing the lead times of certain key suppliers is no longer possible and in certain others (e.g., fashion) where products sell in a concentrated season and responding to the developing actual demand situation on time is not feasible, forecast accuracy wields significant leverage to improving the performance of a supply chain.

Forecasting commonly refers to a combination of an extrapolation of the historical data, aided by mathematical models, and human input based on informed judgements about future events. The role of an unbiased mathematical model to a forecasting process cannot be underestimated as it has the potential, when done right, to completely automate the process of forecasting for a large percentage of items (particularly those that have low demand variability). Although the choice of the statistical model used is a crucial component in the forecasting process, the sophistication of the model should be economically justifiable and in line with the purpose of the forecast (see Fig. 5.69).

Besides the choice of statistical model, another aspect that influences forecast accuracy is the granularity of the historical data on which the forecast is carried out. One of the characteristics of forecasts is that aggregate forecasts are usually more accurate than disaggregate forecasts. This aspect could be used to good effect in choosing the most appropriate level on which to forecast (see Fig. 5.70).

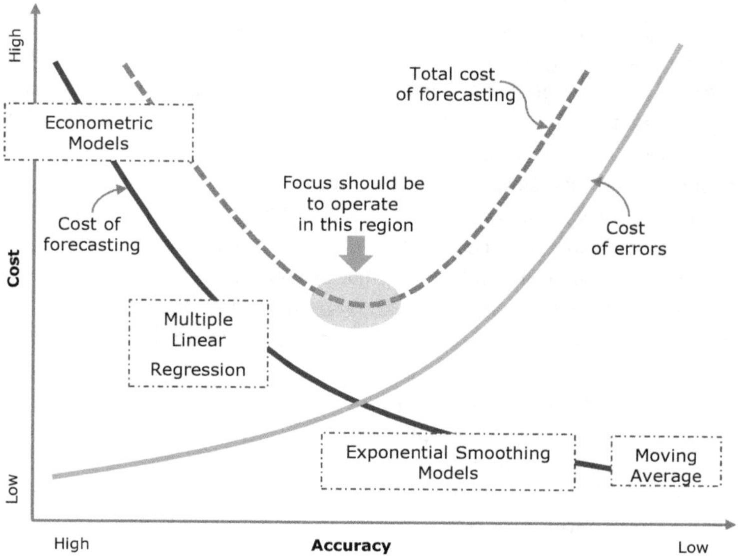


**Fig. 5.69** Balancing cost of forecasting and cost of inaccuracy

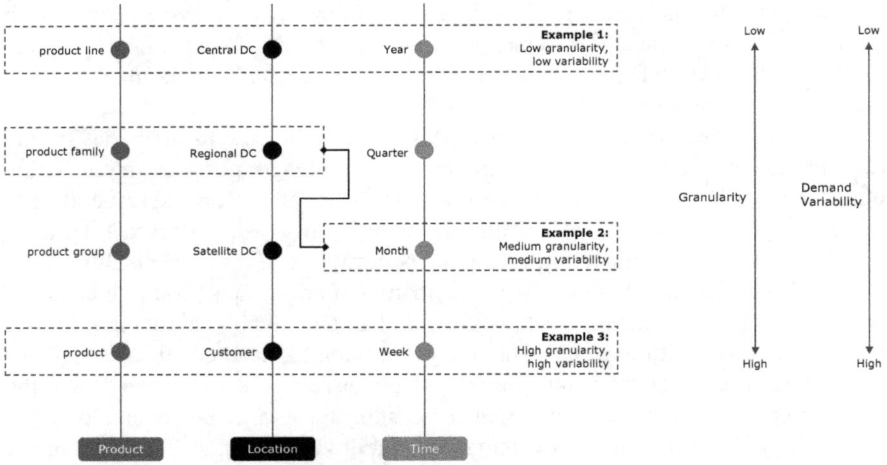


**Fig. 5.70** Relationship between forecast level/granularity and demand variability

In the following paragraphs, we will explore the key steps involved in statistical forecasting with the help of an example modeled on an implementation of statistical forecasting process at a manufacturing client. At this client, it was quite important to strike the right balance between forecast accuracy and workload on the planners. Therefore, the principle of statistical forecasting on an aggregate level, thereby rationalizing workload for the planner as fewer planning combinations had to be analyzed, was employed. The aggregate level chosen was product family. This suited the client as planners had keen insights into demand patterns and product behavior on a product family level. This approach also helped establish a solid first input into the forecasting process as, following the principle stated earlier, aggregate forecasts exhibit lower variability and tend to be more accurate than more granular forecasts. Although the initial statistical forecast was created on a product family level, they had to be broken down to a product level as this is the basis for review and enrichment by demand planners and for subsequent handover to supply planning. For this, statistical forecast automatically generated on product level using "pick best" strategy, whereby the model that results in the lowest error for the chosen measure is selected, was used. The product statistical forecast is then used to calculate distribution factors that are multiplied with the product family forecast finalized by the planner to then calculate the final product level statistical forecast. The steps involved are listed below, and we will review each one in turn along with implementation details.

1. Assessment of cleansing need on a product family level
2. Exception-driven cleansing on a product level
3. Forecast model selection and assignment on a product family level
4. Automatic statistical forecast model selection on a product level
5. Calculation of proportional factors based on product level statistical forecast and calculation of final product level statistical forecast
6. Review of forecast on a product level with help of helpful visualizations

Much more about mid-term and long-term statistical forecasting for seasonal and intermittent products, outlier detection and correction, and short-term demand sensing will be found in the next publication in IBP series.

### 5.2.8 SAP Use Case: Connected Family and Product Level Forecasting

The steps involved in forecasting on family and product level are listed below:

1. Assessment of cleansing need on a product family level
2. Exception-driven cleansing on a product level
3. Forecast model selection and assignment on a product family level
4. Automatic statistical forecast model selection on a product level
5. Calculation of proportional factors based on product level statistical forecast and calculation of final product level statistical forecast

Review of forecast on a product level with help of helpful visualizations

**Step 1** Assessment of cleansing need on a product family level:

Cleansing of historical demand is an important first step in any statistical forecasting process. The purpose is to ensure that demands that form an input to statistical forecasting are valid for extrapolation and are not corrupted as a result of one-off events or as a result of actions that either will not occur again or at least not in the same fashion as they did in the past.

There are several ways by which cleansing can be done, some of them automatic. An automated cleansing process typically involves detection and cleansing of outliers. This approach, although less demanding on planner's time, is error prone. What might be seen as an outlier from a purely statistical standpoint could well be a valid data point that should play a role in the calculation of future forecast. It is advisable to limit the influence of automatic outlier correction (e.g., by setting very high thresholds) and incorporate a manual cleansing step to ensure a sound basis for statistical forecasting.

The approach adopted at this use case involved assessing variation on product family level of most recent historical demand, weighted on volume, vis-à-vis the recent past. The weighted variation was used to rank product families in the descending order of variation. This helped the planner prioritize her/his cleansing activity. For example, in Fig. 5.71, family 023 has the highest weighted variation—that is, the demand in the previous month compared to the previous 3 months' average weighted by volume is the highest among all product families. Weighted variation value is color coded in the tabular display. Visual control played important role in this solution; therefore only top product families are plotted on charts.

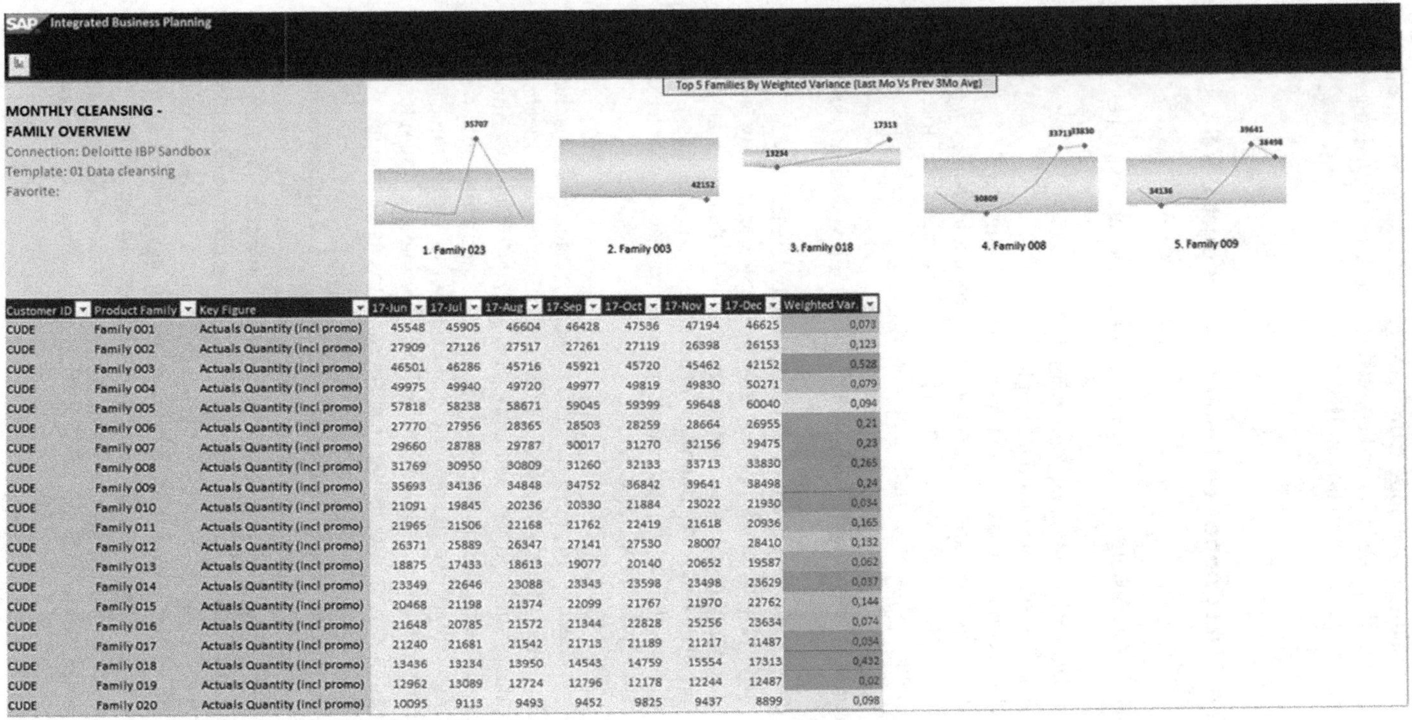


| Customer ID | Product Family | Key Figure | 17-Jun | 17-Jul | 17-Aug | 17-Sep | 17-Oct | 17-Nov | 17-Dec | Weighted Var. |
|---|---|---|---|---|---|---|---|---|---|---|
| CUDE | Family 001 | Actuals Quantity (incl promo) | 45548 | 45905 | 46604 | 46428 | 47536 | 47194 | 46625 | 0,073 |
| CUDE | Family 002 | Actuals Quantity (incl promo) | 27909 | 27126 | 27517 | 27261 | 27119 | 26398 | 26153 | 0,123 |
| CUDE | Family 003 | Actuals Quantity (incl promo) | 46501 | 46286 | 45716 | 45921 | 45720 | 45462 | 42152 | 0,528 |
| CUDE | Family 004 | Actuals Quantity (incl promo) | 49975 | 49940 | 49720 | 49977 | 49819 | 49830 | 50271 | 0,079 |
| CUDE | Family 005 | Actuals Quantity (incl promo) | 57818 | 58238 | 58671 | 59045 | 59399 | 59648 | 60040 | 0,094 |
| CUDE | Family 006 | Actuals Quantity (incl promo) | 27770 | 27956 | 28365 | 28503 | 28259 | 28664 | 26955 | 0,21 |
| CUDE | Family 007 | Actuals Quantity (incl promo) | 29660 | 28788 | 29787 | 30017 | 31270 | 32156 | 29475 | 0,23 |
| CUDE | Family 008 | Actuals Quantity (incl promo) | 31769 | 30950 | 30809 | 31260 | 32133 | 33713 | 33830 | 0,265 |
| CUDE | Family 009 | Actuals Quantity (incl promo) | 35693 | 34136 | 34848 | 34752 | 36842 | 39641 | 38498 | 0,24 |
| CUDE | Family 010 | Actuals Quantity (incl promo) | 21091 | 19845 | 20236 | 20330 | 21884 | 23022 | 21930 | 0,034 |
| CUDE | Family 011 | Actuals Quantity (incl promo) | 21965 | 21506 | 22168 | 21762 | 22419 | 21618 | 20936 | 0,165 |
| CUDE | Family 012 | Actuals Quantity (incl promo) | 26371 | 25889 | 26347 | 27141 | 27530 | 28007 | 28410 | 0,132 |
| CUDE | Family 013 | Actuals Quantity (incl promo) | 18875 | 17433 | 18613 | 19077 | 20140 | 20652 | 19587 | 0,062 |
| CUDE | Family 014 | Actuals Quantity (incl promo) | 23349 | 22646 | 23088 | 23343 | 23598 | 23498 | 23629 | 0,037 |
| CUDE | Family 015 | Actuals Quantity (incl promo) | 20468 | 21198 | 21374 | 22099 | 21767 | 21970 | 22762 | 0,144 |
| CUDE | Family 016 | Actuals Quantity (incl promo) | 21648 | 20785 | 21572 | 21344 | 22828 | 25256 | 23634 | 0,074 |
| CUDE | Family 017 | Actuals Quantity (incl promo) | 21240 | 21681 | 21542 | 21713 | 21189 | 21217 | 21487 | 0,034 |
| CUDE | Family 018 | Actuals Quantity (incl promo) | 13436 | 13234 | 13950 | 14543 | 14759 | 15554 | 17313 | 0,432 |
| CUDE | Family 019 | Actuals Quantity (incl promo) | 12962 | 13089 | 12724 | 12796 | 12178 | 12244 | 12487 | 0,02 |
| CUDE | Family 020 | Actuals Quantity (incl promo) | 10095 | 9113 | 9493 | 9452 | 9825 | 9437 | 8899 | 0,098 |

**Fig. 5.71** SAP IBP product family cleansing view

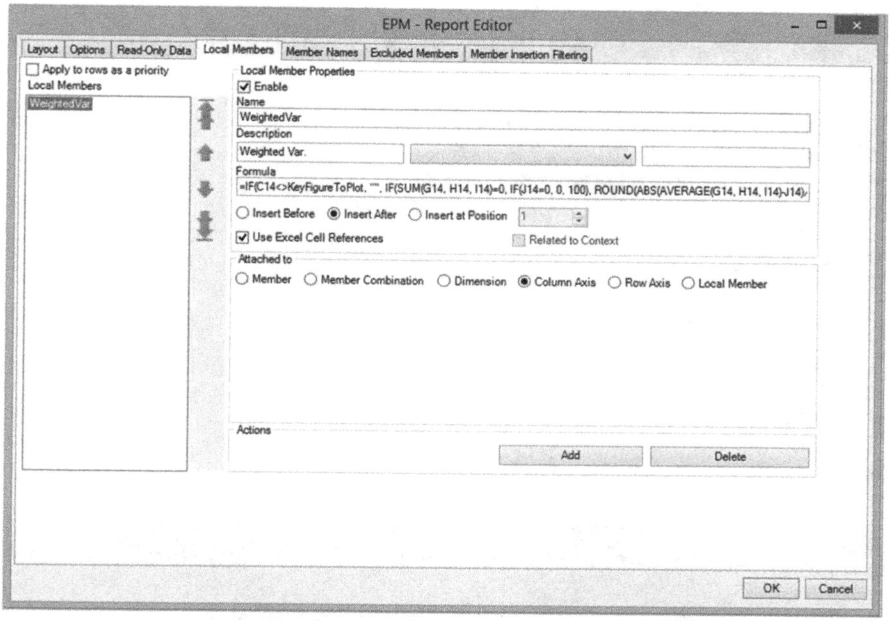


**Fig. 5.72** SAP IBP local member for calculation of weighted variation in actual demand

Weighted variation was calculated using a local member (see Fig. 5.72) in the Excel UI frontend. Once ranked, illustrative graphs were used to visualize the top N families ranked by weighted variation.

Analysis of variation in demand with respect to short-term trend could drive deeper analysis on a product level and subsequent cleansing of demand.

**Step 2** Exception-driven cleansing on a product level:

Product family view was only provided to identify candidates for cleansing. Adjustments to historical demand were only done on a product level. A product level cleansing view was provided to facilitate deeper analysis and the subsequent cleansing activity. An alert was also configured that compares the previous month's demand with historical average to support prioritization on a product level. Adjustments to historical demand were carried out on the cleansed demand key figure, which is different from the actual demand key figure. The actual demand key figure is left intact to serve as reference as it represents what was imported from source system (see Fig. 5.73).

**Step 3**

Forecast model selection and assignment on a product family level

It was much easier and more efficient for planners to monitor and control product family forecast. They have checked level, trend, and seasonality, and it was not disturbed by change of packaging or shipment locations. Product family was supposed to be used as basis for disaggregation; therefore, more attention on statistical forecast model assignment was carried out on this level. Demand planners analyzed

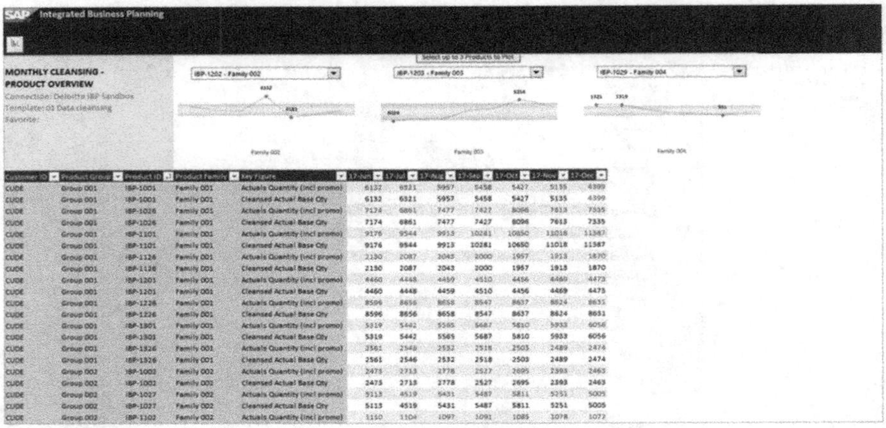


**Fig. 5.73** SAP IBP product level data cleansing

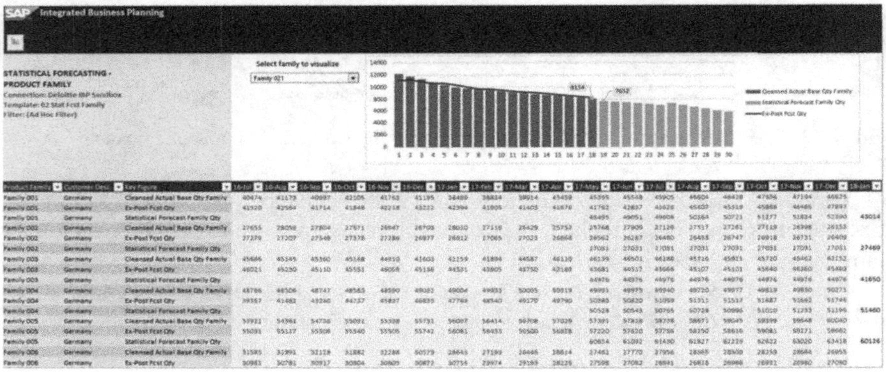


**Fig. 5.74** SAP IBP product family statistical forecast model assignment

data and current forecast assignment and were obliged to assign better model if needed. In this routine system was calculating ex post forecast for them. Planners with use of comparison between ex post forecast and cleansed actuals were able to assess how good statistical forecast family model assignment is (see Fig. 5.74).

Display of ex post forecast plotted over cleansed actuals bars on the chart helped a lot to increase process efficiency.

**Step 4** Automatic statistical forecast model selection on a product level

Demand planner assessed model assignment with the use of spiderweb charts where constant or seasonal model results were plotted. These charts show assignment of products to specific forecasting profiles. This was a way to visualize assignments and to assess spread. For example, "pick best" is the default assignment which represents "best fit" method (automatic model selection). If on the primary

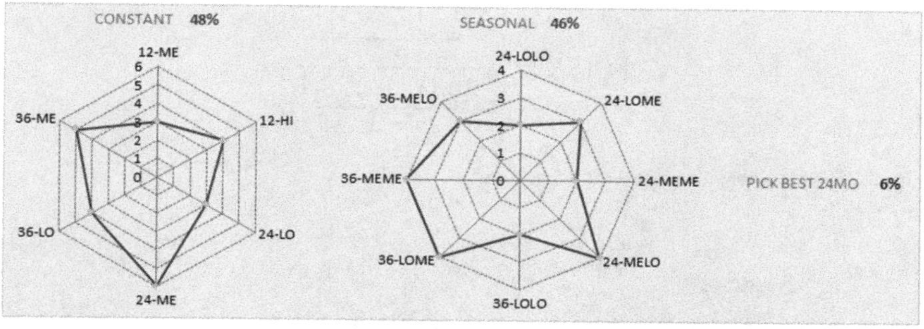


Fig. 5.75 SAP IBP product forecast model assignment spider web chart

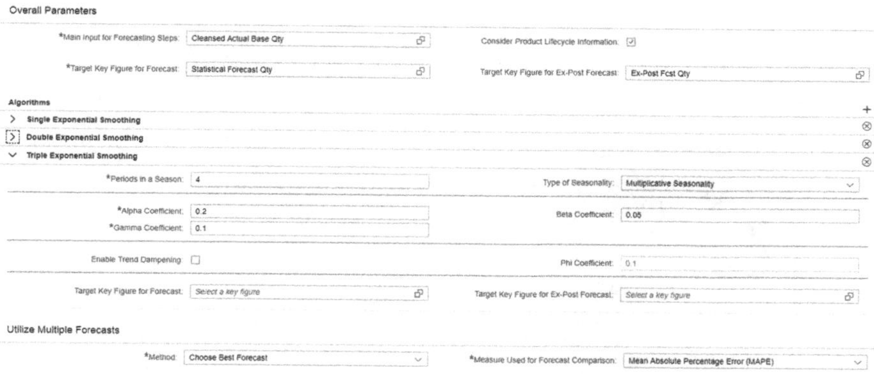


Fig. 5.76 SAP IBP statistical model configuration

forecasting level, planners would see a majority assigned to best fit model, it would be an indication that not too much market knowledge was incorporated into model assignment. It also shows overuse of a certain algorithm/profile (see Fig. 5.75).

SAP IBP configuration was relatively simple since models against best fit were selected had to be parametrized with alpha, beta, and gamma; for data analysis purposes, each model could have target key figure different than "best fit." Best fit model was established based on measure selected by the planner; in this case it was mean absolute percentage error (see Fig. 5.76).

As part of model assignment, analysis of forecast error was done. Performance analysis can be done with use of mean absolute scaled error (MASE). MASE is a ratio between accuracy of current algorithm to use of naïve method (i.e., new forecast = previous period demand) as encapsulated in the MASE formula (Fig. 5.77).

The closer it is to 1, the smaller is the difference to using a naïve method. It means at the end that "naïve" way of forecasting is better if MASE is above 1; the way of improving it should be discussed. Validation of model assignment, brings value and could be done when forecasting on aggregated level, e.g., ABC/XYZ with MASE as measure (Fig. 5.78).

$$MASE = \frac{\frac{\sum_{t=1}^{n}|F_t - Y_t|}{n}}{\frac{\sum_{t=2}^{n}|Y_t - Y_{t-1}|}{n-1}}$$

**Fig. 5.77** Mean absolute scales error formula

| ABC Code | XYZ Code | Mean Absolute Scal... |
|---|---|---|
| A | X | 0.843304 |
| A | Z | 0.856869 |
| B | X | 0.540363 |
| C | X | 0.270619 |

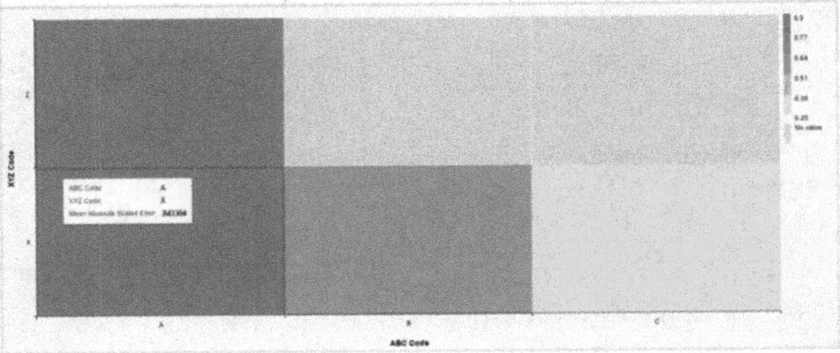

**Fig. 5.78** SAP IBP ABC/XYZ matrix with model assignment measurement

**Step 5** Calculation of proportional factors based on product level statistical forecast and calculation of final product level statistical forecast

Once product family and product level statistical forecast was calculated, special calculation was introduced. As mentioned before product family statistical forecast was easier to control; therefore, it served as basis for disaggregation of the total with use of the proportions of specific product statistical forecast. You may name this method as disaggregation of aggregated stat. forecast with detail stat. forecast. Concept is visualized in Fig. 5.79.

Calculation of ratios was important and was used in disaggregation of family forecast to product level. Family and product level forecast were stored on two different key figures.

**Step 6** Review of forecast on a product level with help of helpful visualizations

Demand planner analyzed product level statistical forecast with use of nano charts positioned in tabular display part of Excel SAP IBP. Nano chart shows in red the

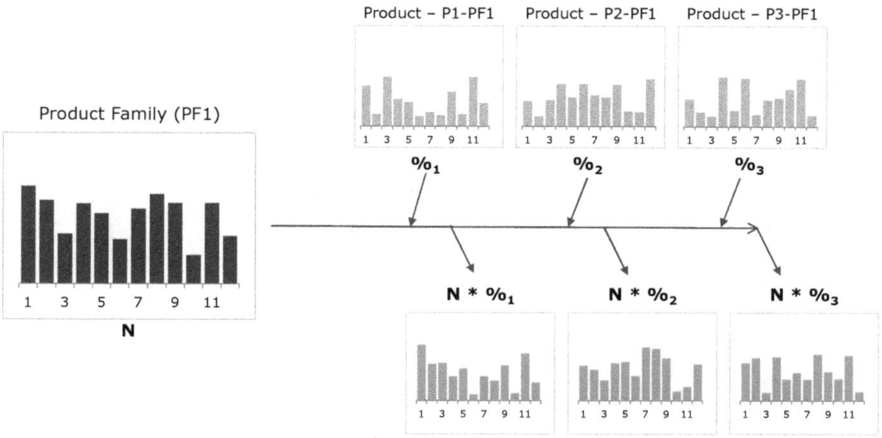


**Fig. 5.79** Product family stat. forecast disaggregation with product statistical forecast

highest peak, in green lowest data point, in gray all other data points in history, and in yellow statistical forecast (Fig. 5.80). It did take much less time to review forecast visually and easier to spot obvious mistakes. Final product level statistical forecast was then used in demand review meeting preparation.

### 5.2.9 Demand Review Meeting Preparation

Capturing demand signal on various level aligned to best insights is key but puts demand review preparation on a spot. Preparation has to be done on detail and aggregated level. This process step should as well validate if automatic disaggregation gives you results which you wanted to have. Review on detail level means that you need to have appropriate functional support from the system to execute exception management. It needs to be clear that responsibility for detail preparation of demand review is assigned to demand planner with consultation or support provided by portfolio managers, sales manager, and finance controllers.

There are many activities from business and analytical perspective which should be done as part of demand review meeting preparation (see Fig. 5.81):

- Access and analyze all forecast inputs in order to validate weighted combined forecast which should be treated as proposal for consensus unconstrained forecast.
- Review forecast input performance vs last unconstrained forecast.
- Review of exceptions/deviation from forecast vs actuals exposed on aggregated level but calculated on detail level.
- List of SKU, exceptions, and questions which need to be validated with sales, marketing, and finance.
- Prepare comprehensive overview of performance (effectiveness, efficiency, process adherence).

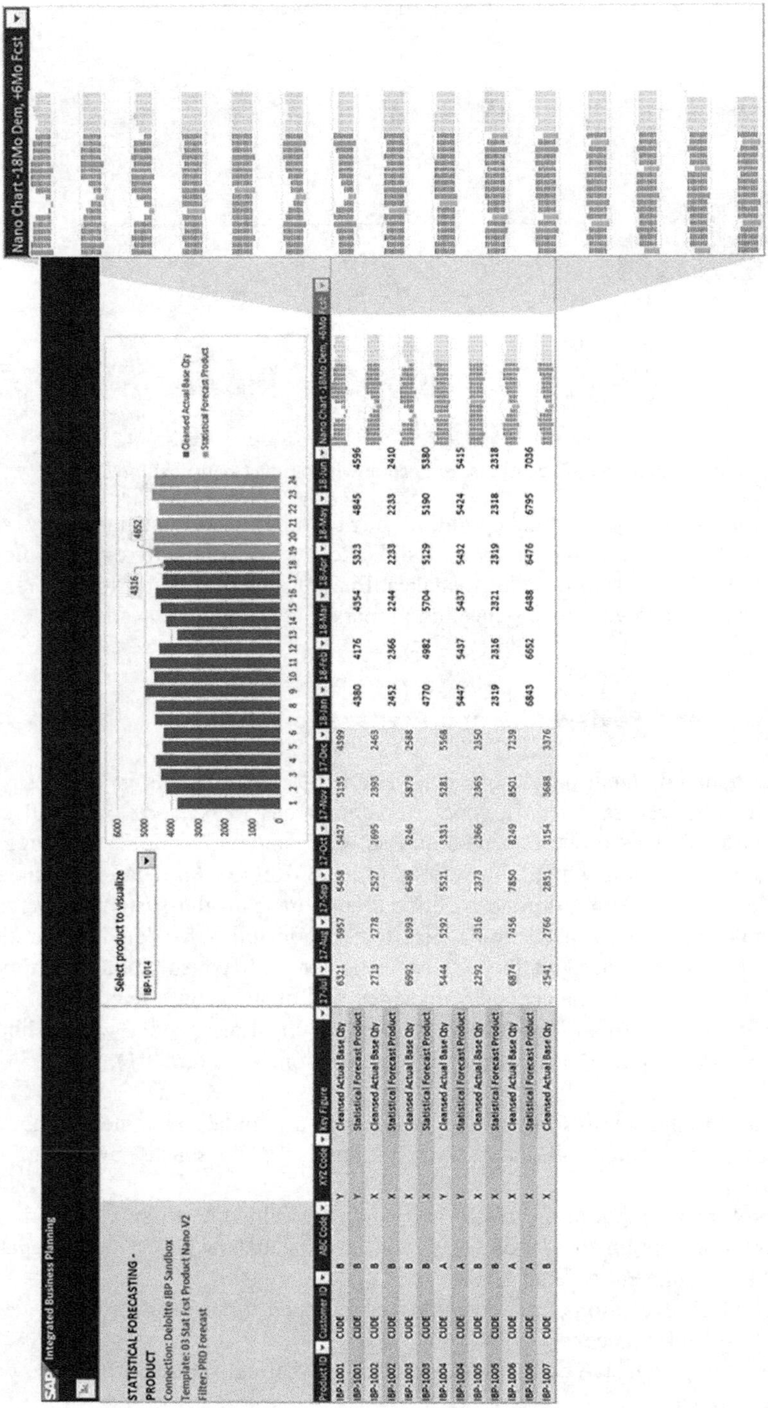


**Fig. 5.80** SAP IBP product statistical forecast visual controls with nano charts

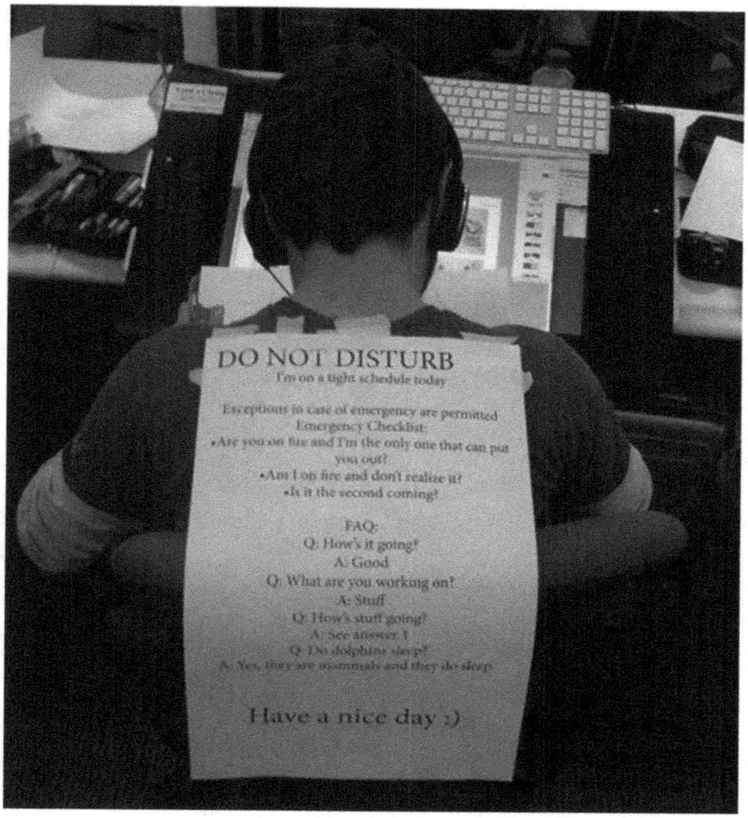


**Fig. 5.81** "Demand planner" focused on demand review preparation

- Collect all inputs for business risk and opportunity impacting volumetric and monetized side of forecast, and prepare inputs and what-if scenario comparison.
- Collect and clarify all assumptions behind scenarios.
- Collect qualitative information about market trends, market share, and competition activities.
- Perform sanity check of new product forecast, phase-in/phase-outs, and samples:
  - Validate with relevant stakeholders nonstandard revenue drivers review, e.g., licenses fees and services fees.
  - Validate with finance high-level credit availability status.
  - Validate with finance currency risks and opportunities.
  - Validate with finance and pricing recent pricing tactics which are captured in the system and which are planned.
  - Compare what has been changed vs last month demand review in volume and value.
  - Perform sanity check on level, trend, and seasonality of consensus forecast.

  - Validate completeness of the forecasting portfolio and sanity check of key master data key attributes, e.g., life cycle and segmentation.
- Agree first draft of demand review assumptions and status vs last month.
- Update status of actions in the last demand review action list.
- Prepare status on trainings and knowledge exchange sessions (if applicable).
- Prepare status on process improvement (if applicable).

#### 5.2.9.1 Demand Planner Hints for Demand Review Meeting Preparation

One of the most important elements of demand review meeting preparation is validation of forecast inputs and validation of changes between current month proposal of consensus forecast and previous month. In the analysis you should use performance measurement; it can trigger corrective actions and help to prepare consensus forecast with removed obvious bias. Demand planner normally asks themselves few questions like, How to spot deviations? What is important? And what is less important?

Let us start from the fundamental principles in your analysis (see Fig. 5.82):

We have expression in Polish which says "Jeden skowronek wiosny nie czyni"; this means "The one skylark does not make a spring" and seems to me it finds a resemblance in forecasting now ☺.

Assessing single event is important when it is really significant and for A class item. The most insightful way to assess performance and learn from it is to combine analysis of:

- wMAPE (weighted mean absolute percentage error)
- Bias (direction of error in %)
- Forecast error (error in value)

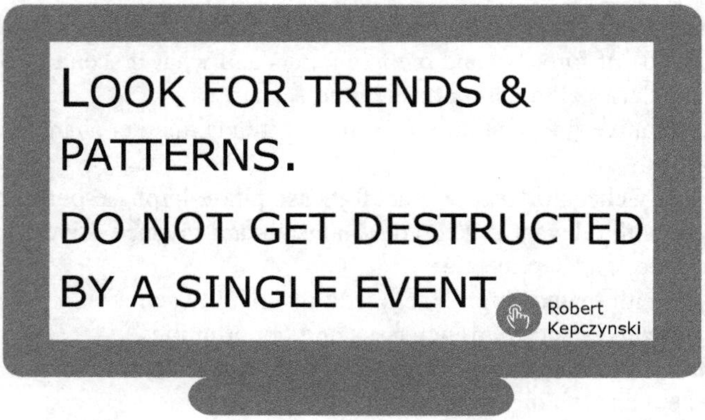

LOOK FOR TRENDS & PATTERNS.
DO NOT GET DESTRUCTED BY A SINGLE EVENT
Robert Kepczynski


**Fig. 5.82** Trends and patters are essential in removing bias in forecasting process

**Trends: Series of Bias Which Is Growing Positively or Negatively (Fig. 5.83)**
You can observe in the forecast obvious trends lines in bias, positive or negative. Try to correct them with following hints.

Corrective actions: check if more than three periods deviate from the objective and form trend line, and consider differentiation of SKU assignment in product segmentation, wMAPE/BIAS objectives, and forecast error showing big magnitude of error (mostly products A or B). Look for trend and pattern in errors. Validate forecast level, trend, and seasonality before introduction of correction action, and check actuals vs forecast and known tangible assumptions behind the forecast. Then if you are above upper objective and you run into over forecasting:

- Check if forecast can be decreased for future periods due to trend in over forecasting, e.g., use year over year.
- If yes, check if forecast level is not to high, and decrease forecast for periods when appropriate.
- If yes, check if forecast trend is not too optimistic, and decrease forecast for periods when appropriate.
- If yes, check if forecast peak season is not overstated, and decrease forecast for periods when appropriate.

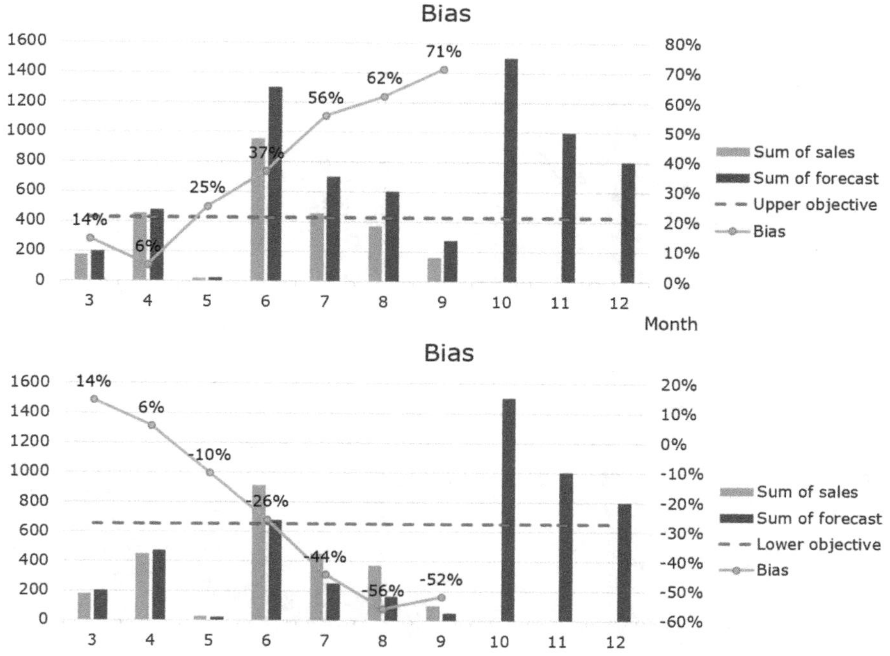


**Fig. 5.83** Bias decline or increase as trend line

If below lower objective and you run into under-forecasting:

- Check if forecast can be increased for future periods due to trend in under-forecasting.
- If yes, check if forecast level is not too low and increase forecast for periods when appropriate.
- If yes, check if forecast trend is not too pessimistic and increase forecast for periods when appropriate.
- If yes, check if forecast peak season is not understated and increase forecast for periods when appropriate.

**Continuous Over-/Under-Forecast: Series of Bias Which Lie Continuously Beyond Objective (Fig. 5.84)**
You can observe in the forecast obvious and continuous over- or under-forecasting. Try to correct them with following hints.

Corrective actions: check if errors form trend line, consider differentiation of SKU assignment in product segmentation and MAPE/BIAS objectives, and forecast error showing magnitude of error (for products A and B, be less forgiving). Then if you are above upper objective and you run into over forecasting:

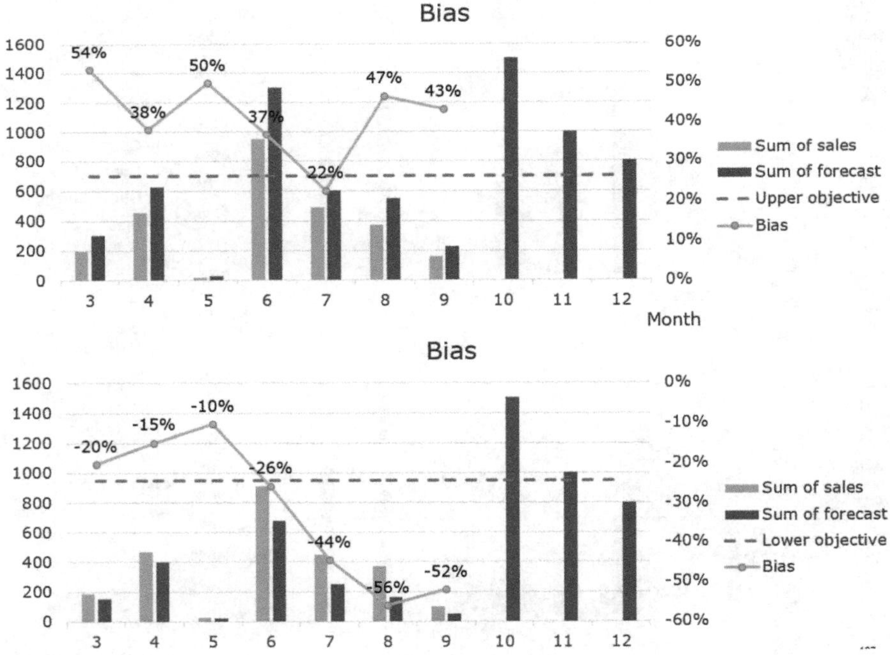


**Fig. 5.84** Continuous over- or under-forecasting bias

- Check if forecast can be decreased for future periods due to constant over forecasting, e.g., use year over year.
- If yes, check if forecast level, trend, or season is not overstated like historical inputs and decrease forecast for periods when appropriate.

If below lower objective and you run into under-forecasting:

- Check if forecast can be increased for future periods due to constant under-forecasting.
- If yes, check if forecast level, trend, or season is not understated like historical inputs and increase forecast for periods when appropriate.

**Continuous Over-/Under-Forecast in the Peak Season and Off the Season (Fig. 5.85)**

You can observe in the forecast obvious over or under-forecasting lined to the peak season and off the season. This happens very often that big mistakes are made for big volume sales. Try to correct them with following hints.

Corrective actions: check if more than two periods out of whole season deviate from objective, consider differentiation of SKU assignment in product segmentation

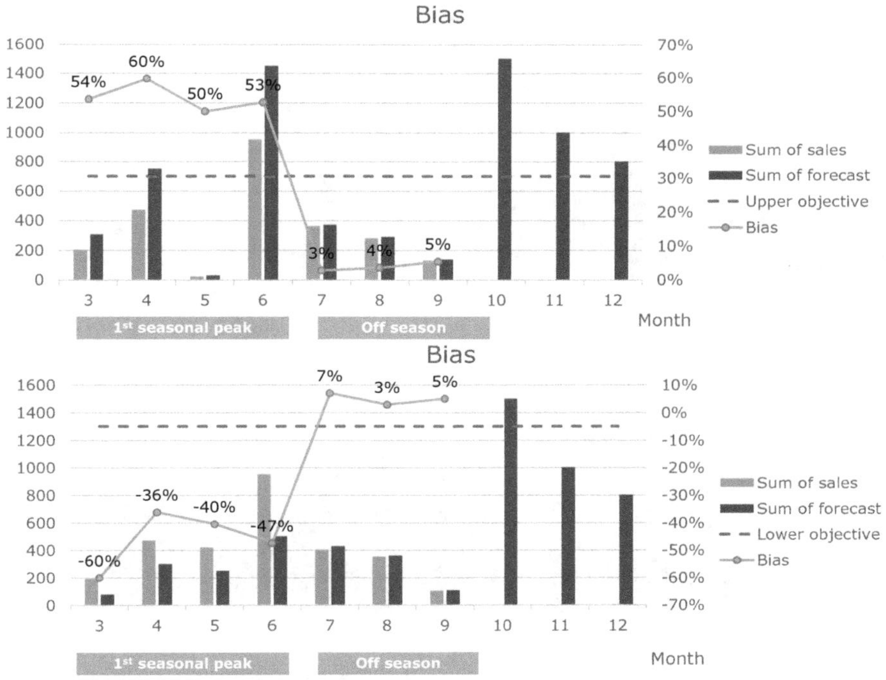


**Fig. 5.85** Off and on season bias trends

and MAPE/BIAS objectives, and forecast error showing magnitude of error. Then if you are above upper objective and run into over forecasting:

- Check if forecast can be decreased for the next season due to constant over forecasting in current season, e.g., use year over year.
- If yes, check if forecast level, trend, or season is not overstated like historical inputs and decrease forecast for periods when appropriate.

If below lower objective and run into under-forecasting:

- Check if forecast can be increased for future next season due to constant under-forecasting in the current season.
- If yes, check if forecast level, trend, or season is not understated like historical inputs and increase forecast for periods when appropriate.

**Importance of Significance (Fig. 5.86)**

You can observe in the forecast event which are significant like big bias for A or B class item. Significance of error is linked to magnitude of error per product segment; error for C class product will be less significant than A or B. Try to correct significant errors with following hints.

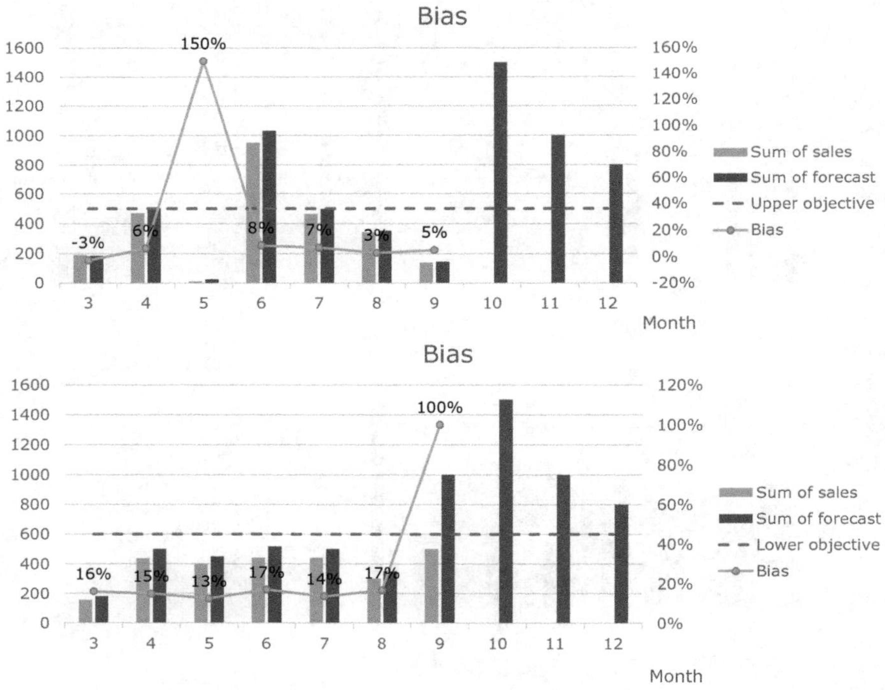


**Fig. 5.86** Bias significance

Corrective actions: check if single data point deviates from objective, and qualify if its significance justifies corrective action. Consider differentiation of SKU assignment in product segmentation and MAPE/BIAS objectives, and forecast error showing magnitude of error. Then if you are above upper objective and run into over forecasting:

- Check if not only bias but also forecast error, which shows volumetric scale of an error, justifies introduction of corrective action. For very small volume and big deviation (%), do not introduce corrective action, set low priorities, or even skip those types of cases. For the example captured in the figure, corrective action was not introduced.

If below lower objective and run into under-forecasting:

- Check if not only bias but also forecast error, which shows volumetric scale of an error, justifies introduction of corrective action. For very small volume and big deviation (%), do not introduce corrective action, set low priorities, or even skip those types of cases. For the example captured in the figure, corrective action was not introduced.

Similar review can be obtained on forecast input level, and this will help you to assess quality of the specific input and will give you important insights which forecast input should be influencing consensus unconstrained forecast. Once you have done analysis and first draft of consensus forecast, please make sure to run sanity checks:

- Check level on aggregated level.
- Check trend on aggregated level.
- Check seasonality on aggregated level.
- Check year-over-year on aggregated level.
- Check current month forecast (proposal) vs current month—1 forecast on aggregated level.

As part of demand review process, you may need to address the challenge of promoting product in the market space vs lowest possible supply chain cost. How the challenge was tackled at Danone:

- Analyze root causes of demand volatility. Determine key actions that could be implemented (investing in statistical forecast metrics and technologies to estimate and reduce demand volatility).
- Evaluate which ones will result in max ROI (Salley 2013).

### 5.2.10 Align Direct and Consignment Sales Forecast

What is so special about making consignment flow and standard direct sales flow aligned in IBP?

- They have two different signals to be reflected in material flows, which inform supply and replenishment.
- They have two different signals to be reflected in financial flows, which inform revenue and profit projections.

Below figure visualizes key elements of direct versus consignment sales forecasting and planning process (Fig. 5.87).

Both cases illustrate material and financial flows for sell-in category, meaning between direct trading partners. We go into more details of information being used and required for consignment forecasting and planning (Fig. 5.88).

Here it is how you should understand above

**Invoiced qty**—illustrates reconciled invoiced qty which follows consumption of stock. In this case reconciliation between declared and real consumption of stock did not result in any discrepancy. It often happens that there are some discrepancies between what is declared by customer and what is really consumed. This signal is constrained by financial flow reconciliation between partners. Invoice qty should serve as base for constrained revenue forecast in IBP.

**Forecasted consignment consumption**—illustrates forecasted consignment consumption of stock at customer location. This data input would be helpful in forecasting unconstrained revenue forecast in IBP. As you imagine actual consumption should be captured as well but for simplification reasons is not mapped on the figure.

**Customer consignment stock**—illustrates balance between opening stock at customer location, fill-up, and forecasted and actual consumption. This is very

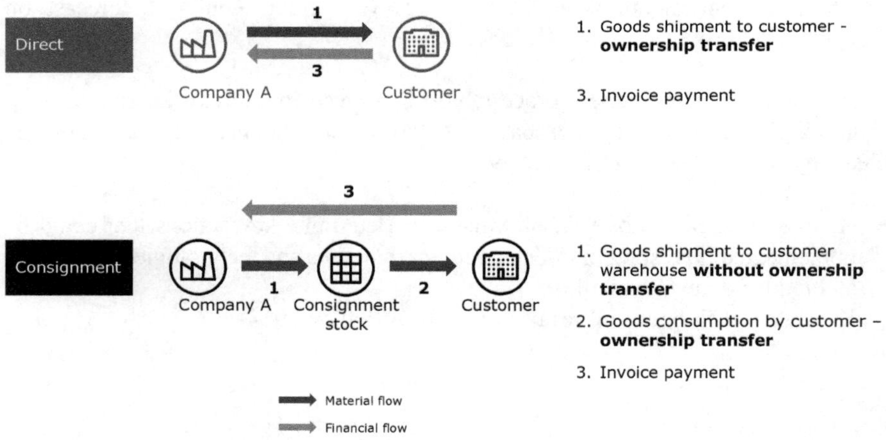


**Fig. 5.87** Consignment vs direct sales forecast

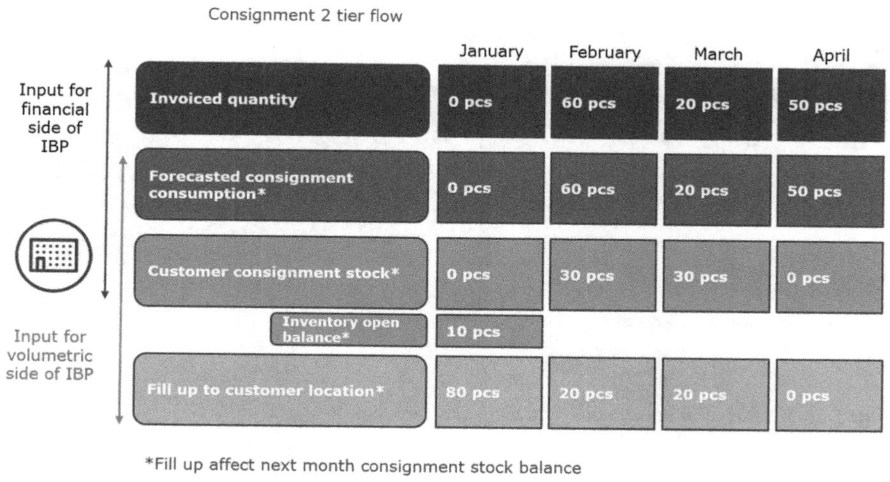


**Fig. 5.88** Consignment sales forecasting in figures

helpful information to be used in reconciliation of consumption and important for planning the fill-up. In case above current month fill-up is considered in next month balance.

**Fill-up to customer location**—illustrates a material flow from your location to customer location. This flow does not change ownership; stock stays in your books but it is at your customer location. This and consignment stock information are key for your supply and replenishment signal.

Challenge of forecasting and planning consignment is behind the fact that when you plan fill-up, you should consider your current stock at customer location and forecast of consumption linked to future invoice qty. This model is very easy to handle for your sales team since once set up it requires less attention. This model is much harder to handle by demand planning, customer service, and finance since it is a two-tier model.

### Alignment Between Direct and Consignment Models

Stakeholders of demand review meeting and integrated reconciliation meeting require consolidated view on both models. Demand review will trigger supply planning and replenishment, and integrated reconciliation will trigger financial, demand, and supply reconciliation. Let us highlight few watch-outs to support your process with right data.

Supply and replenishment signal should consist of common information about what, when, and where needed; therefore direct sales forecast in volume has to be combined with consignment fill-up. Financial side of equation requires direct sales revenue to be combined with monetized forecasted consignment consumption (see Fig. 5.89).

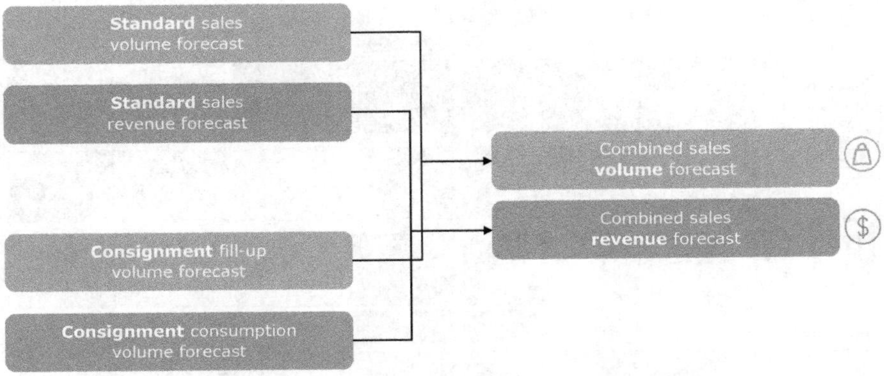


**Fig. 5.89** Combine direct and consignment sales forecasts

In case same SKU can be sold in direct and consignment model, you would need to define a rule for allocation planning which will address a question how to split supply response volume between those direct and consignment models.

### 5.2.11 SAP Use Case: Consignment Forecasting and Planning

Figure 5.88 exemplifies key information which may be used by sales and finance in consignment forecasting and planning. Sales need to focus on information relevant to forecast fill-up and finance on forecast consignment consumption. Demand planner should make sure to coordinate both function in forecasting and planning.

Let us go through what sales need to compare in forecasting fill-up (Fig. 5.90):

- Existing entries for fill-up forecast with what was already shipped to customer location (fill-up shipped qty) to evaluate if shipment are executed according to plan
- What was invoiced/consumed by customer (consumed consignment stock) and what is on stock at customer (actual consignment stock) to plan next fill-ups

As it is shown on the screen (Fig. 5.90), it would make sense to reduce fill-up forecast qty by 50%, for the remaining months of the season. Consumption and even shipments are not according to the plan. Sales in this step do predict returns after the peak season, but do not increase or decrease it yet.

Note that difference between the consumed consign. Stock and the consign. Invoiced qty is generated by the fact that the customer is not invoiced immediately, but fortnightly.

On the other hand, we have the finance closely monitoring the invoiced quantity and predicting the consignment usage forecast volumes until end of the season (Fig. 5.91).

SAP Integrated Business Planning — Consignment Fcst.

| Product | Customer | Key Figure | Jan"18 | Feb"18 | Mar"18 | Apr"18 | May"18 | June"18 |
|---|---|---|---|---|---|---|---|---|
| IBP-100 | CA01 | Fill-up Fcst Qty | 550 | 1,200 | 1,600 | 550 | 220 | 110 |
| | | Fill-up Shipped Qty | 500 | 1,150 | 1,250 | | | |
| | | Consumed Consign. Stock | 200 | 300 | 400 | | | |
| | | Consign. Invoiced Qty | 100 | 200 | 500 | | | |
| | | Actual Consign. Stock | 300 | 1,150 | 2,000 | | | |
| | | Actual Consign. Stock Value | $9,000 | $34,500 | $60,000 | | | |
| | | Sales Consign. Returns FC qty | | | | | 80 | 200 |

**Fig. 5.90** Consignment fill-up forecast

SAP Integrated Business Planning — Consignment Fcst.

| Product | Customer | Key Figure | Jan"18 | Feb"18 | Mar"18 | Apr"18 | May"18 | June"18 |
|---|---|---|---|---|---|---|---|---|
| IBP-100 | CA01 | Fill-up Fcst Qty | 550 | 1,200 | 1,600 | 225 | 110 | 55 |
| | | Consign. Fcst Qty | 500 | 1,100 | 1,400 | 200 | 100 | 50 |
| | | Consign. Fcst Qty Value (Actual + Fcst) | $3,000 | $6,000 | $19,500 | $6,000 | $3,000 | $1,500 |
| | | Consign. Invoiced Qty | 100 | 200 | 650 | | | |

**Fig. 5.91** Consignment usage forecasting 1

SAP Integrated Business Planning — Consignment Fcst.

| Product | Customer | Key Figure | Jan"18 | Feb"18 | Mar"18 | Apr"18 | May"18 | June"18 | Jul"18 |
|---|---|---|---|---|---|---|---|---|---|
| IBP-100 | CA01 | Fill-up Fcst Qty | 550 | 1,200 | 1,600 | 225 | 110 | 55 | |
| | | Fill-up Shipped Qty | 500 | 1,150 | 1,300 | 200 | 100 | | |
| | | Consumed Consign. Stock | 200 | 300 | 600 | 750 | 800 | 40 | |
| | | Consign. Invoiced Qty | 100 | 200 | 650 | 700 | 1,000 | 40 | |
| | | Actual Consign. Stock | 300 | 1,150 | 1,850 | 1,300 | 500 | 340 | |
| | | Actual Consign. Stock Value | $9,000 | $34,500 | $55,500 | $39,000 | $15,000 | $10,200 | |
| | | Sales Consign. Returns FC qty | | | | | 100 | 120 | 150 |

**Fig. 5.92** Consignment usage forecasting 2

Moving toward the end of the peak season, the consumed consignment stock is still behind the fill-up forecast qty. As a measure, the fill-up forecast qty is reduced to zero, and the returns quantity are being increased (Fig. 5.92).

Finance on the other hand would need to assess past consumption of stock and predict future one; final decision should be captured in consignment forecast qty and value.

### 5.2.12 SAP Use Case: Ways of Working Aligned to Best Insights

In the past very often, sales, marketing, finance, and demand planning could not work with data in the system to provide valuable review and updates. Simply because:

> They could not record and analyze data on the level and aggregation which was aligned to their best insights.

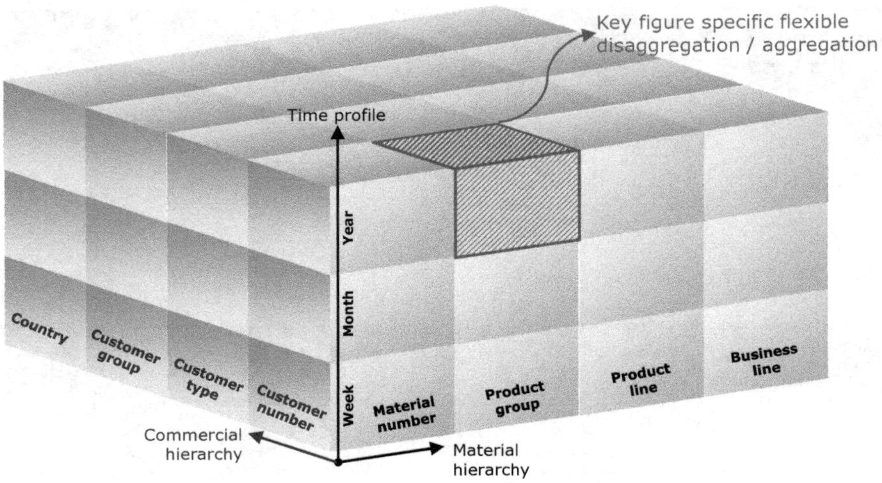


**Fig. 5.93** HANA data model enables you to work with the system on best insights level

Business stakeholders were forced to perform their activities in level which was pre-defined, constrained to the process. Many of the limitations and constraints were caused by poor technology behind the process. Development in the technology enabled many closed doors to be opened. SAP IBP has enabled business users to "work on level aligned to best insights."

We can illustrate that like a "cube" from which you select small piece and you work on it. Data dimensions may be very different but we could say that are few main groups like customer, geographies, product, marketing, supply and operations, financial (Fig. 5.93). In the process design, you will come up with what data you need to update, review, and analyze. Each data element (key figure) can have each own disaggregation and aggregation rule. You can have pre-configured key figures and the ones configured during and after project.

Let us try to explain what flexibility user have on some examples:

Demand review—sales input

- Sales representative goes to customer and discusses his/her requirements. Some of the customer will specify that they want particular packaging, e.g., 1L of the product some will say it is not critical; they may take 1L, 2L, and 5L. Sales representative may enter forecast for specific customer either for specific SKU with 1L packaging or in the other case will enter forecast for specific customer but on packaging type (bottle).
- Sales representative work with distributors which normally buy products in larger volume. Sales representative in this case may enter forecast for sales channel called distributors and will select product group which represents type of products and not specific packaging (bottle, canister, etc.).

Demand review—marketing input

- Product manager wants to review and update the forecast but without going into details since macroeconomic drivers which could not be aligned to particular product group product line did change behavior on the complete country level. Interest rates were much cheaper, and as general rule, there were much more money available. Product manager may enter forecast on product line and country level.

Integrated reconciliation—finance validation of business scenario planning in volume and value

- Finance business partner builds with help of demand manager and supply manager business scenario for management approval. Business scenario considers risk of delay in registration of new product on their market/country and price changes in one of the major sales zones. Finance business manager could increase/decrease forecasted price for product group and sales zone.

All above use cases are translated in the data model. It gives business an opportunity to capture business-relevant information in the granularity/level which speaks to them. It does not necessarily mean that complexity of system solution and costs of implementation to support those use cases (driven by master data/planning level attributes) will be high.

You should not exaggerate with number of dimensions of data, e.g., if complete demand review process has 200 attributes on which forecast can be provided and analyzed; most probably, a lot of them are not really needed in the process. Flexibility comes as well from the fact you could have in SAP IBP global process templates which can be adjusted on regional/country level and even further fine-tuned by users in their favorites. Favorites can be tailored to needs of the particular user to make him/her provide input aligned to his/her best insights and business-relevant information. Global or regional templates defined in blueprint phase may be adjusted by users to their preferences, level on which they want to work (Fig. 5.94).

As business user you can do so many things by yourself and leverage the power that the main user interface of SAP IBP is Excel. It means you can put your own formulas, vlookups beside data being stored/calculated in HANA database. You can view and store data on aggregated level/time horizon and detail in same multi-worksheet template (Fig. 5.95).

You can select and arrange your own data, scenarios, and versions which you work with (Fig. 5.96).

Similar applies to dashboards and analytics. We see that SAP IBP is far more user oriented than its old predecessor SAP APO.

We have seen many times that process improvement was triggered out of S&OP meeting. Here is one example: local S&OP global process owner with demand planner captured actions to cope with adjustments of templates/favorites and reviewed how opportunities will be considered in consensus demand plan (see Fig. 5.97).

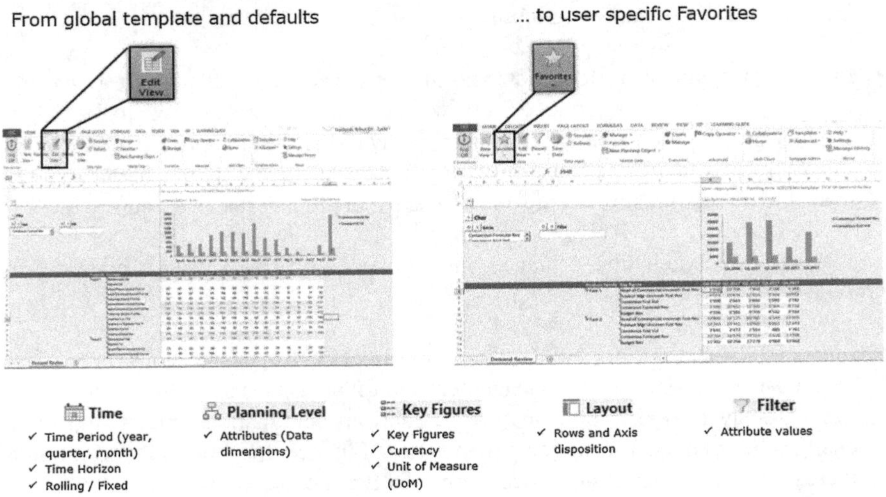


**Fig. 5.94** Global templates and user group or user favorites

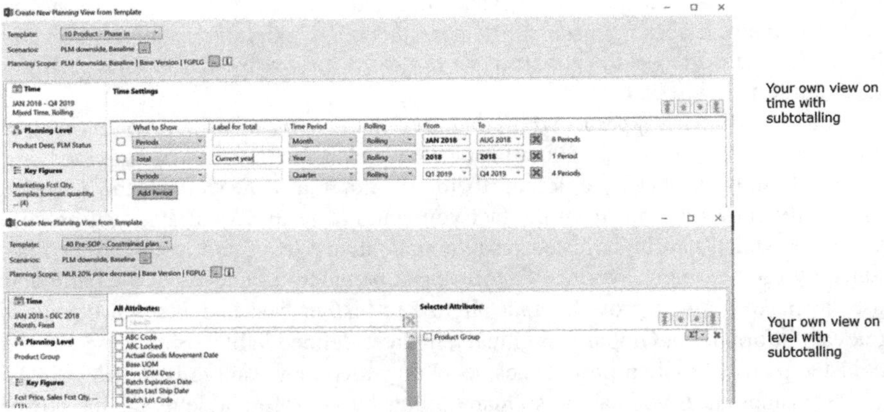


**Fig. 5.95** Your time and level view on data

## 5.2.13 Differentiated Forecasting

Many of us experienced that forecasting and demand planning was:

- Workload intensive especially for qualitative inputs.
- Sales and marketing team do not have enough time for forecasting.
- Overrated basic statistical forecasting.
- Large portfolio of the products.
- Few business models.
- Problematic since not enough focus was introduced.
- Performing below expectations.

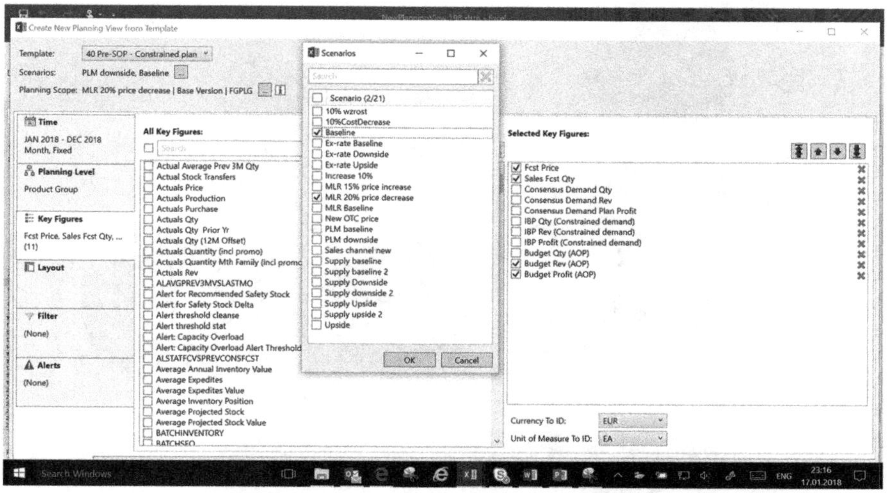


**Fig. 5.96** Your data arranged to your needs

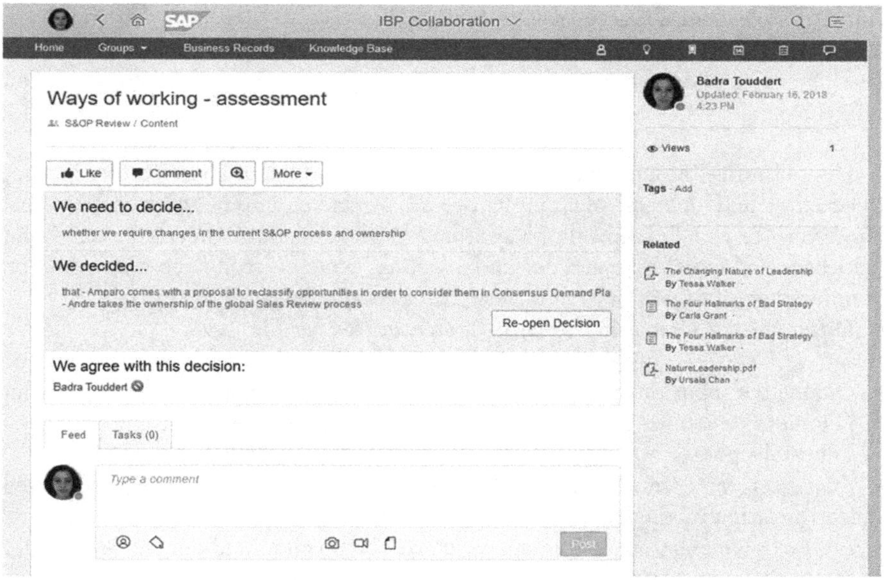


**Fig. 5.97** SAP Jam task to review SAP IBP favorites

Many have faced challenges on how to:

– Distinguish promotions signal from baseline demand and product mix shifts in volume.
– Find the right balance between statistical forecasting and collaborative bottom-up inputs from demand organization.

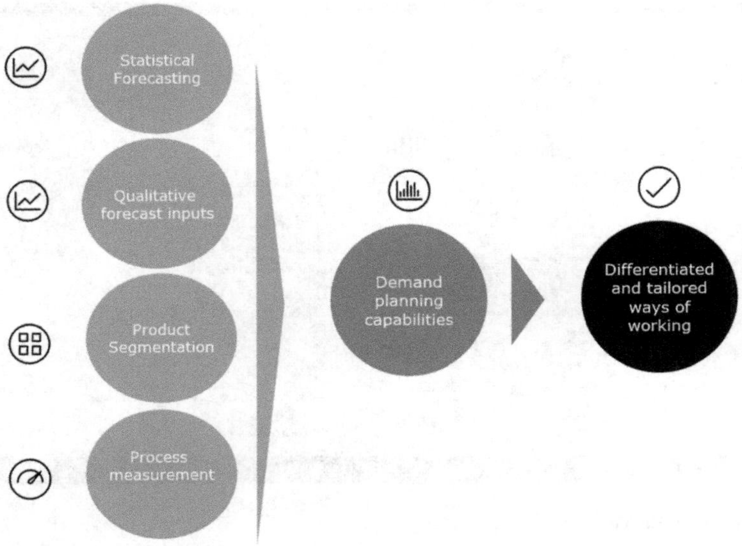


**Fig. 5.98** Differentiated forecasting building blocks

– Make stakeholders more accountable for forecast accuracy (Steutermann et al. 2012b).

How to turn it around and how to become more efficient and effective in your forecasting and demand planning process? To increase process efficiency and effectiveness, you should walk away from "one-size-fits-all" forecasting and build "differentiated forecasting and demand planning" which is really about introduction of tailored ways of working for different product segments.

Differentiated forecasting consists of elements as per Fig. 5.98:

- Qualitative input provided by various functions: sales, marketing, and demand planning, sometimes business development, should provide forecast input aligned to best insights.
- Statistical forecasting: functional system capabilities of basic and advanced statistical forecasting supported by demand planners or data scientists.
- Product segmentation: instrument which will help you to introduce focus on right materials, in a way to be aligned to your strategic objectives (e.g., revenue or profitable growth).
- Process measurement: measurement of all forecasting inputs (qualitative, quantitative) and consensus unconstrained forecast with agreed parameters aligned to S&OP characteristics.
- Demand planning capabilities: analytical and communication skills; for full set of capabilities and skills, please refer to relevant chapter at the beginning of the book.

Segmentation of product portfolio by criteria such as "volume, predictability, channel/customer, promotional and seasonal items" with assigned forecasting type accordingly seem to be very important. Combination of collaborative approach and statistical forecasting is key (Steutermann et al. 2012b).

Rationale for differentiated forecasting, tailored ways of working:

- Balance which function you ask for what type of input. Does it not sound like a waste of time to ask marketing and sales to provide input for extremely easy to forecast stable portfolio which has minor impact on revenue or profitable growth? Can demand planning be responsible for forecasting low-value contribution/high predictability product segments? They should be doing this and sales and marketing only reviewing on aggregated level their efforts, providing guidance.
- Sales team does not need to provide input for all SKUs/customers. Why not to leave in their forecasting portfolio those forecasting combinations which are critical to the business?
- Sales or marketing should own sales forecast, but process design and process improvement should be done by demand planning. Sales and marketing could focus on their core activities and gain time for selling.
- Time being gained from transformation to "differentiated forecasting" can be leveraged for selling, analytical support, and development of business risks and opportunities—in other words, in more value-adding activities. Demand planning plays crucial role in optimizing time being spend on forecasting. This function has to make this change happening.
- Once you have most of building blocks in place, it is most probably inevitable to consider introduction of target setting. Target setting should be as well done based on segment or at least groups of segment, so-called blended targets.

ABC/XYZ visualization matrix is a foundation of differentiated forecasting and can make an impact on how you organize your demand review process, e.g., bottom-up, top-down qualitative forecast inputs, statistical forecasting, and demand review preparation.

In Fig. 5.99, there is an example how you can leverage differentiated forecasting concept:

1. Define leading and supplementary techniques, e.g., input from sales and marketing (S&M), statistical forecasting (STAT), and input from marketing (M).
2. Set forecast performance targets in a more tailored way.
3. Share responsibility across different functions to provide forecast.

Definition of leading forecasting technique should result in list of qualitative or quantitative methods agreed as being the leading one or the only one. Segment BX and CX may be forecasted only with use of statistical forecast, but it should be reviewed maybe even on aggregated level in demand review.

Definition of shared responsibility should result in better balance of workload for input, review, and analysis of the forecast between sales, marketing, and demand planning. It would make sense to allocate forecasting of certain group of products to demand planning but still keep those segments under review in demand review meeting.

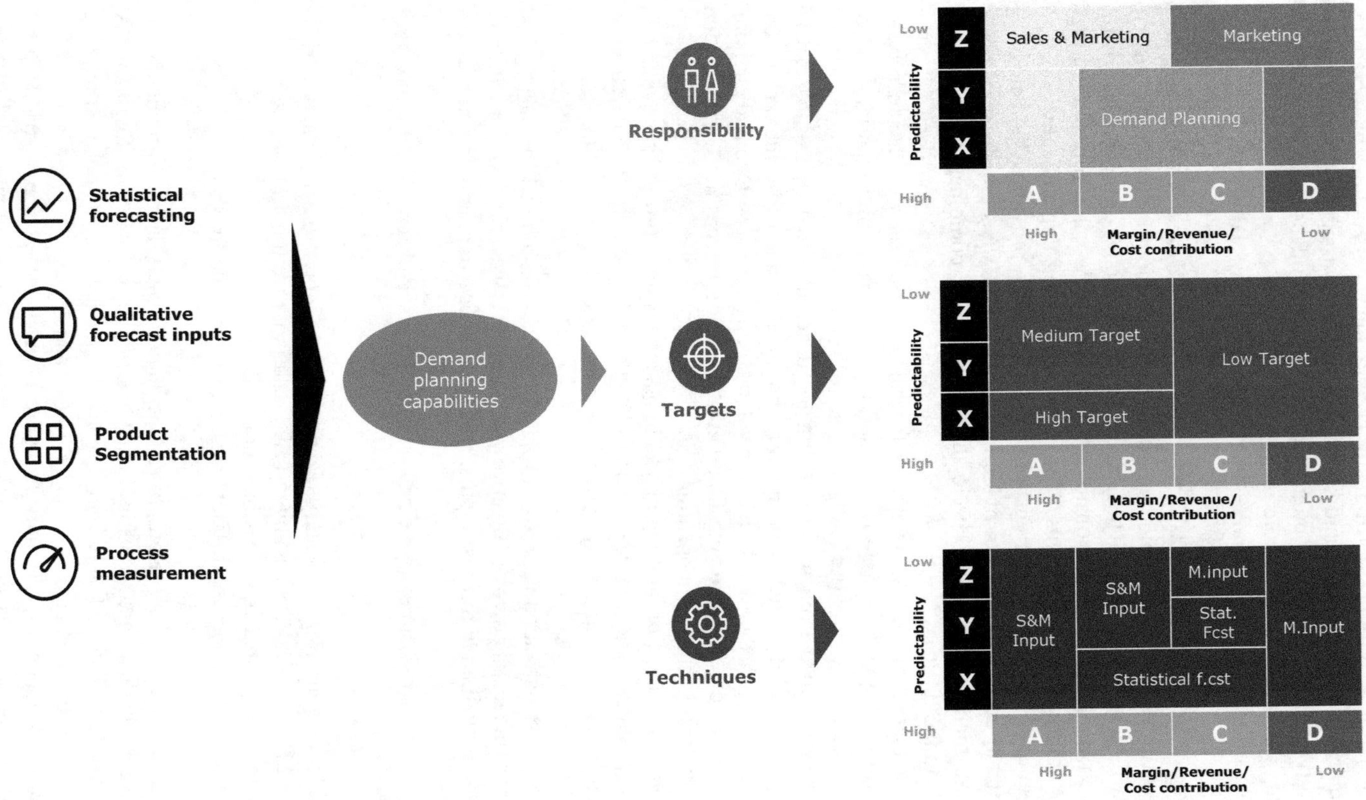


**Fig. 5.99** Differentiated forecasting deep dive

Last but not the least is topic of forecasting performance targets. Targets in differentiated forecasting should be established with a lot of sensitivity, and they should be shared between stakeholder group of sales, marketing, and demand planning. Targets should be challenging but realistic; therefore, you should start your target preparation with data analysis of your past performance. Do not start from visionary target without knowing your current performance. Performance targets need to be prepared based on historical performance with identification of ABC/XYZ; you should analyze time series and full-year view. Differentiated error targets should be set across portfolio.

Once all of the differentiated forecasting building blocks are in place, you will able to map whole solution against ABC/XYZ matrix as per Fig. 5.100.

Let's see how we can leverage above concept in SAP IBP.

We have learned in previous use case who we can build segmentation. With use of segmentation, we will define different ways of working balancing workload efforts, product importance, and demand patterns. Let us extend this with other components of differentiated forecasting.

**Effective Forecasting Strategies**

In this use case, we will generate consensus forecast based on forecasting strategies.

The forecasting strategy will be defined as a characteristic (attribute) of the product/country and will be maintained against ABC/XYZ segmentation, as per Fig. 5.101.

We have defined following strategies (see Fig. 5.102):

- "A"—automatic—consensus forecast defaulted from statistical forecast qty. For "CX" products with small volatility and low-profit contribution consensus forecast will be defaulted from statistical forecast.
- "AM"—automatic and manual—consensus forecast is calculated based on statistical forecast qty and the manual input (s). In our example we combine statistical forecast with demand planner input, but you can combine statistical forecast with many inputs (sales, marketing, demand planning) and use weighted combined forecast concept to combined methods. For "XY" products due to its importance, we decided to combine quantitative and qualitative inputs.
- "M"—manual—consensus forecast in our example will be defaulted to demand planner input but can be as well defined as other or combination of inputs.

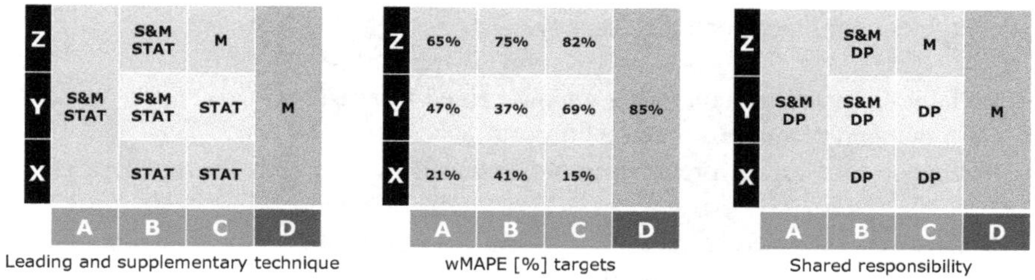


**Fig. 5.100** Differentiated forecasting leading techniques, targets, and shared responsibility

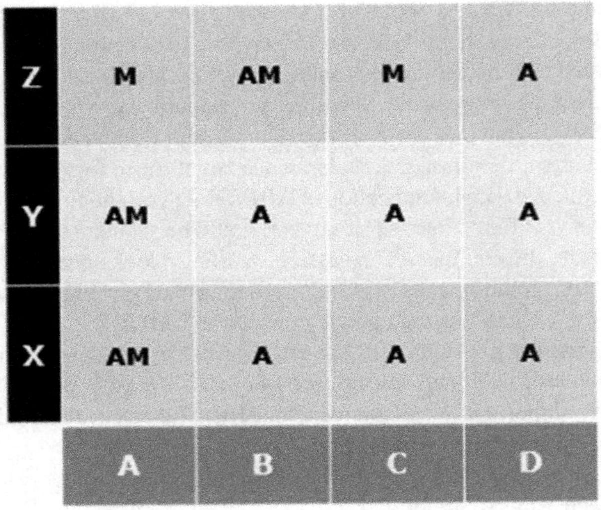


**Fig. 5.101** Forecasting strategies matrix visualization

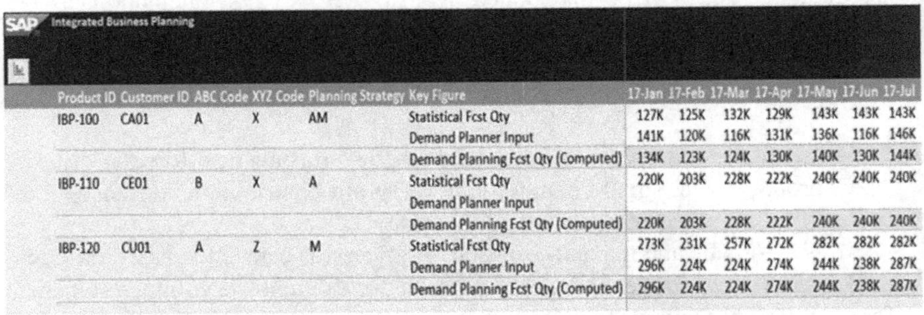


| Product ID | Customer ID | ABC Code | XYZ Code | Planning Strategy | Key Figure | 17-Jan | 17-Feb | 17-Mar | 17-Apr | 17-May | 17-Jun | 17-Jul |
|---|---|---|---|---|---|---|---|---|---|---|---|---|
| IBP-100 | CA01 | A | X | AM | Statistical Fcst Qty | 127K | 125K | 132K | 129K | 143K | 143K | 143K |
| | | | | | Demand Planner Input | 141K | 120K | 116K | 131K | 136K | 116K | 146K |
| | | | | | Demand Planning Fcst Qty (Computed) | 134K | 123K | 124K | 130K | 140K | 130K | 144K |
| IBP-110 | CE01 | B | X | A | Statistical Fcst Qty | 220K | 203K | 228K | 222K | 240K | 240K | 240K |
| | | | | | Demand Planner Input | | | | | | | |
| | | | | | Demand Planning Fcst Qty (Computed) | 220K | 203K | 228K | 222K | 240K | 240K | 240K |
| IBP-120 | CU01 | A | Z | M | Statistical Fcst Qty | 273K | 231K | 257K | 272K | 282K | 282K | 282K |
| | | | | | Demand Planner Input | 296K | 224K | 224K | 274K | 244K | 238K | 287K |
| | | | | | Demand Planning Fcst Qty (Computed) | 296K | 224K | 224K | 274K | 244K | 238K | 287K |

**Fig. 5.102** SAP IBP—forecasting strategies in differentiated forecasting concept

## 5.2.14 Weighted Combined Forecast (WCF)

Demand review is about preparing the most reliable, most realistic consensus unconstrained view of the forecast. Each of the forecast input contains error (see Fig. 5.103).

Weighted combined forecast can serve as:

- Reliable proposal for consensus unconstrained forecast.
- Help demand planner to prepare proposal faster.
- Reference forecast for preparation of consensus unconstrained forecast.

Weighted combined forecast is being recognized by many authors and organizations as one of the methods which can be used to:

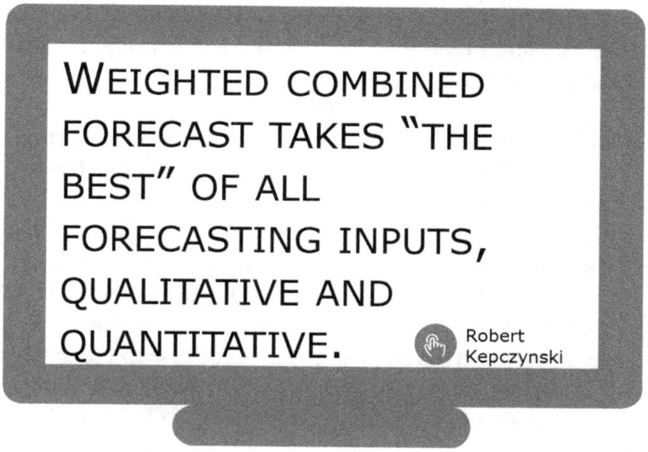

WEIGHTED COMBINED FORECAST TAKES "THE BEST" OF ALL FORECASTING INPUTS, QUALITATIVE AND QUANTITATIVE.
Robert Kepczynski


**Fig. 5.103** Weighted combined forecast takes the best out of the inputs

- Remove "bias" incorporated in qualitative input or some inefficiency of statistical forecasting.
- Increase effectiveness and efficiency of the forecasting process.

Value of WCF:

- The accuracy of the combination of various methods outperforms, on average, the specific methods being combined and does well in comparison with other methods. (Makridakis and Hibon 2000).
- Combining forecasts is especially useful when you are uncertain about the situation, uncertain about which method is most accurate, and when you want to avoid large errors. Compared with errors of the typical individual forecast, combining reduces errors. In 30 empirical comparisons, the reduction in ex ante errors for equally weighted combined forecasts averaged about 12.5% and ranged from 3 to 24% (Armstrong 2002).
- Combing forecasts from different methods offer a powerful strategy for improving forecast accuracy. Evidence from several decades of research including, SAS findings, illustrates that there is significant reduction in the size of the error when forecasts of different models are combined (Chase 2009).

Before getting into the scenarios themselves, let's review some reasons as to why combination forecasts might deliver superior results and also highlight situations where they are not advisable.

By combining forecasts, we are essentially averaging forecast errors. This can often result in accuracy improvements. There are reams of research done on this topic and the conclusion is "unanimous," which is that combining improves accuracy (Clemen, no date). The principle at work is the same as the one that leads to aggregate forecasts being more accurate than granular forecasts. For example, if one of the input forecasts has a high positive bias and another a high negative bias, an optimal combination of the two (e.g., weighted on their individual accuracy) can end up producing a forecast with a very low bias.

Another contributing factor has to do with the assumption of continuity, which is that history is a good indicator of what is to come. Time-series forecasting is done with this assumption, and model fitting (used in the case of statistical forecasting) is carried out looking at past values. If demand patterns should change, thereby invalidating model assumptions, accuracy is impacted. However, by combining forecasts, over-reliance on any one type of demand pattern is reduced, which results in the risk being spread more broadly leading to better accuracy than one would get by simply using one model. There is some debate over the use of combination forecasts in the context of statistical forecasting (more on this topic below). It is easier, though, to justify the use of combined forecasts in the context of judgmental forecasting. As multiple points of view are being collated, it is fair to say each one is based on a set of assumptions and that it is unlikely that any one of them is comprehensive enough. By combining, you might be able to explain that which is being forecasted better.

There is no denying the overwhelming empirical support for the effectiveness of combination forecasts. Having said that there are pitfalls one needs to be mindful of. For one, critics point out that the reason for combining is because no single model is specified comprehensively enough to do a reliable job of predicting the business event in question on its own (see quote below):

From a conventional forecasting point of view, using a combination of forecasts amounts to an admission that the forecaster is unable to build a properly specified model. Trying ever more elaborate combining models seems only to add insult of injury, as the more complicated combinations do not generally perform all that well. (Clemen)

There is merit to this criticism. Use of combination forecast does not preclude the practitioner from trying to do rigorous data analysis and making an attempt to choose the best model and combination of parameters for the job when it comes to statistical forecasting. In fact, when you are dealing with factors both internal and external that remain fairly steady[4] (assumption of continuity holds true), a single model might be sufficient. On the other hand, in the face of high volatility where past behaviors are not reliable indicators of how things will play out, resorting to multiple forecasts based on several different assumptions rather than just one might be prudent. It has been proved empirically that oftentimes a simple combination of forecasts outperforms more sophisticatedly constructed combinations (such as based on optimal weights). Therefore, one needs to carefully evaluate the incremental benefit of choosing different input weights. Judgmental forecasting is definitely a more suitable realm for use of combination forecasts, but here as well caution needs to be exercised. As inputs are more qualitative in nature, we need to consider the impact of

[4]Please note that remaining steady does not mean low variability. It just means the behavior of these factors do not change significantly over time.

the so-called anchoring effect or priming effect on the ultimate result. The anchoring effect is a well-known phenomenon in decision theory, which states that one is prone to suggestions, however unrelated, when estimating an unknown quantity. In reality, this could mean that when a proposal for a consensus forecast is generated automatically using WCF, participants may start anchoring around this number and may neglect factors that may have led them to a different (and potentially a more accurate) conclusion. In summary, although combination forecasts have been empirically proven to be very effective, a careful analysis of pros and cons—key among them discussed above—is called for before employing them in practice.

Weighted combined forecast (WCF) belongs to a class of forecasting methods commonly known as combination forecasts. As discussed earlier, this involves combining multiple forecasts (several time series) to produce a single time series or a composite forecast.

Charles W. Chase (2009) proposes simple formula to illustrate weighted combine forecast:

$$\text{Weighted Combined Forecast} > \beta_1 \text{FM}_1 + \beta_2 \text{FM}_2 + \beta_3 \text{FM}_3$$

where $\beta =$ is weight and FM is forecast method.

There are various methods how to calculate weighted combined forecast which in essence are different in what type of weighting is being used. Many 6 sigma practitioners say that if method is not being understood, it may not be accepted, therefore why not to use for weighing measure the calculation which you already use in your forecast performance measurement. It will help you to explain it to broader group of stakeholders and use wMAPE as simple weighting factor.

There are two popular ways of combining forecasts: one can either use a simple average or use (optimal) weights. This section will focus on WCF, which relies on the use of weights to combine multiple forecasts. In this context, we'll cover two use cases in SAP IBP:

- We will combine the results of multiple statistical forecasting models. The procedure for combining involves using weights that are in inverse proportion to the forecast error measure (say, MAPE values) of the input forecast models.
- We will combine qualitative with statistical forecasts. The result is a forecast proposal, which can serve as the first input into the demand review process.

We'll now turn to the two scenarios listed earlier and discuss how they can be modeled in the system.

### 5.2.15 SAP Use Case: Combining Quantitative and Qualitative Inputs in WCF

In this scenario we will combine statistical forecast, which itself uses a weighted combination and two other qualitative inputs—sales and marketing forecasts,

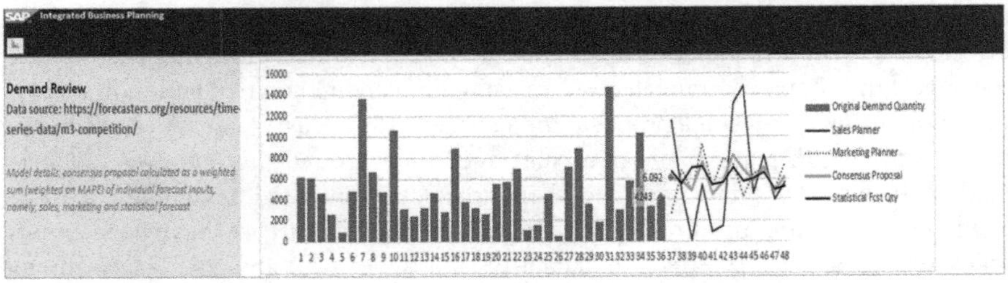


**Fig. 5.104** Generation of consensus proposal from quantitative and qualitative inputs

SAP Integrated Business Planning

| Product ID | Customer ID | Key Figure | JUN 2017 | JUL 2017 | AUG 2017 | SEP 2017 | OCT 2017 | NOV 2017 | DEC 2017 | JAN 2018 | FEB 2018 | MAR 2018 | APR 2018 | MAY 2018 | JUN 2018 | JUL 2018 | AUG 2018 |
|---|---|---|---|---|---|---|---|---|---|---|---|---|---|---|---|---|---|
| IBP_P003 | IBP_C001 | Original Demand Quantity | 10380 | 3360 | 4243 | 2542 | 5512 | 9277 | 7113 | 4367 | 16477 | 7001 | 5661 | 11635 | 8793 | 3821 | 39094 |
| IBP_P003 | IBP_C001 | Cleaned Demand Quantity | 10380 | 3360 | 4243 | | | | | | | | | | | | |
| IBP_P003 | IBP_C001 | Ex-post Forecast Qty | 7008 | 6948 | 6314 | | | | | | | | | | | | |
| IBP_P003 | IBP_C001 | Statistical Fcst Qty | | | | 6700 | 5513 | 7096 | 7125 | 5395 | 5622 | 7033 | 5718 | 5999 | 6652 | 4924 | 5270 |
| IBP_P003 | IBP_C001 | Sales Planner | | | | 11495 | 4700 | 106 | 5408 | 907 | 1410 | 13118 | 14852 | 4571 | 8199 | 3955 | 5609 |
| IBP_P003 | IBP_C001 | Marketing Planner | | | | 2717 | 6764 | 4825 | 9290 | 5220 | 7937 | 7329 | 4306 | 6423 | 7111 | 4815 | 7493 |
| IBP_P003 | IBP_C001 | MAPE Statistical | 55,59 | 55,59 | 55,59 | 55,59 | 55,59 | 55,59 | 55,59 | 55,59 | 55,59 | 55,59 | 55,59 | 55,59 | 55,59 | 55,59 | 55,59 |
| IBP_P003 | IBP_C001 | MAPE SALES | | | | 80,00 | 80,00 | 80,00 | 80,00 | 80,00 | 80,00 | 80,00 | 80,00 | 80,00 | 80,00 | 80,00 | 80,00 |
| IBP_P003 | IBP_C001 | MAPE MARKETING | | | | 60,00 | 60,00 | 60,00 | 60,00 | 60,00 | 60,00 | 60,00 | 60,00 | 60,00 | 60,00 | 60,00 | 60,00 |
| IBP_P003 | IBP_C001 | MAPE TOTAL | | | | 104 | 104 | 104 | 104 | 104 | 104 | 104 | 104 | 104 | 104 | 104 | 104 |
| IBP_P003 | IBP_C001 | WMAPE STATISTICAL | | | | 42,54% | 42,54% | 42,54% | 42,54% | 42,54% | 42,54% | 42,54% | 42,54% | 42,54% | 42,54% | 42,54% | 42,54% |
| IBP_P003 | IBP_C001 | WMAPE SALES | | | | 19,15% | 19,15% | 19,15% | 19,15% | 19,15% | 19,15% | 19,15% | 19,15% | 19,15% | 19,15% | 19,15% | 19,15% |
| IBP_P003 | IBP_C001 | WMAPE MARKETING | | | | 38,31% | 38,31% | 38,31% | 38,31% | 38,31% | 38,31% | 38,31% | 38,31% | 38,31% | 38,31% | 38,31% | 38,31% |
| IBP_P003 | IBP_C001 | Consensus Proposal | | | | 6092 | 5837 | 4887 | 7625 | 4468 | 5702 | 8312 | 6927 | 5888 | 7116 | 4697 | 6186 |

**Fig. 5.105** Result of consensus proposal—numerical data

respectively. The inputs are combined with the help of purpose configured key figures to generate a consensus proposal. The results of this scenario are shown in Figs. 5.104 and 5.105, and the steps followed are described below.

- First, the error measures, MAPE in our scenario, are calculated for each of the input forecasts (see key figures MAPE statistical, MAPE sales, and MAPE marketing in Fig. 5.105).
- Next, MAPE is transformed to an accuracy measure (1—MAPE), and the total accuracy for the three input forecasts is calculated. For Sep 2017, this gives 104 (100 * Number of input forecasts—[$\text{MAPE}_{\text{Statistical}}$ + $\text{MAPE}_{\text{Sales}}$ + $\text{MAPE}_{\text{Marketing}}$] = 300—(56 + 80 + 60) = 104).
- Then the weights are calculated as the ratio between the individual accuracy measure and the total accuracy. This gives 42.54%, 19.15%, and 38.31% for statistical, sales, and marketing forecasts, respectively
- Finally, the consensus proposal is calculated by applying the weights to the respective input forecasts. For Sep 2017, this gives 6092 (42.54% of 6700 + 19.15% of 11,495 + 38.31% of 2717). As we can see from the graph, the consensus proposal is less responsive to the sales planner forecast compared to the other two, which is in line with the weights assigned.

The technical note below shows how the key figures that are needed for the calculations described could be configured.

```
MAPE1UI@MTHPRODCUST    =    "MAPE1@PRODCUST"
```

**Fig. 5.106** Visualizing MAPE

```
ACCUTOTAL@MTHPRODCUST    =    IF( "PERIODID3" >= "$$PERIODID3CU$$" , 300 - ( "WMAPE1UI@MTHPRODCUST" +
                              "MAPESALES@MTHPRODCUST" + "MAPEMARKETING@MTHPRODCUST" ), NULL)
```

**Fig. 5.107** Calculating total accuracy

```
WMAPESALES@MTHPRODCUST    =    (100 - "MAPESALES@MTHPRODCUST" ) / "MAPETOTAL@MTHPRODCUST"
```

**Fig. 5.108** Calculating weights

```
CONSENSUSPROPOSAL      =    ( "WMAPESALES@MTHPRODCUST" * "SALESPLANNER@MTHPRODCUST" ) +
@MTHPRODCUST                ( "WMAPEMARKETING@MTHPRODCUST" * "MARKETINGPLANNER@MTHPRODCUST" ) +
                            ( "WMAPESTATISTICAL@MTHPRODCUST" * "STATISTICALFORECASTQTY@MTHPRODCUST" )
```

**Fig. 5.109** Weighted combined forecast as consensus proposal

**Technical Note:**
How to configure key figures to calculate weighted combined forecast dynamically:

1. The error measure is calculated on a planning level that excludes the time dimension. If it needs to be visualized, it can be done as shown in Fig. 5.106. Here, a calculated key figure is created on a base planning level that is the same as the input planning level except for the fact that it includes a time dimension (MTHPRODCUST vs PRODCUST in the example).
2. The accuracy total of the inputs can be calculated as shown in Fig. 5.107. As this needs to be calculated for each period, the MAPE on a planning level including the time dimension (described in step 1) is used for each of the forecast inputs.
3. The weights are calculated for each of the input forecasts shown in Fig. 5.108.
4. Finally, the weighted combined forecast is calculated using the calculation shown in Fig. 5.109.

### 5.2.16 Demand Review Meeting

Demand review meeting should be positioned as the meeting on which we discuss and agree unconstrained forecast. In order to make the discussion balanced and agreed, sales, marketing, finance, demand planning, and demand manager should be on that meeting.

Meeting should be prepared upfront by demand planner.

Proposed agenda points for demand review meeting:

- Review actions from last meeting.
- Review and sign off new product forecast and samples.
- Review key assumptions for respective team forecast inputs.
- Review forecasting performance indicators (wMAPE, bias, forecast error):
  - Address corrective action for process improvement.
- Review business lines/organizational units/sales channel forecast:
  - Review and assess information gathered in bottom-up, top-down, demand review preparation meetings.
- Review and sign off consensus unconstrained forecast business scenarios:
  - Review price and market tactics.
  - Review promotional activities.
  - Review key initiatives, prospects, and deals captured in scenarios.
  - Review commercial and finance risks and opportunities linked to business scenarios:

    Review on high-level customer credit availability.
    Review on high-level currency risks.
    Review on high-level competition activities.
    Review on high-level volume and value phasing.
  - Achieve agreement on what is the most realistic unconstrained forecast business scenario.
  - Sign off and agree on assumptions behind approved scenario.
  - Define action plan required to make approved scenario happen in real-life business environment.
- Capture and review nonstandard sources of revenue, and ensure complete volume and value market potentials are captured.
- Confirm volumetric and value (revenue projections) of consensus unconstrained forecast incl. consignment model.
- Update and set new actions.

Here are some demand review meeting pitfalls to avoid:

- Review of the forecast input and consensus forecast proposal on very detail level
- Repetition of demand review meeting preparation meeting but with different stakeholders
- Business scenarios build from scratch on the meeting and not on preparation meeting
- One-size-fits-all review, no use of product-customer segmentation
- Lack of graphical presentation of the data
- Lack of review of assumption
- Lack of balance between short- and midterm goals, letting the person who "shouts loudest" to bias consensus decision
- No balanced representation of stakeholders between sales, marketing, demand planning, and finance
- No actions and tasks captured

As you have seen on examples given, forecasting and demand planning is a collaborative and cross-functional process that allows different functions in an organization to work together with the aim of providing a unique, trustworthy, and approved forecast of demand. That should be the ultimate goal of demand review (Penafiel 2016).

You may attempt to create dashboard or one pager overview for key business lines/market or portfolio segments and some detail information. Dashboard may help to review consensus forecast on high level:

- Level
- Trend and cycle
- Seasonality
- Year over year
- Current month vs current month—1
- Consensus demand vs supply availability last month
- Volume and value
- Unconstrained forecast performance
- Forecast input performance

In the other study (Bursa 2014), we see emphasis on focus on high value-added activities:

- A management by exception can be introduced to maximize efficiency, avoid issues, tackle problems, and propose solutions.
- Dashboards can display discrepancies between real and predicted pointing alerts and prioritizing actions.
- Introducing ABC analysis.
- Continuous monitoring and setting up KPIs.

#### 5.2.16.1 Review Demand "Risk and Opportunities"

Demand review meeting should be the forum where key senior stakeholders discuss business uncertainty, which have positive or negative impact on your consensus forecast. As discussed before scenario planning is an instrument which you can use in quick and easy way to capture risks and opportunities and see their impact.

There are many drivers which should be looked at when discussing risk and opportunity for what-if scenario planning:

- Demand increases or decrease due to competition activities
- Demand below/above unconstrained forecast due to own performance
- Promotions and marketing campaigns
- Change in customer pricing/pricing tactics and market price changes
- Demand shift across sales channels/brands
- Macroeconomic leading indicator change

- Change in focus between revenue and profitable growth
- Credit controls/credit availability
- Product rankings and research analysis

There are some activities which you may find relevant when running assessment and impact of what-if scenarios:

- Use baseline set of figures as starting point.
- Define key drivers to be mapped in the business scenario, and assign business scenario owner or even owners.
- Address drivers which impact revenue, cost, and volume.
- Document assumptions for specific scenario/driver, and relate assumptions to figures captured in the system.
- Store scenario in the system as separate versions of the truth.
- Store assumptions for all scenarios, and back up data for validated and approved scenario.
- Prepare comparison of scenarios which shows impact of each of it.

It is not enough to discuss those drivers, but it is critical to capture their expected impact in volume and/or value. There might be several ways how to do it:

- First of all IBP has flexible way to define nonstandard calculation with standard mechanism like key figure calculations. Assuming driver has percentage impact for specific period on consensus forecast in volume, you may introduce a key figure in which you capture driver value, and based on it, consensus forecast will be uplifted or decreased.
- We have seen process where drivers were defined in external systems and were integrated with IBP. Example of it was ranking of specific seed variety provided by independent governmental agency. This ranking was critical in projecting midterm forecast since growers were also using this publicly available information when selecting supplier and specific varieties of seeds. Seed variety with better ranking could give grower higher yield and better profit at the end.
- Last example is when correlation between certain variable, e.g., marketing or sales spend was correlated in the past with sales volume, and this correlation can be used in standard SAP IBP algorithm called multilinear regression model. This statistical model can project increase or decrease of volume projections based on multiple variables including variables for which data comes to IBP from external systems/sources. Key to success in using this method is data analysis and model development which makes sense.

In many life science companies, uncertainty has high impact on their performance (tender orders, regulatory decisions). Those companies should:

- Incorporate uncertainty into demand management using established techniques, such as range forecasts and opportunities.

- Link forecasting, planning for tenders with core supply planning processes to maximize opportunities for flexibility and reuse (Applebaum 2014).

On the other hand, many companies struggle with alignment, so much is required to manage risks and opportunities. What should be done is:

- Leverage S&OP to integrate planning across the organization and accelerate responses to demand shifts.
- Make demand management more assumption-based to drive alignment (Applebaum 2014).

Consensus forecast is an ultimate deliverable of demand review. In the following subchapters, we will discuss in more detail how you can manage demand risks and opportunities with help of SAP commercial applications integrated with SAP IBP.

### 5.2.17 SAP Use Case: Integrate Market Opportunities (SAP C4C Hybris—SAP IBP)

Part of management demand risk and opportunities covers management of tenders, big deals, and market opportunities. We would need to understand that SAP Hybris Cloud for customer is SAP's cloud solution for customer relationship management. It comes with a suite of applications that will help to better know and engage your customers to increase sales and achieve better service. Cloud for Sales comes with multiple features that will help you to transform the selling process and align it to the buying patterns of the consumers:

- Mobility
- Account management and intelligence
- Opportunity management and insight
- Real-time analytics
- Email and notes integration
- Collaboration and social selling
- Sales performance management

Having these features at their finger point, sales people will be able to sell more, reduce the length of the sales cycle, and be more effective in engaging customers.

One of the functionalities of Cloud for Sales is opportunities management. This feature helps you to improve sales effectiveness by gaining better pipeline visibility and ensures a consistent sales process by bringing leading practices methodologies. Here are some of the key features of the solution (see Fig. 5.110):

- Manage opportunity information, sales phase, and status
- Ability to manage sales teams
- Opportunity document flow

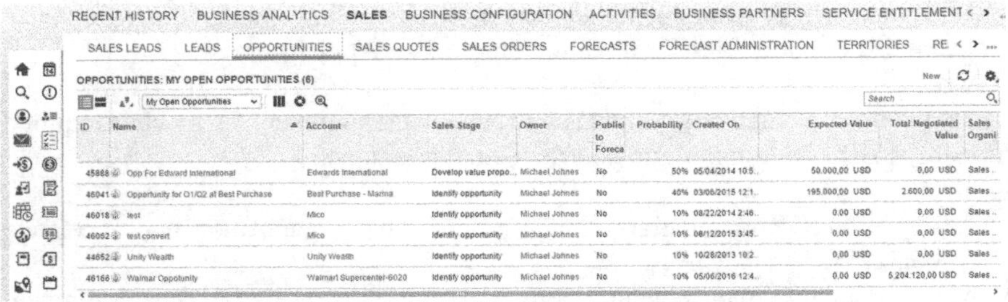


**Fig. 5.110** Cloud 4 sales—management of opportunities

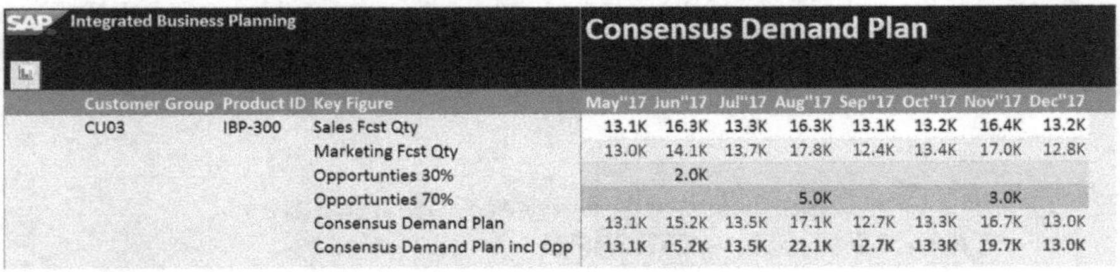


**Fig. 5.111** C4Sales opportunities in IBP

- Embedded collaboration
- Opportunity relationships management, etc.

Visibility over the sales pipeline opportunities and their associated probability of happening can be a key driver of the monthly tactical S&OP process and demand review. Input about opportunities may serve as a basis for what-if analysis to reach the most profitable decisions.

Integrating opportunities in IBP can happen at different levels of granularity, depending on each company in how much detail they would review the opportunities during S&OP process:

- Individual opportunities and their associated probabilities
- Aggregated opportunities and their associated probabilities

We have seen that some customers go for aggregated opportunities rather than individual ones. This is enough for a tactical time-series planning process and it also has advantages from data maintenance perspective. Moreover, it will also save quite a lot of effort during implementation when initialization process will be designed. So now we are going to share an example of how opportunities managed in Cloud 4 Sales can be aggregated and how they can be consumed in the monthly S&OP process.

In Fig. 5.111 we see that opportunities that are coming from Cloud for Sales are aggregated prior to the integration into IBP. In this example, we visualize, analyze, and incorporate them in IBP at the granularity of customer group, product, and

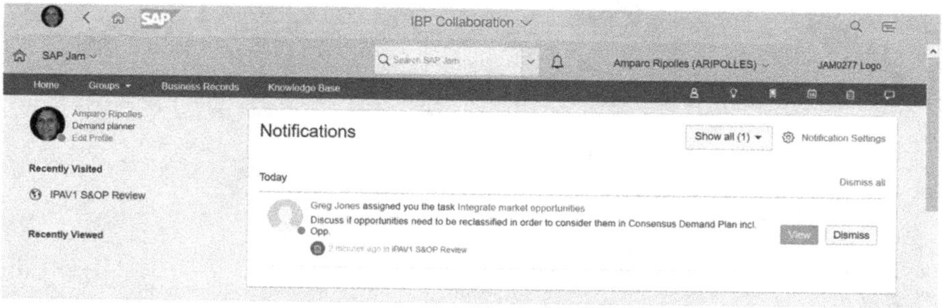


**Fig. 5.112** SAP JAM task to assess opportunities from SAP Hybris

probability. The latter characteristic will divide these opportunities in two categories that are modeled in IBP as two different key figures:

- Opportunities with a chance higher than 30% but lower than 70%. These opportunities are available for analysis, and they can be assessed during consensus demand forecast review but manually added into consensus forecast.
- Opportunities higher than 70% that are automatically added on top of consensus demand forecast.

Having opportunities as part of the consensus demand forecast will help the demand and supply planners to run multiple what-if analyses and anticipate the outcome of opportunities happening probability:

- In case that opportunities get confirmed, how will they impact the delivery capacity?
- Do we have enough stock and/or capacity to fulfill the related demand, or do we need to pre-produce and increase capacity by adding an additional shift, etc.?
- Shall we produce semifinished product for 30% probability opportunities?
- If opportunities are lost, how will this impact projected revenue and profits?

SAP JAM could be used to capture outcome of collaboration and capture inputs from various stakeholders. In this case Amparo was assigned with SAP JAM task to review how opportunities will be considered in consensus demand plan (see Fig. 5.112).

### 5.2.18 SAP Use Case: Integrate Trade Promotions (SAP TTPM—SAP IBP)

In many industries planning of promotions becomes very complex and forms significant part of risk and opportunities linked to demand. Incorporation of trade promotion process outcome into IBP helps to manage end-to-end uncertainties.

SAP Global Trade Management (GTM) solution comes with innovative functionalities that accompany the organizations in their journey from planning to

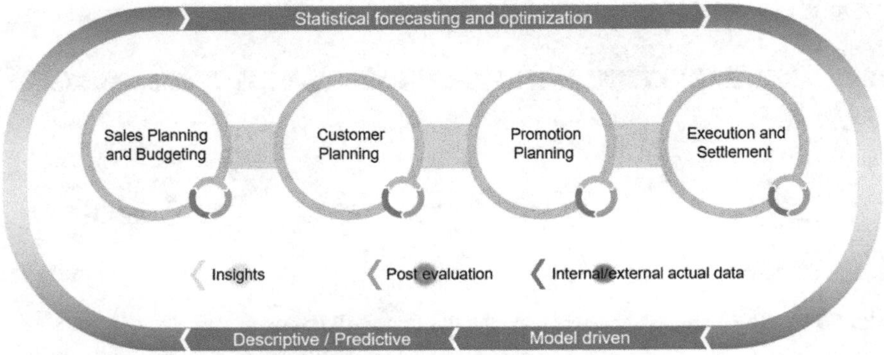


**Fig. 5.113** E2E GTM-IBP process overview

execution by providing support to streamline the sales and budgeting, customer, and promotions planning activities.

The solution combines three functional areas with the aim to build one integrated process driven by real-time visibility, prediction, and optimization capabilities.

SAP Global Trade Management (called GTM) has three applications:

- SAP Trade Promotion Planning and Management (called TTPM)
- SAP Customer Business Planning (called CBP)
- SAP Advanced Trade Management Analytics (called ATMA)

SAP GTM solution blends above capabilities to manage the end-to-end sales process and take the right decisions to balance the promotional and non-promotional volumes, to drive profits and category growth for your customer while increasing the margins.

Figure 5.113 shows an iterative process from target setting through forecasting to execution. Using up-to-date information like shipments, distributor information's for indirect customers, or market research data, the plan gets recalculated; this provides visibility and allows better decisions for the entire organization.

Let us deep dive into how to integrate SAP Trade Promotions Planning and Management application with SAP IBP to achieve cross-functional collaborative forecasting and planning between sales, marketing, supply chain, and finance.

SAP TPPM application provides wide functionalities for planning and managing trade promotions. Mainly for the consumer products industry, the trade promotions effectiveness can be one of the most important pillars for mid- to long-term business growth and increased customer loyalty.

With the SAP software for promotions planning and optimization, the organizations are able to identify the most profitable and strategic promotions. Integrating and analyzing actual data coming from stores or syndicated data allows you to track the promotion execution. In case of a promotion that does not return the expected results, failing both retailer and manufacturer's objectives, you can react on the moment and take corrective actions. Or if the promotion is outperforming, having visibility into promotion as it happens will help you to avoid lost sales due to out of stocks.

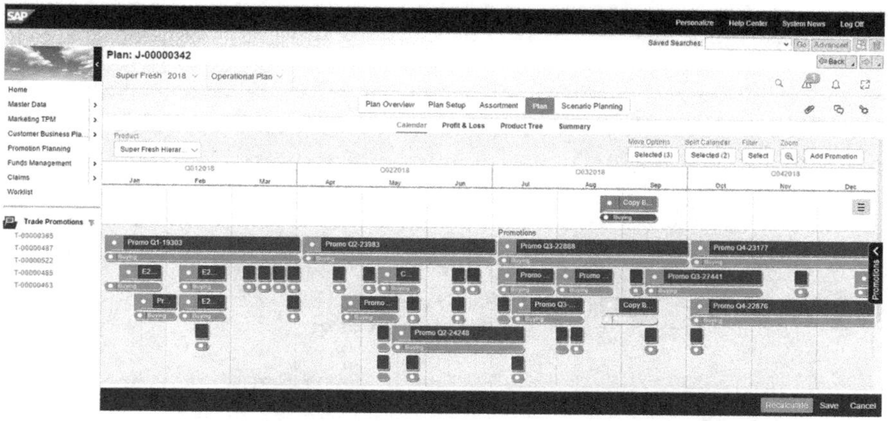

**Fig. 5.114** SAP TPPM, overview of promotions planning

With SAP TPPM we:

- Get reliable recommendations for promotional activity by running what-if simulations based on order history, retail point-of-sale, and market research.
- Predict and optimize promotion outcomes, including revenue and profit, for both manufacturers and retailers through predictive analytics.
- Determine the best way to promote a given product, such as discounts, rebates, or premiums.

We see in Fig. 5.114 that promotions are being planned and visualized on time scale with its length and buying horizon. Promotions are lined to their cost and revenue uplift; therefore, analysis and potential corrective actions can be triggered.

Integrating planned promotions expects to uplift forecast in SAP IBP. It helps to connect relevant information to manage risk and opportunities but not to manage every "connected" process in one application. Planning promotions brings into IBP improved marketing intelligence later used in demand review process but also enables improved supply chain planning of managing promotions, e.g., it helps to:

- Identify the right planning strategy to hedge against stock-outs.
- Generate a more accurate baseline demand plan by identifying the uplift in demand connected with trade promotions.
- Allocate promotions down to distribution centers.

From a technical perspective, the promotion planning integration into SAP IBP covers two dimensions:

- Master data where we include promotions' characteristics such as promotion ID, promotion description, buying periods, number of pre- or post-dip periods, start or end date, etc.

**Fig. 5.115** TPPM—IBP technical integration flow

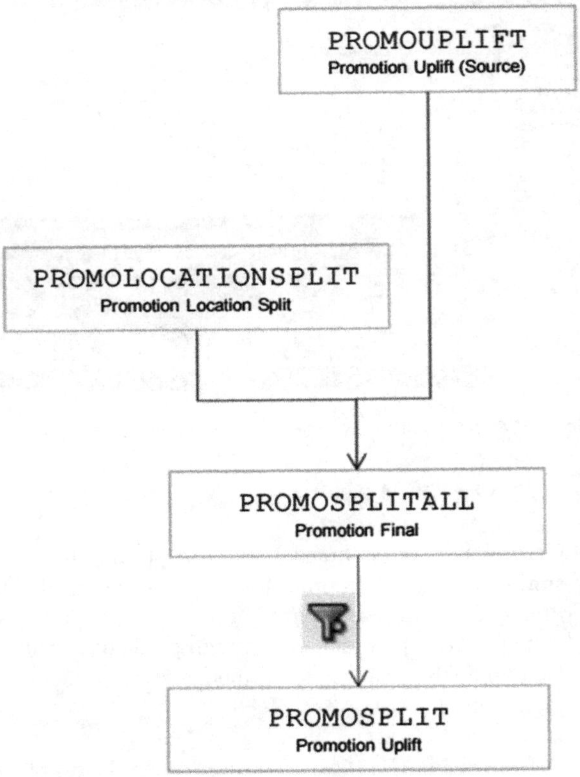


- Time series data that consists of promotion uplift quantities, the sales lift as planned in the promotion planning tool

Figure 5.115 shows the current design where the promotion uplifts are integrated from TPPM on a product-customer granularity to IBP. Further, the uplifts are disaggregated in IBP at location level based on the location sourcing factors. Once the disaggregation to location level is executed, the uplift can be integrated in the generation of the unconstrained consensus demand plan.

Once promotions are integrated into IBP, SAP Fiori app analyzes promotions which are used by planners to visualize and analyze promotions data at a glance as integral part of Integrated Business Planning process. Fiori app Analyze Promotions presents several functionalities:

- Customizable promotion display
- Calculation of maximum and average sales lift
- Overview of transferred promotions plus possibility to dig into details and display data as table or chart

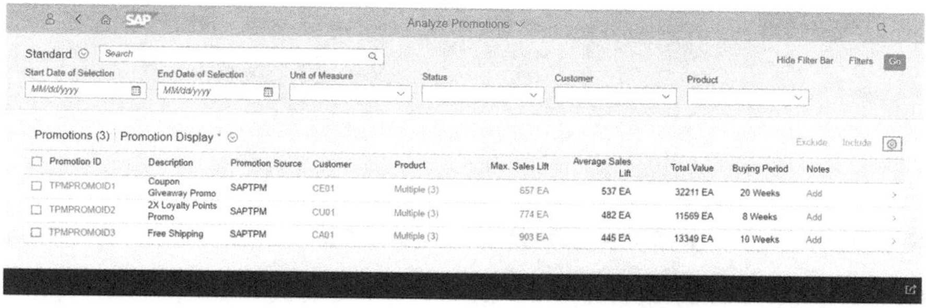


**Fig. 5.116** SAP IBP analyze promotion app overview screen

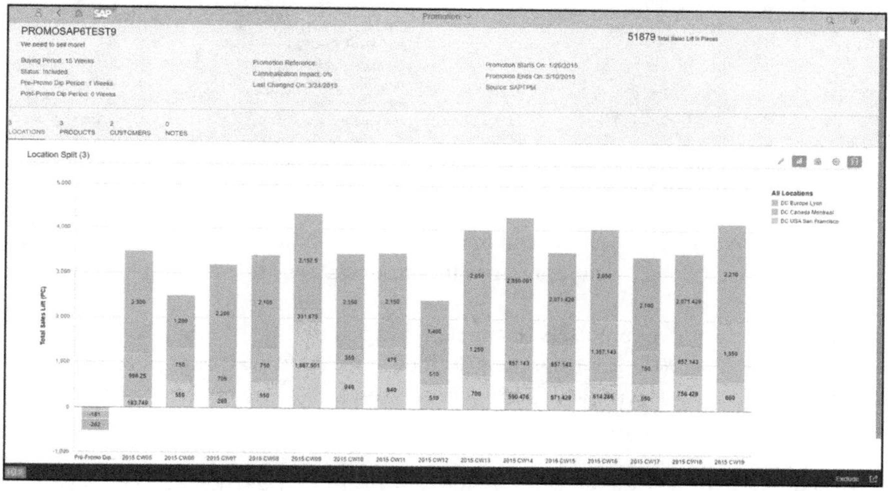


**Fig. 5.117** SAP IBP analyze promotion app detail screen

- Notes creation that can be shared in SAP JAM
- Edit functionality for refinement of promotion allocation to locations

From the promotions overview screen where each user can define his own layout by adding or removing promotions characteristics, one can drill into the details behind each of the promotions by simply selecting the line with the mouse cursor (Fig. 5.116).

The detailed view will show the promotion uplift quantity at the granularity of Prod-Cust-Loc and will allow you to make changes to the distribution—product or location level. For example, you are running a longer promotion and notice that distribution center A is outperforming, while the distribution center B is below the estimated plan. Easily you can adjust the quota of each location from this Fiori app so that you can avoid out of stock in the outperforming distribution centers (distribution center in Fig. 5.117).

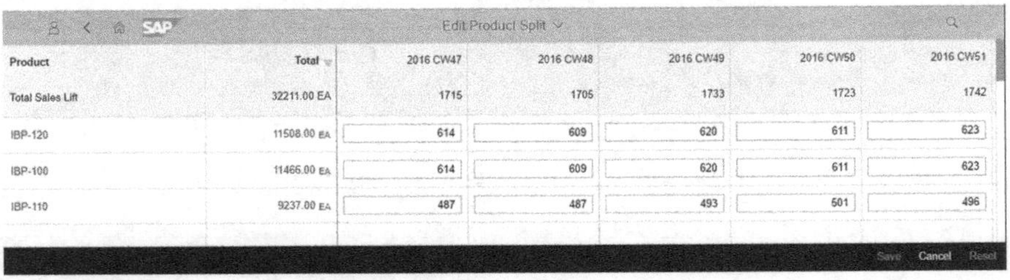


| Product | Total | 2016 CW47 | 2016 CW48 | 2016 CW49 | 2016 CW50 | 2016 CW51 |
|---|---|---|---|---|---|---|
| Total Sales Lift | 32211.00 EA | 1715 | 1705 | 1733 | 1723 | 1742 |
| IBP-120 | 11508.00 EA | 614 | 609 | 620 | 611 | 623 |
| IBP-100 | 11466.00 EA | 614 | 609 | 620 | 611 | 623 |
| IBP-110 | 9237.00 EA | 487 | 487 | 493 | 501 | 496 |

**Fig. 5.118** SAP IBP promotions app—change of promotion sales uplift on product level

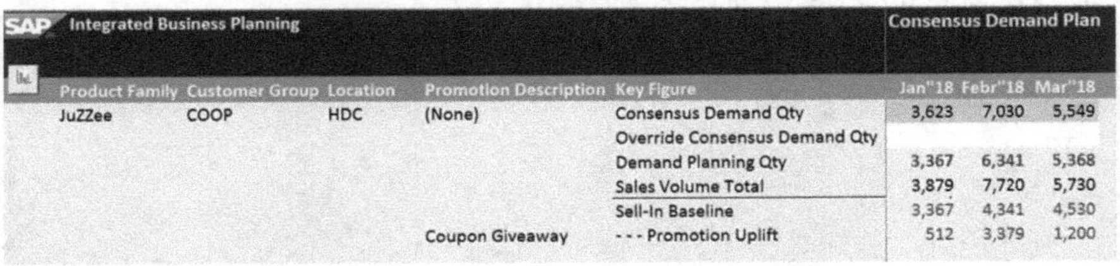


| Product Family | Customer Group | Location | Promotion Description | Key Figure | Jan"18 | Febr"18 | Mar"18 |
|---|---|---|---|---|---|---|---|
| JuZZee | COOP | HDC | (None) | Consensus Demand Qty | 3,623 | 7,030 | 5,549 |
| | | | | Override Consensus Demand Qty | | | |
| | | | | Demand Planning Qty | 3,367 | 6,341 | 5,368 |
| | | | | Sales Volume Total | 3,879 | 7,720 | 5,730 |
| | | | | Sell-In Baseline | 3,367 | 4,341 | 4,530 |
| | | | Coupon Giveaway | --- Promotion Uplift | 512 | 3,379 | 1,200 |

**Fig. 5.119** SAP IBP—adjusted promotion uplift impact

As part of management of risk and opportunities demand planners with marketing can adjust effect of the promotion cross the products and time directly in SAP IBP (Fig. 5.118).

Adjusted and more precisely evaluated impact of the promotion on specific products will lead to a robust unconstrained consensus demand plan based on which inventory and supply planning processes are going to be triggered with improved end-to-end transparency:

- Rough-cut capacity planning for early identification of potential capacity risks
- Explosion of the demand at the component level and integration with ARIBA to see if the suppliers can commit on the forecast
- Inventory optimization
- Constrained supply planning

We see in Fig. 5.119 that promotion uplift is adjusted for better planning.

Having consistent data regarding promotions' uplift is important also for the demand sensing, where the promotions uplift elimination from the sales history is performed automatically as a pre-processing step, to provide a clean baseline for the algorithm run. Demand sensing based on data input with eliminated promotion uplift can improve short-term forecasting and even further improve proper assignment of the forecast to products and locations per time series.

Integrated business plan can be further improved by integration of data from SAP CBP where sales and marketing team manages account plans. On the other hand, integrated business plan which considers commercial, financial, and supply constraints may serve as input to improve account plans stored in SAP Customer Business Planning application (CBP). This will ensure that we close the loop between IBP and CBP.

### 5.2.19 SAP Use Case: Make Account Plans More Realistic (SAP IBP—SAP CBP)

SAP Customer Business Planning is a central management tool that supports the key account managers to handle their customers throughout the year. It will enable the KAMs to have a holistic view across volumes, mix, revenue, margin, promotions, and trade terms.

While SAP Trade Management Promotion Planning and Management is focused only on the promotional activities, the Customer Business Planning (CBP) covers the non-promotional side as well, offering a view on the customer profit and lost information.

SAP Customer Business Planning has the following key functional features:

- Structured target setting process
- Creation of customer-specific planning product hierarchies
- Assortment planning
- Volume planning with building blocks
- Draft promotion planning
- Customer P&L analysis
- What-if scenario planning
- Business-friendly, easy-to-use graphical tool to plan and track annual business with trading partners
- Support for rolling forecasts
- Planning of promoted and non-promoted P&L

In context of account managers and their customers, we need to pay attention what type of selling we talk about, is it "sell-in" or maybe "sell-through?" Please refer to explanation provided in chapter "What Shall You Forecast." Account manager often talks about their sales channels and not always about direct customers.

You may consider to integrate SAP CBP with SAP IBP to support annual planning process. Once per year, in many commercial departments and customer annual plans, targets are defined and assigned to people who will take care of it. In the beginning of the process, account manager who works in CBP will receive the "sell-in" baseline volume projection for 2018. Data will come from disaggregation of IBP plan to customer level. Data will be integrated with use of CPI for time series data. In CBP account manager will execute several activities:

- Updates the assortment with a new product that is going to be introduced and maintains spends for supporting the launch
- Reviews non-promoted plan and adjusts the baseline volumes to reflect the opening of a couple new stores
- Plans 2018 promotions and assesses them in terms of volume, profitability, and trade budget spend
- Determines uplift on the account

We see in Fig. 5.120 that the account manager increases the baseline account plan which was integrated from IBP by 10% between CW09 and CW52 2018. It was done since in week no. 9; there will be new store opened.

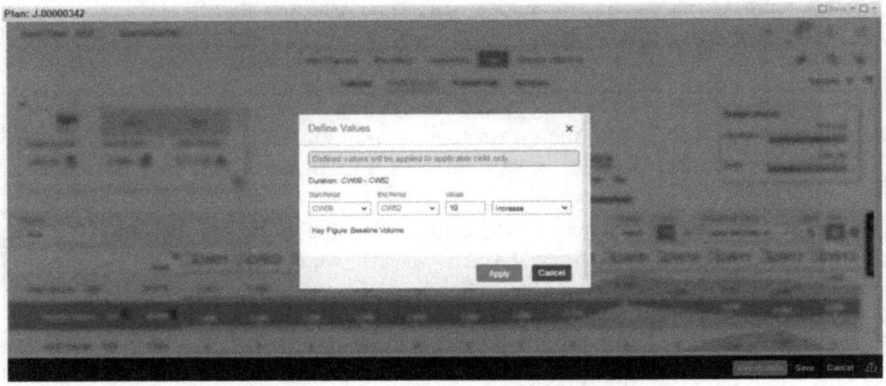


**Fig. 5.120** Baseline account plan increase

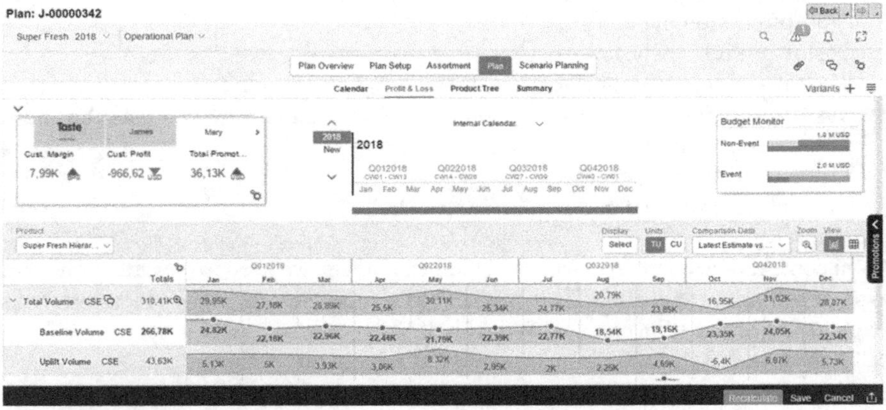


**Fig. 5.121** CBP account plan with promotional uplifts

Account manager further adjusts baseline account plan until it will be confirmed by him. Account manager incorporates promotions for this account to be launched in 2018. First, he checks what is already suggested from bottom-up trade marketing planning executed at headquarter level. He identifies some fits and decides to import them to his plan. Then, he drags and drops some promotions from 2017 that were a real success. While adding the promotions, he can easily keep an eye on the trade spend and ensure he is not overspending. Volumetric account plan and promotions are connected to monetization (Fig. 5.121).

Once the baseline and uplift information in the "sell-in" account plan will be completed, integration between CBP will be triggered to populate validate account plan into IBP. Following data elements can be send to IBP:

- Baseline volume (represented in IBP as KAM forecast input)
- Uplift volume

### 5.2.20 SAP Use Case: Forecast, Supply Data Integration (SAP IBP—ECC, S4)

The master data required by IBP is usually integrated from executional systems like ERP. In many cases companies are growing fast through acquisitions and struggle with many processes and technology challenges, like different systems and applications. SAP provides out-of-the-box templates that can be used as starting point for creating own dataflows to transfer master data objects between SAP ERP, SAP APO, and SAP IBP. These templates include master data types like products, customers, locations, resources, or bill of materials.

Even if IBP allows a very flexible master data management, directly from Excel user interface providing various functionalities like adding, copying, and updating single records or mass changes, IBP is not the master data leading system, so these activities should be allowed only on small scale and restricted to designated user.

Master data maintenance in IBP can be needed for attributes specific to Integrated Business Planning algorithms or processes, attributes that are not available in other systems:

- Updates to ABC/XYZ Lock attribute to restrict segmentation updating the chosen category which can be "D" labeling a special case.
- Updates to time-/not time-dependent sourcing rules
- Another use case is the version-dependent master data where business users can simulate different tactical or strategic decisions.
- New product introductions.
- Network design changes like shifting volumes from one manufacturing location to another.
- Introduction of a new sales channel, etc.

Moving to the transactional data, bidirectional integration between ECC/S4 and IBP is required in most of the cases when IBP is leveraged for S&OP planning. Depending on the customer landscape, the content and the complexity of this integration will vary from one project to another. Most common data to be integrated are measures like actuals, on-hand inventory, or sales forecast price for inbound to IBP or constrained forecast for outbound from IBP. Let's continue with an example of an outbound and inbound interface between IBP and S4.

For the IBP outbound integration scenario, we start from the assumption that we are executing a tactical planning in IBP and require to transfer the plan in ECC or S4 to serve as input for the business execution.

Depending on each customer's specifics, there can be some different integration points.

- For manufactured goods, we may choose to send over the production quantity, available at product-mfg location level.
- For a distribution company or an outsourced product, we may choose to send lane distribution demand (location-dependent demand) available at product-location level.

Most common scenario consists of sending forecast data from IBP as Planned Independent Requirements (PIRs) to execution system. PIR should be used as basis for anticipating the sales before orders are received.

The integration of the time-series data from IBP to ECC/S4 as PIRs can be achieved through SAP Cloud Platform Integration for data services using webservices. For this example, we exposed a Planned Independent Requirements maintenance BAPI as a webservice (see Fig. 5.122).

To avoid duplication, once the actual requirements are received, the corresponding quantity will be subtracted from the forecast. This means that if there is a demand for a specific period generated by both forecast and sales order, the system will subtract the sales order quantity from the forecast (it will consume forecast).

Moving further, for the inbound integration, we will illustrate the transfer the unrestricted-use stock from ECC to IBP, using the SOP_KF_Inventory out-of-the-box template delivered by SAP.

Stock on hand is a standard input key figure that is processed by S&OP heuristic and supply optimizer operators. It contains the available quantity of a product at a specific location at the beginning of the current period. Adding the location receipts (+) and subtracting the supply (−) will generate the projected inventory.

The stock is being retrieved by having the Cloud Platform Integration agent directly connected and reading that from ECC table through RFC connection (see Fig. 5.123).

We see that the available 150 pcs are being transferred in stock on hand key figure, in the current time bucket (Fig. 5.124).

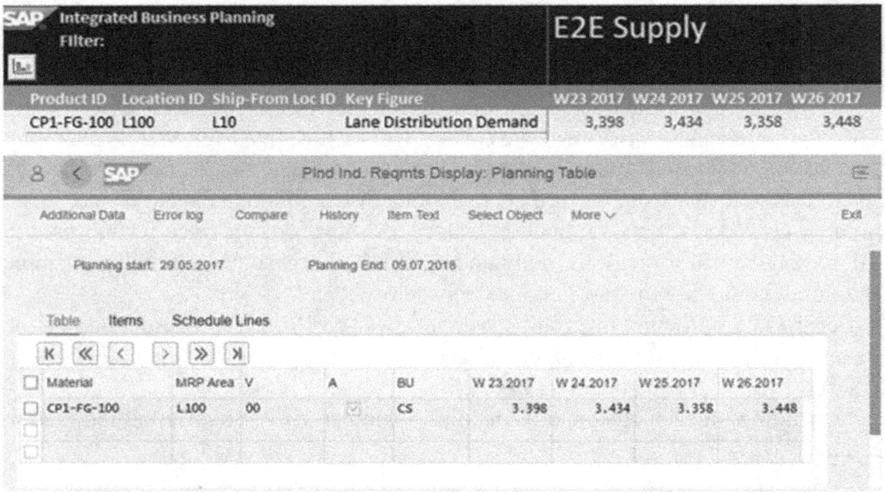


**Fig. 5.122** Integrated forecast into Planned Independent Requirements

| | |
|---|---|
| Table | MARD |
| Short Description | Storage Location Data for Material |
| Number of Entries | 1 |

| MANDT | MATNR | WERKS | LGORT | LABST |
|---|---|---|---|---|
| 800 | IBP-100 | 3200 | 0001 | 150,000 |

**Fig. 5.123** Stock data from ECC

SAP Integrated Business Planning — Inventory Projection

| Product ID | Location ID | Key Figure | W22 2017 | W23 2017 | W24 2017 | W25 2017 | W26 2017 |
|---|---|---|---|---|---|---|---|
| IBP-100 | 3200 | Stock on Hand | 150 | | | | |
| | | Location Total Receipts | 1,955 | 2,167 | 2,640 | 2,287 | 1,987 |
| | | Location Total Supply | 1,827 | 2,152 | 2,329 | 2,315 | 1,990 |
| | | Inventory Projected Stock | 278 | 293 | 605 | 577 | 573 |
| | | Projected Coverage | 0.86 | 0.80 | 0.94 | 1.08 | 1.06 |

**Fig. 5.124** Stock data in SAP IBP

## 5.3 Supply Review

Based on agreed unconstrained but realistic consensus demand forecast, supply planning team does prepare supply plan to match as best as it's possible to demand. There are two typical supply planning modes which are used:

- Unconstrained supply planning which helps to identify gaps and reschedule and change plans manually based on expert knowledge
- Optimized constrained supply planning in which technology solution based on configured optimization criteria and variables proposes optimized supply plan

In this chapter we will highlight key elements of supply planning in tactical horizon.

### 5.3.1 Unconstrained and Constrained Supply Planning

How you make supply planning, how you constrain your supply projections, what criteria and what drivers will influence your calculation, or how you adjust your optimized plans make a huge difference to final integrated business plan.

Taking consensus forecast which is an outcome of demand review process will be the starting point. Demand needs to be propagated and should consider:

- Levels in the bill of material
- Consumptions factors in BoM

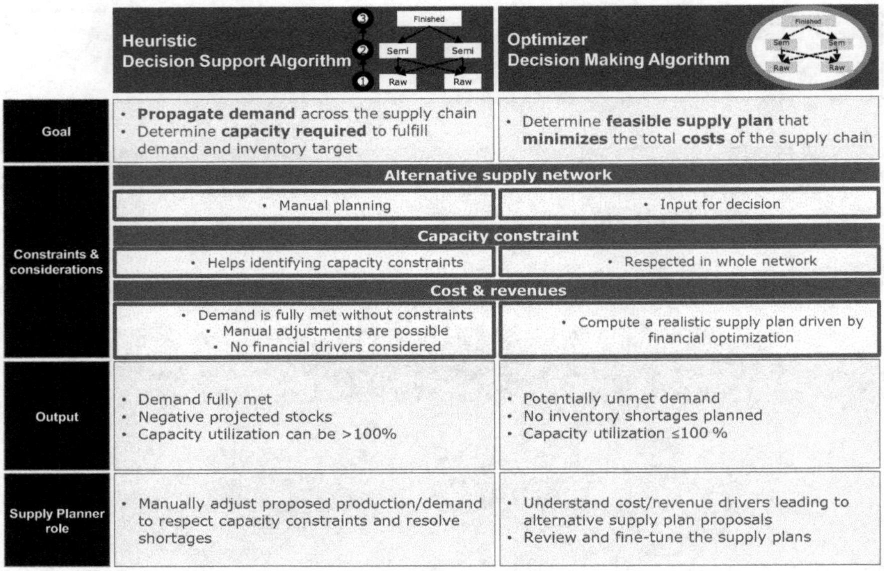
Heuristic
Decision Support Algorithm
Finished
Semi
Semi
Raw
Raw
Optimizer
Decision Making Algorithm
Goal
• Propagate demand across the supply chain
• Determine capacity required to fulfill demand and inventory target
• Determine feasible supply plan that minimizes the total costs of the supply chain
Constraints & considerations
Alternative supply network
• Manual planning
• Input for decision
Capacity constraint
• Helps identifying capacity constraints
• Respected in whole network
Cost & revenues
• Demand is fully met without constraints
• Manual adjustments are possible
• No financial drivers considered
• Compute a realistic supply plan driven by financial optimization
Output
• Demand fully met
• Negative projected stocks
• Capacity utilization can be >100%
• Potentially unmet demand
• No inventory shortages planned
• Capacity utilization ≤100 %
Supply Planner role
• Manually adjust proposed production/demand to respect capacity constraints and resolve shortages
• Understand cost/revenue drivers leading to alternative supply plan proposals
• Review and fine-tune the supply plans

**Fig. 5.125** SAP IBP supply planning algorithms

– Batch sizes
– Supply network
– Lead times
– Stock
– Etc.

As part of demand propagation, utilization of assets (various types of plants) will be calculated; materials' required availability will be calculated considering netting of stocks, in-transits, and work in progress; and collaboration with supplier via SAP Ariba can be triggered to improve preparation of realistic supply plan. In next step you will see supply propagation which will enable communication back of supply plan to demand location (distribution centers, countries, markets) or demand entities (customers, distributors). Supply planning could be executed in unconstrained or constrained mode. In Fig. 5.125 you will find major differences between two methods.

As we see from characteristics describing those two algorithms, we can expect significantly different results of supply planning. One highlights what needs to be done, and second makes proposal of decisions for you automatically for what can be done. There is huge value of using both types of supply planning algorithms.

## 5.3.2 SAP Use Case: Unconstrained Supply Planning

SAP IBP includes two algorithms that are used to compute a tactical supply plan: heuristics in S&OP application and supply optimizer in response and supply application.

The heuristic operator generates an unconstrained plan which is used to determine whether there is enough capacity to address future demand needs. The analysis will provide an overview of the demand potential without taking any constraints into consideration. If constraints are being identified, they can be highlighted locally through alerts, but they are not propagated upstream. You can correct plans manually though.

Most organizations are running the heuristic supply plan with a monthly cadence over a time horizon which usually spans up to 36 months in the future. Heuristics are often used in long-term strategic planning which spans over 5–7 years. If we analyze supply plan generated by heuristic and we will notice that resources are overutilized, it is a good thing since you will have visibility needed to anticipate potential issues to meet the consensus demand plan. The supply planners can then investigate the details behind the issue and identify if there are any adjustments that might overcome or improve the constraint. Using some key IBP capabilities like what-if analysis and ad hoc scenario creation, the planners are empowered to quickly drill up and down the supply network and evaluate the impact of different decisions they might take: change the sourcing rules from one location to another or adjust the quotas, increase the manufacturing or warehouse capacity, etc.

The heuristic algorithm starts from the customer dimension and propagates the demand through the supply chain network based on the given sourcing rules that are maintained for supply and production locations.

The calculation logic consists of the following steps:

(a) Check the consensus demand that is available at product-customer granularity.
(b) Propagate the consensus demand to the locations from where the product can be supplied based on the customer sourcing rules.
(c) For each location, calculate the dependent demand coming from all the customers that have that specific location assigned as a source.
(d) Compute the net demand—total volume that needs to be replenished by supply for a location product. The net demand is computed based on the dependent demand calculated in the previous step and stock on-hand/projected inventory.
(e) Propagate the net demand to the source of supply which can be:
Production process
Transportation
External receipt for procurement from external supplier
(f) Calculate the sum of the receipts that can come from various locations. As we run infinite supply, the total receipt is equal with the net demand, unless an adjusted key figure is used by the supply planner to override the computed value returned for the receipts.
(g) Calculate the supply quantity—everything that is transported from a location directly to the customer or to another location.
(h) Compute the projected stock based on stock on hand (+), receipts (+), and supply (−).

Once the first time period is completed, the steps are iterated for the following periods until the end of the planning horizon is being reached.

Figure 5.126 shows an example of a supply chain network that can be modeled using IBP. During implementation, each organization has the flexibility to design its own network, optional routes, substitutions, etc.

Now that we have explained fundamentals of how the heuristic algorithm works, let's visualize few examples that will make the demand propagation principles easier to follow. For this, we are using a multi-sheet planning view which has the advantage of allowing users to have all the information available in one place and facilitates the end-to-end what-if simulations by providing visibility at different nodes from the network.

We start from the "customer demand" view which shows the consensus demand key figure in a weekly granularity in the first two months and monthly buckets for the remaining horizon defined in the planning view (Fig. 5.127).

The heuristic operator run will first identify the location from where the customer demand is to be met. For this it will check the customer sourcing ratios that are maintained in the customer source master data object (see Fig. 5.128).

Then, following the location sourcing quota, it will propagate the net demand to the location which replenishes the customer facing location. To observe how this is done, we will switch to the next worksheet "transportation lanes" (see Fig. 5.129).

First, we see that the customer demand is being pushed to two different locations 2840 and 3400, one distribution center for each customer. This is done with a shift of 1 week which represents the customer lead time. Then, the demand is further propagated to the source of supply, resulting into lane distribution demand key figure. The distribution center 2840 is linked with a single manufacturing location 2800, while for 3400, it has two sources of supply: 3350 and 3450.

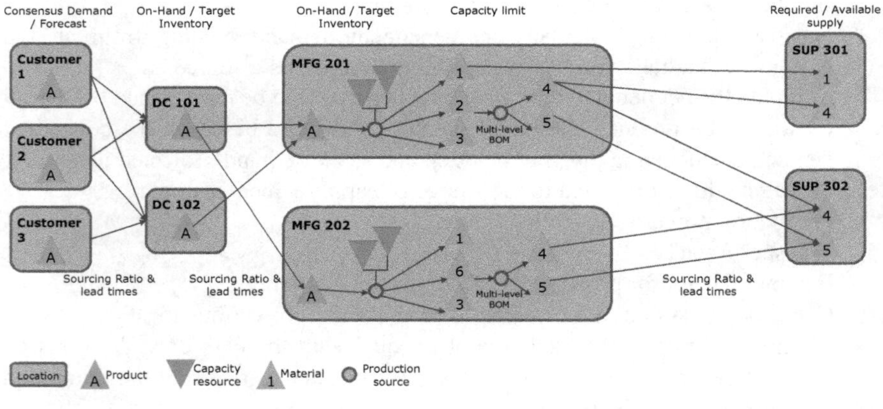


**Fig. 5.126** Demand propagation trough supply network, from market (left) to suppliers (right)

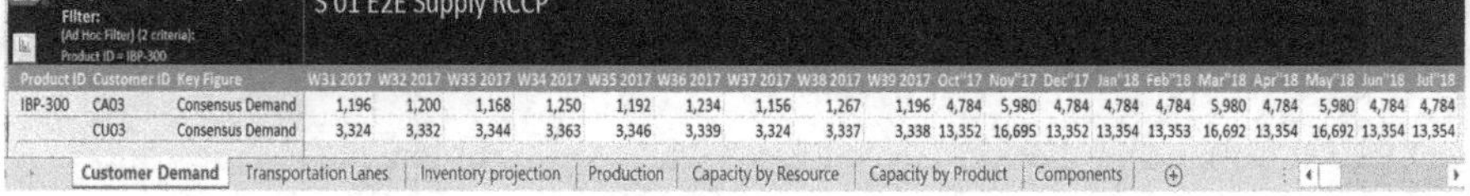


| Product ID | Customer ID | Key Figure | W31 2017 | W32 2017 | W33 2017 | W34 2017 | W35 2017 | W36 2017 | W37 2017 | W38 2017 | W39 2017 | Oct"17 | Nov"17 | Dec"17 | Jan"18 | Feb"18 | Mar"18 | Apr"18 | May"18 | Jun"18 | Jul"18 |
|---|---|---|---|---|---|---|---|---|---|---|---|---|---|---|---|---|---|---|---|---|---|
| IBP-300 | CA03 | Consensus Demand | 1,196 | 1,200 | 1,168 | 1,250 | 1,192 | 1,234 | 1,156 | 1,267 | 1,196 | 4,784 | 5,980 | 4,784 | 4,784 | 4,784 | 5,980 | 4,784 | 5,980 | 4,784 | 4,784 |
| | CU03 | Consensus Demand | 3,324 | 3,332 | 3,344 | 3,363 | 3,346 | 3,339 | 3,324 | 3,337 | 3,338 | 13,352 | 16,695 | 13,352 | 13,354 | 13,353 | 16,692 | 13,354 | 16,692 | 13,354 | 13,354 |

**Fig. 5.127** Consensus demand

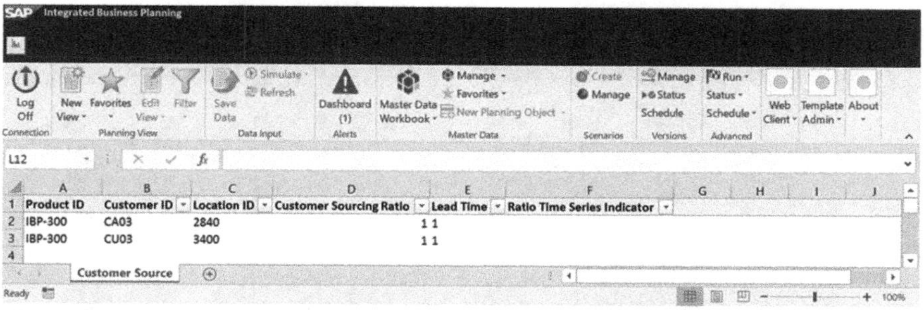


**Fig. 5.128** Customer location sourcing ratio

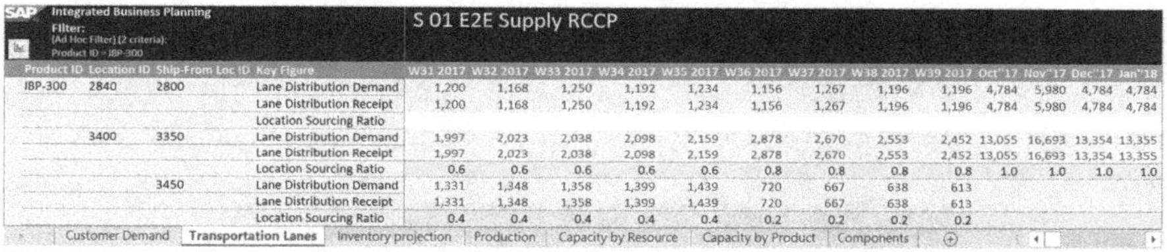


**Fig. 5.129** Transportation lanes

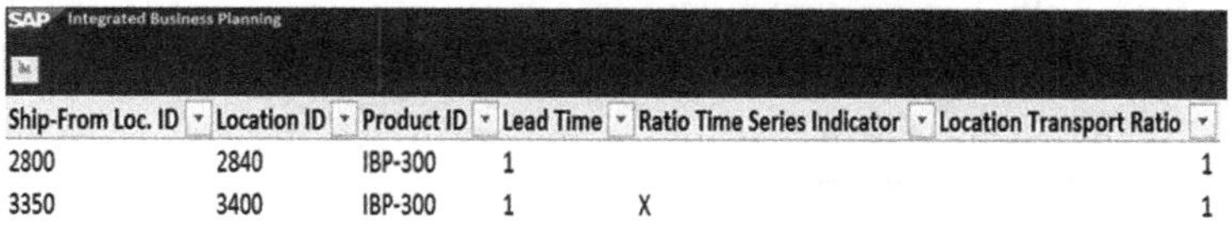


**Fig. 5.130** Location source master data

You might have noticed above that the location sourcing ratios are missing for the location 2840, while for 3400 they are visible and fluctuating over the time axis. The sourcing quotas are reflecting the strategic decision of gradually increasing the capacity in 3350 to be able to absorb the entire net demand of IBP-300 at distribution center 3400 level. This will reduce the product mix in manufacturing location 3450 and free up some capacity that is needed to support the marketing strategy of a different product that is loading same resource.

This modeling approach is possible as the sourcing ratios can be time dependent or independent. When they are time dependent, the same rule is applied over the entire time horizon of the supply plan based on the value that is retrieved from the master data. In case the ratios are not consistent from one time bucket to another, then the sourcing criteria are maintained in the corresponding key figure, location sourcing ratio. Below field from "ratio time series indicator" maintained with a "X" indicated the behavior of the ratio (see Fig. 5.130).

Similarly, the demand is allocated to the manufacturing resources, identifying the needed capacity to fulfill the supply requirements. Switching to the "capacity by product" planning view, we see that the assembly and packaging resources available in manufacturing location 3350 are loaded by two products (see Fig. 5.131).

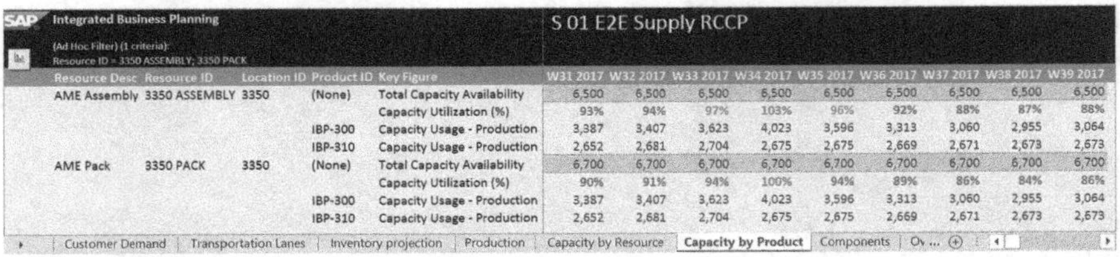

SAP Integrated Business Planning — S 01 E2E Supply RCCP

(Ad Hoc Filter) (1 criteria): Resource ID = 3350 ASSEMBLY; 3350 PACK

| Resource Desc | Resource ID | Location ID | Product ID | Key Figure | W31 2017 | W32 2017 | W33 2017 | W34 2017 | W35 2017 | W36 2017 | W37 2017 | W38 2017 | W39 2017 |
|---|---|---|---|---|---|---|---|---|---|---|---|---|---|
| AME Assembly | 3350 ASSEMBLY | 3350 | (None) | Total Capacity Availability | 6,500 | 6,500 | 6,500 | 6,500 | 6,500 | 6,500 | 6,500 | 6,500 | 6,500 |
| | | | | Capacity Utilization (%) | 93% | 94% | 97% | 103% | 96% | 92% | 88% | 87% | 88% |
| | | | IBP-300 | Capacity Usage - Production | 3,387 | 3,407 | 3,623 | 4,023 | 3,596 | 3,313 | 3,060 | 2,955 | 3,064 |
| | | | IBP-310 | Capacity Usage - Production | 2,652 | 2,681 | 2,704 | 2,675 | 2,675 | 2,669 | 2,671 | 2,673 | 2,673 |
| AME Pack | 3350 PACK | 3350 | (None) | Total Capacity Availability | 6,700 | 6,700 | 6,700 | 6,700 | 6,700 | 6,700 | 6,700 | 6,700 | 6,700 |
| | | | | Capacity Utilization (%) | 90% | 91% | 94% | 100% | 94% | 89% | 86% | 84% | 86% |
| | | | IBP-300 | Capacity Usage - Production | 3,387 | 3,407 | 3,623 | 4,023 | 3,596 | 3,313 | 3,060 | 2,955 | 3,064 |
| | | | IBP-310 | Capacity Usage - Production | 2,652 | 2,681 | 2,704 | 2,675 | 2,675 | 2,669 | 2,671 | 2,673 | 2,673 |



**Fig. 5.131** Capacity utilization by resource and product

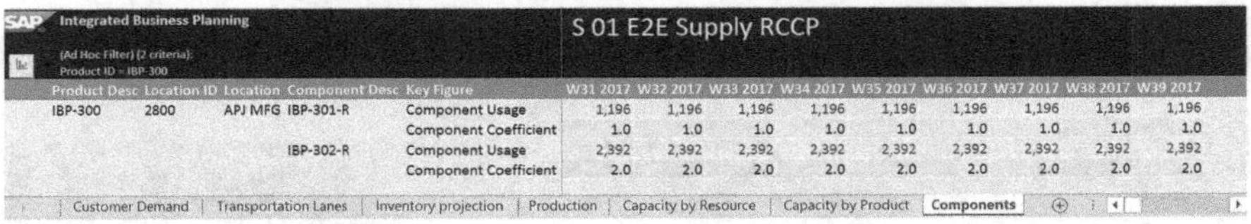

SAP Integrated Business Planning — S 01 E2E Supply RCCP

(Ad Hoc Filter) (2 criteria): Product ID = IBP-300

| Product Desc | Location ID | Location | Component Desc | Key Figure | W31 2017 | W32 2017 | W33 2017 | W34 2017 | W35 2017 | W36 2017 | W37 2017 | W38 2017 | W39 2017 |
|---|---|---|---|---|---|---|---|---|---|---|---|---|---|
| IBP-300 | 2800 | APJ MFG | IBP-301-R | Component Usage | 1,196 | 1,196 | 1,196 | 1,196 | 1,196 | 1,196 | 1,196 | 1,196 | 1,196 |
| | | | | Component Coefficient | 1.0 | 1.0 | 1.0 | 1.0 | 1.0 | 1.0 | 1.0 | 1.0 | 1.0 |
| | | | IBP-302-R | Component Usage | 2,392 | 2,392 | 2,392 | 2,392 | 2,392 | 2,392 | 2,392 | 2,392 | 2,392 |
| | | | | Component Coefficient | 2.0 | 2.0 | 2.0 | 2.0 | 2.0 | 2.0 | 2.0 | 2.0 | 2.0 |



**Fig. 5.132** Component usage coefficient

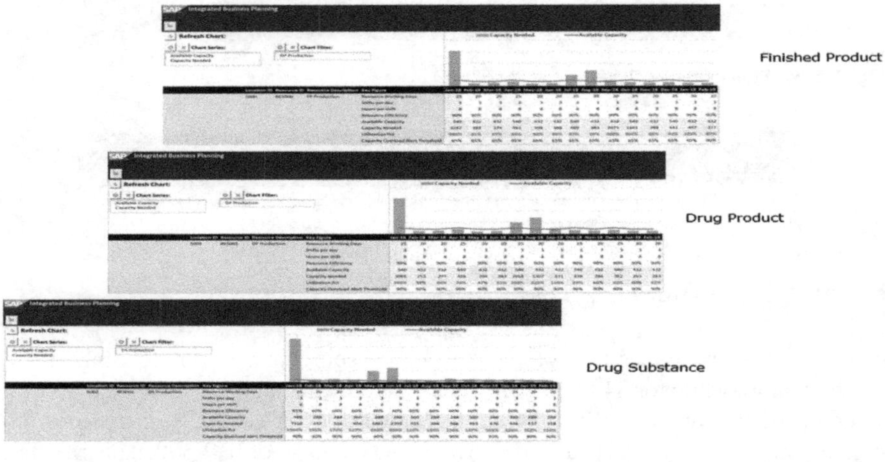



**Fig. 5.133** Demand propagation and resource utilization across BoM levels, resources and shifted with lead time

The heuristic operator is not only propagating the demand through the locations that are part of the network based on the customer and location sourcing rules, but it also explodes the finished good demand at component level. The component coefficients can be fixed over the time axis or defined as time dependent in case the component structure fluctuates (see Fig. 5.132).

On example of pharmaceutical company, we see how from finished product (packed, labeled, and blistered pill for specific country) demand is propagated across BoM to drug product (pill stored in bulk) and to drug substance (active pharma ingredient in the pill, which actually cures you). Demand is propagated and creates utilization load on resources shifted with appropriate lead time (see Fig. 5.133).

### 5.3.3 Constrained Supply Planning

Moving to the time series-based supply planning optimizer, we have a more complex calculation logic that is using mathematical optimization like the simplex algorithm in mixed integer linear program (MILP) to model demand, supply, and cost elements. The outcome of the algorithm is a finite plan that is optimized to maximize its objective function, in this case one of the below two criteria:

- Profit maximization—where profit is the difference between revenue and total costs. The revenue is calculated by multiplying the nondelivery cost rate with the volume shipped to the customers, while the total cost is computed based on costs that are generated during production, holding, and transportation activities. If the total cost is higher than the sales price, the optimizer will classify this demand as unprofitable and choose not to fulfill it.
- Delivery maximization—the goal is to identify the customer demand that can be fulfilled in the presence of various constraints that exist in the supply chain but without taking into consideration the profitability of each product, as the profit maximization mode does.
- The constraints that are considered by the optimizer can be classified in three categories, based on the impact they have on the MILP solver.
- Hard constraints—conditions for variables like resource capacity, stock balance, or maximum inventory that are required to be satisfied.
- Soft constraints—failing to satisfy conditions for variables such as safety-stock violation, inventory holding, or transportation cost is penalized by the objective function. The optimizer will try to keep the constraint violations as small as possible.
- Pseudo-hard constraints—restrictions like adjusted or minimum values that have a very high penalty costs if not fulfilled. Given this, they usually get fulfilled unless there is a limitation like component unavailability.

The most important aspect of setting up the time-series-based supply planning optimizer operator is defining the cost model. There are several supply chain costs, such as transportation, production, or holding inventory costs, that are considered as input into the optimization run. These costs can be modeled as time-independent or time-dependent penalty costs. As the maintenance of the time-independent costs is a setting in the optimizer profile, it provides the implementation team with an easy and fast way of assessing how various costs can influence the optimization's result. However, besides these early stages of the implementation, usually the penalty costs are being maintained as time-dependent key figures.

Below we see the list of the available key figures and their classification between variable and fixed. The variable costs are defined per unit and per time period, while the fixed ones are independent of the quantity.

- Nondelivery cost rate (variable)
- Late delivery costs (variable)

- Transportation costs (fixed and variable)
- External procurement costs (fixed and variable)
- Production costs (fixed and variable)
- Inventory holding costs (variable)
- Safety-stock violation costs (variable)
- Maximum inventory violation costs (variable)

Behind each cost type, it can be a real or an artificial cost. The artificial costs are usually provided to force the optimizer toward a certain planning results. For example, if you don't have a real cost for the safety-stock violation cost rate, you can maintain a value greater than zero to ensure that the optimizer solution will consider the targeted inventory level.

Next, we will review several examples that will make it easier to understand how the time-series-based supply planning optimizer operator works.

### 5.3.4 SAP Use Case: Supply Optimization

We will explain supply planning optimization on pharmaceutical supply chain where finished product is a pill which is blistered and packed with label into box which has country specific text, identification, and certificates to operate. Finished product is being produced at finished product plant where packing, blistering is executed. Pill is being supplied in bulk form to finished product plant from drug product plant. Drug product plant has a key raw material called active pharma ingredient (API, element which actually cures you). API is produced at drug substance plant. Production between nodes takes time captured in specific types of lead time. See whole supply network in Fig. 5.134. We visualize planning on six finished products sold in three markets which are produced from two APIs.

Demand will be propagated from market level to distribution center, netted and with lead time will explode cross other Bill of Material levels, component usage factors, supply network.

In the first step of planning, global demand planner has an overview of all market consensus demand and difference to total constrained qty (constrained supply plan) expressed in demand fulfillment percentage. Supply planner will execute heuristic planning operator to propagate demand across the network, identify constraints, manage constraints, simulate solutions to increase availability in the market, and optimize cost of production. View of consensus forecast is shown in Fig. 5.135. We see that additional demand tenders were not captured, but it would be possible to simulate an impact of the tender with use of scenario planning.

Heuristic planning operator has propagated and netted demand. Planners prepared an overview template to see resource utilization of all three production steps: FP production, finished good production (packaging and packing of pills into blisters); DP production, drug product production (production of pills in bulk form); and DS production, drug substance production of active pharma ingredient. API is the most expensive and normally longest to product element of the medicine.

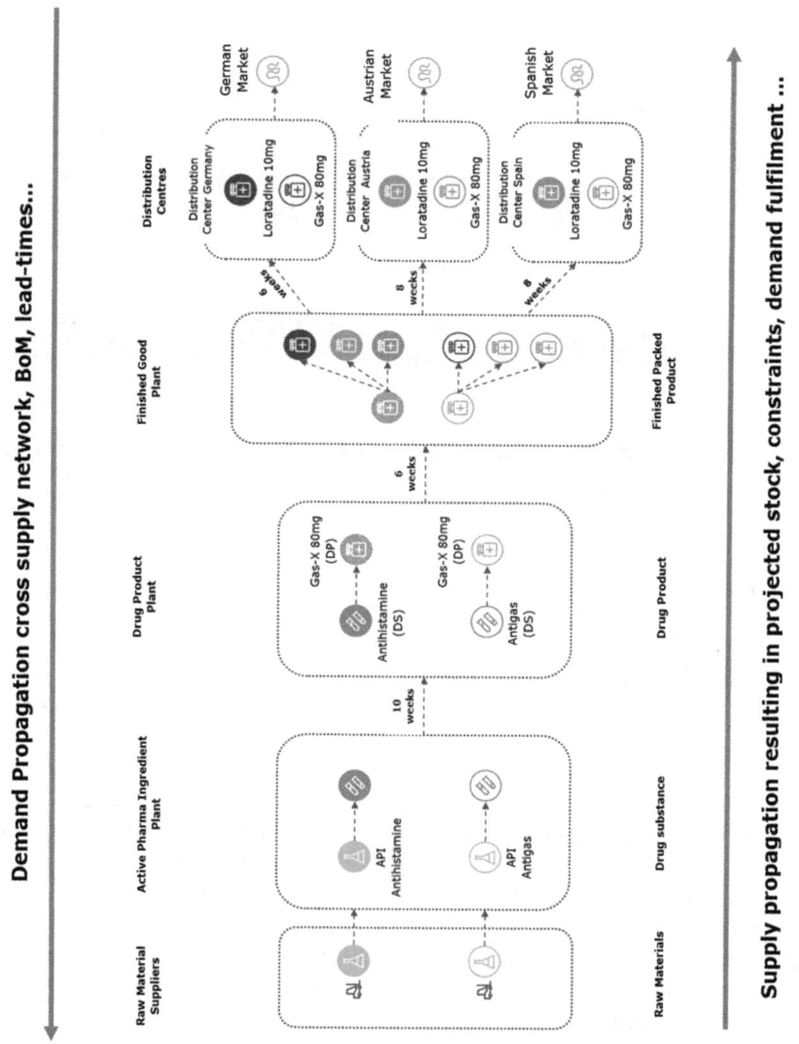


**Fig. 5.134** Example of pharmaceutical supply chain network in SAP IBP

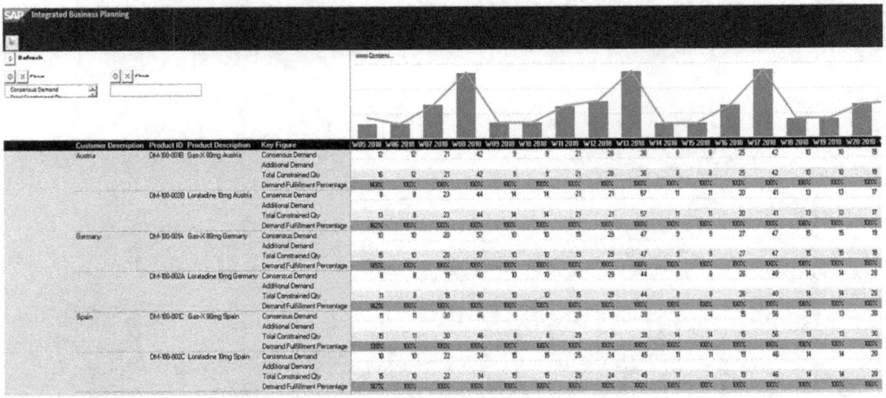


**Fig. 5.135** Consensus demand forecast on market level

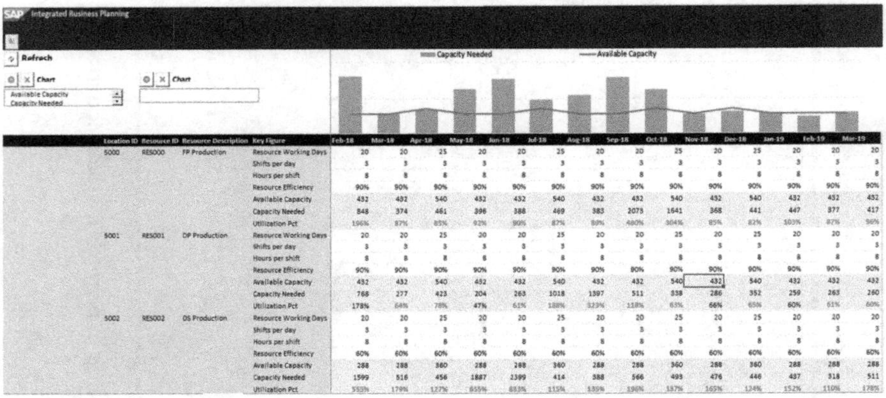


**Fig. 5.136** Rough-cut capacity plan with overutilized resources

In Fig. 5.136 on each level of production, we see how many shifts, hours per shift machine works, what is current machine efficiency, available capacity and capacity needed, and finally capacity utilization percentage. Capacity is overutilized mainly on drug substance production plant and in some periods in finished good and drug product plant.

Supply planner decides to create planning scenario and run supply optimizer. Supply optimizer reschedules production and load capacity utilization with production for products which are more profitable (see Fig. 5.137).

Planner analyzes each production step in more detail to take further actions in planning if needed. In drug substance plant supply optimizer engine did promote more production of the antihistamine against antigas. Cost of production of antigas was much higher (see Fig. 5.138).

Drug substance production needed to be reduced to available capacity and resulted in significant impact on the rest of supply plans. Planner reviewed drug production plants and their proposed production plan (see Fig. 5.139).

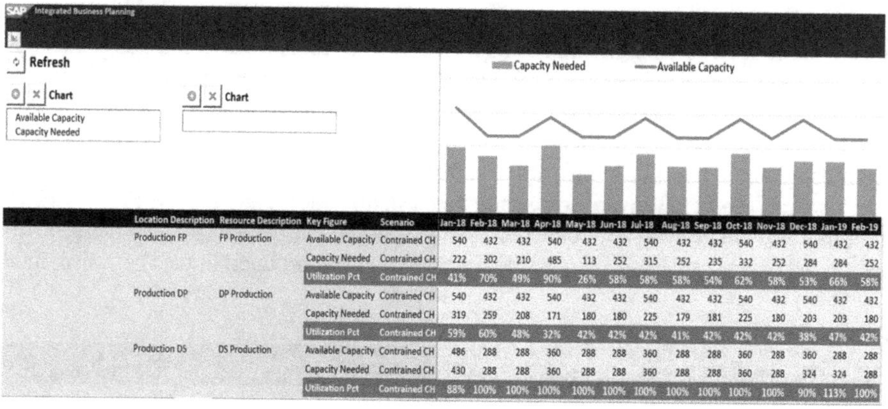


| Location Description | Resource Description | Key Figure | Scenario | Jan-18 | Feb-18 | Mar-18 | Apr-18 | May-18 | Jun-18 | Jul-18 | Aug-18 | Sep-18 | Oct-18 | Nov-18 | Dec-18 | Jan-19 | Feb-19 |
|---|---|---|---|---|---|---|---|---|---|---|---|---|---|---|---|---|---|
| Production FP | FP Production | Available Capacity | Contrained CH | 540 | 432 | 432 | 540 | 432 | 432 | 540 | 432 | 432 | 540 | 432 | 540 | 432 | 432 |
| | | Capacity Needed | Contrained CH | 222 | 302 | 210 | 485 | 113 | 252 | 315 | 252 | 235 | 332 | 252 | 284 | 284 | 252 |
| | | Utilization Pct | Contrained CH | 41% | 70% | 49% | 90% | 26% | 58% | 58% | 58% | 54% | 62% | 58% | 53% | 66% | 58% |
| Production DP | DP Production | Available Capacity | Contrained CH | 540 | 432 | 432 | 540 | 432 | 432 | 540 | 432 | 432 | 540 | 432 | 540 | 432 | 432 |
| | | Capacity Needed | Contrained CH | 319 | 259 | 208 | 171 | 180 | 180 | 225 | 179 | 181 | 225 | 180 | 203 | 203 | 180 |
| | | Utilization Pct | Contrained CH | 59% | 60% | 48% | 32% | 42% | 42% | 42% | 41% | 42% | 42% | 42% | 38% | 47% | 42% |
| Production DS | DS Production | Available Capacity | Contrained CH | 486 | 288 | 288 | 360 | 288 | 288 | 360 | 288 | 288 | 360 | 288 | 360 | 288 | 288 |
| | | Capacity Needed | Contrained CH | 430 | 288 | 288 | 360 | 288 | 288 | 360 | 288 | 288 | 360 | 288 | 324 | 324 | 288 |
| | | Utilization Pct | Contrained CH | 88% | 100% | 100% | 100% | 100% | 100% | 100% | 100% | 100% | 100% | 100% | 90% | 113% | 100% |

**Fig. 5.137** Rough-cut capacity overview after supply optimization

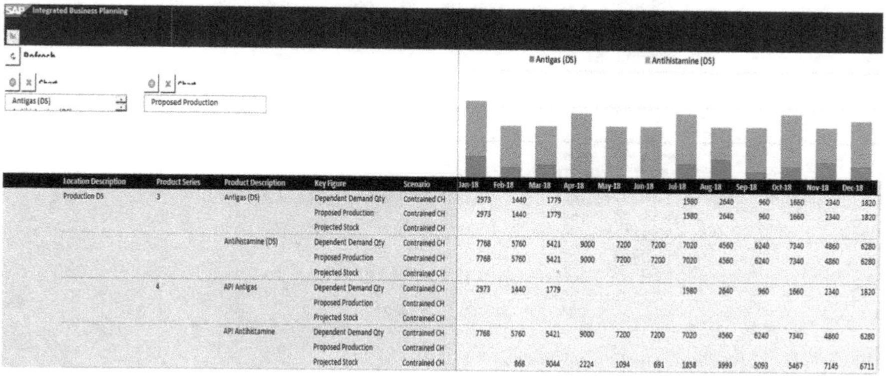


| Location Description | Product Series | Product Description | Key Figure | Scenario | Jan-18 | Feb-18 | Mar-18 | Apr-18 | May-18 | Jun-18 | Jul-18 | Aug-18 | Sep-18 | Oct-18 | Nov-18 | Dec-18 |
|---|---|---|---|---|---|---|---|---|---|---|---|---|---|---|---|---|
| Production DS | 3 | Antigas (DS) | Dependent Demand Qty | Contrained CH | 2973 | 1440 | 1779 | | | | 1980 | 2640 | 960 | 1660 | 2340 | 1820 |
| | | | Proposed Production | Contrained CH | 2973 | 1440 | 1779 | | | | 1980 | 2640 | 960 | 1660 | 2340 | 1820 |
| | | | Projected Stock | Contrained CH | | | | | | | | | | | | |
| | | Antihistamine (DS) | Dependent Demand Qty | Contrained CH | 7768 | 5760 | 5421 | 9000 | 7200 | 7200 | 7020 | 4560 | 6240 | 7340 | 4860 | 6280 |
| | | | Proposed Production | Contrained CH | 7768 | 5760 | 5421 | 9000 | 7200 | 7200 | 7020 | 4560 | 6240 | 7340 | 4860 | 6280 |
| | | | Projected Stock | Contrained CH | | | | | | | | | | | | |
| | 4 | API Antigas | Dependent Demand Qty | Contrained CH | 2973 | 1440 | 1779 | | | | 1980 | 2640 | 960 | 1660 | 2340 | 1820 |
| | | | Proposed Production | Contrained CH | | | | | | | | | | | | |
| | | | Projected Stock | Contrained CH | | | | | | | | | | | | |
| | | API Antihistamine | Dependent Demand Qty | Contrained CH | 7768 | 5760 | 5421 | 9000 | 7200 | 7200 | 7020 | 4560 | 6240 | 7340 | 4860 | 6280 |
| | | | Proposed Production | Contrained CH | | | | | | | | | | | | |
| | | | Projected Stock | Contrained CH | | 868 | 3044 | 2224 | 1094 | 691 | 1858 | 3993 | 5093 | 5467 | 7145 | 6711 |

**Fig. 5.138** Drug substance supply plan, prioritization of more profitable API

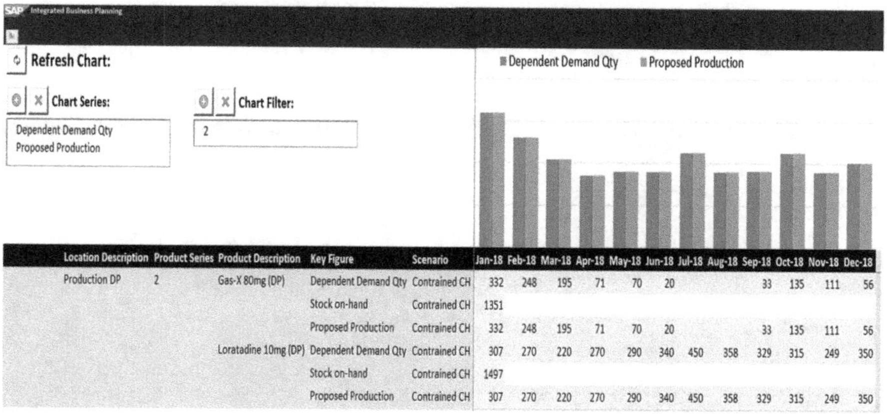


| Location Description | Product Series | Product Description | Key Figure | Scenario | Jan-18 | Feb-18 | Mar-18 | Apr-18 | May-18 | Jun-18 | Jul-18 | Aug-18 | Sep-18 | Oct-18 | Nov-18 | Dec-18 |
|---|---|---|---|---|---|---|---|---|---|---|---|---|---|---|---|---|
| Production DP | 2 | Gas-X 80mg (DP) | Dependent Demand Qty | Contrained CH | 332 | 248 | 195 | 71 | 70 | 20 | | | 33 | 135 | 111 | 56 |
| | | | Stock on-hand | Contrained CH | 1351 | | | | | | | | | | | |
| | | | Proposed Production | Contrained CH | 332 | 248 | 195 | 71 | 70 | 20 | | | 33 | 135 | 111 | 56 |
| | | Loratadine 10mg (DP) | Dependent Demand Qty | Contrained CH | 307 | 270 | 220 | 270 | 290 | 340 | 450 | 358 | 329 | 315 | 249 | 350 |
| | | | Stock on-hand | Contrained CH | 1497 | | | | | | | | | | | |
| | | | Proposed Production | Contrained CH | 307 | 270 | 220 | 270 | 290 | 340 | 450 | 358 | 329 | 315 | 249 | 350 |

**Fig. 5.139** Drug product supply plan

Then planner reviews production plan for packaging plant of the finished products. It is obvious that constraints of the drug substance have impacted packaging plant since in some periods production was not planned due to lack of availability of resources and drug substance/drug product (see Fig. 5.140).

Supply planner reviews market and their distribution centers. For most of the periods, planned maximum inventory in distribution centers is not exceeded. Planner can analyze projected inventory on impacted distribution centers (see Fig. 5.141).

Finally planner analyzes impact on demand fulfillment, which shows planned realization of consensus demand forecast for each market and product. Impact of constrained

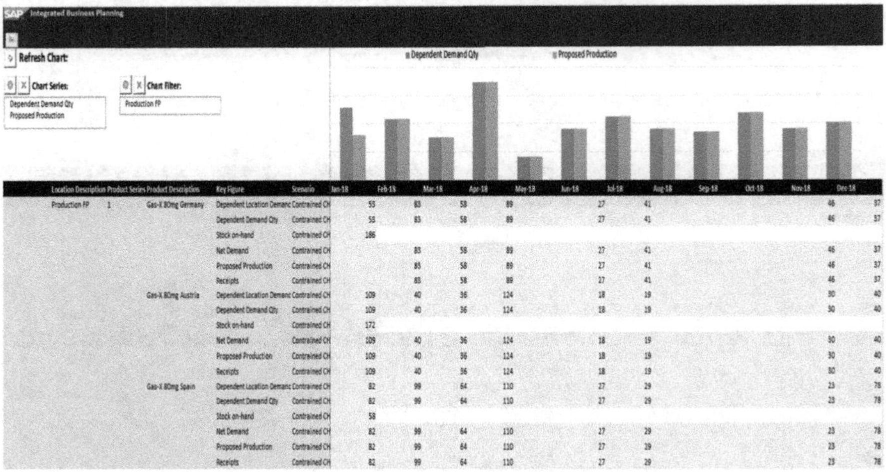


| Location Description | Product Series | Product Description | Key Figure | Scenario | Jan-18 | Feb-18 | Mar-18 | Apr-18 | May-18 | Jun-18 | Jul-18 | Aug-18 | Sep-18 | Oct-18 | Nov-18 | Dec-18 |
|---|---|---|---|---|---|---|---|---|---|---|---|---|---|---|---|---|
| Production FP | 1 | Gas-X 80mg Germany | Dependent Location Demanc | Contrained CH | 53 | 83 | 58 | 89 | | 27 | 41 | | | | 46 | 37 |
| | | | Dependent Demand Qty | Contrained CH | 53 | 83 | 58 | 89 | | 27 | 41 | | | | 46 | 37 |
| | | | Stock on-hand | Contrained CH | 186 | | | | | | | | | | | |
| | | | Net Demand | Contrained CH | | 83 | 58 | 89 | | 27 | 41 | | | | 46 | 37 |
| | | | Proposed Production | Contrained CH | | 83 | 58 | 89 | | 27 | 41 | | | | 46 | 37 |
| | | | Receipts | Contrained CH | | 83 | 58 | 89 | | 27 | 41 | | | | 46 | 37 |
| | | Gas-X 80mg Austria | Dependent Location Demanc | Contrained CH | 109 | 40 | 36 | 124 | | 18 | 19 | | | | 30 | 40 |
| | | | Dependent Demand Qty | Contrained CH | 109 | 40 | 36 | 124 | | 18 | 19 | | | | 30 | 40 |
| | | | Stock on-hand | Contrained CH | 172 | | | | | | | | | | | |
| | | | Net Demand | Contrained CH | 109 | 40 | 36 | 124 | | 18 | 19 | | | | 30 | 40 |
| | | | Proposed Production | Contrained CH | 109 | 40 | 36 | 124 | | 18 | 19 | | | | 30 | 40 |
| | | | Receipts | Contrained CH | 109 | 40 | 36 | 124 | | 18 | 19 | | | | 30 | 40 |
| | | Gas-X 80mg Spain | Dependent Location Demanc | Contrained CH | 82 | 99 | 64 | 110 | | 27 | 29 | | | | 23 | 78 |
| | | | Dependent Demand Qty | Contrained CH | 82 | 99 | 64 | 110 | | 27 | 29 | | | | 23 | 78 |
| | | | Stock on-hand | Contrained CH | 58 | | | | | | | | | | | |
| | | | Net Demand | Contrained CH | 82 | 99 | 64 | 110 | | 27 | 29 | | | | 23 | 78 |
| | | | Proposed Production | Contrained CH | 82 | 99 | 64 | 110 | | 27 | 29 | | | | 23 | 78 |
| | | | Receipts | Contrained CH | 82 | 99 | 64 | 110 | | 27 | 29 | | | | 23 | 78 |

**Fig. 5.140** Finished product supply plans

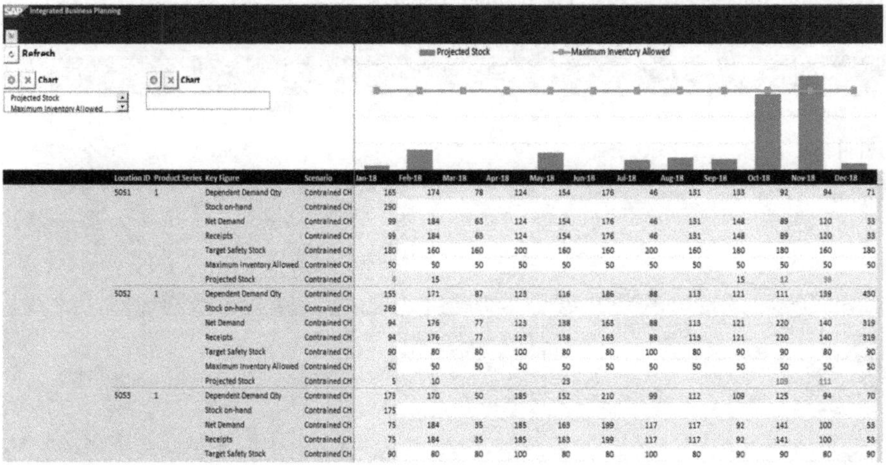


| Location ID | Product Series | Key Figure | Scenario | Jan-18 | Feb-18 | Mar-18 | Apr-18 | May-18 | Jun-18 | Jul-18 | Aug-18 | Sep-18 | Oct-18 | Nov-18 | Dec-18 |
|---|---|---|---|---|---|---|---|---|---|---|---|---|---|---|---|
| 5051 | 1 | Dependent Demand Qty | Contrained CH | 165 | 174 | 78 | 124 | 154 | 176 | 46 | 131 | 133 | 92 | 94 | 71 |
| | | Stock on-hand | Contrained CH | 290 | | | | | | | | | | | |
| | | Net Demand | Contrained CH | 99 | 184 | 63 | 124 | 154 | 176 | 46 | 131 | 148 | 89 | 120 | 33 |
| | | Receipts | Contrained CH | 99 | 184 | 63 | 124 | 154 | 176 | 46 | 131 | 148 | 89 | 120 | 33 |
| | | Target Safety Stock | Contrained CH | 180 | 160 | 160 | 200 | 160 | 160 | 200 | 160 | 180 | 180 | 160 | 180 |
| | | Maximum Inventory Allowed | Contrained CH | 50 | 50 | 50 | 50 | 50 | 50 | 50 | 50 | 50 | 50 | 50 | 50 |
| | | Projected Stock | Contrained CH | 4 | 15 | | | | | | | 15 | 12 | 38 | |
| 5052 | 1 | Dependent Demand Qty | Contrained CH | 155 | 171 | 87 | 123 | 116 | 186 | 88 | 113 | 121 | 111 | 139 | 430 |
| | | Stock on-hand | Contrained CH | 269 | | | | | | | | | | | |
| | | Net Demand | Contrained CH | 94 | 176 | 77 | 123 | 138 | 163 | 88 | 113 | 121 | 220 | 140 | 319 |
| | | Receipts | Contrained CH | 94 | 176 | 77 | 123 | 138 | 163 | 88 | 113 | 121 | 220 | 140 | 319 |
| | | Target Safety Stock | Contrained CH | 90 | 80 | 80 | 100 | 80 | 80 | 100 | 80 | 90 | 90 | 80 | 90 |
| | | Maximum Inventory Allowed | Contrained CH | 50 | 50 | 50 | 50 | 50 | 50 | 50 | 50 | 50 | 50 | 50 | 50 |
| | | Projected Stock | Contrained CH | 5 | 10 | | | 23 | | | | | 109 | 111 | |
| 5053 | 1 | Dependent Demand Qty | Contrained CH | 173 | 170 | 50 | 185 | 152 | 210 | 99 | 112 | 109 | 125 | 94 | 70 |
| | | Stock on-hand | Contrained CH | 175 | | | | | | | | | | | |
| | | Net Demand | Contrained CH | 75 | 184 | 35 | 185 | 163 | 199 | 117 | 117 | 92 | 141 | 100 | 53 |
| | | Receipts | Contrained CH | 75 | 184 | 35 | 185 | 163 | 199 | 117 | 117 | 92 | 141 | 100 | 53 |
| | | Target Safety Stock | Contrained CH | 90 | 80 | 80 | 100 | 80 | 80 | 100 | 80 | 90 | 90 | 80 | 90 |

**Fig. 5.141** Distribution centers overview after constrained planning

planned is visualized in Fig. 5.142. Planners see very fast that gaps in fulfillment exist either visualized on chart or on colored coded demand fulfillment percentage.

Discussion with demand manager and supply manager resulted in further investigation of supply planning. Impact on markets were that significant that supply manager asked for simulation of production line extension which was planned already for drug substance plant (see Fig. 5.143).

Supply planner planned additional resource for drug substance plant in a way that in the first half of the year, we see one shift, and from second-half of the year, we see three shifts. Resource efficiency on main and extended production line was increased. Supply planner reruns supply optimizer and analyzes impact on market level with demand manager again.

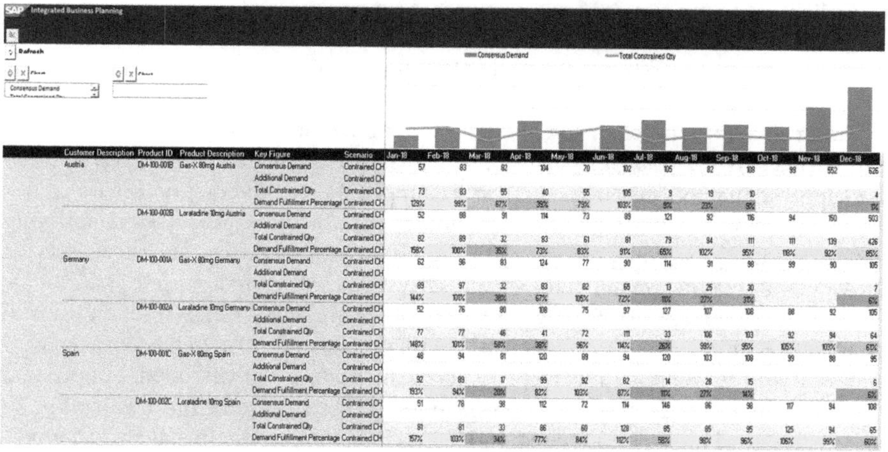


**Fig. 5.142** Market level demand fulfillment after supply plan is constrained

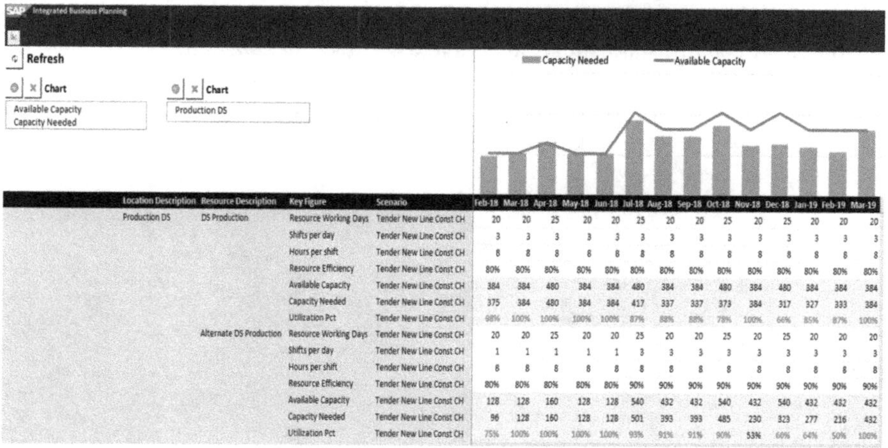


**Fig. 5.143** Drug substance plant resource extension

### 5.3.5 SAP Use Case: Supplier Collaboration (SAP IBP—SAP ARIBA)

With supply chains that are increasing in complexity, incorporating global outsourcing and sometimes tracking up to the third-tier suppliers, companies have to mitigate more diverse risks like supply disruptions caused by economic instability, foreign regulations, longer lead time, volatile exchange rate, etc. Preventing and minimizing such disruptions require visibility not only over their own operations but also across suppliers. It is difficult to make data-driven decisions when there is a high variation in data type and format, having a point to point collection of electronic data interchange (EDI) messages and spreadsheets sent via email. Achieving the necessary visibility is highly dependent on the adoption of the right technology/right supply chain tools that will allow:

- Collaboration with trading partners in real time
- Identification and reaction to supply chain events
- Tracking and assessment of suppliers' performance

As an answer to this challenge, SAP brings together its supply chain expertise and SAP Ariba network of buyers and suppliers to provide a single, cloud-based solution for supply chain collaboration. SAP Ariba supply chain collaboration (SCC) comes as an extension to the supply chain planning and execution processes simplifying and automating the collaboration with the trading partners like suppliers, service providers, or contract manufacturers across systems and geographies.

Further, integrating Ariba SCC with a supply planning SAP IBP solution leads to an effective supply chain management, helping companies to achieve a true end-to-end visibility to support informed decisions in dealing with frequent supply and demand variations. It will enable companies to better predict the availability of supply, improve on-time-to-request (OTTR) KPI, and decrease inventory and working capital expense.

Now let's see how connecting these two systems will help to achieve a faster and more reliable planning cycle.

We will use as an example a company that has a high product mix and is outsourcing 50% of its assembly process to a contract manufacturer.

During S&OP review preparations, it comes out that Q2 turns to be much slower than it was expected, actuals and projected revenue falling short of the budget plan (see Fig. 5.144). Sales, marketing, and demand work together on a new strategy overcome the revenue drop.

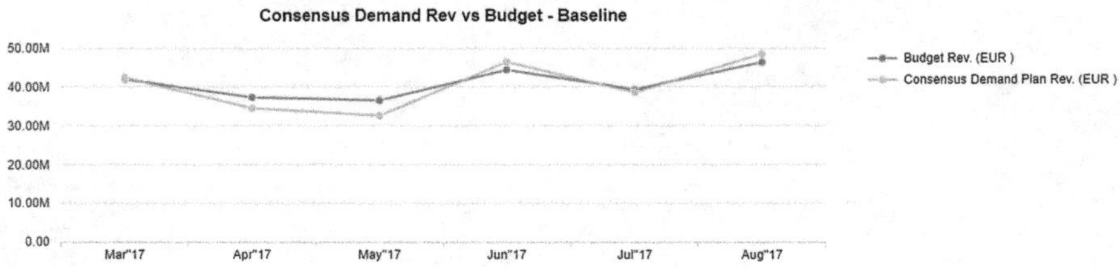


**Fig. 5.144** Demand vs budget comparison

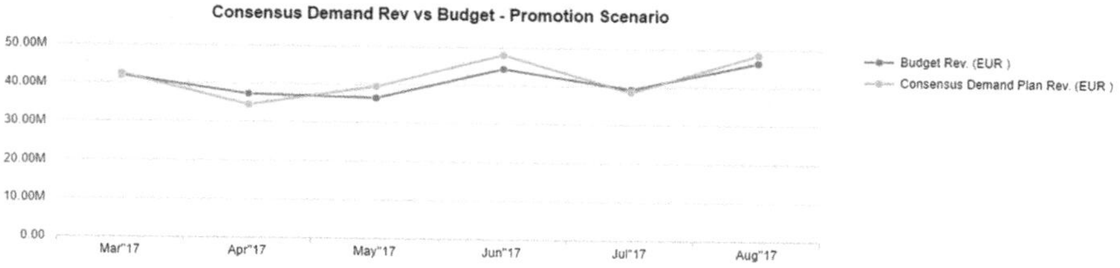


**Fig. 5.145** Promotional consensus demand forecast vs budget

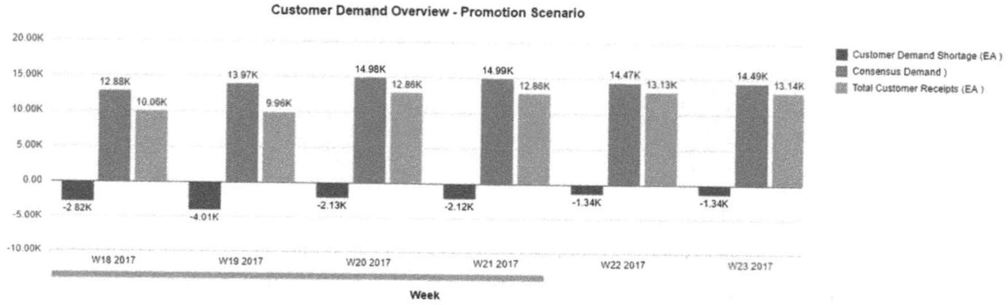


**Fig. 5.146** Supply receipts gap

They plan a promotion in key markets that is expecting to bring the extra demand needed to close the gap (see Fig. 5.145).

Running the promotion is highly dependent on the supply's ability to fulfill the extra demand; otherwise, it would turn into wasted marketing budget and dissatisfied customers.

Once latest demand numbers are committed as part of a scenario, the supply planner is now able to run the promotion numbers and evaluate the gap between projected demand and available quantity. As the chart in supply planner's dashboard highlights, the shortfall is significant and requires to immediately validate the demand spike with the components' suppliers and check whether the total assembly capacity (in-house plus contract manufacturer) is enough to match the plan (see Fig. 5.146).

In the past, this could have triggered a long process of collaboration via emails and spreadsheets, but now the demand for both finished goods and components can be digitally sent to the contract manufacturer and suppliers via IBP Ariba business network collaboration. Having Ariba SCC connected to external partners' own planning system or simply using the planning user interface available in Ariba SCC portal, the latest forecast can be reviewed and the volume commitment can be sent back.

Coming back to our example, one of the main components is purchased from two different suppliers based on a predefined quota of 60% to supplier SA102 and 40% to supplier SA101. Using the Ariba portal, both suppliers input their commitment on the latest forecast. The later one has issues to meet the component requirements and commits a smaller quantity (Fig. 5.147).

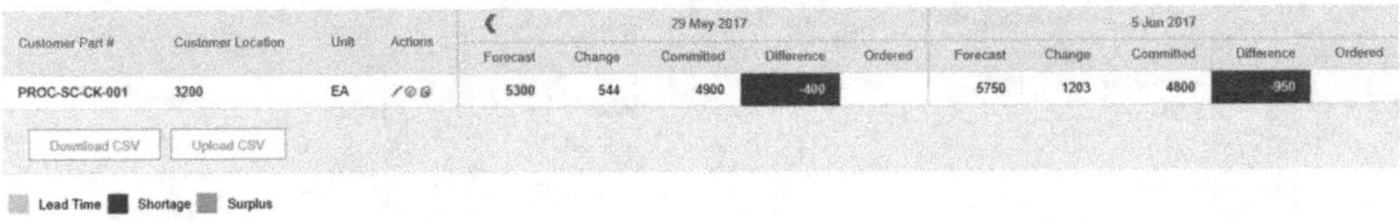


**Fig. 5.147** SAP Ariba supplier commits forecast with differences

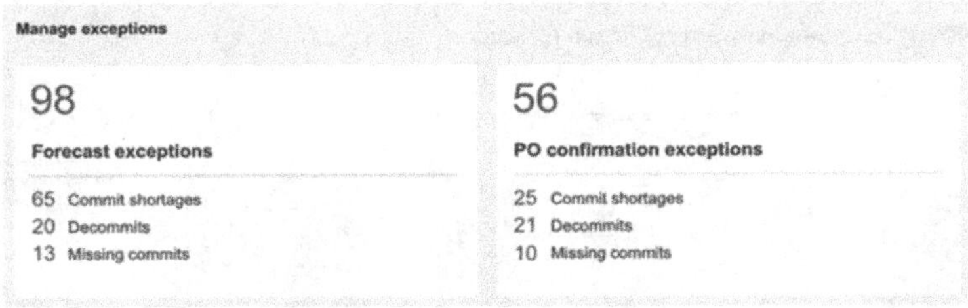


**Fig. 5.148** SAP Supplier forecast and purchase orders deviations

As an outcome of the confirmation, the buyer is immediately informed. He checks the commitments over the entire horizon and sees that the supplier is not able to support the component forecast. Moreover the performance over the past months was constantly dropping, creating many disruptions in the supply chain which ultimately impacted the customer service level (see Fig. 5.148).

The buyer decides to have a closer look to see what can be done to overcome the risk over the mid-long-term horizon:

- Work with the supplier SA101 to increase capacity.
- Increase supplier SA102 quota.
- Find a new supplier.

Before taking a decision, the buyer uses Ariba supplier risk solution to evaluate the threats associated with supplier SA101. With the help of this tool, internal information and syndicated data from thousands of sources, including private and public data sources, are analyzed in real time for a continuous monitoring of the risks to which supplier is exposed:

- Environmental
- Regulatory and legal
- Environmental and social
- Operational
- Financial (see Fig. 5.149)

It seems that the risks linked with this supplier increased a lot over the past horizon, being mainly driven by environmental challenges. Giving more business to the supplier is definitely not a safe decision to take, so the buyer will initiate a sourcing event to find a more reliable supplier.

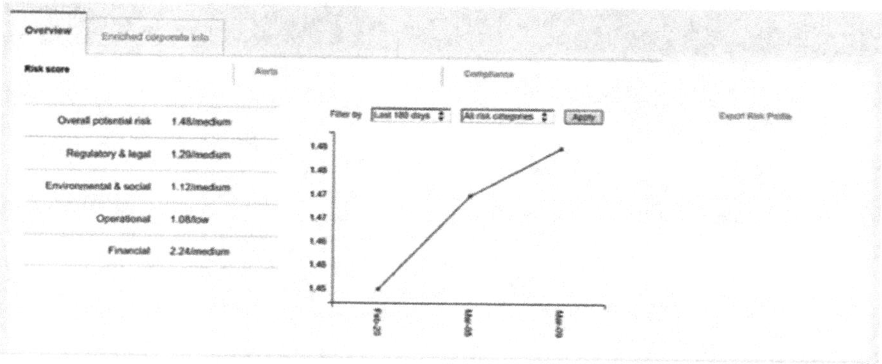


**Fig. 5.149** SAP Ariba supplier assessment

SAP Integrated Business Planning

| Product ID | Location ID | Key Figure | W20 2017 | W21 2017 | W22 2017 | W23 2017 |
|---|---|---|---|---|---|---|
| PROD-SC-CK-001 | SA101 | Supplier Commit | 4,250 | 4,600 | 4,900 | 4,800 |
| | | Supplier Forecast | 5,256 | 5,166 | 5,300 | 5,750 |
| | SA102 | Supplier Commit | 8,000 | 7,700 | 8,000 | 8,500 |
| | | Supplier Forecast | 7,885 | 7,750 | 7,915 | 8,612 |

**Fig. 5.150** SAP IBP supply forecast vs supply commits

In the meantime the supply planner sees the latest commitment integrated in his planning book (see Fig. 5.150). Supply commits are transferred into IBP for constrained supply planning which will consider material availability planned shortages. Supply optimizer will help planner to make realistic plans and communicate impact to sales and marketing in the markets.

### 5.3.6 SAP Use Case: Multisourcing Optimization

Supply planning often faces a challenge of how to execute component sourcing allocation which considers costs. Time-series-based supply planning optimizer operator takes into account for external procurement the following cost drivers:

- External procurement cost rate
- Transportation cost rate
- Component constraint coming from an external source of supply

To illustrate procurement supply optimization, we have a finished good, IBP-210, which has its main component, IBP-211-R, supplied from two different vendors: SA101 and SA102. Even if the procurement cost rate is the same for vendor SA101 and vendor SA102, the transportation cost is higher for SA102. For this reason, the

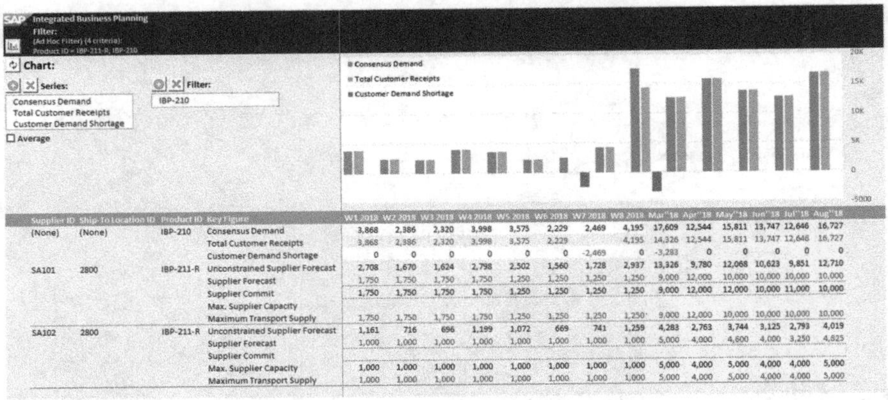


| Supplier ID | Ship-To Location ID | Product ID | Key Figure | W1 2018 | W2 2018 | W3 2018 | W4 2018 | W5 2018 | W6 2018 | W7 2018 | W8 2018 | Mar''18 | Apr''18 | May''18 | Jun''18 | Jul''18 | Aug''18 |
|---|---|---|---|---|---|---|---|---|---|---|---|---|---|---|---|---|---|
| (None) | (None) | IBP-210 | Consensus Demand | 3,868 | 2,386 | 2,320 | 3,998 | 3,575 | 2,229 | 2,469 | 4,195 | 17,609 | 12,544 | 15,811 | 13,747 | 12,646 | 16,727 |
| | | | Total Customer Receipts | 3,868 | 2,386 | 2,320 | 3,998 | 3,575 | 2,229 | | 4,195 | 14,326 | 12,544 | 15,811 | 13,747 | 12,646 | 16,727 |
| | | | Customer Demand Shortage | 0 | 0 | 0 | 0 | 0 | 0 | -2,469 | 0 | -3,283 | 0 | 0 | 0 | 0 | 0 |
| SA101 | 2800 | IBP-211-R | Unconstrained Supplier Forecast | 2,708 | 1,670 | 1,624 | 2,798 | 2,502 | 1,560 | 1,728 | 2,937 | 13,326 | 9,780 | 12,068 | 10,623 | 9,851 | 12,710 |
| | | | Supplier Forecast | 1,750 | 1,750 | 1,750 | 1,750 | 1,250 | 1,250 | 1,250 | 1,250 | 9,000 | 12,000 | 10,000 | 10,000 | 10,000 | 10,000 |
| | | | Supplier Commit | 1,750 | 1,750 | 1,750 | 1,750 | 1,250 | 1,250 | 1,250 | 1,250 | 9,000 | 12,000 | 12,000 | 10,000 | 11,000 | 10,000 |
| | | | Max. Supplier Capacity | | | | | | | | | | | | | | |
| | | | Maximum Transport Supply | 1,750 | 1,750 | 1,750 | 1,750 | 1,250 | 1,250 | 1,250 | 1,250 | 9,000 | 12,000 | 10,000 | 10,000 | 10,000 | 10,000 |
| SA102 | 2800 | IBP-211-R | Unconstrained Supplier Forecast | 1,161 | 716 | 696 | 1,199 | 1,072 | 669 | 741 | 1,259 | 4,283 | 2,763 | 3,744 | 3,125 | 2,793 | 4,019 |
| | | | Supplier Forecast | 1,000 | 1,000 | 1,000 | 1,000 | 1,000 | 1,000 | 1,000 | 1,000 | 5,000 | 4,000 | 4,600 | 4,000 | 3,250 | 4,825 |
| | | | Supplier Commit | | | | | | | | | | | | | | |
| | | | Max. Supplier Capacity | 1,000 | 1,000 | 1,000 | 1,000 | 1,000 | 1,000 | 1,000 | 1,000 | 5,000 | 4,000 | 5,000 | 4,000 | 4,000 | 5,000 |
| | | | Maximum Transport Supply | 1,000 | 1,000 | 1,000 | 1,000 | 1,000 | 1,000 | 1,000 | 1,000 | 5,000 | 4,000 | 5,000 | 4,000 | 4,000 | 5,000 |

**Fig. 5.151** Multisourcing optimization and realistic commitments

optimizer should try to maximize the sourcing from the supplier SA101. Real life is not simple; therefore, in our use case, vendor SA101 has provided a forecast confirmation (commitment) for a quantity that is below the buyer's request (supplier unconstrained forecast). To ensure that the supply optimizer does consider the supplier commit as a hard constraint and it will not forecast receipts above this given limit, we have used the supplier commit as input for the maximum transport supply key figure. This later key figure is part of a category of key figures, maximum key figures that are only computed by the optimizer and not by the heuristics. The maximum key figures' role is to define constraints for the optimizer by limiting the quantities of several output key figures such as projected inventory, customer, transport, or production receipts.

Moving our attention over the supplier SA102, we see that instead of receiving a weekly commitment, we have defined a given maximum capacity up to which the supplier can fulfill the component requirements.

Following the optimization run, SA101 is planned with a lower quantity than initially requested (unconstrained supplier forecast), while the supplier SA102 is requested to deliver in line with its maximum commitment until the end of April (see Fig. 5.151). Unfortunately, this projection indicates a customer shortage in February and March, shortage that the supply planner will further assess.

### 5.3.7 SAP Use Case: Storage Capacity Optimization

With the time-series-based supply planning operators available in SAP IBP, one can model different types of capacity:

- Capacity consumption of the handling resource—e.g., capacity consumed for the good receipt or good issue activity. This type of capacity is available only for the time-series-based supply planning heuristic.

- Capacity consumption of a production resource—e.g., capacity consumed with each unit that is assembled or produced. The time-series-based supply optimizer considers the available capacity of a production resource as a hard constraint, which means that the finite computed solution will not violate the maximum available capacity.
- Capacity consumption of a storage resource—e.g., the warehouse capacity consumed when specific products are stored in. This capacity is modeled as a pseudo-hard constraint to allow the time-series-based supply optimizer to find a solution in situations where the capacity limit must be violated (e.g., huge initial inventories).

We will now stop over the storage capacity and show a typical use case for the tactical planning. We will pick as an example an enterprise that is characterized by a strong seasonal trend, which translates with a big variance of the storage capacity need. To stay competitive, the company must be able to plan how to manage the warehouse space and increase its capacity if needed by lease extra space, if this is an option, or involve a third-party warehouse operator.

The warehouse capacity can be quickly evaluated against the unconstrained storage needs. As part of the rough-cut capacity planning, we are running the unconstrained heuristic operator to see where the bottlenecks are. End of the year is usually characterized by a temporary spike in the demand, and this correlates with an unusual high overload in the warehouse capacity. Notice the warehouse capacity utilization being highlighted in red between W47 and W50 (see Fig. 5.152). As expected, an alert is generated for the warehouse capacity during the two season periods where the demand spike correlates with an unusual high overload in the warehouse capacity. Notice the warehouse capacity utilization being highlighted in red.

We will model the extra capacity requirements during the seasons using the capacity supply extension feature of IBP. This feature can be used for both production resources, where we would like to increase the producing capacity by adding an extra shift, and for the storage facility expansion. The capacity expansion comes with an additional cost rate which will help us to have a more accurate projection of the operating profit. The time-series-based supply planning optimizer will process this cost and will try to find the most cost-effective solution: for example, it could be that late delivery would have a smaller penalty costs than the storage holding value. You also notice that we have an unused capacity at a warehouse contractor. As

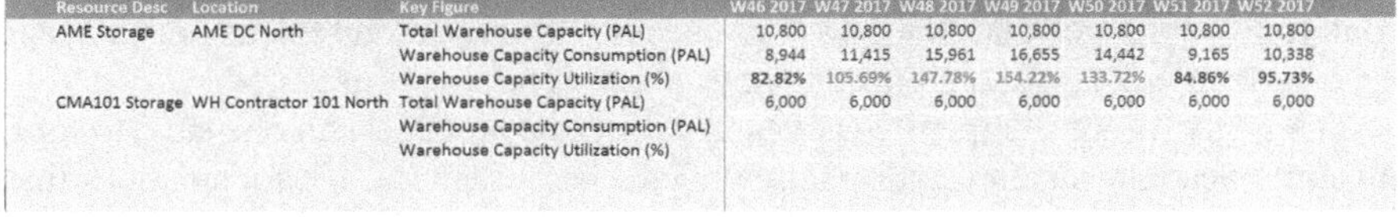
SAP Integrated Business Planning

S 01 End to End Supply

| Resource Desc | Location | Key Figure | W46 2017 | W47 2017 | W48 2017 | W49 2017 | W50 2017 | W51 2017 | W52 2017 |
|---|---|---|---|---|---|---|---|---|---|
| AME Storage | AME DC North | Total Warehouse Capacity (PAL) | 10,800 | 10,800 | 10,800 | 10,800 | 10,800 | 10,800 | 10,800 |
| | | Warehouse Capacity Consumption (PAL) | 8,944 | 11,415 | 15,961 | 16,655 | 14,442 | 9,165 | 10,338 |
| | | Warehouse Capacity Utilization (%) | 82.82% | 105.69% | 147.78% | 154.22% | 133.72% | 84.86% | 95.73% |
| CMA101 Storage | WH Contractor 101 North | Total Warehouse Capacity (PAL) | 6,000 | 6,000 | 6,000 | 6,000 | 6,000 | 6,000 | 6,000 |
| | | Warehouse Capacity Consumption (PAL) | | | | | | | |
| | | Warehouse Capacity Utilization (%) | | | | | | | |

**Fig. 5.152** Warehouse space capacity overutilization

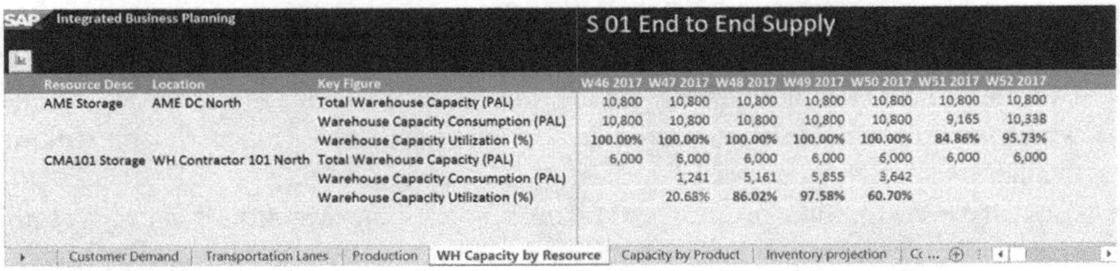



| Resource Desc | Location | Key Figure | W46 2017 | W47 2017 | W48 2017 | W49 2017 | W50 2017 | W51 2017 | W52 2017 |
|---|---|---|---|---|---|---|---|---|---|
| AME Storage | AME DC North | Total Warehouse Capacity (PAL) | 10,800 | 10,800 | 10,800 | 10,800 | 10,800 | 10,800 | 10,800 |
| | | Warehouse Capacity Consumption (PAL) | 10,800 | 10,800 | 10,800 | 10,800 | 10,800 | 9,165 | 10,338 |
| | | Warehouse Capacity Utilization (%) | 100.00% | 100.00% | 100.00% | 100.00% | 100.00% | 84.86% | 95.73% |
| CMA101 Storage | WH Contractor 101 North | Total Warehouse Capacity (PAL) | 6,000 | 6,000 | 6,000 | 6,000 | 6,000 | 6,000 | 6,000 |
| | | Warehouse Capacity Consumption (PAL) | | 1,241 | 5,161 | 5,855 | 3,642 | | |
| | | Warehouse Capacity Utilization (%) | | 20.68% | 86.02% | 97.58% | 60.70% | | |

**Fig. 5.153** Warehouse space optimized with external provider

heuristic is driven by the sourcing rules, it will not check for a solution outside these sourcing rules. Of course, given that the sourcing rules are time dependent, we could adjust the ratio during these time frames.

To come up with a feasible plan which should find way to sort out warehouse space capacity utilization issue, we execute the time-series optimizer operator. It will provide a solution that will shift some of the volumes in the week before where there is available capacity, while the remaining volumes will be allocated to a warehouse storage subcontractor which has a higher inventory holding cost than the one we have in-house. For this reason, the contract manufacturer is the least preferred option, but still it provides a better solution compared with a nondelivery case for the customers and markets (see Fig. 5.153).

External provider warehouse space is now being planned and considered.

### 5.3.8 SAP Use Case: IoT Machine Integration with IBP Supply and S/4 Scheduling

In this use case, we have leveraged SAP Cloud Platform which enabled IoT integration with machine sensors to collect and interpret vibration data and use it in identification of planned shutdown in S/4, connecting to IBP supply planning and optimizing constrained plan with new machine availability.

Talking about the SAP IBP's ability to extend its functionalities, we distinguish between two main areas:

1. Build-in extensibility
2. Side-by-side extensibility

The first one, the build-in extensibility, comes with native capabilities which give customers flexibility to model their supply chain network within SAP IBP, to configure key figures that translate their specific business requirements, or to adapt the user interface layout and its content as per the end users' needs.

The battle for the competitive advantage pushes companies, on one side, to look for simplification, standardization following the best practices, and for solutions that can be quickly deployed. On the other side, it is driving companies to come with unique capabilities or processes that that can serve as industry differentiators. While the software as a service (SaaS) is fully satisfying the first need, it will be challenged by the flexibility needed to maintain uniqueness or to transform ideas into new functionalities. How to satisfy these needs that seem so different, yet complementing each other for defining the business success?

SAP IBP customers don't need to choose the simplification in the detriment of uniqueness. They can extend IBP beyond its usual business scope by using SAP Cloud Platform. SAP Cloud Platform is a platform as a service (PaaS) offering from SAP, targeted to support customers in their journey toward digital transformation by providing:

- An open platform as a service that provides an in-memory database and business services
- Integration technologies that enable integration of processes and high volume of data
- SAP Fiori to create easy-to-use mobile apps

It allows customers and partners to build new personalized application or extend their cloud or on premise applications by providing comprehensive application development services without the requirement of maintaining or investing in on-premises infrastructure.

The side-by-side extensibility given by the SAP Cloud platform is recommended whenever IBP customers or partners are considering to (Fig. 5.154):

- Design and build custom specific applications to run on top or in connection with supply chain processes executed in IBP.
- Enrich existing logic by enabling custom algorithms.
- Enable additional user experience.

We will provide now an example where we used SAP Cloud Platform to build an application that collects and analyzes data streamed by sensors over the Internet. The sensors are attached to the manufacturing equipment from the shop floor to provide a

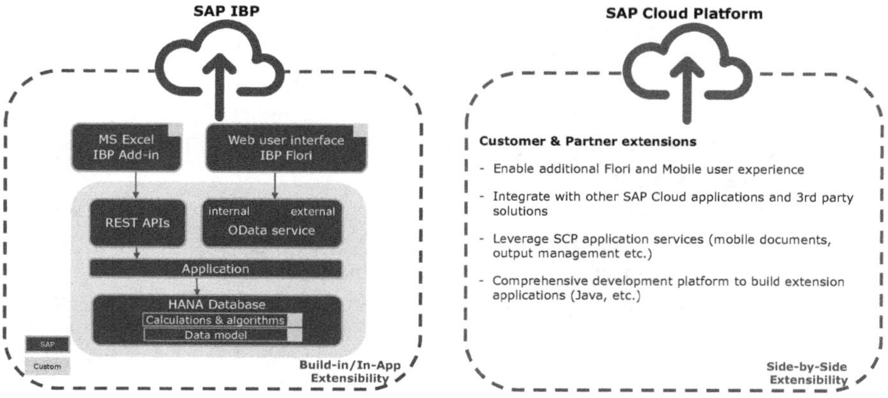


**Fig. 5.154** SAP IBP extendibility with SAP Cloud Platform

real-time insight into the running status of the motors by picking up data on vibration, temperature, or other parameters. The availability of this data can serve as support for taking various decisions on resource optimization, maintenance, or even replacement leading to lower maintenance costs and a reduction of the downtime.

The application we build enables the maintenance engineer to trigger a light or a heavy maintenance downtime that gets integrated either with the executional (S/4 HANA) or planning (IBP) system.

In the main screen (Fig. 5.155), we see a data stream representing a continuous measurement of vibrations emitted by the sensor attached to the monitored equipment. We see a summary which indicates that total number of vibrations outside the usual range and further classified into light and critical based on the intensity. Checking on the last 6-week performance of the resource, we see that scrap rate has increased to 3%.

The maintenance expert can check the last weeks' performance in greater detail and see whether there is any correlation between the critical vibrations and the scrap rate/temperature increase. This kind of analysis requires algorithms that can detect anomalies in very large volume of data, most of the time unstructured. Is there any correlation between the anomaly and the machine performance? What are the trends in the data telling us about the machine time until failure? Is the anomaly precursor to a machine failure?

In our example, based on the recommendation, the maintenance engineer is scheduling a maintenance window (see Fig. 5.156). As you can see, engineer selects the start/finish date and time, and once he hits the Confirm button, a new work order gets created in S/4 HANA Plant Maintenance module.

Further, the downtime corresponding to the recently created work order gets automatically integrated into the S/4 Production Planning module. This way, the production planner can easily visualize the downtime and trigger an action like manually shifting the impacted orders or rerunning the optimization algorithm to consider in detail scheduling new machine availability (see Fig. 5.157).

It can also be the case that the data analysis will indicate the need of a component replacement in the near horizon, which requires a longer downtime of the resource or that shutdown goes beyond short-term horizon.

In our example, we started from the premise that the maintenance engineer planned the component replacement in 6 weeks' time as he does not have the component in stock and there is a considerable lead time to plan. He expects a total downtime of 2 weeks. Once he selects the maintenance horizon, a capacity signal is sent to SAP IBP to indicate that the available capacity will be 0 during that time frame (see Fig. 5.158).

The supply planner gets immediately notified via an alert and assesses the situation. Executing the time-series-based supply planning optimizer, the planner sees there is enough capacity to pre-produce in the weeks before the maintenance window, being able, this way, to secure the customer demand from the prebuild inventory (see Fig. 5.159).

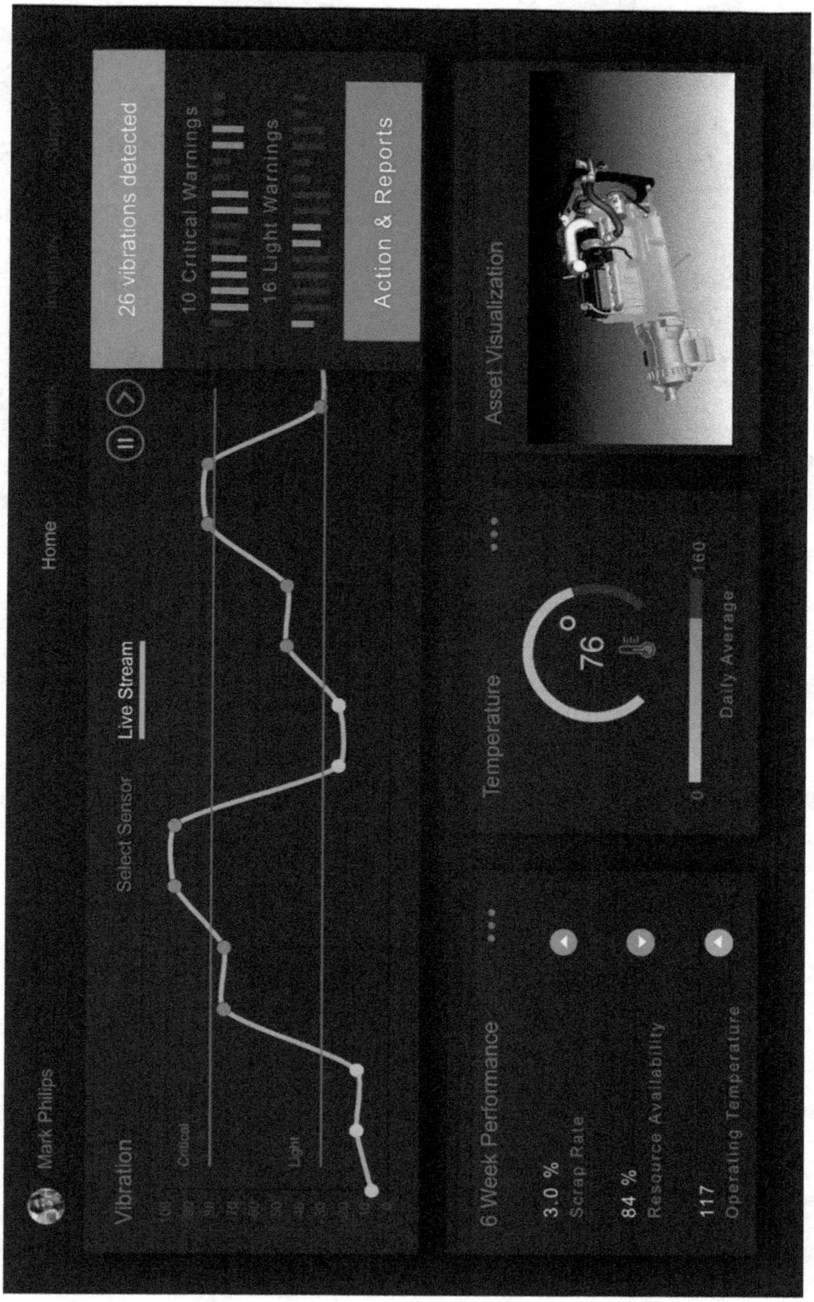


**Fig. 5.155** SAP Cloud Platform customer extended app, connecting machine, IBP, S/4

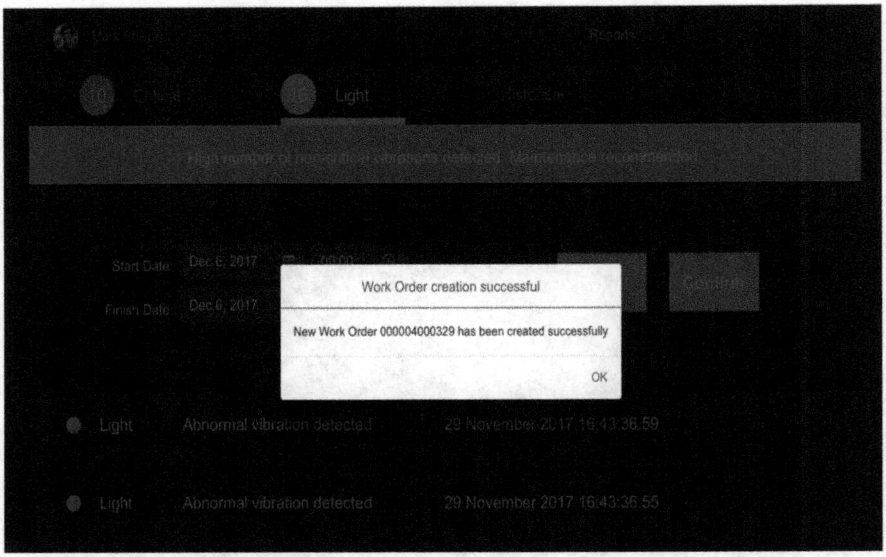


**Fig. 5.156** Work Order is created from the app that was created on SAP Cloud Platform

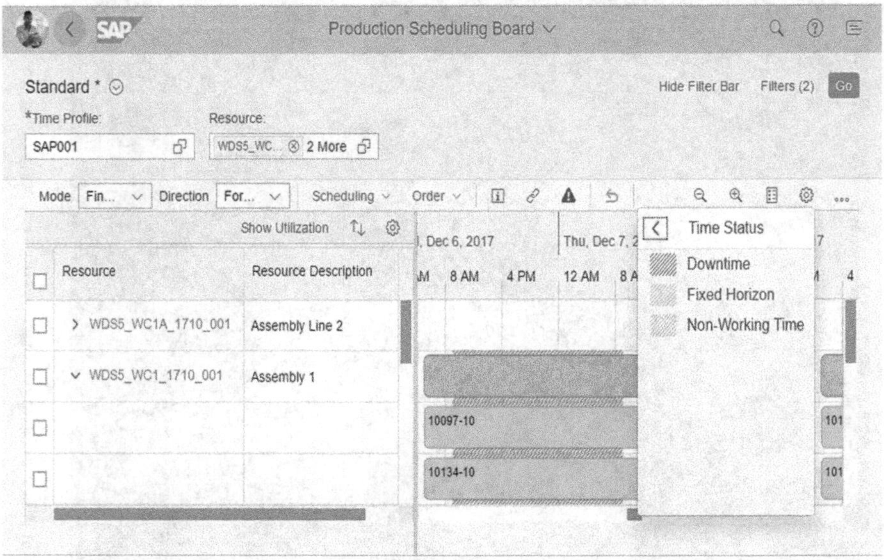


**Fig. 5.157** Downtime reflected in the production scheduling board

However, as expected, this will translate in an increased inventory holding value. The extra inventory value can be evaluated by comparing current projection with the last cycle plan projection which was stored in a version at the end of the S&OP planning cycle (see Fig. 5.160).

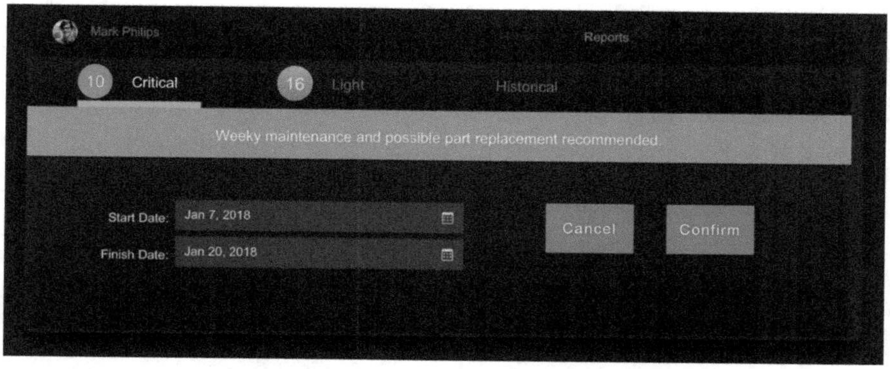


**Fig. 5.158** SAP IBP tactical supply planning is informed about shutdown from SAP Cloud Platform custom app

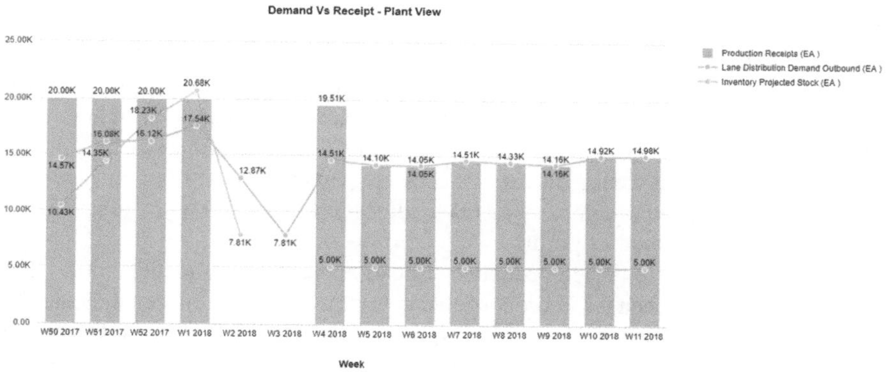


**Fig. 5.159** Pre-production to shutdown planned by optimizer

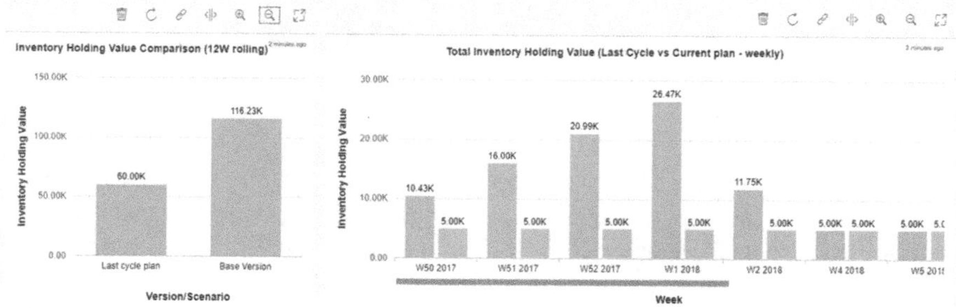


**Fig. 5.160** Inventory holding value increased temporarily because of pre-production

Given there is flexibility in choosing the maintenance window, another tactical use case for IBP would be to evaluate multiple time horizons for the maintenance and choose the one with the least impact on the customer demand, inventory, revenue, and profitability.

But what if the maintenance must occur in the very near horizon and there is no time for a plan B? In this case, the signal could be immediately reflected in IBP response module to run the allocation process but this time on specific orders.

There are obvious benefits of above, e.g.:

- Change the maintenance process from reactive to proactive
- Achieve a connected enterprise

### 5.3.9 Profitable Market/Channel Allocation Planning

As we mentioned earlier, monetization of the forecasts and plans are not only about making it in dollars, euros, and Swiss francs. Very often it is about helping organization to make decisions which are aligned to company strategies, e.g., "achieve profitable growth." Product segmentation or product segmentation weighted with customer segments may be very helpful to achieve link to strategy. One of the dimensions in the segmentation can reflect expected profit contribution, and this dimension can be used to select segments to allocate products based on the strategic driver which was defined as profit.

It will make sense to design profitable allocation planning for tactical (up to 2–3 years) horizon when changes in proportions of volumetric allocation can be linked to changes in profit. In other words if margin can be adjusted on the level where proportion of volume will be adjusted, otherwise impact will be neglectable. What do we mean by that really is if margin is loaded on SKU/country, volumetric allocation plan is adjusted on SKU/country/sales zone level. In this case it is important to align with finance and pricing if margin driven by price or cost can be adjusted on SKU/country/sales zone level.

As part of allocation planning process in tactical horizon, demand manager will have a challenge to address following inputs from demand, supply, and finance in order to:

- Enable proper process integration between commercial, marketing, and supply view, e.g., allocation planning connects demand and supply. Process is often very iterative, since its main objective is to maximize business return. Sales/marketing in country S&OP process needs to know what supply options they can have to plan their activities in the market. On the other hand, supply organization needs to understand what market wants.
- Highlight what kind of commercial flexibility and marketing is to be expected in case of shortages; supply constraints, e.g., if supply can customize the form of the product like pack size; and country label more close to pull

replenishment model (or late customization models) than push (make to stock) replenishment model.
- Understand supply response relevancy for operational, tactical planning, e.g., to classify supply information in short-term impact to long-term impact

Any constraints or excess of availability needs to be clear to demand manager who will need to take a lead and develop most profitable allocation plan and often with cooperation of other functions trigger demand-shaping opportunities. Good information about excess of availability is as much valuable as information about constraints. Both upsides and downside in supply will be used in integrated reconciliation where demand manager and finance controller should lead definition of business risk and opportunities.

Demand organization should be in charge for managing, prioritizing, and communicating demand but in a team, not through individual decisions. There should be some segmentation of planning horizon in place to enable stability zones with decision points. Last but not the least, there should be rules for evaluating how to best fulfill additional demand when supply and demand don't match (Crum and Palmatier 2003).

Supply signal needs to be fully understood by demand manager. Supply plan or supply response normally deviates from forecast. Those deviations may take various forms:

- Shortages
- Excess
- Form of product (often linked to tactical or operational substitutions)
- Granularity of supply plan
- Phasing
- Sourcing location affecting lead time or cost

Shortages, constraints, and deviations from the plan are normally caused by 4M (see Fig. 5.161).

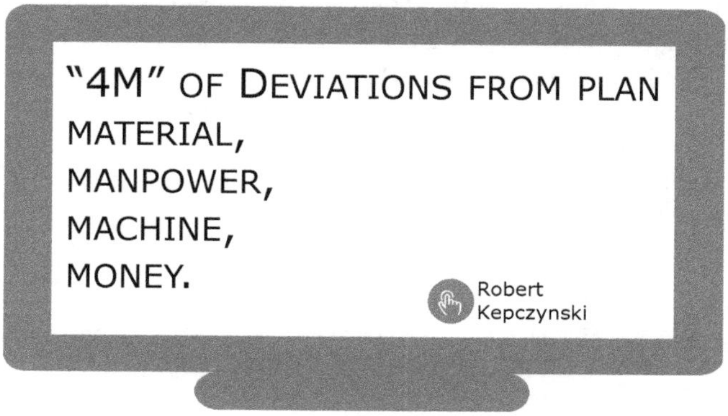


**Fig. 5.161** 4M deviations from plans

Those constraints may have:

- Hard ceiling constraints in which capacity is hardly flexible, e.g., equipment or machinery sets what can be done or skills for the jobs which are hard to train or find.
- Soft ceiling constraints where flexibility can be bought, recruited, or subcontracted.
- Basic difference between "hard and soft" constraints pivots around cost and degree and ease of flexibility (Thacker 2001).

Understanding of deviations comes from data too. Granularity of data and information changes over time in allocation planning in tactical horizon. This implies how demand manager should design process and what type of information to seek. Data may not come in highly granular form for whole horizon, but normally in different granularity linked to different horizons. As we have learned in demand processes, in supply as well, it is important to manage time and granularity in regard to available information.

Let us explain Fig. 5.162 with chemical industry products.

Strategic planning in monthly strategic product planning provides information for current and current year + 1 horizon on aggregated level called "active ingredient." This information needs to be translated to granularity which can be understood by sales and marketing in the markets and regions. Demand manager had to ensure that decision level highlighted above is taking place and that markets will be "allocated" with active ingredient, out of which formulation and finally customized product (SKU) will be produced. SAP IBP data model and functionality will help to work on aggregated and detail level. This is one IBP vs S&OP differentiators. You can define the process and model where you can save allocation quantity on specific form of the product/market combination and once the product is being transformed from low form of customization to higher form of customization like from formulation to packed SKU product (in Fig. 5.162, marked as levels 1, 2, 3).

Monthly process does not really end of seeking an answer to whom to give in case of shortages. In the peak season controlled and monitored through operational planning, it may be required to steer which customer groups/customers should be served with availability and which are not. In this case granularity of information can be even on customer/order level, but in that case, please refer to order-based allocation planning which steers execution of order-to-cash process (discussed in operational planning chapter).

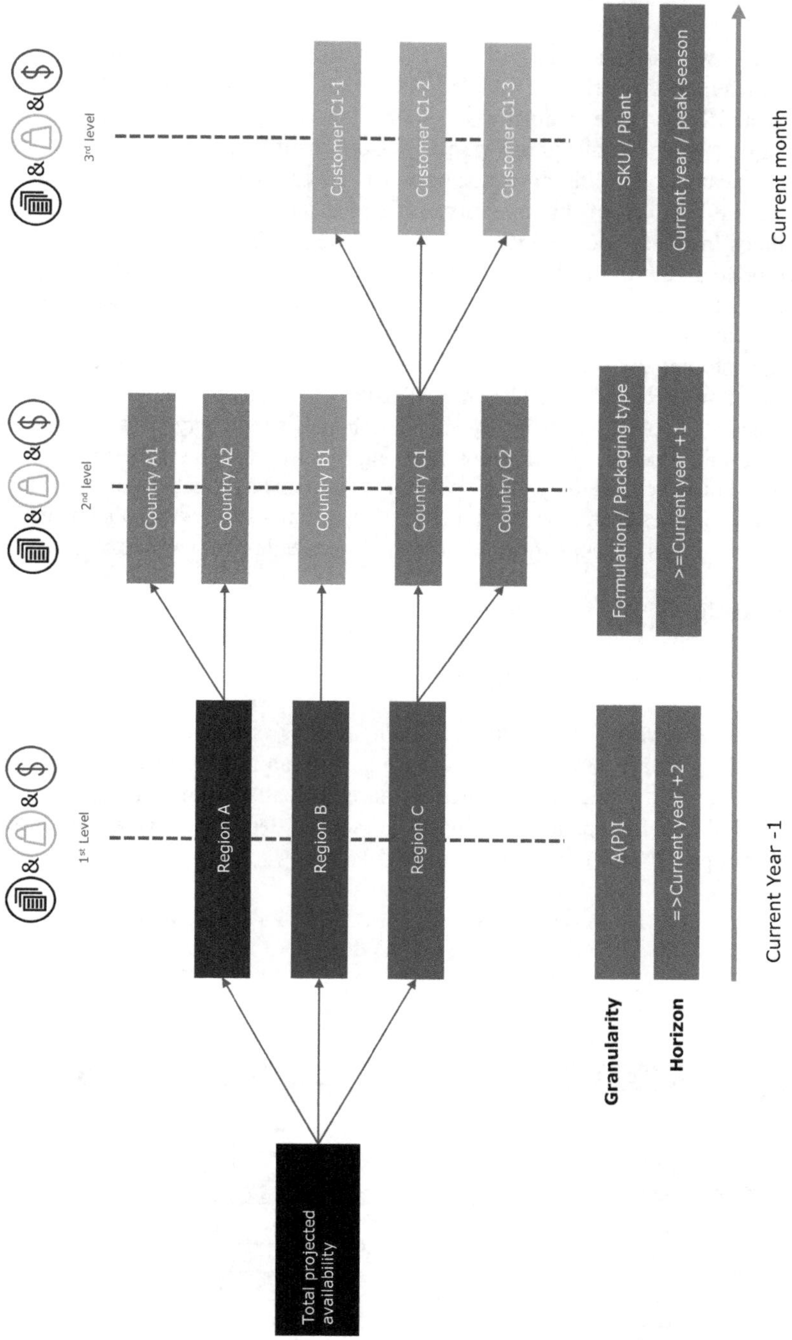


**Fig. 5.162** Allocation planning linked to time horizons and granularity

## 5.3.10 SAP Use Case: Profit-Based Allocation Planning

In this use case we explain in more detail how market allocated quantity can be assigned to different channels and enabled better management of the profit which cab ne extracted from same planned to supplied but constrained quantity. Let us understand the concept visualized in Fig. 5.163. Consensus forecast was 150 kg, but availability allocated to specific market supply was 100 kg. Demand manager had a task to make the best out of this quantity. Cost of the product was the same, but pricing policies in direct and e-commerce channel were different in the respective market (see price and margin). By changing proportion of planned available supply between channels, e.g., scenario baseline no change, scenario upside planning to give more to direct customers, and scenario downside planning to give more to e-commerce customers, we can achieve different profits (see column supply profit).

Let us see how it could look like in SAP IBP. Demand manager has received information about supply availability. It is stored in the supply qty. Based on this availability, he/she needed to run allocation planning in a way to achieve best profit. In the case demand manager will run scenario planning to maximize profit between distributor and e-commerce sales channel. What-if risk and opportunity scenario is about managing different proportions of supply qty and different forecasted prices as per example:

- Scenario baseline: 50/50 split between channels
- Scenario downside: 80% distributors and 20% direct
- Scenario upside: 40% distributors and 60% direct

Proportions can be changed and still demand manager on the bottom of the screen controls if total stays the same between scenarios. Demand manager organized ad hoc meeting with marketing and finance to agree on allocation plan and price adjustments. Results of exercise are being discussed on detail level where we can see revenue and profits and input pricing (Fig. 5.164).

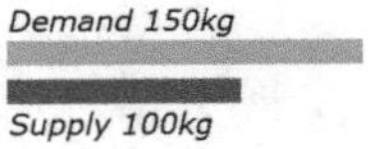


The initial available supply is lower than the demand as it needs to ramped up. Three basic scenarios can be highlighted:

1. Equal distribution between direct and distributor channels - Baseline
2. Higher use of direct (60kg) vs. distributor channels (40kg) - Upside
3. Predominant use of distributor (80kg) vs. direct channels (20kg) - Downside

| Scenario | Price | Margin | Supply revenue | Supply profit |
|---|---|---|---|---|
| *Baseline:* | | | | |
| 50 kg via direct channel | 10 | 5 | 50*10 = 500 | 50*5 = 250 |
| 50 kg via distributor | 8 | 3 | 50*8 = 400 | 50*3 = 150 |
| *Scenario upside:* | | | | |
| 60kg via direct channel | 10 | 5 | 60*10 = 600 | 60*5 = 350 |
| 40 kg via distributor | 8 | 3 | 40*8 = 320 | 40*3 = 120 |
| *Scenario downside:* | | | | |
| 20 kg via direct channel | 10 | 5 | 20*10 = 200 | 20*5 = 100 |
| 80 kg via distributor | 8 | 3 | 80*8 = 640 | 80*3 = 240 |

**Fig. 5.163** Allocation planning by channels resulting in better profits

**SAP** Integrated Business Planning

Chart:
Series:
Distributors
e-commerce

Filter:

Scenarios
**Baseline** — **50% Direct (e-comm) - 50% Distributors**
**Downside** — **20% Direct (e-comm) - 80% Distributors**
**Upside** — **60% Direct (e-comm) - 40% Distributors**

Supply Qty baseline ▪ E-commerce ▪ Distributors
Supply Qty downside ▪ E-commerce ▪ Distributors
Supply Qty upside ▪ E-commerce ▪ Distributors

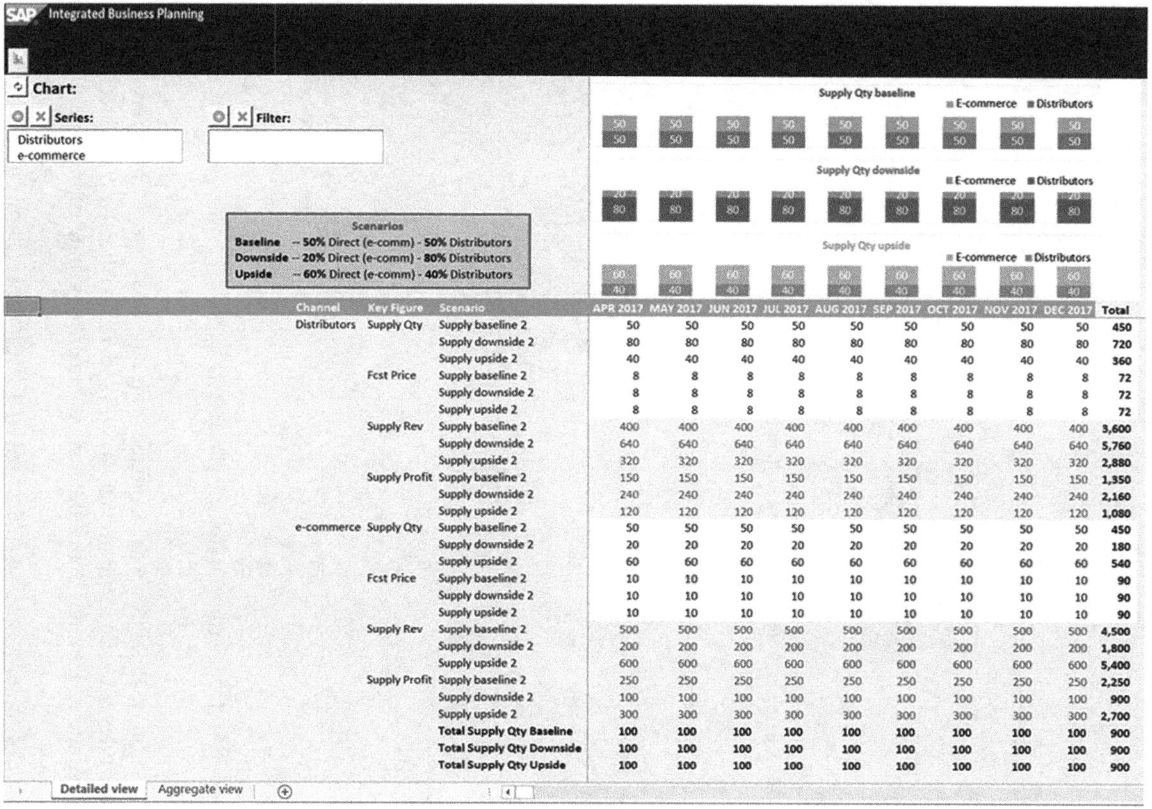

| Channel | Key Figure | Scenario | APR 2017 | MAY 2017 | JUN 2017 | JUL 2017 | AUG 2017 | SEP 2017 | OCT 2017 | NOV 2017 | DEC 2017 | Total |
|---|---|---|---|---|---|---|---|---|---|---|---|---|
| Distributors | Supply Qty | Supply baseline 2 | 50 | 50 | 50 | 50 | 50 | 50 | 50 | 50 | 50 | 450 |
| | | Supply downside 2 | 80 | 80 | 80 | 80 | 80 | 80 | 80 | 80 | 80 | 720 |
| | | Supply upside 2 | 40 | 40 | 40 | 40 | 40 | 40 | 40 | 40 | 40 | 360 |
| | Fcst Price | Supply baseline 2 | 8 | 8 | 8 | 8 | 8 | 8 | 8 | 8 | 8 | 72 |
| | | Supply downside 2 | 8 | 8 | 8 | 8 | 8 | 8 | 8 | 8 | 8 | 72 |
| | | Supply upside 2 | 8 | 8 | 8 | 8 | 8 | 8 | 8 | 8 | 8 | 72 |
| | Supply Rev | Supply baseline 2 | 400 | 400 | 400 | 400 | 400 | 400 | 400 | 400 | 400 | 3,600 |
| | | Supply downside 2 | 640 | 640 | 640 | 640 | 640 | 640 | 640 | 640 | 640 | 5,760 |
| | | Supply upside 2 | 320 | 320 | 320 | 320 | 320 | 320 | 320 | 320 | 320 | 2,880 |
| | Supply Profit | Supply baseline 2 | 150 | 150 | 150 | 150 | 150 | 150 | 150 | 150 | 150 | 1,350 |
| | | Supply downside 2 | 240 | 240 | 240 | 240 | 240 | 240 | 240 | 240 | 240 | 2,160 |
| | | Supply upside 2 | 120 | 120 | 120 | 120 | 120 | 120 | 120 | 120 | 120 | 1,080 |
| e-commerce | Supply Qty | Supply baseline 2 | 50 | 50 | 50 | 50 | 50 | 50 | 50 | 50 | 50 | 450 |
| | | Supply downside 2 | 20 | 20 | 20 | 20 | 20 | 20 | 20 | 20 | 20 | 180 |
| | | Supply upside 2 | 60 | 60 | 60 | 60 | 60 | 60 | 60 | 60 | 60 | 540 |
| | Fcst Price | Supply baseline 2 | 10 | 10 | 10 | 10 | 10 | 10 | 10 | 10 | 10 | 90 |
| | | Supply downside 2 | 10 | 10 | 10 | 10 | 10 | 10 | 10 | 10 | 10 | 90 |
| | | Supply upside 2 | 10 | 10 | 10 | 10 | 10 | 10 | 10 | 10 | 10 | 90 |
| | Supply Rev | Supply baseline 2 | 500 | 500 | 500 | 500 | 500 | 500 | 500 | 500 | 500 | 4,500 |
| | | Supply downside 2 | 200 | 200 | 200 | 200 | 200 | 200 | 200 | 200 | 200 | 1,800 |
| | | Supply upside 2 | 600 | 600 | 600 | 600 | 600 | 600 | 600 | 600 | 600 | 5,400 |
| | Supply Profit | Supply baseline 2 | 250 | 250 | 250 | 250 | 250 | 250 | 250 | 250 | 250 | 2,250 |
| | | Supply downside 2 | 100 | 100 | 100 | 100 | 100 | 100 | 100 | 100 | 100 | 900 |
| | | Supply upside 2 | 300 | 300 | 300 | 300 | 300 | 300 | 300 | 300 | 300 | 2,700 |
| | | **Total Supply Qty Baseline** | **100** | **100** | **100** | **100** | **100** | **100** | **100** | **100** | **100** | **900** |
| | | **Total Supply Qty Downside** | **100** | **100** | **100** | **100** | **100** | **100** | **100** | **100** | **100** | **900** |
| | | **Total Supply Qty Upside** | **100** | **100** | **100** | **100** | **100** | **100** | **100** | **100** | **100** | **900** |

Detailed view   Aggregate view

**Fig. 5.164**  SAP IBP allocation planning per channel detail view

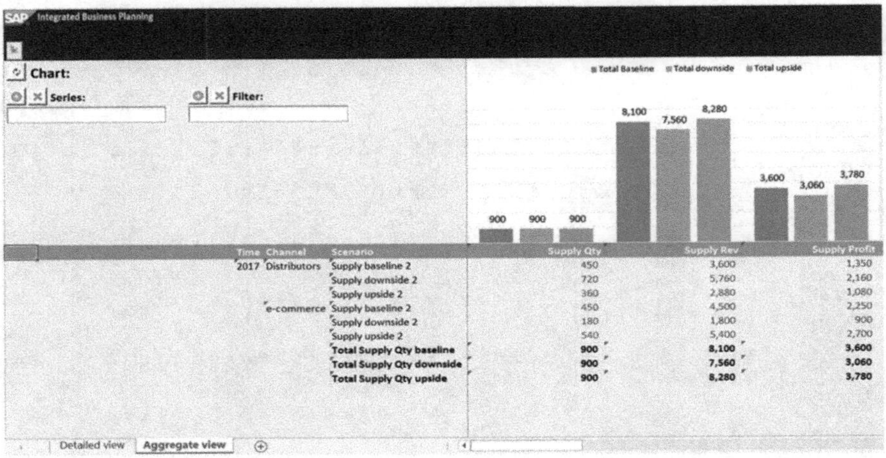


**Fig. 5.165** Aggregated view on allocation planning per channel

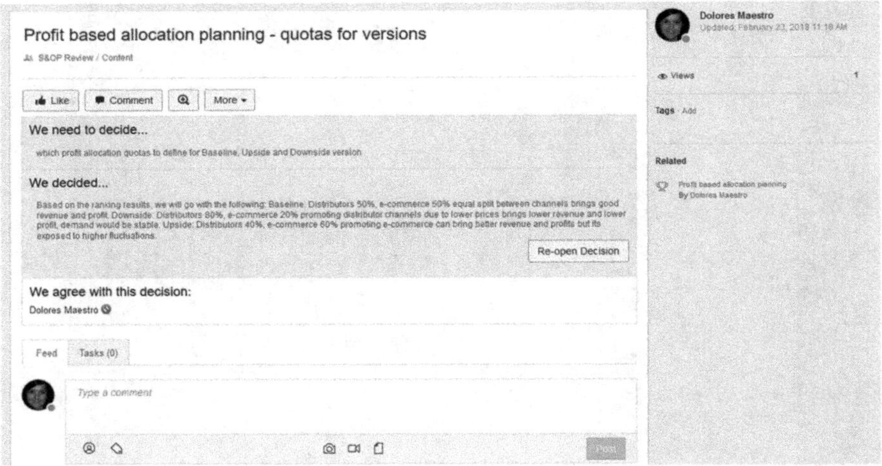


**Fig. 5.166** SAP JAM ranking for scenario planning

Discussion on detail level is facilitated with quick overview which presents data on scenario level for financial impact data (Fig. 5.165). Allocating products more to direct customers (captured in upside) can generate from same supply quantity better profits.

As part of the process, it was decided to discuss the scenarios and decide on the integrated reconciliation meeting which scenario is the best to maximize business return, risks, and opportunities (see Fig. 5.166).

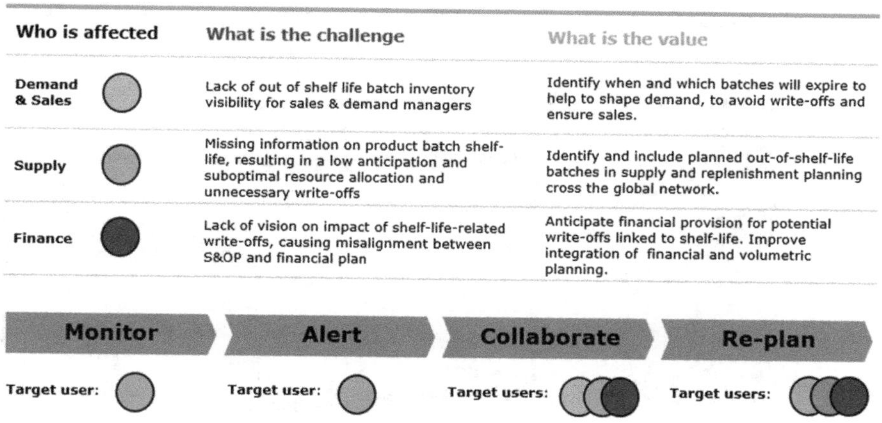

Who is affected
What is the challenge
What is the value
Demand & Sales
Lack of out of shelf life batch inventory visibility for sales & demand managers
Identify when and which batches will expire to help to shape demand, to avoid write-offs and ensure sales.
Supply
Missing information on product batch shelf-life, resulting in a low anticipation and suboptimal resource allocation and unnecessary write-offs
Identify and include planned out-of-shelf-life batches in supply and replenishment planning cross the global network.
Finance
Lack of vision on impact of shelf-life-related write-offs, causing misalignment between S&OP and financial plan
Anticipate financial provision for potential write-offs linked to shelf-life. Improve integration of financial and volumetric planning.
Monitor
Alert
Collaborate
Re-plan
Target user:
Target user:
Target users:
Target users:


**Fig. 5.167** Shelf life planning challenges and process

### 5.3.11 Shelf Life Planning

Products which are controlled with shelf life have a significant impact on supply planning and inventory planning process. Lack of transparency, visibility, and clear process which aims to avoid write-offs may have tremendous negative implication on your company performance. In many industries shelf life of the product plays vital role in availability and can have substantial impact on write-offs effecting integrated business plan in volume and value.

Financial impact of write-offs may be really big and if not managed in proactive manner could be really a nasty type of surprise. Business scenario does explain how proactively you can identify and manage shelf life planning.

In shelf life use case demand planning, sales, supply planning, and finance will collaborate and manage inventory which is foreseen to be obsolete, written off in the future. In many industries (fast-moving consumer, chemical, food and beverages, life science, and healthcare), shelf life of the product affects strongly availability of the product, opportunity to sell, and financial plans (Fig. 5.167).

### 5.3.12 SAP Use Case: Shelf Life Planning and Obsolescence Provisions

It is critical to identify when and what batch will expire and consider it in the planning, in demand shaping. Batch information can be extracted from your ECC, S/4, and ERP system and populated into IBP via SAP cloud integration platform. Visibility of batches and their projected expiration dates globally will need to be addressed (Fig. 5.168).

Planners can define dashboards for their own use or share with others. They can use intuitive functionality to define dashboard specifically for shelf life planning

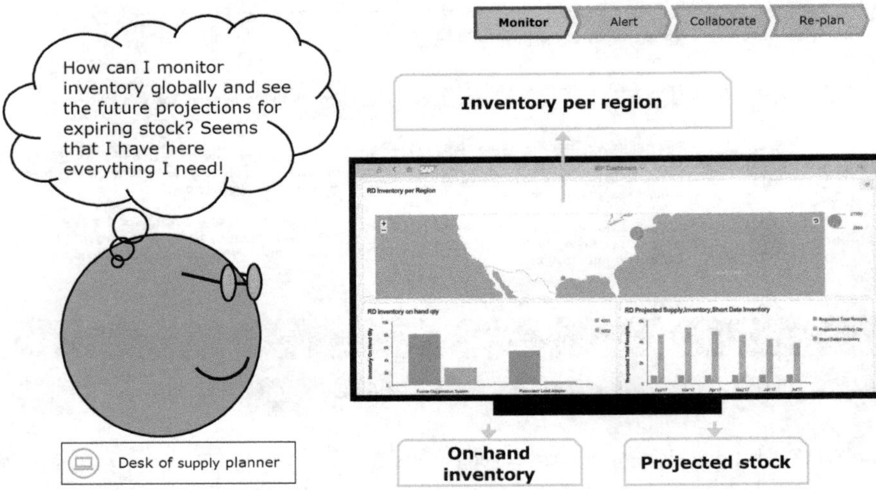


**Fig. 5.168** Monitoring in shelf life planning

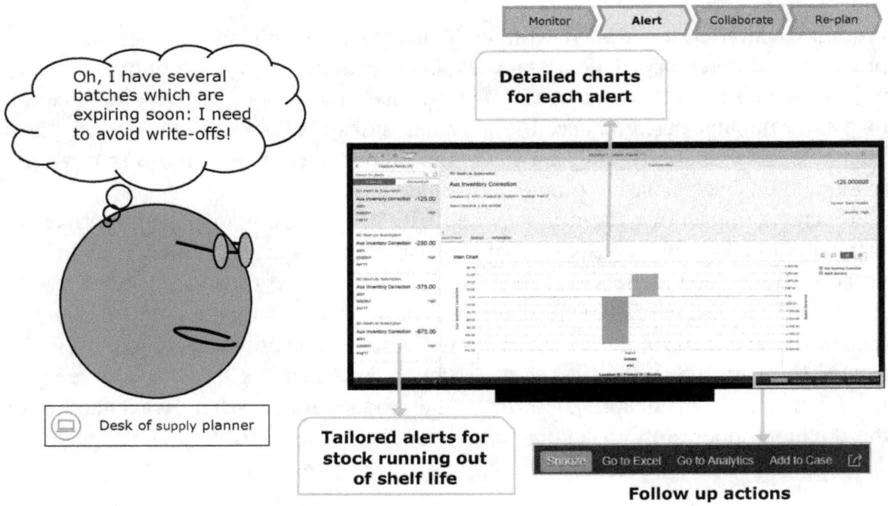


**Fig. 5.169** Exception management, alerts in shelf life planning

where inventory positioned on geo chart, projected out of shelf life stock, and provisions might be displayed.

Number of batches which will be integrated into IBP may be high. Planner would need to be equipped with alerts to help him focus on exceptions, those batches which will expire in near future. Horizons of alerts are fully configurable. Exception management will be introduced with help of supply chain control tower application in SAP IBP.

In Fig. 5.169 custom alert identifies SKUs, batch, and location which will go out of shelf life. On left-hand side of the screen, alerts are listed and on right-hand chart to visualize exception can be displayed. Alerts from SC Control tower will use logic embedded in special key figure. This logic can consider:

- First-expire-first-out logic
- Batch expiration data
- Data when stock should be sold or shipped latest (because of replenishment lead time or storage-time requirement specified by sales channel)
- Projected batch demand
- Actual batch inventory level

And it will result in projecting when and where specific batch will go out of shelf life.

Once exceptions are identified, it is key that supply planner triggers collaboration activities with demand manager and sales representative to sell out stock which will expire in the future. Supply planner may be more centralized since that is how normally manufacturing footprint is organized. Demand manager may be positioned in specific country and would need to trigger jointly with sales and supply some demand-shaping activities. Objectives of those activities will be to sell batches, which are potential threat of being soon out of shelf life in the respective markets. Supply planner may own coordination of selling out the stock before it expires. Strong collaboration and exchange of information is required then; therefore, process will be facilitated with case functionality where actions and progress can be monitored (Fig. 5.170) with use of case management.

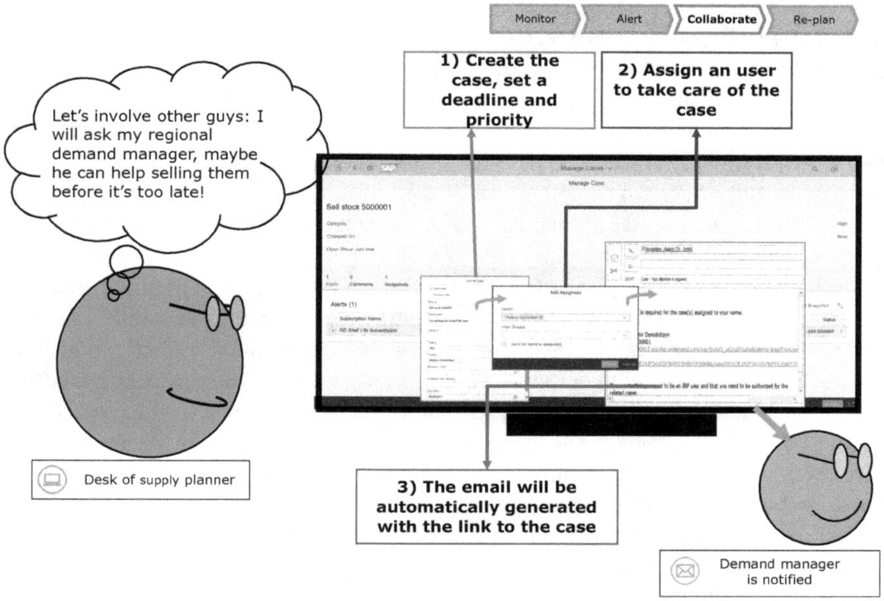


**Fig. 5.170** Collaborate in shelf life planning

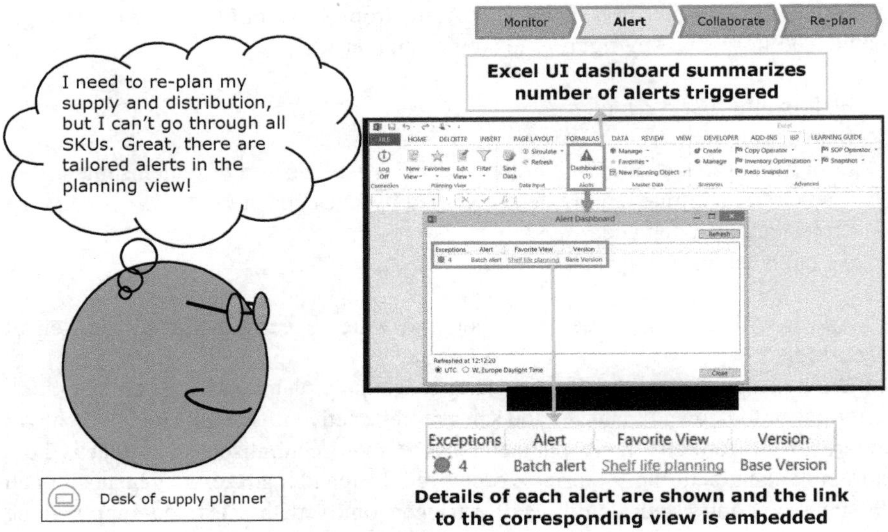


**Fig. 5.171** Alert/Identification in shelf life planning

Once case is created, it becomes a "suitcase" where you put all things related to the issue which can be linked to specific big batch of the product. Supply planner may trigger email notification and specify actions and priorities to ones which should be involved, e.g., demand manager, sales representative, and customer service representative.

Assessment of shelf life planning issues is done in an exception-based manner in the main SAP IBP Excel user interface, while its configuration is done in SAP HANA through the web browser. Alerts are categorized so that users get fast and precise notifications in the planning screen. Once alerts are visualized in planning templates where you can change data, planners need to take some planning activities (Fig. 5.171). Those activities like replenishing short-dated inventory or qualification which batches are really to be considered as the ones which will go out of shelf life are done on planning templates in Excel UI. Planner can start planning with exceptions, exceptions tailored to specific batches. Alerts available in planning view will direct him to specific batches (Fig. 5.171).

At the beginning planner needs to assess if batches with projected out of shelf life inventory are really at risk. In shelf life planning view, planner can evaluate batch by batch the specific product and location. Data is being presented in first-expire-first-out sequence. Batches with earlier expirations data are taken into calculation before the others. Planners are notified with special formatting (red) when which batch will go out of validity dates. On the same screen, planner will see total inventory of all batches of certain product/location which will be out of shelf life in defined horizon. Once on batch level projected out of shelf life inventory is calculated and analyzed by planner, we could consider this in supply planning process (see Fig. 5.172).

Heuristic planning operator works on plant level; therefore, all batches which will expire will be summed up to plant level and visualized in aux. inventory correction key figure later converted into short-dated inventory.

Projected batch stock availability would need to be aggregated to standard SKU-plant level and considered in heuristic supply planning run. Data in short-

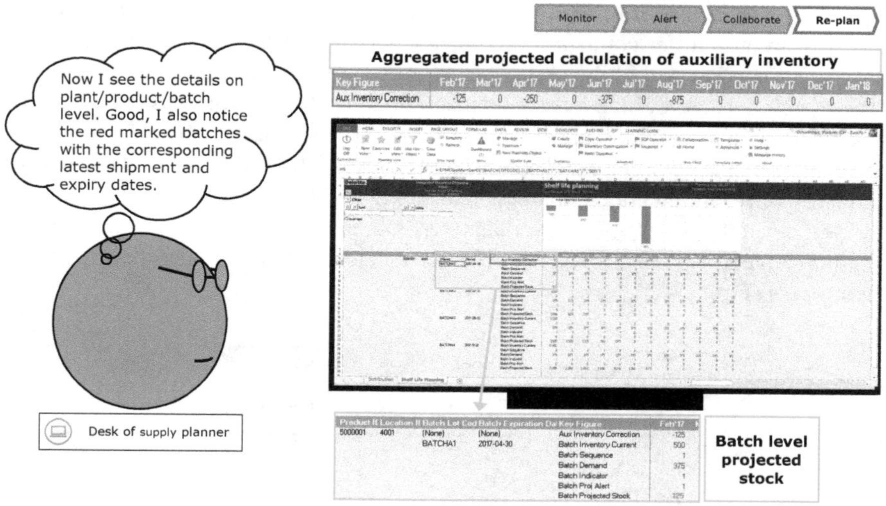


**Fig. 5.172** Batch stock projections in shelf life planning

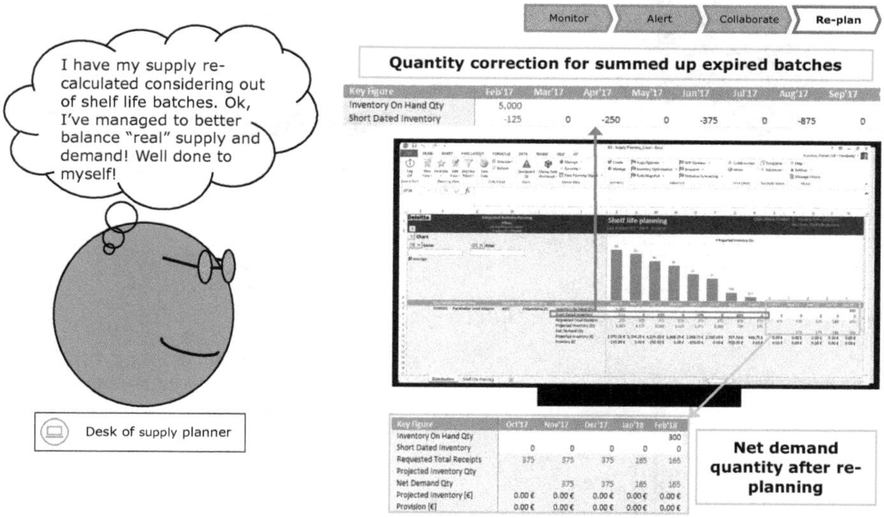


**Fig. 5.173** Re-planning supply in shelf life planning

dated inventory key figure will reduce projected available inventory and will affect supply planning run in a way that it will replenish required missing quantities to keep balance with the demand. This supply run is done to avoid any stock-outs which could be caused by projected out of shelf life inventory (Fig. 5.173).

Information about projected out of shelf life inventory in truly integrated planning will be impacting your financials. We see that "short-dated inventory" is linked to calculation of provisions. Provision does express potential loss caused by planned write-offs of short-dated inventories (Fig. 5.174). We have seen that rules for provisions can substantially differ company to company. We have seen case where degree of provision linked to cost of the product is aligned to time horizon, e.g., first 3 months 80% of cost because of high risk, 6 months 60% of costs, etc. This was done because risk in shorter horizons had higher probability to become real than those far in future.

Finance manage will be able to consider this calculation (done according to your company rules) in integrated business plan (Fig. 5.174).

Last but not the least, supply planner has created dashboard in which he/she monitors inventory on aggregated level and batch level; they can monitor progress in the process (Fig. 5.175).

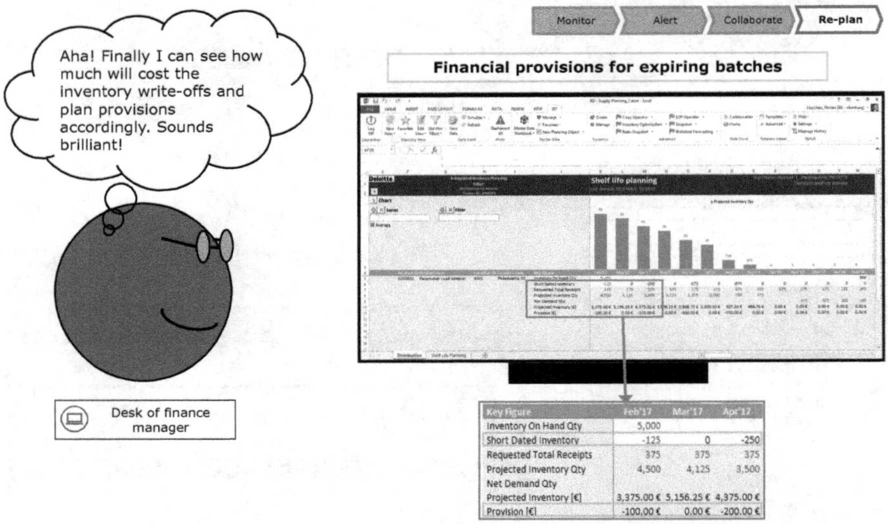


**Fig. 5.174** Calculation of provision in shelf life planning

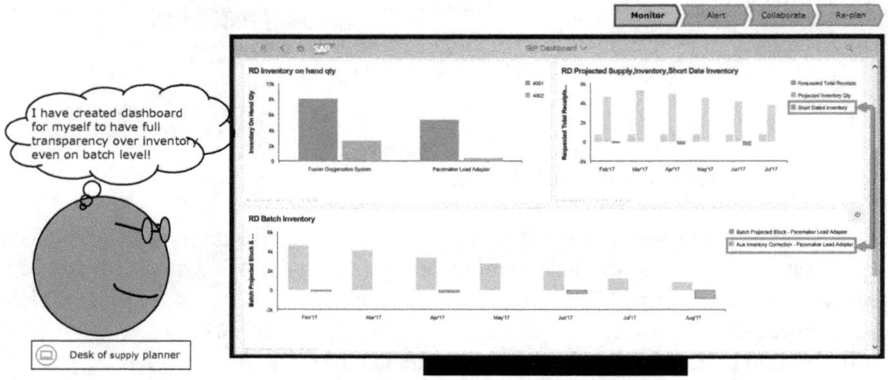


**Fig. 5.175** User-defined shelf life planning dashboard

### 5.3.13 Manage Supply Chain Variability with Inventory Planning

When we look at Fig. 5.176, it becomes quite obvious why inventory optimization is needed and why it is more and more difficult.

Supply chain networks become more complex and sometimes evolve from one large network to set of connected sub-networks. Taking into consideration demand and supply variability which exist cross the entire network(s) is an exercise which is impossible to be executed in Excel spreadsheet. Understanding types of inventory, their drivers become non-Excel spreadsheet exercise, and their coexistence and correlation should become a key task not only of supply manager but demand manager and finance controller.

Let us briefly define types and drivers of inventory visualized in Fig. 5.177.

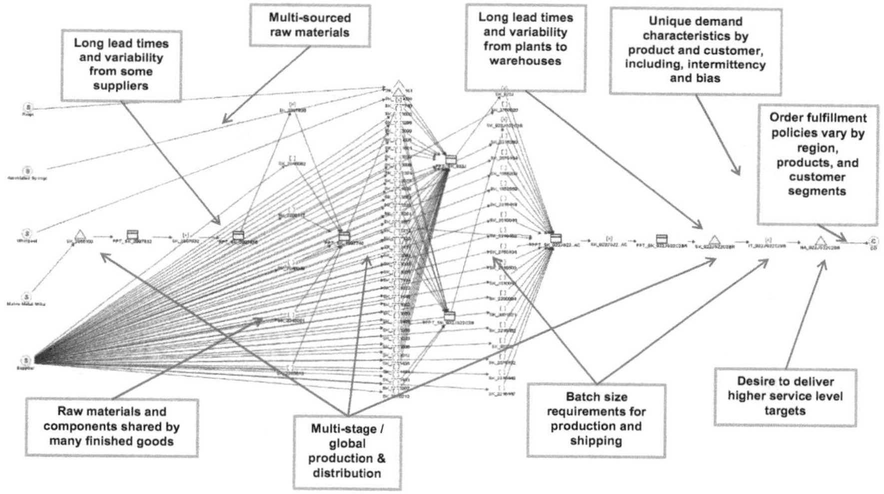


**Fig. 5.176** Supply chain network and typical inventory optimization touchpoints

**Fig. 5.177** Types of inventory

Safety stock is:

- Maintained to avoid stock-out conditions due to demand and supply uncertainty
- Aims to provide a cushion for the exceptional scenario and not to be used as replenishment strategy

Safety-stock drivers are:

- Demand
- Demand uncertainty
- Lead times
- Lead time uncertainty
- Review frequency
- Service level targets
- Service times

Cycle stock is:

- Average amount of inventory required to meet customer demand
- Decreases with consumption against demand

Cycle stock drivers are:

- Demand
- Review frequency
- Batch sizes
- Production rules

Pipeline stock is:

- Stock in-transit
- Increases with the additional sales volume and with longer lead times

Pipeline stock drivers are:

- Order processing lead times
- Transit times
- Demand

We see now how those types of inventory are connected to each other. Technology solution will help to cope with complexity of it. SAP IBP helps you to run inventory optimization in two distinct modes.

Two types of inventory optimization algorithms are illustrated in Fig. 5.178.

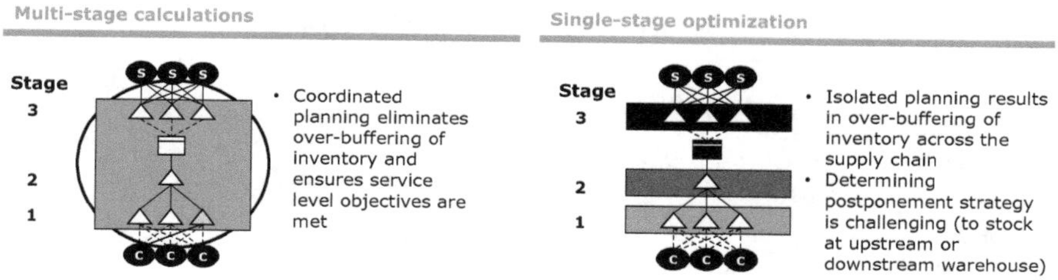


**Fig. 5.178** SAP IBP inventory optimization algorithms

One mode of optimization will check whole network and propose you optimal inventory level considering demand and supply variability mentioned above. This mode is called multistage. The other mode is single-stage optimization which does focus its calculations and proposals for desired level on bill of material (e.g., finished goods only). As the outcome of both calculations, we will see projections of pipeline, cycle, and safety stock for given drivers. Inventory optimization can be done on existing set of parameters or as well with consideration of simulated improvements of inventory optimization drivers.

### 5.3.14 SAP Use Case: Service Level Differentiation Impacting Safety Stock

Inventory optimization engine can produce recommendation of safety stocks which differentiated by product segment specific service levels. If you differentiate service levels for your product categories accordingly, your safety stock will be impacted. Leading practices say that your category A of products should have higher service level than B and C. In our process explanation, we start from recommended safety-stock value by segment, which is for the beginning based on same service level for all product segments. This creates an opportunity for differentiating the inventory strategy with product segmentation and aims to reduce the inventory holding costs (see Fig. 5.179).

Simulation executed with multistage inventory operator but with smaller target service levels for B and C class allows us to save the results into an ad hoc scenario and compare them with the baseline. This operator performs a safety-stock optimization across network driven by several inputs like service level, demand and supply uncertainty, costs, lead time and lead time variability, etc. and returns a significant decrease in the recommended safety-stock value which is correlated with the decrease in target service level differentiated per product segment.

Simulation was executed based on a reduction of target service level starting May onward. New service levels were applied as follows: C class to a new service level of 92% and B class to 94% (see Fig. 5.180).

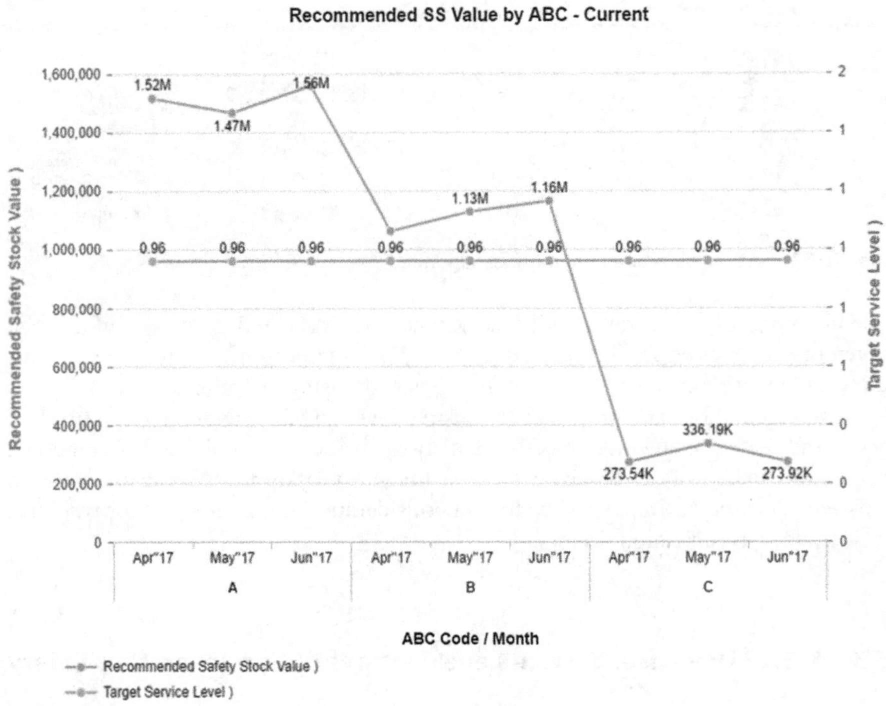


**Fig. 5.179** Inventory management per ABC segments (1), same service level

IO algorithms have returned as well an average of 3.5 safety days of supply decrease for C class and 5.5 decrease of days of supply for B class. Both calculation baseline and with service level differentiated by ABC portfolio segmentation has returned different values of safety stock which can be compared to each other (see Fig. 5.181).

As inventory is more than safety stock needed to hedge against risk and uncertainty in case customer demand comes higher than what was forecasted, we will continue the simulation by running component inventory operator which computes target inventory position which consists of needed inventory to fulfill current period demand (cycle stock), inventory for future period demand until next order is received (pipeline stock), and buffer for uncertainty (safety stock). Translating this in a financial measure, we have the working capital which is strongly driven by target inventory position. And we see in Fig. 5.182 the baseline vs scenario comparison on how working capital is determined based on the new service levels, generating a working capital inventory reduction of ~2M in remaining months of the current year.

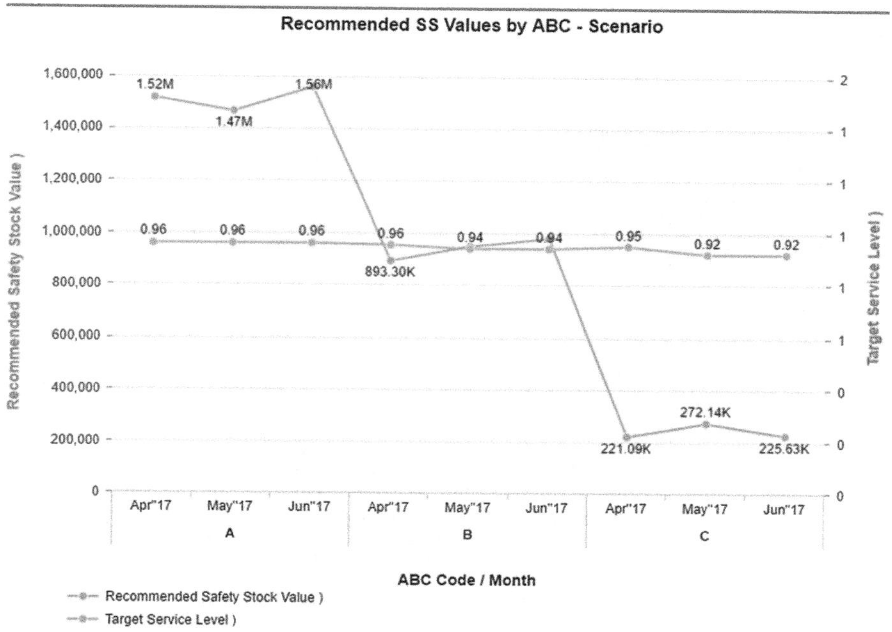


**Fig. 5.180** Inventory management per ABC segments (2), service level decreased for B and C class

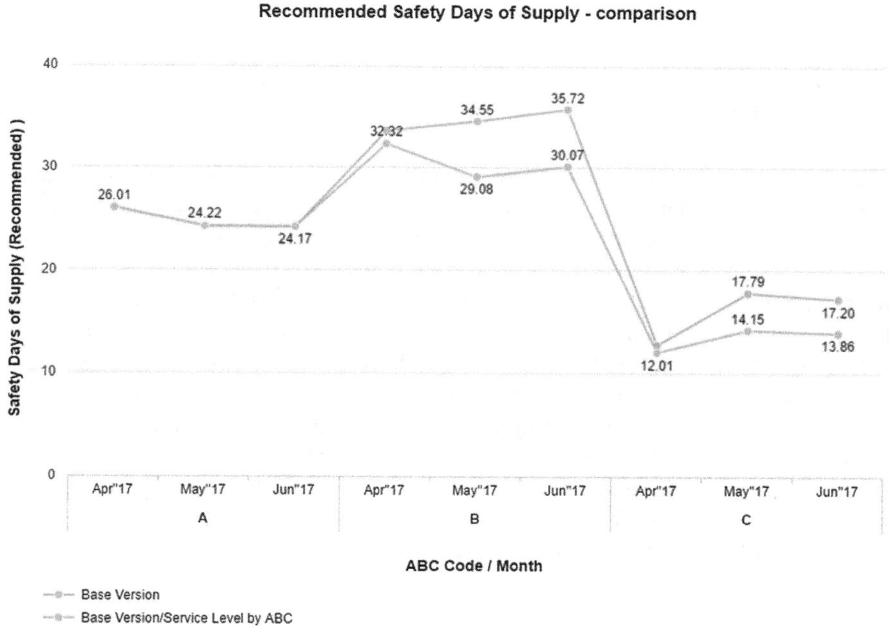


**Fig. 5.181** Inventory management per ABC segments (3), safety-stock per class

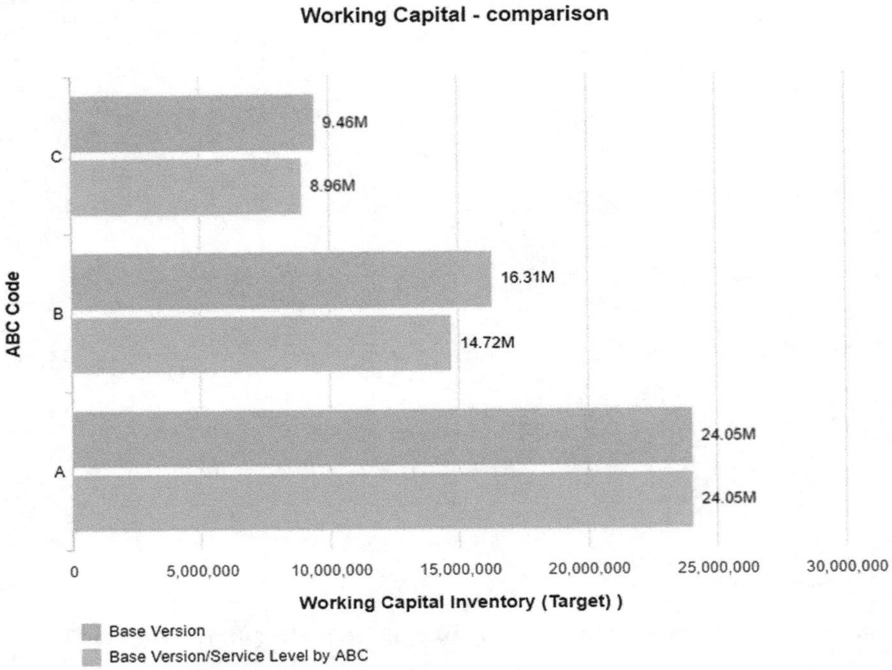


**Fig. 5.182** Inventory management per ABC segments (4), working capital comparison

### 5.3.15 SAP Use Case: Lead Time Reduction Impacting Inventory Optimization

We have seen in the first book several examples of how IBP for inventory can be used to identify and analyze various strategic or tactical supply chain opportunities like the assessment of the customer service level to identify the best trade-off between customer satisfaction and inventory investment (Kepczynski et al. 2018). Moving further with IBP for inventory, we will explore one of the components of the target inventory position, namely, the pipeline inventory. This value is computed both as an average and target by the calculated inventory component algorithm, and it is calculated based on the forecasts of all periods during the order processing and delivery lead time (order processing, transit, production, and good receipt).

In Fig. 5.183 we see the inventory analyst's dashboard representing the weekly inventory components. We notice that the inventory is mainly driven by the pipeline and cycle stock, which gives us some insight into the supply chain network: long lead times, infrequent replenishment, and large batch sizes.

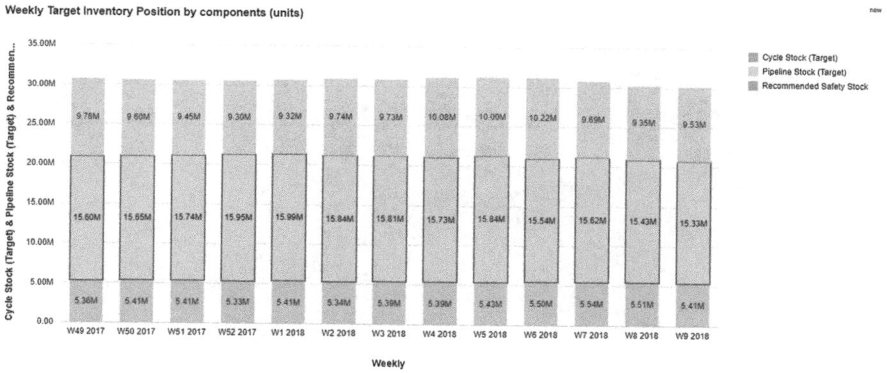


**Fig. 5.183** Target inventory position per week

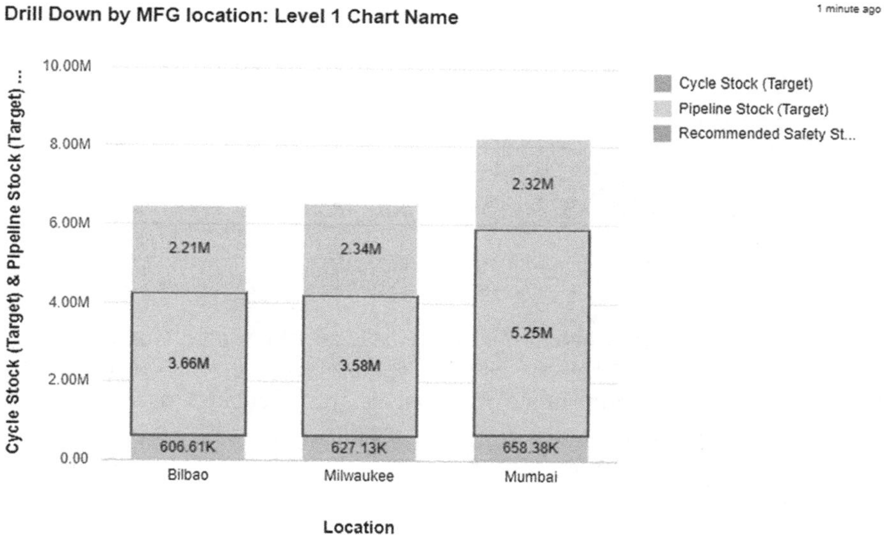


**Fig. 5.184** Inventory position by inventory type and location

Next, we will use the drill down capability to have an extended view of the target inventory components at manufacturing location level (Fig. 5.184).

To complement this chart, we will check the transportation lead time and its associated lead time variability. Using the geographical display, we quickly notice that the transportation lead time and transportation lead time error to Bilbao (Spain), Milwaukee (USA), and Mumbai (India) are very long, hence, the significant share of pipeline inventory in the supply chain (see Fig. 5.185).

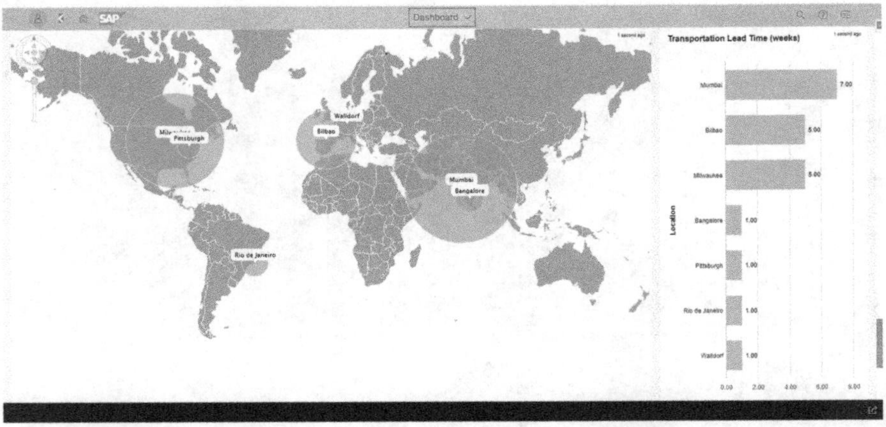


**Fig. 5.185** Transportation lead-time variability influencing pipeline stock.

**Lead Time 20pct reduction analysis on inventory**

| Location | Version/Scenario | Transportation Lead Time | Pipeline Stock (Target) | Target Inventory Position | Pipeline Stock Value (Target) | Working Capital Inventory (Target) |
|---|---|---|---|---|---|---|
| Bilbao | Base Version | 5.00 | 390.19M | 858.81M | 223.97M | 548.94M |
| Milwaukee | Base Version | 5.00 | 395.03M | 872.52M | 223.59M | 551.43M |
| Mumbai | Base Version | 7.00 | 543.49M | 1.02B | 316.81M | 654.39M |
| Bilbao | Base Version/20%LT reduction | 4.99 | 322.43M | 791.23M | 184.66M | 504.72M |
| Milwaukee | Base Version/20%LT reduction | 4.99 | 325.68M | 802.00M | 184.23M | 506.48M |
| Mumbai | Base Version/20%LT reduction | 6.98 | 478.18M | 956.73M | 276.96M | 609.23M |

**Fig. 5.186** Pipeline stock reduction with reduced lead time

Reducing the pipeline inventory can be a great opportunity for decreasing the supply chain costs. To measure this opportunity, we will run the global multistage inventory optimization followed by the calculated target inventory component algorithm to simulate a transportation time reduction of 20%. By saving the simulation results into a scenario, we will be able to answer the following questions:

- How much will the pipeline stock decrease as an implication of the transportation lead time reduction with 20% (see Fig. 5.186)?
- What would be the impact on the working capital requirements (see Fig. 5.187)?

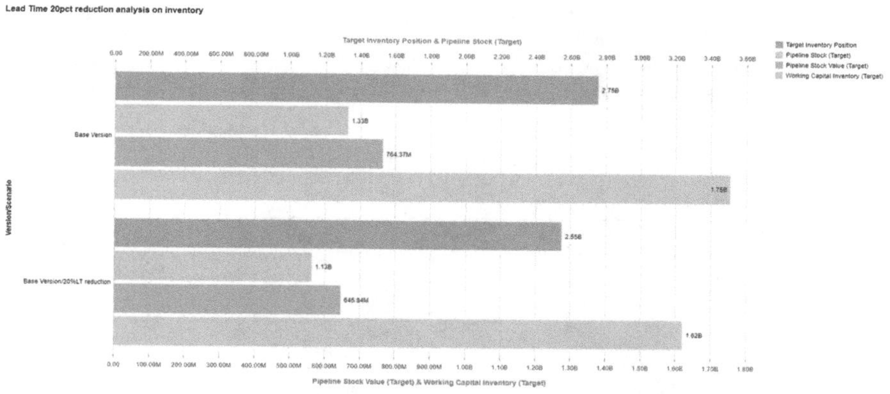


**Fig. 5.187** Working capital reduction based on lead time reduction, comparison of scenarios

## 5.3.16 Distribution (Deployment) Planning

Now that our inventory policy is set via the target stocks described in the previous section, we will take a brief look at how to ensure the right materials are at the right place at the right time.

In the IBP landscape, deployment exists in the world of order-based planning. Most other planning functions highlighted in this text are time-series based. That is, they plan entirely within periods—daily, weekly, monthly, or other sizes of bucket. In IBP, deployment functionality is enabled in order-based planning, which means that the integration with the ERP system involved is much tighter. Deployment results described here can become stock transfer requisitions in ECC, for example, via standard integration.

More examples of order-based planning exist in this text and expand on these concepts—note the sections on allocations, order confirmations, and sales order what if scenarios. IBP order-based planning began with these response-oriented use cases. As the product matures, there are new use cases coming into being. Deployment is a good example of this.

Deployment refers to the process of distributing available supply to demand (see Fig. 5.188).

Deployment plan distributes available stock from central to downstream supply chain stocking points to meet expected service level and demand. In SAP IBP you can use order-based, constrained deployment heuristics which considers priorities, multistage planning, and what-if simulation capabilities and tightly integrate SAP IBP with, e.g., SAP ECC or SAP S/4.

Typically, deployment is relevant within distribution networks, especially hub-and-spoke distribution networks as shown in the figure. Inventory is made available through production at the factory and then moved into the network. While the previous planning runs elsewhere in this chapter typically consider the entire network, deployment is entirely focused on distribution of stock and select supply elements.

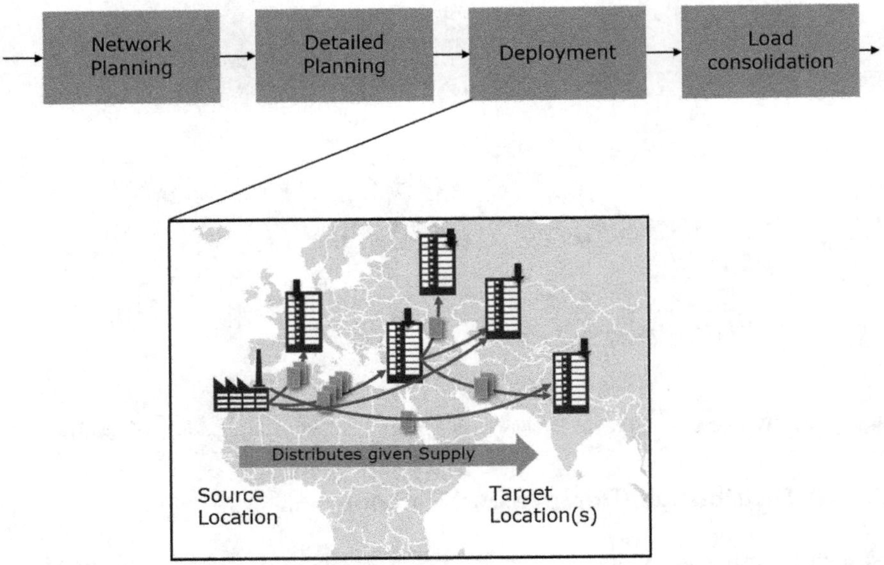


**Fig. 5.188** Deployment distributes available supply to meet demand

Where the response functions like allocations planning and confirmations enable scenarios like those common in high-tech OEMs, deployment has a wider industry scope. Any organization with a distribution network is likely to find a need for deployment of goods through that network.

Commonly, organizations look to use deployment functionality as a "repair" planning process. In this application, the forecast and initial supply plans are created on a less frequent basis—weekly or monthly, for example. As we move into the nearer term (as the supply plan progresses), the planned production becomes actual production, and demands shift from forecasts to sales orders. So, the original plan may have been perfect at the outset, but as supply and demands become more clearly known, the plans give way to near-term choices on where to send which supply.

To solve for this, the deployment run in IBP order-based planning holds production processes firm while matching supply to demand. It considers demands like sales orders and forecasts, as well as safety-stock targets. In Fig. 5.189, the process is illustrated.

Data such as these demands, along with supply requisitions, firmed orders, and stocks, are inputs to the process. The deployment run considers constraints as well. Product allocations (as determined earlier) and the supply itself are potential constraints. Similar to the constrained forecast and confirmation runs, the deployment run matches supply to demand using rules. The deployment plan is then output in the form of deployment stock transfer requisitions. Evaluation tools such as the MS Excel interface and apps like Analyze Supply Usage, View Projected Stock, and Gating factors enable the review of the plan.

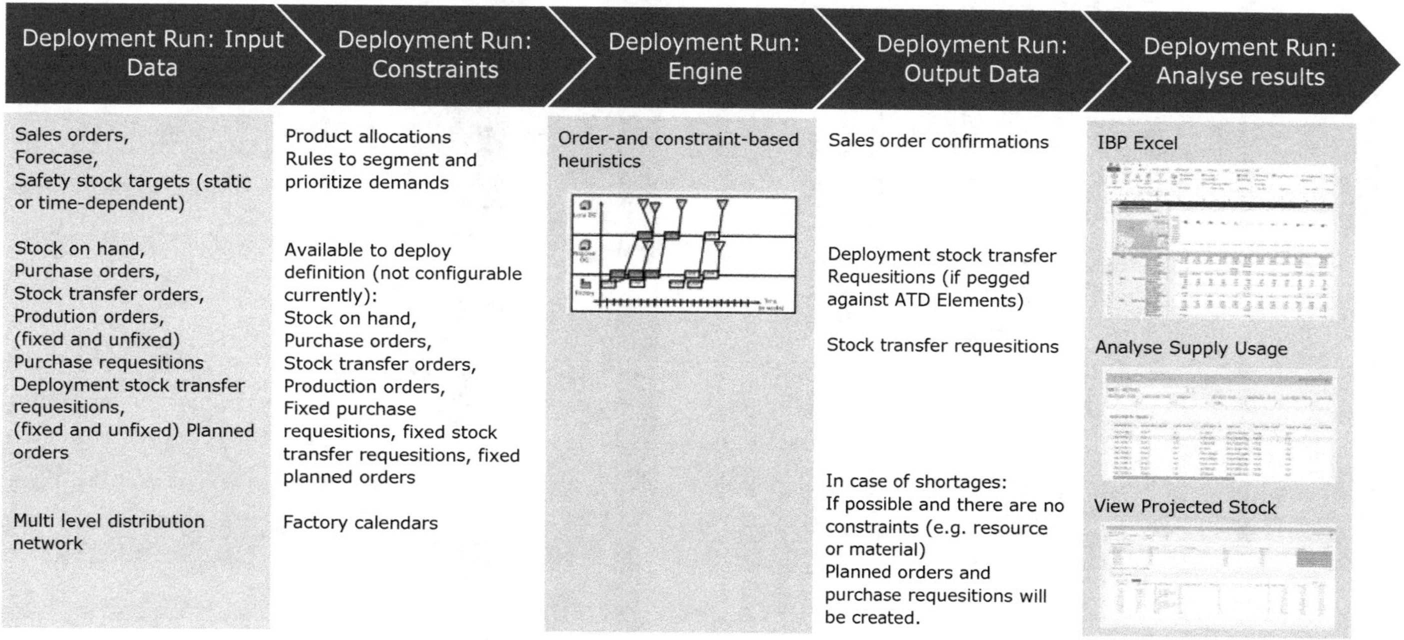
Deployment Run: Input Data
Deployment Run: Constraints
Deployment Run: Engine
Deployment Run: Output Data
Deployment Run: Analyse results
Sales orders,
Forecase,
Safety stock targets (static or time-dependent)
Stock on hand,
Purchase orders,
Stock transfer orders,
Prodution orders,
(fixed and unfixed)
Purchase requesitions
Deployment stock transfer requesitions,
(fixed and unfixed) Planned orders
Multi level distribution network
Product allocations
Rules to segment and prioritize demands
Available to deploy definition (not configurable currently):
Stock on hand,
Purchase orders,
Stock transfer orders,
Production orders,
Fixed purchase requesitions, fixed stock transfer requesitions, fixed planned orders
Factory calendars
Order-and constraint-based heuristics
Sales order confirmations
Deployment stock transfer Requesitions (if pegged against ATD Elements)
Stock transfer requesitions
In case of shortages:
If possible and there are no constraints (e.g. resource or material)
Planned orders and purchase requesitions will be created.
IBP Excel
Analyse Supply Usage
View Projected Stock

**Fig. 5.189** Distribution planning process in order-based IBP planning

## 5.3.17 SAP Use Case: Distribution Plan/Deployment Plan

These deployment plans can be seen in the example of Fig. 5.190.

Note the additional key figures (rows) listed here for distribution demand (lane; deployment), for example. In the case above, this indicates that all 100 units needed at the DC72 facility are to be deployed to that location on time.

In addition to these evaluation tools described previously, new functionality like manual adjustments to the plan was introduced to support deployment planning. Figure 5.191 shows a typical Excel view of manual changes.

Here, we can see that there is a forecast for demand of 120 units and on the next day another 50 units of sales orders at the distribution center named 0001 (the red boxes). The system already deployed 120 units and then another 18 per the available supply from location 0002 (the blue boxes).

In this case a distribution planner decides to override the plan, and push a higher quantity to the location sooner. To do this, the planner makes an adjustment (see Fig. 5.192).

The planner tries to move 150 earlier (the red box). However, there is a problem. There is a lead time of two days between locations, and only 148 units are available at the source location (0002) as of the date needed. The system understands this and lets the planner know (see Fig. 5.193).

Here, the system fulfills nearly what the planner asked for (148 out of 150 units—red boxes), but cannot completely fulfill the planners override. The result is a

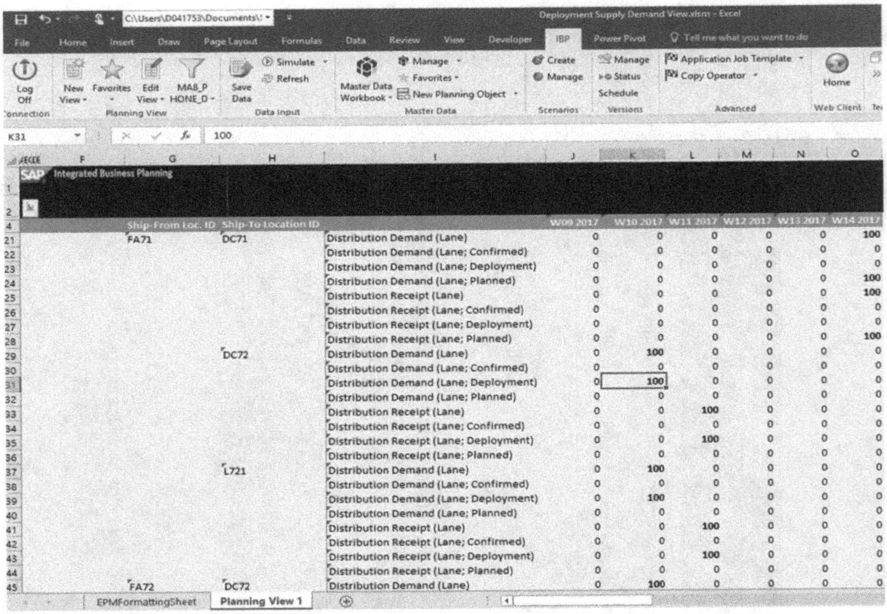


**Fig. 5.190** Distribution (deployment) plan between source and target locations

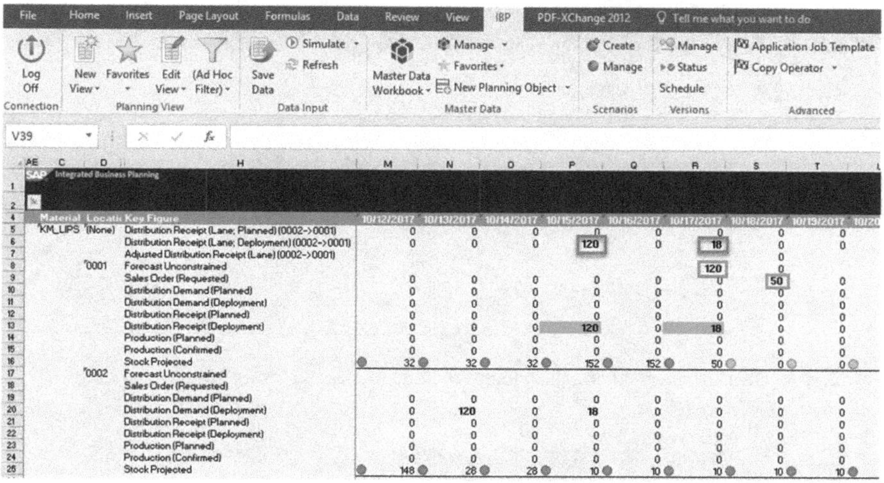

Fig. 5.191 Distribution planner adjusts the plan (1)

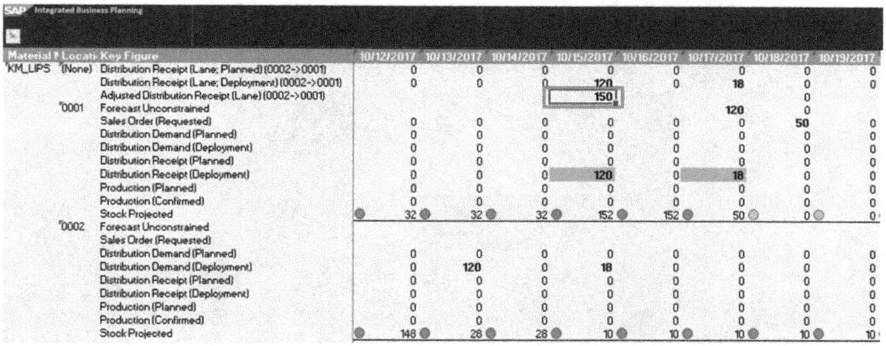

Fig. 5.192 Distribution planner adjusts the plan (2)

feasible plan in response to the override. The system knows that it cannot ship what it does not have available.

Deployment is designed to be used in short-term cases as illustrated in Fig. 5.194, but it can also be used as a midterm distribution planning tool. In any case, deployment functionality will hold the upstream supply as firmed while matching this to the known demand.

Deployment planning use cases:

- Short-term deployment on top of tactical supply plan:
  Create supply plan with IBP response and supply and run IBP deployment as subsequent step. Release results to SAP ECC and S/4.

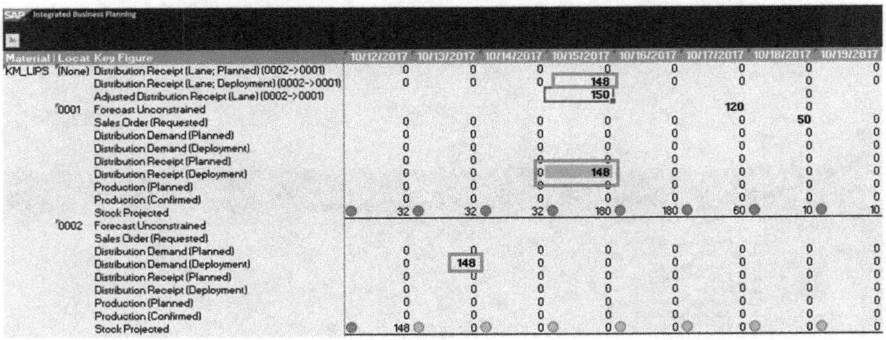

**Fig. 5.193** Distribution planner adjustments are done to feasible level

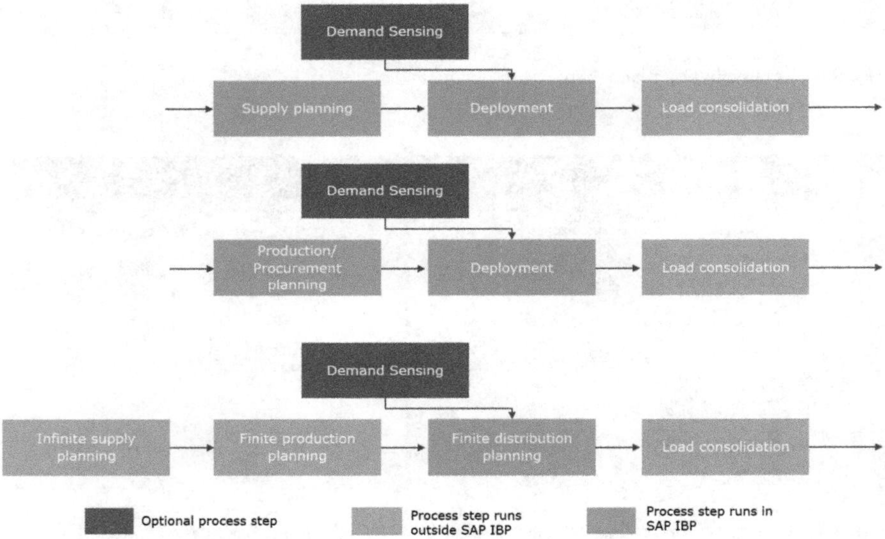


**Fig. 5.194** Use cases for deployment (distribution) planning

– Short-term deployment on top of production and procurement plans: Integrate existing plans with stocks, planned production, or procurement receipts from ERP system. Run deployment in SAP IBP and release plan back to ERP.
– Midterm distribution planning.

## 5.3.18 Supply Planning with Substitutions

Supply and operations may provide signal which in short time horizon (next few weeks, 2–3 months) may not be aligned to requested volume per requested packaging, as, for example, you may have requested, 5 liter packaging but only 1,2, and 10 liter are available.

Packaging supplier may have a molding machine breakdown, and pack may not be available; in this case supply organization may have proposed to use other packaging.

There are few ways to manage this in the process and system. In supply response signal, you might see quantity of 1, 2, and 10 L available in higher quantities then requested. You may define scenario of supply plan in which, based on feedback from demand manager if alternative packaging is accepted by market, supply planner could introduce changes in the firmed supply plan. Demand manager should align with commercial and marketing possibly with finance which packaging is better to sell in higher than desired quantity (1, 2, 10 L) to bridge the gap exposed on 5 L. To make most out of this process, this feedback should be recorded in the system and made transparent to affected stakeholders.

It happens quite often that specific packaging may go out of portfolio and could be phased out. Demand manager with demand planner should ensure that old packaging should be phased out and new one phased in, from desired point in time.

One of the ways to approach that is to introduce like modeling for the product and introduce a forecast for new packaging based on history from old or other SKU which is mapped as "like product"( for details see chapter New Product Forecasting).

### 5.3.19 SAP Use Case: Alternate Supply Plan with Replacements and Substitutions

In SAP IBP, the supply planning optimizer provides product substitution functionality to substitute a product with defined alternative/substituting products in the market, in case of constraints in the supply chain like capacity constraints. From a customer perspective, these alternate products have similar properties as the product being substituted and can be taken in case the substitution product demand cannot be fulfilled.

The supply planning optimizer will find the most profitable way to substitute the product with alternative products. It can choose to substitute all the demand or some portion of the customer demand with the substituting products. The alternative products and quantities that are substituted for the main product can also vary by period depending on how the optimizer computes the profitable alternate products to be shipped to the customer.

SAP IBP master data structures allow to define one or more substitute/alternate products for a given product. Customer source rules can be set up in customer source of supply master date for how the alternate products can be sourced for the customer. For product substitution to take into effect, the customer demand for the main product and customer source for alternative products should be defined.

Let us take a scenario where there is a customer demand for product IBP-100 for a customer 1710001 of 2500ea for the next 12 months. There are other products in the market, i.e., IBP-200 and IBP-300 which could be used to substitute in case the demand for product IBP-100 cannot be met (see Fig. 5.195).

In the initial scenario, the product substitution is not set up, and we see that the demand causes a capacity overload in Plant 1710 with a capacity utilization of 136%. However, there are other plants, e.g., Plant 1010 where the resource capacity can be used to produce alternate products to substitute for the main product to the customer (see Fig. 5.196).

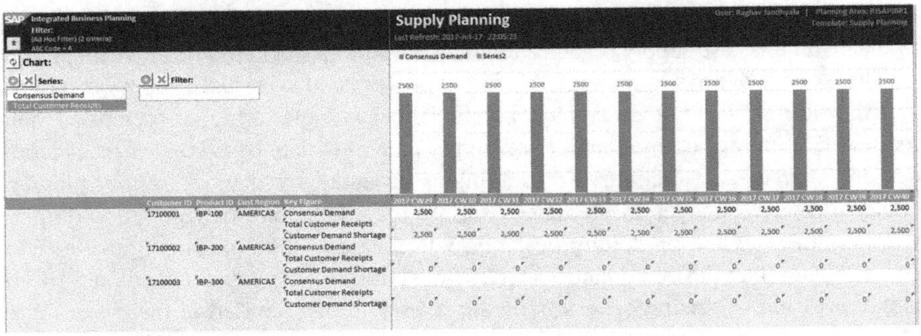


**Fig. 5.195** IBP 100 supply plan may use IBP 200 and 300 products

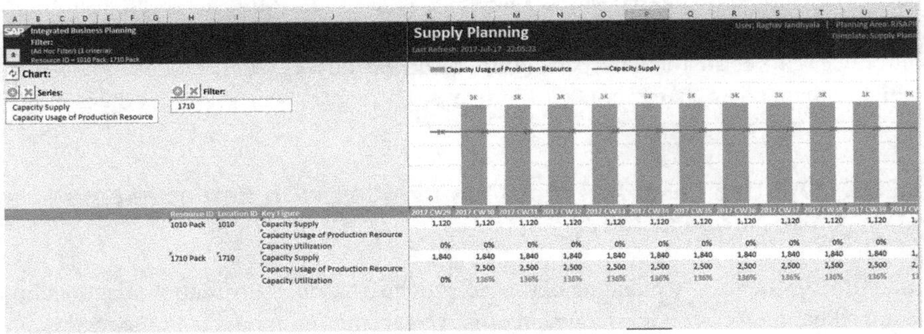


**Fig. 5.196** Capacity overutilization for plan 1710

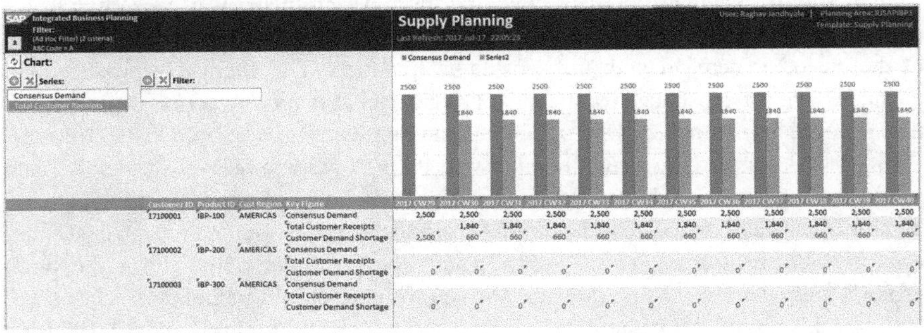


**Fig. 5.197** Reduced supply plan by supply optimizer for IBP 100

Now we run supply optimizer which constraints the capacity usage to the available capacity, and consequently, the customer demand is reduced as shown in Fig. 5.197. Requested demand was 2500ea, whereas the supply is 1840, resulting in a shortage of 660ea.

| Product ID | Substitute Product ID |
|---|---|
| IBP-100 | IBP-200 |
| IBP-100 | IBP-300 |

**Fig. 5.198** IBP 100 product substitutions

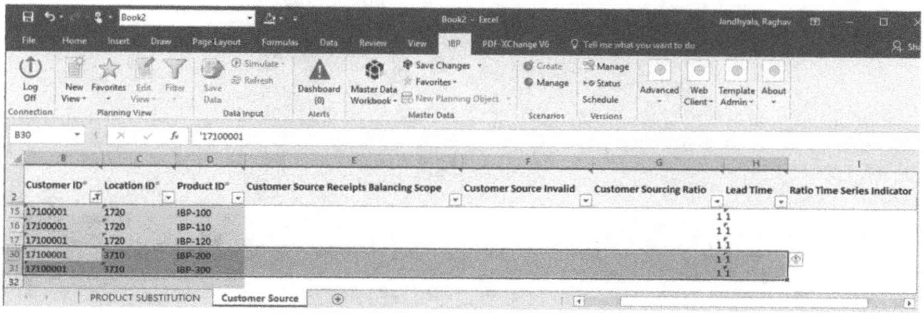


**Fig. 5.199** Alternate sourcing for specific customer/plant

We can then specify a product substitution rule by maintaining entries in SPRODUCT master data type in IBP with the following entries as shown in Fig. 5.198. That means the Product IBP-100 can be substituted by IBP-200 and IBP-300.

Now we need to define customer sourcing for the alternate/substitute products so that the alternate products are considered by the optimizer when there is a shortage situation (see Fig. 5.199).

As shown in Fig. 5.199, the two new sourcing entries are created for IBP-200 and IBP-300. There are other alternate sourcing rules for this customer with products IBP-110 and IBP-120. However, these products are not considered for substitution because they are not defined as alternative products for IBP-100 in the SPRODUCT master data.

Now we run the supply planning optimizer and see that when there is capacity constraint situation for the main product when produced at plant 1710, the alternate products are considered, and corresponding demand is placed on the plant 1010 and produced there (Fig. 5.200).

The capacity by product view shows the capacity usage for the alternative products IBP-200 and IBP-300 because of product substitution configuration for IBP-100 (see Fig. 5.201). These are time-varying based on the results of the profit optimization.

We can finally see how the customer demand of 2500ea for product IBP-100 can be satisfied with the alternative products IBP-200 and IBP-300. The optimizer can also take into consideration the independent customer demand at each of the alternative products along with its nondelivery costs together with product substitution capability (see Fig. 5.202).

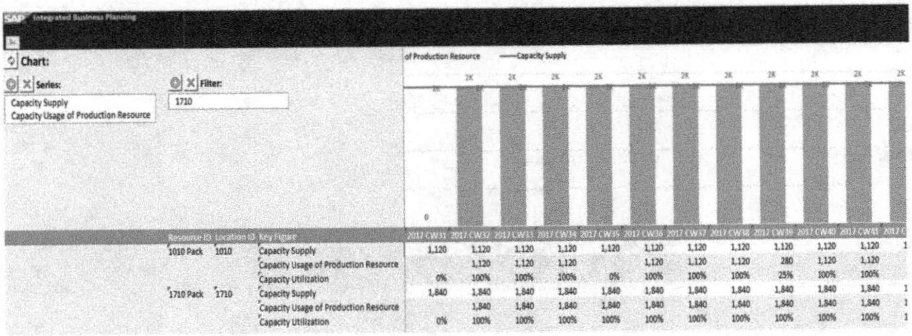


**Fig. 5.200** Alternate sourcing of production from plant 1010

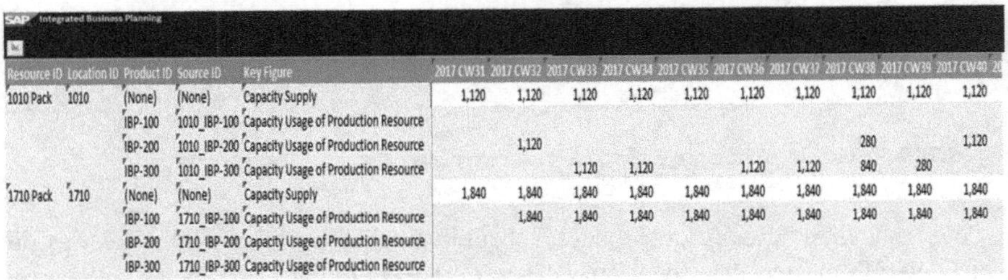


**Fig. 5.201** Alternate products show capacity load utilization

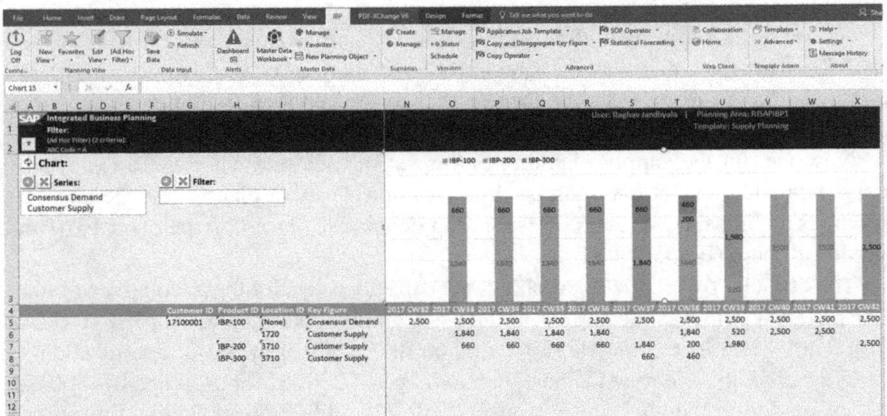


**Fig. 5.202** Multisourcing of IBP 100 and 200, 300 executed with supply optimizer

## 5.4 Integrated Reconciliation and Management Business Review

I had a pleasure to work on one of the projects with Andre Pozza, who used to say that pre-Management Business Review Meeting is similar to cooking; it is about **Cooking Figures** (Fig. 5.203): cooking product, demand, supply, and financial ingredients in one "soup."

Actually to be more precise, it is about preparing few versions of the truth and making recommendation for which "one to go for" in Management Business Review Meeting.

As we go through the IBP process steps, we collect and validate information (see Fig. 5.204).

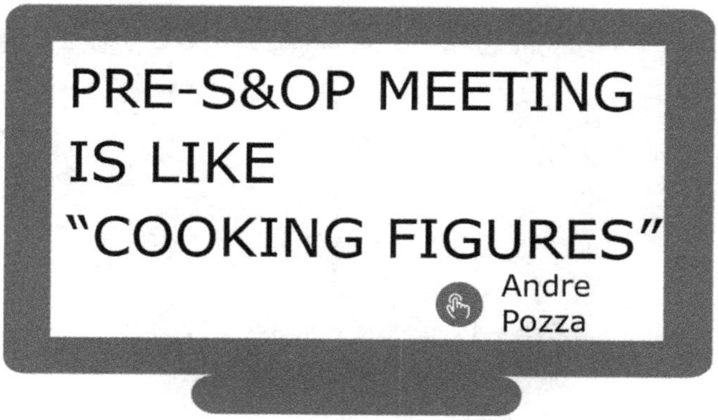


**Fig. 5.203** Integrated reconciliation is like cooking

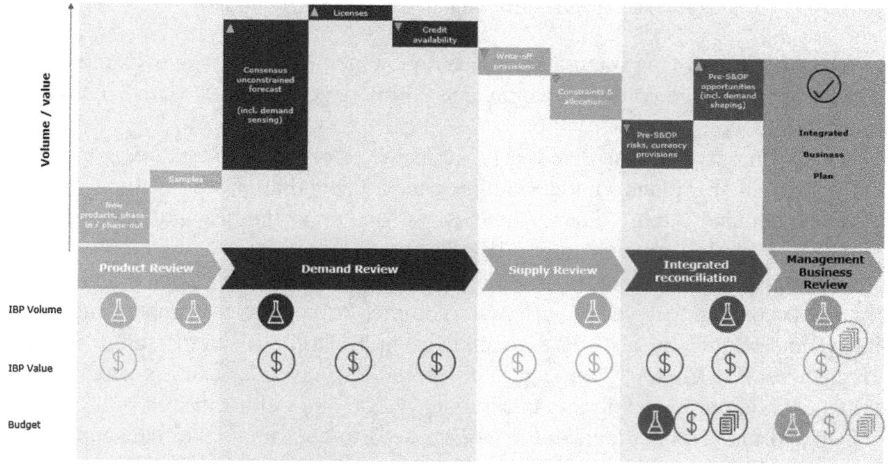


**Fig. 5.204** Tactical S&OP—IBP waterfall

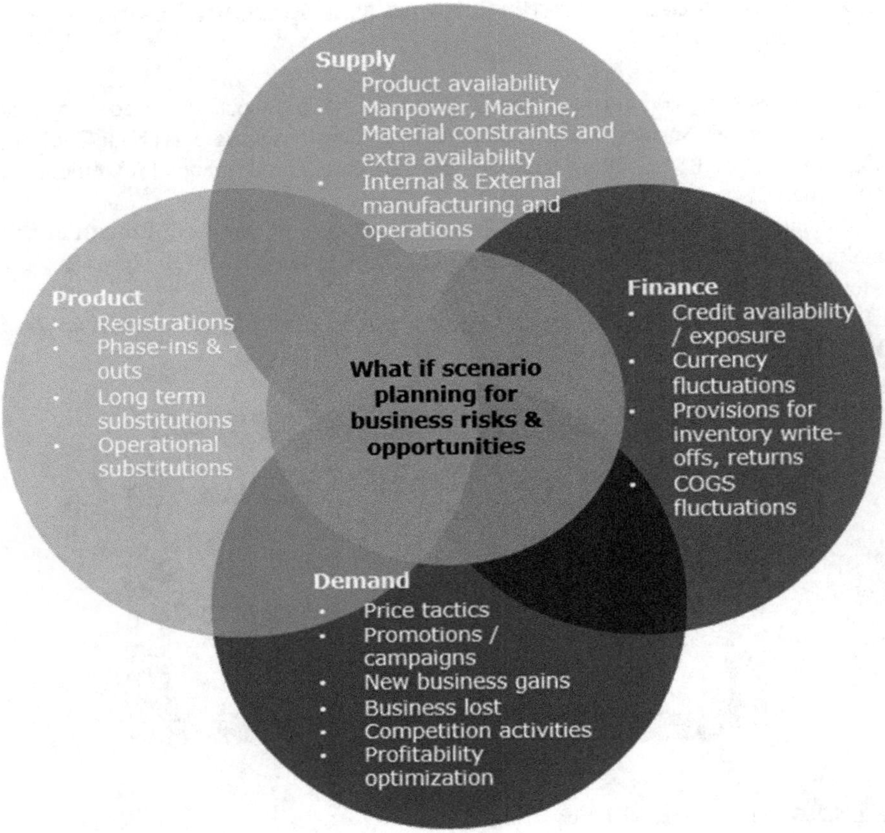


**Fig. 5.205** Business risk and opportunities, product-demand-supply-finance

We start to build your integrated business plan in volume and value. Components of IBP may influence volumetric and value jointly or separately as visualized on the waterfall above.

Once all inputs are considered, it makes sense to compare integrated reconciliation version of IBP plan to budget. In integrated reconciliation we need to focus on balancing demand, supply, financial views, risk and opportunities, and trade-offs for the business model you are running IBP.

Different planning scenarios should arise, as you should segment the planning strategy according to product variability/volume. Probabilistic estimates and decision points should be also used to manage high-variability items (e.g., project-driven) with a risk-based approach. You should also consider using postponement strategies/modularity to mitigate uncertainty (Crum and Palmatier 2003).

Demand planners and demand managers need to coordinate the management of "business risks and opportunities." "Risks and opportunities" are associated with all key dimensions of IBP, meaning product, demand, supply, finance, and reconciliation in the integrated reconciliation. Depending on the case, these can be more volumetric or financially driven (see Fig. 5.205).

The best way to capture uncertainties related to product, supply and demand both in volume or/and in value are through SAP IBP scenario or version planning. I strongly recommend to capture and review assumptions as part of the management of uncertainties. This means that demand planners should take care of capturing assumptions linked to product and demand. Yet, this should be mainly done focusing on the volumetric/financial reconciliation done in the integrated reconciliation phase.

We would like to build on this and enhance their role to integration with finance and business planning. Demand planners and demand managers should play their integration roles in different ways.

Demand planners should integrate sales and marketing to achieve consensus and define the most realistic forecast expressing the company realistic market potential by not being constrained by supply availability.

Demand managers should integrate supply and finance to achieve consensus and define the most profitable plans: those that maximize the business return.

### 5.4.1 End-to-End Business Risk and Opportunities

Final step in preparation of volumetric and financial reconciliation is to address business risk and opportunities. All risk which were validated in previous process steps enriched with availability of financial information come together now.

Risk and opportunities gathered through S&OP process steps can be addressing the following topics (see Fig. 5.206):

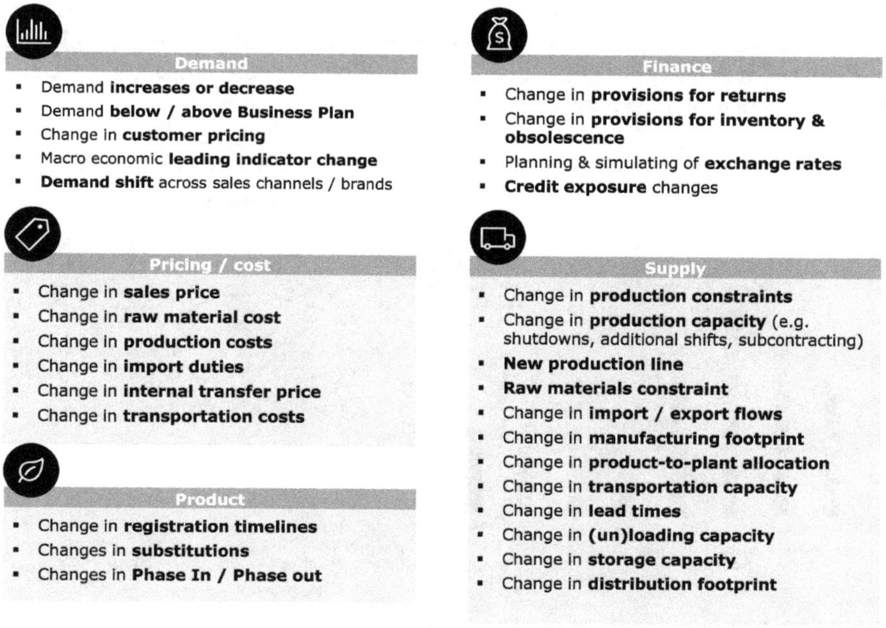


**Fig. 5.206** S&OP risks and opportunities areas—for example

Process, organization, and people capabilities are essential to IBP integration, but system and technology becomes not just as enabler but truly a foundation of management of risk and opportunities. Without easy-to-use, robust technology solution, process to define integrated business plan with all the risk and opportunities can become very time consuming, not transparent, erratic, and not aligned across stakeholders. Leverage SAP IBP to build even ad hoc end-to-end scenario planning.

Statistical forecasting may be used as important instrument to support you in development of scenario planning either in all types of planning in strategic planning, tactical S&OP, and even in operational planning. In operational planning if we integrate point of sales data into IBP via DSiM application, you may use this as variable in multilinear regression (MLR) model. In strategic planning you may use macroeconomic variables which drive growth or decline of the business and build MLR with use of it. Finally in tactical S&OP process and in particular in demand review or integrated reconciliation, more advanced statistical forecast like MLR can generate huge value for the business. When in S&OP process we wanted to create business scenario which describes impact of price changes on volume, revenue, and profit, we always face a problem of huge error caused by judgmental input. We decided to support the process with statistical forecasting. Marketing and sales campaign and its impact were evaluated with the use of MLR algorithm. MLR can work as follows (see Fig. 5.207).

We have selected price as variable which can drive volume, revenue, and profits. We tested that correlation between past volume sales and sales price existed. We have assumed that this correlation will be impacting business in the future as well. Taking this into account, we anticipated that MLR will give us possibility to simulate price changes in the future and see its impact.

Regression algorithms which help model cause and effect scenarios can help to build relationships and evaluate impact of those relationships, for example, on volume linked to many possible variables like marketing spend, temperature, income per capita, price, and many others.

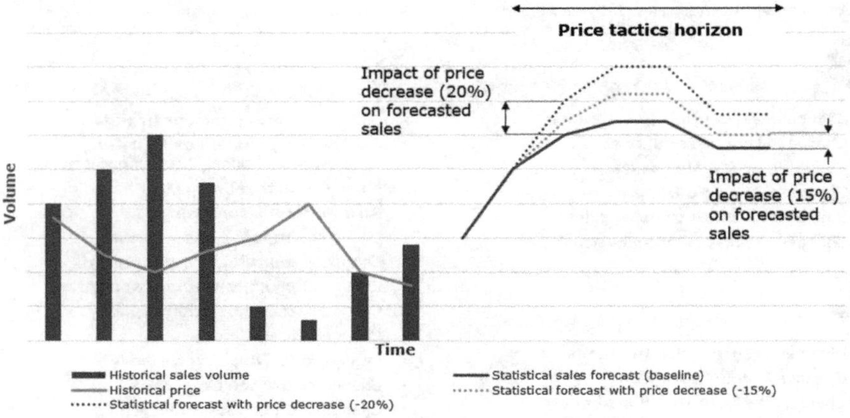


**Fig. 5.207** MLR statistical forecast in what-if simulation of risks and opportunities

Cause and effect algorithm assumes that past correlation between main input variable for modeled scenario existed in the past and will continue to be valid in the future. Those type of algorithms maybe helpful to assess cost to serve.

Cost service analysis (CSA) allows companies to understand the relative size of and the kind of relationship between the supply chain costs and the service levels provided to every kind of customers (internal and external). Use of CSA is growing in size and the trend in familiarity is steadily increasing and most firms use CSA to optimize inventory and pricing strategies. Mature (CSA) models enable useful "what-if" analysis and better understanding of SC trade-off impacts (Aronow and Jr 2011).

### 5.4.2 SAP Use Case: Cause and Effect Model, Price Impact Simulation

Linear regression is an approach to model the linear relationship between a target variable, usually referred to as dependent variable, and one or more variables which explain the target variable, usually referred to as independent variables or predictors.

In linear regression, the quantitative relationship between the dependent variable and the predictors is modeled through linear functions. The parameters of these linear functions are determined from the data by various algorithms.

As an example, the sales of a sort of ice cream are expected to be influenced by both the atmospheric air temperature (positive influence—the warmer it is, the higher the ice cream sales) and by the price (negative influence—the lower the price, the higher the sales).

Using multiple linear regression on historical data of ice cream price and sales volumes and as well on the corresponding weather data, we can construct a linear model that explains in a quantitative manner the ice cream sales numbers (the dependent variable) as a linear function of air temperature and ice cream cost (the predictors).

One question that may appear is what happens when one has more independent variables to choose from, some of which exert an uncertain influence on the dependent variable. Does the amount of rainfall influence ice cream sales? Or maybe the school holidays? Price reductions?. Fortunately, there are regression algorithms which already take this type of situation into account, by offering automatic variable selection. These algorithms look over a range of proposed predictors and select those that are the most relevant for the given dependent variable. This is usually an iterative process. It can start with no predictors in the model and tries to add them one, testing each time if this improves the significance of the model—this is called *forward selection* (see Fig. 5.208)

Alternatively, it can start with all predictors in the model and try to identify which ones have no impact on the significance of the model, if removed—this bears the name *backward selection* (see Fig. 5.209).

IBP employs the multiple linear regression algorithm from SAP HANA Predictive Analysis Library (PAL).

Now let's have a look at an example and see how we can leverage MLR capabilities in a specific business scenario. Assuming we have a price elastic product, we will always expect to have a variation in demand as price fluctuates: a price reduction will

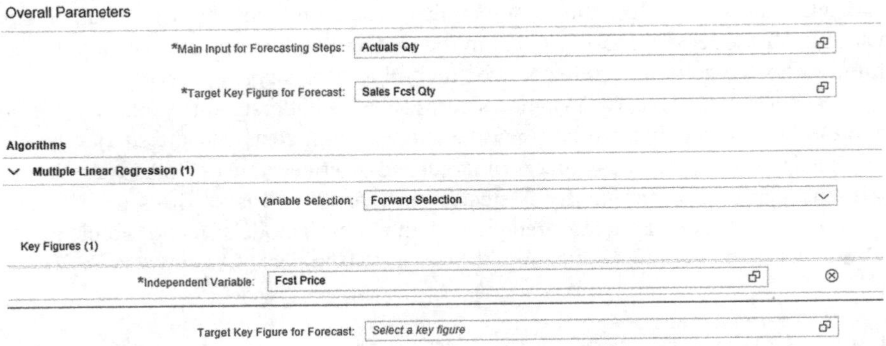


**Fig. 5.208** MLR forward variable selection

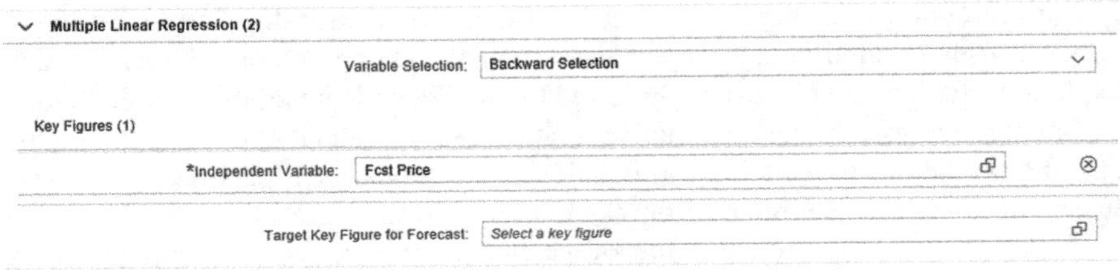


**Fig. 5.209** MLR backward variable selection

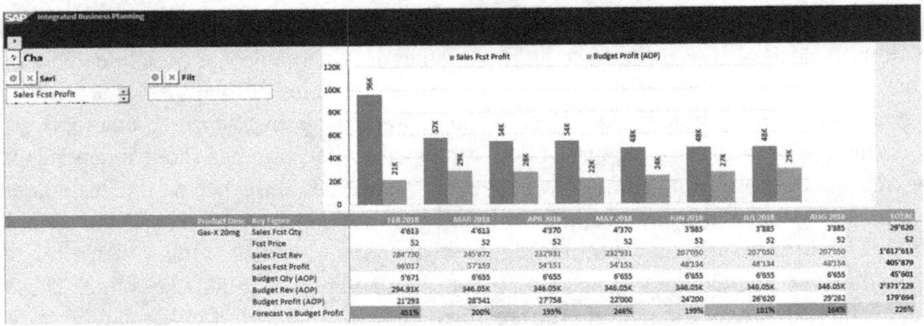


**Fig. 5.210** Initial situation exposes gap to budget

boost demand, while a price increase will create a drop in the demand. But how to find the correct price, which is not too low and not too high and able to secure a good balance between quantity and profit? To find the right answer, one can model forecast-price dependency using multilinear regression algorithm available in IBP Demand.

In Fig. 5.210 from a planning view, you see that sales forecast revenue and sales forecast profit go below the budget revenue and budget profit.

This triggered discussion led by product manager from marketing, demand planner, and finance/pricing to evaluate different measures to bring sales in line

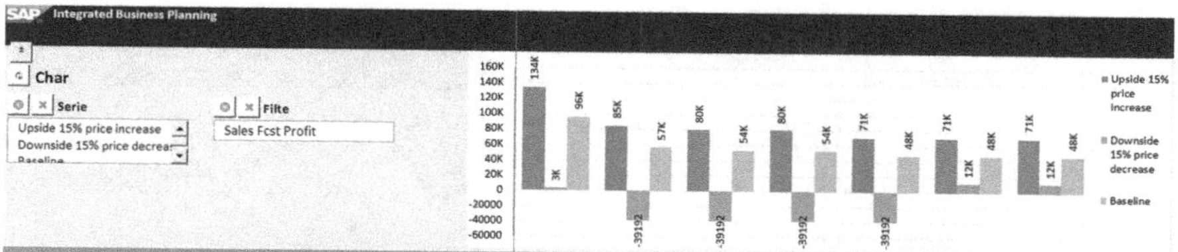


| Product Desc | Key Figure | Scenario | FEB 2018 | MAR 2018 | APR 2018 | MAY 2018 | JUN 2018 | JUL 2018 | AUG 2018 | TOTAL |
|---|---|---|---|---|---|---|---|---|---|---|
| Gas-X 20mg | Sales Fcst Qty | MLR 15% price increase | 4'152 | 4'152 | 3'933 | 3'933 | 3'496 | 3'496 | 3'496 | **26'658** |
| | | MLR 20% price decrease | 5'970 | 7'005 | 7'005 | 7'005 | 7'005 | 7'005 | 7'005 | **48'001** |
| | | Baseline | 4'613 | 4'613 | 4'370 | 4'370 | 3'885 | 3'885 | 3'885 | **29'620** |
| | Fcst Price | MLR 15% price increase | 59 | 59 | 59 | 59 | 59 | 59 | 59 | **59** |
| | | MLR 20% price decrease | 41 | 41 | 41 | 41 | 41 | 41 | 41 | **41** |
| | | Baseline | 52 | 52 | 52 | 52 | 52 | 52 | 52 | **52** |
| | Sales Fcst Rev | MLR 15% price increase | 303'837 | 254'477 | 241'084 | 241'084 | 214'297 | 214'297 | 214'297 | **1'683'372** |
| | | MLR 20% price decrease | 247'429 | 247'381 | 247'381 | 247'381 | 247'381 | 298'698 | 298'698 | **1'834'350** |
| | | Baseline | 284'730 | 245'872 | 232'931 | 232'931 | 207'050 | 207'050 | 207'050 | **1'617'613** |
| | Sales Fcst Profit | MLR 15% price increase | 133'996 | 84'636 | 80'181 | 80'181 | 71'272 | 71'272 | 71'272 | 592'811 |
| | | MLR 20% price decrease | 3'206 | -39'192 | -39'192 | -39'192 | -39'192 | 12'125 | 12'125 | -129'310 |
| | | Baseline | 96'017 | 57'159 | 54'151 | 54'151 | 48'134 | 48'134 | 48'134 | 405'879 |

**Fig. 5.211** Multilinear regression model based on different price tactics generates different forecasted volumes

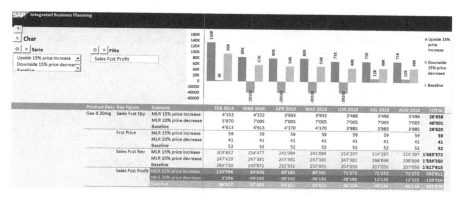

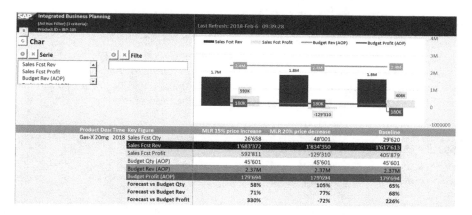

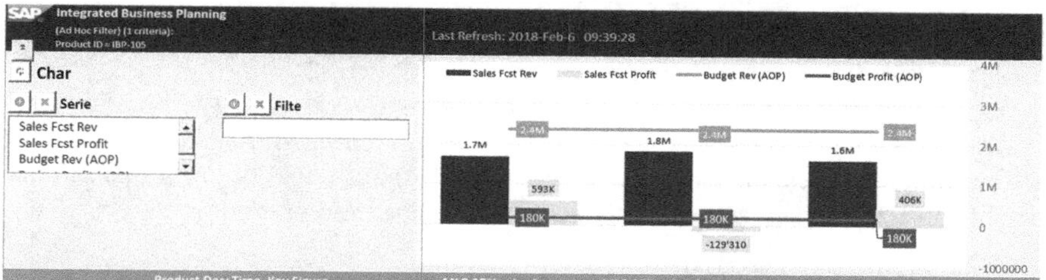


| Product Desc | Time | Key Figure | MLR 15% price increase | MLR 20% price decrease | Baseline |
|---|---|---|---|---|---|
| Gas-X 20mg | 2018 | Sales Fcst Qty | 26'658 | 48'001 | 29'620 |
| | | Sales Fcst Rev | 1'683'372 | 1'834'350 | 1'617'613 |
| | | Sales Fcst Profit | 592'811 | -129'310 | 405'879 |
| | | Budget Qty (AOP) | 45'601 | 45'601 | 45'601 |
| | | Budget Rev (AOP) | 2.37M | 2.37M | 2.37M |
| | | Budget Profit (AOP) | 179'694 | 179'694 | 179'694 |
| | | **Forecast vs Budget Qty** | **58%** | **105%** | **65%** |
| | | **Forecast vs Budget Rev** | **71%** | **77%** | **68%** |
| | | **Forecast vs Budget Profit** | **330%** | **-72%** | **226%** |

**Fig. 5.212** Price tactics scenario on aggregated level

with annual target and balance it with expected profit, especially around summer period. During this exercise, they simulate how demand forecast is shaped by different price tactic like 15% increase and 20% decrease (see Fig. 5.211).

We see that 20% price decrease did not bring us enough of volume to increase revenue and profits against initial baseline scenario. Actually it could be even too dangerous since it did expose impact on lost of profits, while 15% price increase seemed to be the safest option. Let us review scenario and compare gaps to budget in qty and value (see Fig. 5.212).

We see that decision will be not easy since:

- Increase of volume brought be price decrease (scenario MLR 20% price decrease) brings as well extra revenue but profit became negative.
- Increase of profit caused by price increase results in almost same revenue since volume was reduced and capacity utilization will be lower.

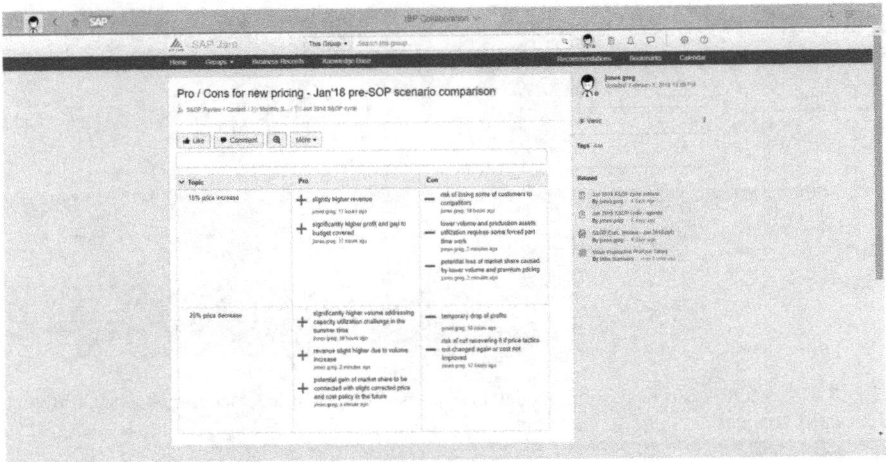


**Fig. 5.213** Risk and opportunities were ranked by team members and recorded

Process coordinator decided to capture pros/cons for scenario (see Fig. 5.213)

Team is inclined to go for price decrease scenario since price and cost initiatives are ongoing and they are sure they will recover temporary loss of profit but will not be able to gain market share (first in volume) if priced too premium.

### 5.4.3 Management Business Review Meeting

Management meeting should aim to:

- Approve or make decisions on each product family, accepting recommendations from integrated reconciliations or choosing another different course of action.
- Authorize changes in cost in production and procurement
- Compare monetized version of the integrated business plan with budget and:
  Initiate sales and marketing, production, and procurement activities.
  Adjust demand or supply plans.
  Adjust final integrated business plan.
- Break ties if integrated reconciliation could manage to find consensus.
- Review critical KPIs from S&OP process steps.
- Define clear actions.

Demand manager and finance controller should support Management Business Review Meeting to:

- Stay focused on most profitable decisions.
- Avoid repetition of product, demand, and supply review.
- Ensure presentation of integrated business scenarios.
- Keep business and not just demand on the spot.
- Present information in aggregated and concise manner.

What demand manager and finance controller should ensure to achieve in Management Business Review Meeting is:

- Sign-off of business scenario (preferable the one recommended in integrated reconciliation).
- Document approved scenario business assumptions, in case they were changed during the meeting.
- Capture expectations or even define high-level action plan, responsibilities, and time lines required to make business scenario happening.
- Record appropriate activities in action log.

We have seen that visualizations of process steps, key information, and scenario planning outcomes to management will be as much important as content which needs to be discussed.

Business risk and opportunity scenarios approval went good when the following elements were visualized:

- Volume
- Revenue
- Profit
- Budget gap
- External factors to be considered
- Assumptions
- Impact on existing plan +/-

It would make total sense if any gap exposed to operating plan (budget) would be combined with:

- Analysis of complete set of budget assumptions (general business atmosphere, market share/industry trends, competition activity)
- Categorization of the gaps (time, volume, geography, customer) (Moon 2013)

### 5.4.4 SAP Use Case: S&OP Dashboard and Analytics

We have found SAP IBP functionality of dashboard and analytics very intuitive.

Understanding of pivot tables in MS Excel or even some basic info about data model will be enough to create your own view on the process. You may pull key information of each process step in S&OP into the dashboards by yourself. Let us review few examples.

**Product Review:**

– Analyze your key indicators, e.g., mean absolute percentage error of the forecast against product segmentation (Fig. 5.214)

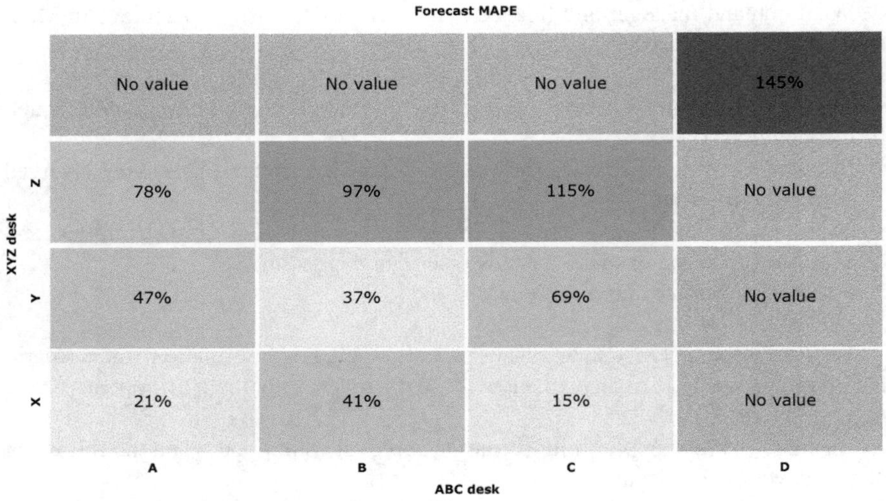


**Fig. 5.214** Product segmentation forecast accuracy

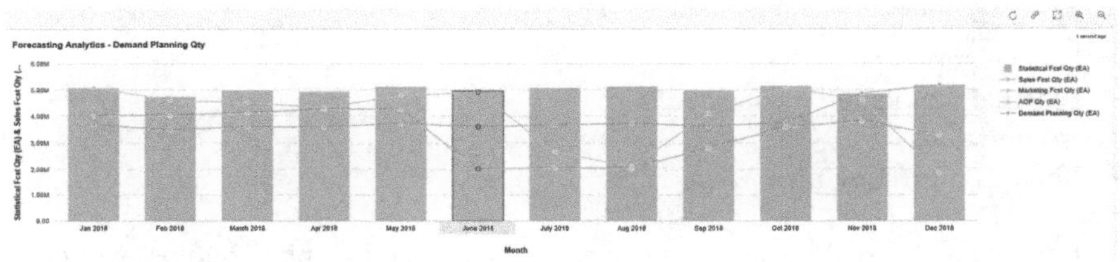


**Fig. 5.215** Forecast inputs vs actuals

You may visualize additional information other measures against this matrix like inventory sales revenue, budget, and inventory forward cover. You may add charts or table data with phase-in/phase-out information, lifecycle status versus data, etc.

## Demand Review

- Compare various forecasting inputs to assess input variability and fluctuation (Fig. 5.215).

You may visualize each input versus actuals to assess trends in actual data versus forecast input trend and its alignment.

- Compare consensus forecast versus actuals last year in year-over-year manner, and look at your customers target realization (Fig. 5.216).

You may integrate as shown in demand review chapter information from SAP commercial applications like TPPM, CBP, and Hybris and visualize key information against IBP data.

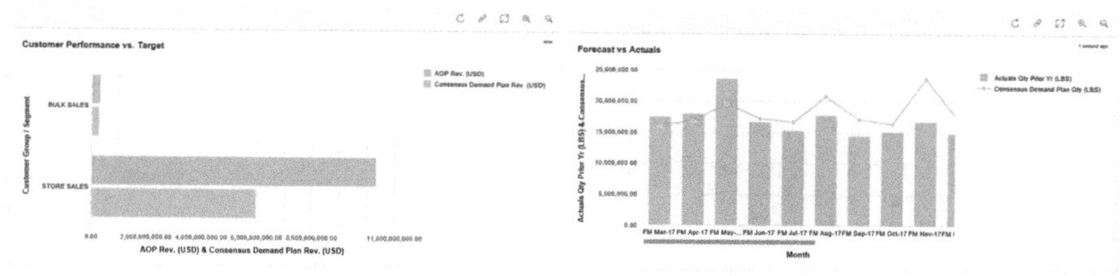


**Fig. 5.216** Forecast vs actuals, customer target realization

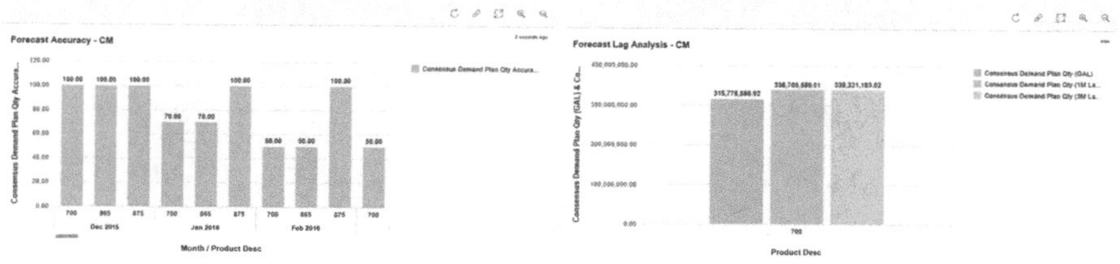


**Fig. 5.217** Forecast accuracy and time lag analysis

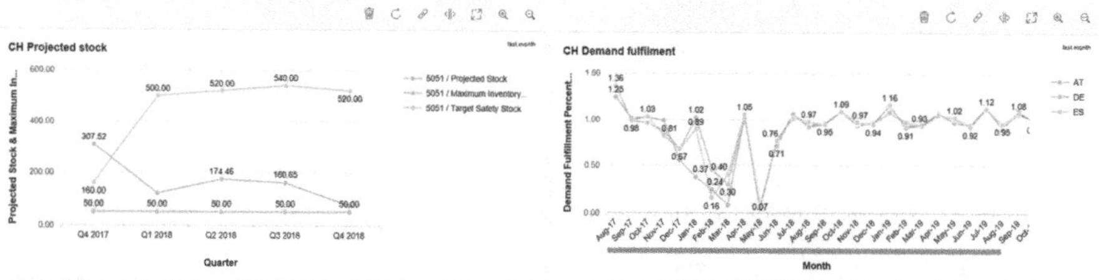


**Fig. 5.218** Stock and demand fulfillment projections

– Analyze you forecast input accuracy and time lag (Fig. 5.217).

You may analyze other forecasting metrics to spot error and trigger corrective actions.

## Supply Review

– Analyze your stock projections on distribution centers and demand fulfillment projections (Fig. 5.218).

We can populate safety stocks, actual and projected stocks, and maximum allowed stocks and assess impact of planning on your working capital.

Impact of planning may be visualized as comparison between consensus market forecast and constrained plan on country level (see demand fulfillment).

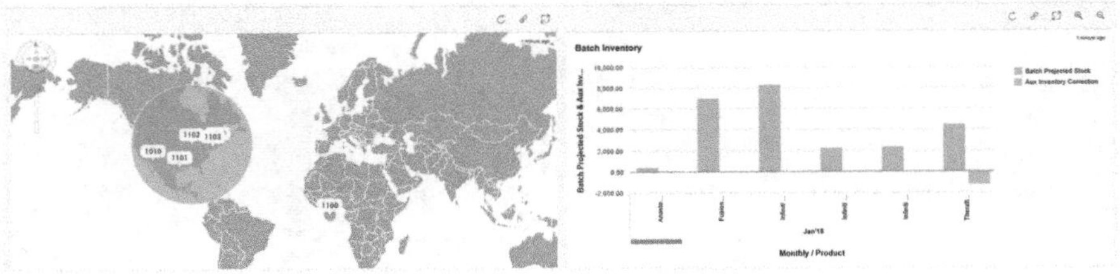


**Fig. 5.219** Inventory analysis

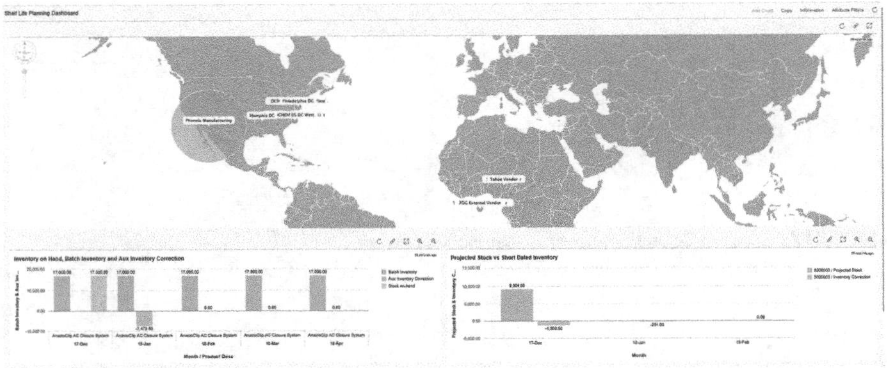


**Fig. 5.220** Shelf life planning overview

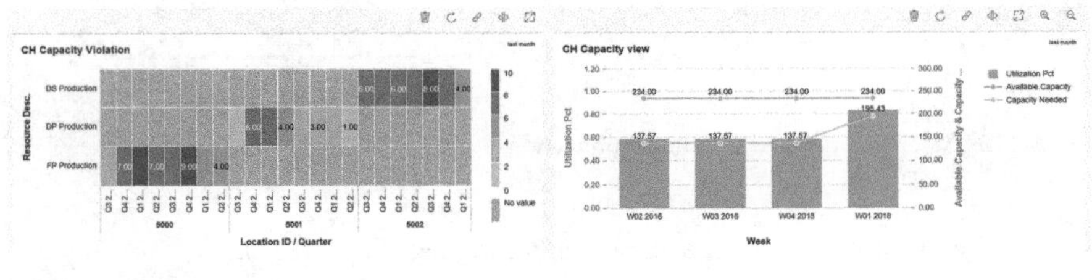


**Fig. 5.221** Capacity utilization

- Analyze your inventory levels and geographical focus of inventory (Fig. 5.219).

In order to use geo charts location, attributes should be mapped with geo coordinates.

- Analyze you shelf life planning process results (Fig. 5.220).

You may easily spot short-dated inventory captured in Aux Inventory Corrections. Specific batch level can be visualized if needed.

- Analyze your capacity utilization (Fig. 5.221).

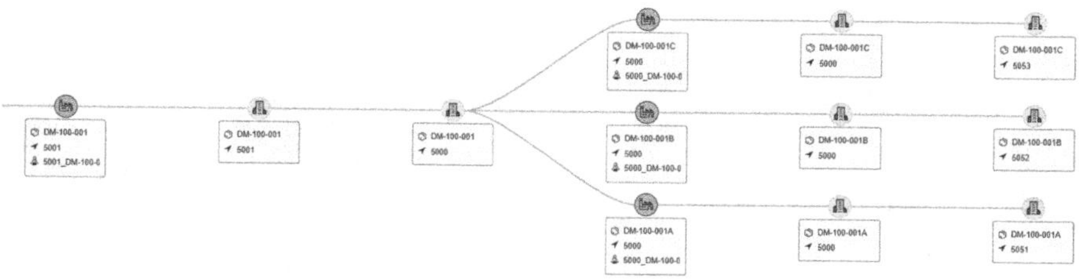

**Fig. 5.222** Key indicators against network

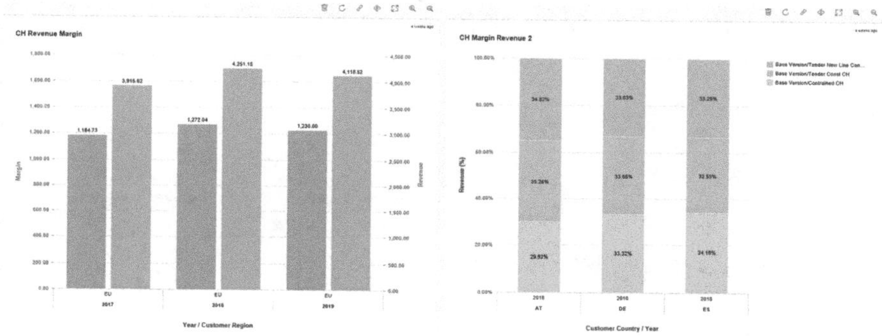


**Fig. 5.223** Revenue and margins and scenario comparison

You may use alert key figure to spot overutilization of capacity on various level of production (FP, finished product; DP, drug product; DS, drug substance in pharma industry).

- Analyze your key indicators (e.g., inventory) against the supply chain network (Fig. 5.222).

Some of data may sense to be displayed at network diagram but some not since exist only in certain nodes.

**Integrated Reconciliation**

- Analyze your revenue and margin/profit, and compare financial impact of the versions/scenario of the plans (Fig. 5.223).
- Analyze profits by product , versions, product, and product line (see Fig. 5.224).

Often in integrated reconciliation, we compare scenario which needs to be approved. Data can be visualized as single ratio, value, or chart (Fig. 5.225).

As you notice there is a lot of flexibility how you want to present data for specific process steps and even cases. Great thing about it is that business users were able to create and adjust dashboards and analytics by themselves.

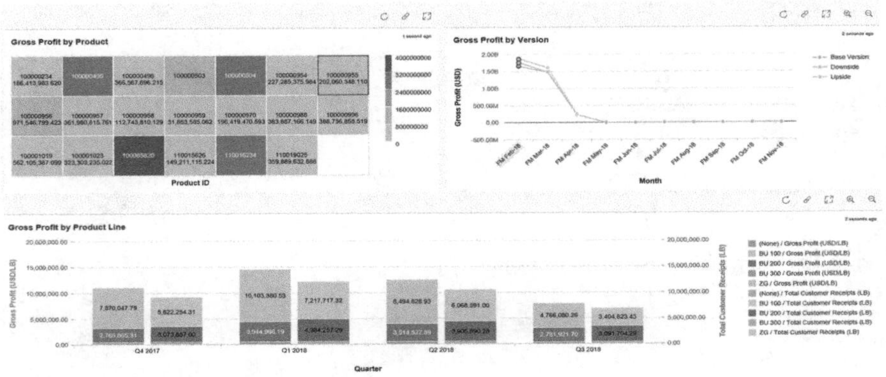


Fig. 5.224 Profit analysis

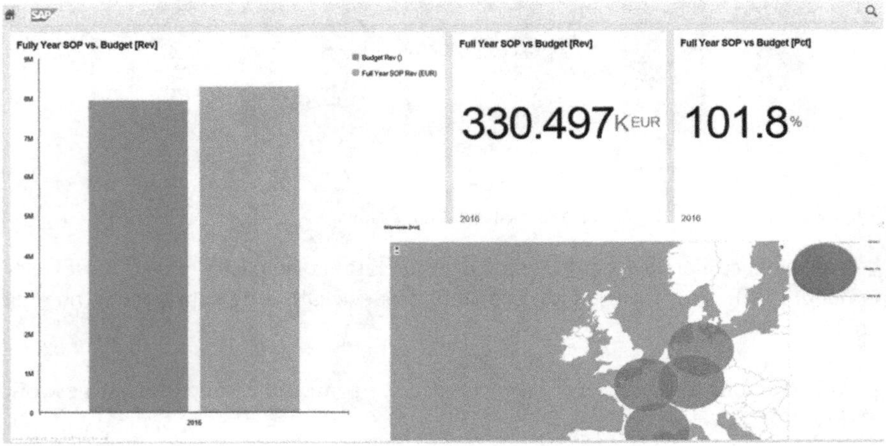


Fig. 5.225 IBP comparison to budget

## 5.4.5 SAP Use Case: S&OP Agenda and Actions

S&OP process reoccurs; output from one cycle normally is reviewed in the next one. We have seen that demand manager or S&OP leader stores normally power point presentation with relevant information gathered from various functions. SAP JAM helps to define agenda and stores file which needs to be reviewed on S&OP meeting.

In Fig. 5.226 we see that January S&OP cycle has its own repository, where files are stored. Meeting takes place normally to agreed agenda which can be stored on JAM as well (see Fig. 5.227).

As the meeting proceeds, demand manager or S&OP leader captures actions and assigns responsible persons (see Fig. 5.228).

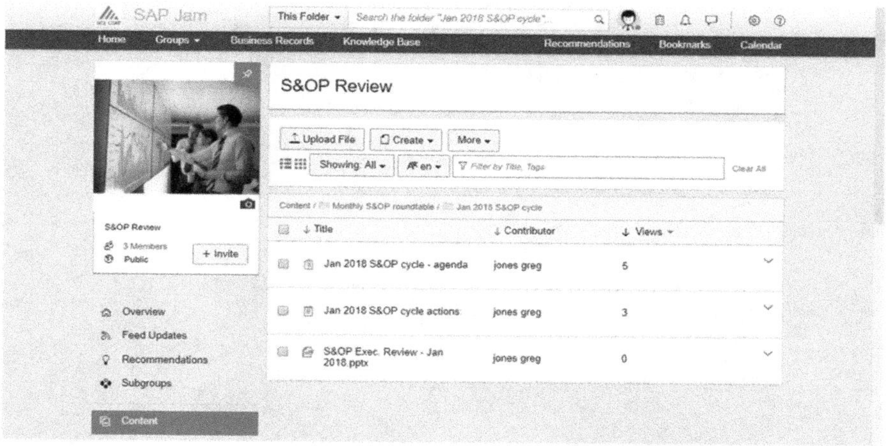


**Fig. 5.226** S&OP meeting collaboration repository

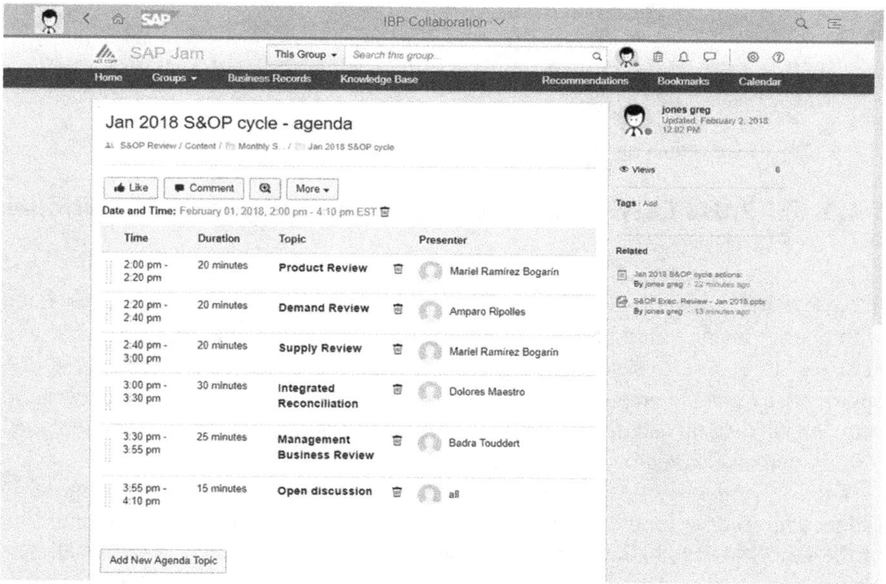


**Fig. 5.227** S&OP cycle agenda

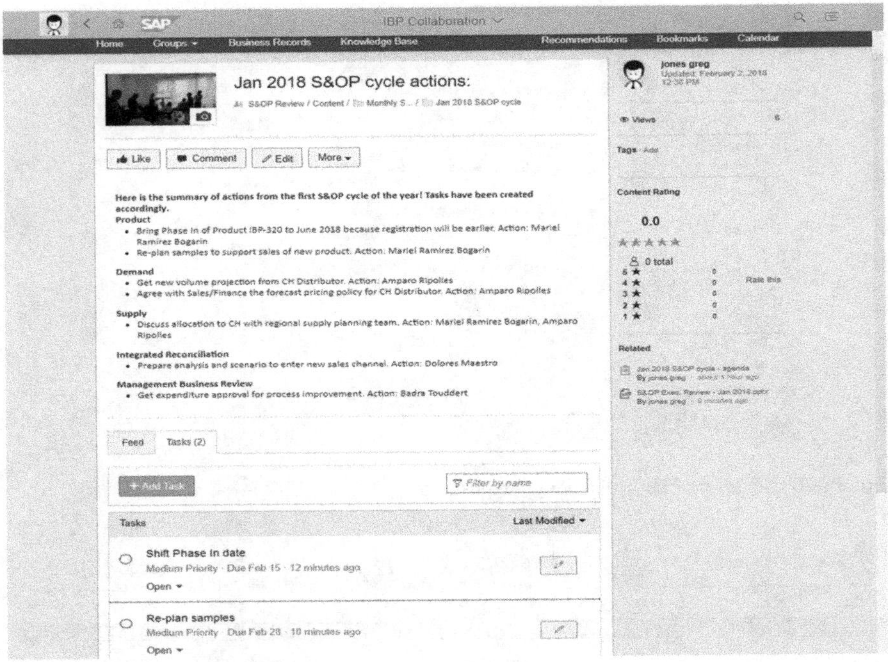


**Fig. 5.228** S&OP actions and tasks

### 5.4.6 SAP Use Case: Integration Between Tactical and Operational Plans

In SAP IBP, the results of the tactical S&OP planning process should be integrated with operations planning process within the same integrated planning model. It will help you to ensure that operational plans follow certain objectives and trade-offs approved by management. Figure 5.229 shows dataflow and process integration between the tactical and operations planning process across several IBP applications: S&OP, demand, inventory, and response and supply.

*Tactical planning:* In IBP S&OP, the tactical planning is performed in monthly cadence for mid- to long-term plan of 3–24 months. The key figures time granularity of the IBP S&OP plan is typically at monthly level or at technical week level. The planning is usually carried out in monthly or weekly level. Further the base planning levels of key figures can be at a lower granular level of product/customer/location, but the planning can be done at an aggregated level. The demand planning process in the tactical plan is typically viewed at an aggregated level of product family and customer region, and these then disaggregate to the lowest planning levels. The supply planning in IBP S&OP which creates production, procurement, and distribution plan is typically at product/location level, product/ship from ship to location, etc. The plans can be viewed at any aggregate level.

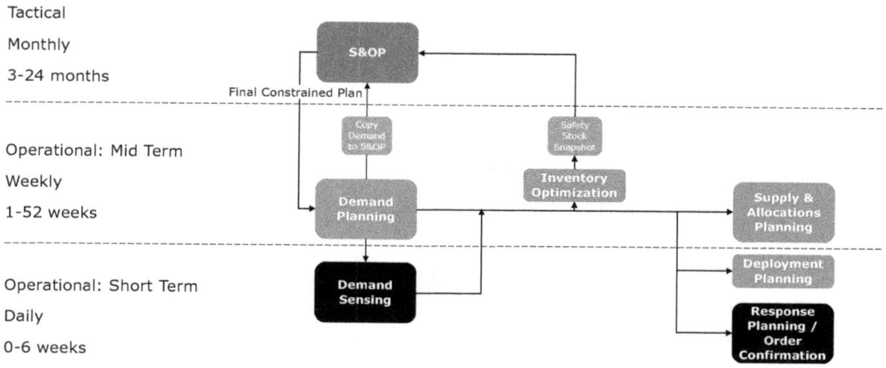


**Fig. 5.229** Tactical and operational planning process integration overview

The *operational plans* like demand sensing and order-based allocation planning are run in a daily or weekly cadence for horizon spanning 1–52 weeks (but really seldom more than 12 weeks). Distribution plans (deployment) may cover bit longer horizon than 12 weeks.

Operational IBP Processes may be used to:

- Manage large marketing/sales campaigns which need support in cross-functional process where monthly drumbeat of tactical S&OP is not sufficient.
- Manage demand/supply balancing for highly seasonal and with short window of sales product incl. limited life offers where tactical S&OP monthly drum bear is not sufficient.
- Enable cross-functional team to make short-term decision with primary objective to make the most out of available resources (inventory, firmed supply orders, logistics, price, margin, orders, inquiries, POS data, etc.).
- Run process on highly granular level compared to other planning types. It has direct link to execution functions like customer service, transportation, sometimes production or tolling with late customization, packing, and production if lead time allows. Time horizon of operational planning is linked typically to sales peak season, large marketing, or product campaign.
- Execute it with significant focus; typically this process is not executed in many steps but rather as very operational meeting, prepared by key stakeholders.

The integration from tactical S&OP to operational planning should happen minimum once per month or more frequently for the horizon window of the operational planning processes as per proposal in Fig. 5.230.

In the overall planning process, the dataflows between the tactical S&OP and operation processes are follows:

### Operational Plans to Tactical Plans

The operational plans flow as input to the monthly tactical planning processes. One such example, as followed in SAP Unified Planning Area (SAPIBP1), is integration

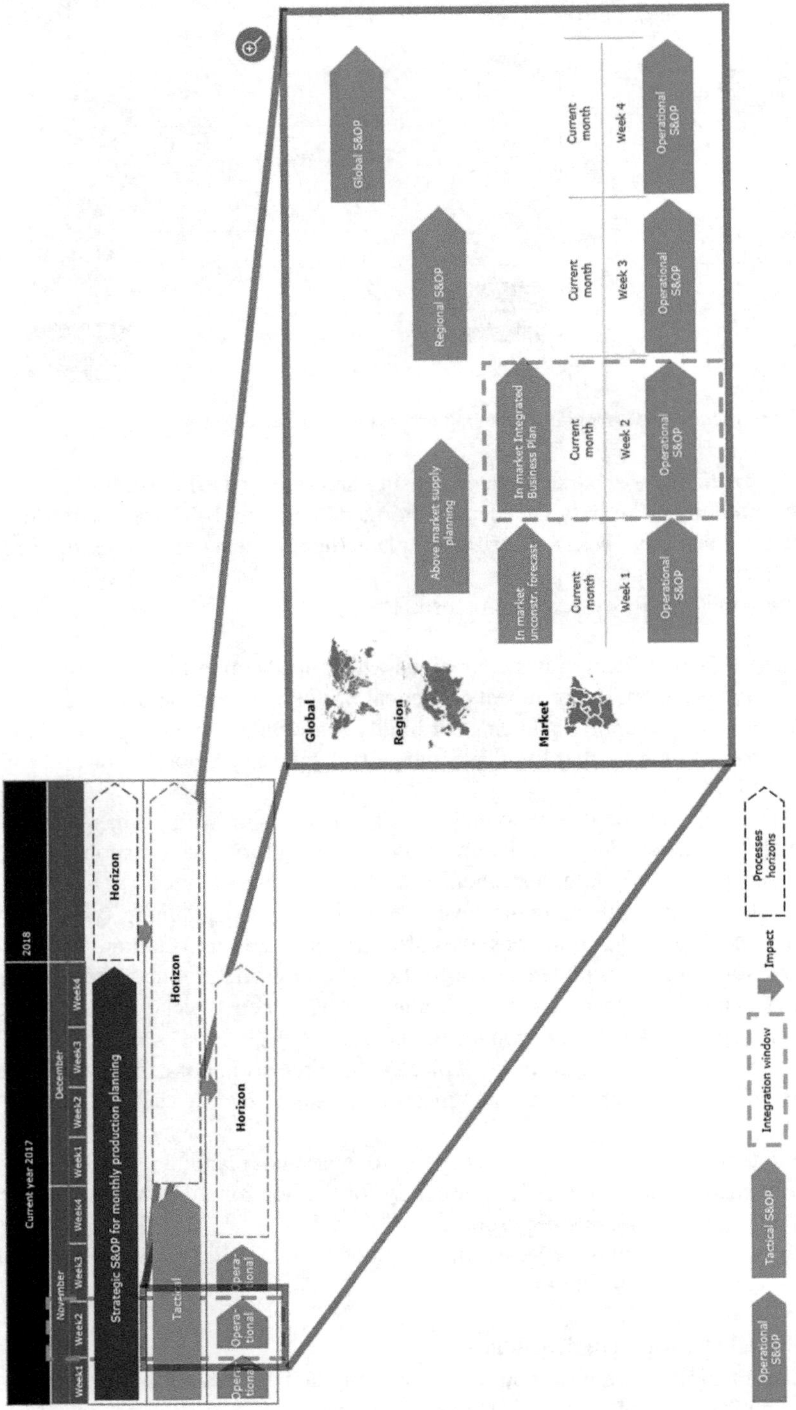


**Fig. 5.230** Tactical S&OP and operational planning integration window

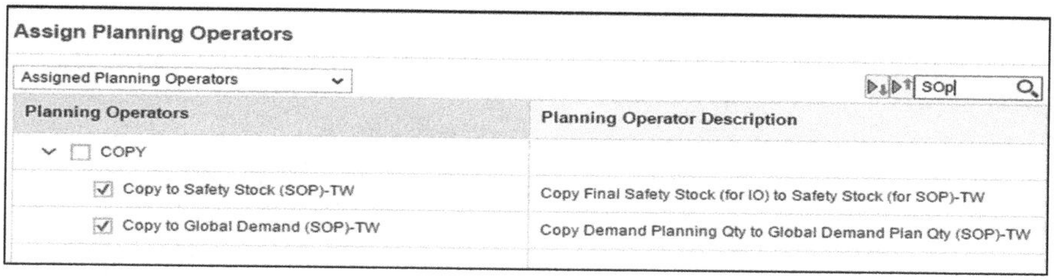


**Fig. 5.231** Copy operators to integrate planning types

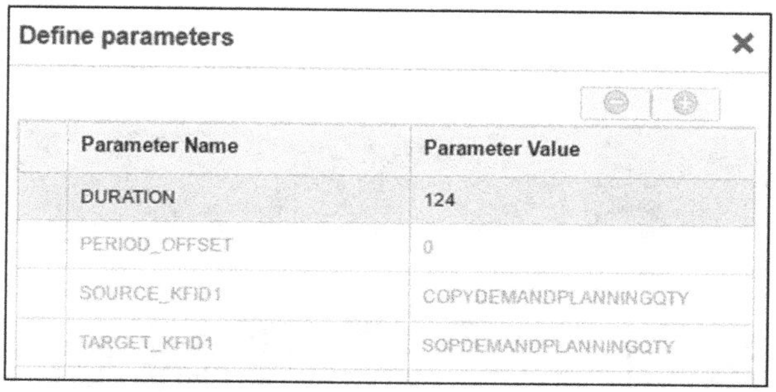

Define parameters
Parameter Name
Parameter Value
DURATION
124
PERIOD_OFFSET
0
SOURCE_KFID1
COPYDEMANDPLANNINGQTY
TARGET_KFID1
SOPDEMANDPLANNINGQTY


**Fig. 5.232** Global demand plan copy operator

of weekly demand plans and inventory targets. These copy functions between key figures are performed by the copy operator. SAPIBP1 has the following two copy operators assigned. The copy operator separate KFs for each of the planning (Fig. 5.231).

1. *Copy to Global Demand (S&OP)*
   The global demand plan qty from weekly demand planning can be copied once a month before the start of the tactical S&OP planning cycle. The copy operator has the following parameters defined for the duration of the plan to be copied along with source and target key figures. In SAP sample planning area SAPIBP1, the global demand plan is managed at technical week/product/customer/location level. This can be copied to key figure SOPDEMANDPLANNINGQTY at technical week/product/customer/location level in S&OP process. However, this can be adjusted based on your requirements. For example, if the input key figures of S&OP process should be at monthly level and at aggregated product/country level, then using the copy operator, the source KF, can be aggregated and copied to the target key figure base planning level stored in weeks and other levels (see Fig. 5.232).
2. *Copy to Safety Stock (SOP)*
   Safety-stock recommendations from weekly inventory optimization can be copied once a month to the tactical S&OP before start of the supply planning review, so that the latest safety targets are considered for supply planning.

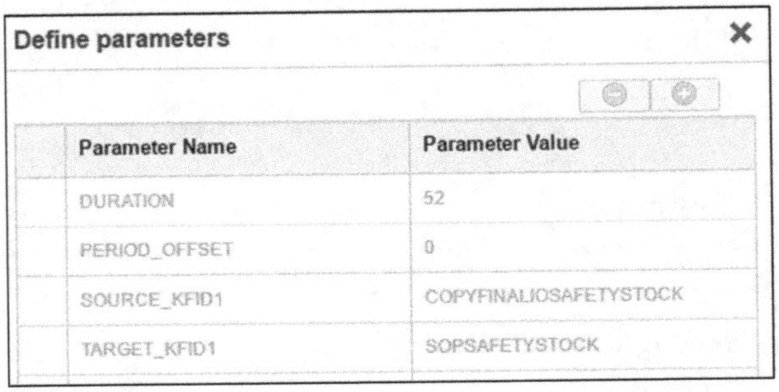


**Fig. 5.233** Safety-stock copy operator

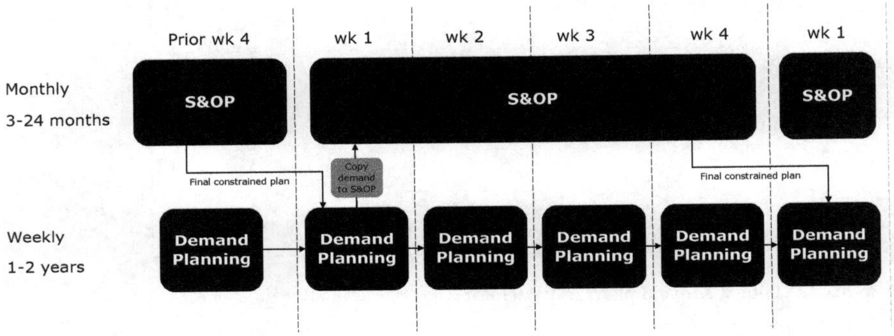


**Fig. 5.234** Managing demand planning data on local and global level as part of global S&OP

The copy operator copies from FINALIOSAFETYSTOCK to SOPSAFERTYSTOCK (see Fig. 5.233). Since the source and target key figures are different, the processes can now run independently, i.e., IO safety targets can continue to be changed in a weekly cycle.

The copy operator thus provides a clear handoff of data between the operational and tactical planning.

### Tactical Plans to Operational Plans

The final constrained plan as a result of management business review in S&OP flows as an input to weekly demand planning processes to shape the weekly global demand plan based on the aggregated S&OP plan. The final constrained plan is updated once a month and readily available for the demand planning processes. In SAP IBP, these processes can be managed in one planning area. Therefore, the key figures from tactical S&OP process are visible in the operational planning process (Fig. 5.234).

In SAP delivered planning area SAPIBP1, both the final constrained demand and global demand plan are at the same planning level, so there is no need to disaggregate. However, if they are at different levels, for example, tactical plan at monthly/product/customer level and operational plan is at weekly/product/customer/location level, and then the aggregated tactical plan can either be disaggregated (using disaggregation operator or split factor configured calculations) or the operational plans can be aggregated to the tactical level for comparison.

## 5.5 Between S&OP Cycles Changes

Many times we have been faced with business scenario which required to trigger actions between monthly tactical S&OP cycles. There is nothing wrong with considering those signals, but there should be some governance about how to introduce change while integrated business plan was agreed and communicated.

Between S&OP cycle changes process should be governed by demand manager and finance controller. Typically those two roles would need to coordinate between "demand," "supply," "finance," and "response" functions to agree way forward on captured signal initiating change request. Between cycle changes process needs to meet objective of keeping responsiveness on one side and midterm objective captured in final integrated business plan on the other side. We see following inputs/triggers for between cycle changes (Fig. 5.235).

Trigger for between cycle changes may come from various groups of sources:

(a) It may be automatically detected as difference between sensed demand and unconstrained forecast.
(b) It may come from simple monitoring dashboard which needs to be reviewed by demand planner on daily basis (if that is the frequency of refreshing data between source system and IBP for "order-to-cash" data).
(c) It may come from sales and marketing who envisage to sell extra volume or lost some opportunities and want to reflect that in short-term plans.

Trigger (a) and (b) would require special approach to exception management and some solution on system side. In SAP IBP supply chain control tower would be an

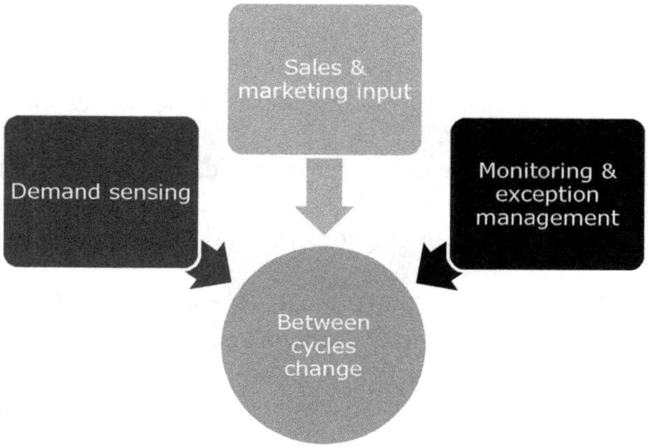


**Fig. 5.235** Between S&OP cycle triggers for change

application to improve visibility, exception management, and SAP IBP demand which has demand sensing engine which improves short-term forecasting.

Exemplary triggers listed above could form a base to capture a demand signal to which you may need to respond. In case there is a way to consider change in the plan and react to it, a question will then pop up, how to do it? Demand planning should work then according to three simple process steps:

– Capture demand signal.
– Analyze demand and supply.
– Deploy agreed supply response.

First of all capture signal coming from different sources, and consult and analyze if it makes sense or is just an erratic event. If signal is not a source of an error, then you would need to analyze if there is a way to respond to it. There should be a discussion done between demand planner or demand manager with supply/operations manager potentially even with finance controller. Expected outcome should be a "what, how, and when" supply response can be provided. Once this is known, you should get full understanding on financial impact of the change. At the end change of demand should be reflected in supply and final IBP plan. Demand manager should be authorized to introduce the change to integrated business plan.

Demand Manager should "hold the keys to updates in IBP plan" and Demand Planner should "hold the keys to updates in consensus unconstrained forecast".

All between S&OP cycles triggers will face same challenge of supply and operations planning fence. Planning fences set borders of responsiveness; they protect specific time horizon from changes. In best way planning fences should consider trade-offs between all main functions and not just production or supply chain which is sort of typical for non-demand-driven organizations. When discussing planning fences, you should ask yourself and other stakeholders:

– Are you able to react to changes in demand without facing any "structural" constraints in supply/logistic network?
– When does it make sense to react to short-term changes in demand and how frequently?
– Shall you stay flexible on demand side without making and pressure on supply time fences, replenishment models, and late customization in your planning and operations area?
– When does it make sense to consider financial constraints?

We wanted to highlight to you two major considerations:

1. Planning fences in IBP should be not just exposing supply chain, operations, and production point of view but holistic view on trade-offs, shared risks, and shared opportunities which are exposed when setting time fences up.
2. Between S&OP cycle changes, process should not impact your forecasting, planning, and execution if you cannot operationalize change and if you cannot react!

# 6 Improve Your Responsiveness with Operational Planning

We have seen that operational planning was introduced in the companies when monthly tactical S&OP process was not granular enough to solve demand-supply-finance imbalances driven by product type, brand, channel, and sales area. Operational planning has a short-term horizon focus and an objective to extract the best value from available assets. Let us see how we may understand operational planning.

## 6.1 Key Characteristics and Value of Operational Planning

**Characteristics**

Operational planning in its nature will focus on enabling a cross-functional team to make short-term decision with a primary objective to make the most out of available resources (inventory, firmed supply orders, logistics, price, margin, orders, inquiries, POS data, etc.).

Operational planning runs on highly granular level compared to other S&OP process. It has direct link to execution functions like customer service, transportation, sometimes production or tolling with late customization, packing, and production if lead time allows. Time horizon of operational planning is linked typically to sales peak season, large marketing, or product campaign.

Operational planning may be used to:

- Manage large marketing/sales campaigns which need support in cross-functional process where monthly drumbeat of tactical S&OP is not sufficient.
- Manage demand/supply balancing for highly seasonal products, with short window of sales product, even for products with limited life offers (like Christmas season) where tactical S&OP monthly drumbeat is not sufficient.

Operational planning typically is not executed in many steps but rather as very operational meeting, prepared by key stakeholders. Let us visualize this in Fig. 6.1:



R. Kepczynski et al., *Implementing Integrated Business Planning*, Management for Professionals, https://doi.org/10.1007/978-3-319-90095-7_6

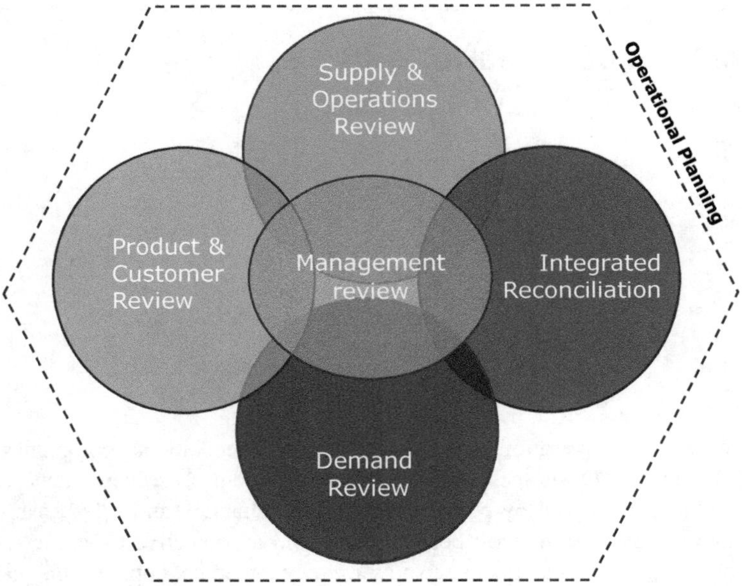


**Fig. 6.1** Operational planning is like "S&OP process" but executed in one step

Operational planning in large extent is framed by outputs from tactical S&OP, expressed in volumetric and value of integrated business plan. We see quite a few similarities to S&OP process steps but executed with different characteristics. We have seen operational planning working within profit-based allocation plan, prepared in tactical S&OP. In other words tactical S&OP sets an objective and rules for operational planning.

The main differentiating characteristics of operational planning vs. tactical S&OP are the following:

- Short term, frequent, and normally but not always time limited
- High pace and high responsiveness
- High granularity
- Demand sensing and shaping switch focus aligned to seasonality
- Stakeholders who perform operational job

We have met business practitioners calling operational planning a control tower. It does not fully work for us since we find it easier to align it to S&OP characteristics like objectives, stakeholders, and tools than to invent different names.

### Frequency, Horizon, and Focus

The frequency of operational planning needs to be aligned to business drivers. Let us describe some of them in the following examples:

- Your products are positioned as commodity where price is a driver, and you need to agree prices and volume frequently with your customers, e.g., on bi-weekly basis, while there is a huge flexibility in production and manufacturing expressed in even so small as 2–5 days' reaction time. Those products can be sold separately, or they form base for the other more complex ones. Assessment of availability on independent and dependent demands linked to demand drivers is essential. Described characteristics suggest to run operational planning on bi-weekly basis.
- Your products are sold through the catalogs in multiple service centers located in big cities. In big cities you have limited storage availability which becomes a critical factor especially at the beginning of sales campaign when products are already visualized in catalogs shown to consumers. You need to assess if it makes sense to establish not daily but even twice a day deliveries to service centers from distribution centers. The focus would be to limit the number of out of stocks and extra costs linked to express extraordinary consumer deliveries. In this case we would recommend to run operational planning on a daily basis at the beginning of the campaign and adjust frequency later as it is required in campaign/season length.
- Your products are sold in a particular part of the year; window of sales is 2–3 months or shorter. External factors like weather drive your demand. In this case operational planning needs to sense when peak happens and when sales start to decline. In large-volume products, implication of that on operations/logistics is substantial; therefore integration achieved by setting up operational planning is very beneficial to manage cost-to-serve and fulfillment. In this case we would recommend to run operational planning at least on a weekly basis in the peak season.

As you see from above examples your business events, characteristics drive key parameters of the operational planning. Visualization of information required to take decision may be different, e.g., you may want to visualize information in daily buckets subtotaled by weeks and month or start from weeks. You may have to visualize data very low in product/commercial hierarchy but at same time to look on totals on brand, product line, and sales zone level.

In all the above examples, business focus is on responsiveness against complete demand picture (sales orders, inquires, sensed demand, consensus constrained integrated business plan, point-of-sales data). Decisions normally are needed to be taken on the meeting, not later, and they are influencing short-term company performance significantly. High pace and high responsiveness may be critical competitive advantage factors; therefore do not limit yourself to tactical S&OP frequency and set up operational planning to gain better control and maximize business return. Do it only when it makes sense and in all aspects of transformation meaning: organization, capabilities, process, and technology. Horizon of operational planning may differ substantially from few weeks to whole year.

**Operational Planning May Have Its Inactive Periods or Different Focus**
It is not unusual that operational planning does not have to run whole year long; it may be linked to specific campaign, event which lifts up demand significantly. You may need to set up a governance when to switch on and switch off operational planning. Trigger to switch on or switch off operational planning normally should come from tactical S&OP decisions. It may be triggered before the limited time campaign, executed for few weeks, and later deactivated.

We have seen operational planning running all year long but with different business objectives (see Fig. 6.2):

- In peak season, the main focus was on sensing when peak starts and declines to effectively manage constraints and making the most profitable allocation plans and decisions.
- Out of the peak season, the main focus was on demand shaping activities so-called sell availability/capacity.

In Fig. 6.2 you can see focus of operational planning which does evolve over time:

- Jan–Mar—demand sensing for increase zone
- Apr–May—demand sensing for decline zone
- Jun onward—demand shaping zone

The same process framework can deliver different results but still aiming to maximize profits (e.g., in chemical industry) or availability (e.g., in pharma). To manage response in peak sales, you need to sense when peak starts and ends. To manage response after peak sales season, you need to establish ways of working enabling better usage of available capacity (manpower, machine, material) against lower market demand; focus is on shaping demand and maximizing business return.

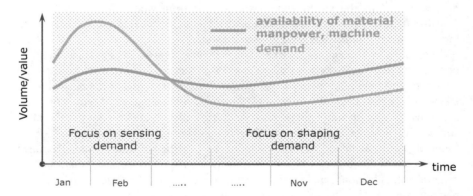

**Fig. 6.2** Demand sensing and demand shaping focus

**Granularity: Data Types**

Granularity of data used in operational planning may vary from daily buckets or at least weekly buckets on SKU-customer (ship-to)-plant level. You would need to assess if information can be provided on that level and even more important if quality and completeness of it are acceptable. In operational planning time/product/ commercial granularity may vary, all depended on business drivers. In product-driven organization, we have seen this process working for specific range of the products (brand) on regional base. In market-driven organization, it was working on country/sales zone level. Mixed granularity model happens very often. There is no golden here, no template! But there are characteristics of your business which you need to understand and evaluate before you take design decisions.

Operational planning requires a lot of high granularity data like:

- Tactical S&OP—integrated business plan in volume and value but disaggregated to daily, weekly buckets.
- Tactical S&OP—consensus unconstrained market forecast in volume and value but disaggregated to daily, weekly buckets.
- Sensed demand—forecast generated based on demand sensing algorithms.
- Sales orders—sales order grouped per processing advancement (e.g., new, confirmed, picked, shipped, delivered, invoiced) in volume and value.
- Sales inquiries—if available sales inquiries are normally included.
- Sales quotas—representing most profitable allocation plan in volume and value (normally not on customer but rather customer group/sales zone level).
- Detail customer and product attributes, e.g., channel, customer type/group, sales zone, sales representative, brand, and SKU description.
- Supply information in volume and value, e.g.:
  - Stock on hand and stock in quality control
  - Supply orders , firmed and planned
  - Intercompany transfer orders
  - Supply location
  - Internal or external relevant manufacturing capacity/availability
- Customization requirement for late labeling and assembly of sets and kits.
- Default price information and price elasticity information.
- Cost and if available margin information but on high customer granularity level.
- Product and customer segmentation attributes.
- Credit availability information.
- Currency exchange rate, relevant in countries where non-base currency contracts exist.
- Service differentiation offering attributes if available (indicating surcharges, delivery service level, and parameters).
- Services requirements.

Normally only a portion of the above operational data is used at once. Which part is used depends mainly on order-to-cash process, your financial information.

**Role of Segmentation**

Operational planning needs an instrument to keep this process focused but aligned to impact which company wants to make, e.g., increase profit or revenue. Segmentation will help you to keep focus on right products/customers because of ABCD dimension and improve effectiveness of your decisions because of XYZ dimension.

There are few ways to approach this topic:

- Use product segmentation to keep focus on important products. Segmentation can be calculated either on market or above market level to reflect market or regional required focus. This segmentation is typically used in product-driven organizations.
- Use product segmentation adjusted (weighted) with customer data to keep balance between product and customer dimension of the business. The best use of it would be if it is calculated on market level. This segmentation is more used in market-driven organizations.
- Use separately calculated portfolio and customer segmentation. To leverage both segmentations efficiently, you may use only ABCD dimension of each of the segmentation. This segmentation could have a broader application where you do not have clear focus on product or market or model is substantially diversified.

Visualization of case 1 and 2 can be done on matrix you are already familiar with (see tactical S&OP product review chapter), and measures behind have to reflect the specific model you want to embed in process execution.

**Organization: Key Roles**

Organizationally local demand manager should take a lead in making operational planning happen. Why demand manager? This role should take care of alignment between tactical and operational planning. Role of demand manager is not easy in this process, since with help of product/brand marketing should balance short term with mid-term objectives. Sales representatives and sales leads will push for revenue, logistics will push for fixed plans, and production will push for fixed production plans. You need to have the right mix of functions to get the best out of operational planning:

- Sales leads/managers (optionally sales representative)
- Customer service
- Logistics and operations
- Supply (own and external)
- Pricing/finance expert
- Demand manager
- Demand planner or analysts
- Product manager/brand manager

Demand manager should take a lead to organize right information and people and ensure decisions are taken. Key representatives are from sales, marketing, and finance. They need to make a most profitable decision, customer service, and logistics to execute them. Demand manager should be a guard which protects optimal cost to serve or profitable decisions. Demand manager should get help from marketing to balance between very short term oriented or "who shouts the loudest" driven decision vs. alignment to tactical or even strategic positioning of the portfolio or customers. Do not be surprised that sales will drive it toward their biggest gaps to sales targets or most opportunistic businesses; that is how it works normally, but demand manager should ensure the right presence of marketing and finance to balance it, to make right trade-offs.

Decision taken in that meeting will affect performance against the targets of the salesforce in the field. They are the ones meeting the customers; therefore whatever decision will be taken in regard to volume, sales team should be informed "who gets what." Demand planners/analyst should ensure the right information is provided.

**Process Fundamentals**

How does operational planning look from process perspective? There are two key considerations to make operational planning executed:

- Right data (detail and overview)
- Right people to make decisions directly on the meeting

We would recommend to have a simple three-step process:

- **Meeting preparation**: demand planners or business analysts would need to prepare data and visualizations of data and organize required inputs from customer service, logistics, finance, marketing, and demand management.
- **Meet and agree decisions**: on the meeting, demand manager should take a facilitator role and co-lead with marketing. Depending on company focus, demand manager should ensure appropriate focus of decisions. Outputs should be recorded in agreed constrained operational planning plan.
- **Communication and follow-up**: demand planner or business analyst should communicate decisions, record decisions in the system, and record actions to follow up.

This process has few key objectives like:

- To whom to give products in case of shortages.
- Review and align logistics and operations plans.
- Make the most profitable decisions or ensure highest availability.
- Balance short-term objective with midterm plans.

Agenda could consider the following points:

- Review of KPI.
- Review of demand pipeline, their status, and probability.

- Review of variances between senses demand, tactical S&OP integrated business plan, and captured demand (sales orders).
- Review available supply and operations constraints.
- Review price and margin tactics.
- Agree to whom to give products in case shortages exist.
- Agree actions to pull supply or inventory in case peek of demand is realistic to materialize.

You may consider the following KPIs:

- Sensed demand forecast error
- Agreed operational planning plan error
- OTIF (on time in full) or OOS (out of stock)

Since process will be executed with high granularity, therefore KPIs should consider that complexity.

You should agree how frequently to measure it in case you would have daily operational planning; my only hint is measure the process outputs but do not overdo it. In case you're running operational planning with weekly drumbeat, it will be most probably feasible to prepare KPIs on the same frequency.

Additional complexity comes if you sell products in sets and kits. Demand for sellable item (which should be forecasted, ordered, sensed) needs to be propagated with use of sales bill of materials (or similar feature) before detailed assessment of availability can be performed. Complexity comes rather from reversing availability of components to complete unit of kit and set.

**Operational, Tactical Planning, and Execution Process Integration**

Tactical S&OP process has optimized forecasts and plans. You've tested the sales projections and found where your shop floor, subcontractors, and vendors will need to change their plans. Costs were tallied. Inventory optimized. And profit approximated. Fantastic.

Now what? You don't care so much about what is supposed to happen, but you are focused on what needs to happen. Tactical and operational plans need to be realized. Forecasts are great—but now we know that we have a capacity constraint next week which was not expected and that key raw material for the most important new product we sell is going to be 6 days late. Those challenges will be addressed in operational planning connected to tactical S&OP (see Fig. 6.3).

This is the purview of tactical and operational planning.

Tactical planning seeks to answer questions like:

- How feasible will the S&OP plan be considering supplier commitments and internal constraints?
- What is the allocation policy I can feasibly put in place to restrict customers to expected (or unexpected) ordering patterns?

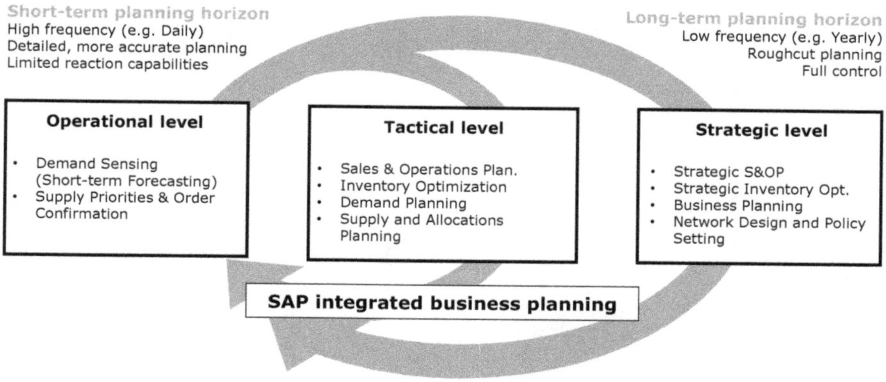


**Fig. 6.3** Integration of operational, tactical, and strategic planning underpinned with SAP IBP

Operational planning seeks to answer questions like:

- Which orders can we fulfill, considering constraints across the supply chain network and bills of material?
- What-if: What is the impact of a new, large order to the mix?
- How can I imprint the plan with my business priorities?
- How closely does the forecast correspond to actual ordering patterns, and what can I do to resolve differences?

For any planning process to be executed successfully, a tight integration with the execution is very much essential. This also allows to analyze the adherence of the plan to execution. There are both inbound and outbound interfaces between execution systems and the SAP IBP. In SAP IBP, the most common integration for the system of record is SAP ECC or S/4 HANA. Figure 6.4 shows the inbound and outbound interfaces to ECC or S/4 for one variant of planning configuration in time series-based planning without the response planning.

From ECC most of the master data flows to the operational and tactical processes. In addition, some of the common data streams for *inbound* from ECC or S/4 to IBP include:

- Sales history for the weekly demand planning process for statistical forecasting
- Open orders for the daily demand sensing process
- On-hand inventory, capacities, consumptions, and other relevant supply master data for tactical S&OP planning
- Firm plan from execution aggregated to time series for the production, distribution, and procurement during the frozen horizon for supply planning

*Outbound* interfaces from the tactical and operational processes from IBP to ECC include the following:

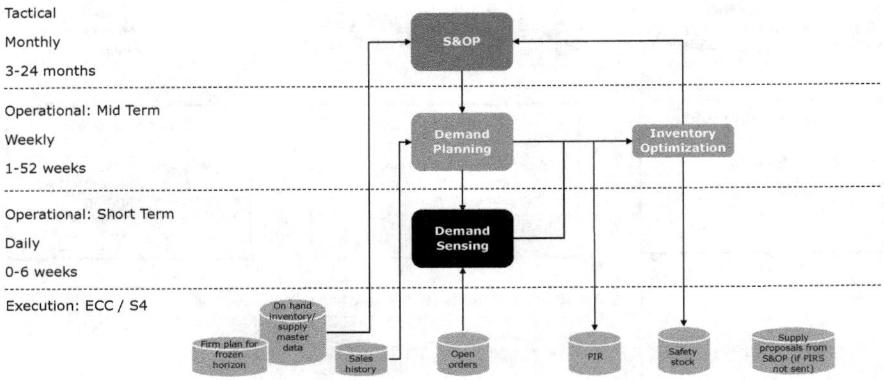


**Fig. 6.4** Technical integration between planning types and execution (time series)

- Safety stock recommendations from inventory optimization.
- Planned independent requirements in ECC from operational/time series-based demand planning and demand sensing plans. Then MRP run in ECC would create the supply plan.
- If the supply plans are sent to ECC, then in such a variant, the PIRs are not sent, but, rather, the time series-based supply proposals are sent to ECC, for example, the distribution plan and the plant level MRP is run in ECC.

In another process variant for response and supply planning, the integration with ECC is based on static model or order data store which allows for tight and near-real-time integration with ECC (see Fig. 6.5).

In such a setup, the inbound data relevant for the processes comes from ECC for the sales orders, supply master data, and other supply elements like production orders, stock transfers, on-hand inventory, etc.

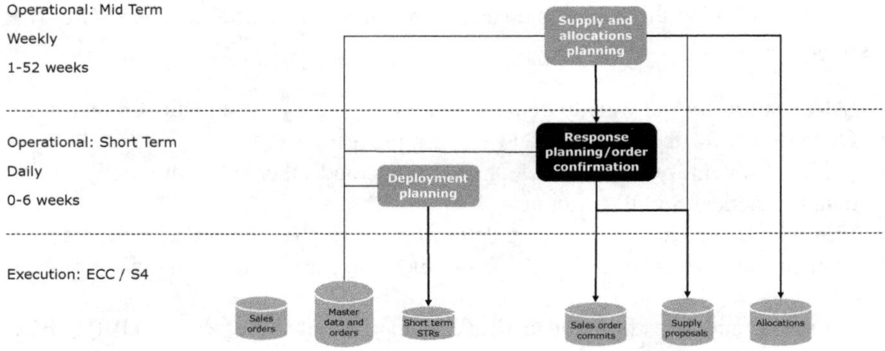


**Fig. 6.5** Technical integration between planning types and execution (order based)

- The operational supply planning (order based) for supply and allocations planning generates supply orders (production, procurement, distribution) as well as allocations to feed to available-to-promise in ERP system.
- Response planning (order based) generates supply orders and sales order confirmation to be sent to SAP ECC-S/4.
- The distribution (deployment) planning re-plans the distribution and creates short-term stock transfer requisitions and sales order confirmations.

### 6.1.1 Demand Sensing and Demand Shaping Interaction

Demand sensing may be understood as process which optimizes forecasting and demand planning but in short-term horizon. This technique can optimize your short-term part of demand plan for many products. You should not expect it will do a magic job for all products though, e.g., for products with intermittent demand patterns.

Demand sensing which runs on pattern recognition algorithms would require substantial amount of data to run optimization. You may start with demand sensing based on your historical and open orders and inquiries and move once tested toward how to leverage PoS data. Historical and open orders though should reflect customer requirement parameters and not your confirmations and constraints.

Demand sensing is about understanding tremendous impact; it can generate on micro- and macro-business drivers of your company. Demand shaping can be seen as technique to become proactive in the market based on insights from the demand sensing (Tohamy et al. 2010).

There are conventional and unconventional levers available to assist with demand sensing; the future demand sensing paradigm requires, e.g., retailers to create demand models not only inclusive of past behaviors but also with the ability to predict future behaviors (Griswold 2012).

When demand sensing works and when does not bring huge benefits:

- In cases in which demand is highly intermittent or window of sales is very short, you may be faced with the challenge that this type of optimization techniques will not bring too much.
- On the other hand, it could bring substantial benefits if you have continuous sales data information.
- It may not bring substantial benefits if your demand planning process produces highly accurate monthly forecast.

Let us position demand sensing as optimization technique which aims to adjust your consensus forecast in the next 4–8 weeks, in order to optimize your ability to respond, affecting:

- Short-term forecast error
- Logistics and distribution and transportation
- Late customization in short term
- Finished product production in short term (Fig. 6.6)

You should ask yourself, what if there are limitations in your supply chain which at the end will block deployment of optimization of the forecast in your supply chain?

Some reasons why optimization may not affect supply chain:

- You may have time fences in the supply chain which cannot be reduced like transportation lead times.
- You may not have ability to change sequence of late customization if at all available.
- You may not have a possibility to produce final product rapidly.
- You may not have enough flexibility in your supply chain network to deploy changes in demand between plants and distribution centers.

Why do we highlight this to you is simply because of, "do not spend efforts and money in demand sensing optimization if you cannot realize it through improved short-term response" (Fig. 6.7).

It has been proven that there is a positive correlation between demand sensing and shaping and forecast accuracy, yet it requires solid demand planning process (Steutermann, Scott and Tohamy 2012). So it is rather about removing obstacles and barriers to enable innovative thinking and leadership to utilize those techniques.

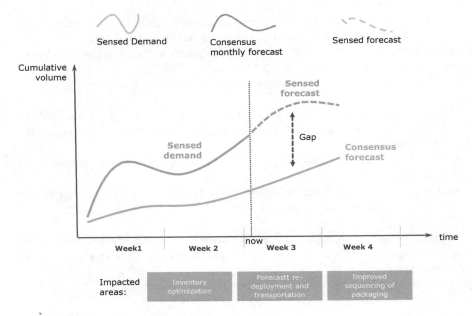

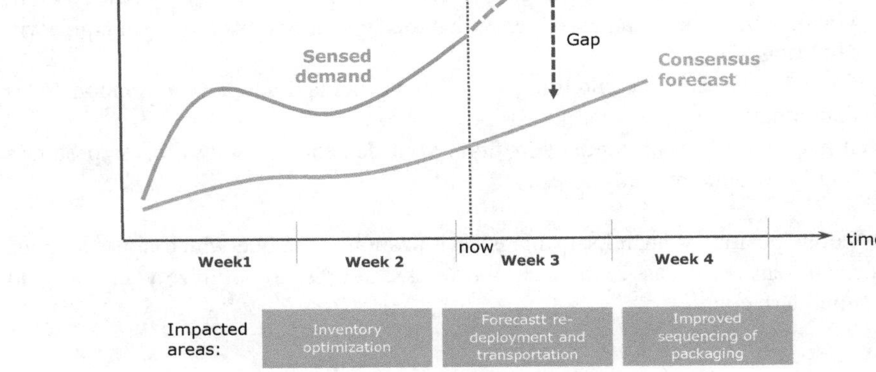


**Fig. 6.6** Demand sensing and impacted process areas

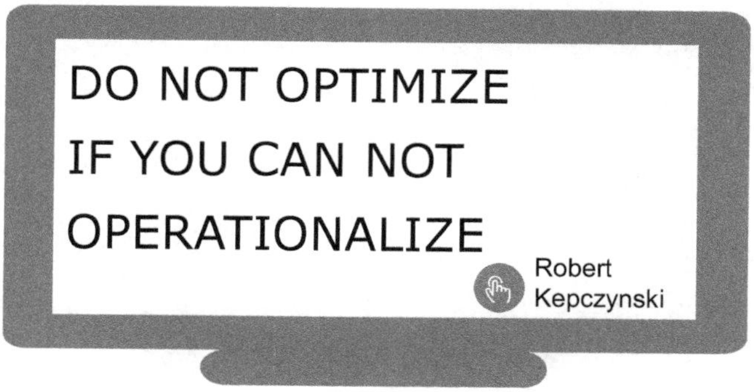
DO NOT OPTIMIZE
IF YOU CAN NOT
OPERATIONALIZE
Robert
Kepczynski

**Fig. 6.7** Do not optimize if you cannot operationalize

Leading practices say that you may need to invest in maturing your S&OP into IBP and in opportunity to leverage demand sensing and shaping (Steutermann 2012). The prevalent answer is to invest in demand sensing technology, especially downstream data acquisition to improve forecast accuracy (Steutermann 2016a).

Let us assume your supply chain can consume benefits of improved short-term sensed forecast. Sensed forecast might serve as indicator or trigger for corrective actions, redeployment of your plans to achieve better responsiveness resulting in maximization of business return.

Demand sensing would facilitate and improve realization of operational planning requirements like high responsiveness, high pace, high granularity, frequent changes, and various delivery models.

Demand sensing and shaping capabilities can improve key metrics like inventory optimization, obsolescence cost, forecast accuracy, and/or service levels. Companies should assess their current master data management (MDM) capabilities as a basis for enhanced decision-making and investigate innovative systems as complementary add-ons to your established ERP and supply chain management (SCM) platform, where intelligent and analytical applications can better assist in identifying demand patterns (Titze and Krasojevic 2012).

Demand planning and demand sensing are directly connected to demand volatility. According to the survey, demand volatility enters top three pain points of companies and influences the forecast accuracy, which is definitely an issue of traditional supply chain design based on order and shipment data. Traditional supply chain was developed to respond but not to sense. Thus it is extremely important to develop adaptable systems capable of sensing and responding to demand volatility, leading to reduction of both bias and error. Consider that you cannot build perfect forecast on imperfect data; therefore focus on understanding demand patterns and demand probability. Start planning from channel and not what you can manufacture (Cecere 2013).

In one of the examples which fit the purpose of operational planning, we were talking about company which had limited warehouse space in their service centers/ shops located in big cities, and their demand at the beginning of the campaign changed a lot (see Fig. 6.8). If you imagine that this company planned marketing campaign of existing product with enough of historical highly granular information,

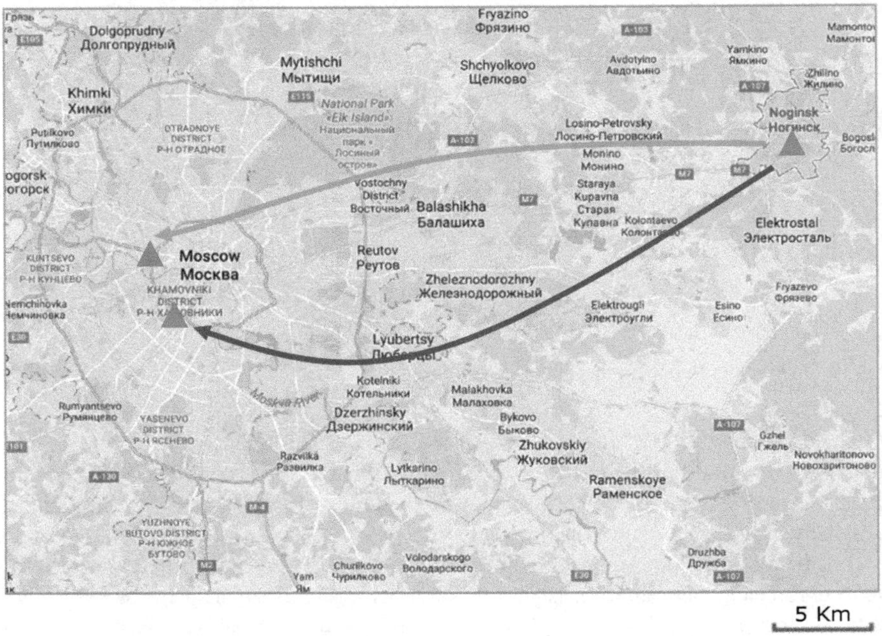


**Fig. 6.8** Frequent replenishment from distribution center to shops, based on demand sensing

then they would be able to replenish their service centers/shops more frequently and more accurately. This would bring increase of revenue and reduction of out of stocks. In this particular example, key enabler would be technology and appropriate transportation mode for replenishment in the big city limits. Possibility to use improved short-term sensed forecast in replenishment process (even twice a day!). Forecasting and supply planning cycle in this case increase dramatically but can bring substantial benefits. Not all of the activities would need to be done with intervention of people; there could be a way to leverage process automation to identify sensed forecast and deploy change easier and faster into operations running from dawn. There is nothing better than the customer who can buy products you promote and he/she wants and nothing worse than the customer who is "upset" when promoted product is not available. This type of pressure is easily transferred into the organization and may cause very costly fire drills.

Example describes shops/service center in downtown of Moscow and distribution center in cite neighborhood.

Demand insights bring advancements, and developing and leveraging demand insights increase the pace of innovation to support growth and responsiveness, the design of supply networks, and the delivery of segmented service strategies (Salley et al. 2016).

Another example of the application of demand sensing could be about figuring out when peak season starts exactly or when peak season starts to decline. Demand sensing algorithm will inform you based on the input data how a particular month will end up. Order intake, PoS data, and sensed forecast projections will give you insights to take decision required to optimize your business return and achieve your plans and targets with short-term focus.

**Demand Shaping/Selling Availability**

Operational planning more than other types of planning does expose an interaction between demand sensing and demand shaping. Those interactions may be exposed differently depending on seasonality of the products. In short horizon and given availability parameters, it is import to collaborate on specific points and interact with customer in increased pace and intensity.

Demand shaping is important and may be understood as the process of modifying the elements that influence demand volume and its related profits and revenues. This process is based on both internal cross-functional integration such as aligning on NPD, pricing policies, advertising, and so on and on external factors such as competitor's activities, economic factors, etc.; demand shaping is becoming an important step of the S&OP process (Chase 2009).

We have observed many times in peak season that availability of the product differed in terms of:

- Quantity—then you would need to figure out if you can sell different products and same product but different pack sizes.
- Timing—then you should explore if you can still sell it at all or at least sell it later with reduced quantity.

Those are attributes of demand shaping related to time and product.

**Demand Sensing Might Help to Identify Risk or Opportunities and Demand Shaping Turns This into Action**

What it means selling availability? We have learned that you can utilize available materials, manpower, and machines. In short-term oriented process, your ability to turn sensed forecast to impact on materials, manpower, or machines is much more limited normally.

You product design, manufacturing, or 4PL capabilities may open doors for late customization of your product, e.g., late labeling. If generic product is delivered to a regional distribution center, you may be able to label it with country, country/brand, or country-/customer-specific label. Signal to label may come based on the orders against supply point in which you will do late customization. In this case instead of costly management of variation of demand on final labeled product, you manage available resources to respond to demand signal and provide late labeling. This example was about static set on how to manage uncertainty and sell available resources.

Selling availability may be as well linked to production processes if manufacturing allows that. Selling of availability works for products where reaction time in manufacturing was counted in days and due to that forecasting and planning cycle were mutually reduced and brought undisputable benefits on utilization of production assets and product availability.

Both example scenario link demand sensing with demand shaping.

Demand management can impact your performance. Demand management involves more than forecasting and planning. Companies with mature demand management practices also incorporate demand sensing, shaping, and fulfilment into their set of capabilities. Demand volatility and lack of demand visibility remain two of the top challenges (Salley et al. 2016).

Connecting demand sensing and shaping is the right direction and leading practice.

We should understand demand management as process based on a mirrored history, but the one it requires demand shaping and demand sensing. Effectiveness of both techniques relies on a maturity of your S&OP. To achieve the best results, demand shaping and demand sensing must be combined together to understand future patterns, to gain insights and visibility, and to improve cross-functional planning and execution. It is worth to mention that demand sensing and shaping differ hugely from sector to sector, and their approach can be strategic, midterm, or operational. The key element of success of demand sensing and shaping is largely based on degree of synchronization between the commercial and supply, since translation of demand insights can enable reactive, agile, and profitable supply responses (Tohamy 2012).

### 6.1.2 Demand Sensing Improves Way to Cope with Demand Trends

Let's start with a general definition of demand sensing provided by Gartner (Steutermann): it is defined as the "translation of demand information with minimal latency to detect who is buying the product, what attributes are selling and what impact demand shaping programs are having." The operative phrase is "minimal latency." If we are able to use the power of analytics to interpret demand signals with minimal latency and turn them into insights, for instance, in the form of more accurate short-term forecasts, we are then able to drive better decisions. The key is leveraging multiple streams of data that help predict future demands at speed and at scale. Clearly, the traditional principle of management by exception alone won't do. IBP's demand sensing algorithms provide the necessary tool support that allows interpretation of demand signals at speed and at scale. The illustration in Fig. 6.9 provides a conceptual illustration of the key principles at work. There are various inputs such as historical orders, historical consensus forecast (also known as consensus revisions—more on this later), and future orders that are captured at multiple lags, meaning at different points in time prior to the actual business event (say, customer order shipment) occurring, which are systematically processed by the demand sensing algorithm to provide a "sensed demand" that encapsulates the insights of the various input streams (Fig. 6.9). With this, one is able to transition from a descriptive/diagnostic (a la alerts) approach that tends to be reactive in nature to a prescriptive/predictive one that is proactive. Of course, real benefits will depend on a supply chain's ability to operationalize the insights gained.

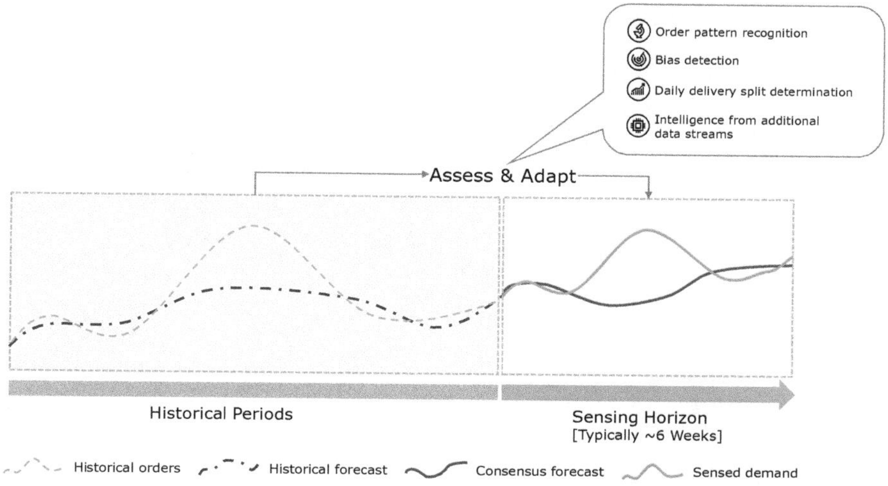


**Fig. 6.9** SAP IBP principles of demand sensing algorithm

**Variability Dampening**

In proliferation of SKUs, deep supply chain networks necessitated by customer proximity are key contributing factors to variability amplification as one gets closer to the customer: from a product structure standpoint, this could mean variability increase as one moves from raw materials to finished products. The increase is particularly pronounced in the case of divergent product flows (a lot more finished SKUs than input materials). From a distribution network perspective, this could mean as moves from suppliers to retainers. From a time granularity perspective, this could be as one switches from months to days. This variability amplification is further exacerbated by the infamous bullwhip effect. This is illustrated in Fig. 6.10.

Demand sensing implies increasing the pulse—that is, systematically reacting to events influencing demand with minimal latency. This approach of using analytical support to process demand signals—both historical and forward looking—to make predictions in the near term leads to lowering of uncertainty "felt" by the supply chain. The dampening effect of increasing the number of demand observations on uncertainty (or variability) can be proved quantitatively (see technical note below).

It can be proved that (Simchi 1999):

$$\text{Variance of orders placed by the retailer at the manufacturer} \,/\, \text{Variance of demand as seen by the retailer} \geq 1 + \frac{2L}{p} + \frac{2L^3}{p^3}$$

where $L$ = lead time and $p$ = number of demand observations.

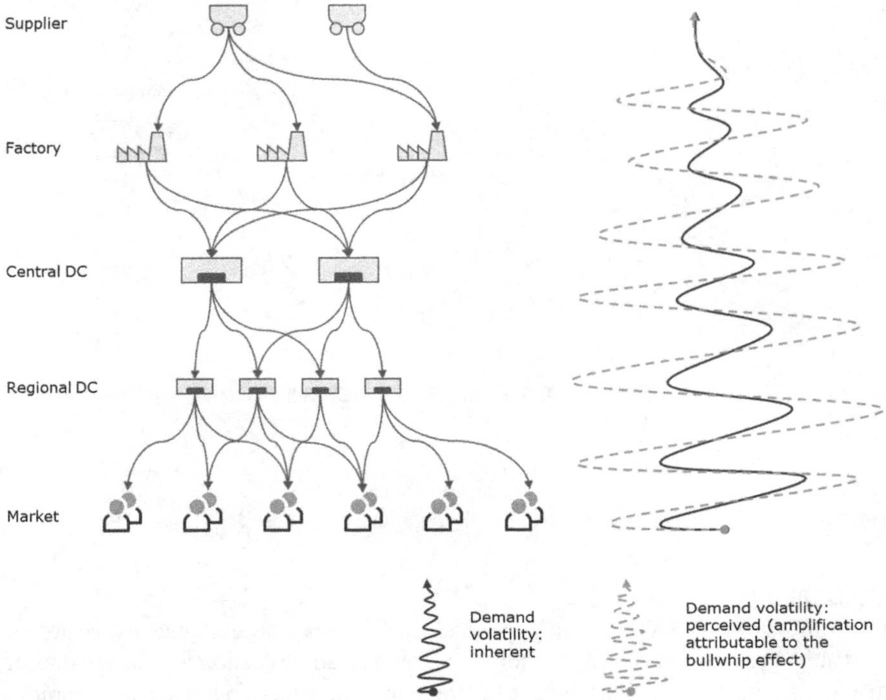


**Fig. 6.10** Variability amplification as one moves closer to customer

## Becoming Demand Driven

Demand-driven principles have been gaining traction with agility becoming more and more important to building "respond" capabilities. One of the core principles of demand driven is enshrined in the phrase "position and pull instead of push and promote" (Debra Smith 2016). This means positioning the decoupling point further downstream, which could potentially lead to grabbing more market share by becoming more attractive (response time-wise) versus competition. The idea is illustrated in Fig. 6.11.

## Working Capital Rationalization

There is also a clear correlation between forecast variability and inventory. The greater the variability, the higher is the required level of stocks to ensure a certain desired service level. As can be seen from Fig. 6.12, this relationship is nonlinear, and this represents a significant opportunity. Improvements in accuracy or reduction in variability can have a positive impact on working capital. One could either offer the same level of service at a reduced inventory or improve the service level keeping inventory investments the same.

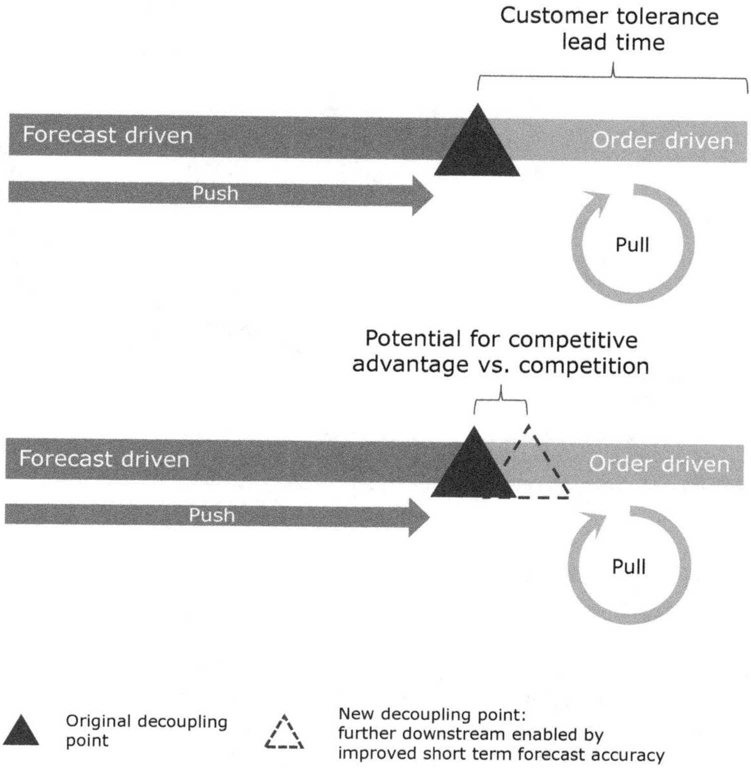


**Fig. 6.11** Near-term forecast accuracy and decoupling point repositioning

**Lead Time Compression**

Reduction of lead times is another area where demand sensing can bring in benefits. This is explained well using a hypothetical bill-of-material (BOM) that consists of parts that are all made-to-order (say, because of high demand variability like in the case of a highly customizable product). Demands for these parts cannot be reliably predicted at higher lags (for instance, 30 days or more). However, let's say, by increasing the cadence and leveraging analytical support, forecast variability could be reduced for some of these parts to a level that makes a switch from make-to-order to make-to-stock viable. If the materials are chosen well, that is if the switch to make-to-stock happens for materials on the critical path (the longest path if one would add up the lead times along this path), the overall lead time would be reduced, and the critical path will change to a new, shorter one. By choosing enough materials on either the original or subsequent critical pats, one could significantly compress the lead time to generate benefits.

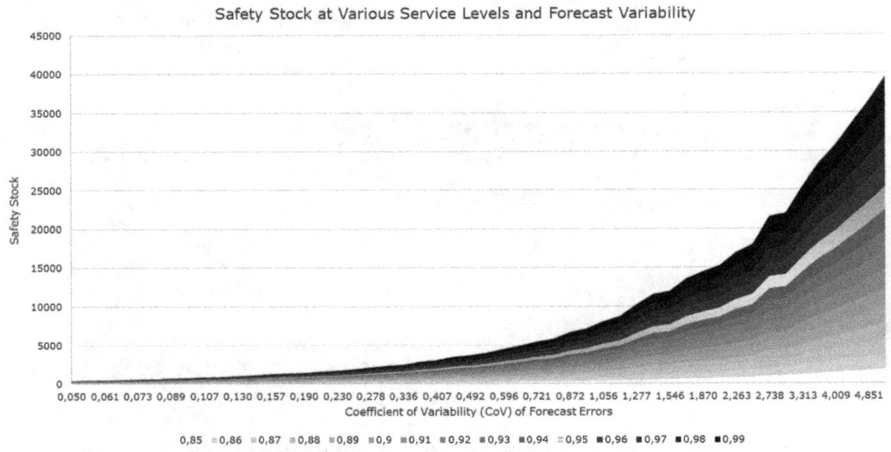


**Fig. 6.12** Forecast variability, customer service level, and safety inventory relationship

## 6.1.3 SAP Use Case: Optimized Short-Term Forecast with Sensed Demand

Although the algorithm itself is proprietary and details of the inner workings are not in the public domain, the main steps can be deduced based on experimental results. The process described below is based on numerous runs of the algorithm for a number of deliberately created datasets to examine its behavior.

The algorithm can be said to consist of four key steps.[1] This is depicted in Fig. 6.13.

We have been running various tests with our customers and wanted to share briefly with you an example of how forecast bias can influence sensed demand quantity. Below figure illustrates that for Distribution Center 1, bias is very low; therefore consensus demand plan and sensed demand are close to each other. Then for Distribution Center 2, gap between becomes bigger, and finally at Distribution Center 3, it is substantial due to growing forecast bias (Fig. 6.14).

**A Tool Du Jour**

We are witnessing major shifts in the way supply chain planning is being done—it has a lot to do with the quantum of data supply chains are having to process. To make sense of all the data, tools that provide strong analytical support are of paramount

[1]This excludes any preprocessing steps. For example, cleansing the consensus demand of promotions is a typical preprocessing step. The assumption made is that the consensus key figure input is one without promotions.

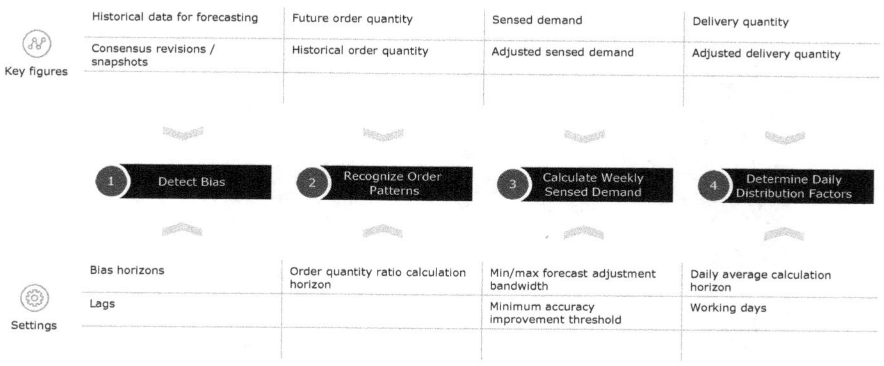


**Fig. 6.13** SAP IBP demand sensing algorithm

importance. In the context of operational or short-term forecasting, demand sensing is a great example of one such instrument that helps predict demands more accurately by processing demand signals at speed and scale with the help of various algorithms. In fact, algorithmic supply chain planning is one trend that is bound to take hold as businesses start to embrace digital more and more. In Payne (2016), the author argues that "competitive advantage will be determined by speed of understanding and adaptive response to environmental signals." Use of demand sensing for short-term forecasting is not just useful but essential for digital businesses to be able to adaptively respond to demand signals. We have talked about how traditional paradoxes are being overcome—particularly the one between cost efficiency and responsiveness. Companies in their efforts to transcend trade-offs and move from "either-or" to "both-and" will need to use any and all means to minimize latency. Demand sensing is in many ways a tool for the times.

That being said, demand sensing in no way diminishes the importance of medium-term forecasting executed as part of tactical S&OP. A good consensus forecast is a prerequisite for an effective demand sensing process. For instance, demand patterns such as seasonality and trend are not detected by sensing. It assumes that these are incorporated in the consensus forecast and relies on insights gained by processing short-term demand signals and analysis of historical forecast performance to adjust consensus forecast (and derive sensed demand).

Blending segmentation into the dynamic demand sensing process can help demand planners to allocate their focus where it matters the most. The faster deviations are identified, the faster the response will come: sensed demand quantity highlighting over performance in some location while in others underperformance—

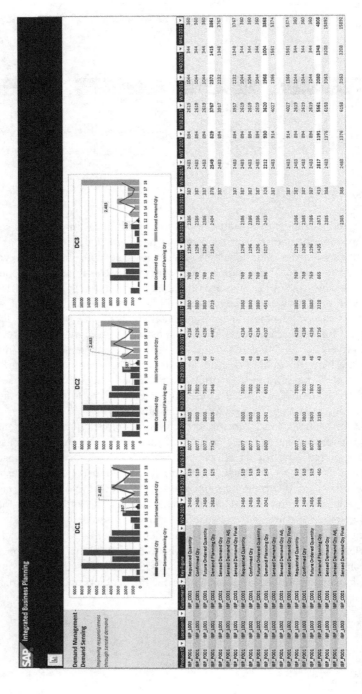

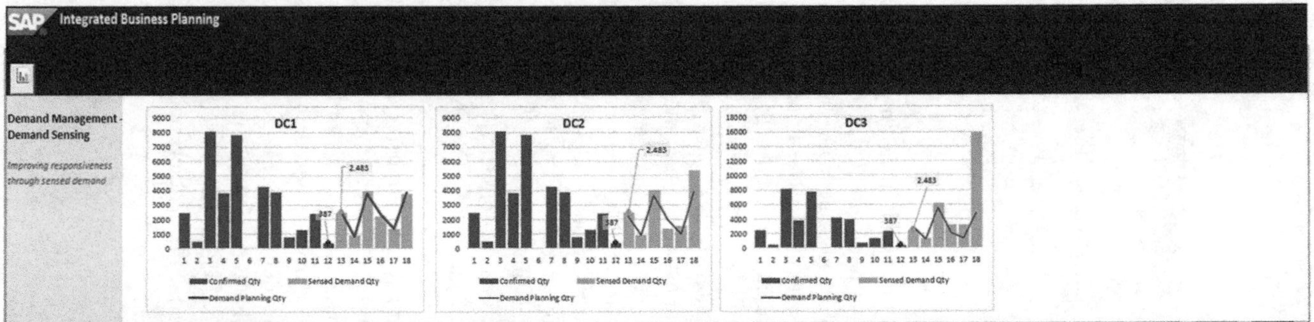


| Product ID | Location ID | Customer ID | Key Figure | W24 2017 | W25 2017 | W26 2017 | W27 2017 | W28 2017 | W29 2017 | W30 2017 | W31 2017 | W32 2017 |
|---|---|---|---|---|---|---|---|---|---|---|---|---|
| IBP_P001 | IBP_L001 | IBP_C001 | Requested Quantity | 2486 | 519 | 8077 | 3803 | 7802 | 48 | 4236 | 3880 | 769 |
| IBP_P001 | IBP_L001 | IBP_C001 | Confirmed Qty | 2486 | 519 | 8077 | 3803 | 7802 | 48 | 4236 | 3880 | 769 |
| IBP_P001 | IBP_L001 | IBP_C001 | Future Ordered Quantity | 2486 | 519 | 8077 | 3803 | 7802 | 48 | 4236 | 3880 | 769 |
| IBP_P001 | IBP_L001 | IBP_C001 | Demand Planning Qty | 2688 | 525 | 7742 | 3805 | 7846 | 47 | 4497 | 3729 | 779 |
| IBP_P001 | IBP_L001 | IBP_C001 | Sensed Demand Qty | | | | | | | | | |
| IBP_P001 | IBP_L001 | IBP_C001 | Sensed Demand Qty Adj. | | | | | | | | | |
| IBP_P001 | IBP_L001 | IBP_C001 | Sensed Demand Qty Final | | | | | | | | | |
| IBP_P001 | IBP_L002 | IBP_C001 | Requested Quantity | 2486 | 519 | 8077 | 3803 | 7802 | 48 | 4236 | 3880 | 769 |
| IBP_P001 | IBP_L002 | IBP_C001 | Confirmed Qty | 2486 | 519 | 8077 | 3803 | 7802 | 48 | 4236 | 3880 | 769 |
| IBP_P001 | IBP_L002 | IBP_C001 | Future Ordered Quantity | 2486 | 519 | 8077 | 3803 | 7802 | 48 | 4236 | 3880 | 769 |
| IBP_P001 | IBP_L002 | IBP_C001 | Demand Planning Qty | 2042 | 545 | 8600 | 3261 | 6932 | 51 | 4107 | 4541 | 896 |
| IBP_P001 | IBP_L002 | IBP_C001 | Sensed Demand Qty | | | | | | | | | |
| IBP_P001 | IBP_L002 | IBP_C001 | Sensed Demand Qty Adj. | | | | | | | | | |
| IBP_P001 | IBP_L002 | IBP_C001 | Sensed Demand Qty Final | | | | | | | | | |
| IBP_P001 | IBP_L003 | IBP_C001 | Requested Quantity | 2486 | 519 | 8077 | 3803 | 7802 | 48 | 4236 | 3880 | 769 |
| IBP_P001 | IBP_L003 | IBP_C001 | Confirmed Qty | 2486 | 519 | 8077 | 3803 | 7802 | 48 | 4236 | 3880 | 769 |
| IBP_P001 | IBP_L003 | IBP_C001 | Future Ordered Quantity | 2486 | 519 | 8077 | 3803 | 7802 | 48 | 4236 | 3880 | 769 |
| IBP_P001 | IBP_L003 | IBP_C001 | Demand Planning Qty | 2998 | 450 | 6806 | 3189 | 6657 | 43 | 3716 | 3228 | 865 |
| IBP_P001 | IBP_L003 | IBP_C001 | Sensed Demand Qty | | | | | | | | | |
| IBP_P001 | IBP_L003 | IBP_C001 | Sensed Demand Qty Adj. | | | | | | | | | |
| IBP_P001 | IBP_L003 | IBP_C001 | Sensed Demand Qty Final | | | | | | | | | |

| Product ID | Location ID | Customer ID | Key Figure | W33 2017 | W34 2017 | W35 2017 | W36 2017 | W37 2017 | W38 2017 | W39 2017 | W40 2017 | W41 2017 |
|---|---|---|---|---|---|---|---|---|---|---|---|---|
| IBP_P001 | IBP_L001 | IBP_C001 | Requested Quantity | 1296 | 2386 | 387 | 2483 | 894 | 2619 | 1044 | 344 | 360 |
| IBP_P001 | IBP_L001 | IBP_C001 | Confirmed Qty | 1296 | 2386 | 387 | 2483 | 894 | 2619 | 1044 | 344 | 360 |
| IBP_P001 | IBP_L001 | IBP_C001 | Future Ordered Quantity | 1296 | 2386 | 387 | 2483 | 894 | 2619 | 1044 | 344 | 360 |
| IBP_P001 | IBP_L001 | IBP_C001 | Demand Planning Qty | 1341 | 2404 | 378 | 2549 | 829 | 3767 | 2372 | 1415 | 3861 |
| IBP_P001 | IBP_L001 | IBP_C001 | Sensed Demand Qty | | | 387 | 2483 | 894 | 3917 | 2232 | 1348 | 3767 |
| IBP_P001 | IBP_L001 | IBP_C001 | Sensed Demand Qty Adj. | | | | | | | | | |
| IBP_P001 | IBP_L001 | IBP_C001 | Sensed Demand Qty Final | | | 387 | 2483 | 894 | 3917 | 2232 | 1348 | 3767 |
| IBP_P001 | IBP_L002 | IBP_C001 | Requested Quantity | 1296 | 2386 | 387 | 2483 | 894 | 2619 | 1044 | 344 | 360 |
| IBP_P001 | IBP_L002 | IBP_C001 | Confirmed Qty | 1296 | 2386 | 387 | 2483 | 894 | 2619 | 1044 | 344 | 360 |
| IBP_P001 | IBP_L002 | IBP_C001 | Future Ordered Quantity | 1296 | 2386 | 387 | 2483 | 894 | 2619 | 1044 | 344 | 360 |
| IBP_P001 | IBP_L002 | IBP_C001 | Demand Planning Qty | 1037 | 2413 | 328 | 2212 | 930 | 3620 | 1968 | 1004 | 3868 |
| IBP_P001 | IBP_L002 | IBP_C001 | Sensed Demand Qty | | | 387 | 2483 | 914 | 4027 | 1366 | 1561 | 5374 |
| IBP_P001 | IBP_L002 | IBP_C001 | Sensed Demand Qty Adj. | | | | | | | | | |
| IBP_P001 | IBP_L002 | IBP_C001 | Sensed Demand Qty Final | | | 387 | 2483 | 914 | 4027 | 1366 | 1561 | 5374 |
| IBP_P001 | IBP_L003 | IBP_C001 | Requested Quantity | 1296 | 2386 | 387 | 2483 | 894 | 2619 | 1044 | 344 | 360 |
| IBP_P001 | IBP_L003 | IBP_C001 | Confirmed Qty | 1296 | 2386 | 387 | 2483 | 894 | 2619 | 1044 | 344 | 360 |
| IBP_P001 | IBP_L003 | IBP_C001 | Future Ordered Quantity | 1296 | 2386 | 387 | 2483 | 894 | 2619 | 1044 | 344 | 360 |
| IBP_P001 | IBP_L003 | IBP_C001 | Demand Planning Qty | 1435 | 2871 | 413 | 2817 | 1191 | 5561 | 2080 | 1348 | 4808 |
| IBP_P001 | IBP_L003 | IBP_C001 | Sensed Demand Qty | | 2385 | 388 | 2483 | 1376 | 6158 | 3163 | 3208 | 15892 |
| IBP_P001 | IBP_L003 | IBP_C001 | Sensed Demand Qty Adj. | | | | | | | | | |
| IBP_P001 | IBP_L003 | IBP_C001 | Sensed Demand Qty Final | | 2385 | 388 | 2483 | 1376 | 6158 | 3163 | 3208 | 15892 |

**Fig. 6.14** SAP IBP—sensed demand impacted by distribution center forecast bias

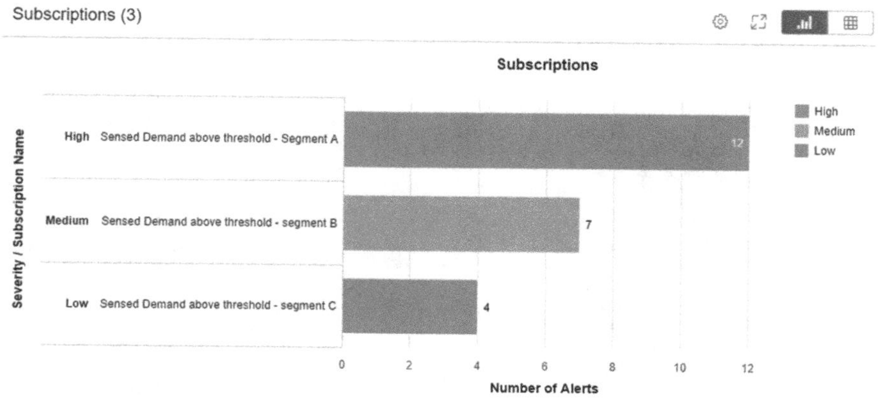


**Fig. 6.15** ABC differentiated alerts for demand sensing

supporting available inventory deployments decisions. In Fig. 6.15 alerts are segmented, enabling differentiated and focus responsiveness.

**Importance of Turning Insights into Action**
The true power of demand sensing cannot be realized unless insights gained cannot be operationalized. Therefore, agile execution processes are important to turn insights into profitable response. In some cases, even if lead times are too long to adapt to demand shifts predicted by demand sensing, early detection of potential issues can itself provide benefits. For example, being able to predict potential shortage might provide an opportunity to explore alternative scenarios, one of which could be switching to a supplier closer to home with a shorter lead time.

You will find far more about short-term forecasting and demand sensing in our next IBP book.

### 6.1.4 SAP Use Case: Demand Signal Integration (SAP IBP-SAP DSiM)

For companies acting in industries like fast-moving consumer goods, high tech, and many others, collecting and analyzing massive volumes of data including real-time demand signals allow them to stay informed and proactively react to market events as they happen which is a critical factor to drive sales performance.

Figure 6.16 shows a representation of a supply chain network which goes beyond the manufacturer's supply chain, including data across customers' stocking points and their supply chain consumption. This allows companies to adopt a demand-

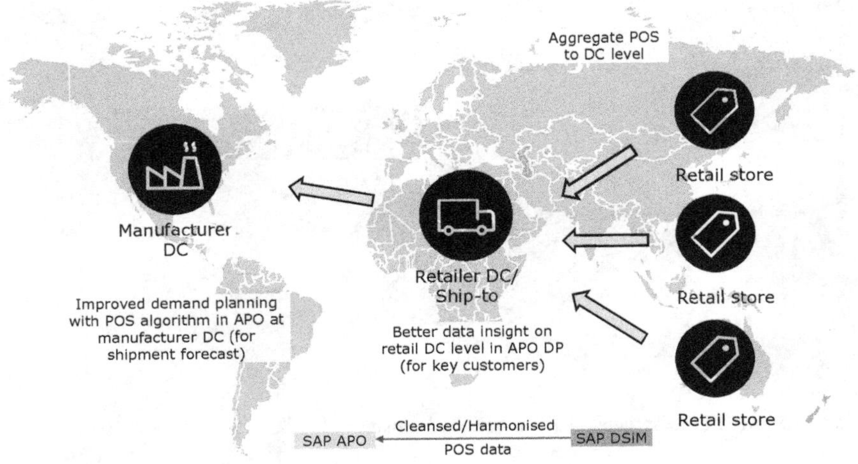


**Fig. 6.16** SAP IBP and SAP DSiM integration of PoS data

driven supply chain by generating their sales forecast on almost near-time information based on market realities.

But until recently, in traditional environments manufacturing companies did not have the right technology to allow retailers to send demand signals, making it nearly impossible for them to respond promptly to various events like stock-out, failed product launches, promotions that don't reach the expected success, etc.

SAP Demand Signal Management (DSiM) serves as a central repository for storing, processing, and harmonization of demand data coming from disparate external sources like points of sales and market research, namely, retail panel or social media data. With an intuitive user interface, which includes pre-delivered analytics and reports, companies are able to analyze and process data almost in real time leading to:

- A deeper understanding of consuming patterns in different markets having a harmonized global view of demand data across the organization
- Forecast accuracy improvement
- Proactive identification of possible stock-outs and replenishment of inventory to avoid lost sales
- Promotions effectiveness monitoring

Moving beyond the borders of SAP DSiM and connecting to IBP, data can be further transformed into actionable insights for the demand planning process. To facilitate the integration, SAP delivers two prepacked interfaces with SAP Cloud Platform Integration for data services:

- IBP_KF_POSSales to extract point of sales and load them in IBP demand planning area: retail store sales quantity, store promotional quantity, and withdrawals from retailers' distribution centers
- IBP_KF_POSStock to extract stock data: retailer store stock and retailer distribution center stock

More integration content can be developed during project implementations in order to incorporate other measures that can be received from the DSiM system like PoS promotional sales, PoS net value, lost sales, etc.

The main use case of integrating recent and current demand signals data to IBP is for improving the accuracy of the short-term forecasting and improving visibility over near-future changes. Points of sales are usually integrated into daily or weekly buckets, at the level of distribution center from where retailers demand is being fulfilled. As not all markets have the capability to provide POS information, for a complete view, POS data is complemented by marketing research that comes in two forms: custom and syndicated.

This information can be leveraged by demand sensing that will compute a sensed demand plan influenced by consumption patterns identified in downstream demand data based on which deployment and inventory planning should be adapted.

A precisely sensed forecast for the immediate future horizon can help to identify and react to fluctuations from the consensus forecast:

- In case of increased demand in one region and short inventory availability in the distribution center that serves this particular region, stock transfer decisions can be made to avoid out-of-stock situations.
- Adapt the packaging or production sequence in case this is needed to support high increases in demand for specific products.

Moving from short- to the midterm horizon, the points-of-sales and market research data can be further used to drive true demand as part of the S&OP process. Usually, the creation of the mid-long-term demand plan starts from the generation of the statistical forecast which runs based on historical data that comprises shipments to the retailer or distributors' centers.

The introduction of several signal influences to be analyzed by multiple linear regression (MLR) algorithms can help in improving the statistical forecast. For example, out of stocks might be correlated with a decline in the forecast, while promotion uplifts with an increase. Depending on the industry, further predictive data like historical weather and predictive temperature and precipitation can be added and analyzed altogether (see Fig. 6.17).

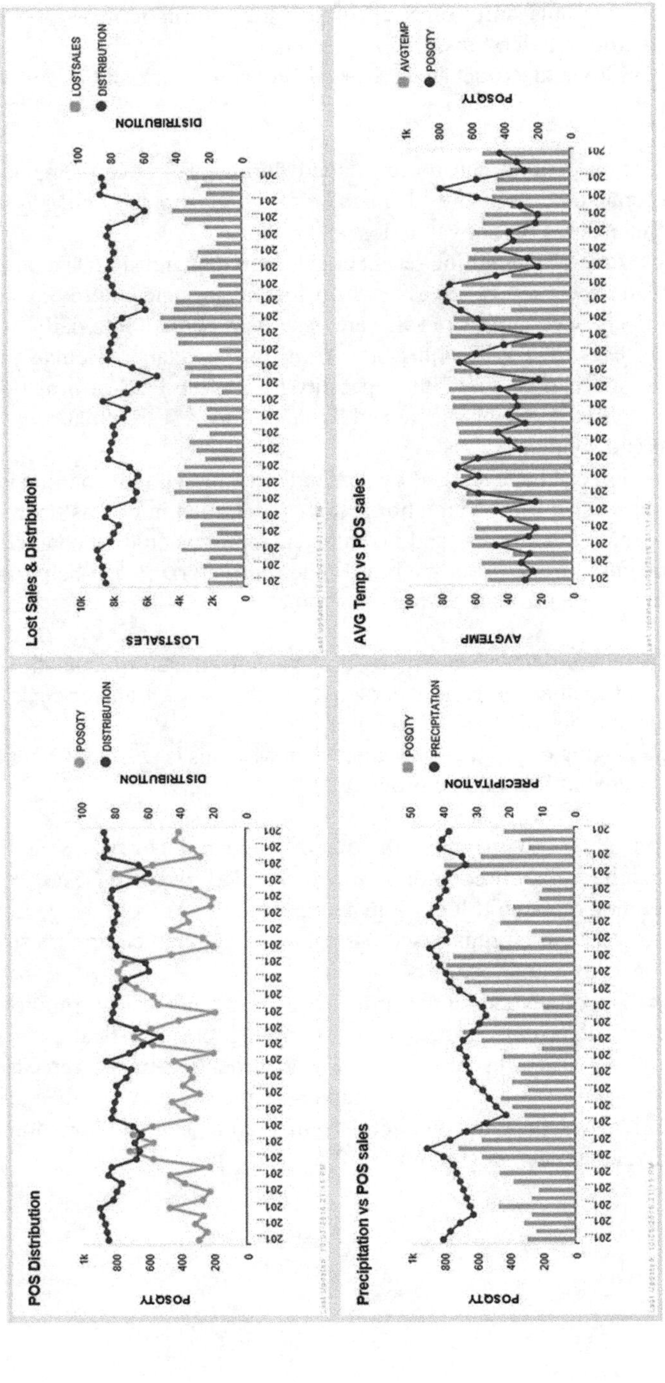


**Fig. 6.17** Point-of-sales data integrated via DSiM

### 6.1.5 High-Tech Industry Order-Based Planning

Point-of-sales data and demand sensing are important ways to understand the volatility of demand. To respond to this, and to set policies on what to do when this volatility occurs, IBP enables response scenarios in order-based planning.

This raises the question: what, exactly, is order-based planning in IBP, and what can it do? Probably the easiest way to answer this is to start with an example.

Response planning is best illustrated in discrete manufacturing scenarios. Because High-Tech Original Equipment Manufacturers (OEMs) have a need to orchestrate a supply chain both in-house and via subcontractors and vendors, work with long lead times for key components (like processors), and have a notoriously difficult time forecasting, this will be the focus of our initial description.

High-Tech OEMs tend to follow a monthly S&OP process, focusing on similar concepts to those shown in Fig. 6.18. They will have a forecast, which is typically afflicted with many new product introductions and short life spans. They will have pass-through forecasts from key customers and input on demand from many sources. They need to constrain based on supplier and subcontractor capacity and consider inventory targets (often determined through mathematical optimization). And, of course, they need to project costs and consider liability clauses of contracts with their subcontractors.

The output of this S&OP plan is a consensus forecast and an idea of what supply requirements are likely to be over the long term. Some of these companies may also pass a component or finished good forecast to their suppliers or CMs (contract manufacturers) within the process and receive back a commit from those business partners.

This isn't the end of the story. Certainly, the planners could stop at this point and allow a simple planning engine like material requirements planning (MRP) to turn this forecast into purchase requisitions, stock transfers, and internal planned production orders. But there is an important piece missing: uncertainty and constraints.

High-Tech OEMs expect the received sales orders to differ widely from the forecast (it's not easy to forecast the next big consumer electronics good—who knows which device will be popular or whether the new version of a product can expect the same reception as the old?). They expect shortages of important materials and need to hold the vendor orders as steady as possible due to the lead times involved.

We enter into response planning. High-Tech OEMs can utilize order-based planning in IBP in two primary ways: product allocations and order confirmations. As shown in Fig. 6.18, these two processes fit between S&OP and execution (tactical and operational planning from our first description at the outset of the chapter).

Utilizing order-based planning in IBP, the product allocations planning run can convert the S&OP forecast into a constrained forecast, allocations policy, and a feasible supply plan simultaneously. Constraints such as the supplier commits, production capacity, and material availability can all be considered. The system enables prioritization against dimensions of the demand such as materials,

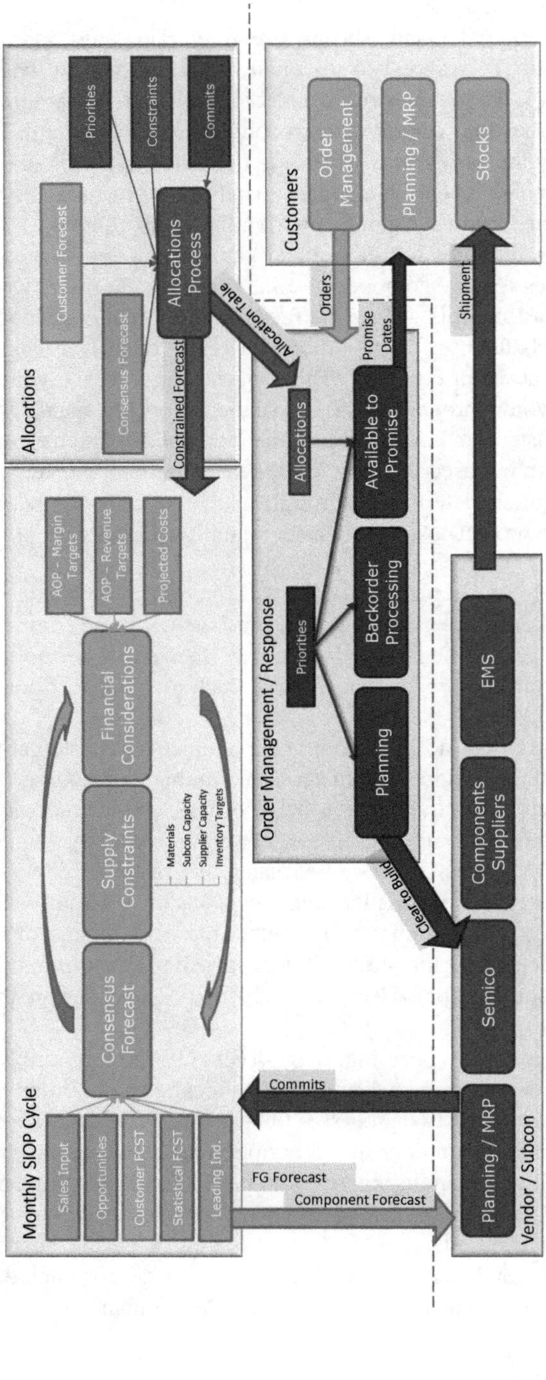


**Fig. 6.18** End-to-end planning including order promising in high-tech industry

customers, and locations to sort out the constraints and holds portions of the demand as highly important and others in less important.

As is clear in the diagram, product allocations are really only a first step. These can constrain the eventual sales orders at point of order, and this would represent an enforcement of the plan made so far.

An even more powerful way to utilize order-based planning in IBP is to support backorder processing. This is shown on Fig. 6.18 in the green boxes. As orders come in, the High-Tech OEM could choose to sequester these orders into groups and then plan the groups periodically considering constraints and priorities. Now, the output purchase requisitions, transfers, and planned production will correspond precisely with the new, feasible order confirmations. In this way, order-based planning supports a multilevel, multi-constraint-based simultaneous backorder processing and planning run. Product allocations and order confirmations can also be combined, as we will discuss.

### 6.1.6 SAP Use Case: Order-Based Demand Analysis

As described in most of the text up to this point, each demand and supply quantity is typically planned in a period—daily, weekly, monthly, quarterly, or other buckets. For processes like Sales and Operations Planning or Inventory Optimization, this is ideal—this limits the amount of data involved in planning and enables quick review, aggregation, and disaggregation across long horizons. It focuses on calculations between rows of data. With operational planning, a more granular approach is needed.

Order-based planning in IBP provides this granularity. Sales orders can be planned as individual orders. Procurement plans are modeled as purchase requisitions, planned production is planned orders, and distribution plans are stock transfer requisitions. This level of planning enables priority considerations and pegging while considering constraints. It also provides order-level modeling which can more easily and precisely be integrated to and from ERP systems.

Most users of IBP find the Excel user interface one of the most attractive aspects of the system. This gives users the ability to interact with plans via the familiar environment of MS Excel. Order-based planning takes full advantage of this feature as well (see Fig. 6.19).

Here, you can see an output of a plan—72 units are due to arrive based on planned distribution receipts in the next few days. And again a few days later, 100 more are planned to arrive. This kind of data is something that an S&OP planner might see but on a longer horizon. However, an account planner/customer service or someone responsible for key customers and for coordinating with planners to fulfil those plans would also certainly notice that there are some sales orders here in the requested row that are not fulfilled right away. The 72 units are coming late. This is an operational planning problem which we will illustrate how to address with use cases.

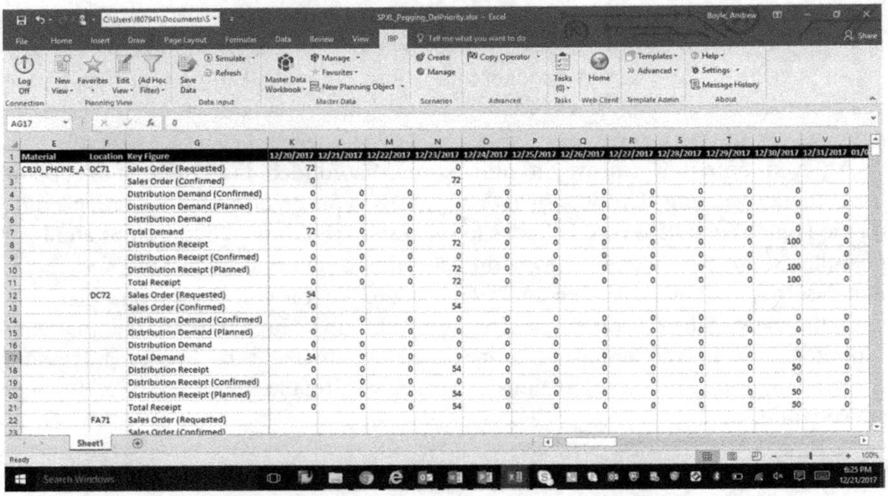

**Fig. 6.19** Simplified order-based data in SAP IBP Excel UI

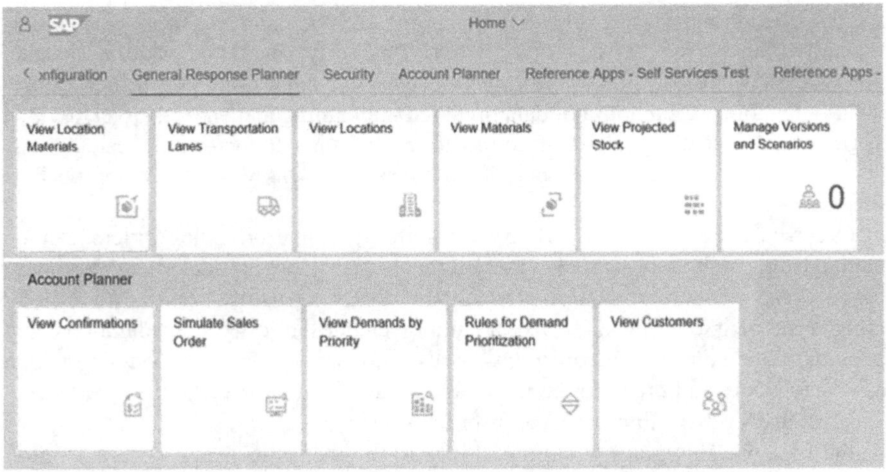


**Fig. 6.20** Fiori apps for customer service/account planner

For more information, the customer service/account planner could use the apps. There are a number of dedicated Fiori Apps designed to promote easy analysis of the order-level plan (see Fig. 6.20).

We will highlight now key apps and their role in solving challenge of those 72 late units. To do so, the account planner reviews the overall demand and supply situation in the View Projected Stock app (Fig. 6.21).

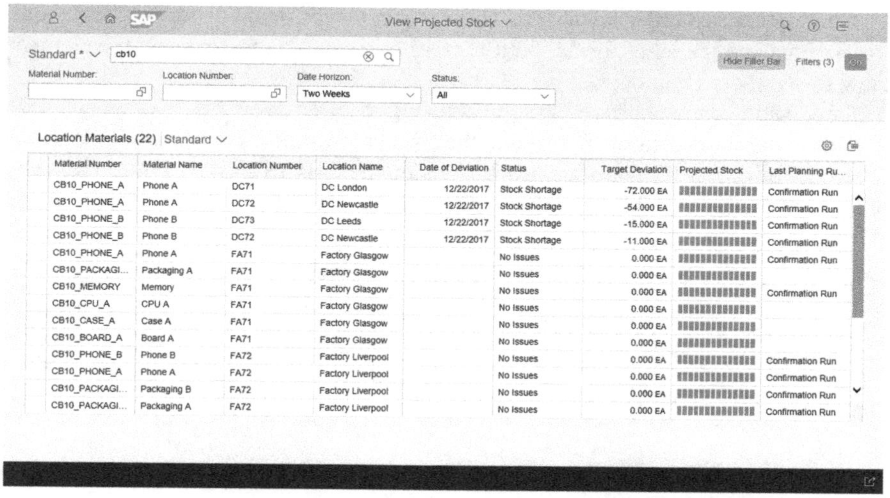


**Fig. 6.21** Projected stock app at summary level

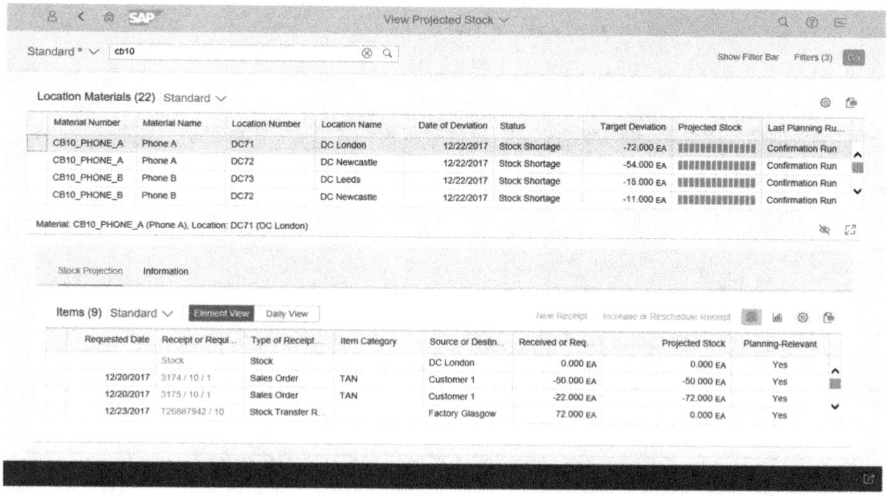


**Fig. 6.22** Projected stock view, detail drill-down to order-level data

Here, we can search for materials that are relevant for our account planner and quickly see where to focus attention—notice the projected stock column with red buckets showing deficits, one of which matches to our 72 units for the phone product in the London location. To drill into more depth, the account planner selects that row and is able to analyze details for marked record on the upper part of the screen (see Fig. 6.22).

Now we can see order-level data. Those 72 units represent late sales orders—one for 50 units and the other for 22, both for Customer 1. We can focus on the element view to see more (Fig. 6.23).

Same view can be analyzed graphically (Fig. 6.24).

This is the same dataset analyzed in the Excel view—just an order-by-order level of detail. In our case, there are stock transfer requests (STRs) to cover the sales orders and additional STRs to cover future requirements. Now, the account planner/

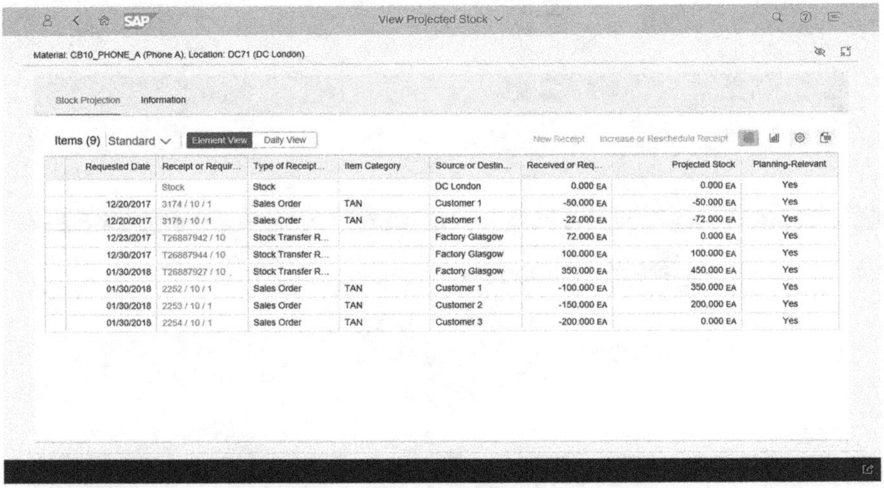


| Requested Date | Receipt or Requir... | Type of Receipt... | Item Category | Source or Destin... | Received or Req... | Projected Stock | Planning-Relevant |
|---|---|---|---|---|---|---|---|
| | Stock | Stock | | DC London | 0.000 EA | 0.000 EA | Yes |
| 12/20/2017 | 3174 / 10 / 1 | Sales Order | TAN | Customer 1 | -50.000 EA | -50.000 EA | Yes |
| 12/20/2017 | 3176 / 10 / 1 | Sales Order | TAN | Customer 1 | -22.000 EA | -72.000 EA | Yes |
| 12/23/2017 | T26887942 / 10 | Stock Transfer R... | | Factory Glasgow | 72.000 EA | 0.000 EA | Yes |
| 12/30/2017 | T26887944 / 10 | Stock Transfer R... | | Factory Glasgow | 100.000 EA | 100.000 EA | Yes |
| 01/30/2018 | T26887927 / 10 | Stock Transfer R... | | Factory Glasgow | 350.000 EA | 450.000 EA | Yes |
| 01/30/2018 | 2252 / 10 / 1 | Sales Order | TAN | Customer 1 | -100.000 EA | 350.000 EA | Yes |
| 01/30/2018 | 2253 / 10 / 1 | Sales Order | TAN | Customer 2 | -150.000 EA | 200.000 EA | Yes |
| 01/30/2018 | 2254 / 10 / 1 | Sales Order | TAN | Customer 3 | -200.000 EA | 0.000 EA | Yes |

**Fig. 6.23** Projected stock view, element view

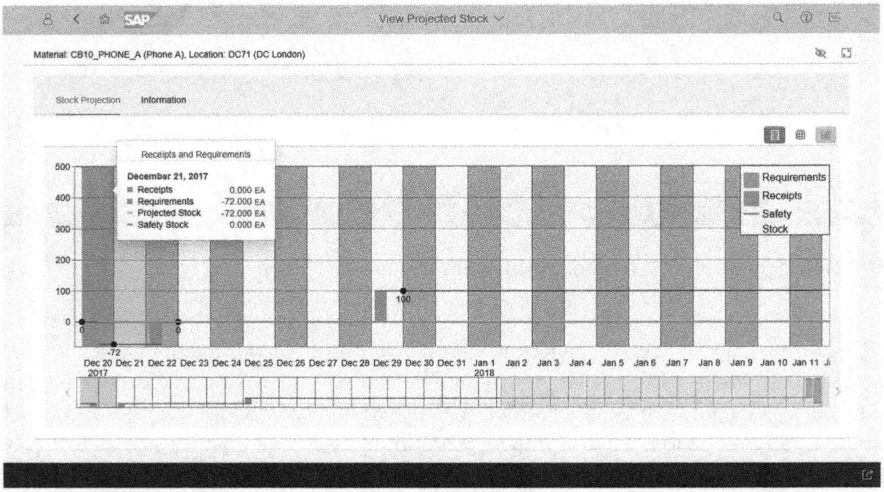


**Fig. 6.24** Projected stock view in graphical form

customer service wants to better understand why the sales orders are expected to be delivered late to the customer. The account planner chooses one of the orders and drills into the details (see Fig. 6.25).

And even further on confirmation lines (see Fig. 6.26).

Here the account planner/customer service sees that there are other competing demands and that we will be able to deliver the 50 quantity, but 3 days late. To understand why, the planner drills into the gating factor analysis (see Fig. 6.27).

And here the account planner/customer service now understands why this order is late. There was insufficient lead time to deliver the stock to this location in time to ship to the customer. Ideally the stock transfer should arrive on the 20th, but it can only arrive on the 23rd. There could be ways to remediate the situation. Perhaps there is stock already pegged to other orders, like those shown in the competing demands section. Maybe a different set of priorities would help us reallocate our available inventory more effectively. If we do re-prioritize, then what would the impact be to orders we would have otherwise confirmed on time? These are the kinds of inquiries order-based planning is in a unique position to help evaluate and solve.

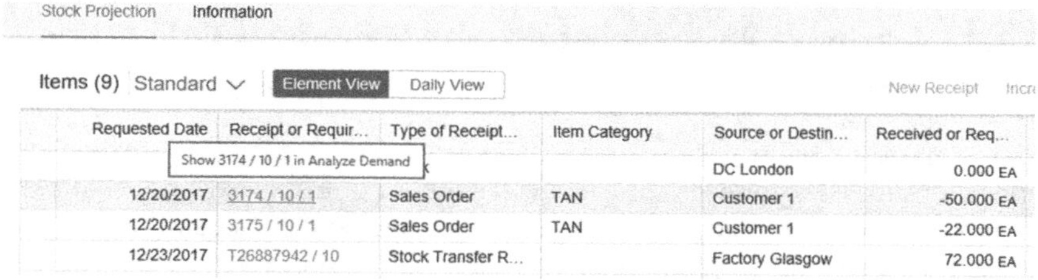


**Fig. 6.25** Sales order details 3174

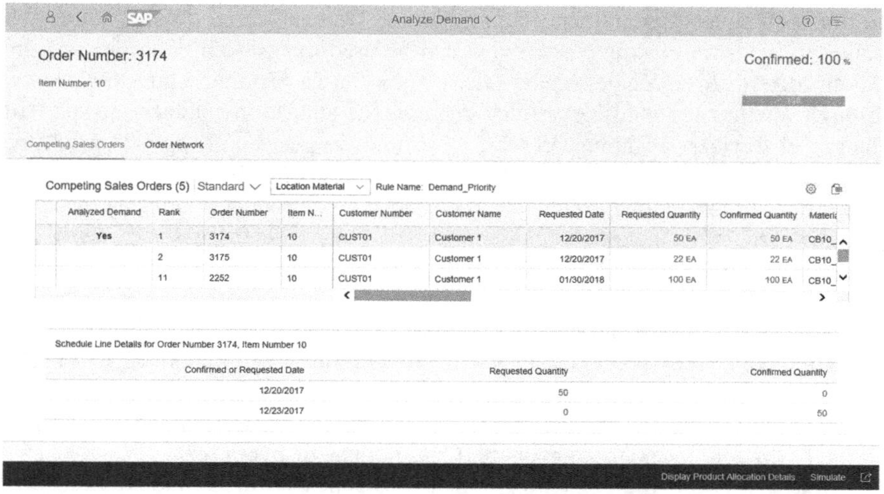


**Fig. 6.26** Sales order 3174 confirmation lines and its deviations

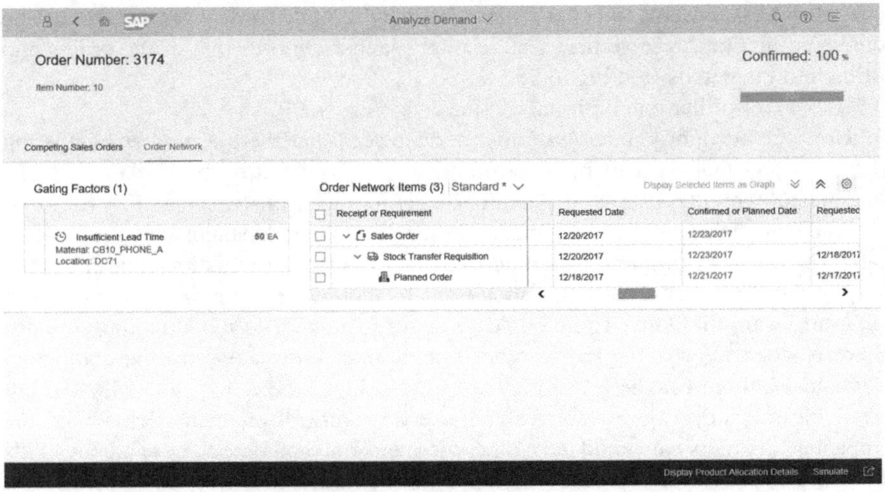


**Fig. 6.27** Sales order 3174 gating factors analysis

## 6.1.7 Maximize Business Return with Order-Based Allocation Planning

In the introduction, we spent some time reviewing concept of creating product allocations for a High-Tech OEM. We will continue with that example in this section.

In order to ensure that product is assembled and sold considering organizational constraints priorities, a High-Tech OEM will determine what customers can buy which product and in what quantity, typically before a sales order is ever received.

As we see on Fig. 6.28 inputs to allocation process are demands, customer, product, organizational priorities, inventory and capacity availability, and supplier and subcontractor commitments/confirmations. Outputs are a product allocation policy in the form of a time series that can be used to constrain later orders from the customers. In a certain extent, it can help you to maximize business returns through alignment to business rules captured in allocation policies. As part of Integrated Business Planning process, you should expect that supply plan will be adapted to support this allocation plan. It can be then submitted to ERP for execution. Many organizations prefer to create and renew product allocations on a set periodic basis, often monthly or as frequently as weekly. As discussed earlier it may be aligned to trigger which drives operational planning, e.g., marketing campaign target for Christmas season. You may use the following process steps to make sure you are able to monitor and improve your responsiveness (see Fig. 6.29).

Here there are key process steps which we will illustrate with use of SAP IBP:

- **Propagate.** Take the finished goods forecast and propagate this demand through the BOM and nodes of the network. Consider existing supply.
- **Collaborate.** Share the resulting component plan with the vendors and receive back a commit.

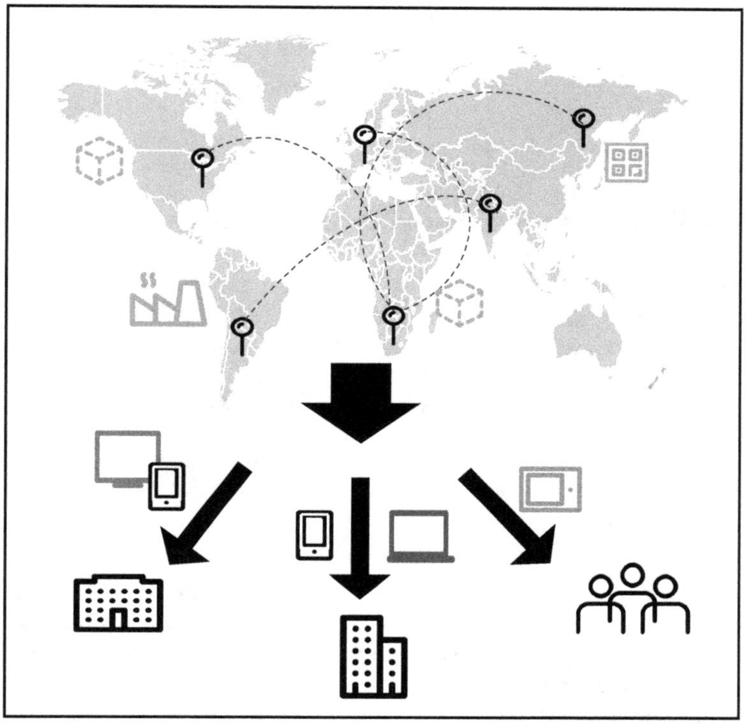

**Fig. 6.28** Product allocation inputs and outputs

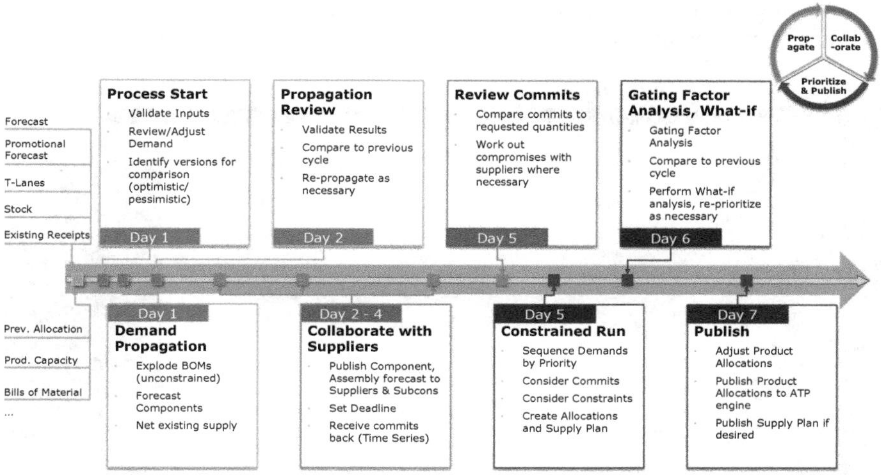


**Fig. 6.29** Weekly cycle for product allocation

- **Prioritize and publish.** Now that all constraints and commits and demands and supplies are included in the model, set company priorities, and run a constrained plan to create an allocation. Analyze the plan, modify as necessary, and publish to ERP (e.g., S/4).

### 6.1.8 SAP Use Case: Rule-Based Order Allocation and Re-planning

**Propagate Demand**

A planner starts the cycle reviewing demand (likely forecast). They may want to add last-minute changes, or represent different versions of a forecast, like optimistic and pessimistic, for the vendors to consider later on. An unconstrained run will then propagate demand through the network and down each level of the bills of material (BOMs). In IBP, the supply heuristic can perform this function. At this point the planner reviews the results and could compare to the previous cycle for obvious changes.

**Collaborate**

Now that the component demand is known, this can be shared with the suppliers. The goal here is to provide a forecast for the suppliers and understand better what those suppliers can commit to. This information is used later to ensure feasible allocations and supply plans.

In recent releases, SAP has enabled integration with collaboration tools in IBP control tower for this purpose. This allows collaboration via the Ariba Network Supply Chain Collaboration tools, for example. Once the forecast is published to the Ariba Network, the vendor can log on and view the data. Offline, the vendor will perform evaluations via their own supply chain planning systems and methods. They can then commit to the forecast (or versions of the forecast), as shown in Fig. 6.30.

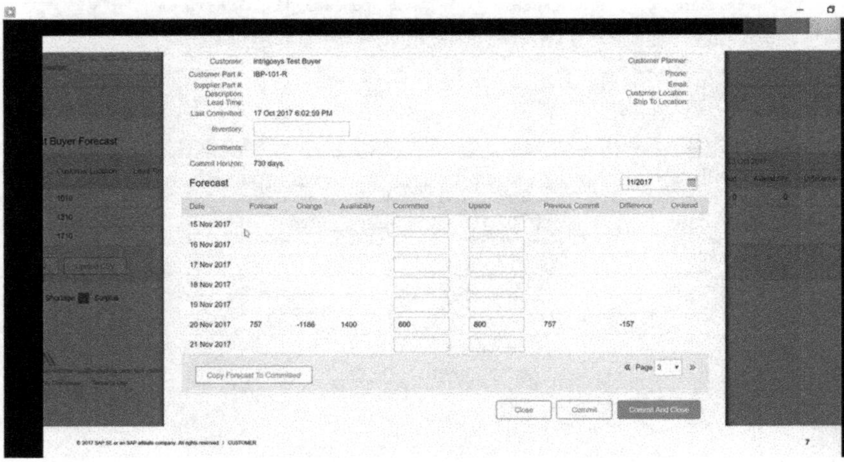


**Fig. 6.30** SAP Ariba supplier forecast confirmation

The forecast commit data will be integrated into IBP. Supplier provides confirmation lower than required quantity exposing gap which needs to be handled in short-term planning process.

**Prioritize and Plan**

Now that the supplier commits are in, we can get down to the business of determining our product allocations policy. We will run the plan, examine the results, and then publish those results. To run the plan, we first examine the organization's priorities.

To keep the example simple and easy to follow, we will focus on four finished goods (smartphones), all of which use similar components. One component in particular, the memory, is common to all of the finished goods. Finally, these products can be bought by two customers. The question to answer here is straightforward:

> Given the constraints on component availability and production constraints, which customers and products should be fulfilled and how will that drive our allocation for future sales orders?

**Demand Prioritization**

To answer this question, we will set up rules which the prioritization heuristic will follow. Each organization can create and support several sets of rules. These can be used under different circumstances or for different what-if analyses. Each rule is made up of segments, which in turn can query and sort demands. This system enables the creation of sophisticated sets of priorities.

As an example, let's say that your organization is looking to first fulfill VIP customer demands at its highest priority, then other customers. And within this approach, you want to also consider that certain products have a higher margin than others. As we've established, these products utilize some of the same key components or production resources. The rules will let the system know which demand to resolve first, second, third, and so on (see Fig. 6.31).

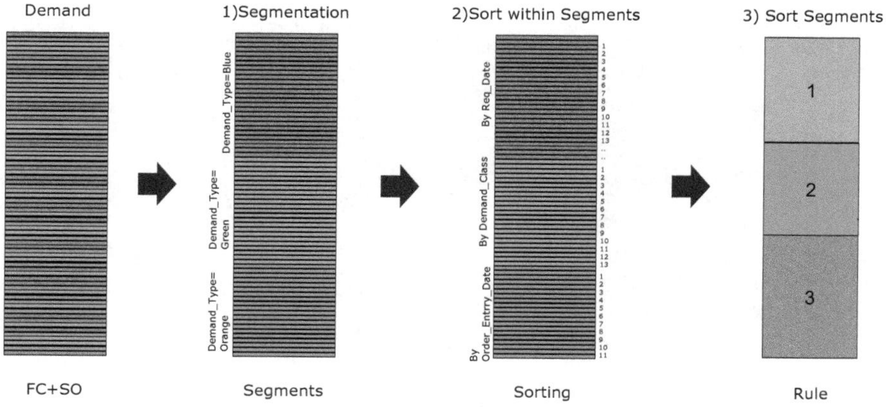


**Fig. 6.31** Demand prioritization rules and segments

Demand is initially a mix of forecasts and sales orders (at least for the confirmation run, discussed later in this chapter), and these have different attributes which might set them apart from one another. In the diagram this is shown by color, but these colors could easily represent other aspects of demand like customers, customer classifications, material groups, delivery priorities on sales orders, and other attributes. Segmentation groups a certain set of attributes together (let's say by customer classification). In that case all customers with classification "01" and "06" could be considered before all other customers.

Within the segment the demands that fit the segment criteria can be further sorted. In the diagram this is represented by sorting by requested date, demand class, and order entry date. These are typical choices.

The easiest way to understand this is with an example. Let's consider our original goal. We want to consider high-priority customers first and for those customers set a higher priority for products that are higher margin. First, we create a segment for the high-importance customers (see Fig. 6.32).

Here, we set a segment condition to query all customers called "CUST01." This is a simple example; this could easily be customer classification instead, or a super user could write a more complex statement looking for only a few customers for a few key materials, all written within the segment conditions. Within the segment, the demands can be further sorted. Here, we first sort by requested date ascending (translation, first demand date is considered first), and then where those dates are the same, we consider material number ascending within that sort.

Using this technique, the organization can specify the exact priority order of one material vs another (as ASP1_PHONE_A is a lower priority than ASX_PHONE_B, despite the alphabetical sequence of the material numbers). This is also maintained in the rules app.

Another segment defines the lower-priority customers (Fig. 6.33).

Again, here we note CUST02 as the lower priority, and within those customer demands, we sort by requested date and then by material number (with the special sequence). Finally we add segment for all the others (see Fig. 6.34).

These segments are arranged in a rule (Fig. 6.35).

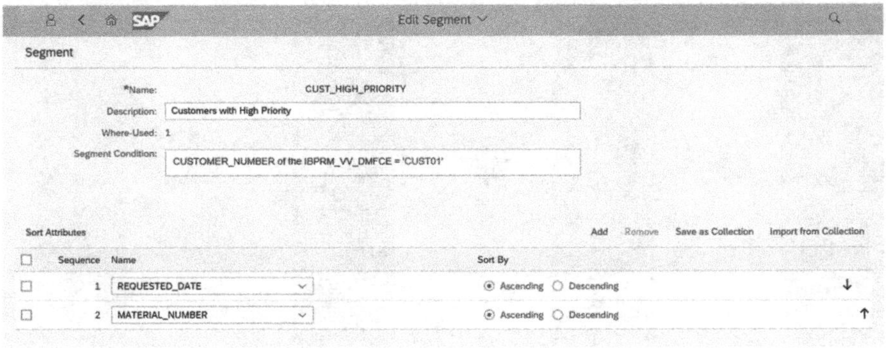


**Fig. 6.32** Segment for high-priority customers

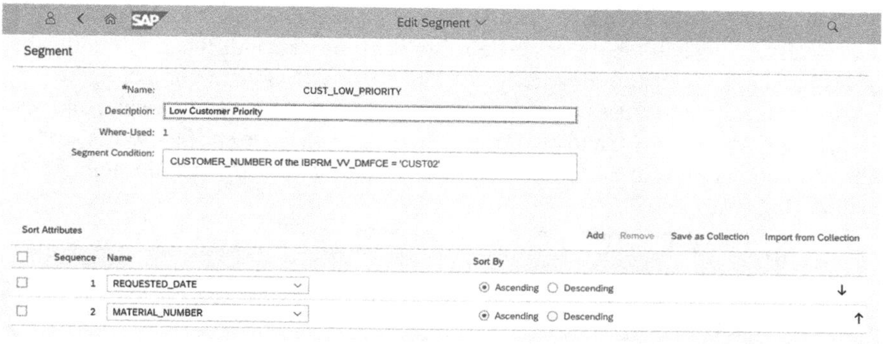


**Fig. 6.33** Lower-priority customers segment

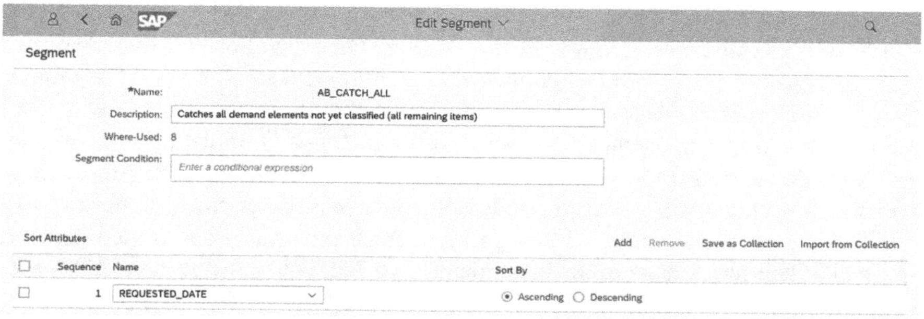


**Fig. 6.34** Other customers segment

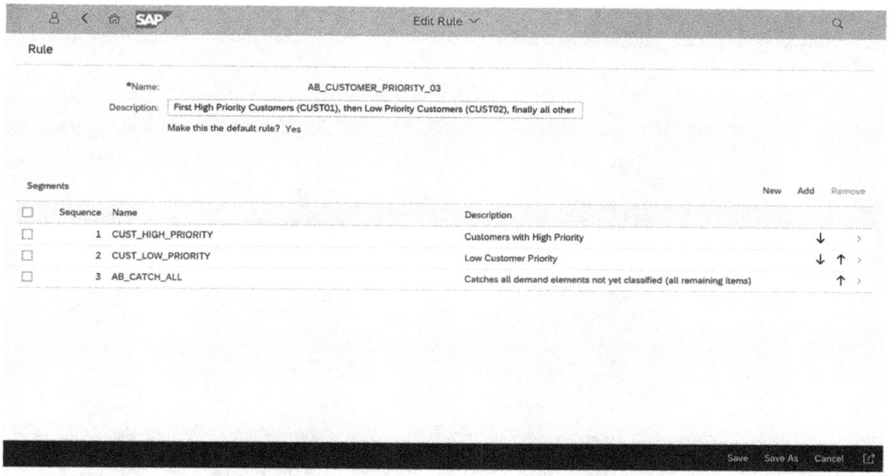


**Fig. 6.35** Rule for higher, lower, and remaining customer demands

This rule specifies the higher-priority customer segment first, then the lower, and then finally a "catchall" segment, designed to plan any demands that don't fit the first criteria (consider a customer other than CUST01 or CUST02 in our example).

An organization that uses order-based planning in IBP can set more than one rule. In fact, a library of rules can be set up ahead of time, and these can be used as needed. This is the function of the Rules for Demand Prioritization app seen throughout this section (Fig. 6.36).

So, our very simple priority rule boils down to:

- CUST01 first—sorted by requested date and then material (ASX1 models before ASP1 models)
- CUST02 second—also sorted by requested date and then material (ASX1 models before ASP1 models)
- Any other demands missed, sorted by requested date

We will use this rule throughout the chapter. Of course, the customer-priority example is just one way to set up demands. In addition to a single forecast key figure discussed below, order-based planning can consider *multiple* key figures (up to five) that represent different categories of demand streams. For example, one stream may represent demand from a previous planning run, while another represents new demand. In this case, the first previous demand would be set to a higher priority than the new demand—the goal being to guarantee previously committed demand first while then moving on to upside demand (see Fig. 6.37).

Another example could be representing forecasts by statistical and promotional forecast data in separate key figures and using those designations to set different priorities.

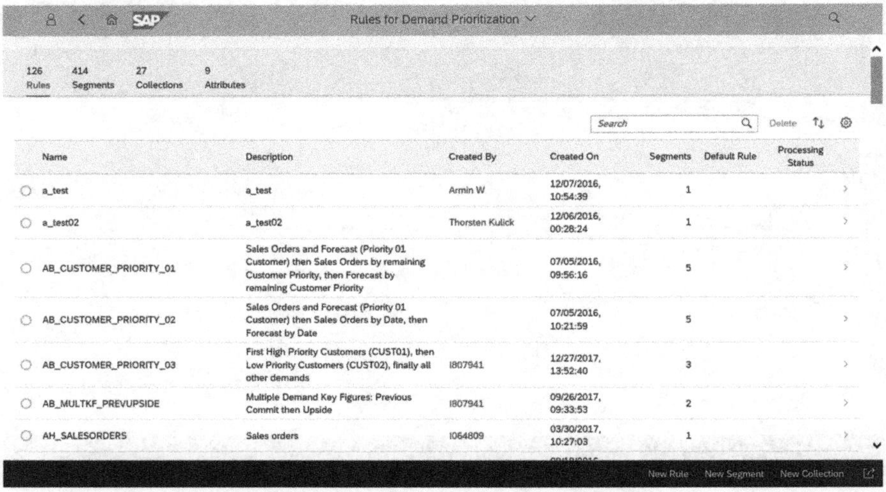


**Fig. 6.36** Rules library in Demand Prioritization app

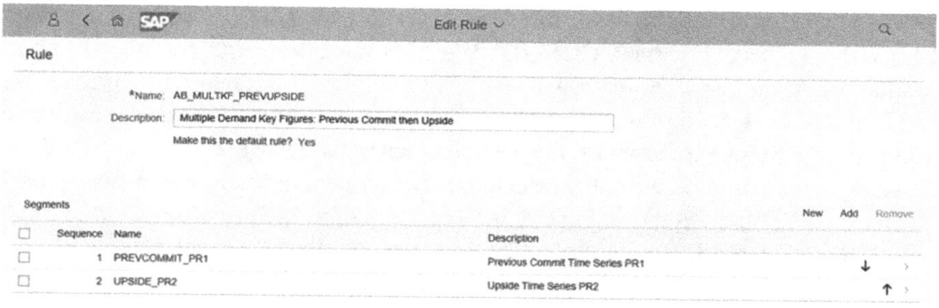


**Fig. 6.37** Previous confirmation then upside segment

A note on APO: Many readers will be familiar with SAP Advanced Planning and Optimization (APO). As those readers might have already noticed, there are some similarities (and some differences) between APO-Supply Network Planning Capable to Match (APO-SNP-CTM) and IBP order-based planning. Note here the simplicity and power in this approach in determining the demand priorities in IBP. CTM's profiles were much more difficult to configure.

### Planning Run

With the organization's priorities now in place, we can turn our attention to the plan itself. We will again use a simple example to illustrate the process.

While in the collaboration phase, our supplier has identified some downtime at their key plant which was previously unexpected. We can now no longer rely on an uninterrupted flow of the memory used to produce our ASP and ASX product lines.

We need to understand how this will impact our allocations and downstream supply plans. To do this, we will first review the plan as it stands from the last weekly cycle (Fig. 6.38).

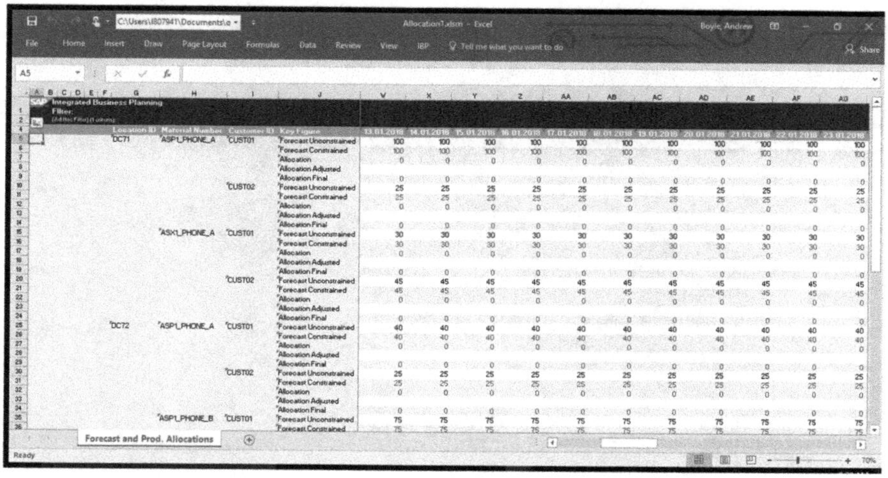


**Fig. 6.38** Original allocation plan

Here, a planner sees that we have forecasts for our two customers, important CUST01 and less important CUST02. We also have forecasts for two different product lines, the less profitable ASP line and the more profitable ASX line. At the end of the last cycle, all of the forecasts (forecast unconstrained rows) were available according to the plan (shown on the forecast constrained rows).

Also, the existing plan requires the memory component as shown in Fig. 6.39.

Here, we see that on the last cycle, the supplier committed to provide up to 2500 units per period, while we only planned to utilize less than half that number.

The new supplier commit (coming back from the Ariba collaboration environment as discussed previously), will include downtime for several days in the near term. This will likely have an impact on our plan. This would either come to us directly from the Ariba collaboration integration or can be edited directly on the Excel view as shown in Fig. 6.40.

The key question now is what this will impact. Of course, in a weekly allocation cycle, there could be many of these kinds of issues. We are actively following these changes here, but in a production environment, there would likely be alerts in place to highlight the week over week changes that a planner would then investigate.

To understand the impact of the supplier confirmation, we will run the plan. This can be done directly from Excel, in a background job, or through the Fiori app as shown on Fig. 6.41.

Note that the rule and materials are chosen directly on the job run—this means that different planning runs can use different rules. For example, the weekly baseline run might always use the same rule, while a what-if analysis against a different version might use a different rule—say one that focuses on a different set of priorities for the end of the quarter. Note that the planning run has respected the new supplier constraints and that the plan now calls for a much higher number of parts prior to the plant shutdown and again immediately after the shutdown. It is likely that our allocations plan has been affected.

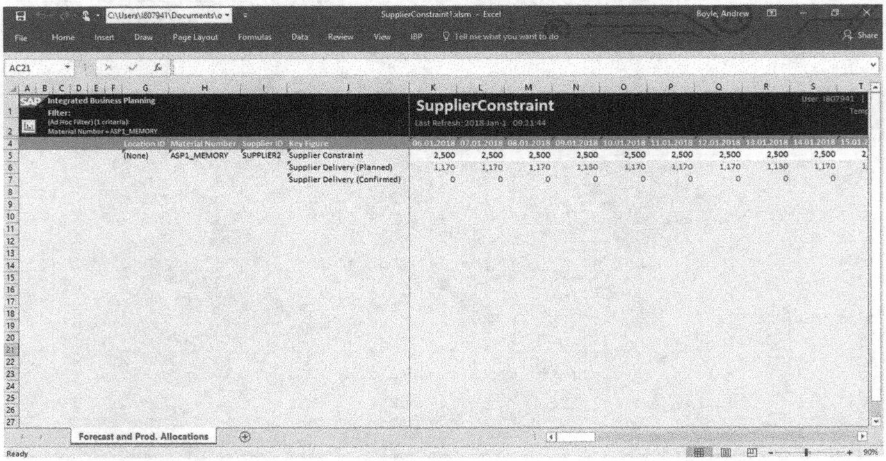


**Fig. 6.39** Supplier constraint and plan prior to changed confirmation

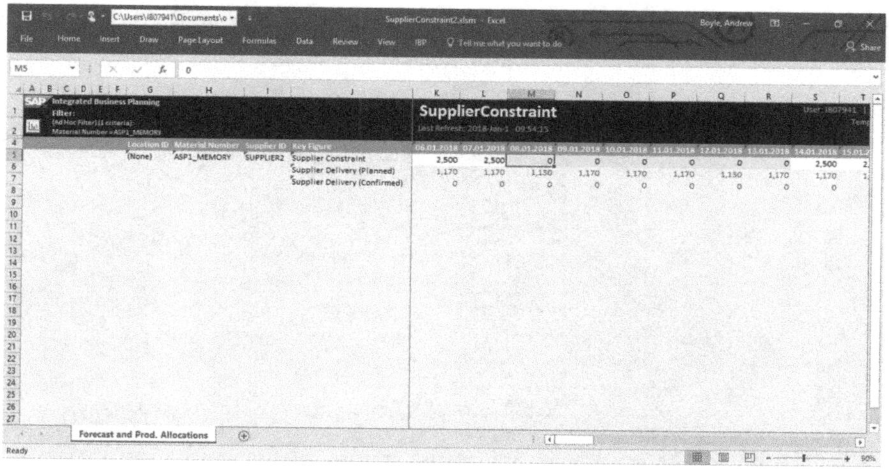


**Fig. 6.40** Supplier confirmation less than supplier forecast

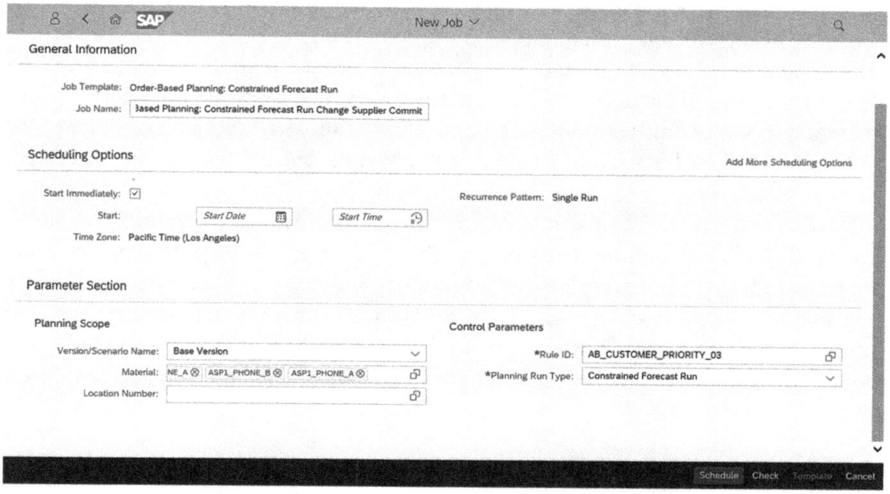


**Fig. 6.41** Constrained forecast run

## Constrained Forecast

The constrained forecast run considers demand in the form of key figure(s) (i.e., forecast) and safety stock targets, existing supply, inventory, and constraints. It outputs both a constrained forecast (which forms the basis for the allocations) and a feasible supply plan simultaneously.

This run considers the demands as they were ranked by the rules. It plans each demand, one by one, while considering constraints and sources of supply across a multilevel bill of material and/or distribution network. Sources of supply (such as production data structures/BOMs and transportation lanes) can also be ranked on the corresponding master data from the source ERP system.

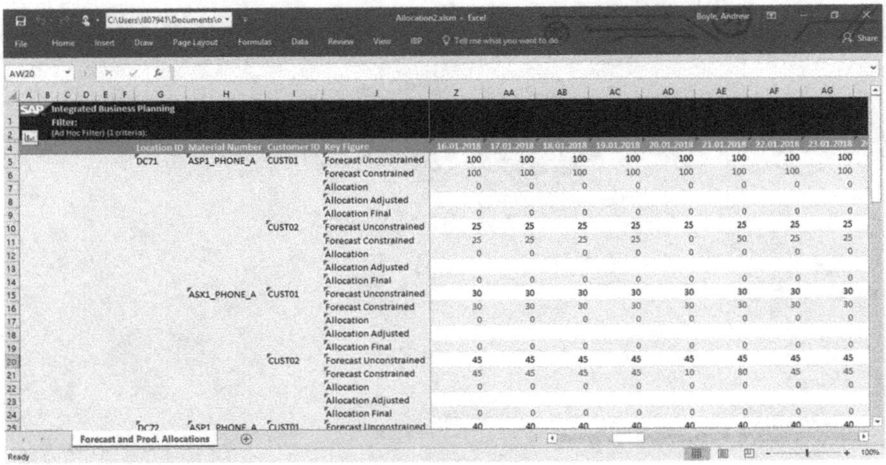

**Fig. 6.42** Constrained forecast was changed, CUST02 got less on 20/01

As a result of our constrained forecast run, we now see that the constrained forecast rows have changed (Fig. 6.42).

Note that there are now instances where the forecast cannot be covered immediately. In the 20th of January, the forecast for ASP1_PHONE_A for CUST02 is not covered but is later covered on the 21st of January. Similarly, the 20th of January for ASX1_PHONE_A for CUST02 is not fully covered, but the balance is covered in the next period.

Why would this be? We know, of course, that our priorities require the plan to first fulfill CUST01 requirements before CUST02. And, those priorities also state that product line ASX be fulfilled before product line ASP. Further, we have already seen that the common component memory is in short supply. These are likely the reasons for this shortage. But how can we be certain? And how can we identify the root cause of issues like these when they are numerous, and where we haven't seen the process at each step?

### Gating Factors Analysis

These are important questions. And the trouble with a typical constrained planning engine is that it can be difficult to ascertain why the system planned the way it did. In order-based planning, however, we can answer these questions easily using the View Gating Factors App. The gating factors app illustrates the constraints that have impacted the plan and links those constraints to the upstream procurement and production plan as well as downstream demand. To illustrate, we will investigate our late forecasts. First, we access the View Gating Factors App as shown in Fig. 6.43.

Here, we can view all or portions of the plan and choose which gating factor type we want to focus on. As the screen shows, we can see issues related to lead times, projected stocks, resource constraints, supplier constraints, incomplete supply chain model (master data), and product allocations (this last will be discussed in the next section). Our planner is investigating the issue with the late fulfillment and runs the plan for the ASP product line for all potential gating factors, as shown in Fig. 6.44.

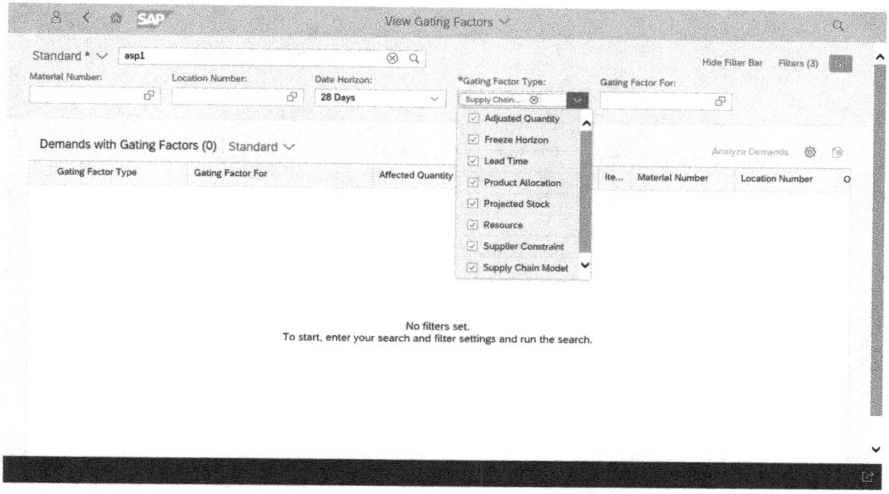


**Fig. 6.43** Gating factor types

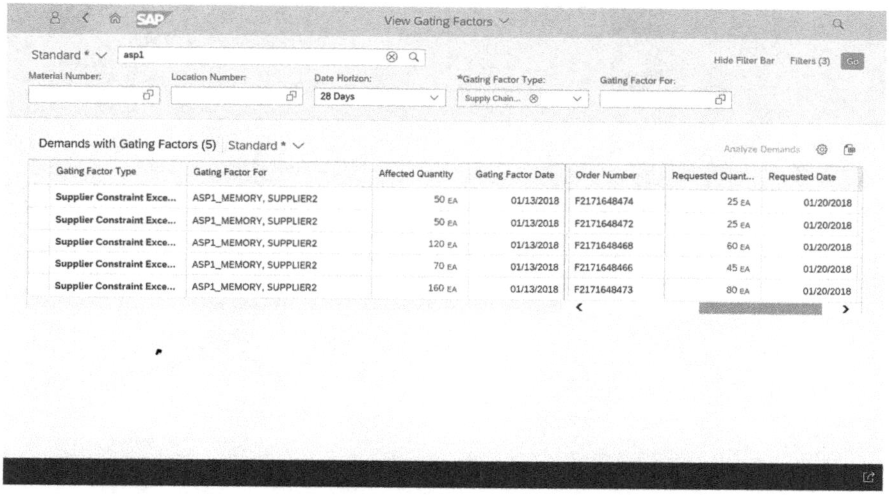


**Fig. 6.44** Gating factors for selected products and supplier

Yes, it's clear that the supplier constraints are indeed the issue. These constraints affect several demands. The planner decides to choose a row and see more details by products and locations dates. Now we come to the Analyze Demand view. It's clear on the left that the supplier constraint change is causing a problem. And on the right, we can see exactly the problem. There is a forecast for ASP Phone A that is now running late. The system shows each level of pegging information between the demand and the supply. A quick scroll to the right shows more detail by date (Fig. 6.45).

The forecast is covered by two stock transfer requests (STRs) from the production location. One is on time (see the green line), and one is 4 days late (see the red line).

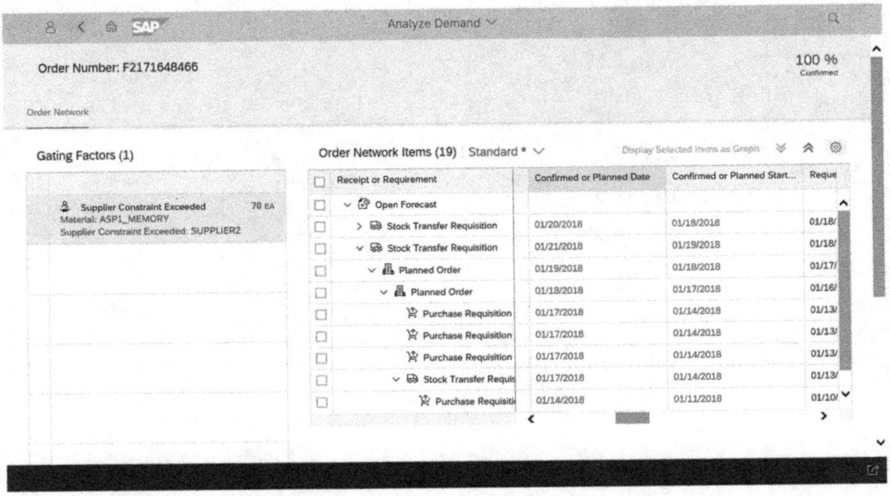


**Fig. 6.45** Requested versus planned dates

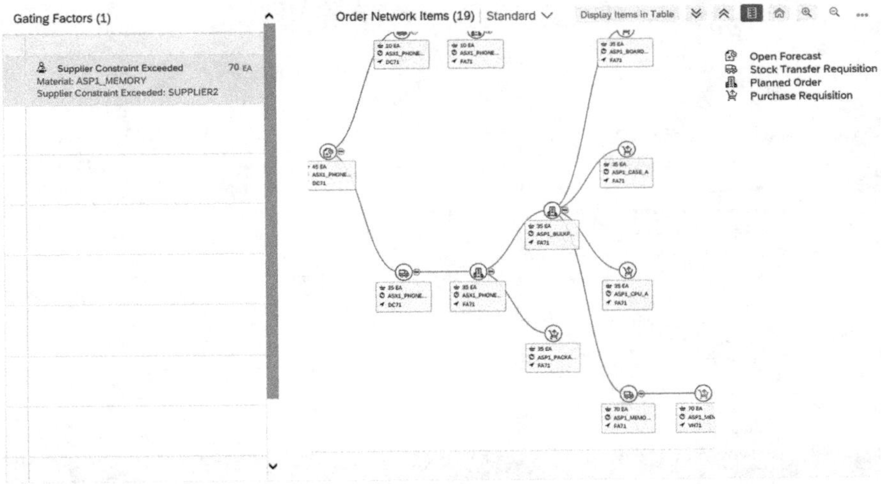


**Fig. 6.46** Demand fulfilment in the graphical form

The STR that is running late is associated with a planned order for final assembly, which is associated with a planned order for subassembly, which finally is associated with several purchase requisitions for components. It can be easier to view this graphically (see Fig. 6.46).

Now the pegging relationships are clearer. Note the red lines leading to the issue. Note the shopping cart is shown in red. This is the purchase requisition that is directly affected by the gating factor. The planner can see this by drilling into details directly on this screen (see Fig. 6.47).

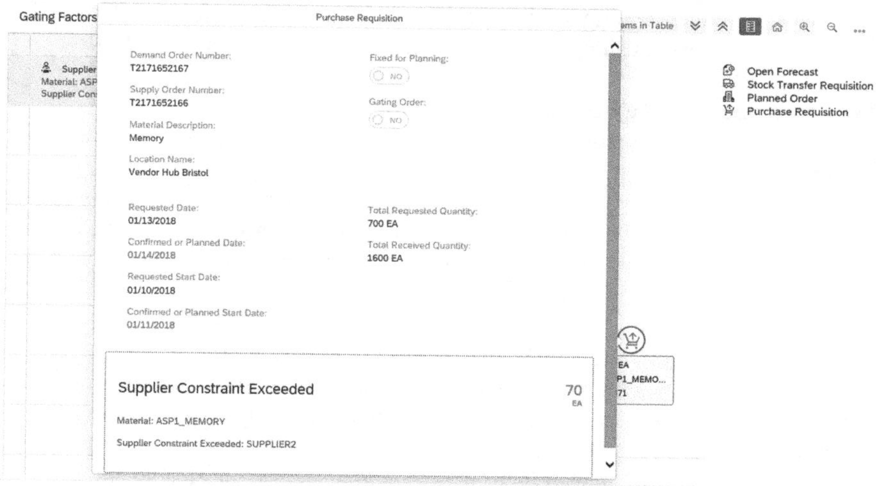


**Fig. 6.47** Drill down into purchase requisition for supplier gating factor

This purchase requisition is a day late, which in turn affects each level of the supply chain back to the demand itself.

## Analyze Supply Pegging

So, now our planner knows that the supplier constraints are an issue. In particular, purchase requisition T2171573896 is now late and is affecting at least one upstream demand. How many other demands might be affected by this?

To find out, our planner opens the Analyze Supply Usage app and investigates the purchase requisition (see Fig. 6.48).

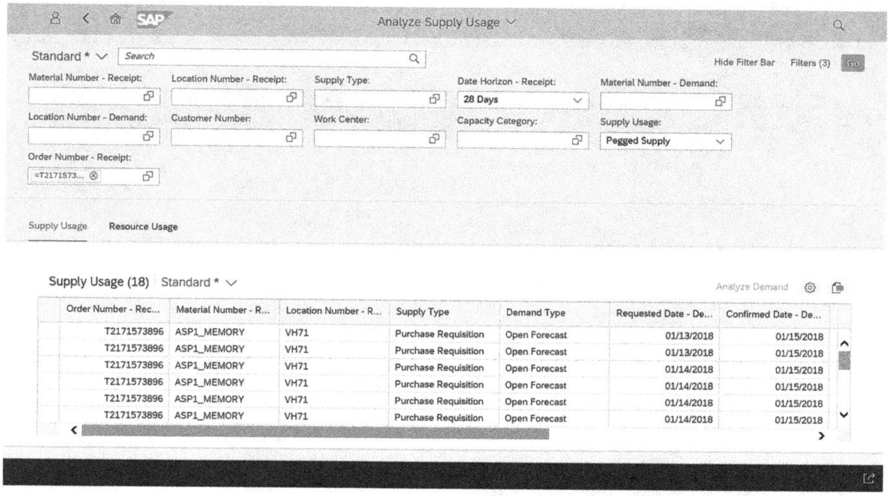


| Order Number - Rec... | Material Number - R... | Location Number - R... | Supply Type | Demand Type | Requested Date - De... | Confirmed Date - De... |
|---|---|---|---|---|---|---|
| T2171573896 | ASP1_MEMORY | VH71 | Purchase Requisition | Open Forecast | 01/13/2018 | 01/15/2018 |
| T2171573896 | ASP1_MEMORY | VH71 | Purchase Requisition | Open Forecast | 01/13/2018 | 01/15/2018 |
| T2171573896 | ASP1_MEMORY | VH71 | Purchase Requisition | Open Forecast | 01/14/2018 | 01/15/2018 |
| T2171573896 | ASP1_MEMORY | VH71 | Purchase Requisition | Open Forecast | 01/14/2018 | 01/15/2018 |
| T2171573896 | ASP1_MEMORY | VH71 | Purchase Requisition | Open Forecast | 01/14/2018 | 01/15/2018 |
| T2171573896 | ASP1_MEMORY | VH71 | Purchase Requisition | Open Forecast | 01/14/2018 | 01/15/2018 |

**Fig. 6.48** Analyze supply which impacts demand, bottom up from purchase requisition

Here, the planner sees that this purchase requisition affects forecast for the 13th and 14th of January, pushing those demands out to the 15th for confirmation.

**Finalize Allocation Results in Planning**

Allocation results can be utilized either within order-based planning in IBP or they can be pushed back to an ERP or other online available-to-promise (ATP) system to constrain orders directly as they arise. Now that the constrained forecast is known, we will promote it to the allocation. This step enables a review process prior to adoption of the allocations plan. Now the allocation key figure is populated (Fig. 6.49).

**Integrating Supply Planning Results to ERP**

As illustrated in the previous pages, the constrained forecast run in order-based planning creates a basis for allocations, and it simultaneously creates the supply plan to support it. This has many advantages, especially as shown above for plan analysis. Now that the allocations cycle is complete, the organization may also want to use the supporting supply plan instead of a material requirements plan (an MRP run) for the materials planned in IBP. This is not a mandatory step (e.g., some organizations will only be interested in the allocations output), but we will show it here to illustrate the integration with SAP ERP and S4.

As shown in Fig. 6.50, we can see the corresponding supply plan created for the previous planning run in Excel. This view focuses on the ASP1_PHONE_A product at a distribution center (DC71). There are distribution receipts planned (i.e., stock transfer requests) of 125 units in each period on the horizon. Figure 6.51 shows the same information in the View Projected Stock Fiori App.

Note again the STRs planned for 125 day over day. Here we can see there is only one STR for each period planned, although this may not always be the case.

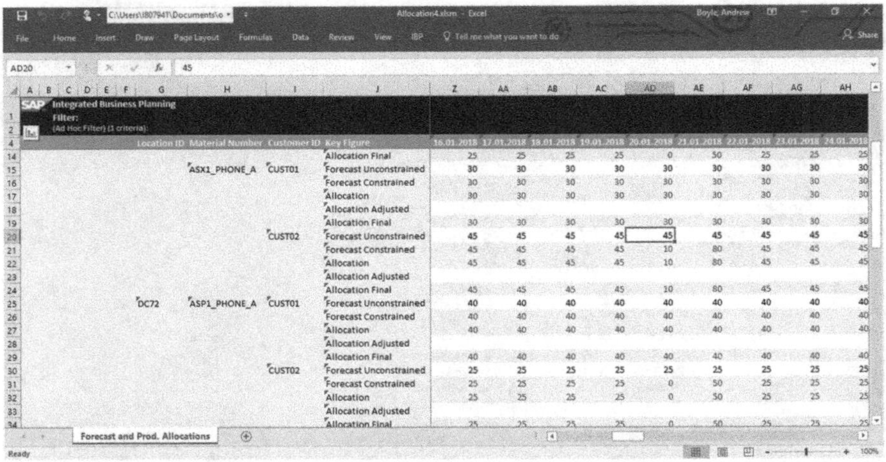


**Fig. 6.49** Allocation is populated

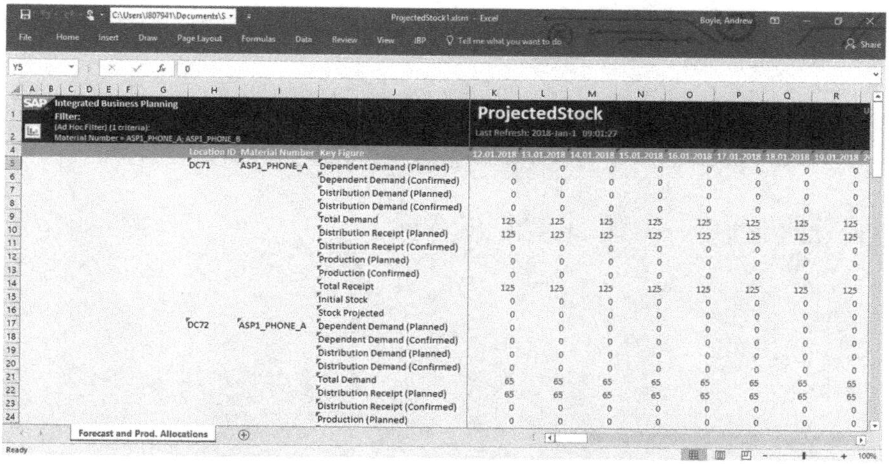


**Fig. 6.50** A view of the plan at a location/material level in the Excel UI

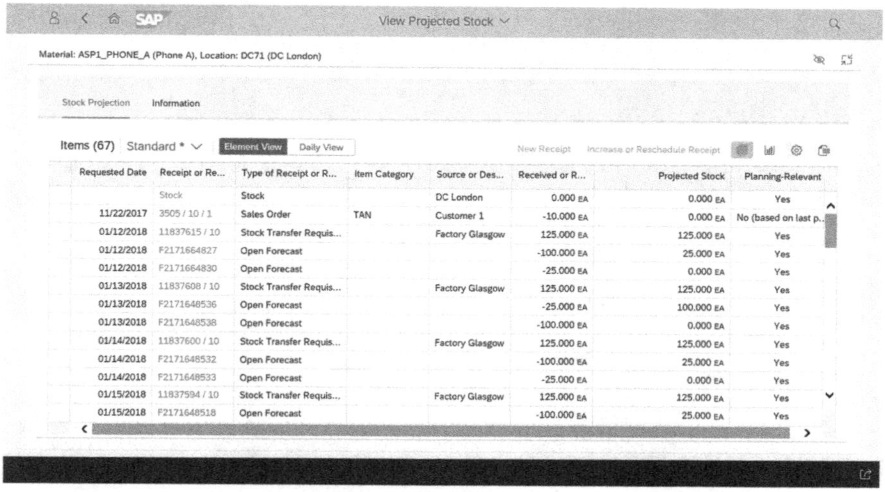


**Fig. 6.51** Supply plan for ASP1_PHONE_A at distribution center

Periodically the supply plan can be integrated with the organization's ERP system. This does not need to be a SAP system and in fact can be another ERP system altogether. For simplicity here we will show the integration with SAP ECC.

Here we can see the Stock Requirements List (Fig. 6.52), otherwise known as transaction MD04. The same purchase requisitions (really STRS) are shown here. You might also note the customer orders present in both the IBP and ECC system. This integration available with ERP extends further. Eventually these stock transfer requisitions will become stock transfer orders (STOs; executable transfer orders).

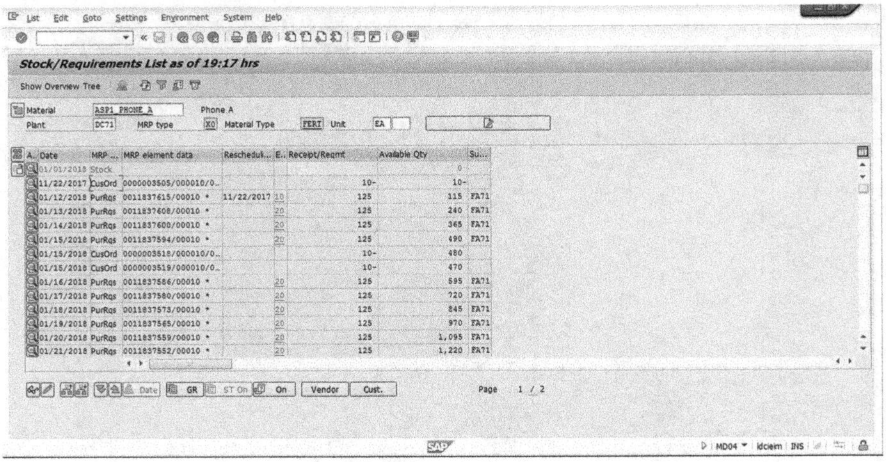


**Fig. 6.52** Stock requirements list showing same material/plan elements like in IBP

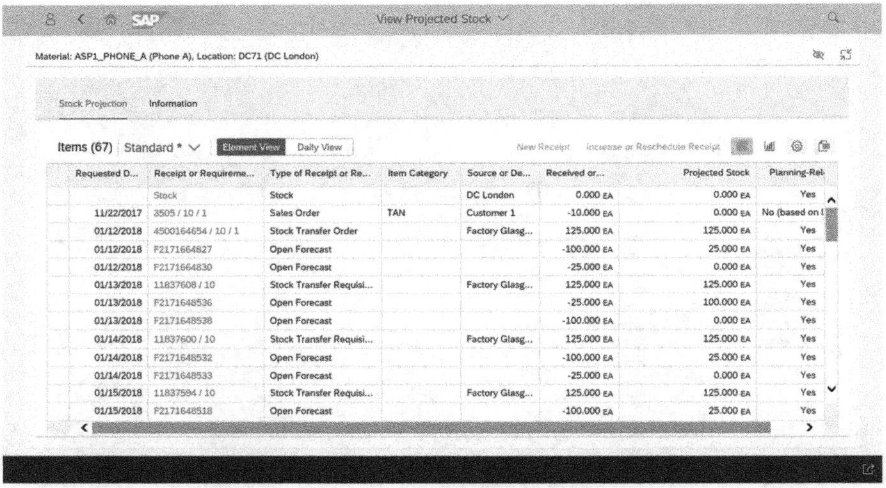


**Fig. 6.53** Stock transfer order 4500164654 is now shown in IBP

And finally, the STO no *4500164654* is passed to the IBP system with the next periodic integration (see Fig. 6.53).

STO 4500164654 will now act as a firmed order during the next supply planning run.

### 6.1.9 Improve O2C and Distribution with Rules-Based Backorder Rescheduling

**Process Overview**

Now that we have determined our product allocations policy, how will we enforce it? What will happen if the orders start to outstrip our anticipated demand? What kinds of analysis can we perform, and how can we drive a new supply and operations plan to respond to the changing supply and demand situation?

To answer these questions, we will focus on backorder rescheduling in order-based planning for IBP.

High-Tech OEMs periodically review and adjust their sales order confirmations via some form of backorder rescheduling. The goal is to adjust the near-term plan (both demand confirmations and unfirmed supply plans) to better fulfill the newly understood demands. The process typically takes the following form (see Fig. 6.54):

- **Periodic data load.** New sales orders and updated inventory, supply, and other demand data are loaded periodically for review.
- **Prioritization.** Organizational priorities are translated into rules.
- **Run plan and analyze results.** Considering constraints, commits, and allocations previously identified, determine which sales orders can be fulfilled and to what degree.
- **Adjust plan.** Planners review the output plan to identify issues and adjust as necessary. This may include multiple runs and comparisons.
- **Publish.** Publish the new plan and order confirmations to ERP for execution.

In the example that follows, the organization runs a backorder rescheduling once every shift (appximately 8 h). In this cycle, a planner will find several sales orders for a lower-priority customer that were not expected. IBP will first suggest that these sales orders not be fulfilled on time, as they exceed the allocation created previously and they outstrip the organizations' resources at the final assembly step. The planner

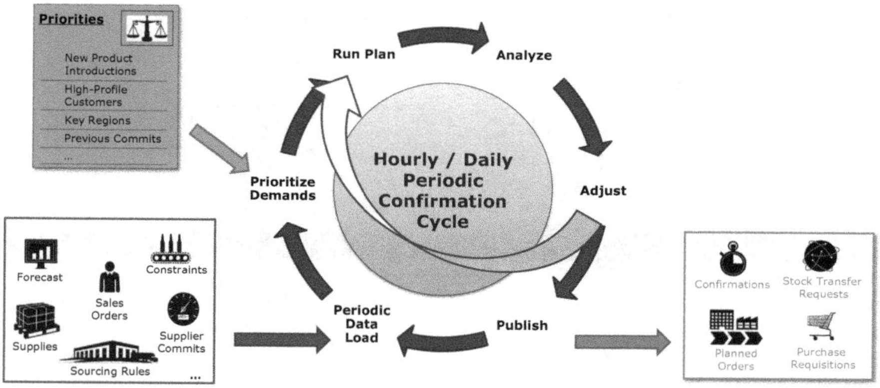


**Fig. 6.54** Periodic backorder rescheduling

will see that there is a problem and decide whether to override the allocations and attempt to fulfill the new orders.

### 6.1.10 SAP Use Case: Rule-Based Sales Order Confirmation

**Demand Prioritization: Set Rules for Sales Orders vs. Forecast, Customer A vs. Customer B, and Other Considerations**

In order-based planning in IBP, the same rules can be used to support both the backorder rescheduling and the allocations planning processes. However, an organization may want to use the segment and sort concept described earlier to better prioritize sales orders versus forecast. CUSTOMER_PRIORITY_03 rule enabled us to prioritize certain customers (CUST01) higher than others (CUST02). CUSTOMER_PRIORITY_01 is a little different (see Fig. 6.55).

Here we can see that high-priority customer sales orders take the first segment, then forecasts for those same customers, and only later sales orders (then forecasts) for lower-priority customers. This means that forecasted demand for the most important electronics retailer will still reserve inventory and resources before customer orders for lower-priority customers. Sales orders for customer priority 01 come first (see Fig. 6.56).

and then its forecast (see Fig. 6.57)

After those segments other customer priorities come served with their orders and forecasts.

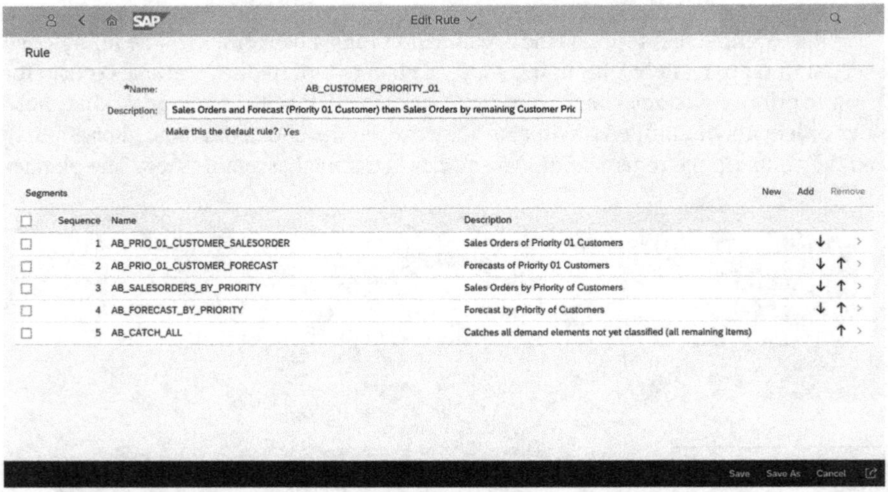


**Fig. 6.55** Sales and forecast for customer priority 1 and then others

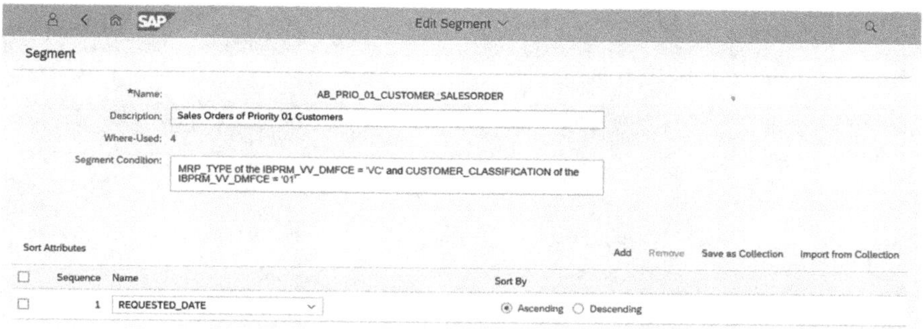


**Fig. 6.56** Sales order for customer priority 01 is fulfilled first

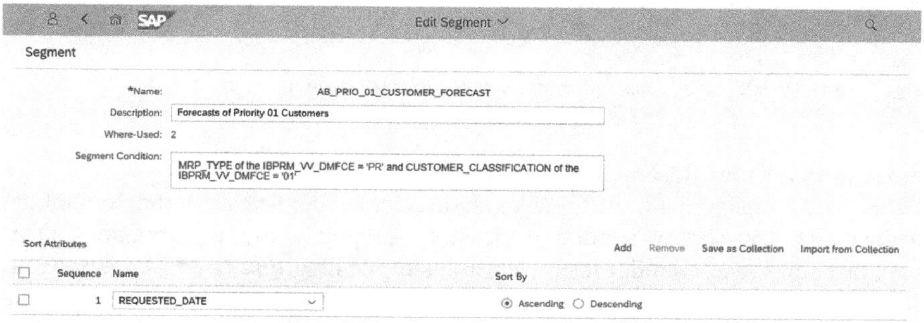


**Fig. 6.57** Forecast for customer priority 01 is fulfilled after its orders

As in the last example, CUST01 is the highest priority customer, while CUST02 represents the second-tier customers. So, if we use this rule, priorities run as follows:

- Sales orders for CUST01
- Forecast for CUST01
- Sales orders for CUST02 and other customers
- Forecast for CUST02 and other customers

### Initial Planning Situation

In our example, several new orders have come in from our CUST02 customer since the last backorder processing run. These orders outstrip our previous plans (see Fig. 6.58).

The original forecasted quantities for this customer for the ASP phone are 25 per period. This was also what we could allocate in the weekly allocations process. However, their actual orders are much higher over the next few days. Also note sales to CUST01's have not been so bad at all, compared with forecast.

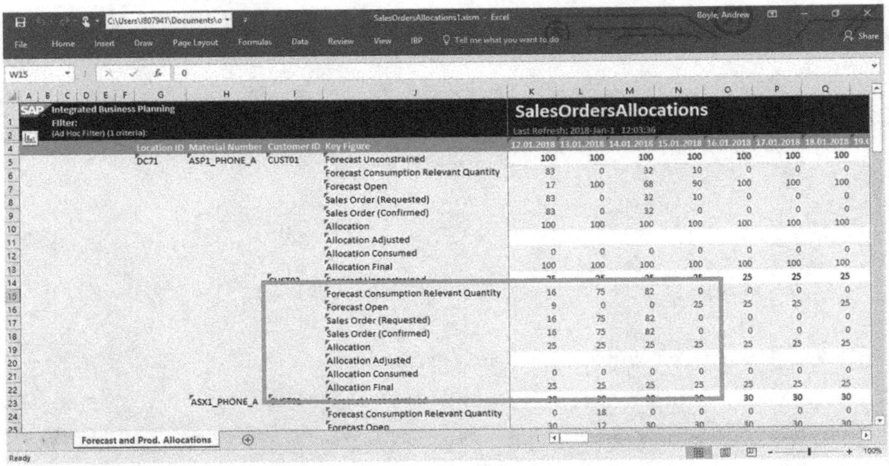


**Fig. 6.58** CUST02's new sales orders exceed the allocated quantities

## Sales Order Rules Based Confirmation Run

Order-based planning in IBP enables a sales order confirmation run to simultaneously re-plan supply needed to feasibly support those confirmations. This planning run is very similar to the constrained planning discussed in the previous section. Like that run it considers demands, customer, product, and organizational priorities, inventory and capacity availability, and supplier and subcontractor confirmations. It also considers product allocations (generated in previous use case) and sales order demands.

The sales order confirmation run outputs can be integrated with ERP, ECC, and S/4:

- Sales order confirmations
- New or updated supply elements necessary to support this plan

The run can be set up as a background job or can be kicked off on demand by a planner with appropriate authorization (see Fig. 6.59).

So, the planner can select the appropriate prioritization rule on each run.

In this case, not all of our new CUST02 sales orders could be confirmed (Fig. 6.60). Note that the sales orders in the first period are fulfilled (all 16 units), but those in the second and third periods could only be partially fulfilled (only up to 25).

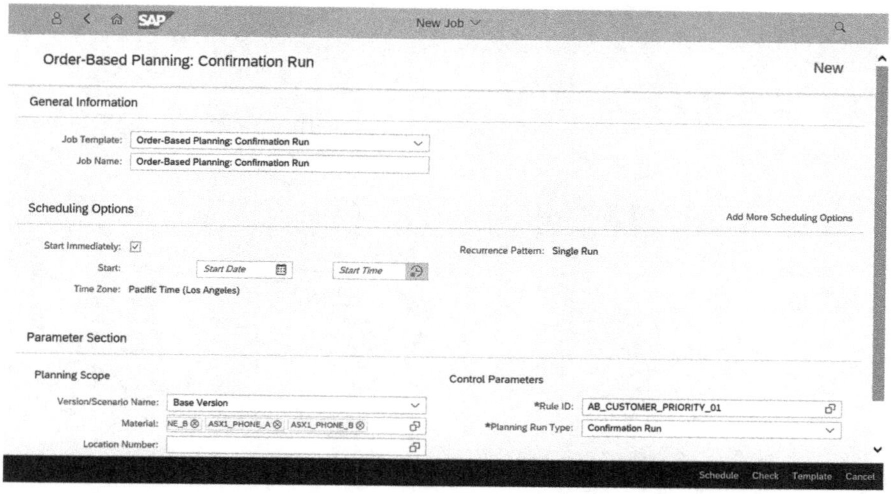

**Fig. 6.59** Sales order confirmation run

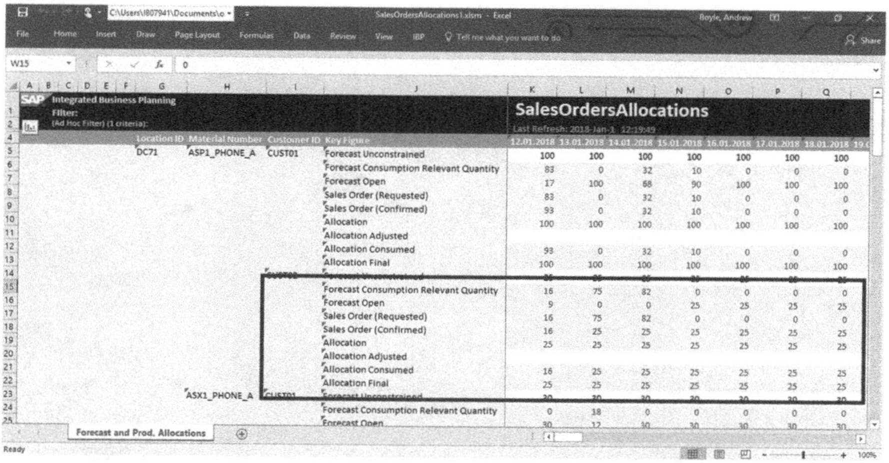

**Fig. 6.60** Order confirmation after run, not all sales orders can be confirmed for CUST02

## View Sales Order Confirmations App

Why were some orders fulfilled, and others not? To evaluate this the planner calls up the View Confirmations App. This Fiori app is designed to review sales orders at a granular level. At first glance (Fig. 6.61), the planner notes that several orders were delayed or not fulfilled.

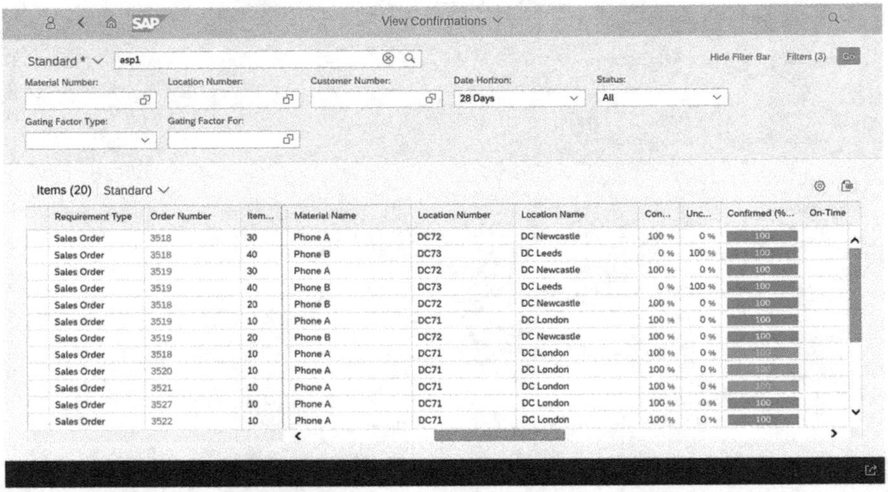


**Fig. 6.61** Sales order confirmation app

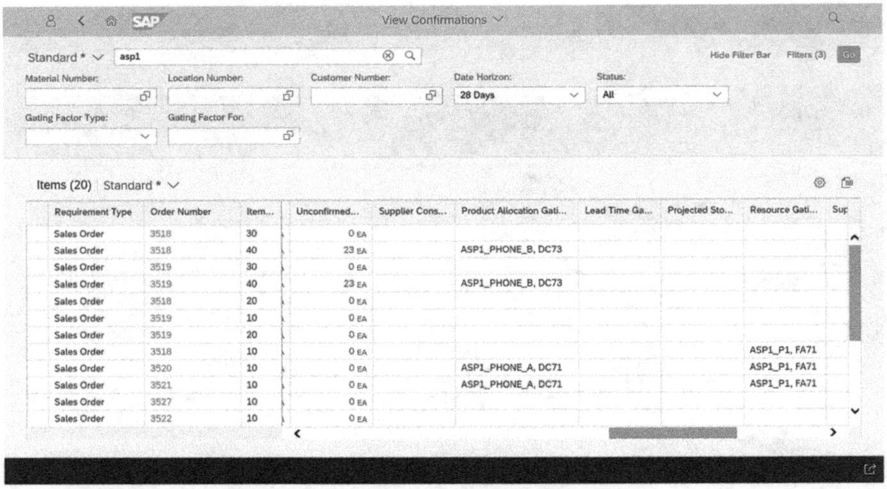


**Fig. 6.62** Gating factors view in sales order confirmation app

Why were these sales orders delayed? One easy way to see more details is to simply scroll to the gating factors section, where we can see what constraints were at play on these sales orders (Fig. 6.62).

So it's clear that some orders (e.g., 3519) could not be fulfilled because of an allocation constraint (see columns versus records). Where others (e.g., 3520) are subject to both an allocation constraint and a resource constraint that were the reason for the lateness of the order.

### Analyze Demand App

A planner wants more detail, chooses a specific order 3523 (showing 93% fulfilled late—Figure BQ), and drills into the Analyze Demand screen (Fig. 6.63).

Here, the planner can see that the order can only be fulfilled partially on time, and most of the quantity will be a day late to the customer. The competing sales order section shows all sales orders that may be using the same resources. The planners see the relative rank of this sales order versus others.

To get more detail on the reasons the order is late, the planner can drill directly to the gating factor analysis (Fig. 6.64).

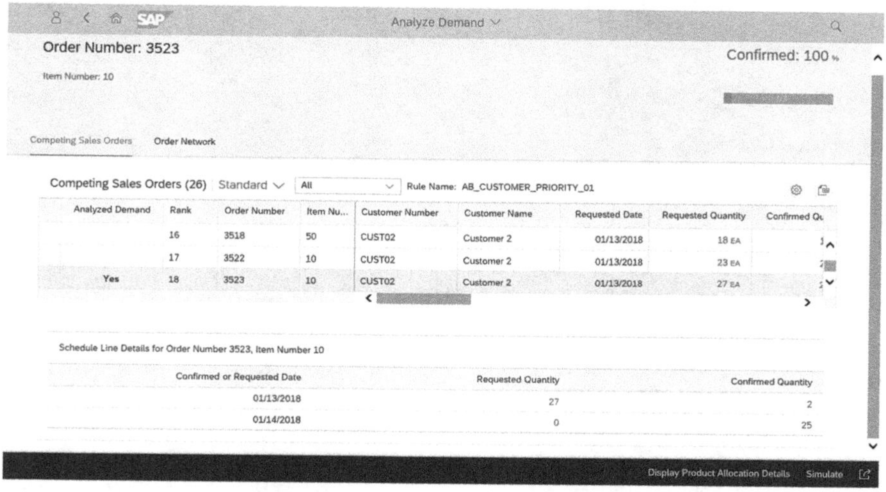


**Fig. 6.63** Sales order 3523—analyze demand app

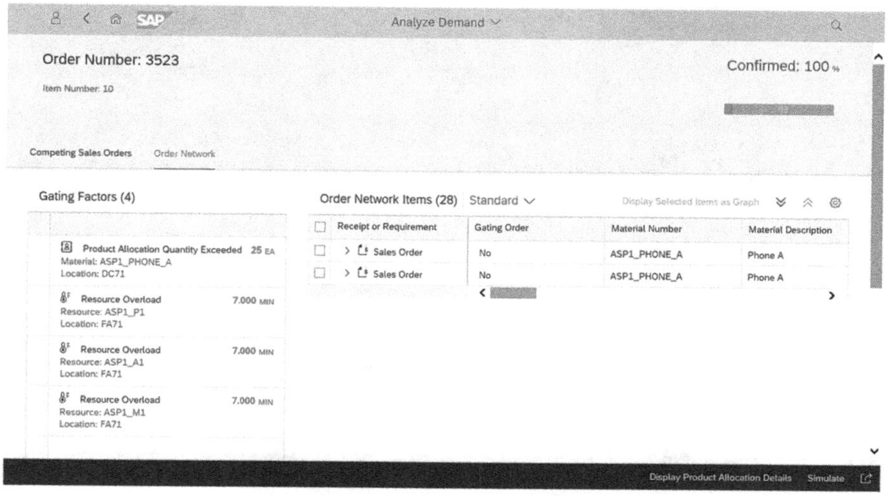


**Fig. 6.64** Gating factors analysis for sales order 3523

**Gating Factor Analysis**
Here, the sales order is subject to an allocation (the 25 units, which has been exceeded, Fig. 6.64). It is also subject to resource overloads at three stages of production. This can be seen well on the graphical view (Fig. 6.65).

Perhaps this resource does cause an issue for much more cases. The planner checks, by navigating to the View Gating Factors App initial screen, there are clearly a number of sales orders (and even now forecast for another product that uses this packaging line) that is impacted because of the resource overload (see Fig. 6.66).

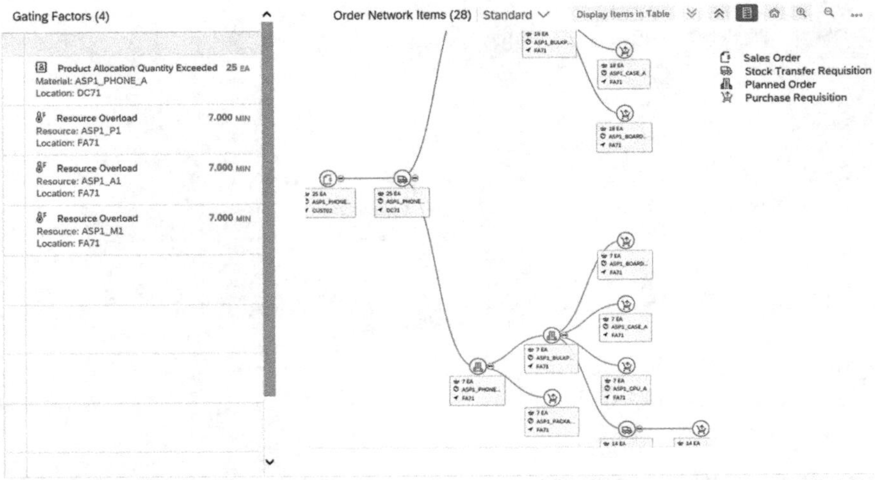


**Fig. 6.65** Pegged demand and supply for problematic sales order

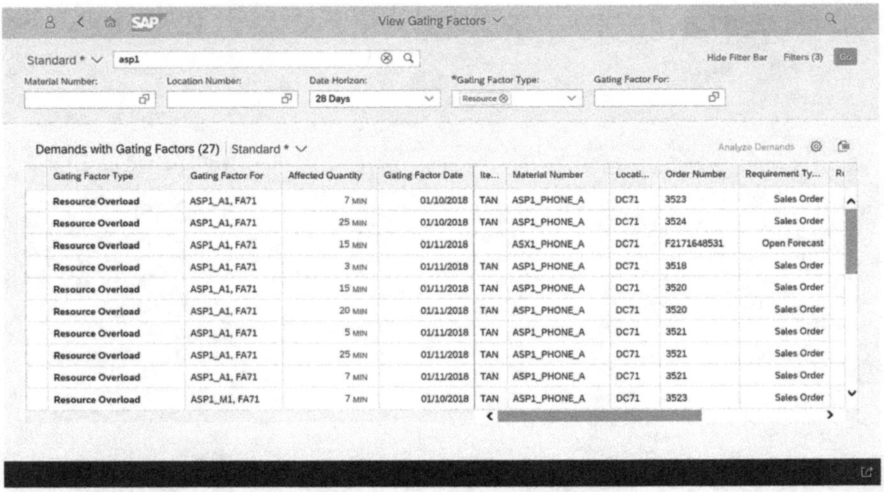


**Fig. 6.66** Resource overload gating factor

So, after a brief analysis, the planner understands a key problem. There more demand on a key resource than the organization can handle, and sales orders exceed forecast and allocation for our lower-priority customer.

**Improving Constrained Plan**

There are a few ways to deal with this. We could change the allocations for our lower-priority customer, "borrowing" some from the higher priority customer for now. The planner may also want to evaluate the impact of changing priorities. If we think the situation is changing and that our customer priorities may shift more permanently, then we could change our rules and review the output. Either way, we still have the overloaded resource to worry about. In this case the planner elects to speak with the line supervisor at the packaging facility. After a brief conversation, the planner discovers it is possible to bring some new resources onto the line for short time. This may resolve the issue, but the planner wants to check to be sure. To do this, the planner will temporarily change the constraints on the plan and see if the sales orders can be fulfilled.

First, the planner changes the resource constraint to adjust for the new temporary workers (see Fig. 6.67).

The planner then runs the sales order confirmation plan again and evaluates the results. Immediately he or she can see that the additional resource capacity is utilized and orders are confirmed and visualized in Excel ui views or confirmation app. A view of the confirmations app confirms that most orders are no longer at risk and that only one still has an issue with a resource constraint. Order 3523 was confirmed now (Fig. 6.68); note that all supply and transportation orders linked to this sales order are also rescheduled and are on time now.

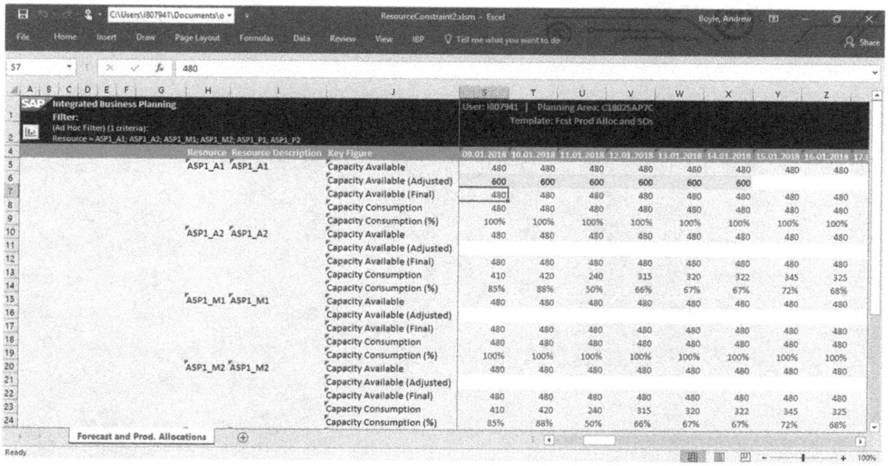


**Fig. 6.67** Planner adjusts capacity to reflect temporary resources confirmed by pack line leader

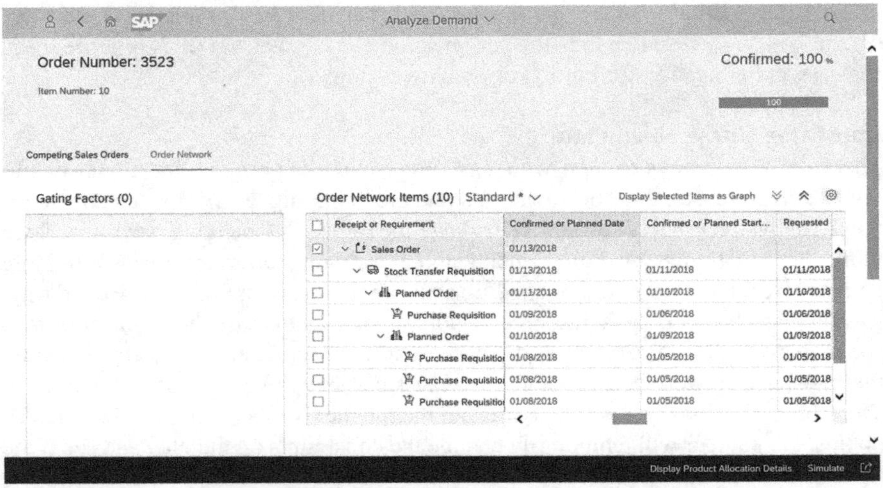

**Fig. 6.68** Increased responsiveness for Order 3523

## New Supply Plan

The plan has some changes from earlier in this unit; now transfers have been planned in accordance with the more granular sales order demand. Previously, the plan called for a daily movement of 125 units to the DC71 location. Now, that is known in more detail, with receipts for different quantities along the horizon. This information is transferred to ERP for execution, as shown in SAP ECC (see Fig. 6.69).

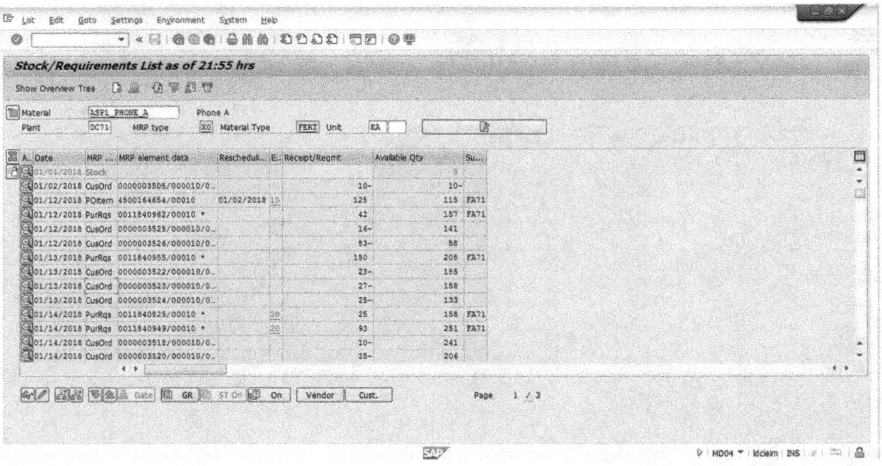

**Fig. 6.69** Needed supply orders to realize sales order confirmation run are transferred to ECC

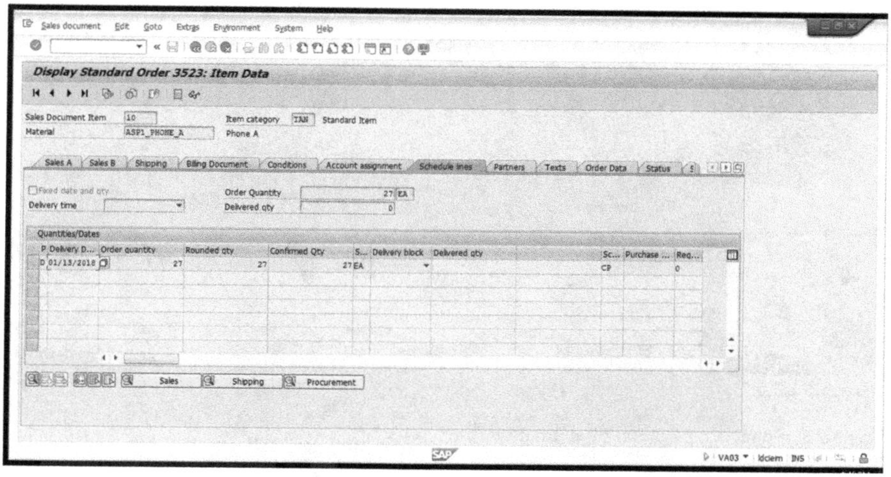

**Fig. 6.70** Sales order 3523 confirmation is transferred to ECC

### Sales Order Confirmations in ERP-S/4

The order confirmations are also transferred to ERP from IBP. Note the new confirmation dates for sales order 3523 (now on time, Fig. 6.70).

The key benefit of this process is the simultaneous supply planning and sales order confirmation process. This enables a feasible plan which is responsive to changes in demand.

## 6.1.11 What-If Analysis to Evaluate Big Deals/Tenders

One of the hardest requests to answer accurately and quickly in all of supply chain is the question of a new, unexpected large order. While this, of course, represents a happy circumstance to the sales department while entertaining this order, in the case of tight capacity constraints, we don't always know whether such an order would be feasible to fulfill. Even if it is feasible, what other orders could be impacted if we decide to fulfill this new order? Which constraints would act as gating factors? How could we manipulate the plan to alleviate these constraints? In the previous sections of this chapter, we focused on creating an allocations plan and working through backorder rescheduling while simultaneously planning supply. As a result, all the data needed to make these kinds of determinations is already available. What remains is to perform the evaluation.

### Process Overview

Our goal is to determine the impact of the new order (Fig. 6.71). To evaluate the new order, we will spin off a new simulation. This will enable us to use data available in the periodic backorder rescheduling process, while also introducing some new

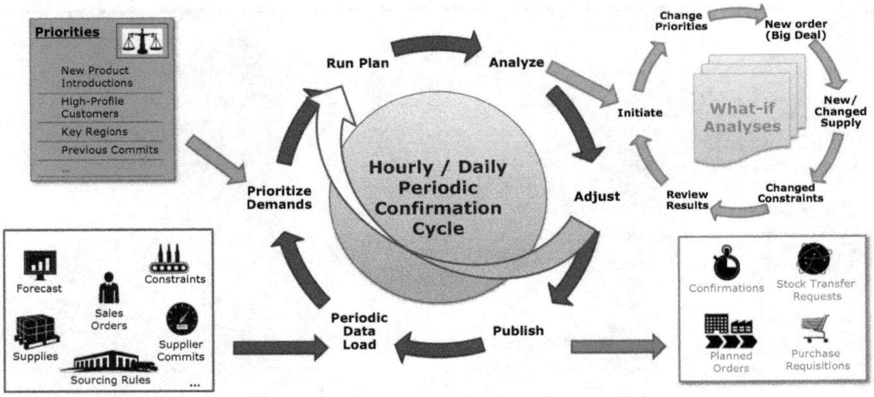


**Fig. 6.71** Tender/big deal order simulation (blue circle)

demands, constraints, or supplies. We can evaluate the order using the same apps that we already examined in previous sections of this chapter.

Along the way, a planner can test certain different ideas. The planner could add a supply order, for example, or modify constraints or even priorities. This could shed light on the appropriate steps to take if such a sales order is received. The planner can even share the scenario with others for their review or input.

If, at the end of the evaluation, the sales order is to be fulfilled, then the focus shifts to active planning. The sales order is added to the source ERP system, and the periodic backorder reprocessing will create confirmations as described in this previous section. The simulated order only existed to enable the what-if analysis; it is not saved back to the ERP system.

### 6.1.12 SAP Use Case: Big Deal/Tender Impact Assessment

**Simulation of Sales Order for Tender/Big Deal**

An important customer is in contact with our account planner/customer service. A question is raised: we could use a new shipment of phones, but only if you can ship it out in the next few days. If not, it will be too late, and we will go to your competitors. Can you deliver the phones on time or not? In this case, the phones are not a make to stock item. We do not have a warehouse full of phones ready to go, but instead these are in pieces at different stages in the supply chain. In addition, most of these components have already been earmarked for existing or expected customer orders.

The account planner logs on to the IBP order-based planning system and chooses the Simulate Sales Order App (Fig. 6.72).

This Fiori app is dedicated to this Big Deal scenario concept. Instead of adding all the details necessary to actually place an order, the account planner/customer service enters only the basics that IBP will need to evaluate the impact of the new demand (see Fig. 6.73).

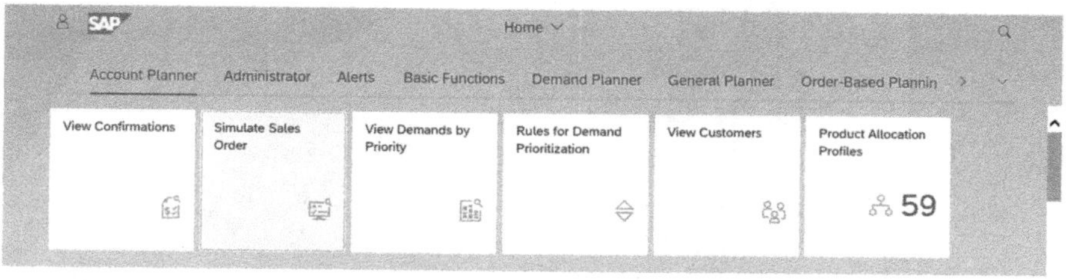


**Fig. 6.72** Account planner (customer service) apps, Simulate Sales Order app

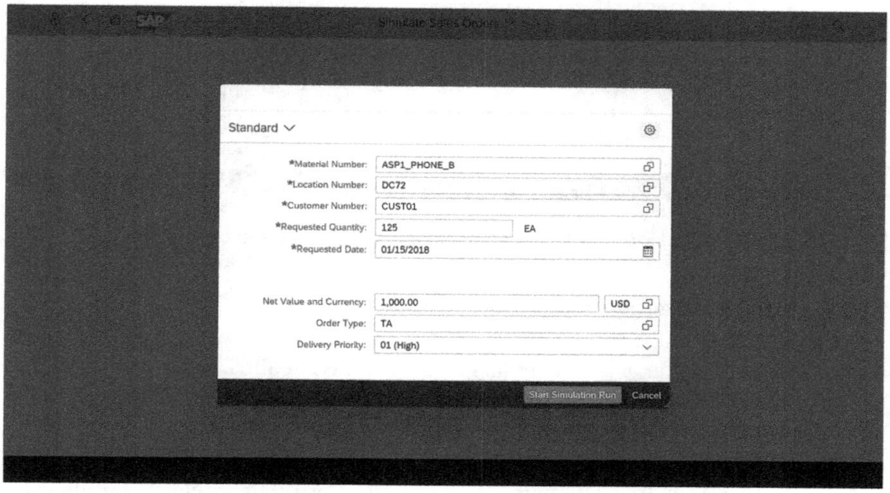


**Fig. 6.73** Simplified simulated sales order pop up

In this case, CUST01 (our high-priority customer as you may recall) wants to purchase 125 phones in just a few days.

The account planner/customer service saves the simulated order, and the system automatically runs a plan to slot this order into the mix. This planning run exists only in a simulation, and does not impact the active plan. Now, the account planner/customer service sees that this new, simulated order can only be partially confirmed on time (see Fig. 6.74).

Sixty-five units could be promised on time and another 60 2 days later. So, the planner now knows that if this order was added to the active cycle, it could only be partially fulfilled under the current constraints, promises, and rules. The account planner/customer service decides to evaluate this further. Why, exactly, was this order promised late? And what can we do to expedite it?

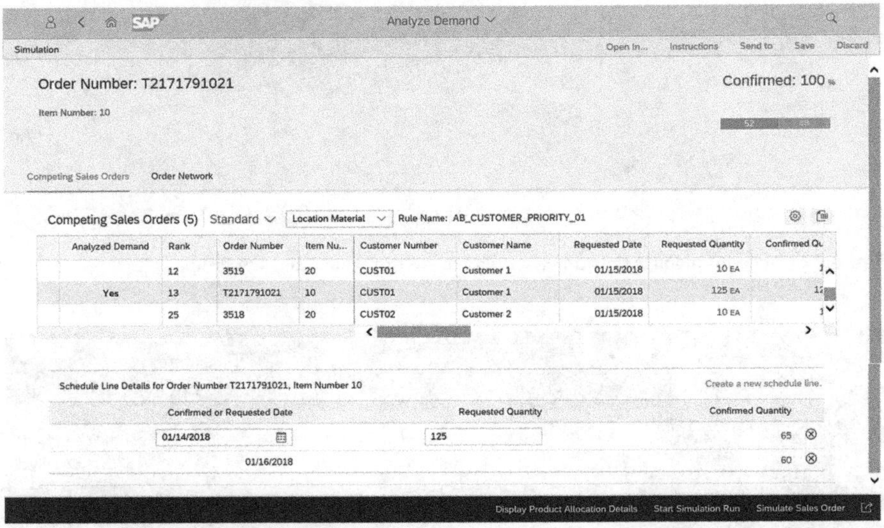

**Fig. 6.74** Simulated order automatically goes into analyze demand and confirmations

**Evaluation of Realization Options**

The planner reviews the set of confirmations related to this new order. Some orders are fulfilled on time, and others are late or not fulfilled at all. The planner drills into the new order and reviews the gating factor analysis. In this case, we can see that the product allocations are the reason the order was delivered late (see Fig. 6.75).

Allocations for 15th and 16th of January restricted the order. A part could be fulfilled on the 15th (the 65 units), and the other 60 units could be fulfilled on the 16th.

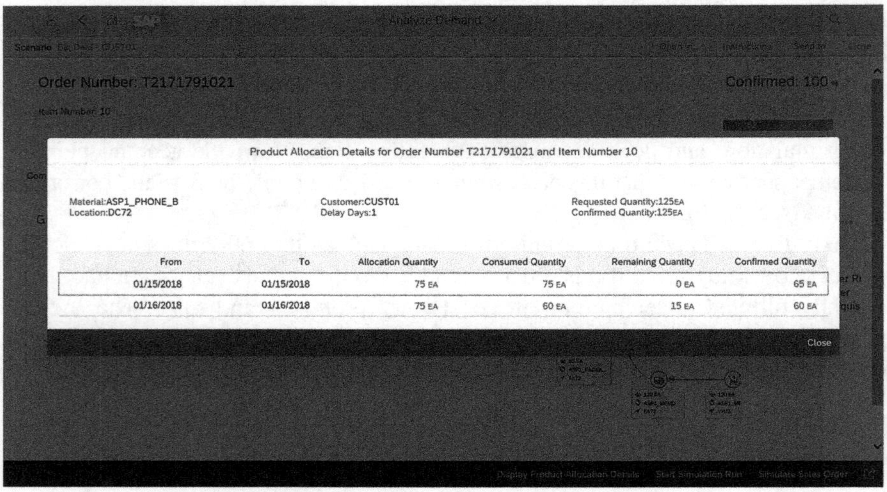

**Fig. 6.75** Simulated sales order gating factor is linked to product allocation quantity

## Modify Supply Plan

As we saw in the previous example in this chapter, we could modify the allocations and see if this solves the problem. In our case, the planner does this and finds that a key component, the packaging, is also acting as a gating factor for our order. To see more details, the planner drills into the projected stock view and sees a deficit for the packaging material (see Fig. 6.76).

It seems as though if we had more of the packaging on time, then the order may be fulfilled. The planner decides to test this hypothesis. Packaging material in Glasgow plant is very easy to prompt as confirmed by packing line leader. Planner enters a single purchase requisition simulation for the packaging (see Fig. 6.77) while on phone with production leader.

The planner places this order for 150 more units of the packaging materials. This is not a real order—it does not represent an actual commitment to buy and will not become a purchase order in the ERP system. This is simply a way for the planner to test this hypothesis: "if we had more of the packaging, could we fulfill the new order on time?" In this case we can. The new simulated purchase requisition is saved, and the planner reviews the order. The product can now be delivered on time. What other sales orders were affected by this change? The planner reviews the confirmations and reviews the column on the app "Revenue at risk" (see Fig. 6.78).

The report shows that some orders are still at risk for nondelivery. These orders, however, are not very large. The planner considers that the large order is likely more important than this downside to a few other orders. As in previous sections, the planner could continue to analyze and could set different priorities to compare results. In this case, however, the planner can conclude that the sales order is feasible and poses no large risk to other demands. To help the planner understand all the changes that went into the simulation, the system provides an instruction sheet which

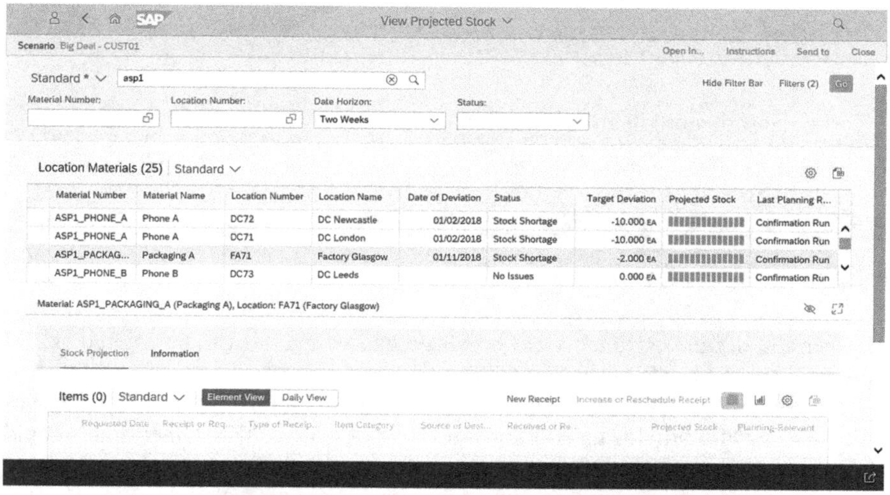


**Fig. 6.76** Packaging material shortage causes an issue

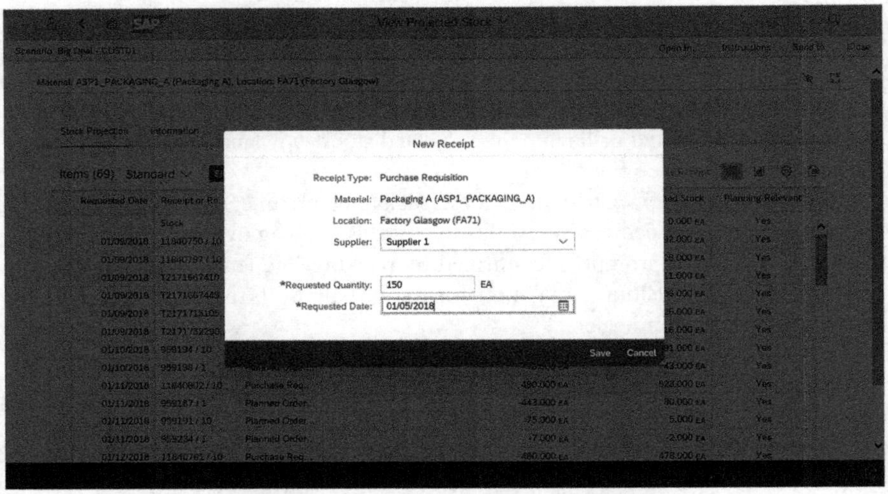


**Fig. 6.77** New purchase requisition for missing packaging material

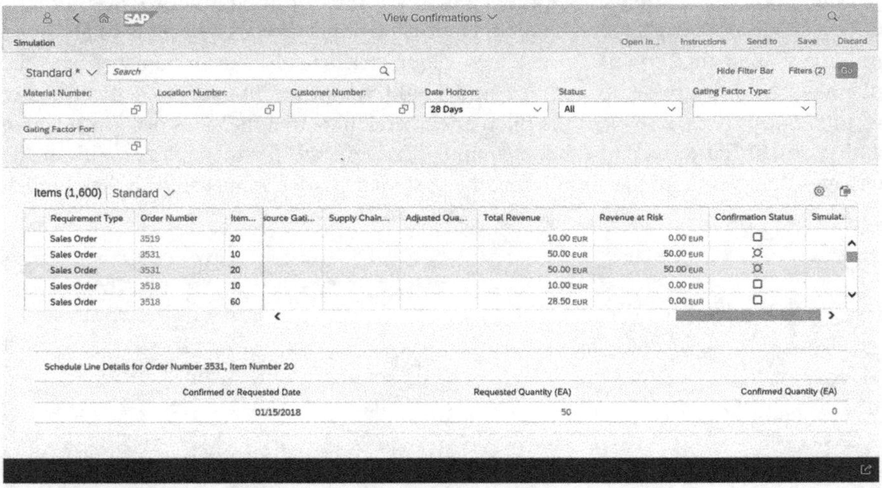


**Fig. 6.78** Some sales orders are still at risk of missing delivery

summarizes all objects which were simulated and would need to be entered as real ones in ERP system/IBP (see Fig. 6.79).

Here, the planner can see that this scenario considered the impact of a single sales order. This would provide an additional revenue of over 1000 €. Other orders could also be added and evaluated in this scenario. To enable this order, it was necessary in this case to add a new purchase requisition for packaging materials. Now that we know that the order is feasible, the next step is to officially accept the order to the

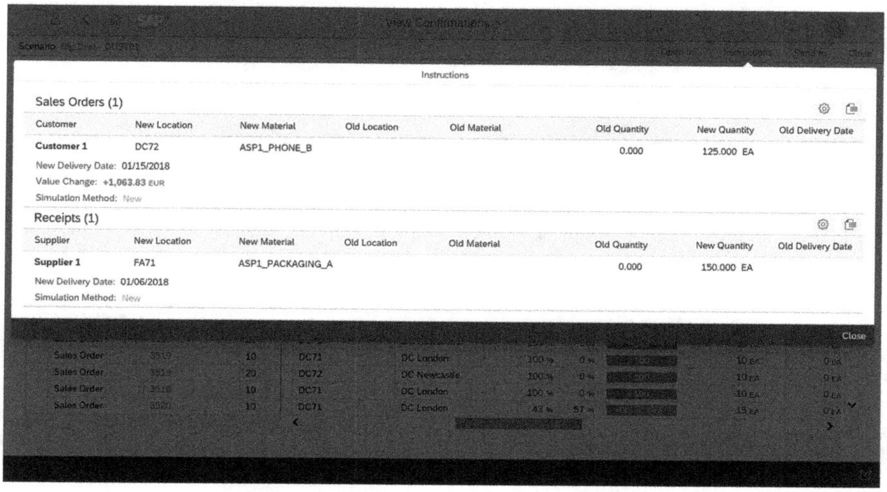


**Fig. 6.79** Instruction sheet for simulated order

customer (i.e., add the order to the ERP system) and make the other changes to the plan per the instruction sheet (in this case create the new, expedited, purchase requisition for the packaging). Using the simulation and scenario functionality in IBP order-based planning, the planner was able to quickly evaluate the new potential sales order and determine it was a feasible goal worth pursuing.

# 7 How to Prepare Process Measurement and Improvement

In this chapter we will highlight our key observations about process measurement and exemplify them on demand planning and forecasting processes.

In simple words, we talk about three dimensions of measurement which are relevant to process measurement and improvement. Once the performance that ought to be measured is clear, the definition of metrics needs to account for the mechanics of the process itself. We'll talk about mechanics in general terms before dwelling on the specific example of demand management. The mechanics are simple enough: a process receives inputs, performs certain activities, and generates outputs. The primary focus when it comes to performance measurement, and consequently, the definition of process metrics, is of course output effectiveness (and associated metrics). However, sole focus on output-centered metrics disregards factors (inputs and activities) that contribute to the observed output (effectiveness) (see Fig. 7.1). Those dimensions need to be linked either to input, process itself, or its outputs.

What can you gain from the measurement of these three aspects?

- Effectiveness measurement, which is a measure of process output, will explain how good you are performing.
- Efficiency measurement, based on process activities and process inputs, will explain how time-consuming or complex your processes are.
- Adherence/quality measurement, which is all about measuring process activities, will help you to understand if process stakeholders provide inputs, review, and decisions on time.

If we put improvement into the context, measurement should feed in information needed to improve process effectiveness (performance). We have observed that you can visualize relationship between process performance and its drivers in the following way (Fig. 7.2).

The diagram is worth to be considered when thinking about process improvement initiatives. There are a lot of examples which prove that effort invested in process improvement may return substantial value for the company. CISCO, where demand



R. Kepczynski et al., *Implementing Integrated Business Planning*, Management for Professionals, https://doi.org/10.1007/978-3-319-90095-7_7

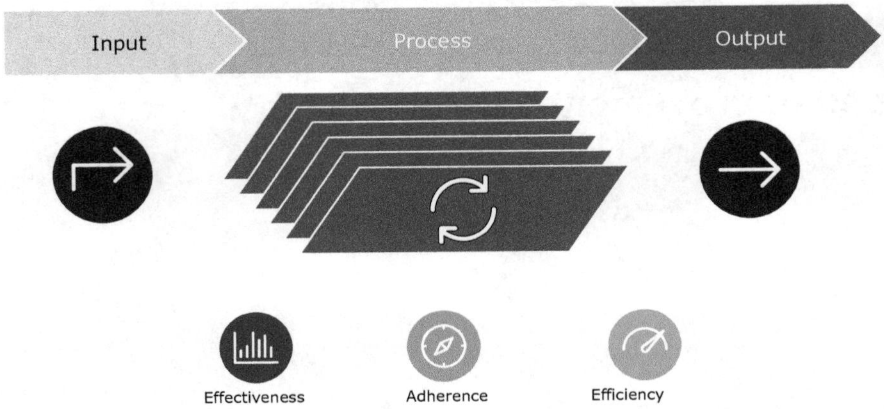


**Fig. 7.1** Three aspects of measurement

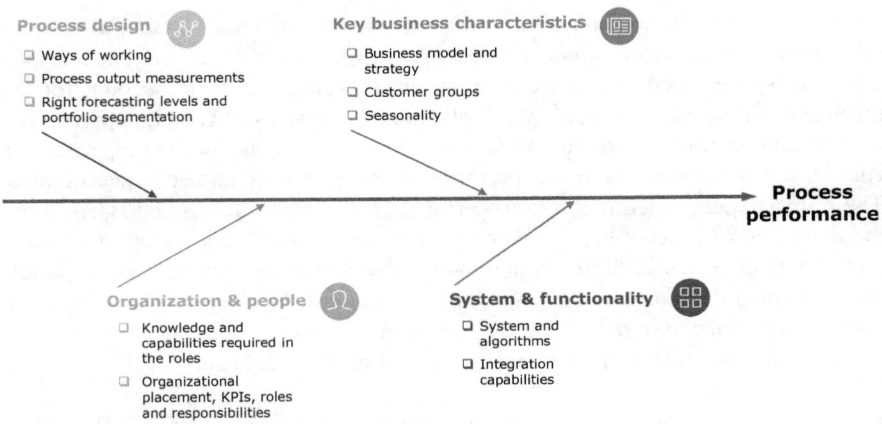


**Fig. 7.2** Process performance fishbone diagram

was very unpredictable and variable, had a global broad market presence and decided to build a dedicated new team with statistical forecasting capabilities, led by forecasting champion who believed in statistical forecasting enabled visibility as well as in value add of inputs and took holistic approach payed back significantly with improvements of:

- Forecast bias reduction of 80%.
- Forecast accuracy improvement of 20%.
- The combination of statistic and business experts represents an added value.
- Great supply and demand balancing thanks to the consensus process (Hostmann 2009).

## 7.1 How to Measure Process Effectiveness, Efficiency, and Adherence

We explain measurement dimensions on demand planning and forecasting. There were a lot of publications about what is the most suitable way to measure forecasting process. Let us deep dive into three dimensions of measurement (Fig. 7.3).

Before we go into how to measure maybe a thought from Charles W. Chase (2009) where he states that "People do not want to be measured, because they are scared of their performances instead of seeing it as an improvement process".

Mentzer and Moon (2005) in *Sales Forecasting Management* set golden rules/ principles where one of them is "Measure, measure, measure" (Mentzer and Moon 2004).

### 7.1.1 Effectiveness

Effectiveness of a process is a measure of performance as they relate to its outputs. Process metrics that measure this aspect of performance rule the most influence on the performance of downstream processes. There are several ways to measure effectiveness and therefore several choices for metrics. When carefully done, a multitude of metrics can actually reveal details about different attributes of performance and together paint a wholesome picture. The analogy of an airplane cockpit, which is often invoked, is entirely apt. Each control in isolation provides a useful but limiting view. However, the cockpit as a whole, which is a collection of these controls, provides great insights regarding the health of the airplane, a prime example of the whole being greater than the sum of its parts.

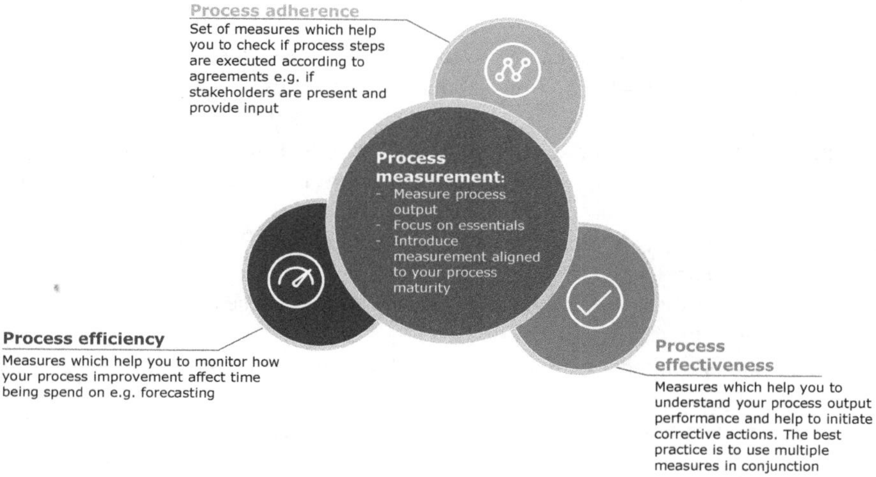


**Fig. 7.3** Process measurement dimensions

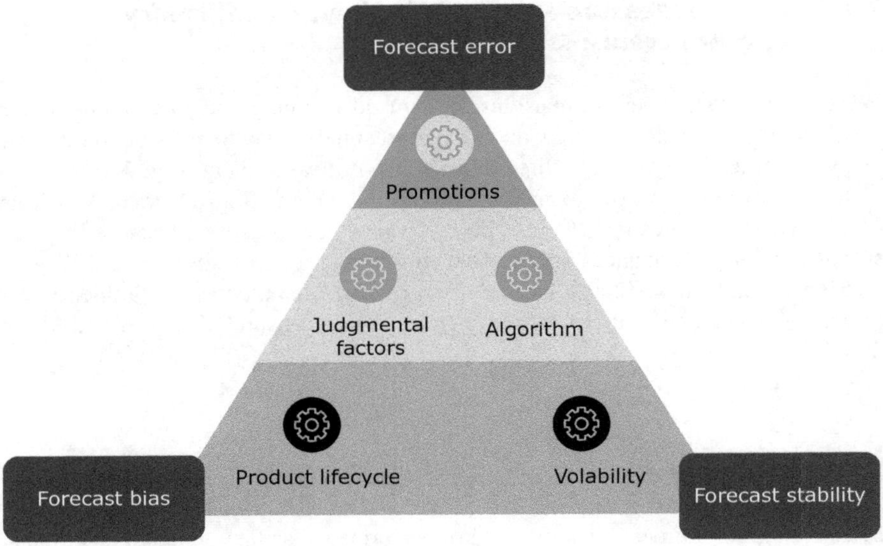


**Fig. 7.4** Effectiveness measures for demand planning

In Fig. 7.4 the three most important effectiveness metrics are depicted, namely, forecast error, bias, and stability. As can be seen within the triangle, the triangle represents decision variables (can be seen as inputs, activities) that contribute to the overall performance as reflected in the effectiveness metrics.

**Forecast Error Metrics** To be able to measure accuracy, one has to quantify errors. Forecast errors are a function of forecast variability and are a key decision variable in the calculation of time, capacity, and inventory buffers to ensure adequate levels of service.

There are many ways to calculate; we highlight some of them in Fig. 7.5.

Let us bring some leaders findings about forecast errors:

- Ninety-two percent of surveyed companies use MAPE as main error KPI. Measurement should be done in a way to identify error sources (Steutermann et al. 2012b).
- Process performance metrics based on percentage (MAPE, RMSPE, etc.) have some deficiencies:
  - If the value of an observation at a certain time is 0, those methods do not react properly.
  - They are not suitable with a meaningful observation of 0, for example, Celsius scale.
  - They impact with a heavier penalty on positive errors compared to negative errors.

| Forecast error metrics | Formula | Guidelines for use |
|---|---|---|
| Mean square error (MSE) | $\frac{1}{n}\sum_{t=1}^{n}(F_t - D_t)^2$ | + Good for penalizing large errors<br>- Not so intuitive to interpret / visualize |
| Mean absolute deviation (MAD) | $\frac{1}{n}\sum_{t=1}^{n}\lvert F_t - D_t\rvert$ | + Intuitive and easy to visualize (same units as demand)<br>+ Good for small numbers |
| Mean absolute percentage error (MAPE) | $\left[\frac{1}{n}\sum_{t=1}^{n}\left\lvert\frac{F_t - D_t}{D_t}\right\rvert\right] * 100$ | - Not affected by magnitude of demand quantities<br>+ Expressed in % - lends itself easily to comparisons<br>+ Good for seasonal patterns<br>+ Good as a leading summary metric |
| Weighted Mean absolute percentage error (MAPE) | $\left(\frac{\sum\lvert Forecast - Sales\rvert}{\sum Sales}\right) * 100$ | + Affected by magnitude of demand quantities<br>+ Expressed in % and easy to understand, used to visualize process error on aggregated level<br>- "Promotes" over forecasting<br>- Not good in handling zero demand or zero forecast |

**Fig. 7.5** Comparison of forecast error measures

- Process performance relative measures (RelMAE) have the advantage to be easily interpreted, but the disadvantage is that they can be difficult and time-consuming to compute. Furthermore computation is made possible only when there are several forecasts on the same time series.
- New proposed solution is scaled error (MASE), which has advantages of independent from the scale of data, and it gives smaller errors and is less sensitive to outliers (Hyndman and Koehler 2005).

Except the metrics which show magnitude of forecast error in %, simple forecast error understood as difference between forecast and actuals is commonly used.

**Forecast Error** Forecast error is measured in volume/value. It shows direction of an error and magnitude. Its formula is like that:

$$Forecast\_Error = Forecast - Sales$$

**Forecast Bias**
Forecast bias is used to uncover systematic biases in the underlying forecasting process leading to consistent over- or under-forecasting. Bias is measured in %, and it has a sign to show direction of deviation.

**Forecast Stability**
Forecast stability measures the stability of the forecast for the same time the bucket is produced in different time horizons. This is visualized in Fig. 7.6. The changes to the

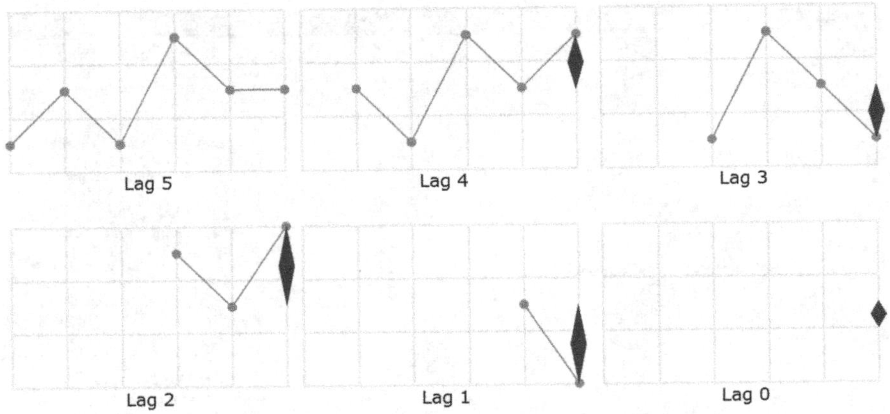


**Fig. 7.6** Visualization of forecast stability metric

forecast from a certain reference point (say, the highest lag; lag 5 in the example visualized) are measured at multiple lags. The height of the red diamonds in the graphic depicts the magnitude of change from the reference point.

Numerically, the following formula can be used to calculate this metric:

$$\text{Forecast Stability} = \left(1 - \frac{\text{Mean Absolute Deviation}}{\text{Mean}}\right) \times 100$$

For example, if lag [1–3] forecasts are 500 PC, 30 PC, and 115 PC, respectively, the mean is 215 PC, and the mean absolute deviation is 190 PC (abs (500 – 215) + abs (500 – 30) + abs (500 – 115)/3 = 190 PC). Therefore forecast stability would be (1 – (190/215)) 10%, which is a very low number as is intuitive, given that the forecast at different lags varies significantly from each other.

**Correlation of Metrics**

As we discussed before, correlation of metrics gives much better insights about forecast error than a single one. Let us illustrate that on selected forecast effectiveness metrics.

We see magnitude of the error is substantial; we understand that we under forecast therefore are exposed to stock outs and finally that we have made an error which may be perceived as big as 1400 tons which in chemical industry may be relatively big. Effectiveness metrics should be analyzed and visualized in year-to-date and time series manner. One measure will not tell you if performance is good or wrong and what corrective actions to introduce. It is always about correlation of few measures which brings understanding of error nature (see Fig. 7.7). When you know the cause, it is easier to trigger and deploy corrective action (Fig. 7.8).

As you have learned from the chapter about preparation to demand review meeting, demand planner should highlight error patterns and trends and not focus on single events only. Should you align forecast inputs provided on level aligned to

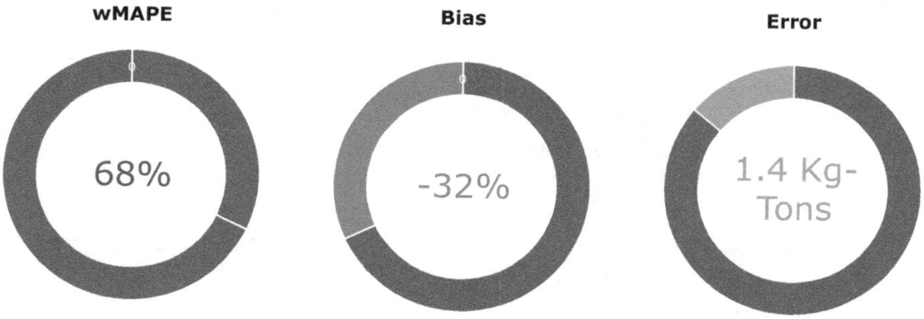


**Fig. 7.7** Correlation of effectiveness measures

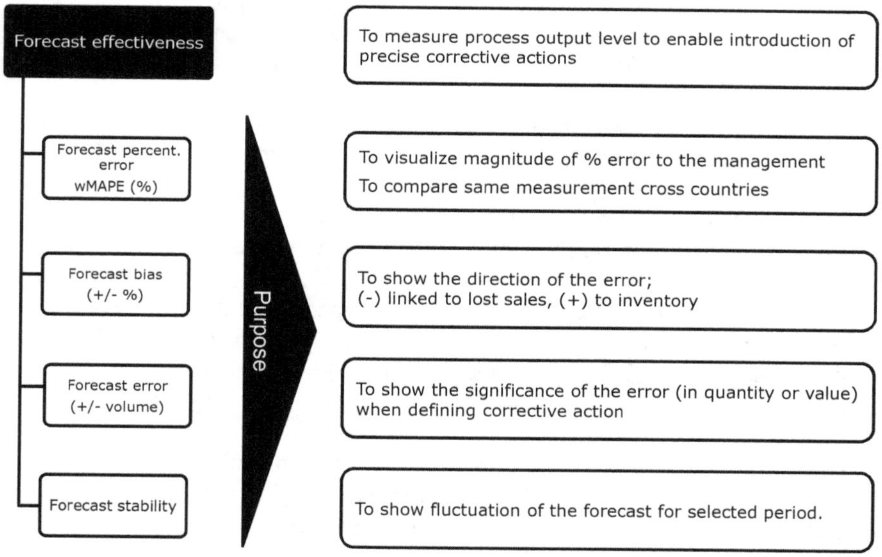


**Fig. 7.8** Forecast effectiveness measures

best insights (e.g., brand by marketing, customer by sales) to measurement level in demand review? The good thing about SAP IBP is that we can work on the level which speaks to us, system will translate it to technical level on which data is stored. You define how key figures are calculated and aggregated. All of those inputs should be automatically translated to level which is common for particular S&OP level (country, regional, global). In tactical S&OP translation may happen to SKU/country/month. Once data is on this common level, you may start to use it in measurement. In the global process design, you may have agreed that each country has to deliver consensus unconstrained forecast by country, by SKU, and by period, and it should be finalized on specific working day (as per S&OP calendar of activities). You may understand this information as demand review meeting output. You should run process effectiveness measurement on this level, but you may visualize it on any higher level in S&OP hierarchy with the use of weighted mean absolute percentage error.

**Parametrization of Metrics**

Let us deep dive a bit into business context of parameters for forecast effectiveness metrics:

- **Measurement level**—level on which process output should be delivered, e.g., by country, by SKU, and by month.
- **Measurement dimension**—volumetric or monetized forecast.
- **Time lag**—should represent average lead time for business impact we want to measure, e.g., 1 month to measure impact on distribution and quality of up-to-date inputs, 3 months to measure impact on production capacity of your critical semifinished products, and 6 months to measure impact on production of your most expensive ingredients and raw materials. Need to be aligned to measurement level.
- **Aggregation window**—should represent cycle on which process is being executed; normally S&OP is done monthly, so aggregation should be 1 month.

  Let's briefly discuss some of the parameters of metrics:
  **Time lag** should represent the forecast issued no of period's prior sales.

In Gartner research (Pukkila, 2015), you will find good illustration of examples why and how to define time lag which will help to measure impact on desired aspect of the business. In Fig. 7.9 you will find slightly modified table based on this Gartner research.

Forecast accuracy measurement should be done by planning horizon; the main purpose of this process is to understand how well the demand planning team can predict the future demand and as a result how performing will be the operations along the entire SC (Pukkila, 2015).

Aggregation Window

In process measurement you may aggregate actuals and forecast data by time, but you should ask yourself why to do that. The main reason of aggregating data should be the cycle on which measured process is being executed and impact of measurement level. Aggregation window for processes which create annual impact and are performed once per year should be 12 (months), but for those processes like monthly tactical S&OP, it should be 1 (month).

**Challenges with Handling Process Effectiveness Measurement**

Few watch outs for how easy is to make process measurement to look better than really is.

| | February | March | April | May | Time lag |
|---|---|---|---|---|---|
| January forecast for Feb sales vs Feb sales | Sales | Measurement | | | 1 month lag |
| January forecast for Mar sales vs Feb sales | Sales | Sales | Measurement | | 2 month lag |
| January forecast for Apr sales vs Feb sales | Sales | Sales | Sales | Measurement | 3 month lag |

**Fig. 7.9** Forecast time lag definition

Forecasting process output level in example below is defined on country level but reviewed often on country group. Below we describe correct and incorrect way of measurement for this case.

Correct way: measurement is done on process output level but aggregated with wMAPE. Error is 12.5% (Fig. 7.10).

Incorrect way: measurement is done on display/review level and not aligned to process outputs, and weighting from wMAPE is not used. Error shows 2.5% (Fig. 7.11).

It is obvious that the second example looks better; it is a fruit which "Eva" from sales or marketing team should not pick up from the tree! The second example does not visualize impact of the forecasting error properly. It is fake measurement. The example above illustrates why we should discuss further parameters of measurement.

It is therefore important, when designing process metrics, to consider the components of measurement described above. In the case of procurement at ACME, for example, forecast accuracy on fabric level that is available at the time of "procurement commit" on monthly basis is what possesses explanatory value to quality of decisions that follow and, therefore, should be the metric that is tracked and included in a functionally oriented dashboard.

You may face a lot of change management challenges when defining your process measurement. There are few examples to illustrate what we mean by that.

### Measure Error Not Accuracy

1. Very often in literature, we see that we should measure process accuracy, but then measures/formulas are for wMAPE, APE, etc. Let us just briefly discuss that. What is more probable in your business, to generate forecast which have more

| Month year | SKU | Country | Country group | Sales | Forecast | Forecast error | Abs forecast error | Forecast bias | APE |
|---|---|---|---|---|---|---|---|---|---|
| 122013 | 15776 | AU | AU/NZ | 200 | 230 | 30 | 30 | 15% | 15% |
| 122013 | 15776 | NZ | AU/NZ | 200 | 180 | -20 | 20 | -11% | 11% |
| Total | | | | **400** | **410** | **10** | **50** | | |
| | | | | | | | | **Weighted MAPE** | **12,5%** |

**Fig. 7.10** Measurement of wMAPE in correct way

| Month year | SKU | Country group | Sales | Forecast | Forecast error | Abs forecast error | Forecast bias | APE |
|---|---|---|---|---|---|---|---|---|
| 122013 | 15776 | AU/NZ | 400 | 410 | -10 | 10 | -2,5% | 2,5% |
| Total | | | **400** | **410** | **-10** | **10** | | |
| | | | | | | | **Weighted MAPE** | **2,5%** |

**Fig. 7.11** Measurement of wMAPE in wrong way

errors or more accurate records? We have seen many companies where probability of delivering error is much higher than delivering accurate records, in this case use error.

2. If you will use error instead of accuracy, you will not limit significance of the error and will not bias measurement system. Let us look at it from Six Sigma perspective, where you need to ensure that your measurement system is validated. In case you would use accuracy, it will show false results since wMPAE error of

120% will be shown as 0% accuracy, why? Accuracy has limit set to 100%, and error does not. Error shows true significance, accuracy not.
3. If you measure error and many of the records are far above 100% wMAPE, your outlier detection preprocessing algorithm will spot "black swans" better.

Measure Process Outputs

1. Sales want to measure monetized forecast, while process delivers volumetric. Unconstrained forecast delivered to production and supply organization is in volume, but sales or marketing wants to see significance exposed in monetary terms. You should protect your measurement system and keep it aligned to outputs. As described above, you may use product segmentation ABC or ABC/XYZ to make a link to financial dimension. You will see right away if you make bigger or smaller error cross more profitable or less profitable SKUs.
2. Measure forecasts in volume and value separately—volumetric projections and value projection as discussed earlier have different drivers. Measure them separately. Both volume and value have its own drivers; do not mix them since you will not understand what drives them.

**How Easy Is to Misuse or Misinterpret Metrics Parameters**

Aggregation Window

1. We have faced the problem that before IBP transformation project, forecast was measured with aggregation window of 3 and in value. Measurement was aggregating 3 months of actuals and running against 3 months of forecast. Results were very nice; it looked like the company did absolutely great job in forecasting. Nobody wanted to switch to the parameters which could align measurement to process output. In this case, to separate volumetric and monetized unconstrained forecast which was revised, it was updated every month. The impact of monthly forecast changes was influencing distribution, redistribution, replenishment from regional supply points, and financial projections including provisions. Sales team wanted to drive measurement parameter toward nicer results (aggregated but not weighted) and not aligned to process impact on the other functions like operations. Unconstrained forecast was updated every month and generated impact on inventory every month; stock was not held on purpose of 3 months versus 3 months of forecast. It would be too expensive for the company to do that but ok for sales to use 3-month aggregation. In this case aggregation window because of the impact forecast did make on supply chain should be 1.
2. In the other company, sales argued to keep 3-month aggregations because many times, actual sales fall into next month by 1 day because of external or even internal factors. Funny was that sales pattern in the month was in shape of ice hockey stick and not too much was sold early in the month.

3. The last example is about how aggregation window was misunderstood. Sales and marketing department wanted to review forecasting KPI on a 3-month basis therefore pushed for wMAPE aggregation window 3.

Time Lag

1. Should current period be taken into consideration when counting time lag? Let us look at it from E2E perspective and not only commercial organization which may want to count current month since they want to introduce change now for current month. Does your company have any time fences in your planning processes? Is it allowed to change anything in the forecast and request commitment from organization which provides response without any buffers, controls? Introduction of forecast changes coupled with redeployment of the forecast followed by redistribution needs to be controlled and very often cannot happen the same month. To cope with that issue, you have between cycle's change processes and not time lag.
2. You submit unconstrained forecast or constrained plan according to S&OP calendar of activities. The whole organization will capture their knowledge and analyze data to come to best conclusion on specific date but with focus on future not current month. Tactical S&OP is not about the next 2-week projections like operational planning; it is a process which does focus on midterm future.

In the studies there were following challenges reported linked to forecasting process measurement:

- The desire to improve forecast accuracy not a SKU level but for aggregating items for improving the bottom line and inventory levels and reaching target fill rates.
- Only 50% of the companies track properly their forecast accuracy mainly due to huge storing data cost, lack of updates, data retention challenge, and lack of metrics and tracking activities (Hoover, 2009).

### 7.1.2 SAP Use Case: Forecast Error Measurement

In SAP IBP with the use of forecast error app, you can define your forecast performance metrics. Once they are defined, they can be used and visualized in Excel UI and Web UI analytics.

You can define performance measurement for any forecast input, e.g., statistical forecast, input from sales team and from marketing, and consensus forecast. Let us describe key elements of configuration. At the beginning we need to define profile which can be combined to the number of forecast error calculation for various inputs and various parameters (see Fig. 7.12).

We need to specify input key figures which will be taken into account; in the example we see corrected actuals and statistical forecast with time lag 1 (see Fig. 7.13) and aggregation window 1.

Once inputs are done, we need to select on which level data will be stored and which metrics we want to have it calculated. There is quite a long list of metrics to

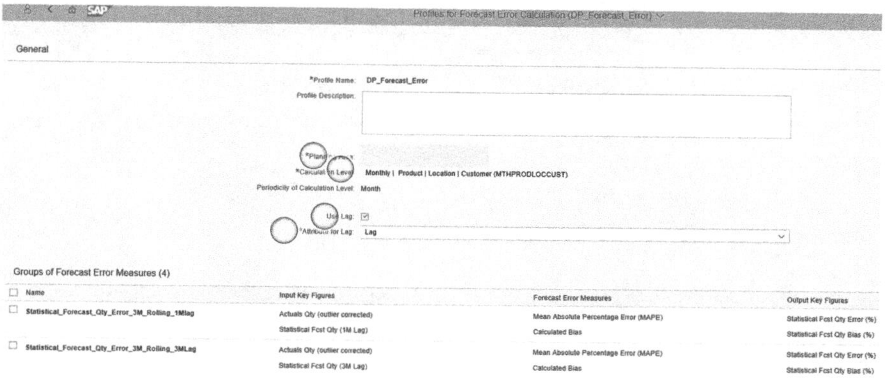

**Fig. 7.12** Forecast measurement profile with multiple forecast performance metrics

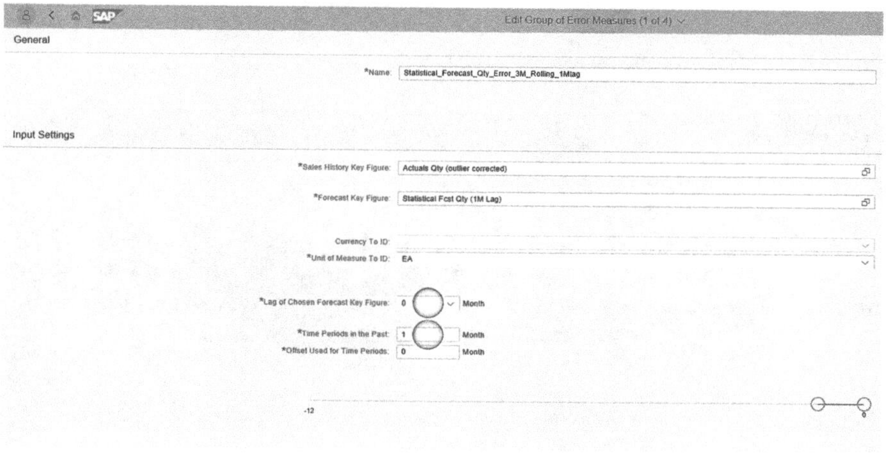

**Fig. 7.13** Forecast measurement configuration (1)—data inputs

see. Note that for one parametrization, multiple output metrics can be calculated. In this case we have statistical forecast error, MASE and Bias (see Fig. 7.14).

Since configuration is done with the app, it can be done normally by business key user. IT need to enable key figures on which outputs will be stored, and business user can make their own decision on forecasting metrics configuration and even add forecast error metrics key figures to their templates and favorites. Visualization of forecast error and metrics should be done in way that it helps demand planner to trigger corrective actions. It means it needs to facilitate assessment of trends in error, one-off events, and main drivers linked to product groups, products, stakeholders, areas, etc. In Fig. 7.15 we visualize sales forecast error (MAPE) and statistical forecast error (MAPE) against input key figures.

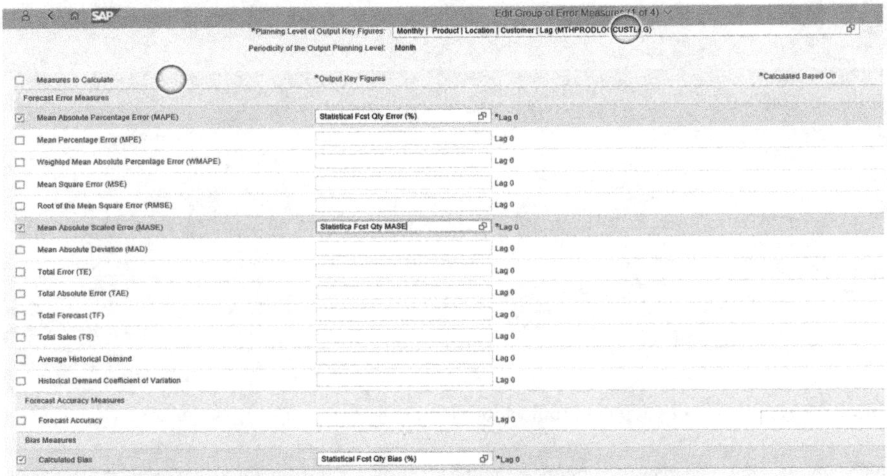


**Fig. 7.14** Forecast measurement configuration (2)—data outputs

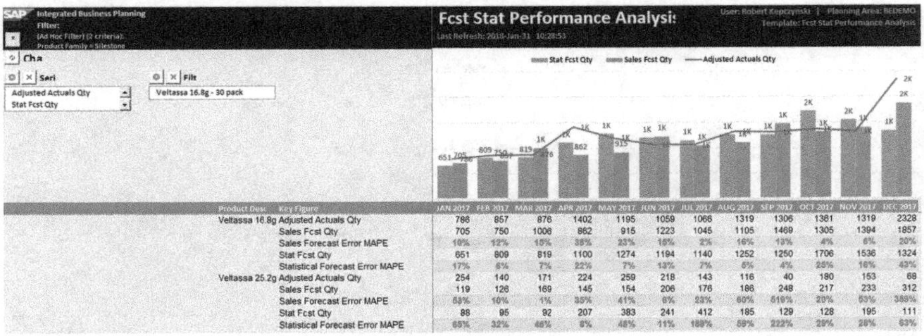


**Fig. 7.15** Forecast error measurement analysis for multiple forecast inputs

Demand planners should focus themselves at errors which make an impact. Therefore it makes sense to visualize forecast error metrics calculation against product segmentation.

In this case we see A (important) and B (less important) product forecast error displayed on the dashboard on separate charts. Charts as you noticed are done with XYZ variability segmentation (Fig. 7.16).

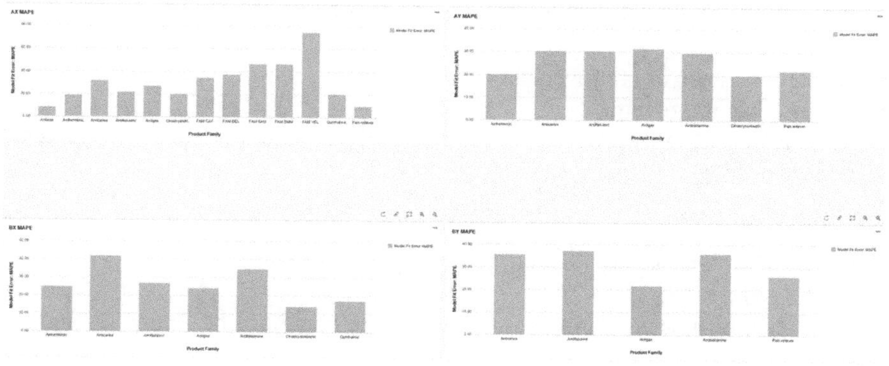

**Fig. 7.16** Forecast error measurement visualization for product segments

### 7.1.3 Efficiency

The measurement of process efficiency can be understood through:

- Value add—metric which should describe what value is generated by specific process steps versus statistical forecasting, naïve. I very often use MASE (mean absolute scaled error) developed by professor Rob J. Hyndman which can measure selected input in reference to naïve forecast.
- Forecasting combinations over time—metric which should help you to describe how many forecasting combination for specific process you have.
- No of phase in vs. phase outs—metric which will help you to understand if product review coordinated by demand planner does produce more and more materials or as well helps to managed long tale of SKUs and removes some SKUs from range.

Measuring efficiency is not easy; you would need to make decision which metric will describe the best way of measuring how efficient your process is.

Some examples:

1. No of forecasting combination—to monitor potential no of touch points available in forecast inputs (sales, marketing, demand planning).
2. No of people providing forecast inputs—to monitor if the no of people providing input does change over time. You may be surprise with the degree of correlation between specific forecast input error and no of people providing forecast input. Very often the more people touching the forecast, the worse it gets.
3. How long does it take to forecast—to monitor how long in average does it take to provide forecast input.
4. Phase in vs. phase outs—to monitor if you only add new SKUs in IBP portfolio and do or do not manage long tail of SKU. Some should be removed from the range.

Why should you measure forecasting process efficiency?

- To identify areas of improvement
- To visualize improvements
- To understand how efforts in collecting inputs are correlated to forecast performance

### 7.1.4 Adherence

Measurement of process quality/process adherence could be understood through:

- Presence on the meeting—it may sound weird to some of you, but especially at the beginning of your IBP journey or improvement, it is quite important to check if stakeholders who either are responsible to provide input or the ones who review it are present on scheduled activities.
- Input provided on time—in large organizations where many inputs are qualitative, you would need to set up time slots by when particular input has to be finalized. You should set up calendar of activities, but as well you should go further and start to measure if inputs are provided against agreed calendar of activities.
- Qualitative inputs up to date—many time you may ask yourself as demand planner if input provided is up to date or not. Visualization of last change time stamp might help to assess it. We are not recommending to update forecast for the sake of updating it, but you may look on forecast input provided by sales rep which is 6 months old differently than on the one which was updated just yesterday.

Measuring process adherence/quality is important. Adherence to process rules may be differently organized in large or small organizations but make very sense. The strength of your process will be described by degree of adherence to the rules you defined with your management.

Some examples:

- Frequency of forecasting combination updates—you may have defined rules how frequently to update forecast for different product segments. It does not stop you to capture changes as needed (new deal, new customer, etc.) but to set up rule how frequently in average it should happen.
- Last forecast update for qualitative inputs—to monitor how up to date the forecast input is. In some cases it may help you to understand reason of forecast input error.
- Process step completeness as per schedule—to monitor individual person routine and compliance with rules.

# References


Amber, S., & Debashis, T. (2015). *Apply the supply chain maturity model for better demand planning*. Gartner.

APICS – Module 2.G – Influencing and prioritizing demand (2015) *APICS – module 2.G – Influencing and prioritizing demand.* APICS.

APICS – Module 3.D – Implementation of demand plans (2015) *APICS – Module 3.D – Implementation of demand plans*. APICS.

Applebaum, T. (2014). *Manage uncertainty and product mix to improve demand management in life sciences*. Gartner.

Armstrong, J. S. (2002). Benchmarks for new product forecast errors. *Innovation*, (December), pp. 1–3.

Aronow, S., & Jr, R. B. (2011, April). *Understanding trade-offs: A practical supply chain cost-service analysis framework and maturity model.* Gartner.

Blosch, M., & Uskert, M. (2011). *Unilever develops demand planning capability in developing and emerging markets*. Gartner.

Bower, P. (2012). Integrated business planning: Is it a hoax or here to stay? *Journal of Business Forecasting*, *31*(1), 11–17. http://www.jaguar-aps.com/pdf/IBP is a Hoax.pdf.

Burkett, M. (2016). *The hierarchy of new product introduction metrics: Grow with new products while managing complexity*. Gartner.

Bursa, K. L. (2014). Achieving demand planning excellence. *European Business Review*. http://www.europeanbusinessreview.com/achieving-demand-planning-excellence/?_sm_au_=irVrqWHpvD54L5PP.

Cecere, L. (2013). A practitioner's guide to demand planning. *Supply Chain Management Review, 14*(2), 40–46. http://www.supplychain247.com/article/a_practitioners_guide_to_demand_planning.

Chase, C. W. (2009). *Demand-driven forecasting: A structured approach to forecasting*. Wiley. https://books.google.com/books?hl=en&lr=&id=iVIbAAAAQBAJ&pgis=1.

Chase, C. W. (2016). *Next generation demand management: People, process, analytics, and technology*. Wiley.

Clemen, R. T. (1989). Combining forecasts: A review and annotated bibliography. *International Journal of Forecasting, 5*, 559–583.

Crum, C., & Palmatier, G. E. (2003). *Demand management best practices: Process, principles, and collaboration*. Oliver Wight, APICS. http://books.google.at/books?id=6l3iWbGM-54C.

Davis, M. (2011). *Customer value analytics for supply chain segmentation*. Gartner.

Davis, M. (2012). *Design the right form of supply chain segmentation for your business*. Gartner.

Debra Smith, C. S. (2016). *Demand driven performance using smart metrics*. McGraw-Hill.

Demand Classification. (2017). Frepple.com

Erhun, F., Gonçalves, P., & Hopman, J. (2007). *The art of managing new product transitions. MIT Sloan Management Review, 48*, 73–80.


 

R. Kepczynski et al., *Implementing Integrated Business Planning*, Management for Professionals, https://doi.org/10.1007/978-3-319-90095-7

Gardner, D., & Tetlock, P. E. (2015). Superforecasting: The art and science of prediction. *New York Times Bestseller*.

Griswold, M. (2012). *Best practices in demand planning: Helping retailers learn from other industries*. Gartner.

Heinonen, T. (2009). *Supporting SOP through finance involvement*. Helsinki School of Economics.

Hoover, J. (2009). *How to track forecast accuracy to guide forecast process improvement*. Foresight.

Hostmann, B. (2009). *Case study: Cisco improves demand forecast accuracy with advanced analytics, domain expertise and a consensus process*. Gartner.

Hyndman, R. J., & Koehler, A. B. (2005). Business statistics another look at measures of forecast accuracy another look at measures of forecast accuracy. *International Journal of Forecasting, 22*(Nov), 679–688. https://doi.org/10.1016/j.ijforecast.2006.03.001.

Kahn, K. B. (2014). *Solving the problems of new product forecasting*. Business Horizons.

Kepczynski, R., Jandhyala, R., Sankaran, G., & Dimofte, A. (2018). *Integrated business planning – How to integrate planning processes, organizational structures & capabilities, and leverage SAP IBP technology*. Springer.

Makridakis, S., & Hibon, M. (2000). The M3 competition: Results, conclusions, and implications. *International Journal of Forecasting, 16*(4), 451–476.

Mentzer Jr J. T., & Moon, M. A. (2004). *Sales forecasting management*. Sage.

Mentzer, J. T., & Moon, M. A. (2005). *Sales forecasting management: A demand management approach*. Thousand Oaks, CA: SAGE Publications.

Moon, M. A. (2013). *Demand and supply integration: The key to world-class demand forecasting*. FT Press. https://books.google.com/books?id=2M9njA9JcMgC&pgis=1.

Mulllick Satinder, K. (1971). *Tecnique, How to choose the right forecasting*. Harvard Business Review.

Palmatier, G. E., & Crum, C. (2003). *Enterprise sales and operations planning: Synchronizing demand, supply and resources for peak performance*. J Ross Publishing.

Palmatier, G. E., & Crum, C. (2013). *The transition from sales and operations planning to integrated business planning*. New London: Oliver Wight. https://www.amazon.com/Transition-Operations-Planning-Integrated-Business/dp/1457518252.

Payne, T. (2016, September). *Digital business requires algorithmic supply chain planning*. Gartner.

Penafiel, W. (2016). *How to design a demand planning process*. MeetLogistics.

Poehlman, J. M. (1987). *Breeding field crops*. Dordrecht: Springer Netherlands.

Porter, M. E., & Millar, V. E. (n.d.). *How information gives you competitive advantage*. Harvard Business Review.

Pukkila, M. (2015). *Align forecast accuracy lag times with supply chain action points to better support decision making*. Gartner.

Reinmuth, J. E. (1974). *Forecasting the impact of a new product introduction*. J.E. JAMS.

Salley, A. (2013). *Building demand management excellence at danone*. Gartner.

Salley, A., Steutermann, S., & Johnson, J. (2016). *Five tenets of demand management are foundational to supply chain transformation*. Gartner.

Shamir, J. (2013). Next-generation forecasting is closer than you might think. *SupplyChainBrain, 17*(5), 52. http://search.ebscohost.com/login.aspx?direct=true&db=edb&AN=91637369&site=eds-live.

Simchi, L. (1999). *Designing and managing the supply chain: Concepts, strategies, and case studies*. McGraw-Hill.

SM Thacker & Associates. (2007). *Demand management*. SM Thacker & Associates.

Steutermann, S. (2010). *Demand planning excellence*. AMR Research.

Steutermann, S. (2012). *Defining demand-planning excellence in consumer products: Structure, talent and technology*. Gartner.

Steutermann, S. (2016a). *Defining demand-planning excellence in consumer products: Structure, talent and technology*. Gartner.

Steutermann, S. (2016b). *Demand forecasting leads the list of challenges impacting customer service across industries*. Gartner.

Steutermann, S., & Suleski, J. (2016). *Take six actions to improve product life cycle management in consumer products*. Gartner.

Steutermann, S., Salley, A., & Lord, P. (2012a). *Demand management elevates value network performance*. Gartner.

Steutermann, S., Scott, F., & Tohamy, N. (2012b). *Building an effective demand-planning process*. Gartner.

Thacker, M. (2001). *Participative sales and operations planning*. MIOM, SM Thacker & Associates.

Titze, C., & Krasojevic, V. (2012). *European SC leaders – What does it really mean to sense and shape demand*. Gartner.

Tohamy, N. (2012). *A broader span for demand sensing and demand shaping across industries and time horizons*. Gartner.

Tohamy, N., Johnson, A., & Davis, M. (2010, October). *Demand sensing and shaping narrow the chasm between commercial and supply chain strategies and goals*. Gartner.

Watkins, R. (2014). *Sales forecasting and demand management*. Delos Partnership.

CPSIA information can be obtained
at www.ICGtesting.com
Printed in the USA
LVHW052047290519
619460LV00002B/54/P

9 783319 900940